New York Chapter,
American Institute of Architects

AIA GUIDE TO NEW YORK CITY

REVISED EDITION

**Norval White
Elliot Willensky**

Collier Books
A DIVISION OF MACMILLAN PUBLISHING CO., INC.
NEW YORK

Collier Macmillan Publishers
LONDON

Macmillan Publishing Co., Inc.
866 Third Avenue, New York, N.Y. 10022
Collier Macmillan Canada, Inc.

Opinions expressed in this book are those of the authors and are not
represented as being those of the New York Chapter, American Institute of
Architects.

Since reference to a structure does not constitute an invitation to visit,
permission (especially in the case of residential properties) should be obtained
beforehand from owner or occupant.

Library of Congress Cataloging in Publication Data

American Institute of Architects. New York Chapter.
   AIA guide to New York City.

   Includes index.
     1. Architecture—New York (City)—Guide-books.
2. New York (City)—Descriptive—Guide-books.
I. White, Norval.   II. Willensky, Elliot.
III. Title.   IV. Title: Guide to New York City.
NA735.N5A78 1977   917.47′1′044   77-21617
ISBN 0-02-626580-X
ISBN 0-02-000980-1 pbk.

Revised Edition 1978

10 9 8 7 6 5

Printed in the United States of America

CONTENTS

MANHATTAN   1

THE BRONX

NECROLOGY

THE CITY

LIST OF MAPS

USING THE GUIDE

The *Guide* is designed to serve a whole spectrum of readers, from the most casual wanderer to the serious historian; from the provincial New Yorker who rarely, if ever, ventures west of the Hudson River, to the visitor who wants to see more than the well-touted monuments, musicals, and museums. From these pages you will be able to select and follow a wide variety of specific walking tours (and automobile tours for the outer reaches of the city), or you may use the book to design your own.

Some of you may explore your own neighborhoods before venturing into unfamiliar places. Braver souls will immediately "go abroad" as tourists in other parts of the city, tasting new and exotic precincts. Some may wish to start at the Battery, working their way geographically or following the chronological development of the city.

For the less athletic, you may leave the *Guide* on your coffee table to leaf through the pages at your leisure, and enjoy excursions of the city in the mind, without ever stepping outside your door. And you will also be able to use the guide to conduct visitors from Paris, Tokyo, San Francisco, or even Hackensack to view and relish not only New York's major monuments, landmarks, and historic districts but also its richness of buildings and precincts in every borough of the city.

Geographical Organization. The *Guide,* like the city, is divided into five boroughs. Manhattan, at whose southern tip the city began, is first. The outlying boroughs (the Bronx, Brooklyn, Queens, and Staten Island) follow in the order they were incorporated into the city. A section entitled "The City" deals with the metropolis as a whole.

The sections of the book are organized to illustrate the complexity and richness of a particular borough, and within that borough its various sectors (e.g., Lower Manhattan, Northern Brooklyn, Northwestern Queens). The sectors, in turn, are often divided into neighborhood areas, called precincts (e.g., Financial District, Greenpoint, Long Island City).

Boroughs, sectors, and precincts are prefaced in the text by a short historical introduction and a capsule description of the area's topography and history of physical development.

Entries. Each listing in the *Guide* is numbered—the numbers appearing within brackets—and identified by name in boldface type. (Sometimes there is also a former or original name or names.) This information is followed by the street address and/or block location, as well as the designer and the date of the building's completion. When no other title follows the name of a designer, it should be assumed to be architect. Throughout the *Guide,* identification lines appear at the bottom of each page. Those at the bottom of left-hand pages indicate the borough and sector being discussed; the identifying letter for the sector (e.g., **N** for Northern, **SE** for Southeastern) keys it to the *Guide*'s maps. Right-hand pages show the precinct being dealt with and the map page on which the entries appear. When several entries are geographically close to one another but are cited individually in the *Guide,* the same number is used for each member of the group, and a letter suffix distinguishes each entry (e.g., **[3a.]**, **[3b.]**). On the maps these groups are usually indicated only by the single number. Bracketed notes (e.g., [see . . .]) refer to entries of related interest.

In a number of cases, buildings were demolished or defaced more rapidly than the conversion of manuscript to printed book. In the interest of the dynamics of the city—even if in a negative sense—they have been overprinted "DEMOLISHED" and "DEFACED," and, frankly, their removal at the last minute to the **Necrology** section (see below) was logistically impossible.

Photographs that illustrate specific listings are captioned, and cited with the same number that identifies the entry in the text. Note that photographs are almost always on the same two-page spread with the building that they illustrate, but not necessarily contiguous with the text. When photographs were not taken recently and show conditions that are not current, the year they were taken is also noted.

Maps. Each borough is described through a specially designed map that delineates its sectors; the sectors use the identifying letters found on left-hand pages. In areas with heavy concentrations of entries, detailed maps for sectors and/or precincts also indicate street systems, subway stations, and major parks and institutions. The numbers on the maps correspond to the bracketed numbers of the text entries. As noted above, however, a single number on the map sometimes refers to a group of geographically adjacent entries mentioned in the text. Special symbols used on the maps throughout the *Guide* are shown below.

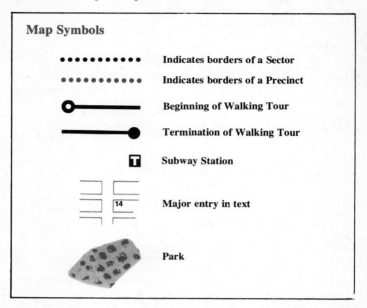

••••••••••	**Indicates borders of a Sector**
••••••••••	**Indicates borders of a Precinct**
O━━━━	**Beginning of Walking Tour**
━━━━●	**Termination of Walking Tour**
T	**Subway Station**
14	**Major entry in text**
	Park

Map Symbols

Walking and Motor Tours. Routes for tours are specified in the text and are shown on the sector maps for the more complex areas. Walking tours are indicated on the maps by solid black lines, their beginning by an open circle and their ending by a solid circle. Where tours are not specifically indicated, the entries are laid out so that by following the numerical sequence of the entries, the reader will naturally trace an easy-to-follow walking or motoring route. Entries located away from the routes of walking tours are indicated at the end of some sections under the heading "Miscellany." For outlying parts of the city, we recommend a good street map. Some of these are available at gas stations (but now for a fee), others at stationery stores (cf., Hagstrom's maps), and still others at map stores (Hammond Map Store, 12 East 41st St.; or Rand McNally, 10 East 53rd St.).

Restaurants, Bistros, and Emporia. Though these have not been numbered, except where they have been included particularly, but not exclusively, for their architectural distinction, they are listed in the index. In the case of restaurants and museums, hours of opening, which often change, have not been included; telephone numbers are provided instead.

Official Landmarks. Items officially designated by the New York City Landmarks Preservation Commission (and confirmed by the Board of Estimate) are identified by a solid star ★. Since designations are being added continuously, we recommend that you write the commission for the most up-to-date information. Designated landmarks and structures lying within designated districts cannot, of course, be demolished or altered without the commission's permission.

Style Symbols. Special symbols in the margin indicate that an entry is a notable example of a building in one of nine significant architectural styles.

Colonial   Literally the architecture of America as a colony, whether of Holland or Great Britain. It implies neither white clapboard nor shutters, and is best exemplified in New York by St. Paul's Chapel (the only "Colonial" building remaining from the New York of 1776) and some of the Dutch Colonial farmhouses of Southeastern Brooklyn.

Georgian/Federal The first (and therefore modern) architecture of the new Federal Republic: a modification of the then-current Georgian architecture of London. Elegant. In both wood and masonry.

Greek Revival The product of both political and aesthetic interests. The Greek revolution made Greece independent of the Turks (i.e., Ottoman Empire) in 1821. The newly won independence recalled, to fascinated American intellectuals, the patrician democracy of ancient Greece and its elegant architecture, created more than 400 years before the birth of Christ. In America, columns and orders were used mostly decoratively. Whole buildings, however, sometimes were recalled (Sailors' Snug Harbor on Staten Island, or the Federal Hall National Memorial on Wall Street are reincarnations of great temples).

Italianate Somewhat obscure in its naming, this style embraces the Renaissance Revival facades of brownstones (pediments, quoins, and console brackets), and the idea of the Italianate villa (Litchfield Mansion in Prospect Park).

Gothic Revival In its purest form it refers to the revival in the 1830s and 1840s, coincidental with that in England, in which interest in the "goodness" of medieval times suggested the emulation of Gothic architecture to achieve a similar goodness now. A re-revival occurred around 1900 and later, particularly for colleges and major churches.

Renaissance/Baroque Revival Drawn from the architecture of 15th through 17th century Italy, France, and England. Italian palazzi, English clubs, and French chateaux became super town houses, American clubs, banks, and government buildings (cf. the Federal Reserve Bank, the James B. Duke House, the Metropolitan Museum, and the old Custom House).

Roman Revival More pompous than Greek Revival, it brought back some of the histrionics of Rome, particularly through elaborate columns, pediments, and sculpture of a grandiose nature.

Romanesque Revival A vigorous style more common in Chicago than New York, but based on the bold arch and vault construction of the early medieval Romanesque. H.H. Richardson was its greatest American exponent, but Frank Freeman of Brooklyn was not far behind.

Modern/Art Deco/Art Moderne The breakdown of "modern" into component styles is a new phenomenon, based on the concept that "modern" as we know it today has its own internal history beginning, in this country, with the works of Louis Sullivan and Frank Lloyd Wright [see Sullivan's Condict Building in Astor Place/East Village], and including such phases as Art Deco (cubistic modern ornament inspired by the Paris Exposition of 1924); Art Moderne (streamlined sleek from the Paris Exposition of 1937); the Bauhaus and/or International Style as imported by Walter Gropius, Mies van der Rohe, and Marcel Breuer (cf. the original Museum of Modern Art, the Seagram Building); and, more recently, individual excursions into a nonhistorical personal architecture.

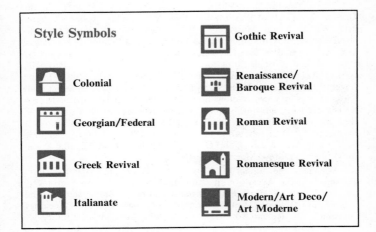

Style Symbols

Colonial

Georgian/Federal

Greek Revival

Italianate

Gothic Revival

Renaissance/Baroque Revival

Roman Revival

Romanesque Revival

Modern/Art Deco/Art Moderne

Necrology. Between the publication of the original edition (for the AIA's one hundredth anniversary in 1967) and the closing date for this third edition in 1978, myriad buildings of distinction have been demolished. A new section, Necrology, remembers them. Entries and photographs in the same format as the main text are included.

Back of the Book. Separate sections included at the "back of the book" are Bridges and Tunnels, Parades and Street Spectacles, and Outdoor Murals. Here are cited the statistics, designers, and locations for all the city's bridges and tunnels; the time and location of the many ethnic and other street festivals which you may wish to attend; and the name, location, and artist for the many public murals that have recently begun to adorn the unused walls of our city.

Most valuable to the serious explorer, whether on foot, by auto, or in the imagination, are the Glossary and Index. The Glossary is a tool to unlock those words that seem esoteric but in fact are shorthand in the language of architecture. The Index is useful not only in the sense of any index, but lists the collected New York works of individual architects and partnerships.

ACKNOWLEDGMENTS

Many people have contributed information, ideas, comments, corrections, and even moral support. Their contributions have ranged from substantial to trivial, but since this book is about both substance and trivia, both are recognized.

The most exceptional contributions have been from Christopher S. Gray, director of the Office for Metropolitan History, acknowledged here for work above and beyond the call of duty. His advice, research, and thoughtful ideas have made this a much better book.

Two others who have made more than substantial contributions are Margaret Latimer, who wrote the Necrology and made many other contributions, and George Salomon, whose continuing on-site research offered many valid corrections.

Lists of buildings and places suggested for inclusion were gratefully received from Dennis Steadman Francis, Larry Levine, Mason Martens, Elliott Nixon, and Jane Carolan.

Among others who contributed major ideas, comments, and corrections were William Alex, Eileen Guggenheim, Andrew Lachman, Robert T. Murphy, Philip Ressner, and John Tauranac.

In addition to all those listed above were legions of supporters who gave anything from a correction of punctuation to a suggestion for a new or corrected entry. We, whose names begin with *W* and are usually listed last, therefore list these supporters in reverse alphabetical order:

Linda Yowell, Marc Willensky, Diana Willensky, William White, Gordon White, Lloyd Westbrook, Robert A. Weinman, Robert C. Weinberg, William J. and Margaret C. Ward, Mrs. Harry R. Van Liew, Michael Strasser, Bayrd Still, Robert A.M. Stern, Rita Stein, Edward Steese, Mrs. P.M. Spanakos, Isaac Schneider, Susan Saybrooke, Virginia Rosen, David Rogoff, Joseph Roberto, Charles Reiss, George E. Pettingill, George P. Pavlos, Mrs. Eugene Pascal, Emma deLong Mills, Donald Loggins, Herbert Lippmann, Sarah Landau, Elfrieda Kraege, Stephen A. Kliment, Gwen Kley, Sydney Starr Keaveney, Lewis Kandel, Robert Kalish, Neil E. Johnson, Stephen Jacoby, Michael M.M. Harris, John Halborg, William Haasters, David L. Gold, Alfred M. Githens, Christine Farquhar, Art D'Lugoff, Anna Maria Dell'Aria, Fred del Pozzo, George R. Collins, Charlotte R. Cole, Giorgio Cavaglieri, Joan Capelin, Susan Braybrooke, Andrew Alpern, Kenneth Agnew.

We thank the staff of the New York City Landmarks Preservation Commission; the Avery Architectural Library of Columbia University; the Brooklyn Collection of the Brooklyn Public Library; the Art and Architecture Division, Map Division, and Local History and Genealogy Division of the Research Libraries of the New York Public Library.

We thank Amanda Vaill, Beth Rashbaum, Ilka Shore Cooper, Pat Buckley, Helen Mills, and Rusty Gutwillig of the Macmillan Publishing Company. Also Vera Schneider for indexing, Barbara Hohol for typing,

Jack Meserole for layout, and Publishing Synthesis Ltd. for map revisions.

We thank all those who have contributed photographs and drawings.

We thank those researchers, writers, designers, and mapmakers who participated in the first edition:

John Morris Dixon, Mina Hamilton, Sophia Duckworth and Henry Hope Reed, Ann Douglass, Roger Feinstein, Richard Dattner. Also Hope Asrelsky, Herb Lubalin, Fran Elfenbein, and Jerome Kuhl.

Special thanks to Andrew Weil for acting like John Garfield long after John Garfield took leave of us.

We thank Maximilian Otto Urbahn and Lathrop Douglass, presidents of the New York Chapter, American Institute of Architects, when the *Guide* was being first privately financed, and then publicly published. And also the chapter's executive directors, H. Dickson McKenna and George S. Lewis.

Organizations and agencies (and their representatives) who contributed photographs, plans, maps, and assisted in other ways include: the following New York City agencies: Department of General Services; Department of Public Works (C. Raymond Devine, William Rome); Parks, Recreation, and Cultural Affairs Administration (Arthur Baker); Department of Buildings (Cornelius Dennis); Fire Department (Community Relations Bureau); Economic Development Administration (George Ira Schulman); and these: the New York Convention and Visitors Bureau (Lois Elias); Housing Authority (Val Coleman, Max B. Schreiber); Transit Authority (Paul Katz); the Board of Higher Education, City University of New York (Henry Motarotti); the New York State Facilities Development Corporation (Lawrence O'Kane); the New York State University Construction Fund (Elwin Stevens); the New York State Urban Development Corporation (Josephine Fisher); Fordham University (William J. Dugan); Columbia University (Frederick H. Knubel); the Brooklyn Public Library (Elizabeth L. White, Marie Cimino Spina, Walter R. McGill); the New York Public Library (Carol Slintak); the Queens Borough Public Library (Davis Erhardt); the Bronx County Historical Society (Janet Butler); the Long Island Historical Society (John H. Lindenbusch, James P. Hurley); and College of Mount Saint Vincent (Sister David).

Between publication of the Revised Edition and its third printing we have received—but have not always been able to accommodate—comments, suggestions, and corrections from the following persons, listed in the order received:

Andrew Lachman, Margaret Latimer, John Tauranac, Joseph Merz, Christopher Gray, Gwen Kley, Bernard Kabak, Paul Goldberger, James Rossant, Erin Drake, Arthur Kortheuer, John Zukosky, Peter Obletz, Paul H. Bonner, Jr., Stephen F. Temmer, Anne E. Finelli, Ms. P. Sanecki, John Diele, Mitchell J. Paluszek, Walter E. Levi, Thomas E. Range, Woodlief Thomas, Jr., Mrs. George E. Dowling, Sidney Horenstein, L.J. Davis, Martin H. Levinson, Jerry Slaff, Ann George, Ernestine Bassman, Stephen Weinstein, Georgia O'Day, Helen Mills, James Kraft, Kevin Bone, Peter Switzer, Dorothy Globus, Peter Freiberg, Jean Wynn, G. Young, Marjorie Pearson, Ernest Ulmer, James M. Ross, Robert B. Snyder, Avis Berman, Vernon and Diana Gibberd, Christopher Forbes, Duncan Maginnis, Francis J. Murray, Mrs. Robert C. Carey, Laurence G. Dengler, Andrew Dolkart, Daniel Nydick, Ava Moncrief, Paul Fritz, R. Michael Brown, Natalie Bunting, Philip I. Danzig, Joseph N. Merola, Michael J. Byczek, Dina Dahbany-Miraglia, Emma Albert, John Margolis, John Pell Lombardi, Deborah Gardner, Ann Bedell, Adriana I. Kleiman, Holly Huckins, Charles Trenowske, Fred Ost, James D. Merritt, Patti Auerbach, Robert Sink, David Ment, Peter J. Bartucca, and Thomas J. Reese, S.J.

1

MANHATTAN

Borough of Manhattan/New York County

To most people, *Manhattan* is New York, a place to **"go to business,"** the *downtown of all downtowns*. This is where the **"action"** is, where money is earned, and, in large part, spent.

To non-New Yorkers, **Manhattan** is known in excerpts from the whole: **Fifth Avenue, Broadway, Greenwich Village, Wall Street,** the *caricatures* of the chic, of bright lights, of the off-beat, of big business; excerpts symbolic of the public power and influence of **Manhattan** as the capital of **banking, corporate headquartering,** the **theater, advertising, publishing, fashion, tourism,** and the **United Nations.** This passing parade of visitors mostly misses **Manhattan's** myriad local neighborhoods with handsome buildings and areas of visual delight. That there are distinguished architecture and urban design in **Harlem,** on the vast **Upper West Side,** or in the loft districts of the **Lower West Side** will startle and, we hope, pleasantly surprise those visitors who have savored only the well-publicized *monuments, musicals, and museums.*

A view of New Amsterdam in 1656. The church was built into the fort in 1642

L

LOWER MANHATTAN

THE FINANCIAL DISTRICT

The **Battery** signals the bottom of Manhattan to most New Yorkers, where tourists are borne by ferry to the **Statue of Liberty,** and "provincial" **Staten Islanders** start their homeward trek to that distant island that turns out to be, *surprisingly,* part of New York. The name for this namesake was a row of guns along the old shorefront line, now approximated by State Street between Bowling Green and Whitehall. During the **War of 1812,** the status of the gunnery was elevated, and **Castle Clinton,** erected on a pile of rock some 300 feet offshore, was known as **West Battery; Castle Williams,** on **Governors Island,** became **East Battery.** Intervening years have seen landfill entirely envelop **Castle Clinton** (*and its various transmogrifications*) forming **Battery Park,** a flat and somewhat confused

MANHATTAN

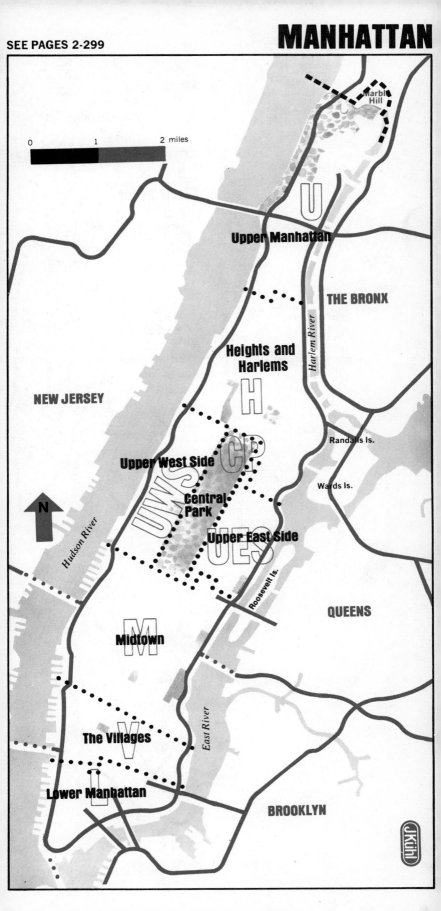

0 1 2 miles

Marble Hill

Upper Manhattan

U

THE BRONX

Heights and Harlems

H

NEW JERSEY

Harlem River

Randalls Is.

CP

Upper West Side

UWS

Central Park

Wards Is.

N

Upper East Side

UES

Hudson River

Roosevelt Is.

QUEENS

Midtown

M

V

The Villages

East River

L

Lower Manhattan

BROOKLYN

JKühl

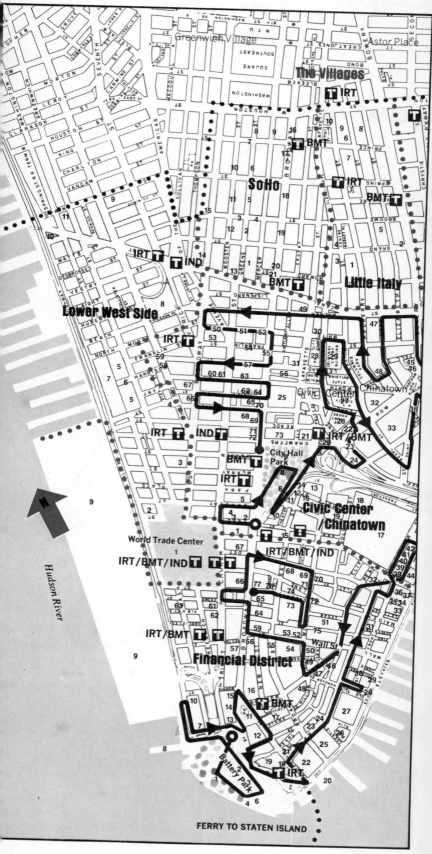

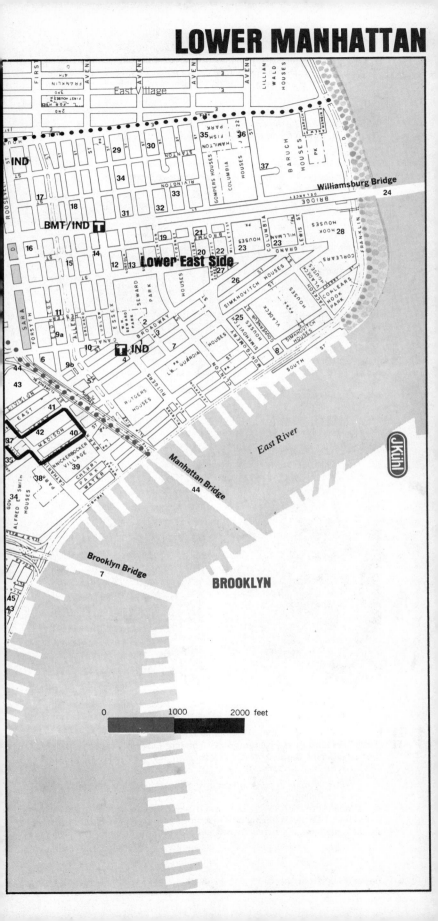

LOWER MANHATTAN

stretch of landscaping that provides greenery and delight to summer New Yorkers from nearby offices. A fresh, if sometimes pungent, breeze from the Upper Bay is an antidote for the doldrums or any bad mood aggravated by heat.

Lower Manhattan Walking Tour: From the **Battery** to **Liberty Street** and **Broadway.** (*IRT Lexington Avenue or Seventh Avenue locals to South Ferry station, or RR train to Whitehall Street.*)

[1.] Gun embrasures, Castle Clinton National Monument/originally W. Battery

[1.] Entrance Portal, Castle Clinton   **[3.]** East Coast Mem'l./Battery Park

[1.] Castle Clinton National Monument/formerly **New York Aquarium** (1896–1941)/formerly **Immigrant Landing Depot** (1855–1890)/ formerly **Castle Garden** (1823–1855)/originally **West Battery** (1807– 1811). John McComb, Jr. ★

Tooled by man to make a rockface brownstone. Until recently, one of the most vitally involved structures in the city's life and history. Built as an island fortification (West Battery—**it** never fired a shot in anger) to complement **Castle Williams** on Governor's Island, it was ceded to the city **12 years later.** As a civic monument it served for reception of distinguished visitors at the very edge of the nation (*General Lafayette, Kossuth, President Jackson, the Prince of Wales*). Remodeled as a concert hall and renamed **Castle Garden,** its moment of supreme glory was the much-ballyhooed **P. T. Barnum-**promoted concert of the **Swedish** soprano, **Jenny Lind,** in **1850.** Only five years later it was transformed once more, into the **Immigrant Landing Depot,** where some 7.7 million new Americans were processed; some into the **Union Army,** others into the **Lower East Side.** Scandal caused its closure and replacement by federal control at the **Barge Office** in **1890** and at **Ellis Island** in **1892.** Not one to be out of the center of action, it juggled its innards, changed its decor, and reentered the fray as the **Aquarium,** much-beloved grotto of **New Yorkers** until **1941.**

Then, apparently doomed by the cut and tunnel for the Battery Park underpass, it was rescued by loud civic noises. Belatedly, Congress dubbed it a *"National Historic Monument"* in **1946.** The aquarium was removed to a new group of buildings at **Coney Island,** perhaps to make the fish comfortable in sight of the sea.

In 1976 a new set of cylindrical piers supports a shingle roof within the remnant brownstone shell, a gutted building: a National Park Service tourist schmaltzification of a lusty place, **in the spirit of lesser restrospective Williamsburgian tourist fantasies.**

Staten Island Ferry, foot of **Whitehall Street** at **Battery Park,** not only ranks as a tourist mecca of great delight but explains the overall arrangement of the city quickly, clearly, and with pleasure. For a quarter you will experience one of the great short water voyages of the world, through the teeming harbor, past **Liberty** and **Ellis Islands,** the **Bayonne Navy Yard,** to the town of **St. George** at **Staten Island's** northeastern shore. If you decide to stay, turn to the **Staten Island section** of this guide. But for free, travel the route in reverse. This is the low-income substitute for a glamorous arrival in **New York** by transatlantic liner, receiving *Liberty*'s salute, and the romantic wedding cake silhouette of Lower Manhattan's skyline. On a lucky day you will surge though the wakes of freighters, tankers, ferries, pleasure craft, and the few extant liners used for cruises: even an occasional warship.

The Ferry Building on Manhattan ranks as the world's most banal portal to joy (*a public men's room en route to Mecca*). Kafka would have had the shivers: a disservice to the celebration of arrival and departure in **New York.**

[2.] Verrazano Memorial, Battery Park. 1909. Ettore Ximenes, sculptor.

A sworded lady guards the bronze-armored verdigris **Verrazano,** Florentine navigator who entered New York Bay in 1524. **Verrazano** was acting for **France** (*Francis I*).

[3.] East Coast Memorial, Battery Park. 1960. Gehron & Seltzer. Sculpture, 1963. Albino Manca.

Eight stolid sawn-granite monoliths (*steles*) with the rolls of those who died at sea off this coast in **World War II.**

[4.] Statue of Liberty Ferry, in Battery Park. BO 9-5755.

Every hour on the hour, year-round, between **9** and **5.** More frequently in summer; **$1.25** adults, children **50¢.** Total time **1** hour **45** minutes, including **1** hour on Liberty.

[5.] Statue of Liberty, Liberty Island/formerly **Bedloes Island,** across the Upper Bay. 1886. Frédéric Auguste Bartholdi, sculptor; Richard Morris Hunt, architect of the base; Gustave Eiffel, engineer.

Perhaps three times the height of the Colossus of Rhodes, which was one of the *"Seven Wonders of the World."* **Liberty** is considered corny these days, but corn is a necessary ingredient here. Like an old shoe to **New Yorkers,** she is always there, has worn and continues to wear well. Take the ferry out to her, ascend the spiral stairway through her innards to the crown, and you will look back on one of the romantic glories of the world: the **New York** skyline. She, up to her own thing, is meanwhile saluting the rising sun of **France.** Located in the base is the **American Museum of Immigration.** Telephone: **RE 2-1286.**

[6.] John Wolfe Ambrose Statue, rear of Staten Island Ferry ticket office, in Battery Park.

The ocean slot for deep-drafted ocean liners was **Ambrose's** channel (and the lightship that marked that channel entrance was named for him as well—now at the **South Street Seaport**).

[7.] Whitehall Building, 17 Battery Place, NE cor. West St. 1900. Henry J. Hardenbergh. Rear addition, 1910, Clinton & Russell.

The best views in **Manhattan** are from this venerable facade.

[8.] Pier A, West St. and Battery Place. 1885. ★

The clock tower at the pierhead memorializes the war dead of **World War I.** It peals ships bells at each half hour.

[9.] Battery Park City, Pier A to Chambers St. on fill between West St. and the Hudson River pierhead line.

The first two residential buildings of this huge fantasy are only foundations: **Harrison & Abramovitz,** architects, under construction **1977. Six million** square feet of future office mythology are advertised here.

[10.] Downtown Athletic Club and adjacent office building, 21 West St., SE cor. Morris St. 1926. Starrett & Van Vleck.

A chromatic range of salt-glazed tile, from burnt oranges to brown. This is the material of which **silos** are frequently made; a natural glaze, resistant to urban "fallout," without the crassness of the popular white-glazed brick of the **fifties** and **sixties.** The arcade with recessed ground floor is composed of corbeled arches, reminiscent of Moorish architecture. Corners are cantilevered, allowing corner windows naturally. An **Art Deco** delight.

[11.] Bowling Green, foot of Broadway; formalized, 1732. Fence 1771. ★ Reconstruction 1976. M. Paul Friedberg & Assocs., landscape architects.

This spot, as an extension of Battery Place (Marcktveldt or Market-field originally), was part of the Dutch cattle market (1638–1647). Then a "parade," it was later leased for the annual fee of one peppercorn, becoming a quasi-public bowling ground (or green) in 1732, for the "beauty and ornament of said streets as well as the recreation and delight of the inhabitants." The fence remaining today was erected in 1771, although its decorative crowns were knocked off by exuberant patriots after the reading of the Declaration of Independence on July 9, 1776. The more telling work of the same patriots was in the pulling down of the statue of **George III,** which was then melted into bullets to shoot *at* the British.

[12.] U.S. Custom House, Bowling Green, State, Whitehall and Bridge Sts. 1907. Cass Gilbert. ★

The *grandest* **Beaux Arts** building of **New York,** now re-loved by modernists searching for renewed meaning in architecture. The four monumental limestone sculptures by **Daniel Chester French** with associate Adolph A. Weinman—French's more famous work is the **Lincoln** of the **Lincoln Memorial,** Washington—are very much part of the architecture of the facade (left to right, **Asia, America, Europe, Africa**). Their whiteness against gray granite is a rich counterpoint of both form and color. **Asia** has a weed (maple tree) growing out of her right toe, **Buddha** in her lap. **America,** a sparrow on her head. **Africa** is sleepy and leaning on a Sphinx. **Europe** is regal, a shrouded figure to her rear.

The oval pavilion within was once a grand salon of bureaucracy—a flat domed space of public importance (1930s murals by **Reginald Marsh**). When the **Customs** vacated in favor of the **World Trade Center,** the challenge became how to make this building a viable participant in community and/or business affairs.

In the position a royal palace might assume in the 17th and 18th centuries, the **Custom House** replaced "Steamship Row," six town houses built as minor mansions and later used for shipping offices. These had earlier replaced the burnt and derelict **Government House,** first built (1790, **John McComb, Jr.**) for **George Washington's** presidency. When the capital was moved to **Philadelphia, Government House** served briefly as the governor's mansion until the state capital also moved, to **Albany. A Dutch,** then **English,** then **Dutch,** then **English,** then **American** fort occupied these same general premises under nine consecutive names, beginning as **Fort Amsterdam,** in **1626,** and ending as **Fort George** (*demolished 1790*). Fort George was the fort of which the **East** and **West Batteries** were outward defenses.

[13.] 1 Broadway, United States Lines Building/formerly **Washington Building,** NW cor. Battery Place at Bowling Green. 1921.

Site of **Kennedy House** (*1771–1882*), once revolutionary headquarters of **Washington** (*1776*), and later **General Howe,** during the **British** occupation.

[8.] Pier A's memorial clock tower   **[12.]** U. S. Custom House, New York

[10.] Downtown Athletic Club and adjacent offices: Art Deco from Paris, 1924

[14.] Bowling Green Offices, 11 Broadway at Bowling Green, W side. 1898. W. G. Audsley.

"**Eclectic**" was invented for confections such as this. The battered "**Egyptian**" pylons framing the entrance are bizarre imports. Above the third floor, however, the spirit changes: strong glazed-brick piers with articulated spandrels have much of the bold verticality of buildings of the "*Chicago School.*"

The Financial District: see map pp. 4–5   **9**

[15.] Cunard Building, 25 Broadway, SW cor. Morris St. 1921. Benjamin Wistar Morris.

This **"Renaissance"** facade, and its neighbors, handsomely surround **Bowling Green** with a high order of group architecture. What matter most at No. **25,** however, are its *great public interior spaces,* now, happily, being altered and preserved by the **Postal Service. Cunard,** the great British steamship company, sold its liners' tickets here **(Queen Mary,** and **Queen Elizabeths I and II).**

The elaborately decorated groined and domical vaults were designed by **Ezra Winter** and executed by imported Italian craftsmen; maps by **Barry Faulkner.**

[16.] 26 Broadway/formerly **Standard Oil Building,** NE cor. Beaver St. 1922. Carrère and Hastings; Shreve, Lamb & Blake.

The curve of this facade reinforces this street's group architecture, working particularly well with its eclectic friend, No. **25.** First **THE Standard Oil Building,** it served until that trust was broken up by federal antitrust action. Then the trust's child, **Socony** (later called **Socony Mobil,** then **Mobil**), lived here until it built its own new building on 42nd Street in **1956** [Turtle Bay/United Nations 3.].

The tower is squared to the grid of the city to the north, rather than to any geometry of the base of local streets. The architects were concerned with it as a skyline element, not a local form, and hence coordinated it with skyline neighbors.

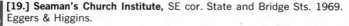

[20.] The Battery Maritime Building   [22.] 1 New York Plaza (office bldg.)

[17.] 2 Broadway, bet. Beaver and Stone Sts. 1959. Emery Roth & Sons.

The great Romanesque Revival **Produce Exchange** by **George G. Post** stood here from **1884** to **1957:** *a miniature extant remembrance is the Long Island Historical Society:* [WC Brooklyn/Brooklyn Heights 28.].

[18.] Rectory of the Shrine of Saint Elizabeth Seton/originally **James Watson House,** 7 State St. bet. Pearl and Whitehall Sts. NE side. 1793–1806. Attributed to John McComb, Jr. ★ Restorations and additions, 1965. Shanley & Sturges.

A single survivor of the first great era of mansions, this facade is original. It is Federal both in the archeological and political senses: it was built in the fourth year of George Washington's presidency of the federal Republic in a style that is separately considered Federal. Slender, elegant, freestanding Ionic columns and delicate late-Georgian detailing.

Mother Seton was canonized as America's first saint in 1975.

[19.] Seaman's Church Institute, SE cor. State and Bridge Sts. 1969. Eggers & Higgins.

A picturesque, plastic, romantic replacement of its antecedent at **Coenties Slip** *(1907–1960).* A public restaurant and exhibits are within. Note the bells in the stair hall. The original institute was a wood **Gothic Revival** chapel on a barge, moored to the **Pike Street** waterfront **(Floating Church of the Saviour).**

"Whitehall," at 1 State Street, NW cor. Whitehall Street (ca. 1657), was **Peter Stuyvesant's** mansion. Renamed **Whitehall** by the first English governor, it occupied a tiny peninsula projecting from the east end of the Battery at this point. One hundred years later **Robert Fulton** was a resident in a different building on the same site.

[20.] Battery Maritime Building (old South Ferry slips), 11 South St., foot of Whitehall St. 1906. ★ Walker & Gillette.

The false front on these aging ferry slips shows a raised porch with 40-foot columns to **Whitehall.** Green paint over sheet metal and steel structural members simulates verdigris copper. The **Governors Island ferry** leaves from here. The only historical style which this inherits *is the very idea* of a colonnade; the columns, however, are original, and relate to the material, sheet metal. Note the **Guastavino** tile soffits under the porch roof.

[21.] U.S. Army Building, 39 Whitehall St. bet. Water and Pearl Sts. ca. 1886.

Victorian brick "fort" with rockface granite; a poor representative of its time, but all that's left locally. It's a hollow doughnut, like the Guggenheim Museum, but rectangular and with flat floors.

[22.] One New York Plaza, Water, Whitehall, South and Broad Sts. 1969. William Lescaze & Assocs.

A behemoth. A thousand interior decorators' picture frames form an unhappy facade for this office building.

Broad Street, ca. 1695: Before it was so named, this was the **Heere Gracht,** a drainage and shipping canal reaching present day **Exchange Place,** where a ferry to Long Island docked. The canal was filled 100 years before the Revolution, but its effect remains in the extraordinary (*for this part of town*) width of the street. The oldest streets of **Manhattan** cross **Broad:** *Bridge* Street, for example, was at the first bridge immediately adjacent to the waterfront at **Pearl.** *Pearl* should be **Mother-of-Pearl,** in fact, for the glistening shells that lined its shores. *Stone* Street was the first to be cobbled. The geometry of public space has not greatly changed, except that **Broad's** meeting with the shoreline is some **600** feet further into the harbor than at the time of the canal's fill, making **Water, Front,** and **South** Streets on man-made land of later date.

[23.] Fraunces Tavern, 54 Pearl St. SE cor. Broad St. 1907. William Mersereau. ★

The tavern of **Samuel Fraunces** occupied this plot and achieved great historic note in the **Revolution:** *for ten days in 1783* it was the last residence of **Washington** as a general. On **December 4** he bade farewell to his officers and withdrew to his estate at **Mount Vernon, Virginia.** He returned six years later and five blocks away to take office as President at old **City Hall,** on Wall Street, by then rebuilt and renamed **Federal Hall.**

The present building is a *highly conjectural* construction (not restoration) based on typical buildings of "the period," parts of remaining walls, and guesswork. With enthusiasm more harmless when attached to genealogy than to wishful archeology, the tavern has been billed as the *real McCoy.* Such charades have caused *"George Washington Slept Here"* architecture to strangle reality in much of suburban **America.**

[24.] 62 Pearl Street, bet. Broad St. and Coenties Slip. 1827.

Here is an architectural workhorse, used and still useable as a loft building, a *valid remnant* of its period; more real than its conjectural neighbor, **Fraunces Tavern.**

The Dutch Stadt Huys, seat of colonial government, stood on the north side of **Pearl St.** (*No. 71*) between **Broad Street** and **Coenties Alley.** During explorations for foundations for a proposed but unbuilt office building on this site, archeologists excavated the foundations, reclaiming many colonial artifacts. Here the old shoreline was so close that tides at times lapped against the **Stadt Huys** steps.

[25.] Four New York Plaza, Water St., bet. Broad St. and Coenties Slip. 1968. Carson, Lundin & Shaw.

A bulky brick brown **"fort"** housing the back office, computer-supported activities for the **Manufacturers Hanover Trust.** A carven monolith.

[26.] Jeannette Park, in Coenties Slip bet. Water and South Sts. 1972. M. Paul Friedberg.

Complicated plaza, bollarded, stepped, stylish, and fussy. Why do we need all the stops pulled out, rather than the serenity, say, of the **Campo** in **Siena?** The prior park here in residence was named for the Arctic sailing ship, *The Jeannette.*

Coenties Slip: As the fill crept seaward, this "slip," a tiny artificial bay for wharfing ships, was created with a diagonal breakwater paralleling the present west boundary. Eventually the breakwater was absorbed as land projected even beyond its former tip.

[25.] Four New York Plaza, a brown brick "fort" for the bank's back offices

[27.] 55 Water Street, bet. Coenties and Old Slips, 1972. Emery Roth & Sons. M. Paul Friedberg, landscape architect.

Parent to **Jeannette Park,** it financed that glory in return for status as the largest private office building in the world (through zoning modifications allowing bonuses because of the contributed park). Escalate from street to an elevated plaza and the downtown branch of the Whitney Museum. *Telephone: 483-0011.*

[28.] First Precinct Station House, N.Y.C. Police Department, bet. South, Old Slip, and Water Sts. 1909. Richard Howland Hunt & Joseph Howland Hunt.

A rusticated **Renaissance** Revival *palazzo!*

[29.] U.S. Assay Building, bet. Old Slip, Front and South Sts. 1930. James A. Wetmore, Acting Supervising Architect, U.S. Treasury.

Its "behind" is what impresses us today: a massively sculptural granite monolith. The front is fussy.

[30.] 77 Water Street, bet. Old Slip, Gouverneur Lane, and Front St. 1970. Emery Roth & Sons. Arcade and roofscape, Corchia-de Harak Assocs., designers.

A simple, sleek, workmanlike building that delivers class and economic success simultaneously. The pools and bridges below give a bit of *eccentric pedestrianism* to the neighborhood: a television-inspired candy store is a theatrical touch.

[31.] 88 Pine Street, bet. Water and Front Sts. N side. 1973. I. M. Pei & Assocs.

A white, crisp elegance of aluminum and glass (*no mullions:* the butted glass fills whole structural bays). The classiest new building in **Lower Manhattan.**

[32.] 127 John Street, NW cor. Water St. 1969. Emery Roth & Sons. Lobby and plaza, Corchia-de Harak Assocs., designers.

No-nonsense building with a **happy-nonsense-**filled lobby and sidewalk. Outside, pipe and canvas structures play with light and shelter pedestrians. Inside, a neon tunnel and other extravaganzas titillate the visitor. An adjacent electric display clock is a building in its own right.

[27.] 55 Water Street (office bldg.)   **[28.]** First Precinct Station House

[29.] United States Assay Building   **[31.]** 88 Pine Street (office bldg.)

[32a.] Excelsior Power Company, 33–43 Gold St., bet. Fulton and John Sts. N side. 1888. William G. Grinnell.

Coal-fired electricity generators once occupied this lusty Renaissance Revival brick monolith.

[33.] Baker, Carver & Morrell/formerly **Hickson W. Field Building,** 170–176 John Street, bet. Front and South Sts. W. side. 1840 ★

An austere granite facade, rare in **New York** in that era, gives a dour face to the street.

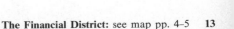

[34.] Baltimore Copper Paint Company/formerly **A. A. Low and Brothers,** 167–171 John St., bet. Front and South Sts. E. side. 1850.

China traders with China clippers parked across the street. **Merchant Abiel** (brother of sometime Mayor and Columbia University President Seth) lived only a ferryboat ride away at **2 Pierrepont Place,** Brooklyn [see WC Brooklyn/Brooklyn Heights 18.]. There is granite under that stucco.

[35.] 159–165 John Street, NE cor. Front St. 1811–1840.

[36.] 181–189 Front Street, 1836. Alterations as late as 1917. **191–193 Front Street,** 1793–1870.

From two to five stories with various transmogrifications.

[37.] Schermerhorn Row, 2–18 Fulton St., 195–197 Front St., 91–92 South St. 1811–1812. ★

Peter Schermerhorn filled the land on these, his "water lots," to a point **600** feet out from the original shoreline. Served by these buildings, among many others, **South Street** was lined with ships, parked bowsprit in, oversailing the wheeled and pedestrian traffic below. (The line of the bulkhead was approximately the line of the west or inner row of columns supporting the vehicular viaduct.)

These were **Georgian-Federal** ware- and countinghouses, with high-pitched, loft-enclosing roofs, built as an investment by the Schermerhorn family. No storefronts at first: an arched business entry of brownstone, quoined, and a double-hung window for light, now show. Later **Greek Revival** and **cast-iron** shopfronts brought a merchandising cast to serve the great crowds brought by the **Fulton ferry,** starting in 1814.

Don't miss the South Street Seaport Museum at 16 Fulton and the Museum Book and Chart Shop across the street at No. 25. Museum Telephone: 766-9020.

The South Street Seaport Museum, developed under the leadership of **Peter Stanford,** has masterplanned the restoration of these precincts to their early 19-century glories and has collected great ships that are now moored at the **South Street Seaport** piers, projecting into the river at the foot of Fulton Street. Floating architecture here is honored by the **Peking** *(1911. Steel bathtub of a square-rigger: bathtub to keep the water out rather than in);* the old humanoid **Ambrose Light Ship** *(1908. Its successor is electronic.);* the **Lettie G. Howard** *(1893), a venerable oysterman; and others.* **Bring children.** The cast is in a state of flux.

[38.] 207–211 Water Street. 1836.

Greek Revival warehouses. The **South Street Seaport Museum Model Shop** is at **207.** A reincarnated **19th**-century printer, **Bowne & Co.,** at **211.**

[39.] 213–215 Water Street. 1868.

Cast iron below, cut stone above.

[40.] 243 Water Street/formerly **Schermerhorn Ship Chandlery,** 1799. Alterations through 1912.

[41.] 251 Water Street, SE cor. Peck Slip. 1888. Carl F. Eisenach.

Romanesque Revival terra cotta and brick: its keystones bear faces surveying the street.

[42.] Former **Joseph Rose House and Shop,** 273 Water St. 1773.

Modeled, remodeled, and moss-covered remnant, the third-oldest building on Manhattan Island.

[43.] 211 Front Street, NE cor. Beekman St. 1885. George B. Post.

A cornice of cockleshells, tierods with starfish rather than stars, and keystones with fish in bas-relief are the seafood motifs supplied by Post, better known for the New York Stock Exchange, the Long Island Historical Society, and City College.

[44.] 203 Front Street. 1816. Remodeled 1883. Theobald Engelhardt.

The South Street Seaport Museum offices are upstairs, the Museum Ship Chandlery below. After 1883 it was William Wainwright's Hotel.

[45.] Meyers' Hotel, 116–119 South St. SW cor. Peck Slip. 1873. John B. Snook.

Elegant, ornate Victoriana. Still a hotel and bar.

[46.] European-American Bank/formerly **Franklin National Bank,** 132 Pearl St. at Hanover Sq. 1962. Eggers & Higgins.

The client called for "Georgian." The result is an awkward, inflated place; the real Georges, lacking elevators, built two- and three-story buildings.

[34.] Baltimore Copper Paint Co.   **[47.]** India House (a private club)

Peking, a square-rigged steel "bathtub" to keep the water out rather than in

Hanover Square was the original printing house square. At **81 Pearl, William Bradford** established the first printing press in the **Colonies** in **1693.** The *Great Fire of 1835* substantially destroyed all buildings in an area of which this square was the center: the area between **Coenties Slip, Broad, Wall,** and **South Streets,** excepting the row facing **Broad,** and those facing **Wall** between **William** and **Broad.**

[47.] India House/originally **Hanover Bank, N.Y. Cotton Exchange, and W. R. Grace and Co.,** 1 Hanover Sq. bet. Pearl and Stone Sts. 1851–1854. Richard J. Carman, carpenter.

Florentine "palazzo," typical of many brownstone commercial buildings that once dotted this area, now replaced by newer and denser construction. The style is so associated with the New York brownstone *row house* that we almost do a double take on seeing it clothing a **Wall Street** building. Now a club, it harbors a maritime museum. Handsome stripped-Corinthian columns. **Carman,** the carpenter (as he oddly listed himself in the City Directory), was later responsible for **Carmanville,** a village located at the present location of **Columbia University.**

Stone Street, between Hanover Square and Broad Street, ca. 1657: paved with cobbles, the name changed from Brouwer to Stone Street in a society that was naively and happily literal. Its curve merely reflects the profile of the original shoreline.

[48.] Delmonico's (the restaurant)   [50.] Originally Merchants' Exchange

[48.] Delmonico's Restaurant/now **Oscar's Delmonico,** 56 Beaver St. at William St. 1891. James Brown Lord.

Occupying, like the **Flatiron Building,** the valuable but awkward triangular space left between two converging streets. A distinguished restaurant for a century and a half, **Lord** designed this palatial headquarters at the height of **Delmonico's** prestige and popularity. Try to remember another **New York** restaurant (without hotel) which is more than the outfitting of commercial "store space." Orange terra cotta and brick, suitably flanked across the street (at 1 William) by the palace of **Lehman Brothers (Francis Kimball** and **Julian Levi).** The portal behind **Delmonico's** porch is *reputed* to have been brought from Pompeii by the **Delmonico brothers.**

[49.] Canadian Imperial Bank of Commerce/formerly **First National City Trust Co.**/originally the **City Bank Farmers' Trust Co.,** 22 William St. bet. Beaver St. and Exchange Place. 1931. Cross & Cross.

A slender **57**-story tower of limestone, from the awkward period of architectural history between buildings-as-columns and steel cage construction. *Art Moderne vs. the neo-Renaissance.*

Wall Street: The Dutch **wall** of **1653** (a palisade of wood palings) was built as protection against attack from **English** colonies to the north. The **English** took it down, but the name remains.

[50.] Citibank/formerly **First National City Bank**/lower portion formerly the **Custom House** (1863–1899)/originally the **Merchants' Exchange,** 55 Wall St. bet. William and Hanover Sts. 1836–1842. Isaiah Rogers. Remodeled and doubled in height, 1907. McKim, Mead & White ★

Smoked granite. After the destruction of the **first Merchants' Exchange** in the *Great Fire of 1835,* **Rogers** erected a three-storied **Ionic** "temple" with a central domed trading hall on the same site. Later used as the **Custom House,** it was remodeled in 1907 (after the Fed's removal to Bowling Green) as the head office of the **National City Bank:** another tier of columns, this time **Corinthian,** was superimposed to double the cubic content.

[51.] 60 Wall Tower, 70 Pine St. bet. Pearl and Cedar Sts. N. side. 1932. Clinton & Russell.

Addressmanship at its most blatant: the tail on **Wall** used to wag the body on Pine, and now a parking lot has replaced **60 Wall.** This is a skyline building, with a **"Gothic"** crown only to be appreciated as part of the skyline from a great distance or from a neighboring eyrie.

[52.] 40 Wall Street/originally **Bank of the Manhattan Company,** bet. William and Nassau Sts. 1929. H. Craig Severance and Yasuo Matsui. Ground floor remodeled, 1963. Carson, Lundin & Shaw.

Another skyline bank building, now best observed from an upper floor of the composite bank to which it has moved its quarters: the **Chase Manhattan** on Chase Manhattan Plaza to the north. The pyramidal crown was the strong and simple symbol of the original bank. Chartered originally (i.e., **The Manhattan Company**) as a water company and the first quasi-public utility, it became redundant in **1842** when the **Croton Reservoir** system began to feed **Manhattan** with water. Always permitted by a clause in its charter to engage in banking, it continued, after **1842,** solely as the *Bank* of the Manhattan Company, the latter, parent, organization becoming incidental to its offshoot.

[53.] Federal Hall National Memorial (Washington took the oath near this site)

[53.] Federal Hall National Memorial/formerly **Subtreasury Building,** 1862–1925/originally **Custom House,** 1842–1862, 28 Wall St. NE cor. Nassau St. 1834–1842. Town & Davis, with John Frazee and Samuel Thompson. ★

A **Doric-**columned temple, this, and Staten Island's **Sailors' Snug Harbor** are the stars of New York's **Greek Revival.** The **Wall Street** facade is a simplified **Parthenon,** without the sculptured frieze or pediment. Carved from marble quarried in Westchester County, it is raised on a high base to handle the change in grade from **Pine** to **Wall.** Inside is a very non-Greek rotunda, *the principal, and startling, space,* analogous to finding a cubical body in a conch shell. Pale blue paint and gilt are, perhaps, archeologically correct within. If so, those **revived Greeks** had garish bad taste in paint.

The old **Assay Office** (*Martin Thompson, 1824*) was next door to the east until the building's demolition to make room for bigger things; its facade was rescued and installed at the **Metropolitan Museum's American Wing.**

The current name, **Federal Hall National Memorial,** commemorates the building on the same site in which **Washington** took the oath of office as president. It had been remodeled by **Pierre L'Enfant** from the shell of the **old City Hall** to which local government had been removed in **1701** from the Dutch **Stadt Huys** on **Pearl Street.**

J(ohn) Q(uincy) A(dams) Ward's statue of **Washington** (*1883*) stands on the approximate spot where the man himself took the oath, in 1789.

[54.] Morgan Guaranty Trust Company/formerly **J. P. Morgan & Co.**, 23 Wall St. SE cor. Broad St. 1913. Trowbridge & Livingston. ★

Interesting more for its contents than its architectural envelope: **J. Pierpont Morgan** epitomized Wall Street to *capitalists, communists, radicals,* and *conservatives* alike. And, of course, when **Wall Street** was to be bombed, this was considered its sensitive center of control: on **September 16, 1920,** an anarchist ignited a wagonload of explosives next to the **Wall Street** flank. **33** persons were killed, **400** injured. The scars are still visible in the stonework.

[55.] New York Stock Exchange, 8 Broad St. bet. Wall St. and Exchange Place. 1903. George B. Post. Addition, 1923. Trowbridge & Livingston. Pediment sculpture, J. Q. A. Ward and Paul Bartlett.

One of the few great architectural spaces *accessible* to the public in this city. Guided tours are available to the galleries.

The original **Roman** temple facade by **Post** is a far cry from his **Queen Anne style Long Island Historical Society** *27* years before. [see WC Brooklyn/Brooklyn Heights 28.]. The **Columbian Exposition** of **1893** had swept such earth-colored picturesque architecture under the rug. The rage for **neo-Classical** architecture and cities was compelling even to those who had been the *Goths of architecture.* The original mythological figures of the pediment became so deteriorated that their stone was replaced with sheet metal, secretively, so that the public would not know that any facet of the Stock Exchange was vulnerable.

[56.] Irving Trust Company, 1 Wall St. SE cor. Broadway. 1932. Voorhees, Gmelin & Walker. Addition, 1965, Smith, Smith, Haines, Lundberg & Waehler.

Ralph Walker's experiments with the *plastic molding* of skyscraper form, both in massing and detail, include this one example in limestone, and three in brick: two for the **Telephone Company** (*140 West Street and 32 Sixth Avenue*), and one for **Western Union** (*60 Hudson Street*).

[57.] Empire Building, 71 Broadway, 1894. Renwick, Aspinwall & Tucker.

An ornate wall, backdrop to **Trinity Churchyard.**

[58.] Trinity Church, Broadway at the head of Wall St. 1846. Richard Upjohn. ★ **William Backhouse Astor Memorial Altar and Reredos,** 1876. Frederick Clarke Withers. **Chapel of All Saints,** 1913, Thomas Nash. **Bishop Manning Memorial Wing,** 1965. Adams and Woodbridge. **Churchyard.** 1681–now.

The attached chapel must not be confused with **Trinity's** *colonial* chapels, which were, in fact, separate and remotely located church buildings serving this immense **Episcopal** parish. Typical of the latter is **St. Paul's Chapel** at **Fulton** and **Broadway.** The parish is an *enormous* landowner (Fulton to Christopher Streets, Broadway west to the river was its original grant from Queen Anne, 1705). Thus, the proselytizing of the faith through missionary activities could be financed comfortably (**St. Augustine's** and **St. Christopher's Chapels** on the Lower East Side are further examples).

Nestled in the canyons of **Broadway** and **Trinity Place,** its tiny form is totally comprehensible to the pedestrian: on the axis of **Wall Street** the canyon walls read as surfaces, while **Trinity** sits importantly, an anthracite jewel, bedded in a green baize cemetery. The cemetery offers a green retreat for summer-tired office workers at noontime. Bronze doors designed by **Richard Morris Hunt** were executed by **Charles Niehaus, Karl Bitter,** and **J. Massey Rhind.** (*Left entrance, main entrance, and right entrance, respectively.*)

Cemetery monuments of particular note include the *pyramid* of **Alexander Hamilton, Robert Fulton's** bronze bas-relief, and that of **William Bradford.**

The original **Trinity** Church was founded in **1696,** erected **1698,** enlarged and "beautified" **1737,** burned to the ground **1776;** second building constructed **1788–1790,** demolished **1839.**

[59.] Bank of Tokyo/formerly **American Surety Company,** 100 Broadway, SE cor. Pine St. 1895. Bruce Price. Alterations, 1975, Kajima International.

Kajima, through designer **Nobutaka Ashihara,** has recycled Price's *"rusticated pillar"* into modern and economic elegance. The Italians excelled at this in the 1950s (as at the **Sforza Palace** in Milan, converted to a museum); the Japanese now equal the Italian best in New York.

The ladies above, by sculptor **J. Massey Rhind,** are a stern Athenian octet.

[56.] Irving Trust & Trinity Church   **[58.]** Trinity Church at Wall Street

[59.] Price's "rusticated pillar" recycled into modern economic elegance

[60.] Trinity and U.S. Realty Buildings, 111 and 115 Broadway, at Thames St. W. side. 1906. Francis H. Kimball.

Rich buildings, from top to bottom, their narrow ends at **Broadway** are broken **Gothic** forms with strongly scaled details. They have a great deal of personality vis-à-vis the passing pedestrian. Unlike the blank austerity of **1 Wall,** the temple entrance of **100 Broadway,** or the modern openness of **Chase Manhattan's** vast transparent lobby for bureaucrats en masse, these are buildings for individual people. One could feel possessive about them. **Bully.**

[61.] Nichols Hall, N.Y.U. Graduate School of Business Administration, 100 Trinity Place bet. Thames and Cedar Sts. W side. 1959. Skidmore, Owings & Merrill.

Stylish in **1959,** Nichols has, in retrospect, become a dull, white-speckled brick ancestor to **Merrill** (below).

[62.] Charles E. Merrill Hall, N.Y.U. Graduate School of Business Administration, SW cor. Church and Thames Sts. 1975. Skidmore, Owings & Merrill.

An *off-black* monolith incised for strip windows. A classic background modern monument.

[63.] 90 West Street, bet. Albany and Cedar Sts. 1905. Cass Gilbert.

Limestone and cast terra cotta. increasingly interesting and complex the *higher you raise your eyes:* designed for a view from the harbor, or the eyries of an adjacent skyscraper, rather than the ordinary **West Street** pedestrian. A similar, but less successful, use of terra cotta than **Gilbert's** spectacular **Woolworth Building.**

[62.] Charles E. Merrill Hall, N.Y.U.   **[63.]** 90 West Street (office bldg.)

[64.] The Equitable Building, a behemoth that triggered the 1916 zoning law

[64.] Equitable Building, 120 Broadway bet. Pine and Cedar Sts. 1915. Ernest R. Graham (of Graham, Anderson, Probst and White, successors to D. H. Burnham).

This is more famous for what it caused than what it is. An immense volume, it exploited the site as no building had before: **1,200,000** square feet on a plot of just under an acre, or a floor area of almost **30** times the site's area. The hue and cry after **Equitable's** completion led to the adoption of the first zoning resolution, in **1916,** which permitted, a maximum floor area of **12** times the site's area, with all special bonuses. (**Chicago,** however, still achieves **30** times the area on occasion, and with architectural *style!*)

[65.] Marine Midland Bank, 140 Broadway, E. side bet. Liberty and Cedar Sts., Broadway and Nassau St. 1967. Skidmore. Owings & Merrill.

A taut skin stretched over bare bones. The sleek and visually flush facade is in melodramatic contrast to the ornamented environment surrounding it. Matteness of black spandrels breaks up the reflections of the neighbors into more random, mysterious parts. The plaza at Broadway is a perfect size to have a major impact on the feel of this neighborhood. (The same architects' Chase Manhattan Plaza next door on Pine suffers from an amorphous shape, and a separation by elevation from the street life around it, except at the Nassau Street end.)

The sculpture on the plaza's lap at **Broadway** is a teetering vermilion cube (by **Isamu Noguchi**) gored by a cylindrical punch.

[66.] A gloomy cadaverous hulk replaces Ernest Flagg's great Singer Building

[66.] 1 Liberty Plaza, Broadway, Liberty, Maiden Lane, and Church Sts. 1974. Skidmore, Owings & Merrill.

A gloomy, articulate, cadaverous extravaganza of steel: handsome and somber as the renaissance of Florence. It replaces the great **Singer Building** (*1908–1970*) by **Ernest Flagg,** an eclectic palace-tower, and the tallest building ever to be demolished. The *actual* structural steel of 1 Liberty is exposed (*i.e., the webs, or vertical faces, of the beams*).

Bollards and chains surround the low, depressed basement that seems designed, consciously, to crush the passer and enterer (compare the great **Fosse Ardeatine** monument in **Rome**). A hovering hulk.

Across **Liberty Street** to the south is a plaza dedicated to the public, part of the zoning calculations, which allowed the developers (U.S. Steel) to add bulk to their behemoth. The plaza links, in a chain, that of **140 Broadway** to the **Chase Manhattan Plaza** to the east, and to the **World Trade Center** to the west.

[67.] American Telephone and Telegraph Building, 195 Broadway bet. Dey and Fulton Sts. W side. 1917. William Welles Bosworth.

The *layer cake* of **New York:** eight **Ionic** colonnades (embracing three stories within each set) are stacked on a **Doric** order. All is surmounted by the famous telephone company symbol: **Spirit of Communication,** by **Evelyn Longman.** Handsome parts are assembled into a bizarre whole: more columns than any stone facade in the world. The columns within the enormous public lobby continue the record setting.

[68.] Annex, Federal Reserve Bank, Nassau St. bet. Maiden Lane and John St. E. side. 1978. Roche, Dinkeloo & Assocs.

Twenty-four stories of bank facilities will hover over a plaza, supported by four great **13**-story-high steel columns. The skin will, like graph paper, be without scale, an abstract envelope.

[69.] John Street United Methodist Church, 44 John St., bet. Nassau and William Sts. 1840–1841. ★

The first church in **America** of the **Irish Wesleyans** was here in **1766,** later replaced by this building. The congregation is, therefore, the *oldest* **Methodist Society** in **America.**

Nassau Street Shopping Area: From **Maiden Lane** to **Beekman Street, Nassau** serves as a most active local shopping strip: medium- to modest-priced chain stores, discount houses, and small, specialized shops. Panty-hose, radio equipment, dresses, shoes, all of the *personal and portable items* that a noontime lunch-shopper would be most inclined to inspect and purchase. The ground-floor activity and clutter of show windows and signs keep the eye at street level. The form and detail of buildings above, no matter how tall, is rarely noticed, amost never observed. *Closed to vehicles midday to fulfill its pedestrianism.*

[70.] 100 William Street, SE cor. John St. 1973. Davis, Brody & Assocs.

Green schist (split from natural geological strata) slate. A diagonal gallery slashes the form with a four-story, stepped street-volume: a *humanist* place, rich, natural, and elegant.

[71.] Home Insurance Company, 59 Maiden Lane, NW cor. William St. 1966. Office of Alfred Easton Poor.

A small plaza again shows that public space contained by buildings can *benefit from being small;* increasing the size would diminish rather than enhance its quality. The back of the **Federal Reserve** forms a foil and wall for this space.

The **H. V. Smith Museum** occupies the **15th** floor and has the nation's most complete collection of equipment, art, and history of fire fighting and fire insurance (*open to the public—telephone: 530-7051*).

[72.] 90 Maiden Lane, bet. William and Pearl Sts. 1865.

A cast-iron remnant.

[73.] Chase Manhattan Bank and Plaza, 1 Chase Manhattan Plaza, bet. Nassau and William, Liberty and Pine Sts. 1960. Skidmore, Owings & Merrill.

David Rockefeller and his fellow board members, through their act of faith in building this Gargantua, here cried *"Excelsior,"* and the flagging spirit of the **Financial District** took courage. Architecturally less successful than the newer and more sophisticated **Marine Midland** by the same firm, it provides, however, the first gratuitous plaza hereabouts. Many have appeared since: the **Home Insurance Company, Marine Midland, Liberty Plaza, the World Trade Center,** and so forth.

A sheer **800** feet of aluminum and glass rises from the paved plaza surface, which is accessible from both **Nassau** and **Pine Streets.** The topography unfortunately forces the **Liberty** and **William Street** sides down, detaching them from participation in the plaza's space.

A sunken circular courtyard is paved with undulating forms of granite blocks, crowned with sculpture, and caressed in summer by a fountain and pools: all by sculptor **Isamu Noguchi.** Goldfish were resident at first, but the urban fallout and sentimentalists' *"coins in the fountain"* destroyed even those resilient carp.

The **Dubuffet** (sculpture), on the axis of **Cedar Street,** looks papier mâché, but isn't: it gives out a *temporary, expendable* feeling.

[74.] Federal Reserve Bank of New York, 33 Liberty St. bet. William and Nassau Sts., Liberty St. and Maiden Lane. 1924. York & Sawyer. Samuel Yellin, ironworker. ★

A **Florentine** "palazzo" conserves within its dungeons more money than **Fort Knox.** This is a great neo-Renaissance building of rusticated

Indiana limestone, Ohio sandstone, and elegant ironwork. A *bank for banks,* this is the great stabilizer and equalizer of their separately erratic activities. Nations have rooms in the five levels below the street, where their gold is stored, and moved, in the balance of trade, from nation to nation, without ever leaving the building. (*Free tours available by appointment.*) Telephone: 791-6130.

The stony south wall, on **Liberty Street,** is a magnificent foil to the crystalline glass and aluminum of the Chase Manhattan Bank. We hope that the **Federal Reserve** will live forever. (Florence, not having the luxury of *15th-century elevators,* couldn't imagine such large-scaled grandeur!)

[73.] Chase Manhattan Bank and Plaza   **[74.]** Federal Reserve Bank of N.Y.

[73.] Chase Manhattan Executive suite views **[52.]** 40 Wall Street tower

[75.] Down Town Association, 60 Pine St. bet. William and Pearl Sts. N side. 1887. Charles C. Haight.

Anonymous, understated, this *appropriately somber* club serves many distinguished financial executives. principally for lunch.

[76.] Liberty Tower, 55 Liberty St. NE cor. Nassau St. 1909. Henry Ives Cobb.

Glorious terra cotta, similar to **Cass Gilbert's** gothicized **90 West Street,** over limestone as high as a person can reach.

[77.] Chamber of Commerce of the State of New York, 65 Liberty St. NW cor. Liberty Place 1901. James B. Baker. ★

Rich, ornate **Beaux Arts;** a minor palace of imposing scale and rich detail. Rusticated, **Ionic** columns, mansard roof, oval porthole windows.

End of Tour. Nearest subway at either Wall Street or Fulton Street and Broadway (IRT Lexington Avenue Line) or at Fulton Street for IND Eighth Avenue Line, IRT Seventh Avenue Line.

[77.] N.Y. State Chamber of Commerce

[1.] World Trade Center, looking east

The Full Stomach

Sweet's Restaurant, 2 Fulton St. at South St. WH 2-9628. A la carte. Closed weekends, holidays, and the first two weeks of July.

For those Latins or Russians who cannot bear to dine before 10, this must be stricken from the list. *Sweet's refuses admission after 8 P.M.* At the foot of **Schermerhorn Row** [see 37.], this venerable seafood restaurant (est. **1845** as a "refectory") occupies an even more venerable **1811** building.

Fraunces Tavern, 54 Pearl St. SE cor. Broad St. BO 9-0144. 12–9 P.M. weekdays only. [For the building, see 23.]

Not fascinating gastronomically, but the competition is limited. This is the cuisine of the American suburban roadhouse: steak, roast beef, scampi.

Oscar's Delmonico, 56 Beaver St. at S. William St. BO 9-1180. 11:45 A.M.–10:15 P.M. Closed weekends and holidays.

This, the downtown restaurant of the **Delmonico** family, has served, in two guises and two buildings, six generations of New Yorkers (*since 1836*). **Oscar** provides **North Italian** cuisine of high quality. Very expensive. Very elegant.

Chez Yvonne L'Escargot, 54 Stone St. bet. Broad St. and Hanover Sq. 944-9887. Open until 8 P.M. (kitchen closes at 7.). Closed weekends and holidays.

Yvonne the Snail, not surprisingly, specializes in snails as an appetizer—they are notable. *Rare lamb,* another notable rarity in **America,** is also available.

Sloppy Louie's Restaurant, 92 South St. bet. Fulton and John Sts. 952-9657.

Bouillabaise extraordinaire. Fish, crustaceans, and mollusks galore. Don't eat the soup. Closes at **7:45 P.M.** No liquor.

Jimmy's Greek American Restaurant, 6 Water St. 952-9607.

A do-it-yourself, inexpensive, **Greek,** menu-less, and pleasant experience. Bring your own wine.

Harry's Restaurant, 1 Hanover Sq., SW cor. Stone St. WH 4-9251. Closes 9:30 P.M. (for dinner), the bar at 12 P.M.

Within part of the west flank of **India House,** this public restaurant shares some of the volume of that private club. Schnitzel, hasenpfeffer, dumplings, and other goodies devised to adjust the jowls to bankers' proportions. Good and inexpensive.

ZUM ZUM, 74 Broad St., SW cor. Marketfield St.

Another in the happily spreading empire of crisp, clean, and elegantly designed **German** short-order restaurants. Soup, salad, sausages, and beer are standard. Inexpensive.

Manhattan Landing, along the **East River** between the **South Street Seaport** and **Whitehall Street.** This ambitious planning proposal occupies the space between South Street and the pierhead line, **500** feet out (on platforms over water). Tens of thousands of apartments and a new **Stock Exchange** were suggested, then tabled in the economic recession starting in **1973.** Reincarnation is inevitable.

LOWER WEST SIDE

After the Civil War, shipping shifted from the **East** to the **North (Hudson) River.** The many-bowsprited streets on the east flank of Manhattan were abandoned for the many-berthed piers of steam-powered transatlantic shipping on the west flank. In much later years auto traffic needs caused the Miller Highway, that elevated portion of the West Side Drive to 72nd Street, to dominate West Street. The Miller is now closed, due to deterioration, with contracts awarded for demolition of a portion of it. A new highway (named **Westway**) is proposed over water at the pierhead line.

Battery Park City, a giant landfill development between **Battery Place** and **Chambers Street,** displaces the river outward from **West Street.** A proposed urbanization of dwellings and workplaces, it is largely moribund in the city's financial crisis: two apartment buildings (Harrison & Abramovitz, architects) are under construction. [See Financial District 9.]

[1.] World Trade Center, West, Washington, Barclay, West Broadway, Vesey, Church, and Liberty Sts. 1962–1977. Minoru Yamasaki & Assoc., and Emery Roth & Sons.

Twin **110-**story buildings flank low buildings and a plaza larger than the **Piazza San Marco** in **Venice.** From the harbor, Brooklyn, or New Jersey, this pair dominates the Lower Manhattan skyline; stolid, banal monoliths overshadowing the cluster of filigreed towers that still provide the romantic symbolism that once evoked the very thought of "skyline."

Ten million square feet of space here are offered: seven times the area of the **Empire State Building,** four times that of the **Pan Am Building.** The public agency that built them **(Port Authority of New York and New Jersey)** ran *amok* with both money and aesthetics.

[2.] New York Telephone Company, 140 West St., bet. Barclay and Vesey Sts. 1926. McKenzie, Voorhees & Gmelin.

This *distinguished* monolith borders the **World Trade Center:** an early experiment in massing large urban form within the zoning "envelope" permitted in the then-new law of **1916.** The arcaded sidewalk **along Vesey Street** is handsome and pleasant: why not elsewhere in **New York** to protect the pedestrian from inclement weather and to enrich the architectural form of the street? (Down the road a piece, **21 West Street** has a brief arcade as well; and **Roosevelt Island's** Main Street uses pedestrian arcades as the *very armature* of pedestrianism.)

The decoration is both **Art Deco** and **Mayan Revival,** with bas-reliefs of babies, bears, parrots, and panthers. Test the echo under the **Guastavino** vaults (at the joining arch).

[3.] 75 Murray Street, bet. West Broadway and Greenwich Sts. ca. 1865. Attributed to John Gaynor.

An ornate **Palladian** cast-iron facade.

[4a.] 171 Duane Street, NW cor. Staple St. ca. 1865.

Cast iron of an *offbeat* design.

[4b.] 173 Duane Street, bet. Greenwich and Staple Sts. ca. 1885.

Another brick monolith. Note the naturalistic incised terra-cotta archivolts banding the great arches.

[4c.] Duane Park, bet. Hudson, Duane, and Staple Sts. 1795. Reconstructed 1940.

Annetje Jans' farm was here after 1636. Family farmers included **Roeloff Jans,** whose widow married a **Bogardus.** The farm was later sold to **Governor Lovelace;** then the **Duke of York** confiscated it and gave it to **Trinity Church.** The city purchased it as a public park in **1795** for **$5!**

[4d.] 172 Duane Street, bet. Greenwich and Hudson Sts. S side ca. 1870.

Elliptical over semicircular cast-iron arches. Elegant. **Brunelleschi** was simply but handsomely remembered here. Note the curved triangles in the spandrels (*i.e., the space between the arches*).

Cast-Iron Buildings, constructed in **1849** by **James Bogardus,** stood at the northwest corner of **Washington** and **Murray Streets.** Carefully disassembled, their facades were to be reerected as part of **Manhattan Community College [7.]** to the north. Stored on an empty lot, the parts were spirited away in the dead of night and sold for scrap (by *scrap-nappers?*), but the **doughty police** pursued and captured the thieves, reclaiming some but not all of the stolen parts. Is this the first building ever stolen? or at least the first historic monument?

The first cast-iron building in New York City by engineer James Bogardus

[5.] Independence Plaza North, Greenwich, Duane, Washington, and North Moore Sts. 1975. Oppenheimer, Brady & Vogelstein, John Pruyn. Associated Architects.

Middle-income **blockbusters** of brick and striated concrete block. Their **40**-story towers are made *plastic* by cantilevered and increasing bulk, and *toothy* by balconies silhouetted against the sky.

[6.] 25 Harrison Street, ca. 1804. **37, 39, 41 Harrison St.,** 1828. (Formerly 314, 329, 331, and 337 Washington St. around the corner.) John McComb, Jr., and friends. Restored 1975. Oppenheimer, Brady & Vogelstein.

These were elegant *Federal* houses, recycled as meat-market buildings on the now-extinct **Washington Street.** Their reincarnation included moving two from **Washington** to **Harrison Street.** They are lovely (perhaps *too perfectly* restored: cf. Williamsburg, Va.). McComb *lived* in one.

[7.] Manhattan Community College, Washington, Duane, West, and North Moore Sts. Construction halted 1976. CRS (Caudill, Rowlett, Scott and Assocs.).

One of the **superbuildings** programmed by the City University to house its burgeoning population.

[8.] Old Saint John's Square. Laight, Varick, Ericcson, and Hudson Sts. 1803.

A space now occupied by the exit roadways of the Holland Tunnel, this was once a *square* in a class with **Washington Square** and **Gramercy Park.** Its owners (the perimeter houses surrounding it were grand **Federal** and **Greek Revival** places), experiencing decline, sold the great space to **Commodore Vanderbilt** for a railroad terminal (*1869*). Later the railroads moved uptown (*passengers*), and to the north and west (*freight*), and the railroad's abandonment made it a found-place for the car to penetrate **New York's** edge by tunnel.

A handsome Georgian-Federal church (**St. John's.** *1807–1918.* John McComb, Jr.) stood at the east side of the square (*Varick Street*) and gave the place its name. An *Evening Post* of **1847** lyrically describes **St. John's Park** as a "spot of eden loveliness . . . it seems as if retiring from the din and tumult of the noisy town to enjoy its own secret solitude." At this, amidst the noise and tumult of belching autos, we heave a historical (and sometimes hysterical) sigh.

[5.] Independence Plaza North (apts.)

[6.] John McComb Jr.'s Federal houses

[9.] 284 and 288 Hudson Street, bet. Dominick and Spring Sts. ca. 1820.

Federal remnants, their forms (simple bodies with pitched roofs and dormer windows) remain: now commercial places where the **early American** middle class once dwelled.

[10.] Miller Highway Bridge, over Canal St. at West St.

An elegant steel arch suspends the defunct **Miller Highway** across this intersection.

[11.] James Brown House, 326 Spring St., bet. Greenwich and Washington Sts. 1817. ★

Columbia College (*originally* King's College) occupied the blocks between **West Broadway, Barclay, Church,** and **Murray Streets.** The river's edge was then **250** feet away, approximately at **Greenwich Street,** offering a view and sea breezes to the then-rural student and faculty bodies. In **1857** the college moved north, occupying the former buildings of the **New York Deaf and Dumb Asylum** between **49th** and **50th Streets, Madison** and **Park Avenues.**

Windows on the World, 107th Floor, World Trade Center, North Building. 938-1111. 1976. Warren Platner.

Sensual, view-filled, **expensive:** the crown of restaurant fantasies. The stepped arrangements allow nearly all to enjoy a simultaneous view. Bring your *thickest* wallet, or just stop for a drink.

Delphi Restaurant, NE cor. West Broadway at Reade St. Monday–Sunday, 10 A.M.–11 P.M.

A pleasant and inexpensive **Greek** restaurant. Wine and beer.

CIVIC CENTER/CHINATOWN

The flavor of city life rests largely in the sharp juxtaposition of different activities—government, commerce, industry, housing, entertainment—with differing ethnic and economic groups. These precincts are a caricature of that thought.

Spreading out from City Hall, the neighborhood's center of gravity, are government offices (**federal, state,** and **city),** middle-income and public housing, commercial warehousing, the fringes of the financial district, **Chinatown,** and that ancient viaduct that made New York's consolidation with the City of Brooklyn possible: **the Brooklyn Bridge.**

These streets are some of New York's most venerable, but only a smattering of the structures that originally lined them remain: slowly the blocks have been consolidated, and larger and larger single projects of all kinds built or planned—housing projects, government structures, and a college campus.

Civic Center

Walking Tour: From Fulton Street and Broadway to Chambers Street and Broadway via City Hall Park, the Civic Center, and Chinatown. (IRT Lexington Avenue Subway to the Fulton Street Station, or the IND Eighth Avenue Subway to the Broadway-Nassau Station.)

[1.] St. Paul's Chapel and Churchyard, bounded by Broadway, Fulton, Church, and Vesey Sts. 1764–1766. Thomas McBean. Tower, steeple and porch, 1796. James Crommelin Lawrence. ★

New York's *only* extant pre-Revolutionary building. Although the city's present territory contains a dozen other buildings that old or more, they were isolated farmhouses or country seats that bear no more relation to the city than do still-rural 18th-century houses in outlands surrounding the enlarged city. Unlike **Fraunces Tavern, St. Paul's** is as close to the original as any building requiring maintenance over **200** years could be.

McBean was, perhaps, a pupil of **James Gibbs,** whose **St. Martin's-in-the-Fields** (London) was undoubtedly a prototype for **St. Paul's.** Stone from the site (Manhattan schist) forms walls that are *quoined, columned, parapeted, pedimented, porched,* and *towered* in **Manhattan's** favorite **18th-** and **19th-**century, masonry: **brownstone.**

A gilt weathervane forms a finial to the finial of a tower crowning a "Choragic Monument of Lysicrates" (Hellenistic Greek monument for Renaissance and neo-Renaissance copycats).

The graveyard is a green oasis, dappled with sunlight, an umbrella of trees over somber gravestones. Ivy. Squirrels. Lovely.

It is rumored that **Pierre L'Enfant,** the soldier-architect who designed the **Federal Hall,** America's *first* capitol [see Financial District 53.], designed the golden sunburst (gloire) over the high altar.

Governor Clinton's and **President Washington's** pews are within.

[2.] New York County Lawyers' Association, 14 Vesey St., bet. Church St. and Broadway. 1930. Cass Gilbert.

Law in America is based on **English** *common law,* and what better tie to the fount than to club together in a **London** club; here a *watery* neo-Georgian.

[3.] Garrison Building/formerly **New York Evening Post Building,** 20 Vesey St., bet. Church St. and Broadway. 1906. Robert D. Kohn. Gutzon Borglum, Sculptor. ★

The interest here is at the top: sculptured limestone and copper **Art Nouveau.**

[4.] St. Peter's Church (Roman Catholic), 22 Barclay St. SE cor. Church St. 1838. John R. Haggerty and Thomas Thomas. ★

A granite **Ionic** temple. The wood-framed pediment and roof structure are sheathed in sheet metal molded to the appropriate profiles.

[1.] St. Paul's Chapel & Churchyard   **[5.]** Neo-Gothic Woolworth Building

[4.] St. Peter's Roman Catholic Church: a Greek Revival temple in granite

[5.] Woolworth Building, 233 Broadway, bet. Park Pl. and Barclay St. 1913. Cass Gilbert.

Much maligned for its **eclectic Gothic** detail and **charcoal Gothic** crown, this sheer shaft is one of the most imposingly sited skyscrapers of New York. Rising almost **800** feet from the street, it soars; only the **Seagram** and **CBS Buildings** have the combination of articulate architecture and massing to achieve similar drama. The lobby is clothed in Skyros veined marble. Horace Walpole, who built a **Gothic "castle"** at "Strawberry Hill" and wrote the *Castle of Otranto,* could have set his action here.

[6.] City Hall Park/formerly the **City Common.** ca. 1700.

The bounds were determined by the two main post roads from **New York** (the city extended barely to Wall Street at this time): the westerly one to the north island village of **Bloomingdale** (near present Columbia University); and the easterly one to **Boston.**

Buildings, seemingly for random purposes at random locations, occupied pieces of this turf from time to time. One of special note was **Vanderlyn's Rotunda** (near the southwest corner of Chambers and Centre Streets), a mini-Pantheon for the display of panoramic views, such as that of Versailles, which, in a pre-photography, pre-electronic world simulated the experience of being there very nicely. The *biggest* guest building was the **Post Office** by **Alfred Mullet,** much maligned at the time: in retrospect it was a rich building inspired by Napoleon III's Paris. **Mullet's** more famous, and preserved building, is the **Executive Office Building** in **Washington.**

Assorted sculpture is also present: **Nathan Hale** (1893. Frederick MacMonnies, Sculptor; Stanford White, Architect of the Base.) is looking into the **BMT** for his tardy date; **Horace Greeley** (1890. J. Q. A. Ward.) is grandly seated before the **Surrogates Court.**

[7.] Brooklyn Bridge, spanning from City Hall Park to Brooklyn's Cadman Plaza

[7.] Brooklyn Bridge, City Hall Park, Manhattan, to Cadman Plaza, Brooklyn, 1867–1883. John A. and Washington Roebling. ★

A walk across the raised central boardwalk to **Brooklyn Heights** is one of the *great* dramatic walks of New York. As a side tour from **City Hall,** it is a unique experience, viewing **Brooklyn, Manhattan,** their skylines, and the harbor through a filigree of cables.

The steel and cables have been repainted their original sprightly colors—beige and light brown—instead of the somber battleship gray that gloomed for a misguided generation.

A walk across at sunset, passing down the **Brooklyn Heights Esplanade, Joralemon** and **Fulton Streets** to Gage and Tollner's Restaurant, is unbeatable.

[8.] City Hall, City Hall Park bet. Broadway and Park Row. 1802–1811. Mangin and McComb. ★

A mini-palace, crossing **French Renaissance** detail with **Federal** form, perhaps inevitable where the competition-winning scheme was the product of a **Frenchman** and a **Scot. Mangin** (who had worked in Paris with **Gabriel** on the **Place de la Concorde)** was the principal preliminary designer and theorist; **McComb** supervised construction and determined much of the detailing.

Interiors were restored and refurbished between **1902** and **1920** under **Grosvenor Atterbury,** and the exterior peeled off, reproduced in new Alabama limestone (piece by piece), and restored under **Shreve, Lamb, and Harmon** in **1959.** The soft original **Massachusetts** marble had badly eroded by joint attacks of pollution and pigeons (the rear of the building had been built in brownstone to save money!).

The central domed space leads past the offices of mayor and city councilmen, up twin spiral, self-supporting marble stairs to the Corinthian-columned gallery serving both the **City Council Chamber** and **Board**

of Estimate. The **Governor's Room,** originally for his use when in New York City, is now a portrait gallery replete with portraits by *Sully, Inman, Jarvis, Trumbull,* and others.

A bronze tablet in front of City Hall commemorates the commencement of construction of the first viable subway system in the world: the **IRT** (*Interborough Rapid Transit*) in **1900.** At the foot of the entrance stairs to the **IRT,** at the **SE** cor. of **Chambers** and **Centre Streets,** is a *second* ornate plaque (**Gutzom Borglum,** sculptor) honoring the subway's constructors, led by Chairman **August Belmont, Jr.** (his daddy, né **Schönberg,** on his *Americanization* in a time of **German** unpopularity, changed his name to literal French: **Schönberg** = beautiful mountain = **Belmont**).

Under City Hall Park, and sealed like King Tut's tomb, is the world's most beautiful (former) subway station at the south edge of the loop that turns the **Lexington Avenue IRT** *locals* around from **"Brooklyn Bridge"** pointed south to **"Brooklyn Bridge"** pointed north. **Heins & La Farge** were architects (*1904*). You can sneak a peek by staying on a southbound local at Brooklyn Bridge and looping with it, instead of getting off at the "end of the line."

[9.] Old New York County Courthouse ("Tweed" Courthouse), Chambers St. bet. Broadway and Centre St. 1878 John Kellum, Leopold Eidlitz.

A building maligned and praised at one time: maligned perhaps mostly because of the great scandal in its construction (the **Tweed Ring** apparently made off with **$10** of the **$14** million construction "cost"); and praised because of a new understanding of, and interest in, **Victorian** architecture.

Another view could consider this a late **Victorian** version of an **English Renaissance** country house.

[10.] Park Row Building, 15 Park Row, bet. Ann and Beekman Sts. 1899. R. H. Robertson.

Twin towers for the romantic businessman; guarded by four caryatids on the fourth floor.

[8.] New York's grand City Hall crosses French Renaissance with Federal form

[11.] Potter Building, 38 Park Row, NE cor. Beekman St. 1883. N. G. Starkweather.

An elaborately ornate confection in cast and pressed terra cotta, an early use in **New York** of a material that was to become the rage, producing repetitive elaboration economically. The invisibly used structural steel of this building is the first in **New York** to be fireproofed by terra cotta.

[12.] Pace University/originally **The New York Times Building,** 41 Park Row bet. Beekman and Spruce Sts. 1889. George B. Post. Altered 1905. Robert Maynicke.

Rusticated granite, but dull as dishwater. **Post's** perigee.

[13.] Pace University, New Building, Nassau, Frankfort, Gold, and Spruce Sts. 1970. Eggers & Higgins.

An ungainly form is, unhappily, squeezed between its neighbors.

[14.] Benjamin Franklin, Printing House Square. 1872. A. Plassman.

The patron "saint" of **American** printing.

[15.] Bennett Building, 99 Nassau St. bet. Fulton and Ann Sts. 1873. Arthur Gilman.

A glassy building with a bold structural grid. The hectic shops of the ground floor distract the eye; few notice its overhead quality.

[15.] Bennett Bldg., a glassy grid   **[22.]** Metropolitan Correction Ctr.

[18.] A delicate concrete cage at 100 Gold Street for Bache Halsey Stuart

[16.] 150 Nassau Street Building/formerly **American Tract Society,** SE cor. Spruce St. 1896. R. H. Robertson.

The fascination here is at the roof, where giant **"Romanesque"** arches provide a geometry of architecture separate from the rusticated granite below.

[17.] Southbridge Towers, Gold, Frankfort, Water, and Fulton Sts. 1969. Gruzen & Partners.

The charm of this scheme is in the contained urban spaces surrounded by **6**-story buildings—new at the time in publicly assisted housing. This is a **"Mitchell-Lama"** middle-income housing project.

[18.] 100 Gold Street, SE cor. Frankfort St. 1969. Gruzen & Partners.

A delicate concrete cage reminiscent of **Aalto.** A pleasant and glassy understatement.

[19.] Beekman Downtown Hospital, bet. Spruce, Gold, Beekman, and William Sts. 1971. Skidmore, Owings & Merrill.

The forbidding base gives this humane place an inhuman posture.

[20.] Municipal Building, Chambers St. at Centre St. 1914. McKim, Mead & White (William M. Kendall and Burt Fenner). ★

This is urban architecture, boldly straddling a city street. In those days the ways of traffic were entwined with architecture (see **Warren & Wetmore's Grand Central Terminal of 1913**). The "Choragic Monument" atop this composition is, in turn, surmounted by *"Civic Virtue,"* now newly gilt, by **Adolph A. Weinman.**

[21.] Hall of Records/orig. Surrogate's Court, with Ward's *Horace Greeley*

[21.] Surrogate's Court/Hall of Records, 31 Chambers St., NW cor. Centre St. 1899–1911. John R. Thomas and Horgan & Slattery. ★

Civic monuments were designed to *impress* the citizen in those days (not merely humor him, as is most often the case today). Therefore his records were kept in a place of splendor. Go in. The central hall is worthy of **Charles Garnier's** earlier **Paris Opera.**

[22.] Metropolitan Correction Center, bet. Park Row, Duane and Pearl Sts. 1975. Gruzen & Partners.

An annex to **Cass Gilbert's** U.S. Courthouse provides offices and a detention center. It forms a happy fòil to the same firm's **Police Headquarters** and plaza adjacent.

[23.] Police Headquarters, bet. Park Row, Pearl, Henry, and New Sts. 1973. Gruzen & Partners, Architect; M. Paul Friedberg, Landscape Architect.

The most urbane civic building for **New York** since the **City Hall** of **1812,** largely because of its elegant plaza, stepped pedestrian passageways, and terraces that form an interlock for people in this car-laced area. A brown-brick cube of office space hovers over special police facilities below.

Five in One, a sculpture by **Bernard (Tony) Rosenthal** in self-weathering (consciously rusty) steel, looms over the **Municipal Building** end.

[24.] Murry Bergtraum High School, 411 Pearl St., S cor. Madison St. to Avenue of the Finest. 1976. Gruzen & Partners.

A sleek, purple-brown triangular "fort," complete with corner turrets, financed, through the Educational Construction Fund, by the overwhelming telephone building next door. (The **air rights** of the school provide **zoning credit** for the telephone building; the latter, in return, pays off the bonds that built the school.)

[25.] U.S. Federal Building and Customs Courthouse, 1 Federal Plaza (Foley Sq.), bet. Duane and Worth Sts. W side. 1967. Alfred Easton Poor, Kahn & Jacobs, Eggers & Higgins, Associated Architects. Broadway addition, 1976. Same cast.

An ungainly checkerboard of granite now extended westward with a continuing heavy hand.

[26.] U.S. Courthouse, Foley Sq., SE cor. Pearl St. 1936. Cass Gilbert and Cass Gilbert, Jr. ★

Capped by another Gilbert gold pyramid (cf. the **New York Life Insurance Company Building**). Dour granite.

[24.] Murry Bergtraum High School   **[27.]** New York County Courthouse

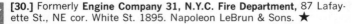

[27.] New York County Courthouse, Foley Sq., bet. Pearl St., Hamill Place, and Worth St. E side. 1926. Guy Lowell. ★

This **"Hexagon"** anticipated the **Pentagon** by **30** years. Lowell's scheme won a 1912 competition (but wasn't built until much later), in the spirit of both City Hall and the Municipal Building. The imposing Corinthian portico is **handsome Roman archeology,** but doesn't measure up to the vigorous planning of the building. It is a **grand form** to view from above.

[28.] Civil and Municipal Courthouse, City of New York, 111 Centre St., SW cor. White St. 1960. William Lescaze and Matthew Del Gaudio.

A **sleek but dull cube** fills the site facing an open plaza, not for people, but for judges' parking. Bas-reliefs by William Zorach.

[29.] Criminal Courts Building and Prison, 100 Centre St., bet. Leonard and White Sts. E side. 1939. Harvey Wiley Corbett.

The **"Tombs"** after its "Egyptian" Revival two-generation ancestor across the street. This is a ziggurated construction overlaid with stylish detail of the thirties: **Art Moderne,** as at the **Paris Exposition of 1937.**

[30.] Formerly **Engine Company 31, N.Y.C. Fire Department,** 87 Lafayette St., NE cor. White St. 1895. Napoleon LeBrun & Sons. ★

This *was* a house for fire engines, disguised as a **Loire Valley chateau:** now a surplus landmark awaiting a friendly use.

[31.] Family Court, City of New York, 60 Lafayette St., bet. Leonard and Franklin Sts. 1975. Haines, Lundberg & Waehler.

A **fashionable** new form: intended to look as if its incised cubism was carved away from a polished black granite monolith. Somber, pretentious: a wide miss.

[32.] Chatham Towers (apartments), 170 Park Row, bet. Park Row and Worth St., N side. 1965. Kelly & Gruzen.

Sculpted concrete, this joins the ranks of distinguished housing architecture: the **Dakota, Butterfield House, 131 East 66th Street, Williamsburg Houses,** and **East Midtown Plaza** are its peers from all eras. All are participants in the city's life and streets, as opposed to towered *islands,* as in most public housing. And like all strong architectural statements, **Chatham Towers** rouse great admiration and great criticism.

[28.] The Civil and Municipal Court **[30.]** Old Engine Co. 31, Fire Dept.

[32.] Chatham Towers (apartments) **[33.]** Chatham Green (apartments)

[33.] Chatham Green (apartments), 185 Park Row, bet. St. James Place, Park Row, Pearl, and Madison Sts. 1961. Kelly & Gruzen.

A great undulating wall: open access galleries are served by vertical circulation towers. **Barney Gruzen** designed it after seeing **Alfonso Reidy's** undulating slabs at **Pedregulho** in Brazil.

Castilla's Restaurant, 35 Madison St., bet. St. James Place and James St. Telephone: BE 3-9492.

An adventure in **Spanish food** (cooked principally for local Spanish-speaking residents). A full bar available, and reasonable prices. Open seven days a week.

[34.] Governor Alfred E. Smith Houses, N.Y.C. Housing Authority, bet. South, Madison, and Catherine Sts. and St. James and Robert F. Wagner, Sr., Places. 1952. Eggers & Higgins.

Al Smith lived a short stone's throw away: his turf. These are typical of New York's public housing of the forties and fifties: **dull warehouses** for people; expensive for the taxpayer, cheap for the poor, and well maintained. For school and recreation center on northeast boundary of site, see [38.].

[35.] St. James Church, Greek Revival   **[43.]** Confucius Plaza (apartments)

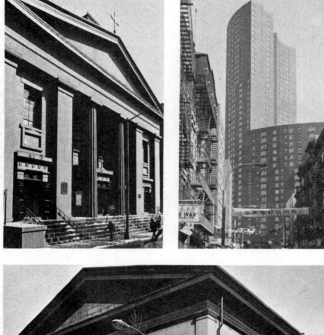

[37b.] Mariners' Temple/form. Oliver Street Church: Ionic distyle in antis

[35.] St. James (Roman Catholic) Church, 32 James St., bet. St. James Place and Madison St. 1837. Attributed to Minard Lafever. ★

Brownstone Doric Greek Revival. Distyle (two columns) in antis (between flanking blank walls). Compare it to **Mariners' Temple** below.

[36.] First Shearith Israel Graveyard, 55 St. James Place, bet. Oliver and James Sts. 1683–1828. ★

The *only* people-shaped remnant of New York's 17th century, this bears the remains of **Sephardic Jews** (of Spanish-Portuguese extraction) who emigrated from **Brazil** in the mid-17th century.

[37a.] St. Margaret's House/originally **Robert Dodge Residence,** 2 Oliver St., bet. St. James Place and Henry St. 1820. James O'Donnell. Third floor added, 1850.

A **Federal** house, now attached to the work of adjacent Mariners' Temple.

[37b.] Mariners' Temple (Baptist)/formerly **Oliver Street Church,** 12 Oliver St., NW cor. Henry St. 1842. Minard Lafever. ★

A stone, **Greek Revival Ionic** temple. *Servicios in Espãnol and Chinese.* A wide cross section of communicants worships in a sailors' church that might well be a **temple to Athena.** Peeling.

[38.] Public School 126 Manhattan, The Jacob Riis School, and **Alfred E. Smith Recreation Center,** 80 Catherine St., bet. Cherry and Monroe Sts. W side. 1966. Percival Goodman.

A neatly articulated school and community recreation center, both of high design quality. Note the murals.

[39.] Knickerbocker Village (apartments), Catherine to Market Sts., Monroe to Cherry Sts. 1934. Van Wart & Ackerman.

A **blockbuster,** with **1,600** apartments on three acres (New York City public housing averages 80 to 100 units per acre). The central courtyards are reached through gated tunnels and seem a welcome relief by contrast with their dense and massive surroundings. This was the *first* major housing project even partially aided by public funds. It maintains its well-kept middle-class air today. **Stolid and solid for modern burghers.**

[40.] 51 Market Street/originally **William Clark House,** bet. Monroe and Madison Sts. 1824. ★

A *rare* four-story **Federal** house: they were almost always two or three (plus basement and/or dormered attic). Its entranceway is Federal at its most superb.

[41.] Sea and Land Church/The First Chinese Presbyterian Church/formerly **Market Street Church,** 61 Henry St., NW cor. Market St. 1819. ★

A **Georgian-Federal** body punched with Gothic Revival windows; of dressed Manhattan schist, with brownstone surrounds (enframement) and trim.

[42.] Chinatown Mission/Church of Our Saviour (Protestant Episcopal), 48 Henry St., bet. Market and Catherine Sts. 1830.

Two houses saved by churchly missionary needs (as a chapel of **Trinity Church** downtown). The roof balustrade is from a **Georgian** country house, the doorway elaborated **Federal** carving, encrusted with blurring paint layers (cut through the rings of paint to tell the age, as you would a tree).

[43.] Confucius Plaza (apartments) and Public School 124 Manhattan, bet. the Bowery, Division St., Chatham Sq., and the Manhattan Bridge approaches. 1976. Horowitz & Chun.

A "dual use" construction of school and housing interlocked. The curved slab is arbitrary, but a pleasant skyline form.

[44a.] Manhattan Bridge, bet. Canal St. and the Bowery in Manhattan and Flatbush Ave. Ext. in Brooklyn. 1905. Gustav Lindenthal, engineer.
[44b.] Arch and Colonnade, at entrance to bridge. 1905. Carrère & Hastings.

A regal and monumental horseshoe-shaped colonnade which has somehow overcome all attempts by highway engineers to remove it. Long may it last!

Chinatown

In most major American cities **Chinese** have formed enclaves that are sought by tourists and relished by city dwellers with an interested palate. New York's **Chinatown** is centered in eight blocks bounded by Canal, Worth, and Mulberry Streets, the Bowery, and Chatham Square. Its "main street" is still Mott, along whose flanks the Chinese population is rapidly expanding north of Canal into what *was* exclusively Little Italy.

Looking north on Mott Street, center of Chinatown, at the turn of the century

 [45.] OTB Parlor (Off Track Betting)/originally **Edward Mooney House,** 18 Bowery, SW cor. Pell St. 1785–1789. Alterations, 1807. Restoration, 1971. ★

Built *after* the **Revolution** but *before* Washington's inauguration.

[46.] Olliffe's Pharmacy, 6 Bowery, bet. Pell and Doyers Sts. W side. 1803. Remodeled later.

The **oldest** drugstore in **America.**

[47.] Chinese Merchant's Association, 85 Mott St., SW cor. Canal St. 1958.

Grauman's Chinese Theater architecture: on this *both* **Mao** and **Chiang** might have agreed.

 [48.] Church of the Transfiguration/formerly **Zion Episcopal Church,** 25 Mott St., NW cor. Park St. 1801. ★

Like **Sea and Land [see 41.],** a Georgian church with Gothic windows, although here with Gothic tracery, there with small-paned double-hung windows. Dressed Manhattan schist makes neat building blocks, with brownstone detail. The octagonal tower, copper sheathed, is of a later date.

Entertainments and a Full Stomach

Mandarin Inn, 14 Mott St. Telephone: 962–5830.

Cue: "The food at *both* of these restaurants [see below] is great. There are [*sic*] a wide selection of dishes from mild to fiery."

Mandarin Inn, 23 Pell St. Telephone: 267-2092.

See notes on **Mandarin Inn,** 14 Mott Street, above.

Quong Yee Wo Co. (merchandise), 38 Mott St., SE cor. Pell St.

The tan-and-green-topped white roots that form the *nucleus* of **Chinese vegetarianism** are featured here, as are seeds and candy to complement.

Joy Luck Coffee Shop, 57 Mott St. Telephone: 267-3056.

No telephone. *No* booze. *No* reservations. The food is excellent and cheap.

Hong Fat Restaurant, 63 Mott St. Telephone: WO 2-9588.

Gall *and/or* Chinese are needed here, but what they may command is exotic. Either intimidate the waiters or ply them with Cantonese.

Wing Wo Lung Co., 50 Mott St., SE cor. Bayard St.

Vegetables and dried goodies press against the glass, compartmentalized as an index of Chinese gastronomy.

Bo Bo's Restaurant, 20½ Pell St., opp. end of Doyers St. Telephone: WO 2-9458.

Unlikely. Disguised as an unattractive commercial storefront, this crowded, popular, reasonably priced restaurant is a mecca for the sophisticated but penurious college student. Try a plate of Chinese dumplings, the assorted knishes of Chinatown. No booze.

Wo Ping, 24 Pell St. Telephone: RE 2-0847.

Craig Claiborne of the *Times* described it as "noisy as a gong, and earthy as a ginger root." Snails, crabs, fish: what the Chinese cannot grow underground, they catch underseas.

King Wu Restaurant, 18 Doyers St. Telephone: WO 2-8480.

Straightforward, excellent, inexpensive. No liquor served. In a cellar.

Bo-Bo's Restaurant: For the penurious but sophisticated dumpling eater

Cast-Iron District 1 (South of Canal Street)

Cast iron gave an inexpensive means of reproducing elaborate detail, previously possible only as carving in stone. More Corinthian, Ionic, Doric, Composite, Egyptian and *Lord-knows-what-else* columns were cast for New York facades of the 1850s and 1860s than Greece and Rome turned out in a thousand years. The two great centers were between Broadway and West Broadway, Canal to Duane (here described), and to the north, Crosby Street to West Broadway, Canal to Houston Streets, now rechristened **SoHo** (*South of Houston*). [SoHo is a separate precinct, below.]

These handsome loft spaces are used by assorted commercialdom, principally for warehousing, sometimes for light manufacturing, and for studios by the many real or would-be artists who have penetrated these precincts.

[49.] 254 Canal Street, SW cor. Lafayette St. ca. 1865.

Cast iron over chaos, it gets few complimentary glances.

[50.] White Street, West Broadway to Church St.

No. 2. 1809. ★ A genuine *Federal* liquor store, now propped by a steel pipe-column: a real building with a real, and current, use. **Nos. 8–10.** Elaborated Tuscan columns. Watch for the neo-Renaissance trick of foreshortening each floor in height to increase the apparent height.

[51.] White Street, Church St. to Broadway.

No. 46. 1865. Formerly Woods Mercantile Building. A set of buildings organized by its pediment. **No. 52.** Note the appropriate sign. **Nos. 54–56.** Italianate brownstone over cast-iron ground floor. **Nos. 55–57.** ca. 1865. James Kellum & Son. Mutilated ground floor. **Nos. 60–66.** 1869. Ground floors mutilated at **Nos. 64–66.**

[52.] Shaare Zedek Synagogue (Civic Center Synagogue), 49 White St., bet. Church St. and Broadway, S side. 1967. William N. Breger Assocs.

A **ribbon** of marble undulates to a garden behind: unhappily (due to modern security needs) barred from the passerby by wrought iron fencing.

[53.] 221 West Broadway, bet. Franklin and White Sts. E side.

A good solo sandstone over cast-iron Corinthian banded columns. Note **228 West Broadway** opposite, with delicate vegetation in the spandrels: rusty steel *here* becomes aesthetic.

[54.] Franklin Street, bet. Church and Broadway. 1860s.

More white, brown, and simulated (cast-iron) stone. Savor the Corinthian capitals, the glassy windows, the rich and variegated variations on a theme. A somewhat tired but elegant block that would blossom with paint and washed windows. It is said that Renwick and Co. did **No. 71. Nos. 112–114,** a rich stone and cast-iron set.

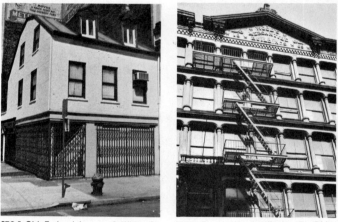

[50.] Old Federal house, 2 White St. [51.] Form. Woods Mercantile Bldg.

Teddy's Restaurant, 219 West Broadway, bet. Franklin and White Sts. Telephone: WO 6-2180.

White stucco Italian, busy, moderately expensive. A full bar, lunch and dinner, save Sundays. Reservations advisable. Credit cards accepted.

Klimataria (i.e., Grapevine) Restaurant, SE cor. W. Broadway and White St.

Baklava, moussaka, souvlaki, Greek salad, pita bread, liquor. A **Greek Grandma Moses** painted this blue and violet primitive mural: a **bit of life** in these business precincts.

[55.] 361 Broadway/originally **James S. White Building,** SW cor. Franklin St. 1882. W. Wheeler Smith.

[56.] 346 Broadway/originally **New York Life Insurance Company,** bet. Broadway, Leonard, Catherine, and Lafayette Sts. 1870. Griffith Thomas. Remodeled and expanded, 1890s. McKim, Mead & White.

New York Life's headquarters until 1928. M, M & W lifted Mr. Thomas's Italianate face (at the Broadway end only) with some larger-scaled neo-Renaissance trappings. The **clock tower** overlooking Broadway is the home of the avant-garde **Clocktower (gallery),** of the **Institute for Art and Urban Resources.**

[57.] Leonard Street from Broadway to Church Street. 1860s.

Limestone (white), brownstone and cast iron; the game is to look closely to separate them: the iron tends to be more slender than the brittle stone. **No. 85, ★,** was James Bogardus' own warehouse; **Nos. 87–89** are similar but simpler, and of stone, matching Bogardus' cast iron (all 1862). **Nos. 80–82.** 1862. James H. Giles. **No. 73.** 1863. James F. Duckworth. **No. 71.** 1860. S. A. Warner.

[52.] The Civic Center Synagogue   **[56.]** Old N.Y. Life Insurance Co.

[57.] 85–89 Leonard Street buildings: which is stone, and which cast iron?

The Chinese Analogy: "All Chinese look alike" is a classic American comment based on lazy eyes and a lazy mind, a state of affairs that obtains for classic buildings (Renaissance Revival, Classical Revival, Georgian, etc.) as well; but with knowledge and friendship, identity becomes apparent of buildings as well as of people: a closely packed vernacular of minor variations on a theme. Variety within discipline is far more fascinating than rampant originality. Such disciplined variety is here elegantly expressed in this glassy cast-iron world. Keep a scorecard: stone versus cast iron, Corinthian versus Doric; proportions, rhythm, glassiness, vintage, color, texture, patina.

[58.] New York Mercantile Exchange, 6 Harrison St., NW cor. Hudson St. 1884.

Monolithic brick and granite, rusticated pilasters at its base. A hearty pile: study the tower.

[59.] Powell Building, 105 Hudson St., NW cor. Franklin St. ca. 1898.

Dirty Renaissance Revival in brick and terra cotta, an American transposition of the original Italian stone. A **Blimpie** in its base.

Note the rusticated marshmallow columns across the street at the northeast corner: **Victorian Baroque.**

[58.] New York Mercantile Exchange   "Marshmallow" Baroque columns

[62.] American Telephone & Telegraph Company Long Lines Building, Worth St.

[60.] 39–41 Worth Street, bet. W. Broadway and Church St., N side. 1860. S. A. Warner.

The first floor has been castrated by a banal "modernization."

[61.] 47 Worth Street, bet. W. Broadway and Church St., N side. ca. 1860.

A victim of "Colonializing" by an **innocent admirer** of history, who, unfortunately, misunderstands architecture.

[62.] American Telephone & Telegraph Long Lines Building, Church St., bet. Thomas and Worth Sts. E side. 1974. John Carl Warnecke & Assocs.

A giant electronic complex *in the guise* of a building. Pink, textured (flame-treated) Swedish granite sheaths a stylish leviathan that looms over the city with **architectural eyebrows.** The **only bow** to the neighboring humanity is a **bleak plaza** to the east. **Ma Bell,** why not leave the air for people, and place your electrons underground?

[63.] 65–85 Worth Street, bet. Church St. and Broadway, N side. ca. 1865.

This **handsome remnant** row of neo-Renaissance whitestone buildings once faced a fabulous cast-iron row (replaced by [62.] above).

[64.] 319 Broadway, NW cor. Thomas St. 1865.

A **sentinel** marking the entrance of **Thomas Street,** marred seriously (as usual) by **grossly unsympathetic** commercial alterations at the street. Very elaborate, this is a cast-iron gem of the first order.

 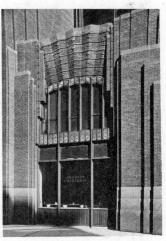

[63.] Neo-Renaissance "whitestones"   **[67.]** The Western Union Building

[65.] 8 Thomas Street, bet. Broadway and Church St., S side. 1875. J. Morgan Slade.

An **elaborate confection** composed of Romanesque, Venetian Gothic, brick, sandstone, granite and cast-iron parts, worthy of **John Ruskin,** whose polemics inspired such thoughts [cf. the Jefferson Market Courthouse, Greenwich Village 28a.].

The **Thomas Street Inn** occupies the ground floor: a sensitive adaptation for lunch and early dinner. Beer and wine. Telephone: 349-6350.

[66.] 62 Thomas Street, bet. W. Broadway and Hudson St., S side. 1867.

A **rare** neo-Gothic cast-iron building suitably painted dark brown: note the polygonal columns.

[67.] Western Union Building, 60 Hudson St., bet. Thomas and Worth Sts., and West Broadway. 1930. Voorhees, Gmelin & Walker.

Nineteen shades of brick from brown to salmon form a subtly shaded palette. Note the handsome signs at the ground floor.

[68.] N.Y.C. Fire Department Museum (Engine Company 7, Ladder Company 1), 100 Duane St., bet. Church St. and Broadway. 1905. Trowbridge & Livingston.

An **English** version of an **Italian** palazzo with double-hung windows and fire engines. Filled with artifacts for fire buffs of all ages and with old equipment, too. Open to the public free of charge; for hours, call 744-1000, extension 230.

[74.] The Marketplace purveys fruit, art, and pizza in a cast-iron classic

[69.] **National Council of the YMCA,** 291 Broadway, NW cor. Reade St. 1910. Clinton & Russell.

Some pleasant Renaissance trappings near street and cornice.

[70.] **Langdon Building,** 305 Broadway, NW cor. Duane St. 1890s.

Handsome clustered Romanesque Revival colonnettes form piers that as ornament are equal to the natural incised bas-reliefs of **Louis Sullivan.**

[71.] **287 Broadway,** SW cor. Reade St. 1872. J. B. Snook.

A glassy mansarded, wrought-iron-crested, Ionic- and Corinthian-columned cast-iron delight. **Lovely.**

[72.] **Broadway Chambers Building,** 277 Broadway, NW cor. Chambers St. ca. 1900. Cass Gilbert.

Carefully stacked Renaissance Revival. A Nedick's hot dog stand once scarred the corner, now **carefully restored** by the **Manufacturers Hanover Trust Co.** (note the carefully matched and replaced granite).

[73.] **280 Broadway/**formerly **Sun Building/**originally **A. T. Stewart Dry Goods Store,** NE cor. Chambers St. 1846. Trench & Snook. Ottavio Gori, stonemason. Additions.

Here **Stewart** founded the *first* great department store of America, later to occupy grand premises at Broadway, 9th–10th Streets (known to recent generations as Wanamaker's, who bought out all of Stewart's enterprises). **Henry James** and **Anthony Trollope** both lavished words of wonder on these premises. Later the *Sun* was published here. Now, in part a discount house, with city offices above.

Suerken's Restaurant, 27 Park Place, at Church St. Telephone: 233-9595.

Cast-iron Corinthian columns face the local home of **dumplings, Löwenbräu, sauerbraten:** weight watchers, beware, the delights here offered are tempting, a caloric Garden of Eden.

Job Lot Trading Company, 140 Church St., bet. Warren and Murray Sts.

A mecca for bargains and gadgets. Irresistible devices from **thingamajigs** to **whatchamacallits** fill racks and bins, enticing the gadgeteer into buying all sorts of things he never knew he wanted or needed before. Regular hardware, paints, and other more normal goodies are here in variety and quantity. It is a bazaar.

Note the flaglike wall mural overhead [see **Outdoor Murals**].

[74.] The Marketplace/formerly **The Cary Building,** W side of Church St., bet. Chambers and Reade Sts. 1856. King & Kellum. Altered, 1972.

Art, pizza, and **fruit** are here intermingled in a pleasant canvas-canopied extension of the classic cast-iron building. A refreshing bit of moneymaking. The Church Street wall was first exposed with the mid-1920s street widening; the storefronts date from 1972.

SOHO

SoHo (or South of Houston), as an acronym, is **stretching** it, recalling the **"Greenwich Village"** of London: *Soho.* These 20 blocks between Canal and Houston ("how-ston") Streets, West Broadway and Broadway are a rich architectural resource, a high point in urban commercial architectural history. They are, largely, not to be noticed as individual monuments, but as parties to whole streets and blocks that, together, make the *most glorious* urban commercial groupings that New York has ever seen. Mostly **Italianate,** some might be termed **Palladian:** they are surprising precursors of the exposed structural expression in concrete seen at **Kips Bay Plaza** and the **American Bible Society.**

Once these were called **"Hell's Hundred Acres"** because of the many fires in overcrowded, untended warehouses filled with flammables. Now given over in large part to artists' (and would-be artists') studios and housing, the once-empty streets and buildings are a **lively, urbane place, much tended and loved,** and hence no longer a potential lonely inferno. Huge "lofts" here give possibility of great space for large paintings or sculptures, and equally great space for living.

The richest single street is **Greene,** then **Broome,** but wander throughout. Not only the revived architecture, but shops and stores of elegance and delight abound.

SoHo Cast-Iron Historic District, The center lines of Canal and Howard Sts. to W. Houston and E. Houston Sts., W. Broadway to Crosby St. and to Broadway below Howard St. District designated, 1973. ★

Within the 26 blocks of this historic district are concentrated, as the designation report states, "the **largest concentration** of full and partial cast-iron facades **anywhere in the world.**" Their protection under law was a great victory of the landmarks preservation activists.

Note: All numbered entries in the SoHo precinct are within the historic district unless *otherwise* noted.

[1.] Greene Street, bet. Canal and Grand Sts.

Nos. 10–14 Greene St. 1869. J. B. Snook. Tuscan columns and pilasters. **Nos. 15–17** Greene St. 1895. S. A. Warner. Delicate Corinthian pilasters. **Nos. 16–18** Greene St. 1880. S. A. Warner. He was architect of the Marble Collegiate Church [see **Four Squares** 25.]. **Nos. 19–21** Greene St. 1872. Henry Fernbach. Bold Tuscan columns by the architect of Central Synagogue. **Nos. 20–26** Greene St. 1880. S. A. Warner. Two buildings in grand Corinthian. **Nos. 23–25** Greene St. 1873. James F. Duckworth. Sparsely leaved Corinthian. **Nos. 28–30** Greene St. Blue leafless Corinthian, with a Second Empire roof. **No. 31** Greene St. 1876. Christian DaCunha. Extraordinarily ornate. **No. 32** Greene St., 1873. C. Wright. Leafless Corinthian. **No. 34** Greene St. 1873. C. Wright. Tuscan. **Nos. 83–87** Grand St., SW cor. Greene St. 1872. Serene Tuscan over elaborate Corinthian.

[2.] Greene Street, bet. Grand and Broome Sts.

No. 33 Greene St., NW cor. Grand St. Composite columns above, Tuscan below. **Nos. 37–43** Greene St. 1884. R. Berger. Green composite columns over a Corinthian base. **No. 45** Greene St. 1882. J. Morgan Slade. Rusting delicate composite Ionic.

[3.] Broome Street, bet. Greene and Wooster Sts.

No. 484 Broome St., NW cor. Wooster. Grand Romanesque Revival brick and rockface brownstone. Entwined serpents form corbeled arch supports in sandstone. **No. 480** Broome St. 1885. R. Berger. Composite Ionic columns. **No. 478** Broome St. 1885. Griffith Thomas. Green Corinthian. **No. 481** Broome St. 1885. E. Shiffin. Corinthian. **No. 475** Broome St. 1873. Griffith Thomas. Note the rich Corinthian foliage and the elegant curved and glazed corner.

[4.] Broome Street, bet. Greene and Mercer Sts.

No. 467 Broome St. 1873. James F. Duckworth. Tuscan. **No. 461** Broome St. 1871. Griffith Thomas. Tuscan encore. **No. 455** Broome St. 1873. Griffith Thomas. Corinthian.

[5.] Greene Street, bet. Broome and Spring Sts.

No. 60 Greene St. 1871. Henry Fernbach. Bold Corinthian. **No. 62** Greene St. 1872. Henry Fernbach again. Bulky Composite Ionic. **No. 66** Greene St. 1873. J. B. Snook. **No. 65** Greene St. 1873. J. B. Snook. Bold Tuscan. **Nos. 67, 69, 71, 75, 77, 81** Greene St. 1873. Henry Fernbach. All bold Tuscan. **Nos. 72–76** Greene St. 1873. James F. Duckworth. The king of this block: projecting pedimented porch of magnificent Corinthian columns and pilasters. **No. 75** Greene St. 1878. Henry Fernbach. **No. 80** Greene St. 1873. Griffith Thomas. Blue Tuscan base supports simplicity.

[6.] Greene Street, bet. Spring and Prince Sts.

Nos. 93–99 Greene St. 1881. Three buildings sport Composite Ionic. **No. 96** Greene St. 1879. Tuscan. **No. 100** Greene St. 1880. "Corinthionic!" **No. 105** Greene St. 1879. Modified Corinthian. **No. 112** Greene St. 1884. Seedy brown Ionic. **Nos. 114–120** Greene St. 1882. Two buildings in composite Ionic. All by Henry Fernbach.

[7.] Prince Street, bet. Greene and Wooster Sts.

Nos. 112–114 Prince St. 1889. Remodeled, 1975. Hanford Yang. A City Walls, Inc., photo-realistic painted facade by **Richard Haas** extrapolates lush architecture to the side wall. **No. 109** Prince St. 1889. J. Morgan Slade.

[8.] Greene Street, bet. Prince and Houston Sts.

No. 121 Greene St. 1883. Henry Fernbach. A cream-colored and classy Corinthian. Savor the monolithic granite sidewalks, self-curbed, an old and disappearing local amenity. **Nos. 132–140** Greene St. 1885. A. Zucker. Three buildings wear a rusty, free-spirited Ionic facade (capitals turned sideways). **No. 135** Greene St. 1883. Henry Fernbach. A delicate Tuscan-ordered building. **No. 142** Greene St. 1871. Henry Fernbach. Bulky Tuscan. Residents include Azuma Gallery and Sculpture Now. **No. 139** Greene St. ca. 1824. Brick Federal house hopefully on its way to reincarnation.

SoHo's north edge is bounded by the expressway-scaled Houston Street, that, having been widened for the IND Sixth Avenue Subway, caused the body of **SoHo** to face a ragged edge to **Greenwich Village** on the north. Gas stations, lots, and unkempt buildings' sides are all that **SoHo** here offers of its inner splendors.

[9.]. Originally **Firemen's Hall,** 155 Mercer St., bet. Prince and W. Houston Sts. 1854. Field & Correja. Altered.

At the time this building was built the city's fire laddies were volunteers. Most of the original ornate trim and moldings are gone, but some of its early form is visible in the quoins.

[10.] Originally **Engine Company 13, N.Y.C. Fire Department,** 99 Wooster St., bet. Spring and Prince Sts. W side. 1881. Napoleon LeBrun.

A cast-iron bottom supporting a masonry top. The two piers carry shields which once contained the engine company's insignia.

[11a.] 64 Wooster Street, bet. Broome and Spring Sts. E side. 1899. E. H. Kendall. **[11b.] 80 Wooster Street.** 1894. G. A. Schellenger. **[11c.] 84 Wooster Street.** 1896. Albert Wagner.

Seven- and eight-story Renaissance Revival warehouses. Arches and cornices here creep into these cast-iron precincts: **larger and more pretentious** than their neighbors.

[12.] 46 Wooster Street, bet. Grand and Broome Sts., E Side. 1895. F. S. Baldwin.

Brick Romanesque Revival, with rockface brownstone and cast iron in concert. Here **the attempt is at grandeur,** more than the spartan elegance of cast iron alone.

[13.] 2 Wooster Street, NE cor. Canal St. 1872. W. H. Gaylor.

All of a piece, the **Corinthian** capitals have mostly rusted away.

Canal Street becomes a Casbah between the Avenue of the Americas (Sixth Avenue to everyone) and Broadway. Here shops spill into the street; their wares—"bargains" real or apparent—abound: radio and TV parts, tools, dresses, plastic, whatever. A great place for the browsing gadgeteer, or the serious bargain hunter familiar with his needs.

[14a.] St. Alphonsus Church (Roman Catholic)/originally **Church of St. Alphonsus Liguori,** 312 W. Broadway, bet. Canal and Grand Sts. W side. 1872. **[14b.] Rectory,** 308 W. Broadway. ca. 1878. **[14c.] Church Hall,** 320 W. Broadway. ca. 1885. All outside the historic district.

A sprightly combination of facades dominated by the central work, the asymmetric Lombardian Romanesque church facade.

[15.] West Broadway, bet. Canal and W. Houston Sts. West (even-numbered) side of street not included in historic district.

No. 380 W. Broadway, bet. Prince and Spring Streets, west side. Prosperous cast iron: cream-colored renovation; neat but without pizazz. No. 386 W. Broadway, bet. Prince and Spring Streets. Stacked gray Tuscan cast-iron columns in descending sizes from first to fifth floors. No. 420 W. Broadway, bet. Prince and Spring Streets, west side. Cut granite over black Tuscan stone: somber elegance containing the galleries of **André Emmerich, John Weber, Sonnabend,** and **Leo Castelli. No. 468** W. Broadway, bet. Prince and Houston Streets, west side. Brick Romanesque Revival on a grand scale. Note the cast-iron swags in the spandrels.

Kenn's Broome Street Bar, 363 W. Broadway, cor. Broome St. Telephone: 925-2086.

In a late Federal (ca. 1830) house, advertised with elegant Victorian gilt lettering: a pleasant pseudo-vintage eating and drinking place. Plants. Ceiling fans. Stained glass.

162 (restaurant and bar), 162 Spring St., cor. W. Broadway. Telephone: 431-7637.

A place to eat and/or drink in surroundings designed on the bias. Moderate.

Jaap Rietman (art and architecture books), 167 Spring St., cor. W. Broadway.

One flight up to a wonderland of books on the local as well as the worldwide art scene. A good section on architecture, too.

Let There Be Neon, 451 W. Broadway, bet. Prince and W. Houston Sts.

Neon as an art form, flashing, bubbling, blinking: camp to serious. For sale, or attend their neon-bending school and **light your own way.**

The Ballroom, 458 W. Broadway, bet. Prince and W. Houston Sts. Telephone: 473-9367.

White paint, white globes, and green plants bring a cool grace to this restaurant. John Canaday: "The food is good and the price is right."

[16.] 600 Broadway, bet. Prince and E. Houston Sts., E side. ca. 1886.

Corinthian columns of descending heights for each successive floor. The ground floor alteration is by **local philistines.** Cleaned, and painted white, it would be a smasher.

[17.] Paul Building/originally **Singer Building,** 561 Broadway, bet. Spring and Prince Sts., W side facing both Broadway and Prince St. 1907. Ernest Flagg.

Steel, glass, and terra cotta, avant-garde for its time, the forerunner of the curtain wall, that light metal-and-glass skin in which much of commercial New York of the fifties and sixties is clad—grossly, it seems, when compared to this **70-year-old charmer. Flagg's** other local palace of delight is the Fifth Avenue store for Scribner's.

[18a.] 502 Broadway, bet. Broome and Spring Sts. E side. 1860. John Kellum.

Tall, slender arches in stone, not cast iron.

[18b.] Haughwout Building, 488 Broadway, NE cor. Broome St. 1857. J. P. Gaynor. Iron by Badger Iron Works. ★

Palladio would have been proud of this offspring in cast iron, a rich participant in the urban scene. A proud and handsome, but not egocentric, building here proves that quality does not demand originality for its own sake. It also houses the *first* practical safety elevator, installed by **Elisha Graves Otis,** founder of that famous, ubiquitous elevator company.

The Corinthian columns flanking arches are sometimes remembered as Serlian, for their advertisement through the writings of **Sebastiano Serlio:** he, however, lifted them from **Palladio,** most elegantly displayed at the **Basilica in Vicenza.**

[19a.] Roosevelt Building, 478 Broadway, bet. Grand and Broome Sts. E side. 1874. Richard Morris Hunt.

Filigreed iron, with cast Composite columns on a huge scale. **Hunt** is best known for the **Metropolitan Museum of Art's** central building and entrance.

[17.] Paul Bldg./orig. Singer Bldg.   **[19a.]** Roosevelt Bldg. (cast iron)

[19b.] 462 Broadway, NE cor. Grand St. 1879. Griffith Thomas.

Mutilated.

[20.] European-American Bank & Trust Co./originally **Franklin National Bank,** 433 Broadway, NW cor. Howard St. 1967. Eggers & Higgins, architects. Zion & Breen, landscape architects.

A **neo-Georgian** "suburban" bank building provides a tree-canopied plaza. The impulse to provide amenities is commendable, but the result a strange and inappropriate one in this virile cast-iron environment. Incidentally, the **Georges** never used the hexagon for building: that is a later, Greek Revival game.

[21.] A.J. Dittenhofer Building, 427 Broadway, SW cor. Howard St. 1870. Thomas R. Jackson.

Circular arches on black Corinthian columns face this lusty, glassy place.

LITTLE ITALY

Canal to Houston Streets, Lafayette Street to the Bowery, is still, in large part, the most important old **Italian** center of New York: but now with *old* Italians, as the newest generation has made the move to suburbia. They return, however, for festivals and family festivities: marriages, funerals, feasts, and holy days. Meanwhile, the **Chinese** have slowly moved north across the former cultural moat of **Canal Street** and partially share this turf. (It is rumored that the Chinese and Italians at their negotiating table have agreed that the Chinese movement northward will be acceptable as long as the signs bear Roman characters rather than ideographs.)

[1.] Paolucci's Restaurant/originally **Stephen van Rensselaer House,** 149 Mulberry St., bet. Hester and Grand Sts. 1816. ★

A **Federal** two-story, dormered brick house, a surprising remnant in these tenemented streets. The color scheme of green and white signals "Italian Federal."

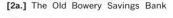
[2a.] The Old Bowery Savings Bank   **[4.]** Old N.Y. City Police Hdqtrs.

[2a.] Bowery Savings Bank, 130 Bowery, bet. Grand and Broome Sts. 1894. McKim, Mead & White. ★ **[2b.] Grand St. Branch, Citibank/** originally **Bowery Bank,** 124 Bowery, NW cor. Grand St. 1902. York & Sawyer.

Roman pomp wraps around **Renaissance luster** on the Bowery, at the edge of Little Italy. They have served as **architectural and economic anchors** through the Bowery's years of hard times. The interior of the Bowery bank is one of the **great spaces** of New York. Go in.

[3.] 165 Grand Street/originally **Odd Fellows Hall,** SE cor. Centre St. 1849. J. B. Snook.

The somewhat bedraggled palace of the **Odd Fellows,** a high rise in brownstone second only to the Cooper Union [Astor Place/East Village 31.]. **Snook** contributed many cast-iron buildings to the SoHo district to the west.

[4.] Originally **New York City Police Headquarters,** 240 Centre St., bet. Grand and Broome Sts., and Centre Market Place. 1909. Hoppin & Koen. ★

In the manner of a French *hôtel de ville* (town hall), this is tightly arranged within the city's street system, not isolated palatially (as is City Hall or most any state capitol). Ornate **Renaissance Revival** architecture is laced with bits of **Baroque.** The shape of the building even follows that of the wedge-shaped plot it occupies.

The Feast of San Gennaro fills Mulberry Street from Canal to Spring Streets after the middle of September. Happily, autos are exiled. Arcaded with a filigree of electric lights, the street becomes a vast al fresco restaurant, interspersed with games of chance, for the benefit of this **venerable Neapolitan saint.** Fried pastries and sausages steam the air, and for one evening you may become part of the gregarious Italian public life (are those vendors really **Italian? Greek? Jewish? Limbos?**). **St. Anthony of Padua's** festival in June is also a delight [see Parades and Street Spectacles].

[5.] Engine Company 55, N.Y.C. Fire Department, 363 Broome St., bet. Mott and Elizabeth Sts. 1898. R. H. Robertson.

Ornate, eclectic Renaissance Revival.

Milan Laboratories, 57 Spring St., bet. Mulberry and Lafayette Sts.

The center for vinocultural chemistry: both for ingredients and equipment. Here one can outfit oneself to produce **Chianti in the cellar.** Apparatus and advice are available, as well as spices.

Grotta Azzurra (restaurant), 387 Broome St., cor. Mulberry St. Telephone: 226-9283.

The **grandest spot** of Little Italy. Those who have made the big time luxuriously return here to enjoy their old neighborhood. No reservations. No credit cards. You descend to a cellar: appropriate for a grotto.

 [6.] Old St. Patrick's Cathedral (Roman Catholic), 260–264 Mulberry St., bet. Prince and E. Houston Sts. E side. 1815. Joseph Mangin. Restored after a fire in 1868. Henry Engelbert. ★

The *original* **Roman Catholic** cathedral of New York. Present St. Patrick's uptown replaced it after a disastrous fire. Restored, this building was demoted to parish church status. The interior is a grand, murky brown "Gothicized" space, with cast-iron columns supporting a timber roof. The original (prefire) shell is in the Gothic-decorated Georgian tradition of **Sea and Land,** or the **Church of the Transfiguration,** both in the **Civic Center/Chinatown area.**

[7.] Old St. Patrick's Convent and Girl's School, 32 Prince St., SW cor. Mott St. 1826. ★

A **Georgian-Federal** building with a *classy* **Federal** entryway. Here the vocabulary of a Federal house was merely inflated to the program requirements of a parish school.

[8.] Originally **Fourteenth Ward Industrial School/Astor Memorial School,** 256–258 Mott St., bet. Prince and E. Houston Sts. E side. 1888. Vaux & Radford.

Gothic Revival forms give this somber relic **class** on an otherwise reserved block. Adaptively reused as a residential co-op.

[9.] St. Michael's Chapel (Roman Catholic), 266 Mulberry St., bet. Prince and E. Houston Sts. ca. 1850. ★

Neo-Gothic brownstone and brick built in a shape and location as if on a tenement lot.

[10.] Puck Building, 295 Lafayette St., bet. Houston, Jersey, and Mulberry Sts. 1885. Addition, 1892. Albert Wagner.

A gold-leafed **Puck** holds forth from the third-story perch at the corner of Mulberry Street. Monolithic red brick **Romanesque Revival.** Note the handsome gilt signs of the **Superior Printing Ink Company** across the ground floor. Smell the ink along Mulberry!

LOWER EAST SIDE

Far more significant historically than architecturally, this area harbors the legions of tenement buildings that **warehoused the arriving immigrants** of the 1880s, 1890s, and **up to World War I.**

Six-story masonry blocks covered **90** percent of the lots in question, offering no light and air except at the 90-foot-distant ends of these railroad flats and through minuscule sidewall air shafts. (Rooms strung end to end like railroad cars gave rise to the term "railroad flats.")

Hester Street at the turn of the century: tenements and seething humanity

On a 25- by 100-foot lot, ten to twelve families were the standard. Post-1930s **reaction against overcrowding** has produced an **unhappy over-compensation.** The density per acre remains the same or greater, but the edges of the Lower East Side have become dominated by high-rise, freestanding structures (it seems the taller and further apart the better). Project dwellers are supposed to **yearn for light and air,** or at least the apparent virtues of light and air. In that cause **they sacrifice the urbanity** that exists, say, in **Brooklyn Heights, Greenwich Village,** or **London's Bloomsbury** in the name of great sweeping lawns (that you can't touch, or cavort upon).

If there is a **significant** building type in this precinct it is **the syna-gogue.** In the years before World War I, some 500 Jewish houses of worship and *talmud torahs* (religious schools) were built here. Now few remain and fewer still are in use. A sampling follows, together with other landmarks of the community.

Seward Park to the East River:

[1.] Forward Building, 175 E. Broadway, bet. Rutgers and Jefferson Sts. S side. 1912.

The citadel of Yiddish thought and culture (once). Yiddish lettering in polychrome terra cotta on the roof parapet still reads *Forward* despite the relocation of New York's (and America's) **foremost Jewish language newspaper** to Harper & Row's old space on East 33rd Street. The build-ing's twelve stories housed not only the editorial offices of the newspaper but the main headquarters of a distinguished social organization, the *Arbiter Ring* **(Workmen's Circle)** and those of many other Jewish social and benevolent organizations and burial societies.

Garden Cafeteria, 165 E. Broadway at Rutgers St. Telephone: AL 4-6962.

A *true* New York cafeteria. When you enter you must **take a check** from a machine (gong!) scrupulously guarded by an employee who makes certain you take at least one and not two or more. The check gets presented to the counterman for punching as you accrete the dishes of your meal at the various stations of the counter. And what dishes! **All of a culture**—Eastern European Jewish. And all of a type—*dairy* (including fish)—as contrasted with *meat:* the two don't mix in a strictly kosher eating place, which this is. Here, **in the shadow** of the former Forward Building is where **politics** are still debated and **gossip** shared. Certainly the *Forward's* editor, Abraham Cahan (1860-1951), ate here; rumor has it that Leon Trotsky did too, while he lived in New York.

Seward Park: A bit of green (3 acres) at the intersection of East Broadway and Canal and Essex Streets **seems less rare today** than it did in the years before urban renewal when tenements were cleared and towers were placed on lawns. The park was named for Lincoln's secretary of state, **William H. Seward** (1801-1872).

[2a.] Recreation Building, in Seward Park. 1939. Department of Parks.

A Greek temple **updated** in the style of the Paris Exposition of 1936. Limestone with an ultramarine blue terra-cotta frieze (and lots of calligraphic grafitti—added later).

[2b.] Seward Park Branch, N.Y. Public Library, 192 E. Broadway opp. Jefferson St. W side. 1909. Babb, Cook & Welch.

A **palazzo for book users** (on the exterior at least). When built the area was bulging with people and land was scarce, hence the roof was planned as an outdoor reading area—note the balusters and verdigris beginnings of a trellis.

[3.] David Sarnoff Building, Educational Alliance, 197 E. Broadway SE cor. Jefferson St. 1889. Remodeled, 1969. David Kenneth Specter.

A **Romanesque Revival** settlement house with its spirit extended by the great new entrance arch.

[4.] St. Teresa's Roman Catholic Church/originally **First Presbyterian Church of New York,** 16–18 Rutgers St., NW cor. Henry St. 1841.

An ashlar church **in the tradition** of the others nearby, which antedate 1850. This one conducts services in **three languages:** English, Spanish, and Chinese.

[5.] Congregation B'nai Israel Kalwarie (synagogue), 15 Pike St., bet. E. Broadway and Henry St. E side. 1903.

A **humble** but lovely house of worship.

[6.] St. Barbara Greek Orthodox Church/originally **Kol Israel Anshe Poland (synagogue),** 27 Forsyth St. S of Canal St. E side. ca. 1895.

A **proud** religious edifice seeing reuse as a church.

[7.] Gouverneur Hospital, N.Y.C. Health and Hospitals Corporation, 327 Madison St., bet. Jefferson and Clinton Sts. N side. 1972. Charles B. Meyers, succeeded by Viola, Bernhard & Philips. Katz, Waisman, Weber & Strauss, architects and engineers; Blumenkranz & Bernhard, consultants.

A **fussy red brick prism** with buff pilasters that reach all the way to the roof. Note how the window size and placement are **irregular,** reflecting the **complex floor plans** of a modern-day hospital center.

[8.] Old Gouverneur Hospital, Franklin D. Roosevelt Drive bet. Gouverneur Slips E. and W., N side. 1901. Attributed to McKim, Mead & White.

The tiers of **curved, screened verandas** that jut out toward the Drive are familiar to the thousands of motorists who pass this **old city hospital** every day. Surpassed medically by its modern replacement [7.], its architectural merits remain. Can an adaptive reuse be found? If not, its future is a **wrecker's ball.**

The Great Shopping Area: The Bowery to Essex Street; Division Street north to East Houston.

Urban renewal has barely invaded here. Yet many of the tenements are vacant—but neatly boarded up. The explanation is the flourishing retail trade on the ground floors which injects economic vitality into the area. Best time to visit: Sunday.

[9a.] Congregation K'hal Adath Jeshurun (synagogue), 12–16 Eldridge St., bet. Forsyth and Canal Sts. E side. 1887. Herter Bros.

Eclectic: **Flamboyant Moorish** embellishment and a Gothic **wheel window** as well. This ornate facade, **the finest** of any of the Lower East Side synagogues, makes the tenements of Eldridge Street look **even more squalid.** Unfortunately, vandalism has taken its toll of the stained glass.

[9b.] Originally **Electrical Substation, Manhattan Railway Company,** 100 Division St. NW cor. Allen St. ca. 1900.

The elevated rapid transit ran above city streets because they offered a readily available and **inexpensive right-of-way.** When turns from one narrow thoroughfare into another were required, **private land** had to be purchased over which the viaduct would curve. When electrification came to the "els" these private sites also became the location for electrical substations, as is this one, skewed to clear the curve of the now-removed viaduct. [Also see Harlem 2.] This facility served the **Second Avenue elevated,** which clattered east out of Chatham Square along Division Street and turned northward into Allen Street (only **fifty feet wide** until 1930!). Allen Street's **perpetual darkness** and **noise** made it an undesirable place—it was one of the city's most notorious **red light districts** as a result.

Orchard Street on a recent Sunday

[9a.] Congr'n. K'hal Adath Jeshurun

[10.] Originally **S. Jarmulovsky's Bank,** 54–58 Canal St., SW cor. Orchard St. ca. 1912.

There are those who consider the domed, columned "temple" atop this building's twelve stories **a local architectural landmark.** But to those who know the saga of this bank, it is **a historical landmark.** Jarmulovsky's was established (in 1873 as the bronze lettering over the entrance still proclaims) as a local bank catering to the growing number of non-English-speaking immigrants being drawn to the area. As assets rose, largely from the working-class depositors' self-denial, **rumors began to spread** about insolvency. With the coming of World War I many wished to withdraw deposits to help relatives caught in Europe. Soon **runs** on this and other local banks developed, and then **actual riots.** For the Lower East Side, **black Tuesday** was August 4, 1914, when this and another bank were ordered closed as being "in an unsound and unsatisfactory condition." Thousands **lost their savings;** The Jarmulovskys received a suspended sentence.

The marketplace: Ethnically the Lower East Side has changed markedly since the beginning of the century. From what was once a community almost **entirely Jewish** has evolved a **mixed settlement** pattern: **Chinese** settling along East Broadway and environs, **Hispanics** moving in north of Delancey Street, and so on. But as these changes occur one quality remains, that of the citywide marketplace, particularly on Sundays—most of the shops are closed between Friday afternoon and Sunday morning in observance of *shabbos,* the Hebrew sabbath.

Grand Street between the Bowery and Chrystie: wedding gowns and tuxedoes; east of Forsyth: linens. **Canal Street** and lower **Eldridge Street:** religious goods such as *yarmulkes* (skull caps), *tallisim* (prayer shawls), and special items like *dreydlach* (spinning tops for Chanukah) and all manner of books in English, Yiddish, and Hebrew which deal with all facets of Judaism. **Allen Street:** brasswear. And most hectic and famous of all, **Orchard Street:** clothes, shoes, *shmatas* ("rags"), and fabrics (frequently remnants). The attraction which brings thousands back to this area to shop: bargains. Don't expect genteel salespeople or elegant displays—this is New York's most exciting bazaar.

[11.] Hester-Allen Turnkey Housing, N.Y.C. Housing Authority, 45 Allen St., NW cor. Hester St. 1973. Edelman & Salzman.

Simple, straightforward concrete and ribbed block housing with some thoughtful detailing at the ground plane.

[12.] Seward Park Extension (west part), N.Y.C. Housing Authority, 64–66 Essex St. bet. Grand and Broome Sts. E side. 1973. William F. Pedersen & Assocs.

One of two tall tan slabs [see 19.] whose design is **concentrated** in one **rich, plastic, three-dimensional, balconied facade,** this one facing south. Adjacent is an outdoor court and a low recreation building. Handsome.

[16.] Seventh Day Adventists Church   **[17.]** Cong. Adath Jeshurun of Jassy

B'nai B'rith: A plaque on the courtyard wall of the public housing calls attention to the birth at that site of B'nai B'rith, the nation's first national service agency, on October 13, 1843.

[13.] Beth Hamedrash Hagodol (synagogue)/originally **Norfolk Street Baptist Church,** 60–64 Norfolk St. bet. Grand and Broome Sts. E side. 1850. ★

Smooth stuccoing and a cream paint job with brown trim make the facade **a cartoon** of the original Gothic Revival design.

The Full Stomach:

Galishoff's (dairy restaurant), 81 Rivington St., W of Orchard St. Telephone: 473-6366. Kosher; closed Friday evening and all day Saturday.

They make their own *blintzes* here, thin dough filled with cheese and topped (if you wish) with sour cream. Try the cheese bagel, a warm, sticky sweet pastry which has only a vague relation to the bagel. Inexpensive.

Bernstein-on-Essex-Street (meat restaurant), 135 Essex St., bet. Rivington and Stanton Sts. Telephone: GR 3-3900. Kosher; closed Friday evening through Saturday evening.

Superbly corned, smoked, and spiced meats in the style of a Jewish delicatessen. But Kosher Chinese food as well! No pork, of course, but beef spareribs that could fool an expert. And for those whose eating habits are as eclectic as their taste for architectural styles, bread and pickles are served with Chinese meals upon request. Moderate. Chinese food, however, is considerably more expensive than in an equivalent Chinese restaurant and is only fair. Beer and wine available.

Katz's Delicatessen, 205 E. Houston St., cor. Ludlow St. Telephone: AL 4-2246. Non-Kosher.

Famous and busy but a far cry from the days when its reputation was made.

Guss Pickle Products, 42 Hester St., W of Essex St. Telephone: GR 7-1969. Kosher. Closed for the sabbath.

They line up on the sidewalk here, alongside the pickle barrels (plastic now; no longer of wood staves) to buy half-sours, sour tomatoes, sweet red peppers, and sauerkraut. Buy something to munch on the street as you walk, or buy some to take home . . . jars are available to send you home with both pickles *and* their garlic-flavored brine.

Gertel's (bakery and coffee shop), 53 Hester St., W of Essex St. Telephone: 982-3250. Kosher. Closed for the sabbath.

While primarily a bakeshop there are tables in the rear where you can enjoy a pastry and coffee (or tea). Try some *ruggalach,* tiny rolled pastries which become more flavorful the more you chew.

[14.] Bell Yarn/originally **Eastern Dispensary**/later **Good Samaritan Dispensary,** 75 Essex St., NW cor. Broome St. ca. 1895.

Today, four stories of yarn; once the eastern outpost of a dispensary system for Lower Manhattan [see Northern Dispensary, Greenwich Village 43.]. Stately golden-brown and salmon brick.

[15.] Originally **E. Ridley & Son (dry goods),** 319–321 Grand St., SW cor. Orchard St. ca. 1870.

Before and after the Civil War, Grand Street east of the Bowery was the **center of women's fashions** in the city. **Lord & Taylor,** at Grand and Chrystie Streets, and **Edward Ridley's,** at Orchard, were the two **most popular** dry goods stores. Of the two, only Ridley's building remains. Its facade is of cast iron and still plays a role today in the Lower East Side shopping bazaar.

[16.] Seventh Day Adventists Church of Union Square/originally **Poel Zedek Anshe Ileya (synagogue),** 128–130 Forsyth St., SE cor. Delancey St. ca. 1895.

This house of worship is reached by a symmetrical flight of steps on the Forsyth Street sidewalk, thus permitting retail establishments to occupy the ground floor on Delancey Street. The combination of worship (sacred) and business (profane) did well.

[17.] Originally **Congregation Adath Jeshurun of Jassy (synagogue)**/later **First Warsaw Congregation,** 58–60 Rivington St., bet. Eldridge and Allen Sts. N side. 1903.

A magnificent eclectic facade with bits and pieces from a variety of styles and influences. Damaged by vandalism, its days may be numbered. **Worth an extra trip** anyway.

[18.] Congregation Shaarai Shomoyim First Roumanian American Congregation (synagogue)/originally **Allen Street Methodist Church,** 83–93 Rivington St., bet. Orchard and Ludlow Sts. S side. ca. 1885.

Solid, stolid Romanesque Revival flattened by paint and soot.

Deep down: At Delancey and Eldridge Streets is Shaft XX of the Catskill Water System, the city's third aqueduct. It is notable in that it is the deepest shaft, 740 feet into the earth's crust.

Grand Street and environs: From Essex Street to the East River

[19.] Seward Park Extension (east part), N.Y.C. Housing Authority, 154–156 Broome St., E of Clinton St., N side. 1973. William F. Pederson & Assocs.

The sibling of 64–66 Essex Street [see 12.] but minus a community facility annex. This slab's rich facade faces east to the river.

[20.] St. Mary's Roman Catholic Church, 438 Grand St., W of Pitt St. N side. 1833. Enlarged, present facade added, 1871. P.C. Keely.

The **oldest** Roman Catholic church structure **in all of the city**—the somber gray ashlar rear portion, that is. The amusing red brick front and its twin spires are by the prolific church architect Patrick Charles Keely.

[21.] 7th Precinct Station House, N.Y.C. Police Department, and Engine Company 17, Ladder Company 18, N.Y.C. Fire Department, 19½–25 Pitt St. NW cor. Broome St. 1975. William F. Pedersen & Assocs.

Articulated form, each function with its special shape and view, the **antithesis of Mies van der Rohe.** Specific, plastic, slotted, revealed: a unique building for unique uses. Note the use of clinker bricks to develop a subtle texture seen only up close.

[22a.] Arts for Living Center, Henry Street Settlement and Neighborhood Playhouse, 466 Grand St., bet. Pitt and Willett Sts. N side. 1975. Prentice & Chan, Ohlhausen.

An urban exedra, these buildings make a civic space in this *wasteland* of amorphous streets. A high moment of architecture that brings a suggestion of urbane Manhattan (cf. **Greenwich Village, Gramercy Park**) to this Rego Park-styled area.

[22a.] Arts for Living Center, Henry Street Settlement and Neighbd. Playhouse

[22b.] Bialystoker Synagogue/originally **Willett Street Methodist Church,** 7–13 Willett St., bet. Grand and Broome Sts. W side. 1826. ★

Manhattan schist, brownstone and whitestone. Shifting ethnic populations cause changing uses of venerable buildings such as this. Originally a **rural Protestant church,** it now serves the dense Jewish population in this neighborhood.

[23a.] Amalgamated Dwellings, 504–520 Grand St., NW cor. Abraham Kazan Street, through to Broome St. 1930. Springsteen & Goldhammer.
[23b.] Hillman Housing, 500, 530, and 550 Grand St., bet. Willett and Lewis Sts. 1951. Springsteen & Goldhammer.

Two generations ago, the late **Abraham Kazan,** as president of the **United Housing Foundation,** explored the world of mass housing on behalf of the Amalgamated Clothing Workers, providing, in concert with his architects, these pioneer projects. Times have changed: his **15,500**-unit **Co-op City** in the Bronx is not in the same class of avant-garde thinking as these antecedents.

The pre-Depression project, a hollow rectangular donut, was heavily influenced by the work of the founder of the School of Amsterdam style, **Michael de Klerk** (1884–1923), and early 1920s public housing of **Adolf Loos** (1870–1933) in Vienna. The parabolic arched opening from Broome Street offers a view into the fine central courtyard. The post-World War II project begins to reflect the tower on the lawn approach. It comes off poorly in comparison.

[24.] Williamsburg Bridge, from Delancey and Clinton Sts. in Manhattan to Washington Plaza in Brooklyn. 1903. Leffert L. Buck, chief engineer.

To the former **City of Williamsburgh,** now part of Brooklyn. The unusual **(straight)** cables on the land side of the towers result from the fact that support is by truss and pier, rather than pendant cable as in the Brooklyn Bridge: the latter's land-side cables hang in a **catenary curve,** in contrast.

[22b.] The Bialystoker Synagogue   **[26a.]** The Henry Street Settlement

[25.] St. Augustine's Chapel, Trinity Parish (Protestant Episcopal)/originally **All Saints' Church,** 290 Henry St., bet. Montgomery and Jackson Sts. S side. 1828. Attributed to John Heath. ★

Georgian body with Gothic Revival windows. Compare Chinatown's **Church of the Transfiguration,** or the **Sea and Land Church** [see Civic Center/Chinatown 48. and 41.]. Built with Manhattan schist and crisp white pediments.

[26a.] Henry Street Settlement/originally **Nurses Settlement,** 263–267 Henry St., bet. Montgomery and Grand Sts. N side. 1827–1834. ★

Greek Revival town houses now happily preserved by a distinguished private social agency, founded by **Lillian Wald** (1867–1940), who is personally memorialized in the public housing bearing her name between East Houston and East 6th Streets on the river. **No. 265** is the *star*.

[26b.] Engine Company 15, N.Y.C. Fire Department, 269 Henry St., bet. Montgomery and Grand Sts. 1883.

Virtuoso facade of brick over a cast-iron ground floor. Particularly enlivening are the pair of corbeled cornice brackets and marvelous, textured spandrels.

[27.] Ritualarium (mikveh)/formerly **Young Men's Benevolent Association,** 313 E. Broadway, W of Grand St. 1904.

This ornate facade clads a building now used for the **ritual baths** which Orthodox Jewish women are required to take prior to the marriage ceremony and monthly thereafter. According to the Scriptures the water must be unadulterated—when possible it is rainwater captured in cisterns.

[28.] East River Houses/ILGWU Cooperative Village (International Ladies Garment Workers Union)/originally called **Corlear's Hook Houses,** N and S of Grand St., bet. Lewis and Jackson Sts. to Franklin D. Roosevelt Dr. 1956. Herman Jessor.

Five thousand people dwell in these carven brick monoliths that excel their descendants at **Co-op City** in cost, in architecture, and in views.

[29.] Old Congregation Anshe Chesed   [37.] The DeWitt Reformed Church

[36.] A square doughnut on stilts: JHS 22, Manhattan, with adjacent library

Delancey to Houston Streets: From Essex Street to the East River

[29.] Originally **Congregation Anshe Chesed (synagogue)**/later **Ohab Zedek**/later **Anshe Slonim,** 172–176 Norfolk St., bet. Stanton and E. Houston Sts., E side. 1849. Alexander Saeltzer.

With the exception of this distinguished house of worship—now in a state of painful disrepair—all Lower East Side Jewish congregations that occupied buildings built before 1850 had purchased and converted **existing churches.** This edifice, the city's **oldest** and for a time its **largest** synagogue (and its first Reform temple), was built by an established Jewish community whose members **moved northward,** together with their Christian neighbors, as the area became a refuge for Eastern European immigrants. **Anshe Chesed** is today in the Upper West Side.

[30.] Congregation Chasam Sofer (synagogue)/originally **Congregation Rodeph Sholom,** 8–10 Clinton St., bet. Stanton and E. Houston Sts., E side. 1853.

The second oldest surviving synagogue in the city [after 29.]. Rodeph Sholom left these parts in 1886. Today its temple is on West 83rd Street.

Matzos and wine: Two important industries remain along Rivington Street in the heart of the Lower East Side, Shapiro's Wine Company (No. 126), and Streit's Matzoth Company (No. 150). Both prepare their products for sacramental purposes, although many who live in the community (and many others) enjoy them throughout the year. Need one add that they are prepared under rabbinical supervision and are kosher.

[31.] Loew's Delancey Theater, 140–146 Delancey St., NW cor. Suffolk St. ca. 1922.

An unusually attractive maroon brick box is capped by a polychrome terra-cotta frieze under a projecting cornice. The marquee has been updated.

[32.] Originally **Congregation Dukler Mugain Abraham (synagogue),** 87 Attorney St. bet. Delancey and Rivington Sts. W side. ca. 1898.

A humble Roman Revival temple.

[33.] Public School 142 Manhattan, 100 Attorney St., SE cor. Rivington St. 1975. Michael Radoslavitch.

A fashionable form in plan, a banjo, fails to come to life as architecture.

[34.] Intermediate School 25 Manhattan, 145 Stanton St., bet. Norfolk and Suffolk Sts. S side. 1977. David Todd & Assocs.

A powerful combination of creamy white concrete horizontals with dark red giant brick infill all embraced by the strong forms of the stair towers at the corners. Will the materials withstand the grafitti?

[35.] Originally **Hamilton Fish Park Gymnasium and Public Baths, N.Y.C. Parks and Recreation Department,** 130 Pitt St., bet. Stanton and E. Houston Sts. E side. ca. 1905. Carrère & Hastings.

An **oompah** Beaux Arts pavilion built to serve the needs for **recreation and bathing** of the immigrants who crowded this precinct after the turn of the century. Though monumental *in scale,* it surely failed to be large enough *in size.*

[36.] Junior High School 22 Manhattan, The Gustave V.E. Straubenmuller School, and **Hamilton Fish Park Branch, N.Y. Public Library,** 111 Columbia St., SE cor. Houston St. 1956. Kelly & Gruzen.

A **square doughnut** on stilts and an adjacent, earthbound library. Its modern materials wore poorly. Stylish in its time, it is now dated.

[37.] DeWitt Reformed Church, 280 Rivington St., NE cor. Columbia St. 1957. Edgar Tafel.

A simple brick box that contains a space of used brick and a cross of tree trunks: **rustic and humane charm** amidst overpowering housing.

V

THE VILLAGES

GREENWICH VILLAGE

Nonconformist: In its street grids (they differ from each other as well as from those of the rest of Manhattan), in the life-styles it tolerates (or is it *nurtures?*), and in its *remarkable* variety of architecture, **Greenwich Village** is a concentration of contrasts in a city of contrasts. But in the **Village's** case, these contrasts have long been synonymous with its identity: *bohemia.* This is less true today than when both aspiring and successful artists and writers gravitated to this crooked-streeted, humanely scaled,

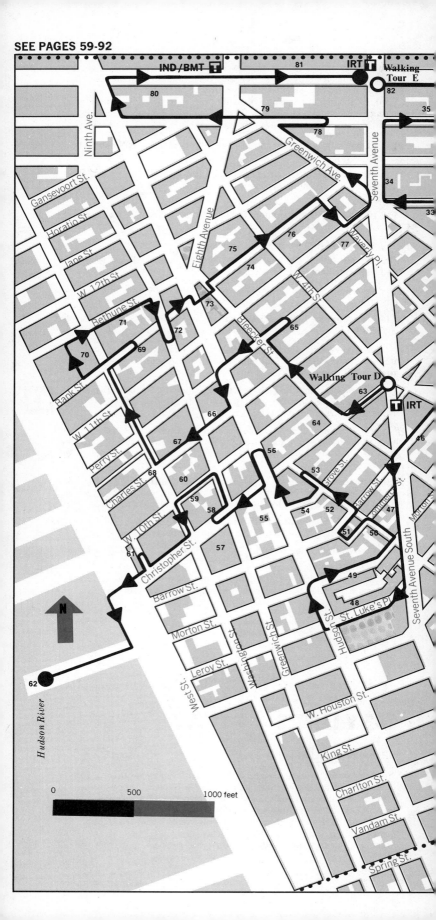

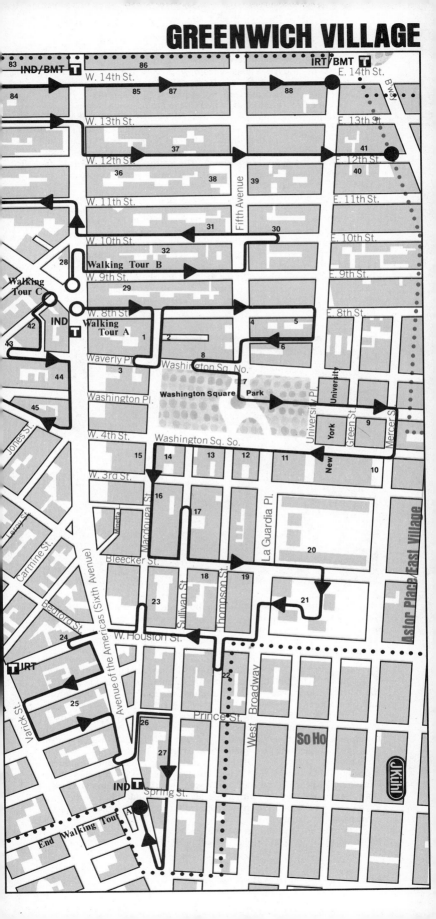

GREENWICH VILLAGE

out-of-the-way, low-rent enclave passed over by the city's growth northward. Actually, today's **Village** encompasses **both** the long-fashionable side streets along **lower Fifth Avenue** as well as those *irregular byways* to the south and west that are featured in picture postcard views.

Since the turn of the century the **Village** has been not only a proving ground for new ideas among its creative residents but also a symbol of the forbidden, the free life, the **closest thing to Paris** that we have in this country. With the opening up of Sixth and Seventh Avenues and the subways beneath them, the area became accessible to more and more visitors. After the hiatus caused by the **Depression** and **World War II,** the Village once again attracted interest, this time from high-rise housing developers, from smaller entrepreneurs who created little studio apartments whose minispaces were inversely proportional to their high rents, and from tenants who left the "duller" (meaning the outer) parts of the city to taste a *forbidden* life. Creators were swept out by observers (middle-class doctors, dentists, cloak and suiters, and other vicarious residents). The people of the visible Village changed—leaving West Village families, such as those written about by urbanist **Jane Jacobs,** and those of the South Village (the Italian community), to go about their own business, largely unnoticed. In the fifties, it was the *beat* **generation;** since then it has had an increasingly large representation of **the drug culture,** a situation not helped by the **greedy commercialization** around Eighth and MacDougal Streets.

As its nostalgic glamour fades, however, it continues to fulfill a variety of seemingly conflicting roles: a genteel place to live, a fashionable step up the professional ladder, a spawning ground for movements such as feminism and gay liberation, a singles' haven, a place to raise a family, in short, a *perplexing* **but certainly not colorless** community.

Heritage: Always a village, the first one was an Algonquin community, **Sapokanikan.** The **Dutch,** upon their arrival in **1626,** quickly kicked out the natives, taking over the fertile rolling farmland for their own profit and pleasure.

Growth was leisurely since the village was completely separated from the bustling community concentrated at the lower tip of the island; its stature, though, rose suddenly in the **1730s** with the land purchases of socially prominent naval **Captain Peter Warren.** When **Captain Warren** bought a large parcel in **1731,** he was the first of a long line of affluent individuals to settle in the Village. His mansion was soon followed by **Richmond Hill** (owned by Aaron Burr, among others), **Alexander Hamilton's estate,** and the **Brevoort** homestead. **Richmond Hill** was the best known of these homes which, for nearly 100 years, gave the Village an unsurpassed social status.

The city commissioners, having already contemplated the future growth of Manhattan, appointed **John Randel, Jr.,** who from **1808** to **1811** prepared maps and plans for the present gridiron of Manhattan's streets. The Village escaped most of this layout, however, since it was simply too difficult to impose it over the well-established pattern. The **commissioners,** though, had their way with the hills; *leveling* them all by **1811,** and taking with them the grandeur of the old estates. These properties were then easily divisible into small city lots, and by 1822 the community was densely settled, many of the settlers "refugees" from a series of "downtown" epidemics.

Sailors' Snug Harbor and Trinity Parish have both had leading roles in the **Village's** growth.

The **Harbor** was founded in 1801 when **Captain Robert Richard Randall** deeded in perpetual lease 21 acres of land (around and north of Washington Square), together with a modest cash grant, for the support of a home for aged seamen. It was moved to **Staten Island** in **1833,** and since then has received its *income* from its leased Village land. Prior to the 1920s, its property had been divided into small lots, rented mainly for individual residences. Since then, land values have skyrocketed, and the **Harbor** understandably sought to increase its income from its holdings. In doing so, however, it leased rather indiscriminately, permitting the demolition of many historic and architectural treasures and their replacement by mediocre works, to the detriment of the area.

Trinity Parish made great contributions to the development of the **West Village** in the **19th** century, encouraging respectful care and beautification of its leased land. In **1822** it developed a residential settlement around **St. Luke's Church** which to this day is a positive influence upon the neighborhood.

The Residents: Perhaps as important as the architectural heritage are the *people* the **Village** has attracted; the artists and writers, entertainers, intellectuals, and bohemians who have made their homes alongside long-established but less conspicuous Village families. But the artist in his garret is today more legend than reality. The well-established Hollywood actor, "Madison Avenue gallery" painter, and copy writer have replaced the *struggling* painter and writer; we find **Dustin Hoffman, Robert Rauschenberg** (perhaps self-serious, but certainly "art" motivated), and **Leontyne Price** more typical residents. **Eugene O'Neill** and his group at The Provincetown Playhouse; **Maxwell Bodenheim; Edna St. Vincent Millay;** the delightful, "spirited" **Dylan Thomas** at Hudson Street's White Horse Tavern; and quiet **Joe Gould** accumulating material for his "oral history" at the Minetta—these were the ones who once made the Village reputation international. Their forerunners were writers of the **19th** century who took up residence here, attracted by modest rents, the leisurely pace, and the delightful streets and houses. They included **Poe** and **Melville, Mark Twain,** and **Henry James.**

Though the future "writers-in-residence" of the **Village** will, more frequently than not, be well-paid *copy* writers, they will, more than likely, seek out the same **Federal** and **Victorian** row houses and back-alleyed, converted stables to live in that attracted the **Mark Twains** and **E. St. V. Millays** years ago.

The Village, though no longer bohemian, still represents the unconventional, a reputation supported by its winding streets, its tiny houses sandwiched between impersonal behemoths, its charming shops and eateries.

Greenwich Village Historic District: It took more than four years and seven public hearings to decide upon one contiguous historic district for the Village—at one point eighteen separate districts were considered— and the enormous irregular shape of the hundred-plus block area defies simple description in words. Suffice to say that it stretches *west* from **University Place** to **Washington Street** in the **West Village.** Its *southernmost* border, again in the **West Village,** is **St. Luke's Place,** but in the *east* it begins with **Washington Square Park.** On the *north* the district approaches, but never quite encompasses, **Fourteenth Street.** And, to complicate matters further, there are two *other* official historic districts in the southern reaches of the Village [see **23.** and **25.**].

District designated, 1969. ★

Note: The first four walking tours include *some* buildings in the **Greenwich Village Historic District;** they are identified at the start of each of those tours.

Walking Tour A: Eighth Street, Washington Square, N.Y.U., and the South Village. From West Eighth Street at Sixth Avenue to the Charlton-King-Vandam Historic District. Begin at Village Square (IND Sixth and Eighth Avenue Subways to the West Fourth Street Station).

Note: Only entries 1–8 on this tour lie within the Greenwich Village Historic District. ★

West Eighth Street may have seen its heyday, for today the shops seem a bit worn, and the quality of the goods offered between Sixth Avenue and Fifth is, more often than not, a more expensive, poorer variation of what can be found elsewhere in the area. Yet there are **noteworthy exceptions** among the tourist traps. The **West Side Book Store**, No. 26, and **E. S. Wilentz's Eighth Street Bookshop**, No. 17, are havens for both local habitués and the serious reader. Toward Fifth Avenue the New York Studio School, No. 8, marks **the original site of the Whitney Museum** of American Art—it began in the bohemian Village and has twice moved uptown, as if itself keeping pace with swiftly changing styles.

[1.] Tenth Church of Christ, Scientist   [2.] The entrance to MacDougal Alley

Frederick J. Kiesler's Eighth Street Playhouse (52 West Eighth Street) is barely recognizable today, its succession of owners having failed to value his visionary designs, though they were applauded and applied by theater architects throughout the world. Here, in 1928, he made provisions for **simultaneous slide projections** on the side walls and created a main screen where the projection surface area could be altered in size—film projection concepts that are still considered avant-garde. The exterior bears no trace of his hand.

[1.] **Tenth Church of Christ, Scientist,** 171 MacDougal Street, bet. W. 8th St. and Waverly Place. W side. 1967. Victor Christ-Janer.

Great corbeled brick openings in an austere facade give this a **monumental scale** in these small streets.

[2.] **MacDougal Alley,** at MacDougal Street, bet. W. 8th St. and Washington Sq. N., E side.

This *charming* cul-de-sac (less charming when filled with residents' cars) is jointly owned by property holders on **Washington Square North** and on the south side of 8th Street. The twenty-storied bulk of No. 2 Fifth Avenue looms over it, overwhelming its space and diminishing its small-scaled delight.

[3.] **108 Waverly Place,** bet. Sixth Ave. and Washington Sq. W., S side. 1826. Altered, 1906. Charles C. Haight. Garage entrance removed, 1927.

In this pleasantly Classical street, this eccentric and dour granite house wears crenellations (presumably to protect the skylight against insurrection).

[4a.] 1 Fifth Avenue (apartments), SE cor. E. Eighth St. 1929. Helmle, Corbett & Harrison and Sugarman & Berger.

A stepped-back pinnacle of cool brown brick which has been a **visual landmark** on lower Fifth Avenue and Washington Square ever since it was built. On its Eighth Street frontage is:

[4b.] 1/5 (One Fifth Avenue Bar/Restaurant), 1976. Kiki Kogelnik, designer. Telephone: 260-3434.

A restaurant and bar outfitted with Art Deco remnants of the Cunard liner *S.S. Caronia*'s first-class dining room, rescued from her wreckage. Great for Sunday brunch or drinks. Moderate to expensive.

[5.] 4–26 East Eighth Street (converted apartments), bet. University Place and Fifth Ave. Remodeled, 1916. Harvey Wiley Corbett.

A set of brick houses made picturesque by the addition of bold decorative eaves, brickwork inlaid in a stucco ground, and bits of wrought ironwork. A **stage set,** symbolic of the "village" of a bohemian artist but **not typical** of its Federal/Greek Revival architectural reality.

A walk-through Belgian-block-paved Washington Mews (private, but pedestrians are not discouraged) is the best way to sense this alley's space:

[6.] Washington Mews, from University Place to Fifth Ave., bet. E. Eighth St. and Washington Sq. N.

A **19th-century mews** lined on its uptown side with converted stables that once served the brownstones on Eighth Street and Washington Square and that now, in the case of many, serve **New York University.** The buildings on the south side were built in the 1930s and almost all were stuccoed in concert, causing an unfortunate regimentation.

[7.] Washington Square Park, at the foot of Fifth Ave. Reconstructed, 1971. John J. Kassner & Co., engineers. Robert Nichols, landscape architect. Service buildings, 1971. Edgar Tafel & Assocs. Patchwork mosaic plaza, 1971. Cityarts Workshop. **[7a.] Washington Arch,** 1892. McKim, Mead & White. Winged figures, Frederick MacMonnies. West pier, *Washington in Peace,* 1918. A. Stirling Calder. East pier, *Washington in War,* 1916. Herman A. MacNeil.

Originally marshland with **Minetta Brook** meandering through, then a potter's field, and later the site of the hanging gallows; in the **1820s** a less sadistic citizenry converted it to a public park and parade ground for the military. With this change, building quickly began on all sides of the park,

[7./7a.] Washington Square Park and Arch, **[4a.]** 1 Fifth Avenue in background

the north side with its **"Row"** [see **8.**], and the east, which became the site of the first **N.Y.U.** building in **1837.**

The **Memorial Arch** (1892) was first erected in wood in **1876** for the centennial celebration by **McKim, Mead & White.** It was so well liked that pianist **Jan Paderewski** gave a benefit concert to help finance the permanent arch. The statue of Washington as a civilian on the west pier was sculpted by mobile-maker **Alexander Calder's** father, **Alexander Stirling Calder** (1870–1945).

In 1964, local and citywide groups achieved a victory in their battle to keep an underpass from being built beneath the park. They later managed to free the park *entirely* of vehicular traffic—Fifth Avenue buses had for years used the space around the fountain as a turnaround, idling their engines there between runs. These accomplishments were later escalated into a full-blown redesign of the park, which kept the canopy of trees and added a circular pedestrian plaza ringing the old central fountain, a fresh interpretation of **the European plaza.**

Despite substantial involvement of the community in the redesign, the physical changes have been the subject of great controversy. Some of this is the result of major demographic population shifts in the adjunct community—an outflow of families and an influx of outcasts.

Best seen from the park:

[8.] "The Row," Nos. 1–13, Nos. 21–26 Washington Square North (originally Nos. 1–28). ca. 1831. Nos. 21–26, Martin E. Thompson of Town & Davis.

When built, these housed the most socially prominent New Yorkers, such as the **Delano family.** Later, **Edith Wharton, William Dean Howells,** and **Henry James** all lived and worked at No. 1. In this century **John Dos Passos** wrote *Manhattan Transfer* in No. 3; others living there have been **Edward Hopper** and **Rockwell Kent.** No. 8 was once the official residence of the mayor.

The first six (Nos. 21–26) at the west end of today's row (also remembered in **Henry James'** *Washington Square*) established the overall style, a bold Ionic Greek Revival, leaving the others which followed to other architects or builders. Over the years community pressure and artful illusion have maintained **The Row** in a fairly whole condition. Those from **7 to 13,** to the east of Fifth Avenue, retain the shell of their front and side facades only: **Sailors' Snug Harbor** *gutted* them for multiple-dwelling housing, and entrance to these now N.Y.U.-owned apartments is via a pergola facing Fifth Avenue. On the west side of Fifth, when the huge No. 2 Fifth Avenue apartment tower was being planned, citizens put up an outcry, and a *neo-neo-***Georgian** wing was designed for the Washington Square frontage, conspicuously lower than the adjacent *real* **Greek Revival** row houses.

Sailors' Snug Harbor Headquarters, 262 Greene St., bet. E. Eighth St. and Waverly Place. The administrative center of a compact real estate empire (within a short walk of this building) funded by Capt. Robert Richard Randall in 1801 to endow a home for aged seamen. The sailors' home on Staten Island [see Staten Island 3.], an elegant Greek Revival landmark, was vacated in 1976 in favor of new facilities in North Carolina.

New York University: N.Y.U.'s avaricious land grabbing has created an empire *larger* than the Village holdings of Sailors' Snug Harbor, consisting of **loft buildings, apartment houses, and Greek Revival rows** on and around Washington Square. Once the bane of Villagers' existence, N.Y.U.'s empire-building was tamed in the **1970s** by economic realities. Philip Johnson and Richard Foster had been commissioned to create a unified urban campus where none had existed before. Their plans called for rebuilding and refacing buildings around the east side of Washington Square with the vivid red sandstone visible in the master plan's only fruits: the **Bobst Library,** the **Tisch building,** and the **Meyer physics building.** Happily, the rest of this grandiose scheme has been abandoned.

Grey Art Gallery, N.Y.U., 33 Washington Place, E of Washington Sq. E. Telephone: 598-3479.

One of N.Y.U.'s bright spots: an offbeat gallery with high standards of quality. Note the grid of white-painted Doric columns on the interior around which the exhibitions are arranged.

The Triangle Fire: A polite bronze plaque at the northwest corner of Washington Place and Greene Street refers discreetly to "the site" of the Triangle Shirtwaist Company fire, a tragedy which took **146 lives**, mostly those of young women, on the Saturday afternoon of March 25, 1911. The loft building which stands today on this corner, originally called the **Asch Building,** is the very building in which the holocaust took place; Triangle occupied the upper three floors of the ten-story building.

[9.] Ten Washington Place Building, N.Y.U./originally **loft building**, bet. Mercer and Greene Sts. 1891. Richard Berger. Facade restored, 1972.

The loss of its cornice has not seriously diminished the delicate character of this loft building's orange terra-cotta, black cast-iron, and pink granite facade carefully restored by N.Y.U. upon the advice of master planners Johnson and Foster.

[10.] Warren Weaver Hall, N.Y.U., 251 Mercer St., bet. W. 3rd and W. 4th Sts. W side. 1966. Warner, Burns, Toan & Lunde.

An early N.Y.U. attempt at architectural identity via a new building—now dated.

[8.] "The Row," Washington Square N.   **[10.]** Warren Weaver Hall at N.Y.U.

The Redskins:

[11.] Elmer Holmes Bobst Library, N.Y.U., 70 Washington Square S., bet. W. Broadway and Washington Sq. E., S side. 1972. Philip Johnson and Richard Foster.

Johnson is here experimenting with a free neo-Classicism (the "columns" are voids rather than volumes). The redskin facade thus produced is, however, bulky and mannered. Inside, a great atrium brings light and a sense of space to its users, while the outside shades the park. Though Bobst was begun first, in 1968, it took the longest to complete and was beaten to completion by two other bulky works:

[11a.] André and Bella Meyer Physics Hall, N.Y.U., 707 Broadway, SW cor. Washington Place. W side. 1971. **[11b.] Tisch Hall, N.Y.U.,** 40 W. 4th St. at Greene St. S side. 1972. Both by Philip Johnson and Richard Foster.

Two more "redskins," this time *without* meaningful inner spaces. Note in front of Tisch Hall the Gothic finial from N.Y.U.'s original building on Washington Square. Removed during the demolition in 1894, it had been at N.Y.U.'s Bronx campus [see W Bronx **34.**] until N.Y.U. pulled out in 1974.

[12a.] Loeb Student Center, N.Y.U., 566–576 LaGuardia Place, SE cor. Washington Sq. S. 1959. Harrison & Abramovitz, architects. Reuben Nakian, sculptor. **[12b.] Holy Trinity Chapel, Generoso Pope Catholic Center at N.Y.U.,** 58 Washington Sq. S. SE cor. Thompson St. 1964. Eggers & Higgins.

Two awkward attempts at "modern architecture."

[13a.] Judson Memorial Baptist Church, 55 Washington Sq. S. ★
[13b.] Judson Hall and Tower, 53 Washington Sq. S., bet. Thompson
and Sullivan Sts. 1892. McKim, Mead & White, architects. John La
Farge, stained glass. ★ Herbert Adams, marble relief, south wall of
chancel (after plans of Saint-Gaudens).

An *eclectic* **Romanesque Revival** church and tower (in a spirit and
scale as if built by a Roman) that once dominated Washington Square,
but now is dwarfed by many bulbous neighbors. Its ornate and pompous
detail, en masse, recalls such inflated Roman churches as St. Paul's
Outside-the-Walls. Look inside. The tower and adjacent buildings are
now a dormitory.

[13a.] Judson Memorial Church/Tower   **[13c.]** Hagop Kevorkian Center, N.Y.U.

[13c.] Hagop Kevorkian Center for Near Eastern Studies, N.Y.U.,
50 Washington Sq. S., SE cor. Sullivan St. 1972. Philip Johnson and
Richard Foster.

A classy but overscaled granite building matching in size the adjacent
"town house." It would have been a *happier* neighbor to the Judson
complex were it in brick.

[14.] Vanderbilt Law School, N.Y.U., 40 Washington Sq. S., bet. Sullivan
and MacDougal Sts. 1951. Eggers & Higgins.

A blockful of fake Georgian building, trying to be neighborly, but
succeeding only in being banal.

[15.] 127–131 MacDougal Street, bet. W. 3rd and W. 4th Sts. W side.
1829.

These Federal houses were built for **Aaron Burr.** The pineapple
newel posts on the ironwork at No. **129** are one of the few such pairs
remaining in the Village.

MacDougal Street: This street and vicinity between West Third and
Bleecker was one of the most colorful and magnetic to tourists out for an
evening in the Village. With the advent of the drug scene its activities took
a turn to the bizarre, and many of its restaurants, coffee houses, jewelry
boutiques, and folk song emporia disappeared. Some still remain or have
been reincarnated:

Granados Restaurant (Spanish), 125 MacDougal St., cor. W. 3rd St.
Telephone: OR 3-5576.

Gracious dining amidst Goya prints. Try the familiar, such as *arroz
con pollo,* or more tantalizing dishes. *Sangria* and a full bar are available,
as well. Dinner only, alas. Moderate.

[16.] 130–132 MacDougal Street, bet. Bleecker and W. 3rd Sts. E side.
1852. ★

Twin entrances and ironwork portico are uncommon. **Louisa May
Alcott** once lived here.

Minetta Tavern, 113 MacDougal St., SW cor. Minetta Lane. Telephone: 473-9119.

A **drinking man's museum** of Greenwich Village. The walls are crammed with photographs and other mementoes of the famed characters who claimed the Minetta as a second home during the heyday of the Village. Note especially the **Joe Gould memorabilia.** Italian cooking, moderate prices.

Monte's (Italian restaurant), 97 MacDougal St., N. of Bleecker St. Telephone: OR 4-9456.

Downstairs, cramped, colorful. Tasty Italian food at bargain prices. Cash only.

Coffeehouses:

Caffè Reggio, 119 MacDougal St., S of Minetta Lane. Telephone: GR 5-9557. **Café Borgia,** 185 Bleecker St., cor. MacDougal St. Telephone: 674-9589. **Le Figaro,** 186 Bleecker St., cor. MacDougal St. Telephone: 677-1100. **Caffè Dante,** 81 MacDougal St., S of Bleecker St. Telephone: 674-9261.

The oldest and most authentic is Reggio with a nickelplated brass *mácchina* spewing forth steamed espresso or other coffee, cocoa, or milk combinations. Dante's special contribution is a giant color photo mural of Florence from **San Miniato.** But all have pastries, hot and cold beverages, and conviviality.

[17.] Originally **Lower West Side Children's Center, Children's Aid Society (Sullivan Street School)**/now **William Church Osborn Club,** 219 Sullivan St., bet. W. 3rd and Bleecker Sts. E side. 1892. Vaux & Radford.

Rich interplay of brick and brownstone (now stucco), solid and void, arches and angles: its details have since been smoothed by less-skilled craftsmen.

[15.] 127–131 MacDougal St. (l to r)   **[18.]** The Atrium (apts.) (photo 1967)

[18.] The Atrium (apartments)/originally **Mills House No. 1,** 160 Bleecker St., bet. Thompson and Sullivan Sts. S side. 1896. Ernest Flagg. Altered, 1976.

Reclaimed by the middle class as apartments, the structure was built originally as a hostel for poor "gentlemen" (the room rate was only **20¢** a night, but the expenses were covered by profits on the **10¢** and **25¢** meals). The building was a milestone in concept and plan: **1,500** tiny bedrooms either on the outside or overlooking the two grassed interior courts open to the sky. Eventually the courts were skylighted and paved and the structure became a *seedy* hotel, **The Greenwich.** The two courts, now neatly rebuilt with access balconies to the apartments which ring them, are the inspiration for the project's new name. In the basement and on street level:

Village Gate (theater-nightclub)/Top of the Gate (restaurant). Telephone: 982-9292.

An ancient, by Village standards, downstairs showplace (1958) with cabaret above and restaurant between, the theater-nightclub noted for its avant-garde and traditional entertainment.

[19.] Bleecker Street Playhouse/formerly **Mori's Restaurant,** 146 Bleecker St., bet. LaGuardia Place and Thompson St. Restaurant alteration and current facade, 1920. Raymond Hood.

Hood, soon to gain recognition in the *Chicago Tribune* Tower competition, converted a pair of old row houses to one of the Village's best-known Italian restaurants of the period, **Mori's.** He and his wife also lived here briefly in a tiny apartment over the premises.

[20.] Washington Square Village, Nos. 1 and 2, W. 3rd to Bleecker Sts., W. Broadway to Mercer St. 1956–1958. S. J. Kessler; Paul Lester Weiner, consultant for design and site planning.

Superbuildings on superblocks. The antithesis of Village scale and charm. The appliqué colors are decorative and not part of the architecture; the self-conscious roof forms are dated.

[21.] Originally **University Village,** 100 and 110 Bleecker St., and 505 LaGuardia Place. Bleecker to W. Houston Sts., bet. Mercer St. and LaGuardia Place. 1966. I. M. Pei & Partners. Central sculpture, 1970. Pablo Picasso. (Large-scale translation by Carl Nesjar.)

Three **pinwheel-plan** apartment point blocks visible for miles. What is exceptional for high-rise housing is that one can grasp the size of individual apartments because of their articulated form. Inside, corridors are short—not the usual labyrinth—and handsomely lit and carpeted. Outside, the technology of cast-in-place concrete had advanced then to the point where it is hard, even today, to believe that the project's intricate forms and smooth surfaces could be achieved despite the vicissitudes of on-site casting. The two **Bleecker Street** units **(Silver Towers)** are N.Y.U. owned; the other is a co-op.

Added later in the center of the project is the 36-foot-high enlargement, in concrete and stone, of **Pablo Picasso's** small cubist sculpture, *Portrait of Sylvette.* Despite sensitive craftsmanship, the work loses much in translation.

[21.] Orig. University Village (apts.)   **[24b.]** The Barney Rossett Residence

[22.] 140 Thompson Street (lofts), bet. Prince and W. Houston Sts. E side. ca. 1885.

Tall brick arches worthy of a Roman aqueduct carry a "cornice" of small, windowed spaces. Strangely prescient of Kallmann, McKinnell & Knowles' **Boston City Hall** (1970).

[23.] MacDougal-Sullivan Gardens Historic District, bet. MacDougal and Sullivan Sts., W. Houston and Bleecker Sts. ca. 1923. 170–188 Sullivan St., E side. 1850. 74–96 MacDougal St., W side. 1844. Altered, 1921. Arthur C. Holden, District designated, 1967. ★

The whole-block renovation started with the idea of **William Sloane Coffin** (then a director of the family business, the W. & J. Sloane furniture house) to develop from a slum neighborhood a pleasing residence for middle-income professionals. He formed the **Hearth and Home Corporation** which bought the block, renovated it, and, by 1921, the following year, had rented nearly all the houses. Coffin's dream of a private community garden was realized around 1923; each house has its own low-walled garden that opens onto a central mall with grouped seating for adults and, at one end, a small playground. The garden is for residents only.

Joe's Restaurant, 79 MacDougal St., bet. Bleecker and W. Houston Sts. Telephone: 473-8834.

Excellent home-cooked Italian meals. Specialties are hot antipasto, shrimp in wine sauce, *zabaglione* à la Joe. Wide price range.

[25.] Charlton-King-Vandam Historic District: a view along Charlton Street

[24a.] Avenue of the Americas Improvement, Sixth Ave., bet. Canal and W. 4th Sts. 1975. N.Y.C. Department of Highways; Frank Rogers, director of urban design.

As Seventh Avenue South was cut through the West Village during World War I, the extension of Sixth Avenue **below Carmine Street** in the twenties resulted in more *urban surgery.* The widenings and narrowings of the avenue's irregular swath through the South Village's already confusing grids created a speedway for cars and trucks, a battlefield for pedestrians. This sensitive municipal improvement, a half-century later, places "careful consideration of pedestrian amenities on a par with the orderly flow of traffic," in the words of the **Municipal Art Society,** "turning a no-man's land into a community resource for sitting, playing, talking, and enjoying the city."

[24b.] Barney Rossett Residence, 196 W. Houston St., bet. Bedford St. and Seventh Ave. S. Altered, 1969, Eugene Futterman.

A cool, geometric facade of handsome brown-glazed structural tile units. Today it houses both the offices of **Grove Press** and its publisher's home.

[25.] Charlton-King-Vandam Historic District, 9–43, 20–42 Charlton St., 1–49, 16–54 King St., 9–29 Vandam St., 43–51 MacDougal St. District designated, 1966. ★

This historic district, **minute in size** when compared with that of Greenwich Village to the north, is New York's **greatest display** of Federal style row houses. The two best (*and best preserved*) examples are Nos. **37 and 39 Charlton,** whose exquisitely detailed entrances with original doors and leaded glass side lights convey many of the style's most distinctive qualities.

Richmond Hill, a country mansion built in 1767, once enjoyed magnificent views from its 100-foot-high mound near today's intersection of Charlton and Varick Streets. **George Washington** briefly used it as his headquarters during the Revolution; **John Adams** occupied it as vice-president, later when the city was the nation's capital; **Aaron Burr** still later bought the elegant structure to lavish entertainment upon those who might further his political ambitions. It was **Burr** who recognized the value of the surrounding 26 acres. He had them mapped into 25- by 100-foot lots in 1797 and, after this and other Village hills were leveled by the Commissioners' Plan of 1811 to their present flatness, saw the development by **John Jacob Astor** of the row houses still extant in the Charlton-King-Vandam district. Meanwhile the mansion itself, literally knocked off its "pedestal," lost its status and was finally demolished.

[26a.] Quartermaster Storehouse, N.Y.C. Police Department/originally **10th Precinct Station House,** 194 Sixth Ave. (originally 24 MacDougal St.), bet. Spring and Prince Sts. E side. 1893.

A dour, pressed brick and granite police station with great rusticated voussoirs around the arched entrance portal.

[26a.] Police Quartermaster Stores   **[26b.]** 203 Prince Street (row house)

[26b.] 203 Prince Street (row house), bet. MacDougal and Sullivan Sts. N side. 1834. ★

An overly careful restoration of the old facade adds a **"restoration village" look** to this commercial street's appearance.

[27a.] James S. Rossant Residence, 114 Sullivan St., bet. Spring and Prince Sts. 1832.

A Federal *gem* on an otherwise unprepossessing block. Architects of high-rise modern housing (like Rossant) tend to spend their private lives residing in low-rise houses like this. 116 is a landmark. ★

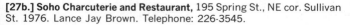
[27b.] Soho Charcuterie and Restaurant, 195 Spring St., NE cor. Sullivan St. 1976. Lance Jay Brown. Telephone: 226-3545.

Gourmet foods (retail) in front; French restaurant in back. Charming and mouth-watering. Expensive.

[27c.] 83 and 85 Sullivan Street, bet. Broome and Spring Sts. E side. ca. 1819. Altered later. ★

A pair of **Greek Revival** row houses with Victorian cornices.

End of tour: Nearest subway is the IND Eighth Avenue's Spring Street Station (at Sixth Avenue); next closest is the IRT Seventh Avenue's Houston Street Station a few blocks northwest at Varick Street.

Walking Tour B: From Jefferson Market Library to Twelfth Street and University Place. Begin at Village Square (IND Sixth and Eighth Avenue Subways to the West Fourth Street Station).

Note: Only entries 28–38 on this tour lie within the Greenwich Village Historic District. ★

[28a.] Jefferson Market Lib. in 1967   Jefferson Market's orig. fire tower

[28a.] Jefferson Market Branch, N.Y. Public Library/originally **Third Judicial District (or Jefferson Market) Courthouse,** 425 Sixth Ave., SW cor. W. 10th St. 1877. Vaux & Withers. Exterior restoration, interior remodeling, 1967. Giorgio Cavaglieri.

A **Neuschwansteinian assemblage** (after Ludwig II of Bavaria's mock castle, Neuschwanstein) of leaded glass, steeply sloping roofs, gables, pinnacles, **Venetian Gothic** embellishments, and an intricate tower and clock make this one of the city's most remarkable buildings. Endangered when no use could be found for it—it had remained vacant **since 1945**— local residents went into action. Led by *indefatigable* **Margot Gayle,** they first repaired and lighted the clock and eventually persuaded city fathers to restore the entire structure as a regional branch library. Budgetary limitations meant the loss of the polychrome slate roof shingles, but the exterior did get a thorough cleaning and repair.

Today's prominent tower served originally as a fire lookout, replacing a tall clapboard version, around which the Jefferson Market's sheds, dating from 1833, clustered. In **1877** the courthouse, and its adjoining jail along Tenth Street, were completed from Frederick Clarke Withers' designs. In **1883** a masonry market building designed by Douglas Smyth filled the remainder of the site, replacing the market's old sheds. Both jail and market were demolished in **1927** in favor of the high-rise **Women's House of Detention** (1931. Sloan & Robertson), in turn demolished in 1974.

The Jefferson Market Greening, on Greenwich Avenue between Christopher and West Tenth Streets, is the official name for the fenced formal park that occupies the site of the old market and of the more recent Women's House of Detention. The *greening* was started (and continues to be maintained, with help from The Vincent Astor Foundation) by members of the local community. It forms a verdant foreground to the amusing forms of the Jefferson Market Library.

La Crêpe (restaurant), 15 Greenwich Ave., bet. Christopher and W. 10th Sts. Telephone: 243–2555.

Over 100 varieties of crêpes (French pancakes)—from *beurre d'escargot* to those filled with caviar. All served in the neat decor of Brittany. Part of a chain, this unit has always prided itself on its French-speaking (and Brittany-costumed) waitresses. Wine only. Reasonable.

[28b.] Patchin Place, off W. 10th St., bet. Greenwich and Sixth Aves. NW side. 1849. **[28c.] Milligan Place,** Sixth Ave., bet. W. 10th and W. 11th Sts. W side. 1848.

In **1848** and **1852,** respectively, Patchin and Milligan Places were built as *second-class* boarding houses for the **Basque** waiters and workers at the **old Brevoort Hotel** on Fifth Avenue. Charming not for the quality of their architecture but rather as peaceful pedestrian cul-de-sacs that contrast with the agitated ebb and flow of Village Square crowds only a block to the south.

In the 1920s Patchin Place became famous for its writer residents, though **Theodore Dreiser** lived there as early as 1895. Its most renowned tenant was **e. e. cummings,** who lived at No. 4.

[29a.] 54, 56, and 58 West Ninth Street (row houses), bet. Fifth and Sixth Aves. 1853. Reuben R. Wood, builder.

A **distinguished** group: pairs of half-round arched windows set within segmental arched openings.

[29b.] The Portsmouth (apartments), 38–44 W. 9th St., bet. Fifth and Sixth Aves. 1882. **[29c.] The Hampshire,** 46–50 W. 9th St. 1883. Both by Ralph Townsend.

Lusty Victorian flats embellished with rich terra-cotta spandrels (and, in the case of The Hampshire, diminished by festoons of fire escapes).

[30a.] Originally **Lockwood de Forest Residence,** 7 E. 10th St., bet. University Place and Fifth Ave. 1887. Van Campen Taylor. **[30b.] Apartment house,** 9 E. 10th St. 1888. Renwick, Aspinwall & Russell.

Unique in New York is the exotic, unpainted, and intricately carved teakwood bay window which adorns No. **7.** Its infectious forms influence the other **east Indian** details of this town house as well as those of the apartment building to the east, designed about the same time. Note how the exterior teakwood here has withstood the rigors of the city's atmosphere better than the brownstone of neighboring row houses.

[31.] Church of the Ascension (Protestant Episcopal), 36–38 Fifth Ave., NW cor. W. 10th St. 1841. Richard Upjohn. Interior remodeled, 1885–1889. McKim, Mead & White. Altar mural and stained glass, John La Farge. Altar relief, Augustus Saint-Gaudens. **[31a.] Parish House,** 12 W. 11th St., bet. Fifth and Sixth Aves. 1844. Altered to present appearance, 1889. McKim, Mead & White.

Random brownstone ashlar in **Gothic Revival** dress. One of the few churches that lights up its stained glass at night, allowing evening strollers on lower Fifth Avenue to enjoy the colors. If you're wondering about the inconsistent quality of the stained glass, you're correct: not all the windows are La Farge's.

[32a.] 12 West Tenth Street, bet. Fifth and Sixth Aves. 1846. Extensive renovations, 1895. Bruce Price.

Breaking from the more popular Italianate town house style, this one is unique. There have been several renovations; one of them was the subdivision into four apartments, one for each daughter, by one owner, architect **Bruce Price.** One of those daughters, **Emily Post,** tells of having President Wilson to Thanksgiving dinner (and it is rumored he proposed to his second wife here).

[32b.] 14, 16, and 18 West Tenth Street, bet. Fifth and Sixth Aves. 1855–1856.

Grand mansions for the small-scaled Village. No. **14** maintains the crust of its original brownstone detail. No. **18** is more serene. No. **16,** in the middle, was neatly stripped.

[32c.] "The English Terrace Row," 20–38 West 10th St., bet. Fifth and Sixth Aves. 1856–1858. Attributed to James Renwick, Jr.

The first group of row houses in the city to abandon the high, Dutch "stoop," placing the entry floor only two or three steps up from the street. Being the first builders in Nieuw Amsterdam, the Dutch had followed the home style—stoops high above the canal or streetlevel to protect against periodic flooding—despite no equivalent threat from the waters here.

Terrace does not refer to the handsome balcony that runs the length of these houses, but is the English term for a *row* of houses, such as found in the **Kensington** and **Paddington** districts of London of the **1840s, 1850s,** and **1860s.** New Yorkers visiting England were impressed with this style, and saw good reason to adopt it upon their return.

[32d.] 50 West Tenth Street, bet. Fifth and Sixth Aves. Post–Civil War.

The upper stories of this former stable use brick in a bold, straightforward fashion to ornament as well as to support and enclose (in contrast with the smooth nondecorative planes of brickwork elsewhere on the block).

[32e.] 56 West Tenth Street, bet. Fifth and Sixth Aves. 1832.

Among the oldest houses in this part of the Village, it has much of its original detail: **pineapple posts** (indicating welcome), with segmented ironwork in mint condition, door with fluted Ionic colonnettes and leaded lights. The cornice and dormer trim came later.

Rhinelander Gardens: In 1955, P. S. 41 Manhattan, on the south side of West Eleventh Street, just west of Sixth Avenue, replaced James Renwick, Jr.'s, **Rhinelander Gardens.** These were a one-of-a-kind group of eight wrought-iron balconied row houses, in the manner of New Orleans' Bourbon Street. For nostalgia's sake a bit of the wrought iron was saved and applied to the school's rear facade—*barely* visible across the bleak asphalt play area from Greenwich Avenue.

[30a.] Orig. Lockwood de Forest Res.

[32b.] 14 West Tenth St. (row house)

[33a.] The Greta Garbo Home for Wayward Boys and Girls, 146 W. 11th St., bet. Sixth and Greenwich Aves. 1836. Aaron Marsh, builder. Altered.

A Victorian row house with a weird brass plaque on its door. Weird because (a) it's **Greta Garbo,** and (b) *who* calls boys and girls "wayward" these days?

[33b.] The Second Cemetery of the Spanish and Portuguese Synagogue, Shearith Israel, in the City of New York, 72–76 W. 11th St., bet. Fifth and Sixth Aves. 1805–1829.

The *original* Shearith Israel cemetery is at Chatham Square [see Civic Center/Chinatown 36.]. Burials began here in 1805, in what was a much larger, square plot extending into what now is the street. The Commissioners' Plan had established the City's grid in 1811, but not until 1830 was West Eleventh Street cut through, at that time reducing the cemetery to its present tiny triangle. The disturbed plots were moved farther uptown to the **Third Cemetery** on West 21st Street [see Chelsea **14b.**]. In 1852, City law forbade burial within Manhattan and subsequent interments have been made in Cypress Hills, Long Island.

Elephant & Castle (restaurant), 68 Greenwich Ave., SE of Seventh Ave. Telephone: 243-1400.

Omelettes and such. Closely packed tables. Frothy atmosphere. No liquor.

[34a.] Main Building, St. Vincent's Hospital, 157 W. 11th St., NE cor. Seventh Ave. 1899. Schickel & Ditmars.

The most distinguished element in St. Vincent's bulky main complex: dark red brick set off by loads of light-colored stone trim.

[34b.] Edward and Theresa O'Toole Medical Services Bldg., St. Vincent's Hospital

[35.] The Village Community Church   **[37b.]** Butterfield House (apartments)

The Village Green: The triangle of land bounded by Seventh and Greenwich Avenues and West 12th Street was once the site of the **Loew's Sheridan,** a vast barn of a movie theater, demolished in the seventies to make way for the expansion of St. Vincent's. The **West Village Committee** took advantage of a hiatus in the building schedule to plant (and maintain) the charming garden which enriches the scene behind a high wire fence. In the wake of the **Earth Day** movement, the Village Green Recycling Team rescues tin cans, bottles, and paper at the rear of the site.

[34b.] Edward and Theresa O'Toole Medical Services Building, St. Vincent's Hospital Center/originally **National Maritime Union of America, AFL-CIO,** 36 Seventh Ave., bet. W. 12th and W. 13th Sts. W side. 1964. Albert C. Ledner & Assocs. Altered, 1977. Ferrenz & Taylor.

In the *wake* of Frank Lloyd Wright's **Guggenheim Museum** [see UES 31a.], this huge double-dentured monument is without precedent. It suffered from the same rough concrete work as its **Upper East Side cousin** and so was later veneered with the small white-glazed tesserae which cover the building today. Compare with its **sibling** on West 17th Street. [See Chelsea 22a].

[35.] Village Community Church (Presbyterian)/originally **Thirteenth Street Presbyterian Church,** 143 W. 13th St., bet. Sixth and Seventh Aves. 1846. Attributed to Samuel Thompson. Rebuilt after fires, 1855, 1902.

The *best* **Greek Revival** church in the city, modeled after the **Theseum** in Athens. The columns and pediment resemble stone but are actually of wood; the walls brick and stucco. The porch is most inviting, as is the light and airy interior with its clear glass windows. The church, now empty and up for sale, is threatened with alteration or demolition.

Rum, Romanism, and Rebellion: The characterization of **Grover Cleveland's** Democratic Party as one of rum, Romanism, and rebellion cost Republican candidate **James G. Blaine** the presidency in 1884. The fiery speech, containing the phrase that antagonized the (Roman) Catholic Irish in New York City, was delivered by **Dr. Samuel D. Burchard,** long minister of what is today the Village Community Church. The adjacent row house at 139 West Thirteenth Street was built in 1846 as the manse for Dr. Burchard when he became the church's first rector.

For the Evangeline Residence see [84b.].

[36a.] The New School for Social Research, 66 W. 12th St., bet. Fifth and Sixth Aves. 1930. Joseph Urban. **[36b.] Jacob M. Kaplan Building, Eleventh Street Building,** and **Interior Court,** additions to the west and southwest. 1958. Mayer, Whittlesey & Glass; William J. Conklin, associate partner in charge of design.

The New School became the "university in exile" for the intelligentsia fleeing Nazi Germany in the 1930s. The original (east) building is a precocious design for New York in its restrained use of strip windows and spandrels whose brick courses set back slightly from the street as they rise. These subtleties make it appear shorter, less imposing, more in scale with the adjacent row-house residences on this street. The auditorium within is a dramatic example of Urban's theatrical talents. The school's additions to the south are linked across a rear sculpture court by an impressive glassed-in two-story-high bridge.

[37a.] 45 West Twelfth Street (row house), bet. Fifth and Sixth Aves. 1846.

Look carefully at the east side of this building for the acute angle. The side wall slants back because it originally faced the once-above-ground **Minetta Brook.** Frank Lloyd Wright's sister, Mrs. William Pope Barney, owned and lived in the house at one time.

[37b.] Butterfield House (apartments), 37 W. 12th St., bet. Fifth and Sixth Aves. 1962. Mayer, Whittlesey & Glass; William J. Conklin, associate partner in charge of design, and James S. Rossant.

The *friendly* neighborhood high-rise. On residential Twelfth Street, this cooperative apartment rises to **only seven stories;** varied windows, projected bays, and balconies break up the facade and relate it to the prevailing **19th-century residential scale** of the street. A glazed courtyard passage to the north wing shares its neighbors' backyard charm. On Thirteenth Street, though, with numerous lofts and **20th-century** apartment towers, the building's flat wall rises agreeably (and economically) to thirteen stories.

[37c.] 35 West Twelfth Street, bet. Fifth and Sixth Aves. 1840. Altered 1868; right half removed in 1893.

Originally about **25** feet wide; the building of Nos. 31–33 consumed half of this house, leaving a curious but not unpleasing reminder.

[37d.] The Ardea (apartments), 31–33 W. 12th St., bet. Fifth and Sixth Aves. 1895, 1901. J. B. Snook & Sons.

This dark crusty facade, lyrically set off by delicate ironwork balconies, is one of many structures in the city *wrongfully attributed* to **McKim, Mead & White.** Buildings of great character, as this one, were designed by many distinguished firms. The client here was **George A. Hearn,** the department store magnate, whose dry goods emporium was once a showplace nearby on Fourteenth Street.

[37e.] Originally **Macmillan Company Building**/now **Forbes Magazine Building,** 60 Fifth Ave., NW cor. W. 12th St. 1925. Carrére & Hastings.

For some four decades, Macmillan conducted its publishing business from this pompous limestone cube whose boring surfaces are embellished here and there with echoes of Rome's glories. Following Macmillan's relocation to an anonymous midtown tower, Forbes Magazine assumed ownership of the stodgy pile.

Dauber & Pine Bookshops, 66 Fifth Ave., bet. W. 12th and W. 13th Sts.

Browsers are welcome in the ground floor shop where books seem always to be 25 percent off the marked price. But habitués make a beeline downstairs where there are thousands more at various prices. Bookshops, plural, yes: **Pine** reigns upstairs; **Dauber** below.

[38a.] First Presbyterian Church, 48 Fifth Ave., bet. W. 11th and W. 12th Sts. W side. 1846. Joseph C. Wells. South transept, 1893, McKim, Mead & White. Chancel added, 1919. **[38b.] Church House.** 1960. Edgar Tafel.

A stately, crenellated, coursed, and dressed ashlar **central tower** of brownstone; set well back from Fifth Avenue, it is **the bold form that identifies** this church. Embellishing the walls of that tall prism is a Gothic Revival tracery of quatrefoils which also forms the motif for the adjacent, properly reticent, church house, built **more than a century** later. Note the handsome fence which rings the site—partly of cast iron and, **surprisingly,** partly of wood.

Boom! For years a tall wooden fence enclosed the property at 18 West Eleventh Street. Between 1845 and 1970 a Greek Revival row house stood here, similar to its neighbors on either side. On March 5, 1970, the street was rocked by an explosion. When the smoke cleared, little was left of the house—its cellar, it turned out, was being used by a radical group as a **bomb manufactory.** An attempt soon afterward, by architect **Hugh Hardy,** to build a contemporary replacement was picked to death by a combination of governmental red tape and rising construction costs. His scheme was later revived for another client (1978. Hardy Holzman Pfeiffer Assocs.).

[39.] Salmagundi Club/originally **Irad Hawley Residence,** 47 Fifth Ave., bet. E. 11th and E. 12th Sts. E side. 1853. ★ Telephone: 255-7740.

The **Salmagundi Club** is America's oldest artists' club (founded in 1870). This private, all-male club moved to Fifth Avenue in 1917; members included **John La Farge, Louis C. Tiffany,** and **Stanford White.** Painting exhibitions open to the public are sometimes installed on the parlor floor, a superbly preserved interior of the period.

[40.] Youth Aid and Property Clerk Divisions, N.Y.C. Police Department/originally **Girls' High School,** 34½ E. 12th St., bet. Broadway and University Place. 1856. Thomas R. Jackson.

Beautifully preserved Italian **Renaissance Revival** painted brownstone and painted brick. Proper but gloomy.

[41.] East Twelfth Street (lofts), bet. Broadway and University Place. N side. ca. 1895.

Big and bold Romanesque Revival row, each multistory loft out-doing the other. Look up at the rich stone and brickwork.

Bradley's (bar and restaurant), 70 University Place, bet. E. 10th and E. 11th Sts. Telephone: 228-6440.

A pleasant, quiet place to sip or eat. Moderate prices.

End of Tour: For more nearby, see **Astor Place/East Village.** If you're calling it a day, the nearest IRT and BMT Subways are uptown a few blocks at Union Square.

Walking Tour C—The Lower West Village: Village Square to Morton Street Pier. Begin at Village Square (IND Sixth and Eighth Avenue Subways to West Fourth Street Station).

Note: Only entries 42–56 on this tour lie within the Greenwich Village Historic District. ★

There are so many early **19th century houses** in this section of **the Village,** one is tempted to say "when you've seen one, you've seen 'em all." Not so. There are always surprises; some are squashed between six-story lofts, others are tucked away in back yards, often they are bedecked with destructive but nostalgic wisteria vines. It is this rich texture that makes them such a valuable contribution to **the Village**—take away the contrasts and **the Village** would be a dull place indeed.

[37d.] The Ardea (apartment building) **[42a.]** 18 and 20 Christopher Street

[38b.] Church House, First Presbyterian Church: motifs echo adjacent edifice

[42a.] 18 and 20 Christopher Street, bet. Gay St. and Waverly Place. SE side. 1827. Daniel Simonson, builder. Alterations: storefronts.

A **Federal** pair with superdormers.

[42b.] 10 Christopher Street, SE cor. at Gay St. 1903. Jardine, Kent & Jardine. Altered, 1939, 1975.

This tall, simple loft contrasts beautifully with the tiny houses around the corner on Gay Street. Its back wall curves to match the bend in the side street.

[42c.] Gay Street, bet. Christopher St. and Waverly Place. Houses, 1827–1860.

My Sister Eileen territory. A handful of little **Federal** houses, delightful for being so close to the street. More superdormers.

[43.] Northern Dispensary/originally **Northern Dispensary Institute,** 165 Waverly Place on triangle with Waverly Place and Christopher St. 1831. Henry Bayard, carpenter; John C. Tucker, mason. Third floor added, 1854.

An austere vernacular **Georgian** building with sheet-metal lintels and cornice of a later period. Remarkable for having continuously operated as a public clinic since its founding in **1827.** Edgar Allen Poe was treated here for a head cold in 1837—without charge, as are all who can't afford the fee.

Northern Dispensary,
Waverley place, corner Christopher street.

The triangular **Northern Dispensary** is the only building in New York with one side on two streets (**Grove** and **Christopher** where they join) and two sides on one street (**Waverly Place,** where it forks to go off in two directions).

The Lion's Head (restaurant and bar), 59 Christopher St., bet. Waverly Place and Seventh Ave. Telephone: WH 9-0670.

Originally a coffeehouse in the West Village, now relocated. A gathering place for younger pols, sports writers, and others of the fifth estate.

[44a.] Residence of the Graymore Friars/formerly **St. Joseph's Church Rectory,** 138 Waverly Place, bet. Sixth Ave. and Grove St. S side. 1895. George H. Streeton.

A brick and brownstone **Gothic Revival** outpost in this **mostly Greek Revival** place.

[44b.] St. Joseph's Roman Catholic Church, 365 Sixth Ave., NW cor. Washington Place. 1834. John Doran.

This church is one of the dwindling group of Greek Revival "temples."

[44c.] St. Joseph's Washington Place School, 111 Washington Place, bet. Sixth Ave. and Grove St. N side. 1897. George H. Streeton.

A five-story facade embellished by ornament borrowed from **Greek** temples, **Italian** Renaissance palazzi, and Baroque country houses.

[45.] 175–179 West Fourth Street (row houses), at Jones St. N side. 1833, 1834.

Three Federal houses whose parlor floors and basements gracefully house elegant shops. Look up to the exquisite dormers—No. 175 had them too until altered.

Sheridan Square, bounded by Washington Place and West Fourth, Barrow, and Grove Streets, is the most unused public space in the Village, marked out with a striped asphalt triangle stanchioned with "no parking" signs, surrounded by bland towers of housing. The Square is frequently confused with Christopher Park around the corner where a statue of Civil War **General Philip Sheridan** (for whom *this* square is named) happens, in fact, to stand. It causes havoc when fire engines respond to the wrong place.

Buffalo Roadhouse (bar and restaurant), 87 Seventh Ave. S., N of Barrow St. Telephone: 675-9875.

Its dusty name contrasts with its neat environment. Pleasant for lunch. Dinner very busy and "in." In warm weather it sports a tiny outdoor patio right on the avenue.

Seventh Avenue South: Before the construction of the West Side **IRT** Subway *below* **Times Square,** around **World War I,** Seventh Avenue began its northward journey at Greenwich Avenue and West Eleventh Street. The building of the Seventh Avenue Subway to connect with Varick Street and the creation of Seventh Avenue South as a surface thoroughfare made **huge scars** through these West Village blocks that left the backs and sides of buildings crudely exposed. Isolated triangles of land are now filled with dingy gas stations and parking lots. Seventh Avenue South opened for traffic in 1919.

[44b.] St. Joseph's Catholic Church   **[47.]** Simo Service Sta., a '20s relic

[46a.] 15 Barrow Street, bet. W. 4th St. and Seventh Ave. S., SE side. 1896. H. Hasenstein.

Originally a four-story stable—note the horse's head protruding from just below the cornice.

[46b.] Greenwich House, 29 Barrow St., bet. W. 4th St. and Seventh Ave. S. SE side. 1917. Delano & Aldrich.

The building, an ill-kempt Georgian Revival, is most significant for its works: **social reform.** At the turn of the century when Greenwich House was founded, Jones Street, a block to the east, was home to 1,400 people—975 to the acre—then the **highest density** in this part of Manhattan. These were **second-generation Irish, first-generation Italian, some black, some French.** From Greenwich House, founded in 1901 by **Mary Kingsbury Simkhovitch,** daughter of an old patrician family, came the **Greenwich Village Improvement Society,** the **first** neighborhood association in the city.

[47.] Simo Service Station (Getty), 48 Seventh Ave. S., bet. Commerce and Morton Sts. W side. ca. 1919.

Occupying a triangle of real estate amputated by the extension of Seventh Avenue is this grimy one-room temple to petroleum left over from the early days of the motor car, an endangered reminder of the not-too-distant past when gas stations only pumped gas. A coat of paint could do wonders.

Bleecker Street between Seventh Avenue South and Sixth Avenue (Father Demo Square), a colorful Italian shopping street:

Tavola Caldo da Alfredo (restaurant), 285 Bleecker St., near Seventh Ave. S. Telephone: 924-4789.

Italian cooking in a light, casual setting, greened by plants and ferns. Good food; no liquor.

Second Childhood (antique toys), 283 Bleecker St. Telephone: 989-6140.

Aptly named and disarming, but antiques can be very expensive, even (*or especially*) antique toys.

A. Zito & Sons (bakery), 259 Bleecker St., at Cornelia St. Telephone: WA 9-6139.

Loaves, long, round, sesame seeded or not, and all crusty. **Mmmm.**

Zampognaro's (food market), 262 Bleecker St., opp. Cornelia St. Telephone: WA 9-8566.

Cheese, quiches, pâtés, and coffees.

Faicco's (sausages), 260 Bleecker St. Telephone: CH 3-1974.

Homemade sausage since 1927. *Tipico Italiano.*

Rocco's Pastry Shop, 243 Bleecker St. opp. Leroy St. Telephone: CH 2-6031.

Great Italian ices for a summer stroll. The Italian rum cake (with luscious frosting!) is not to be believed.

Changing street names in midstream: St. Luke's Place assumes its name halfway between Seventh Avenue South and Hudson Street—at the bend to be precise. The eastern portion is officially **Leroy Street,** a lesser thoroughfare to those who are snobbish about such things.

[48.] 6–13 St. Luke's Place, bet. Leroy and Hudson Sts. N side. 1852–1853.

This well-kept row of handsome brick and brownstone Italianate residences seems an eerie stage set in this world of industrial lofts visible across **James J. Walker Park**—named for the city's **colorful mayor** who lived at No. 6. Fortunately, when the street's two rows of gingko trees green they form a graceful arbor, giving form to a street only **"one-sided"** in winter. The land occupied by the park, between 1812 and 1895, was part of Trinity Parish's cemetery until it was moved up to 155th Street [see U Manhattan **1.**].

[48.] 6–13 St. Luke's Pl. (row houses)   **[50b.]** The Isaacs-Hendricks House

[49.] Morton Street, from Hudson to Bedford Sts.

If there is a *typical* Village block, this is it. It **bends.** It has a **private court** with its own, out-of-whack numbers (Nos. 144A, 144B). It is full of **surprising changes of scale, setbacks, facade treatments.** No. **66** has a bold bay; No. **59** has one of the finest Federal doorways in the Village. Old Law tenements interrupt the street, greedily consuming their property, right out to the building line. In them live Italians and Irish, groups that remind their more affluent neighbors of an earlier, less moneyed Village.

[50a.] "Narrowest house in the Village," 75½ Bedford St., bet. Morton and Commerce Sts. W side. 1873.

It's 9½ feet wide; originally built **to span an alley** to the rear court (where its main entrance is). Though narrow by any standards, it was **wide enough** for the carriages that used to pass through. Unfortunately it has been defaced with a fake brick coating. This is one of several residences of **Edna St. Vincent Millay** which remain in the Village. She lived here in 1923–1924.

Edna St. Vincent Millay (1892–1950): This poet, closely identified with the Village in the twenties, was given her middle name after St. Vincent's Hospital here, this despite the fact that she was born in Rockland, Maine. It seems that the hospital had saved the life of a relative.

[50b.] Isaacs-Hendricks House, 77 Bedford St., SW cor. Commerce St. 1799. Alterations, 1836, 1928.

Significant only for its early date; remodeling has destroyed original Federal style and left it more like an abandoned warehouse. The **original clapboard** walls are visible to the side and rear.

[51.] 39 and 41 Commerce Street, at Barrow St. E side. 1831 and 1832, respectively. Mansard roofs, 1870s. D. T. Atwood.

This extraordinary **one-of-a-kind pair** proclaims the elegance once surrounding this and neighboring St. Luke's Place. A **local legend holds** they were built by a **sea captain** for his two daughters; one for each because they could not live together. The **records show** they were built for a **milkman,** one Peter Huyler.

Chumley's (restaurant), 86 Bedford St., bet. Barrow and Grove Sts. NE side. Telephone: 989-9038.

Famed ex-speakeasy whose reputation still lingers; there is still **no sign nor any other outside indication** that this is a pub. Today's side entrance leads to a backyard off Barrow Street called **Pamela Court.** During Prohibition this was the **discreet entry**—the Bedford Street front having been disguised as a garage entrance. Its days as a literary rendezvous are recalled by dusty book jackets along the walls. Simple food and drink. Medium prices.

[51.] 39 and 41 Commerce Street: mansarded twins embracing a green space

[52.] Originally **J. Goebel & Co.,** 95 Bedford St., bet. Barrow and Grove Sts. W side. 1894. Kurzer & Kohl.

A stable once used by a wine company, as the lettering on the facade clearly indicates; converted into apartments in 1927.

[53a.] 17 Grove Street, NE cor. Bedford St. 1822. Third floor added, 1870. **[53b.] 100 Bedford Street,** bet. Grove and Christopher Sts. 1833.

William Hyde built this as his house. He was a sash-maker and later put up a small building around the corner on Bedford Street for his workshop. His home is the *most whole* of the few remaining wood-frame houses in the Village. A **grand wisteria** seems to hold up the facade.

[53c.] "Twin Peaks," 102 Bedford St., bet. Grove and Christopher Sts. E side. 1830. Renovation, 1925.

The renovation was the work of a local resident, Clifford Reed Daily; it was financed by the wealthy Otto Kahn whose daughter lived here for some time. Daily considered the surrounding buildings "unfit for inspiring the minds of creative Villagers," and set out to give them this "island growing in a desert of mediocrity." Great fun for the kids—**pure Hansel and Gretel.**

[54a.] 14–16 Grove Street, bet. Bedford and Hudson Sts. S side. 1840. Samuel Winant and John Degraw, builders.

A pair of vine-clad Greek Revival houses in pristine condition. Until altered in 1966, No. **14** was believed to have been the last *completely* untouched **Greek Revival** residence in the city.

[54b.] Grove Court, viewed bet. 10 and 12 Grove St., bet. Bedford and Hudson Sts. S side. 1853–1854. Alterations.

This charming cul-de-sac lined with story-book brick-fronted houses hints at the irregularity of early 19th century property lines. Evidence of similar holdings can be glimpsed throughout the West Village. These houses were built for working men; the court was once known as **"Mixed Ale Alley."**

[54c.] 4–10 Grove Street, bet. Bedford and Hudson Sts. S side. 1827–1834. James N. Wells, builder.

An excellent row of houses—brick-fronted with clapboard behinds.

Honest and humble. The Federal houses at 4–10 Grove Street represent the prevailing style of the 1820s. Americans then had few architects; instead, the local carpenters and masons copied and adapted plans and details from builders' copybooks. In translation, the detailing is less pretentious, adapting to the needs of their American merchant and craftsman clients; nonetheless, there is a faint, pleasant echo of **London's Bloomsbury.**

[53c.] "Twin Peaks," 102 Bedford St.   **[55a.]** St. Luke in the Fields Church

[55a.] Church of St. Luke in the Fields (Protestant Episcopal)/formerly **St. Luke's Episcopal Chapel of Trinity Parish,** 485 Hudson St., bet. Barrow and Christopher Sts. at Grove St. W side. 1822. James N. Wells, builder. Interior remodeling, 1875, 1886.

An austere country church from the time when this was "the country" to New Yorkers living on the tip of Manhattan Island.

The original church was founded independently by local residents, with some **financial help** from the **wealthy, downtown** Trinity Parish. With the influx of immigrants to the area in 1892, the **carriage-trade congregation moved uptown** to Convent Avenue to found a St. Luke's there [see Hamilton Heights 3a.]. This St. Luke's **reopened** the next year, now under the auspices of downtown Trinity Parish, which had bought the property in the interim.

[55b.] 473–477, 487–491 Hudson Street, flanking St. Luke's Chapel, bet. Barrow and Christopher Sts. W side. 1825. **90–96 Barrow Street,** bet. Hudson and Greenwich Sts. N side. 1827. James N. Wells, builder.

Only six houses remain of a total of fourteen originally symmetrically arrayed, seven to the north of the church and seven to the south, planning made possible because the entire tract of land was developed under a lease from the **Trinity Church Corporation.** The houses are bleak Federal.

[56.] 510–518 Hudson Street (houses), bet. Christopher and W. 10th Sts. E side. 1827. Isaac Hatfield, carpenter and builder.

Five **Federal** row houses of which No. 510 (except for its altered ground floor and tasteful 1970s paint job) shows the original appearance.

Cozinha Brasileira/Brazilian Cuisine (restaurant), 501 Hudson St. at Christopher St. Telephone: 924-2705.

A handsome example of the modern sign painter's art identifies this simple restaurant's less-than-elegant interior. As the sign indicates, the food is Rio-style. No liquor.

[57.] Originally **U.S. Appraiser's Stores**/then **U.S. Federal Archives Building,** 641 Washington St., Washington to Greenwich Sts., Barrow to Christopher Sts. 1899. Willoughby J. Edbrooke. ★

A *smooth* brick ten-story-high monolith in the **Romanesque Revival** style of **H. H. Richardson.** Great brick arches form a virile base, and arched corbel tables march across the cornice against the sky. The building, originally a customs appraiser's warehouse, is scheduled for recycling for community and residential uses.

[57.] Original U.S. Appraiser's Stores   **[58.]** St. Veronica's Catholic Church

[63.] St. John's Evan. Luth. Church   **[65a.]** The Hampton (apartments)

[58.] St. Veronica's Roman Catholic Church, 153 Christopher St., bet. Greenwich and Washington Sts. N side. ca. 1900.

Here are squat towers worthy of **Prague's Old City.**

[59.] Village Community School/originally **Public School 107 Manhattan,** 272 W. 10th St., bet. Greenwich and Washington Sts. 1885.

A five-story schoolhouse from the late 19th century. In a building this height the stairway was important enough to put behind an enormous multistory arched window, which surprises its otherwise symmetric, polychromed brick facade.

[60.] Converted apartments/originally **Everhard's Storage Warehouse,** 667 Washington St., NE cor. W. 10th St. ca. 1894. Conversion, 1978. Bernard Rothzeid & Partners.

A cousin to the old Appraiser's Stores building [57.], a block away. Here, giant granite arches support a brick **Romanesque Revival** facade.

West Village Houses, along Washington Street's west flank below Christopher Street and above West Tenth are covered on **Tour D.** [See **68.**]

Between Washington and West Streets lies a one-block-long, north-south thoroughfare known as Weehawken Street:

[61.] 6 Weehawken Street, bet. Christopher and West 10th Sts.

This little oddity reveals skeletal remains of the 18th century—its appearance shouldn't be taken seriously as architecture, but valued more for the wonder that anything remains of it at all.

[62.] Morton Street Pier/originally **Pier 42 North River,** Hudson River at West St.

"Renovated" because of local demand, the flat pier is graced with the black hulls of two **Board of Education Maritime High School ships** and neat and humorously painted bollards warning smokers to puff elsewhere. Nonetheless, it's crowded almost year-round with West Villagers desperate for any open space, flowing water, and the smoke-stacked panorama of New Jersey.

End of Tour: Walk back to West 10th Street, where the eastbound crosstown bus will take you to Greenwich Avenue and Village Square.

Walking Tour D—The West Village: Sheridan Square, Westbeth, Bank Street, the Gansevoort Market and Spanish Fourteenth Street. Begin at Christopher Street and Seventh Avenue South (IRT Seventh Avenue local to the Christopher Street/Sheridan Square Subway Station).

Note: Only entries 63–66 and 71–79 on this tour lie within the Greenwich Village Historic District. ★

[63.] St. John's Evangelical Lutheran Church/formerly **St. Matthew's Protestant Episcopal Church**/originally **The Eighth Presbyterian Church.** 81 Christopher St. bet. Seventh Ave. S. and Bleecker St. N side. 1821. Altered.

A **Federal cupola** over a painted brownstone and sheet metal Romanesque brownstone body. The parish house to the west, next door, is stolid brick **Romanesque Revival.**

[64.] 95 Christopher Street (apartments), NW cor. Bleecker St. 1931. H. I. Feldman.

Using a palette of browns, this striped brick Art Deco multiple dwelling is a forceful contrast to the more typical Village scale.

The Gay White Way: Christopher Street, between Bleecker and Hudson Streets, is the 1970s Broadway for homosexual New Yorkers, particularly after dark.

[65a.] The Hampton (apartments), 80–82 Perry St., bet. W. 4th and Bleecker Sts. S side. 1887. Thom & Wilson.

A red brick and brownstone super tenement with **Moorish** "keyhole" lintels at the ground floor windows.

[65b.] 70 Perry Street (row house), bet. W. 4th and Bleecker Sts. S side. 1867. Walter Jones, builder.

The architectural gem of this block in a superb state of repair. Tooled brownstone and stately proportions give it a grand scale in the style of the French **Second Empire.** As a result, it seems larger than its neighbors. . . it isn't.

"Dog of the Ilk": This inscription and a coat-of-arms embellish the gable of 43 Perry Street, a travertine curiosity altered in 1967 (Simon Zelnick) from an 1850s stable.

[66.] Sven Bernhard Residence, 121 Charles St., NE cor. Greenwich St. Relocated, 1968, William Shopsin.

This petite white frame mongrel has occupied at least two other sites before stopping in this unlikely spot. Its beginnings are unknown, but it wound up as a back house uptown on York Avenue and 71st Street some time in the 19th century. When it was threatened with demolition in the 1960s, its owners had it rolled through five miles of city streets to this West Village location.

[67a.] 131 Charles Street (row house), bet. Greenwich and Washington Sts. N side. 1834. ★

A beauty of a **Federal** house whose delicate scale contrasts—in a not unpleasant way—with the oompah details of the old police station adjacent. Note the oval window over the second doorway leading to No. 131½, a back house.

[67b.] Form. 6th Pct. Station House

[72.] Orig. Helmut Jacoby Residence

[67b.] Formerly **Sixth Precinct Station House, N.Y.C. Police Department,** 135 Charles St., bet. Greenwich and Washington Sts. N side. 1895. John Du Fais.

A **mélange** of many styles, this ungainly four-story dowager was the Village's police station until 1971 when operations moved to a new, **bland low-rise replacement** at 233 West 10th Street, today's Sixth Precinct, truly a visual catastrophe.

[68.] West Village Houses (apartments), along Washington St. bet. Bank and W. 10th Sts., Christopher and Morton Sts. W side. Also along side streets. 1974. Perkins & Will.

The scene of the **great war** between the **defenders** of "Greenwich Village scale" and the **establishment,** which proposed another high-rise housing project. The David in this case was critic Jane Jacobs; the Goliath, Robert Moses, then the city's urban renewal czar. A **pyrrhic victory** for David: the 5- and 6-story red brick products are dumpy, dull, and expensive.

The Other Side of the Tracks: The old deserted N.Y. Central Railroad freight viaduct west of Washington Street (built in 1934) for all appearances forms the western boundary of the Village. But scattered beyond this gloomy elevated structure are quite a few 19th-century houses—some restored, others decaying—originally built for speculation or in the rush to house those fleeing the epidemics of lower Manhattan. An area to investigate if you have lots of time. Don't miss **Charles Lane,** between **Charles** and **Perry Streets** off **Washington.**

Mother Courage (feminist restaurant), 342 W. 11th St., bet. Greenwich and Washington Sts. Telephone: 924-9728.

Named for the character in **Bertolt Brecht's** drama. It serves simple fare in a pleasant, unpretentious atmosphere.

[69.] 128 and 130 Bank Street (row houses), bet. Greenwich and Washington Sts. S side. 1837 and 1833, respectively.

Two **Greek Revival** houses, the most perfect examples in a longer row. Note the windows in the frieze.

It is usually possible to walk north through Westbeth from the entrance court on Bank Street to the Bethune Street entrance.

[70.] Westbeth Artists' Housing, 155 Bank St., bet. Washington and West Sts. Altered, 1969. Richard Meier & Assocs.

The old **Bell Telephone Laboratories,** a block filler, reincarnated as **artists' loft housing.** The exterior is a 40-year mélange of loft buildings embracing a bleak entrance court on Bank. The **inner court,** closer to Bethune, is a dark canyon festooned with fire egress balconies.

[71a.] 19–29 Bethune Street (row houses), bet. Greenwich and Washington Sts. 1837. Henry S. Forman and Alexander Douglass, builders. **[71b.] 24–34 Bethune Street,** 1845. Alexander R. Holden, builder. **[71c.] 36 Bethune Street,** 1847. Altered, 1928.

A block of small-scaled and handsome mongrels. Note the diminutive windows at the third floor (servants' rooms) typical of early **Greek Revival.**

[72.] 767 Greenwich St./originally **Helmut Jacoby Residence,** bet. W. 11th and Bank Sts. E side. 1965. Helmut Jacoby, designer; Leonard Feldman, architect.

A modern town house, one of only a half-dozen in Manhattan. As crisp as a rendering but lacking passion.

Trattoria da Alfredo (Italian restaurant), 90 Bank St., cor. Hudson St. Telephone: 929-4400.

Popular small restaurant (seats 38), whose owner, Alfredo Viazzi, takes pride in the quality of its food. It lacks not for customers, so its waiters can be gruff. Bring your own wine. Moderate.

[73.] Abingdon Square Park and Playground at Hudson, Bank, and Bleecker Sts. Rebuilt, 1966, Arnold Vollmer, landscape architects and engineers, with a committee of community architects.

Here we see evidence of an imaginative playground, one of the earliest chinks in the armor of the city's Parks Department, long dominated by Robert Moses' retardaire policies. It *can* be fun to play.

[74.] 68 Bank Street (row house), bet. W. 4th and Bleecker Sts. S side. 1863. Jacob C. Bogert, builder. **[75a.] 74 and 76 Bank Street (row houses),** 1839–42. Andrew Lockwood, builder. **[75b.] 55 and 57 Bank Street (row houses),** N side. 1842. Aaron Marsh, builder.

An especially felicitous group of houses.

The Front Porch Restaurant, 253 W. 11th St., NE cor. W. 4th St. Telephone: 243-9262.

An old drugstore converted to a soup and open-sandwich restaurant. Eat in the company of apothecary fixtures that still remain. Tiny, sunny, green with plants. Just right for a snack.

[76a.] 48 Bank Street (town house), bet. Waverly Place and W. 4th St. 1969. Claude Samton & Assocs.

Severe brown brick and linseed-oil-brushed copper distinguish this 20th-century town house, a rarity along the Village's **Federal** and **Victorian** blocks.

[76b.] 37 Bank Street (row house), bet. Waverly Place and W. 4th St. N side. 1837.

One of the best of the Greek Revival style in the Village. The block is a striking one—despite the curious lintel details (Nos. 16–34) and some ghastly refacing across the street.

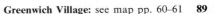

[77a.] St. John's-in-the-Village Church (Protestant Episcopal), Waverly Place, SW cor. W. 11th St. 1974. Edgar Tafel & Assocs. **[77b.] Parish House/**originally **South Baptist Church,** 224 Waverly Place bet. Perry and W. 11th Sts., W side. ca. 1854.

An austere red brick box disguised with a pediment and a brow of giant pseudo-Greek details. It replaced **a true Greek Revival "temple"** destroyed in a fire. A glimpse of its predecessor's style is visible in the parish house.

Ye Waverly Inn, 16 Bank St., SW cor. Waverly Place. Telephone: WA 9-4377.

Quaint, New England-style restaurant, tucked away in the basement nooks and crannies of a house dating from 1845. No lunches served on weekends. Liquor available. Moderate prices.

Caffè da Alfredo, 17 Perry St. at Waverly Place. Telephone: 989-7028.

Olive green decor with giant multicolored ceramic floor tiles and tables on antique cast-iron pedestals set the **visual tone** for this coffee-house. Delicious. *Tramezzini* (Roman sandwiches), *antipasti* (salads), and *pasta* (pasta) set the **gustatorial tone.** Moderate to immoderate.

[78.] Food and Maritime Trades Vocational High School/originally **Public School 16 Manhattan,** 208 W. 13th St., bet. Seventh and Greenwich Aves. Center portion, ca. 1869. Extensions, ca. 1879, ca. 1877, ca. 1899.

A fine example of the **Italianate** school buildings built by the city in the third quarter of the **19th** century. The school ships moored at the Morton Street Pier [see **62.**] are annexes of this school.

The Jackson Square Area: Greenwich and Eighth Avenues and West Thirteenth Street.

[79b.] Orig. Jackson Square Library

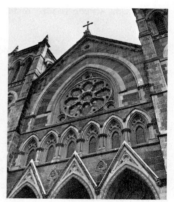

[80.] The R.C. Church of St. Bernard

[79a.] IND Electrical Substation, 253 W. 13th St., NE cor. Greenwich Ave. 1930.

The city's own subway system, the **Independent** (independent at that time of the privately owned **IRT** and **BMT**), arrived on the scene about the time **Art Deco** influences did. Hence utilitarian structures such as this were ornamented in that style. They can be found all over the city.

[79b.] The Great Building Crack-Up/International Headquarters of the First National Church of the Exquisite Panic, Inc./originally **Jackson Square Branch, N.Y. Public Library,** 251 West 13th St., bet. Greenwich and Seventh Aves. N side. 1887. Richard Morris Hunt. Altered 1971. Paul Rudolph.

A benefaction of **William K. Vanderbilt,** this former library building resembles an old **Dutch guildhall.** Its original leaded glass windows, so important in establishing scale, have been removed in a conversion to a residence and gallery. Inside the now recessed (and metal screened) ground floor space is a large plaque worth reading—a mystical statement on the relationship of architect and client.

Gansevoort Market Area, a detour west from Jackson Square, lies roughly between Ninth Avenue and the Hudson, from Gansevoort Street north to Fourteenth. Busy, chaotic, earthy from before sunrise well into the day . . . empty, eerie, scary at night. From these wholesale meat markets comes the meat for most of Manhattan's restaurants and institutions. **Herman Melville** (1819–1891) worked here on what was then the Gansevoort Dock as an outdoor customs inspector for 19 years. He came to this job, discouraged and unable to earn a living as a writer. It was sometime during these years that he completed *Moby Dick.*

[80.] The Church of St. Bernard (Roman Catholic), 330 W. 14th St., bet. Eighth and Ninth Aves. 1875. P. C. Keely.

Two-tone brownstone **Ruskinian Gothic Revival,** with a wheel-window overlooking 14th Street.

[81.] Iglesia Catolica Guadalupe (Roman Catholic), 229 W. 14th St., bet. Seventh and Eighth Aves.

An extraordinary brownstone conversion from row house to humble **Spanish Catholic** church. Its Iberian ancestry is expressed both in the language of its services and in its new world **Spanish Baroque** facade.

Casa Moneo (Spanish and Latin American imports), 210 and 225 W. 14th St., bet. Seventh and Eighth Aves. Telephone: 929-1644.

No. 210 is *the* Spanish *bodega,* crammed with all the makings for such Latin treats as *enchiladas, mariscadas,* and *flan.* No. 225 across the street specializes in nonedibles: books, records, cooking pots two feet wide, wine carafes (both the portable *botas* and the glass *parrones*) are just a sampling.

Oviedo Restaurant and Bar (Spanish), 202 W. 14th St., bet. Seventh and Eighth Aves. Telephone: 929-9454.

An unpretentious family restaurant with well prepared food at very moderate prices. Low keyed, leisurely. No atmosphere. Bar and wine. Try the shrimp in green sauce or the *paella á la Valenciana.*

For more of Fourteenth Street, see **Walking Tour E.**

End of Tour: The Seventh Avenue IRT is at the corner; the INDs can be found at the Sixth and Eighth Avenue intersections.

Walking Tour E—Fourteenth Street: Seventh Avenue to Union Square (IRT Seventh Avenue Subway to the 14th Street Station).

Note: No entries on this tour lie within the Greenwich Village Historic District.

Fourteenth Street, west as well as east, has seen better days, when the magnetism of Wanamaker's department store radiated from Broadway and East Ninth Street throughout the area. Today, much of the street from Seventh Avenue to Union Square is crowded with shoppers bargaining for the cheap merchandise which spills out onto the wide sidewalks from a variety of small shops. Above the bustle are the great facades from an earlier era, well worth considering and enjoying. West of Seventh Avenue [see **80-81.**] is a healthy Spanish neighborhood with a variety of Latin shops and restaurants.

To make the best of this tour of Fourteenth Street, **walk on the uptown side**—most of the tall facades are best seen from across the street.

[82a.] 154–160 West Fourteenth Street (lofts), SE cor. Seventh Ave. 1913. Herman Lee Meader.

A rich display of glazed and colored terra-cotta decoration with some flavor of the older Art Nouveau (the frieze at the second floor), and yet anticipating the later Art Deco at its cornice. [Also see Meader's **Cliff Dwellers' Apartments,** Riverside Drive 15.]

[82b.] 138–146 West Fourteenth Street (lofts), bet. Sixth and Seventh Aves. ca. 1899.

A Roman Revival loft building encrusted with elaborate terra-cotta detail; inspired by the **World's Columbian Exposition** (Chicago World's Fair) of 1893.

[82c.] 132–136 West Fourteenth Street (lofts), bet. Sixth and Seventh Aves. ca. 1887.

A robust **Romanesque Revival loft building,** with delicate foliate cast-iron and terra-cotta ornamentation.

[83.] 42nd Division Armory, N.Y. National Guard, 125 W. 14th St., bet. Sixth and Seventh Aves. 1971. N.Y.S. General Services Administration; Charles S. Kawecki, State Architect.

A gross and overbearing modern drill hall that replaced a 19th-century fantasy fort of rich detail (ca. 1895. W.A. Cable).

[84a.] Salvation Army Centennial Memorial Temple and Executive Offices, 120 W. 14th St., bet. Sixth and Seventh Aves. 1930. **[84b.] John and Mary R. Markle Memorial Residence/Evangeline Residence, Salvation Army,** 123–131 W. 13th St. 1929. All by Voorhees, Gmelin & Walker.

Art Deco on a monumental scale gives entrance to the Centennial Memorial Temple. The interior is as splashy. To the west and south (on Thirteenth Street) are related but more subdued adjuncts.

[85.] 56 West Fourteenth Street, bet. Fifth and Sixth Aves. ca. 1899.

This thin building, pompously laden with Beaux Arts eclectic detail, now sports the sign of the Bunnie's Children's Center and Steffie's Dresses, Pant Suits—typical of the odd juxtaposition of a once-elegant past and today's aging honky-tonk.

[86.] Painting Industry Welfare Building, 45 W. 14th St., bet. Fifth and Sixth Aves. 1960. Mayer, Whittlesey & Glass, William J. Conklin, associate partner in charge.

In 1967, the *AIA Guide* said: "Hopefully, this witty and elegant refacing of a tired facade will inspire its neighbors to follow." **They didn't.**

[87.] Originally **Ludwig Brothers Dry Goods Store,** 34–42 W. 14th St., bet. Fifth and Sixth Aves. 1878. W. Wheeler Smith. Enlarged, 1899. Louis Korn.

A subdued cast-iron building with cheap stores below.

[88.] Originally **Baumann's Carpet Store,** 22–26 E. 14th St., bet. University Place and Fifth Ave. 1880. D. & J. Jardine.

A rich embroidery of cast iron—Composite columns, anthemia, garlands, festoons, floral bas-reliefs—embraces four tiers of enormous double-hung windows. The economics of keeping Fourteenth Street green (with money) has erased the results of the pattern maker's craft at street level in favor of a cheap five-and-dime.

End of Tour: The BMT and Lexington Avenue IRT Subways are at Union Square.

ASTOR PLACE/EAST VILLAGE

For one brief generation in the changing fashions of New York, **Lafayette Street** (then Lafayette Place) was its **most wealthy and elegant residential precinct.** Then running only from Great Jones Street to Astor Place, it was a short, tree-lined boulevard, flanked by town houses of the **Astors, Vanderbilts,** and **Delanos.** Now the trees are gone, and only **Colonnade Row** (LaGrange Terrace) remains, albeit in shoddy condition. Its character is so strong that it still suggests the urbane qualities present up until the **Civil War.** Mostly developed in **1831,** the street's construction replaced **Sperry's Botanic Gardens,** later **Vauxhall Gardens,** a summer entertainment enclave, where music and theatrical performances were presented in the open air. **John Lambert,** an English traveler of **1808,** noted it as a "neat plantation . . . the theatrical corps of New York City is chiefly engaged at Vauxhall during the summer." Only twenty years after this residential development in the 1830s, the street's principal families moved away to Fifth Avenue. At the same time the **Astor Library** (later to become a major part of New York's Public Library) and the **Cooper Union Foundation Building** were built (started in **1854** and **1853,** respectively), seeding the precinct with different uses: Lafayette became primarily a light-manufacturing and warehousing street, with erratic or isolated physical remnants of past moments in its varied history. The

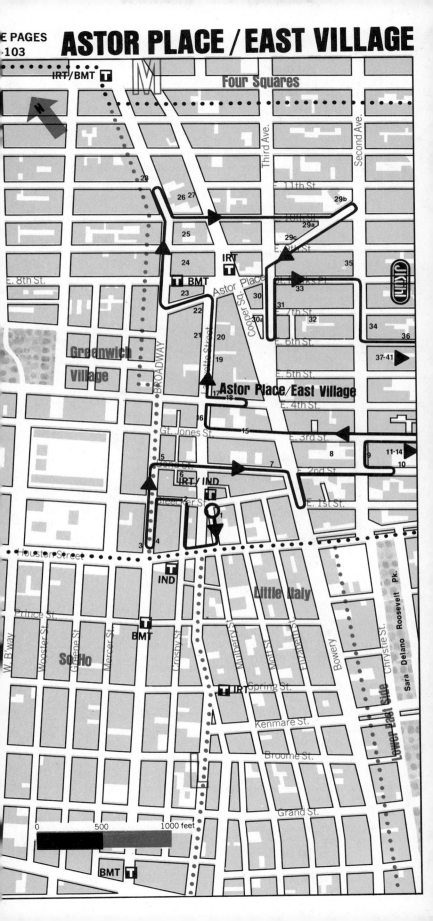

Astor Library was bought by **HIAS** (Hebrew Immigrant Aid Society), but in the late 1960s it was converted into a clutch of indoor theaters for Joseph Papp's **New York Shakespeare Festival**—a usage which brings the street back to the mainstream of human activity.

[1.] St. Barnabas House, 304 Mulberry St., SE cor. Bleecker St. 1949. Ketchum, Giná & Sharp.

A **modern pioneer** in these precincts, badly maintained. It houses a shelter for homeless women and children.

[2.] Bayard Building/formerly **Condict Building,** 65 Bleecker St., opp. Crosby St. N side. 1898. Louis H. Sullivan. ★

This was a radical building in its time, a direct confrontation with the architectural establishment that had embraced American Renaissance architecture after the **Columbian Exposition** (Chicago World's Fair) of **1893. Sullivan,** the principal philosopher and leading designer of the Chicago School, was the employer and teacher of **Frank Lloyd Wright** (who referred to him romantically as *Lieber Meister*). The sextet of angels supporting the cornice were added, over Sullivan's objections but still by his hand, at the request of his client, **Silas Alden Condict.** The building had little influence in New York, for, as Carl Condit has stated: "Who would expect an aesthetic experience on Bleecker Street?"

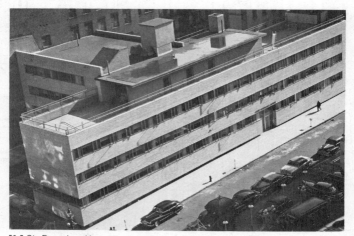

[1.] St. Barnabas House: once a contrast to the tawdry area (1949 photo)

[3.] Originally **The Cable Building,** 621 Broadway, NW cor. Houston St. 1894. McKim, Mead & White.

Wishy-washy for these usually vigorous architects. The ladies stroking the oval window over the entry are stiffs. The building's name refers to the fact that it was built as headquarters for and was one of the power stations of Manhattan's not inconsiderable cable car empire—the slots between the running rails later made it possible to convert to underground electric feed around the turn of the century.

[4a.] 620 Broadway (lofts), bet. Houston and Bleecker Sts. E side. 1858. J. B. Snook.

Vigorous Corinthian cast iron over a ravaged ground floor.

[4b.] Originally **New York Mercantile Exchange,** 628 Broadway, bet. Houston and Bleecker Sts. E side. 1882. Herman J. Schwartzmann.

Delicate **Tuscan** cast-iron columns by the chief architect of Philadelphia's Centennial Exhibition of 1876.

[5.] 670 Broadway/originally **Brooks Brothers Store,** NE cor. Bond St. 1874. George E. Harney.

A romantic commercial structure at the third of five sequential locations of **Brooks Brothers. Eastlakian** (after Charles Eastlake, one of the 19th century's most ornate designers).

[6.] 1 Bond Street/formerly **Robbins & Appleton Building,** SE cor. Jones Alley. 1871. S. D. Hatch.

Five white-painted stories of elegant Corinthian cast iron occupying the site of the house of **Albert Gallatin,** Jefferson's Secretary of the Treasury, later minister to France. It is capped by a **Second Empire** mansard roof and dormers.

[2.] Louis Sullivan's Bayard Building

[3.] Orig. The Cable (office) Building

[5.] Orig. the Brooks Brothers Store

[6.] 1 Bond St./Corinthian cast iron

A detour to the east [or skip to 15.].

[7.] Bouwerie Lane Theater/originally **Bond Street Savings Bank Building,** 330 Bowery, NW cor. Bond St. 1874. Henry Engelbert. ★

A **more intricate composition** of columns than on most cast-iron buildings.

[8.] New York Marble Cemetery, interior of the block bet. E. 2nd and E. 3rd Sts., Second Ave., and the Bowery. Entrance on Second Ave. bet. E. 2nd and E. 3rd Sts., W side. ★

One of the earliest sophistications of burial practices, anticipating, and therefore preventing, a marble orchard; the **interred are noted by tablets** inlaid in the perimeter brick wall. [Also see 10.]

[9.] Church of the Nativity, (Roman Catholic), 46 Second Ave., bet. E. 2nd and E. 3rd Sts. E side. 1970.

A **modern architectural cartoon exhibiting a gross** idea without detail. It replaces an elegant Greek Revival building (1832. Town & Davis. Demolished, 1970).

[10.] New York City Marble Cemetery, 52–74 E. 2nd St., bet. First and Second Aves. 1832. ★

President **James Monroe** was briefly interred in this, one of two remaining cemeteries [see 8.] in a part of town that contained many in the **1830–1850** period.

[15.] Engine Co. 33, NYC Fire Dept.   **[16.]** 376 Lafayette St. Rom'sqe pier

[11.] Originally **Rectory, St. Nicholas Roman Catholic Church,** 135 E. 2nd St., bet. First Ave. and Avenue A. ca. 1890.

An essay in late Gothic Revival mannerism. Swell stone trim around the tiers of pointed arch windows.

[12.] First Houses, N.Y.C. Housing Authority, 29–41 Avenue A, SW cor. E. 3rd St., 112–138 E. 3rd St., bet. First Ave. and Avenue A. Reconstructed into public housing, 1935. ★

The *first* houses built, or rather rebuilt in this instance, by the city's housing authority. In a block of tenements every third was demolished, allowing the remaining pairs light and air on three sides. This, as a remodeling, and **Williamsburg Houses,** as new construction, are still the brightest lights in the history of this city's early public housing. Walk through the urbane cobbled and tree-filled space behind.

[13.] Most Holy Reedemer Roman Catholic Church and Rectory, 161–165 E. 3rd St., bet. Avenue A and Avenue B. ca. 1905.

A stiff, high-collared limestone edifice which is among the tallest structures (except for the "projects") in the community.

[14.] NENA Comprehensive Health Service Center, Northeast Neighborhood Association, 279 E. 3rd St., bet Avenue C and Avenue D. 1976. Edelman & Salzman.

The facade of this multistory health center enjoys the monumentality once reserved for cathedrals. Within, the spaces (and the muted color scheme) establish a scale more appropriate to community health care.

Note that the picture windows are "glazed" in transparent polycarbonate plastic sheets (which have high impact resistance to vandal's missiles). Ordinary glass in adjacent tenements fares considerably less well here.

[15.] Engine Company 33, N.Y.C. Fire Department, 44 Great Jones St., bet. Lafayette St. and the Bowery. N side. 1898. Ernest Flagg and W. B. Chambers. ★

A grand Beaux Arts arch bears a cartouche. Once the **fire chief's headquarters.**

[16.] 376–380 Lafayette Street, NW cor. Great Jones St. 1888. Henry J. Hardenbergh. ★

Free-swinging **Romanesque Revival** by the architect who has graced New York with more romantic symbolism than any of his competitors (cf. the **Plaza Hotel, Art Students' League,** and the **Dakota Apartments).**

[17.] Originally **DeVinne Press Building, 399 Lafayette Street,** NE cor. E. 4th St. 1885. Babb, Cook & Willard. ★

Roman brickwork worthy of the Roman Forum's **Basilica of Constantine.** The waterfront of Brooklyn is graced with the poor country cousins (the Empire Stores) of this magnificent pile. Certainly this is a sample of "less is more"—especially when juxtaposed with (and compared to) **376** down the block.

[18a.] Old Merchant's House/originally **Seabury Tredwell House,** 29 E. 4th St., bet. Lafayette St. and the Bowery. 1832. Attributed to Minard Lafever. ★

A relic from New York's Federal past, when blocks surrounding this spot had houses of equal quality. Open to the public by appointment. **The original house is all here.**

[17.] Orig. DeVinne Press Building   [18a.] Orig. Seabury Tredwell House

[18b.] Samuel Tredwell Skidmore House, 37 E. 4th St., bet. Lafayette St. and the Bowery. 1844. ★

Greek Revival. These Ionic columns are unequaled in this vintage.

[19.] Durst Building, 409 Lafayette St., bet. E. 4th St. and Astor Place. E side. ca. 1890.

Ornate cast iron and brick **Romanesque Revival.** The three freestanding columns form a virile base.

[20.] Public Theater/formerly **Hebrew Immigrant Aid Society/**originally **Astor Library,** 425 Lafayette St., bet. E. 4th St. and Astor Place. E side. 1853–1881. South wing, 1853. Alexander Saeltzer. Center section, 1859. Griffith Thomas. North Wing, 1881. Thomas Stent. Conversion into theater complex, 1967–1976. Giorgio Cavaglieri. ★

A timid red-brick and brownstone Romanesque Revival exterior houses seven exciting modern and revived theater spaces. **John Jacob**

Astor here contributed New York's first free library, later combined with its peers (**Lenox Library,** which was sited where the **Frick Collection** is today, and the **Tilden Foundation)** to form the central branch of the **New York Public Library at 42nd Street.** These are the theaters of **Joseph Papp,** whose outdoor Shakespeare Festival in Central Park made these its indoor habitat.

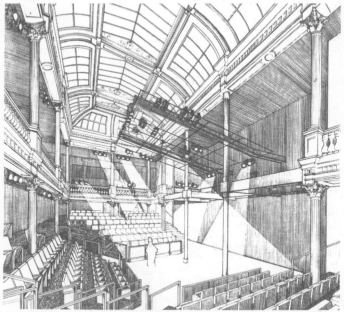

[20.] Papp's Public Theater, where the great rock musical *Hair* first opened

[21.] **Colonnade Row/**also known as **LaGrange Terrace,** 428–434 Lafayette St., bet. E. 4th St. and Astor Place. W side. Attributed to Seth Greer. 1833. ★

Four of nine houses built speculatively by **Seth Greer** in **1831.** Five at the south end were demolished for the still existing Wanamaker warehouse. An elegant urban arrangement of private structures subordinated to an imposing Corinthian colonnade (compare the **Rue de Rivoli** or the **Place des Vosges** in Paris). **Delanos, Astors,** and **Vanderbilts** lived here, until their game of social musical chairs sent them uptown.

[22.] **444 Lafayette Street (lofts)** SW cor. Astor Place. ca. 1885.

Brick and painted limestone eclectic Eastlake.

[23.] **District 65 Building (Distributive Workers of America)/**formerly **Mercantile Library Building,** 13 Astor Place, bet. Lafayette St. and Broadway. N side. 1890. George E. Harney.

Harney's **ode to Ruskin** at 670 Broadway 16 years earlier is here replaced by an establishment Harney.

The District 65 Building rests on the site of the Astor Place Opera House, where, in **May 1849,** rioting between the competing claques of the American actor Forrest and the English actor Macready caused the death of 34 stalwarts. The Seventh Regiment, quartered in an armory on the site of the present Hewitt building of Cooper Union, quelled the passions forcibly.

[24.] Originally **Wanamaker Annex,** Broadway to Fourth Ave., E. 8th to E. 9th Sts. 1903. Daniel H. Burnham & Co.

This squat and stolid 15-story monolith contains approximately as much space as the **Empire State Building!** No courtyards intervene, for this was built as a windowless selling store. It is used by the federal government today for its own mysterious purposes.

[25.] Stewart House, 70 E. 10th St., bet. Broadway and Fourth Ave. 1961.

This site was once graced by the finest cast-iron, post–Civil War building in New York: the "old" **Wanamaker** Store. Built around a central court rising through the building to a huge skylight, it was the most gracious shopping space in New York, in the European tradition: a **bazaar** comprehensible as a whole, yet subdivided into articulated specialty shops. The replacement is a gross white brick apartment house.

[26a.] Grace Church (Protestant Episcopal), 800 Broadway, Broadway to Fourth Ave. at E. 10th St. 1846. James Renwick, Jr. ★ Front garden, 1881. Vaux & Co., landscape architects.

A magnificent Gothic Revival church, **designed by an engineer** who studied the copybooks of the **Pugins,** the great English Gothic Revival theorists and detailers. At the bend of Broadway, its tower dominates the vista from the south.

[21.] Colonnade Row/LaGrange Terr.   **[26a.]** Grace Prot. Episcopal Church

[26b.] 808 Broadway, opposite E. 11th St. E side. 1888. Renwick, Aspinwall & Russell.

A Gothic Revival wall forms a visual backdrop for Grace Church, built 42 years after the church's completion by Renwick's successor firm.

[27.] The Grace Church Houses: [27a.] The Clergy House, 92 Fourth Ave., bet. E. 10th and E. 12th Sts. W side. 1902. Heins & La Farge. ★ **[27b.] Grace Memorial House/Huntington House,** 94–96 Fourth Ave. 1883. James Renwick, Jr. ★ **[27c.] Neighborhood House,** 98 Fourth Ave. 1907. Renwick, Aspinwall & Tucker.

A trio in the Gothic Revival tradition established by the elder Renwick at Grace Church on the Broadway side of the block. Endangered in the 1970s for improvements to the school, the facades were finally saved. In this case landmark designation *followed* the threat of loss.

[28a.] The Cast Iron Building/originally **James McCreery Dry Goods Store,** 67 E. 11th St. NW cor. Broadway. 1868. John Kellum. Converted, 1971. Stephen P. Jacobs. **[28b.] 49 East Twelfth Street (apartments)**/formerly **St. George Hotel,** bet. Broadway and University Place. Converted, 1977. Stephen P. Jacobs.

Two buildings converted to apartments. The old McCreery's cast-iron Corinthian columns and almost endless arches both enrich and discipline the facade—though concern for historic preservation waned at the upper stories. The old hotel is an interesting array of windows and half-round exit balconies whose reused old brick gives it the look of a slice of salami.

[29.] St. Mark's Historic District, 21–35 and 42–46 Stuyvesant St., 106–128 and 109–129 E. 10th St., 232 E. 11th St. and St. Mark's-in-the-Bowery Church. District designated, 1969. ★

This historic district, subdivided and partly developed by Governor Peter Stuyvesant's grandson, includes two landmarks established earlier, St. Mark's and the Stuyvesant-Fish house, as well as the "Renwick" Triangle.

[28a.] The Cast Iron Bldg. (apts.)   **[29c.]** Stuyvesant-Fish Residence

[29a.] Renwick Triangle: (bwnstones), St. Mark's-in-the-Bowery Church at right

[29a.] "Renwick" Triangle, 114–128 E. 10th St., 23–25 Stuyvesant St., bet. Second and Third Aves. 1861. Attributed to James Renwick, Jr.

Buildings with differing plans but uniform facades (within, buildings vary *in depth* from **16** to **48** feet, *in width* from **16** to **32** feet) make a handsome grouping, carefully restored by new owners as one- and two-family houses. **Stanford White** once lived at 118 East 10th Street.

[29b.] St. Mark's-in-the-Bowery Church (Protestant Episcopal), Second Ave., NW cor. E. 10th St. 1799. Steeple, 1828. Ithiel Town. Cast-iron portico, 1854. ★

This **Federal** body, **Greek Revival** steeple, and **Civil War** portico stand on the site of a garden chapel of **Peter Stuyvesant's** estate.

The interior is typical of many handsome churches of the pre– and post–Revolutionary War period (cf. **St. Paul's Chapel, Mariners' Temple).** The graveyard, containing Stuyvesant's vault, is now remodeled in undulating cobblestones for play purposes.

Governor Peter (Petrus) Stuyvesant's mansion sat roughly at the intersection of Tenth and Stuyvesant Streets and Second Avenue. The Bowery was then the Bouwerie (Dutch for "farm") Road, bounding the southwest flank of the Stuyvesant estate (which extended north to 23rd Street, east to Avenue C, and south to 3rd Street). Stuyvesant Street was the driveway from the Bouwerie Road to the ex-governor's mansion.

[29c.] Stuyvesant-Fish Residence, 21 Stuyvesant St., bet. Third and Second Aves. 1804. ★

A **fat Federal** house, of width unusual for its time: only five years younger than the body of St. Mark's down the block. The house was built by Governor Stuyvesant's great grandson as a wedding gift for his daughter, who was to marry Nicholas Fish, hence its hyphenated name. It suffers from "over-restoration," giving it a bland cast.

[30.] Cooper Union Foundation Building, E. 7th St. to Astor Place, Fourth Ave. to the Bowery, at Cooper Sq. 1859. Frederick A. Peterson. ★ Interior reconstructed, 1975. John Hejduk.

A high-rise brownstone, **Cooper Union** is the oldest extant building framed with steel beams in America. **Peter Cooper,** its founder and a benefactor in the great Victorian paternalistic tradition (he gave presents to Cooper Union on his birthday), was a partner of **Samuel F. B. Morse** in laying the first Atlantic cable and was the builder of the **Tom Thumb** steam locomotive; also an iron-maker, he rolled the first steel railroad rails. Such rails were used by Cooper as beams, spanning brick bearing walls. In turn brick floor arches jumped between rail and rail. The facade is in the same **Italianate brownstone** tradition popular at the time with cast-iron designers, but heavier-handed, as it is in masonry except at the ground floor.

The remodeling is almost entirely internal, with simultaneous conservation of **Peterson's** brownstone facade, and fulfillment of **Cooper's** original designs: a round elevator finally rides in his clairvoyantly round shaft.

[30a.] Peter Cooper Statue, in Cooper Square, S of E. 7th St. 1897. Augustus Saint-Gaudens, sculptor; Stanford White, architect of the base.

Cooper seated in front of his benefaction.

The Bowery, popularly known as a skid row populated by "bums," is much more complex than that. South from Cooper Square to Canal Street the vista includes the center of commercial kitchen equipment distribution for New York, and one of the principal wholesale-retail lighting fixture sales places for the city. Interspersed are the hotels (flophouses to some), resting places of the unwanted, the alcoholic, the derelict.

[31.] Cooper Square Assembly of God/formerly **the Metropolitan Savings Bank,** 59 Third Ave., NW cor. E. 7th St. 1868. Attributed to Carl Pfeiffer. ★

Marble parallel to the then-current cast-iron world: such material denoted class (cast iron was used to gain elaboration inexpensively). The church use is a happy solution to the problem of preserving a grand old neighborhood friend. Not too old, however: **McSorley's (Wonderful) Saloon** down the block is **14** years its senior [see below].

[32a.] St. George's Ukrainian Catholic Church (old building), E. 7th St., bet. Hall Place and Second Ave. ca. 1840.

A **Greek Revival** temple in stucco, with a mini-onion dome.

[32b.] St. George's Ukrainian Catholic Church (new building), E. 7th St., SE cor. Hall Place. 1977. Apollinare Osadca.

A domed symbol of the parish's wealth and burgeoning membership: **Miami Beach on 7th Street** replaces the real Greek Revival thing.

Entertainment, Stimuli, and the Full Stomach

To appreciate the buildings and urban design of this, or any, area, the native cuisine and/or artifacts add greatly:

McSorley's Old Ale House/formerly **McSorley's Saloon,** 15 E. 7th St., bet. Cooper Sq. and Second Ave.

Opened in **1854,** the year construction on **Cooper Union** started, it was made famous by painter **John Sloan** and the *New Yorker* stories by **Joseph Mitchell.** Ale, brewed to their own formula, is sold in pairs of steins. Lunch is cheap, and good.

The Surma Book and Record Company, 11 E. 7th St., bet. Cooper Sq. and Second Ave.

A fascinating **Ukrainian** store (books, records, decorated Easter eggs) retains the flavor of this old neighborhood's **Eastern European society.**

Di Roberti's Pasticceria, 176 First Ave., bet. E. 10th and E. 11th Sts.

A coffeehouse from the old world. Its interior is surfaced with mosaic tiles worthy of Ravenna. The capuccino is frothy; the homemade ices are flavorful.

Booksellers' Row, up Fourth Ave. and Broadway from Cooper Sq. to Union Sq.

Lined with bookshops with old, frequently fascinating, and sometimes rare, books. The **Strand,** at **Fourth Avenue** and **East 12th Street,** sells quantities of reviewer's copies at half price; and all have books sorted by topic. The least expensive are displayed on racks along the street, a **browser's delight,** particularly in balmy weather.

Hammer's (dairy restaurant), 243 E. 14th St., bet. Second and Third Aves. Telephone: 473-9805, or GR 7-4760.

A relic of earlier years when there were many Jews in the community. No meat is served here but it can be amazing to taste the substitutes such as vegetable cutlet. Fish is served, however. Try the cold pike. Moderate. No liquor.

St. Mark's Place, although the standard width (60 feet) in theory, is actually wider, as most of the buildings are built (unusual for Manhattan) back from their respective property lines. Cast-iron stairs once modulated the space, jumping from street to parlor floors as matter-of-fact pop-sculpture: scarcely any remain, save that at **No. 7.** Basement shops of considerable design elegance now line both sides of the street, including those for **dresses, jewelry, beads, buttons,** and **posters.** A somewhat seedy "Turkish" bath rounds out this block, the first "swinging" area of what is now called Village East, but now in decline.

[33a.] Deutsch-Amerikanische Schuetzen Gesellschaft, 12 St. Mark's Place bet. Second and Third Aves., S side. 1885.

A **German shooting club** reveled here, and shot elsewhere.

[33b.] Originally **Daniel LeRoy House,** 20 St. Mark's Place, bet. Second and Third Aves. S side. 1832. ★

Greek Revival swings again as the Grassroots Tavern.

[34.] Isaac T. Hopper Home, 110 Second Ave., bet. E. 6th and E. 7th Sts., E side. 1839.

A **very grand** late Federal building. "Wayward" girls, to use the Horatio Alger term, are here given a chance to rehabilitate themselves.

[35a.] Ottendorfer Branch, N.Y. Public Library/originally **Freie Bibliothek und Lesehalle,** 135 Second Ave., bet. St. Mark's Place and E. 9th St. W side. 1884. William Schickel. ★

Originally a free German public library in the period of heavy German immigration to the surrounding streets. **An architectural confection.**

[35b.] Stuyvesant Polyclinic/formerly German Polyklinik, 137 Second Ave., bet. St. Mark's Place and E. 9th St. W side. 1884. William Schickel. ★

Originally the downtown dispensary of the German Hospital (today's Lenox Hill) at Park Avenue and East 77th Street. (It lost its "German" appellation as a result of anti-German feelings which were rampant here during World War I.) The ornate facade of this building is (unfortunately) painted white.

[36.] Community Synagogue Center/originally **United German Lutheran Church,** 323 E. 6th St., bet. First and Second Aves. 1848.

Brick Romanesque Revival.

Leshko Coffee Shop, 111 Avenue A, cor. E. 7th St. Telephone: 473-9208.

Polish cooking in a formica setting. Try the *pirogi.* Available either boiled or fried, filled with meat, potatoes, or sauerkraut.

[37.] Tompkins Square Park, E. 7th to E. 10th Sts., Avenue A to Avenue B.

Another **English** (Bloomsbury) park surrounded by high-density, low-rise housing. Sixteen *blessed* acres in these tight and dense streets.

[38.] St. Nicholas Carpatho Russian Orthodox Greek Catholic Church/originally **St. Mark's Memorial Chapel,** 288 E. 10th St. SW cor. Avenue B.

Gothic Revival in exuberant red brick and matching terra cotta.

[39.] Originally Newsboys' and Bootblacks' Lodging House, Children's Aid Society, 127 Avenue B, NE cor. E. 8th St. 1887. Vaux & Radford.
[40.] Originally Sloane Children's Center, Children's Aid Society, 630 E. 6th St., bet. Avenue B and Avenue C. 1890. Vaux & Radford.

Two of a series of industrial schools/lodging houses which Calvert Vaux turned his attention to after his Central Park-Prospect days were behind him.

[34.] Isaac T. Hopper Home of the Women's Prison Association of New York

[41.] Riis Houses Plaza, in Jacob Riis Houses, N.Y.C. Housing Authority, E. 6th to E. 10th Sts., Avenue D to the East River Dr. 1966. Pomerance & Breines, architects. M. Paul Friedberg, landscape architect.

This is well worth the trip. Public space, between buildings, is usually filled with either traffic or parked cars, or grassed and fenced off from the pedestrian. Here space is made available in a construction to delight all ages: pyramids to climb on for the small, an amphitheater that spans all age groups, places to **sit, stand, walk, talk, hop, skip, scoot,** and **tag.** Given an asphalt street down the block from a local park, kids will most frequently pick the street to play: Riis is planned to be the alternate to streets and is where the action is, in these parts, these days. **A grand place.**

M

MIDTOWN MANHATTAN

If Manhattan is the center of the city, midtown is **the center of the center.**
Here are most of the elements one expects to find in a city core: the **major**
railroad and bus stations, the **vast majority** of hotel rooms, the **biggest**
stores, the **main** public library and post office. Of the **four major activities**
that have traditionally sustained New York, two—the offices of nationwide corporations and the garment industry—are concentrated in midtown. Another of the four—shipping—has declined to a point where
freight, largely in the form of container shipping, has moved to where
space is available, in Staten Island and Brooklyn. Transatlantic passenger
travel, once cause of **grand experiences of arrival and departure** on West
Side piers, has become **almost extinct,** the new West Side passenger
terminal a place for catching cruises, rather than a ride to Europe on the
France or *Michelangelo* or their equals. Only one of Manhattan's major
commercial activities—the financial center—is concentrated in another
part of the island.

Social status in midtown once followed a clear-cut pattern: all the
fashionable shops and living quarters ran **up a central spine** along Fifth
and Park Avenues. But Central Park, by **driving a cleft** between this spine
and the Upper West Side, **diverted** fashionable Manhattan **a bit to the
east,** and the purposeful development of Park Avenue in the 1920s shifted
the weight a bit further, encouraging some colonies of high society to
move far to the east. With the construction of the United Nations Headquarters on the East River, **a whole new profile** took shape.

CHELSEA

Almost a century and a half of ups and downs have left Chelsea a
patchwork of town houses, tenements, factories, and housing projects. The
name was originally given by **Captain Thomas Clarke** to his estate, staked
out in 1750, which extended roughly from the present 14th to 24th Streets,
from Eighth Avenue west to the Hudson, boundaries which still apply,
except that the northern one is now at about 30th Street and the eastern
one is Seventh Avenue.

Captain Clarke's grandson, **Clement Clarke Moore** (1779–1863), who
grew up in the family mansion near the present corner of 23rd Street and
Eighth Avenue, was the one who **divided the estate** into lots about 1830.
Moore, noted as a **scholar of languages** in his time, is remembered now
mainly for his poem *A Visit from Saint Nicholas,* which sealed the
unscholarly but **imperishable connection** between Saint Nick and Christmas. Moore donated one choice block for the General Theological Seminary, which is still there, and the surrounding blocks prospered as **a
desirable suburb.** Then the **Hudson River Railroad** opened along Eleventh
Avenue in 1851, attracting slaughterhouses, breweries, and so on, followed quickly by the shanties and tenements of workers.

In 1871 the dignity of town house blocks still unaffected by the
railroad was shattered by the steam locomotives of New York's **first
elevated railroad,** which ran up **Ninth Avenue.** In the 1870s, a declining
Chelsea was brightened by the blossoming of the city's **theater district**
along West 23rd Street. For a decade or so, these blocks were **ideally
convenient** to both the **high society** of Madison Square and the **flourishing
vice district** along Sixth Avenue in the upper 20s and 30s. When the
theater world moved uptown, artists and literati stayed on to make Chelsea New York's **bohemia;** early in this century bohemia moved south to
Greenwich Village, but the writers never quite deserted 23rd Street.

Around 1905–1915, a **new art form,** the **motion picture,** was centered
in Chelsea, whose old lofts and theaters made economical studios, but the
sunshine of **Hollywood** soon lured the industry away. In the 1920s and
1930s, Chelsea got a lift from some **impressive new industrial buildings**
near the piers and some luxury apartments inland. But the greatest im-

provements were on the grade-level freight line, long since part of the New York Central, which ran along Eleventh Avenue (there was a *Death Avenue Cowboy* on horseback, carrying a red flag of warning ahead of each train); it was replaced by an inconspicuous **through-the-block** elevated line just west of Tenth Avenue. Just prior to World War II the rattling Ninth Avenue "el," the direct descendant of the city's first **above-the-streets rapid transit** line, was shut down.

In the 1950s and 1960s public housing and urban renewal **uprooted** some large chunks of slum housing, and rehabilitation of Chelsea's many fine town houses followed **a slow upward trend.**

Chelsea Walking Tour A: From West 23rd Street between Seventh and Eighth Avenues (23rd Street Stations of IRT Seventh Avenue or IND Eighth Avenue Subways) to Seventh Avenue and 27th Street (one block south of IRT Seventh Avenue 28th Street Station).

J. B. & J. M. CORNELL,

IRON

Buildings.
Bridges.
Roofs.
Fronts.
Girders.
Beams.
Stairs.
Columns.
Etc.

141 Centre Street, N.Y.

[1.] Chelsea Hotel: detail of balcony railings cast by J.B. and J.M. Cornell

[1.] Chelsea Hotel, 222 W. 23rd St., bet. Seventh and Eighth Aves. 1884. Hubert, Pirsson & Co. ★

Built as one of the city's first cooperative apartment houses, the Chelsea became a hotel in 1905 but has a high ratio of permanent tenants even today. The 12-story brick **bearing wall** structure has been called Victorian Gothic, but its style is hard to pin down. The most prominent exterior features are the delicate iron balconies (made by J. B. and J. M. Cornell) that screen the hefty brickwork. Plaques at the entrance honor writers who have lived here: **Thomas Wolfe, Dylan Thomas,** and **Brendan Behan,** three of a long list that runs from **Mark Twain** and **O. Henry** to **Tennessee Williams** and **Yevgeni Yevtushenko.** Guests from other arts have included **Sarah Bernhardt, Virgil Thomson, John Sloan,** and **Jackson Pollack. Edgar Lee Masters** wrote a poem about the Chelsea, and **Andy Warhol** made it the scene of his movie *Chelsea Girls*. The lobby is a bit of a letdown, but the rooms are reported to be well-kept and full of Edwardian atmosphere—and quite reasonable in price, at least by midtown standards.

Grand Opera House stood on the northwest corner of 23rd Street and Eighth Avenue until 1960, when land was cleared for the surrounding Penn Station South [see Chelsea 10.]. Bought by the notorious financier, impresario, and bon vivant "Jubilee" Jim Fisk in the late 1860s, it did double service as head office of his Erie Railroad. It withstood repeated assaults by irate Erie stockholders (with steel doors reputed to be 12 inches thick) and was the scene of Fisk's funeral in 1872, after he was shot by Edward S. Stokes, hot-blooded third party of a triangle whose apex was the famous actress Josie Mansfield, Fisk's onetime mistress.

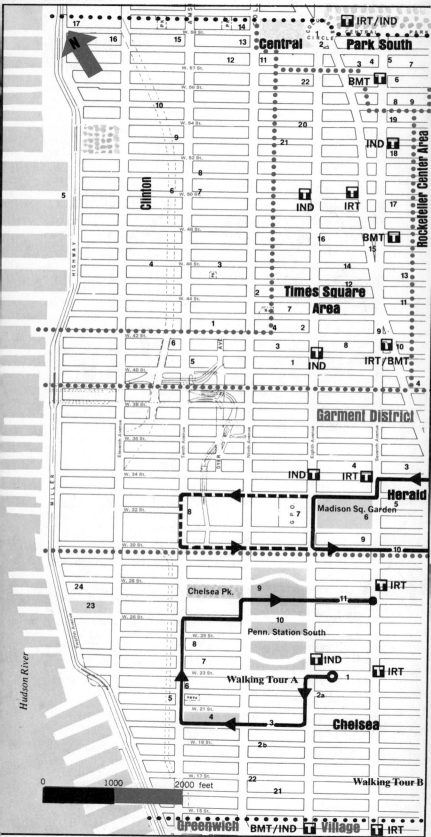

[2a.] 260 West 22nd Street (apartments), bet. Seventh and Eighth Aves. 1969. **[2b.] 365 West 19th Street (apartments),** bet. Eighth and Ninth Aves. 1970. Both by Robert Ostrow.

Their owner/architect rebuilt these row houses with **wit and imagination.** His rich exterior modeling of dark brick, glass, and ribbed metal roofing reflect equally intricate interior spaces. After completing these gems, however, he became fed up with the city and moved to **Stateline, Nevada.**

[3.] Chelsea Historic District, generally between W. 20th and W. 22nd Sts., Tenth Ave. and points E. of Ninth Ave. District designated, 1970. ★

This historic district is **a condensation** of the best qualities of Chelsea with architecture from all its periods: Greek and Gothic Revival, Italianate, and 1890s apartment buildings by such firms as C. P. H. Gilbert and Neville & Bagge.

[3a.] St. Peter's Church (Protestant Episcopal), 344 W. 20th St., bet. Eighth and Ninth Aves. 1836–1838. James W. Smith, builder, after designs by Clement Clarke Moore. **[3b.] Rectory.** 1832. Both included within the historic district.

These two buildings form **a remarkable study** in the **popular adaptation** of styles. The rectory, which apparently served first as the church, is in a very stripped-down Greek Revival style, but its fine proportions give it dignity. By the time the much larger church was built, the congregation was ready to make it one of New York's **earliest ventures** into the Gothic Revival. Its fieldstone walls, massively buttressed, with spare trim of cut granite, give it a military look.

The third building in the group, the hall east of the church, is an example of later **common brick Gothic,** started in 1854 and given its strangely churchlike front in 1871. The wrought iron fence along the street is older than any of the buildings. It dates from about 1790 and was **a hand-me-down** from venerable Trinity Church, which was putting up its third ediffice in the 1830s.

Around the church are many interesting town houses.

[4a.] General Theological Seminary, bet. W. 20th and W. 21st Sts., Ninth and Tenth Aves. **Main buildings,** 1883–1900. Charles C. Haight. **[4b.] West Building,** Nos. 5 and 6 Chelsea Square, W. 20th St., bet. Ninth and Tenth Aves. N side. 1836. Included within the historic district. ★

The stoutly fenced full city block of the seminary is accessible through the building (1960. O'Connor & Kilham) on the Ninth Avenue front, but the major buildings can be seen from West 20th Street. The **West Building,** one of the oldest examples of Gothic Revival in the city, was modeled after an even earlier, matching **East Building** (built, 1827; razed, 1892). Haight's surrounding dour red brick and brownstone structures are, for their period, quite simple in massing and ornament.

Shop Ninth Avenue: Between West 20th and West 22nd Streets are some of Chelsea's most diverting antique shops: **Yesterday** (174A), **Early Halloween** (180), and **Sideshow** (184). Also a delightfully informal place to snack.

[4c.] The Cushman Row, 406–418 W. 20th St., bet. Ninth and Tenth Aves. 1840. Included within the historic district. ★

Built by dry goods merchant **Don Alonzo Cushman** (Don was his first name), a friend of Clement Moore's who became a millionaire developing Chelsea. The row houses' fine Greek Revival detail, except for losses here and there, is intact: tiny, **wreath-encircled** attic windows; **deeply recessed** doorways with brownstone frames; **handsome** iron balustrades, newels, and fences.

[4d.] 446–450 West 20th Street, bet. Ninth and Tenth Aves. 1855. **[4e.] 465–473 West 21st Street,** NE cor. Tenth Ave. 1853. Included within the historic district. ★

Eight *exceptional* **Italianate** houses facing the austere side walls of the seminary across the street.

[5.] Church of the Guardian Angel (Roman Catholic), Tenth Ave., NW cor. W. 21st St. 1930. John Van Pelt.

Its simple brick and limestone **Italian Romanesque** facade merges with the **Tuscan village forms** of auxiliary buildings to the north in a well-related group.

[6a.] Clement Clarke Moore Park, W. 22nd St., SE cor. Tenth Ave. 1968. Coffey, Levine & Blumberg, architects and landscape architects. Included within the historic district. ★

A friendly, understated green adjunct to the row-housed district.

[6b.] Empire Diner, 210 Tenth Ave., NE cor. W. 22nd St. 1943. Altered, 1976. Carl Laanes.

The reincarnation and *ultimate homage* to the **American diner.** Stainless steel never looked better, set off by black and chrome furnishings. Moderate. Never closes. Telephone: 243-2736.

[7.] London Terrace (apartments), W. 23rd to W. 24th Sts., Ninth to Tenth Aves. 1930. Farrar & Watmaugh.

This vast brick pile, in **protomodern planar style** with faintly Gothic verticality, is actually two rows of connected apartment buildings enclosing a block-long private garden. All in all it contains 1,670 units, with swimming pool, solarium, and shops and banks in the avenue fronts. The name comes from a row (*terrace* is what the English call such) of four-story houses that once stretched along the same West 23rd Street frontage, facing the **18th-century Clarke mansion.** When the present complex was new, doormen were dressed as London bobbies as a play on the name.

For the home: Two standbys occupy rebuilt old buildings across Tenth Avenue. The original **Pottery Barn** branch (231) sells all manner of first- and second-quality wineglasses, china, enameled pots and what have you on three floors. Next door is Walkaway Workbench (229) where informal furniture is informally and colorfully displayed.

~~OUT OF BUSINESS~~

[8a.] 437–459 West 24th Street (row houses), bet. Ninth and Tenth Aves.

A row of late Italianate brick houses unusual in their large setback from the street. No. 461 next door is an earlier Federal house.

[8b.] 242–258 Tenth Avenue, bet. W. 24th and W. 25th Sts. E side.

An **Italianate** commercial row.

[9.] Church of the Holy Apostles (Protestant Episcopal), 300 Ninth Ave., SE cor. W. 28th St. 1848. Minard Lafever. Transepts, 1858. Richard Upjohn & Son. ★

This **remarkably independent work** fits into no stylistic slot. It has been called an early effort at Romanesque Revival, but its brick details, bracketed eaves, and unique bronze and slate spire—completely dominating the low nave—mark it as an equally early appearance of the Italianate style, rarely seen in churches. The interior has the simple barrel-vaulted geometry of early Italian Renaissance, without the classical details. The windows, by **William Jay Bolton,** are as unusual as the building, if less vigorous; each is composed of square panels of colorful abstract design, with central medallions painted in delicate monochromatic and realistic style.

[10.] Penn Station South (apartment complex), W. 23rd to W. 29th Sts., Eighth to Ninth Aves. 1962. Herman Jessor.

This **2,820-**unit urban renewal development is a cooperative sponsored by the **International Ladies' Garment Workers Union** ("ladies" here refers to the *garments*), conveniently located at the southwest corner of the **Garment District** (which extends north to West 40th Street and east to Sixth Avenue).

[11.] Fashion Institute of Technology, W. 26th to W. 28th Sts., bet. Seventh and Eighth Aves. **[11a.] Administration and Technology Building,** and **[11b.] Morris W. & Fannie B. Haft Auditorium,** both on W. 27th St. N Side. 1958. **[11c.] Nagler Hall (dormitory),** W. 27th St. S side.

1962. **[11d.] Shirley Goodman Resource Center,** Seventh Ave., bet. W. 26th and W. 27th Sts. W side. 1977. **[11e.] Arts and Design Center,** Seventh Ave., bet. W. 27th and W. 28th Sts. W side. 1977. **[11f.] David Dubinsky Student Center,** Eighth Ave., bet. W. 27th and W. 28th Sts. E side. 1977. All by DeYoung & Moscowitz.

This complex was planned as the training ground for acolytes to New York's garment industry. As in dresses, coats, and suits, fashions change every season, as did the style of the architecture over the score of years this campus took to complete.

Belly Dancing Center of the Western World: Around Eighth Avenue between West 28th and West 29th Streets. Exotic nightclubs, remnant of a 19th-century Greek colony that later spread north up Eighth Avenue, are housed in a rich variety of Victorian buildings. Their names—**Grecian Cave, Ali Baba, Egyptian Gardens, Port Said,** and **Istanbul**—show some geographical confusion, which extends to the dancers themselves, many reported to be just plain American, although quite accomplished.

End of Chelsea Walking Tour A.

Chelsea Walking Tour B: From West 23rd Street and Sixth Avenue (Avenue of the Americas) south to West 14th Street. IND Sixth Avenue Subway to 23rd Street station.

Sixth Avenue Magasins: The old **Stern's** dry goods store on West 23rd Street and the other block-long ghosts lining what is officially **Avenue of the Americas** recall the latter part of the 19th century, when this was **fashion row.** Though now all used for loft and office space, their splendor is still quite evident.

[15.] Orig. Hugh O'Neill Dry Goods Store: dean of Sixth Avenue's gray ghosts

[12.] Originally **Stern's Dry Goods Store,** 32–36 W. 23rd St., bet. Fifth and Sixth Aves. 1878. Henry Fernbach. 38–46 W. 23rd St. 1892. William Schickel.

A **resplendent** cast-iron emporium for "New York's first merchandising family."

[13.] Originally **Ehrich Brothers Dry Goods Store,** 695–709 Sixth Ave., bet. W. 22nd and W. 23rd Sts. W side. 1889. Alfred Zucker & Co.

An **elegant** cast-iron facade.

[14a.] Originally **Adams Dry Goods Store,** 675–691 Sixth Ave., bet. W. 21st and W. 22nd Sts. W side. 1900. DeLemos & Cordes.

A late arrival to retail row. Note the **ADG monograms** amongst the ornament.

[14b.] Third Cemetery of the Spanish-Portuguese Synagogue, Shearith Israel, 98–110 W. 21st St., bet. Sixth and Seventh Aves. 1829–1851.

Contained by painted brick loft buildings on three sides, this is a handsome, though private, oasis graced with a venerable ailanthus tree. This cemetery is **one of three** on Manhattan Island, and the youngest of the trio. [See Civic Center 36. and Greenwich Village 33b.]

[15.] Originally **Hugh O'Neill Dry Goods Store,** 655–671 Sixth Ave. bet. W. 20th and W. 21st Sts. 1875. Mortimer C. Merritt.

Cast-iron **Corinthian** columned and pilastered facade with almost full cylindrical towers once crowned with domes interlocked at its two corners. The name remains clearly visible in relief at the pediment.

[16.] Church of the Holy Communion (Protestant Episcopal), 49 W. 20th St., NE cor. Sixth Ave. 1846. Richard Upjohn. ★

More notable because Upjohn *did* it than because of its intrinsic architectural quality. *Endangered.*

[17.] Originally **Simpson Crawford Dry Goods Store,** 641 Sixth Ave., bet. W. 19th and W. 20th Sts. W side. 1900. William H. Hume.

Seven stories of limestone, a sober work of architecture.

Witches and Warlocks: The **Magickal Childe,** at 35 West 19th Street, vends amulets, talismans, herbs, roots, and spices, ostensibly to bring protection, good luck, and/or love. Telephone: 242-7182.

[18.] Originally **B. Altman Dry Goods Store,** 621 Sixth Ave., bet. W. 18th and W. 19th Sts. W side. 1876. D. & J. Jardine. Addition to S, 1887. William H. Hume. Addition on W. 18th St., 1910. Buchman & Fox.

B. Altman's (or **Baltman's** to some) forsook this cast-iron emporium in 1906 for its imposing stone edifice at Fifth Avenue and 34th Street.

[19.] Originally **Siegel-Cooper Dry Goods Store,** 616–632 Sixth Ave., bet. W. 18th and W. 19th Sts. E side. 1895. DeLemos & Cordes.

Fifteen-and-a-half acres of space are contained in this latecomer to the area. Elaborately embellished in glazed terra cotta, it clearly bears the stamp of the **Chicago World's Fair of 1893.** At one time it was a favored meeting place, the phrase "Meet you at the fountain!" referring to the jet of water graced by the figure of the *Republic* by **Daniel Chester French** (now reposing at California's Forest Lawn Cemetery). After a brief but turbulent retailing history, it was converted to a military hospital during World War I. In recent years it has served as a loft for the construction of television scenery.

End of Chelsea Walking Tour B: The **Sixth Avenue IND 14th Street** Station is the nearest, although a short walk along the street will get you to a wide range of rapid transit.

Sixteenth Street east of Sixth Avenue contains a wealth of architectural styles and building types.

[20a.] 31 West 16th Street (row house). Altered, 1971. Stephen B. Jacobs.

Syncopated rhythms mark the window placement in this altered row house.

[20b.] Church of St. Francis Xavier (Roman Catholic), 30 W. 16th St. 1882. P. C. Keely.

The monumental porch of this **neo-Baroque** church spills onto the sidewalk. Inside is an equally monumental **Baroque** space.

[20c.] IRT Electrical Substation, No. 41, 27–29 W. 16th St. 1917.

A chaste tapestry of brick embellished by an intricate verdigris cornice. The facade is further enhanced by two early street lights with fuschia-shaped milk glass globes.

[20d]. 17 West 16th Street (row house). ca. 1846. ★

A **Greek Revival** residence to which Margaret Sanger moved her Birth Control Clinical Research Bureau in **1930.** Its swell-front (and those of its neighbors at Nos. 5–9) was a common characteristic of **Boston's Greek Revival** (as around Louisburg Square) but was rare in New York.

Miscellany:

[21.] Originally **Port of New York Authority Commerce Building/Union Inland Terminal No. 1,** 111 Eighth Ave. bet. W. 15th and W. 16th Sts. through to Ninth Ave. 1932. Abbott, Merkt & Co., engineers and architects.

An **enormous** inner-city warehousing facility occupying a full city block, **a whale of a structure** but only **a little brother** to Starrett-Lehigh [see 23.]. Before occupying space in its World Trade Center, this was the headquarters of the Port of New York Authority (today, Port Authority of New York and New Jersey).

[22a.] National Maritime Union of America, Joseph Curran Annex, 346 W. 17th St., bet. Eighth and Ninth Aves. 1966. **[22b.] Joseph Curran Plaza,** 100 Ninth Ave., bet. W. 16th and W. 17th Sts. Both by Albert C. Ledner & Assocs.

A startling white tile-faced, porthole-pierced front wall sloping **$8\frac{1}{2}$ degrees** from vertical was the architect's way of meeting the setback requirement of the old Zoning Resolution. As novel on the exterior as the union's former main building [see Greenwich Village 34b.], it is efficiently laid out inside to accommodate medical and recreational facilities for union members.

[23.] Starrett-Lehigh Building, W. 26th to W. 27th Sts., Eleventh to Twelfth Aves. 1931. Russell G. and Walter M. Cory. Yasuo Matsui, associated architect.

Literally miles of strip windows and bands of brick, **streaking and swerving** around this block-square, 19-story factory-warehouse structure have made it **a landmark of modern architecture** ever since it rose over the air rights of the former Lehigh Valley Railroad freight terminal.

[24.] Central Stores, Terminal Warehouse Company, W. 27th to W. 28th Sts., Eleventh to Twelfth Aves. 1891.

Twenty-four acres of warehousing within a brick fortress composing 25 separate buildings crowned with Tuscan detail. A close relative of the Rossiter Stores at West 57th Street [see Clinton 17.].

Famous Players in Famous Plays: Adolph Zukor, who originated this title, produced a number of old films in Chelsea. Nor was his the only studio, others being **Kalem, Charles O. Bauman & Adam Kessel Films, Reliance, Majestic,** etc. The **Famous Players Studios** was at 221 West 26th Street; its roster of stars contained such names as Mary Pickford and John Barrymore.

THE FOUR SQUARES

More than a hundred years ago, the laying out of **Gramercy, Union, Stuyvesant,** and **Madison Squares** gave promise of urbane residential precincts for wealthy New Yorkers: all speculative developments in the spirit of **London's Bloomsbury** (where the Dukes of Bedford developed farmland into a precinct of Georgian architecture and garden "squares").

Union Square: First Union Place, it joined the **Bloomingdale Road** (Broadway), from the north, to the **Bowery Road** (Fourth Avenue), from the south. Before the Civil War, it was a grand residential square, with a private park, locked and gated for the residents surrounding it (as Gramercy Park still is today). In **1854,** the first glimmer of its future as a new theatrical district appeared with the opening of the **Academy of Music** (opposite its movie palace namesake of today, and where now are the Consolidated Edison offices). When it later became the center of radicalism, thousands of protestors here waited news of the execution of **Sacco and Vanzetti.** May Day celebrations were centered here, the precinct of the *Daily Worker,* and many other more or less radical publications and organizations were in the neighborhood.

Note: The entries are arranged in three corridors: the **western,** from Union Square northward to Madison Square and beyond; **central,** Irving Place, Stuyvesant Square, Gramercy Park, and the area of the armory and the Belmore Cafeteria; and **eastern,** east to Stuyvesant Town, Peter Cooper Village, Kips Bay, and the East River.

WEST CORRIDOR

Union Square and Vicinity

[1.] Union Square Park, E. 14th to E. 17th Sts., Union Square W. to Park Ave. S.

The park's present, raised configuration dates from the era of World War I when the construction of the BMT subway station, with its maze of passages, caused its total reconstruction to allow for adequate clearances.

Small crowds still assemble here around their favorite debater to heckle, support, or berate him: New York's **"Hyde Park"** was made a sacred precinct for orators and agitators after police excesses in repressing Depression unemployment rallies in **1930.**

Washington (H. K. Brown, Sculptor), a copy of the Houdon original (on horseback), dates from 1856. **Brown** also contributed *Lincoln* in 1866; and in 1876, **Bartholdi,** sculptor of the Statue of Liberty, left *Lafayette* as token of Franco-American relations (early in his indefatigable campaign to raise funds for *Liberty*).

[2.] Former **S. Klein's,** 6 Union Sq., bet. E. 14th and E. 15th Sts. E side.

The old discount department store is **a clutch of small buildings** which once served the most modest women's budget, and occasionally yielded **high style** for those who searched the racks frequently and with sharp eyes. Sold for recycling by a new owner, will there be a sleek new facade cladding the quasi-medieval maze behind?

[3.] United Mutual Savings Bank/originally **Union Square Savings Bank,** 20 Union Square E., NE cor. E. 15th St. Henry Bacon.

A classy **Corinthian colonnade** is, in these precincts, somewhat forlorn. **Bacon's** best remembrance is the **Lincoln Memorial.**

[4a.] Guardian Life Ins. Co.: neo-Renaissance tower with sleek modern annex

[4a.] Guardian Life Insurance Company/originally **Germania Life Insurance Company,** 201 Park Avenue S., NE cor. E. 17th St. 1911. D'Oench & Yost. **[4b.] Annex,** 105 E. 17th St., bet. Park Ave. S. and Irving Place. 1961. Skidmore, Owings & Merrill.

The multistory mansard-topped tower was called **Germania Life** until World War I anger persuaded the board of directors to rename it. They picked a name with as large a number of **reusable** letters as they could find, *Guardian.* The tower's crowning glory, its mansard, is best seen from the park.

Next door is the sleek annex, a simple grid of aluminum and glass, infilled with white blinds.

[5.] Originally **The Century Building,** 33 E. 17th St., facing Union Square Park bet. Park Ave. S. and Broadway. 1881. William Schickel.

This red brick and whitestone charmer is where the popular **Century** and **St. Nicholas** magazines were published, back before the turn of the century.

[6.] McIntyre Building, 874 Broadway, NE cor. E. 18th St. ca. 1892.

Unspeakable Eclectic: a murmuration of Byzantine columns, Romanesque arches, Gothic finials and crockets: the designer used the *whole* spectrum of history in one shot.

[7.] Originally **YWCA (Young Women's Christian Association)/**formerly **Rand School,** 7 E. 15th St., bet. Union Sq. W. and Fifth Ave. ca. 1889. R. H. Robertson.

Romanesque Revival buried in shadow by its taller 20th-century neighbor.

Between Union and Madison Squares

[8.] Originally **Arnold Constable Dry Goods Store,** 881–887 Broadway, SW cor. E. 19th St., through to Fifth Ave. 1869. Extended, 1873, 1877. All by Griffith Thomas.

Lovers of marble walls, cast-iron facades, mansard roofs, **rejoice!** There is something here for *each* of you. The Broadway facade, the oldest, is of marble. The extension on Fifth Avenue, the youngest, is of cast iron. And, in between, the two-story-high **miraculous mansard** roof appeared over the early part and was extended later when the addition was made. Among the city's **most wonderful** relics.

[8.] Orig. Arnold Constable Store   [13.] Orig. Methodist Book Concern

[9.] 889–891 Broadway (lofts), NW cor. E. 19th St. 1883. Edward H. Kendall.

The skyline is *desperately* labored to achieve a varying picturesque profile: bits and pieces of roof interlock at random with the brick facade.

[10.] 900 Broadway (lofts), SE cor. E. 20th St. 1887. McKim, Mead & White.

Limestone supports a brick polychromy of arches. The cornice has been removed.

[11.] Theodore Roosevelt Birthplace, National Park Service, 28 E. 20th St., bet. Broadway and Park Ave. S. Original building, 1848, demolished. Replicated, 1923. Theodate Pope Riddle. ★

After the property was recaptured by the **Theodore Roosevelt Association,** this structure was built to reproduce the one Roosevelt knew (he was born here in **1858,** and died elsewhere in **1919**). Open to the public. Telephone: 260-1616.

[12.] Originally **Lord & Taylor Dry Goods Store,** 901 Broadway, SW cor. E. 20th St. 1869. James H. Giles.

Exuberant cast-iron facade, unusually capped with a single-storied, dormered mansard roof. The corner pavilion is reminiscent of the **Ren-**

aissance castle architecture of Prague. The ground floor has been remodeled for selfish commercial purposes with no respect for its uppers.

[13.] Originally **The Methodist Book Concern,** 150 Fifth Ave., SW cor. E. 20th St. 1889.

Romanesque Revival in brick: the ground floor entrance has been modernized with misunderstanding. The brick rests on a rockface granite podium.

[14.] Hotel 21, 21 E. 21st St., bet. Broadway and Park Ave. S. 1878. Bruce Price.

A socialite architect, **Price** planned Tuxedo Park, N.Y., a wealthy suburban private community, and designed many of its shingle style houses. (His daughter was **Emily Post.**) Now a seedy example of **American Queen Anne,** it is a picturesque composition ornamented with original metalwork: note the finial at its gable. The stoop railing is bronze, now painted a bilious green.

[15.] Originally **Scribner Building,** 153–157 Fifth Ave., bet. E. 21st and E. 22nd Sts. 1894. Ernest Flagg. ★

The **first headquarters** built for publishers Charles Scribner's Sons by an architect who would later build for them a second headquarters [Fifth Avenue 4a.], a printing plant [Times Square 7.], and a residence [Upper East Side 10c.]. It is a **chaste** facade which once sported a broad, **semi-ellipsoidal** cast-iron and glass canopy, in the Parisian mode.

Madison Square and Environs

[16.] Originally **Western Union Telegraph Company Building,** 186 Fifth Ave., SW cor. W. 23rd St. 1884. Henry J. Hardenbergh.

An amazing holdover from Hardenbergh's Dakota period—this from the same year [see Central Park West 15.]. This is one of Fifth Avenue's earliest commercial buildings.

[17.] Flatiron Building/originally **Fuller Building,** E. 22nd to E. 23rd Sts., Fifth Ave. to Broadway. 1902. D. H. Burnham & Co. ★

The diagonal line of Broadway formed triangular buildings here and at Times Square. Burnham was master of architectural ceremonies at the **World's Columbian Exposition** (Chicago World's Fair), **1893,** an architectural event that **changed the course of civic architecture** for a generation: Roman and Renaissance Revival architecture gave a face of pomp to government buildings.

Rusticated limestone uniformly detailed from ground to sky, in the **manner of an Italian palazzo.** The acutely angled corners give it a dramatic perspective.

[18.] Madison Square/formerly known as **The Parade/**formerly **a potter's field,** Fifth to Madison Aves., E. 23rd to E. 26th Sts. 1847.

The city crept past this point just prior to the Civil War. Madison Avenue springs from the east flank of the square at 23rd Street. The **Commissioners' Plan of 1811,** establishing a surveyor's grid for the city, showed a parade from Third to Seventh Avenues, 23rd to 34th Streets. The present space is all that remains of that idea: **replaced in scale by Central Park,** which had not been a part of the commissioners' scheme.

Statuary: *Chester A. Arthur,* 1898. George Bissell. *Admiral David G. Farragut,* 1880. Augustus Saint-Gaudens, sculptor. Stanford White, architect. A great and melancholy memorial. *Roscoe Conkling,* 1893. J. Q. A. Ward. Republican political leader. *William H. Seward,* 1876. Randolph Rogers. Seward was Lincoln's Secretary of State: here, owing to unsuccessful fund-raising, the sculpted body is one that Rogers modeled of Lincoln. With Seward's head attached, it holds the emancipation proclamation.

[18a.] Worth Monument, W. 25th to W. 26th Sts., Fifth Ave. to Broadway. 1857.

General William J. Worth, hero of the Seminole and Mexican Wars, is buried here—in the middle of the intersection under a Renaissance obelisk!

A brief detour to the west:

[19a.] Serbian Orthodox Cathedral of St. Sava/originally **Trinity Chapel,** 15 W. 25th St., bet Fifth and Sixth Aves. 1855. ★ **[19b.] Clergy House,** 16 W. 26th St. 1855. Both by Richard Upjohn. ★ **[19c.] Parish House**/originally **Trinity Chapel School,** 13 W. 25th St. 1860. J. Wrey Mould. ★ In Church: Swope Memorial reredos, 1892. Altar, 1897. Both by Frederick Clarke Withers.

A complicated midblock complex. The **somber** brownstone church and clergy house and the **playful** Ruskinian Gothic polychromed parish house to the east form **an unexpected pedestrian shortcut** from 25th to 26th Streets. A century of grime **conceals** the detailing and color of all three works.

A statue of **Michael Idvorsky Pupin** (1858–1935), a noted physicist of Croatian background, stands in the walkway. Pupin Hall, at Columbia, is named for him.

[20a.] Metropolitan Life Insurance Company, Main Building, 1 Madison Ave., bet. E. 23rd and E. 25th Sts. E side. 1893. **Tower,** 1909. Both by Napoleon LeBrun & Sons. Entire complex altered, 1961. **[20b.] North Building,** 11–25 Madison Ave. bet. E. 24th and E. 25th Sts. E side. 1932. Harvey Wiley Corbett and D. Everett Waid.

Stripped of its ornament and retained as a symbol after its adjacent base was rebuilt, the tower is now used as storage for company records. At the **North Building,** two marks to note are the polygonal modeling of the upper bulk to make it less ponderous—an early *search for form* in the history of modern architecture—and the vaulted entrance space at each of its four corners.

[21.] Appellate Division, N.Y. State Supreme Court, NE cor. E. 25th St. and Madison Ave. 1900. James Brown Lord. ★

This **small marble palace** is the reincarnation of an English 18th-century country house. The sculpture is **extravagant:** *Wisdom* and *Force,* by Frederick Ruckstahl, flank the portal; *Peace,* by Karl Bitter, is the central figure on the balustrade facing the Square; *Justice* (fourth from the left on 25th Street) is by Daniel Chester French.

[22.] Child Study Association of America, Inc./originally **American Society for the Prevention of Cruelty to Animals,** 50 Madison Avenue, NW cor. E. 26th St. 1896. Renwick, Aspinwall & Owen.

A **proper London Club** in delicately tooled limestone. Note the elaborately worked cornice. The blank space in the stonework over the entrance once contained an elaborately carved escutcheon of the A.S.P.C.A.

North of Madison Square

[23.] New York Life Insurance Company, 51 Madison Ave., E. 26th to E. 27th Sts., Madison Ave. to Park Ave. S. 1928. Cass Gilbert.

Limestone Renaissance at the bottom, birthday cake at the top. Gilbert was obsessed with pyramidal caps for his buildings: compare the **Woolworth Building** (1913), and the **Federal Courthouse** at Foley Square (1936).

This site has a rich history. Originally it was occupied by the New York terminal of the New York and Harlem Railroad: its Union Depot. After 1871, the old Union Depot's shell was converted into Barnum's **Hippodrome** (the first Grand Central Depot had been built to replace Union), then to the first **Madison Square Garden.** Stanford White (McKim, Mead & White) designed a lavish replacement complete with a tower copied from the **Giralda** in Seville. White was shot on the roof garden in 1906 by Harry Thaw, whose wife, the former Evelyn Nesbitt, was reputedly (before Thaw's marriage to her) White's mistress. One added irony is the fact that the Madison Square Garden's newest quarters, two buildings later, are on the site of demolished Pennsylvania Station, McKim, Mead & White's *greatest* New York work.

[24a.] 250 Fifth Avenue, NW cor. W. 28th St. 1907. McKim, Mead & White.

One of the few McKim, Mead & White office buildings [cf. the **Cable Building,** Astor Place/East Village 3.]: no great shakes, it is awkwardly proportioned limestone and brick.

[24b.] 256 Fifth Avenue (lofts), bet. W. 28th and W. 29th Sts. W side. ca. 1892.

Terra-cotta virtuosity maximized in a **neo-Gothic phantasmagoria,** at least *above* the first floor.

[25.] Marble Collegiate Church, 272 Fifth Ave., NW cor. E. 29th St. 1854. S. A. Warner. ★

Sharp-edged limestone Gothic Revival, contemporary with Grace and Trinity Churches. Most noted for its former pastor, **Norman Vincent Peale,** whose many books try to span popular religion and popular psychology; **Richard Nixon** attended this church in his lawyer days, between his Vice-Presidency and Presidency.

[22.] Child Study Assn. of America   **[25.]** The Marble Collegiate Church

---

Holland House: The adjacent loft building at the southwest corner of Fifth Avenue and West 30th Street is the old and famous Holland House Hotel, spruced up in the early 1920s for use as a mercantile establishment. In its original incarnation (1891. Harding & Gooch) it had an opulent interior of marble, brocade, and lace, and was considered the equal of any hotel in the world.

[26.] Church of the Transfiguration/"The Little Church Around the Corner" (Protestant Episcopal), 1 E. 29th St., bet. Fifth and Madison Aves. **Church, Rectory, Guildhall,** 1849–1861. ★ **Lich Gate,** 1896. ★ Frederick Clarke Withers. **Lady Chapel, Mortuary Chapel,** 1908. ★

Its notorious nickname has stuck since 1870, when a fashionable, local pastor declined to officiate at the funeral of George Holland, an actor, and suggested the obsequies be held at **"the little church around the corner."** It has been a church for those in the theater ever since. Pleasant small scale with a garden.

[27.] American Academy of Dramatic Arts/originally **The Colony Club,** 120 Madison Ave., bet. E. 30th and E. 31st Sts. 1905. McKim, Mead & White. ★

Georgian-Federal Revival seemed appropriate for venerably connected and socially prominent ladies. Unusual brickwork, with the headers (short ends) of brick facing out. The false balcony is an irritating mannerism from a firm of talent.

[28.] 121 Madison Avenue (apartments)/originally **Hubert Home Club,** NE cor. E. 30th St. 1883. Hubert, Pirsson & Co. Altered, 1940. Mayers, Murray & Philip.

Pre–World War II alterations to this relative of the **Chelsea Hotel** [Chelsea 1.] disguised its once picturesque skyline. Nevertheless, its bulk, color (red), and what remains of its original detail distinguish it.

Irving Place to Stuyvesant Square

[29.] Consolidated Edison Company Building/originally **Consolidated Gas Company Building,** 4 Irving Place, NE cor. E. 14th St., 1915–1929. Henry J. Hardenbergh. Tower, 1926. Warren & Wetmore.

Hardenbergh's last significant and dullest work: the vigor of his creativity (the **Dakota,** the **Plaza**) here gives way to a profitable establishment client. A landmark clock tops this, Con Ed's GHQ, on the site of the old **Academy of Music;** its namesake, a now-decrepit movie palace, is opposite.

[32a.] Tuesday's/form. Joe King's

[35.] Friends' (Quaker) Meeting House

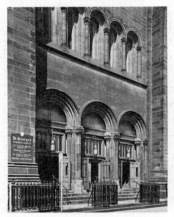

[36.] St. George's Episcopal Church

[36.] St. George's Parish House

[30.] Lüchow's (restaurant), 110 E. 14th St. opp. Irving Place.

Once one of the great gourmand, if not gourmet, landmarks of New York. This is **North German,** not Chinese. With an **ancient band** playing *Tales from the Vienna Woods,* **aged and mellowed mahogany,** and **mirrors, sauerbraten, dumplings,** and **draft German beer.** An alternate scenario provides **Oompah,** stained glass skylights, and Liebfraumilch. The quality of the atmosphere outweighs that of the food. Moderate to expensive.

[31.] "Washington Irving" House, 122 E. 17th St. SW cor. Irving Place. 1845.

Irving's connection with this house is but the wishful thinking of an ancient owner. In the real world, **Elsie de Wolfe** and **Elizabeth Marbury** lived here from **1894** to **1911.** They maintained a salon where notables from all walks of life gathered amidst the "white decor" that was the beginning of Elsie's career as America's first paid—highly paid—interior decorator. Later, as **Lady Mendl,** she gave parties with as much élan as her decor.

Paul and Jimmy's Place, 54 Irving Place, bet. E. 17th and E. 18th Sts. Telephone: OR 4-9463.

Superb southern Italian cooking in a small, popular restaurant. Cocktails and wine.

[32a.] Tuesday's/formerly **Joe King's Rathskeller,** or **German-American**/originally **Scheffel Hall.** 190 Third Ave., bet. E. 17th and E. 18th Sts. 1894. Weber & Drosser.

German-American eclectic Renaissance Revival. A generation ago this was an in-town place for collegians to drink beer, sing, and make out. Before the collegians, it expressed the aspirations of a massive local immigrant German population.

[32b.] Wilburt's (home furnishings), 194 Third Ave., bet. E. 17th and E. 18th Sts. 1964. Space Design Group.

Housewares, glass, china, pottery, candles, and endless details of good design are sold here. The D/R of Gramercy Park. The shop is as handsome as its contents: unpretentious, elegant.

[33.] Stuyvesant Square Historic District, generally including the square, its entire frontage on Rutherford Place, partial frontages on E. 15th St. and E. 17th St., and parts of E. 15th, E. 16th, E. 17th, and E. 18th Sts. bet. Second and Third Aves. District designated, 1975. ★

A complex area: the side streets are graced by groups of homogeneous row houses; the frontages around the square contain religious buildings and (outside the district) hospitals. Third Avenue, to which the district barely extends, is the neighborhood shopping strip.

[34.] Stuyvesant Square, Second Ave., bet. E. 15th and E. 17th Sts., Rutherford and Perlman Places. 1837. Reconstructed, 1936. N.Y.C. Department of Parks. Included within the historic district.

This split, handsome square, a gift of Stuyvesant, benefitted the city as well as the owners of the surrounding land: the first in urban graces, the latter in future profits. Statuary: *Peter Stuyvesant,* 1936. Gertrude Vanderbilt Whitney (founder of the Whitney Museum), sculptor.

[35.] Friends' Meeting House and Seminary, 221 E. 15th St., facing Stuyvesant Square. (Rutherford Place), bet. E. 15th and E. 16th Sts. 1860. Charles T. Bunting. ★ Included within the historic district.

Appropriately plain **Quaker** architecture. Spartan designs of the Civil War era speak well to modern architects: red brick, brownstone quoins, white trim.

[36.] St. George's Church (Protestant Episcopal), Rutherford Place, NW cor. E. 16th St. facing Stuyvesant Square. 1856. Blesch & Eidlitz. ★ **Parish House,** 207 E. 16th St. 1888. Cyrus L. W. Eidlitz. **Chapel,** 4 Rutherford Place. 1911. Matthew Lansing Emery and Henry George Emery. **Henry Hill Pierce House**/originally **Rectory,** 209 E. 16th St. Early 1850s. Leopold Eidlitz. All included within the historic district.

J. P. Morgan's church. Stolid brownstone, cut and dressed. The chapel is not in the same bold class as its parent: it is *overdressed,* in the Byzantine-Romanesque fashion.

The parish house is in rockface brownstone: **heavy, towered Gothic Revival.**

[37a.] Salvation Army/originally **St. John the Baptist House,** 231–235 E. 17th St., bet. Second and Third Aves. E part, 1877. E. T. Littel. W part, 1883. Charles C. Haight. Included within the historic district.

Picturesque, asymmetrical Victorian Gothic.

[37b.] Originally **Sidney Webster Residence,** 245 E. 17th St., bet. Second and Third Aves. 1883. Richard Morris Hunt. Included within the historic district.

A *single* house, rare in these parts and unique in this district. Brick and brownstone interpretation of the French Renaissance.

[38.] New York Infirmary (hospital), Nathan D. Perlman Place, bet. E. 15th and E. 16th Sts., E side. 1950. Skidmore, Owings & Merrill.

A pristine white prism entered through a restrained black canopy. Anywhere else its refinement would be admired; in this precinct it feels out of place.

[39.] St. Mary's Catholic Church of the Byzantine Rite, 246 E. 15th St. SW cor. Second Ave. 1964. Brother Cajetan J. B. Baumann.

Essentially a **stained glass concrete-framed box,** ornamented with sculpture and mosaics.

Gramercy Park and Environs

[40.] Gramercy Park Historic District, an irregular area including the park, and the W, S, and part of the E frontages on the park; much of the N side of E. 18th St. and both sides of E. 19th St., bet. Irving Place and Third Ave.; and Calvary Church. District designated, 1966. ★

[41.] Gramercy Park, Gramercy Park E. and W., Gramercy Park N. and S. Its axis is Lexington Ave. to the N., Irving Place to the S. 1831. Samuel Ruggles. Included within the historic district.

Enlightened self-interest graced this neighborhood with a park. Although private and restricted to the tenants occupying the original plots that surrounded it, it is a handsome space for all strollers to enjoy. This was built with the same attitude the **Dukes of Bedford** employed in London, where **Bloomsbury** and **Covent Garden,** speculative housing precincts, were made not only more delightful, but more profitable, by the addition of varied parks and squares and a consistent architectural quality control. **Union Square** had a similar role with its once-surrounding private mansions.

Edwin Booth (who lived at 16 Gramercy Park South) stands as placed by sculptor **Edmond T. Quinn** in 1916.

[42.] 34 and 36 Gramercy Park East, bet. E. 20th and E. 21st Sts., E side. ca. 1883 and 1905, respectively. Included within the historic district.

Two **venerable elders** (red brick fortified, and white terra-cotta bay-windowed Gothic, respectively) whose uptown brethren have been mostly demolished to build apartments with more floors and lower ceilings.

[43.] The Brotherhood Synagogue/originally **Friends' Meeting House,** 28 Gramercy Park S., bet. Irving Place and Third Ave. S side. 1859. King & Kellum. ★ Remodeled as a synagogue. 1975. James Stewart Polshek. Included within the historic district. ★

An appropriately spartan brownstone box built for the Quakers, now used by another religious group.

[44.] The Block Beautiful, E. 19th St. bet. Irving Place and Third Ave. Remodeled as a group. Frederick J. Sterner. Included within the historic district. ★

A **handsome, picturesque architectural unit,** more notable for the sum of its parts than the parts themselves. No single building is of great note: in spite of this, it is one of the **best places** in New York: tree-lined, with limited traffic, it is quiet, serene, urbane.

Pete's Tavern, 129 E. 18th St., NE cor. Irving Place. Telephone: GR 3-7676.

A social landmark in a corner bar that is not garish and has the patina of age and a sophisticated clientele. In summer a shallow sidewalk café bounds two sides. Inside old and bare brick brings a vintage experience: common Italian food and burgers; booze and wine. Moderate.

[45a.] The Players, 16 Gramercy Park S., bet. Irving Place and Park Ave. S., S side. 1845. Remodeled, 1888. Stanford White. ★ Included within the historic district.

Edwin Booth bought this house to found a club for those in the theater (as loosely defined). He was a star in a sense not easily conceivable today, when stars are neither so rare nor influential. A **superbrownstone,** with a two-story Tuscan porch bracketed by great wrought iron lanterns.

[45b.] National Arts Club, 15 Gramercy Park S., bet. Irving Place and Park Ave. S., S side. 1884. Calvert Vaux. ★ Included within the historic district.

Here the **Vaux** (say "Vawx") of **Olmsted & Vaux** reverted to a single architectural commission for **Samuel J. Tilden,** outspoken opponent of the Tweed Ring and later governor of New York. In 1876 **Tilden** ran for president against **Rutherford B. Hayes;** he won the popular vote by 250,000 but lost in the electoral college. Fearful of his personal security in a time of riots, **Tilden** had rolling steel doors built into the Gramercy Park facade (behind the windows), and a tunnel to 19th Street for a speedy exit in case the doors failed. Gothic Revival in the manner of **John Ruskin.** Brownstone and polished black granite trim.

[39.] St. Mary's Catholic Church   [45b.] Orig. Samuel J. Tilden House

[46.] 3 and 4 Gramercy Park West, bet. E. 20th and E. 21st Sts. W side. 1846. Alexander Jackson Davis. Included within the historic district.

The iron work is *notable* here, over plain brick bodies. Davis was one of America's most versatile 19th-century architects.

[47a.] Calvary Church (Protestant Episcopal), 273 Park Ave. S., NE cor. E. 21st St. 1846. James Renwick, Jr. **[47b.] The Sunday School Building.** 1867. James Renwick, Jr.

Second-rate Renwick; its wooden towers long since removed because of deterioration. The adjacent Sunday school pavilion, now rented to a theater group, is a charming surprise on Park Avenue South.

[48.] Protestant Welfare Agencies Building/originally **Church Missions' House,** 281 Park Ave. S., SE cor. E. 22nd St. 1894. R. W. Gibson and E. J. N. Stent.

A glassy, articulated stone office building worthy of commercial buildings of the **Belgian** and **Dutch Renaissance.** Lovely.

[49.] The New York Bank for Savings, 280 Park Ave. S., SW cor. E. 22nd St. 1894. C. L. W. Eidlitz. Altered, 1933, 1954.

The handsome home office of New York State's **oldest savings bank.** Its corner entrance is not original—and unfortunate.

[50.] Originally **United Charities Building,** 287 Park Avenue S., NE cor. E. 22nd St. 1891. R. H. Robertson and Rowe & Baker.

A bulky but boring work.

[51.] Gramercy Towers (apartments)/originally **Russell Sage Foundation,** 4 Lexington Ave., SW cor. E. 22nd St. ca. 1914. Grosvenor Atterbury. Tower added, ca. 1919. Converted to apartments, 1975.

Converted into apartments and other uses, this handsome detailed Renaissance Revival building bears clear traces of its utilitarian heritage, e.g., the frieze: FOR THE IMPROVEMENT OF SOCIAL AND LIVING CONDITIONS. Among the early works of the philanthropic foundation was Forest Hills Gardens [see C Queens 19.].

[52.] Mabel Dean Bacon Vocational High School/originally **Manhattan Trade School For Girls,** 129 E. 22nd St. NW cor. Lexington Ave. 1919. C. B. J. Snyder.

No nonsense here: ten stories of loft space for vocational education. The exterior does have some handsome terra-cotta detailing.

[53.] 134 East 22nd Street (apartments), bet. Lexington and Third Aves. Converted to apartments, 1975. William B. Gleckman.

A stylish seven-story brown brick apartment house that would be **at home in Milan.** The cross-over balconies (for fire exits from the duplexes) provide large-scaled architectural form.

Armory/Belmore: Twenty-third to Thirty-fourth Streets; Lexington to Second Avenues.

[54.] Originally **69th Regiment Armory,** 68 Lexington Ave., bet. E. 25th and E. 26th Sts. W side. 1905. Hunt & Hunt.

The armory of the **"Armory Show"** of 1913, the bombshell entry of cubist painting to America. A brick, mansarded palace with **gun bays surveying Lexington.** The drill hall behind the Lexington Avenue facade shows its barrel form to the street, ribbed and buttressed with an exposed, articulated structure.

Belmore Cafeteria, 407 Park Avenue S., N of E. 28th St. Telephone: LE 2-0510.

Taxi drivers' **haven and heaven.** Filled with Formica, cigar smoke, and **cabbies' tales of woe.** A local institution.

[55.] St. Stephen's Church (Roman Catholic), 149 E. 28th St. 1854. James Renwick, Jr., Extended to N, 1865. P. C. Keely. Restored, 1949. School, ca. 1902. Elliott Lynch.

Brownstone Romanesque Revival: an airy hall, slender cast-iron (plaster encased) columns with elaborate foliated capitals supporting multiribbed vaulting. The transepts have unusual galleries overseeing the nave. Interior mural by Constantino Brumidi, "decorator" of the Capitol in Washington. Unfortunately, the whole has been smoothed over in brownstone-colored smooth stucco. The extension onto East 29th Street is more tempestuous and in the original brick and stone.

Presidential inauguration: Such ceremonies normally take place in Washington. But on September 20, 1881, Chester A. Arthur was sworn in as president here at his home at 123 Lexington Avenue, north of East 28th Street. The assassination of James A. Garfield unexpectedly promoted Vice-President Arthur to the higher post.

[56.] "I Love You Kathy" (apartments), 160 E. 26th St., SW cor. Third Ave. Altered, 1975. Stephen B. Jacobs.

An unusual solution to "fire escapes" when altering an old tenement. The 26th Street facade is a stuccoed sculpture. (The building's name refers to the developer's private life.)

[57.] Caliban's (bar and restaurant), 360 Third Ave., bet. 26th and 27th Sts. 1966. Haroutiun Derderian.

An elegant modern bar: its exposed brick in counterpoint with a rich Victorian bar-counter. Spacious, richly austere. The wine list is extensive.

Newsstand, E. 29th St., SE cor. Third Ave.

A rare holdout. This one is *not* at a subway entrance and is *not* a minuscule "doghouse" at the curb. Large and boldly occupying globs of sidewalk space, it leans against the brick wall of the building, its prime means of (physical) support. Economic support is provided by the purchasers of the magazines and newspapers which **plummet forth** from all directions. It doesn't offer much of a living so its days are numbered—unless Hollywood preserves it for its upcoming **nostalgia** films about Gotham.

Trinacria Importing Company, 415 Third Ave., cor. E 29th St.

Mostly food (although Turkish coffee makers are amongst their wares), and wide ranging: **Greek, Armenian,** and other **Near Eastern** delights, magnificent heroes: have your lunch al fresco. If it isn't time for lunch, walk in and inhale!

[58.] 203 East 29th Street (converted stable), bet. Second and Third Aves. ca. 1860.

It is a rarity to find a *wood frame* stable in Manhattan, particularly right on the street and not hidden in some out-of-the-way backyard. **Here it is!**

A touch of India: Twenty-ninth Street (and adjacent thoroughfares) between Madison and Third Avenues is a center for purchase of exotic foods, fabrics, and other delicacies from the Indian subcontinent. **Spice & Sweet Mahal** (135 Lexington Ave., cor. E. 29th St.), for example, purveys freshly prepared snacks and desserts for sidewalk feasting, as well as the normal stock of canned and packaged foods. Diaphanous fabrics for saris are available elsewhere in this area.

Old Print Shop, 150 Lexington Ave., bet. E. 29th and E. 30th Sts.

Appropriately humble, like the rich wearing old clothes, it is a mine of maps and prints, from modest to very expensive.

[59.] First Moravian Church, 154 Lexington Ave., SW cor. E. 30th St. ca. 1845.

A plain brick box with gabled roof and tall, narrow, half-round arched windows. **A modest** gem.

[55.] St. Stephen's Catholic Church   **[62.]** The Kips Bay Branch Library

[60.] Pratt-New York Phoenix School of Design/originally **New York School of Applied Design for Women,** 160 Lexington Ave., NW cor. E. 30th St. 1909. Pell & Corbett.

A great tour-de-force of *Grecian* design. A veritable 20th-century **temple to the arts.** Note the witty, *single* polished gray marble column (in antis) on the Lexington Avenue facade. It is said that designer Harvey Wiley Corbett's atelier of fledgling architects worked on the drawings. [See WC Brooklyn/Fort Greene 12a. for another kind of temple.]

[61.] Originally Madison Square Church Mission House, 432 Third Ave., NW cor. E. 30th St. ca. 1898. Howells & Stokes.

Four stories of golden brown brick windowed with **severe** (no trim) half-round arched openings. Down at street level are **tiny** terra-cotta **checkerboards** used to rusticate the plane of the wall. A **noble building** vacant for years.

[62.] Kips Bay Branch, N.Y. Public Library, 446 Third Ave. SW cor. E. 31st St. 1971. Giorgio Cavaglieri.

A sculptured corner-turner along Third Avenue. Just enough of a widened sidewalk to invite its users to enter.

[63.] Push Pin Studios/originally **Democratic Party Clubhouse,** 207 E. 32nd St., bet. Second and Third Aves. ca. 1900.

Beaux Arts pomp and circumstance orphaned when the remainder of its row was removed for an apartment house plaza and a school yard. **Push Pin,** the internationally renowned graphic arts combine, occupies space here—for a time **New York Magazine did,** too.

EAST CORRIDOR

Town and Village and Environs: Fourteenth to below Twenty-third Streets; Second Avenue to the East River.

[64.] 326, 328, and 330 East 18th Street (row houses), bet. First and Second Aves. 1850s. ★

Deep front yards have caused this tiny trio to be overlooked but certainly not neglected. The charming original cast-iron work is reminiscent of New Orleans.

[65.] Immaculate Conception Church (Roman Catholic)/originally **Grace Chapel and Dispensary (Protestant Episcopal),** 406–412 E. 14th St., bet. First Ave. and Avenue B. 1894. Barney & Chapman. ★

These **François I** style buildings were built as an outpost of Grace Church [Astor Place/East Village 26a.] and were purchased by the Roman Catholic archdiocese in 1943. Their picturesque forms might be found in the **Loire Valley,** as might those of their uptown descendant, Holy Trinity [Yorkville 10.].

[66.] Stuyvesant Town (apartment complex), E. 14th to E. 20th Sts., First Ave. to Franklin D. Roosevelt Dr. 1947. Irwin Clavan and Gilmore Clarke.

Tax abatement allowed this Metropolitan Life Insurance Company project to supply middle-income housing to the returning serviceman from World War II. Huge, dense (8,755 families), the 30-year-old trees now soften its early brutality.

[67.] Peter Cooper Village (apartment complex), E. 20th to E. 23rd Sts., First Ave. to Franklin D. Roosevelt Dr. 1947. Irwin Clavan and Gilmore Clarke.

More space and more rent make this the **rich stepbrother** of Stuyvesant Town.

[68.] Church of the Epiphany (Roman Catholic), Second Ave., SW cor. E. 22nd St. 1967. Belfatto & Pavarini.

Highly styled brown brick: this is the *phoenix* of a 19th-century church on this site destroyed by fire. It is the most positive modern religious statement on **Manhattan Island** to date.

Kips Bay and Environs: Twenty-third to Thirty-fourth Streets; Second Avenue to the East River.

[69.] Phipps Plaza (apartment complex), Second Ave. bet. E. 26th and E. 29th Sts. E side. 1976. Frost Assocs.

Red brick that caught some styling from East Midtown Plaza to the south. Polygonal diagonal.

[70.] East Midtown Plaza (apartment complex), E. 23rd to E. 25th Sts., bet. First and Second Aves. 1972, 1974. All by Davis, Brody & Assocs.

Brown brick, **cut, carved, notched and molded:** the "balconies" are architectural spaces and forms, not paste-ons. Urbane street architecture, with the terraces of Babylon; this is **an ode to brick.**

Amy's Restaurant, 210 E. 23rd St., E of Second Ave. Telephone: 889-2720.

Self-service Middle Eastern dining—sometimes to the accompaniment of a guitarist-folk singer. Unpretentious. Paper plates. Inexpensive.

[71.] Public Baths, City of New York, E. 23rd St., NE cor. Asser Levy Place. 1906. Arnold W. Brunner and William Martin Aiken. ★

Roman pomp was particularly appropriate for a public bath, a Roman building type we reproduced indiscriminately for *other* functions

[68.] Church of the Epiphany (R.C.)　　**[71.]** Public Baths, City of New York

[70.] East Midtown Plaza: urbane street architecture, this is an ode to brick

(cf. the now demolished Pennsylvania Station modeled on the **Baths of Caracalla**). These public baths are, in that sense, our **Baths of Roosevelt** (Teddy), or, on a local level, the **Baths of McClellan** (mayor of New York).

[72.] United Nations International School, 2450 Franklin D. Roosevelt Dr. opp. E. 25th St. S of Waterside. 1973. Harrison, Abramovitz & Harris.

A bulky, white precast concrete block hugging the East River shore and **Waterside:** an **illogical site** for students in need of public transportation at a large volume.

[73.] Waterside (apartment complex), Franklin D. Roosevelt Dr. bet. E. 25th and E. 30th Sts. E side. 1974. Davis, Brody & Assocs.

Brown towers of a **cut and carved cubism** mounted on a platform tucked in a notch of the East River. Sixteen hundred units, shopping, restaurants, and pedestrian plazas give a share of Manhattan's glorious waterfront **back to the people.** Wander about, and to the water's edge.

[74.] Bellevue Hospital Center, E. 25th to E. 30th Sts., First Ave. to Franklin D. Roosevelt Dr. 1908–1939. McKim, Mead & White. **[74a.] Psychiatric Hospital,** Charles B. Meyers and Thompson, Holmes & Converse.

Its old brick hulk is now squeezed between the parking garage addition on First Avenue and a giant 22-story "wing" facing the river. The top floors and roof contain the only serious architectural embellishments: Roman brick Corinthian columns, pitched tile roofs. **"Belle Vue"** was the name of a farm that originally occupied this site.

[74b.] New Building, Bellevue Hospital, E. 27th to E. 28th Sts. 1974. Katz, Waisman, Weber, Strauss; Joseph Blumenkranz; Pomerance & Breines; Feld & Timoney. Parking garage, 1965.

A **behemoth.** Each floor is an acre and a half of loft space served by 20 elevators. It's the white cube you see from FDR Drive.

[73.] Waterside (apartment complex)   **[75.]** N.Y.U.—Bellevue Medical Center

[75.] New York University-Bellevue Medical Center, E. 30th to E. 34th Sts., First Ave. to Franklin D. Roosevelt Dr. 1950. Skidmore, Owings & Merrill. Additions through 1977.

A teaching hospital can attract staff and faculty of the highest stature. Here they are provided for in a facility complementing **Bellevue Hospital,** designed in a single master plan by **SOM,** and constructed over a number of years. White glazed brick and aluminum sash.

[75a.] Jesse Stanton Developmental Playground for Preschool Handicapped Children, Institute of Rehabilitation Medicine, N.Y.U.-Bellevue Medical Center, E. 34th St., bet. First Ave. and Franklin D. Roosevelt Dr., S side. 1971. Richard Dattner & Assocs.

A specially designed playground for the handicapped, just barely visible from the sidewalk.

[76.] Kips Bay Plaza (apartment complex), E. 30th to E. 33rd Sts., First to Second Aves. South Building, 1960. North Building, 1965. I. M. Pei & Assocs. and S. J. Kessler.

New York's *first* exposed concrete apartment houses, joined soon after by **Chatham Towers** (1965, Kelly & Gruzen), and Pei's own **University Plaza** (1966).

The vast open space compensates for the huge 21-story building slabs. These are stepchildren of Le Corbusier's **Marseille Block:** the giant and beautifully detailed concrete building in a park. Here, the **city planning decision** is more important than architectural detail (although the latter is careful, but boring). Do buildings define urban pedestrian space—streets, boulevards and plazas—or shall they be freestanding objects in a park? In 1960 the latter proposition seemed to be gaining currency; these days **the streets are winning** again.

[77.] St. Vartan Cathedral of the Armenian Orthodox Church in America, Second Ave., bet. E. 34th and E. 35th Sts. E side. 1967. Steinmann & Cain.

A huge (to accommodate cathedral-sized congregations) version of early **Romanesque Armenian** churches in Asia Minor.

HERALD SQUARE AREA

In the **1870s** and **1880s** the whole area between the respectability of Fifth Avenue and the slums of **Hell's Kitchen** (west of Seventh Avenue), from the 20s through the 30s, was New York's **Tenderloin.** The present Herald Square was right in the middle of it. Dance halls and cafes were lined up under the "el" along Sixth Avenue, with bordellos on the shady side streets, all flourishing under the Tammany Hall political machine. A brief period of reform in the 1890s **dimmed the gaiety** of the Tenderloin, and it slowly faded away. Both the theater and the press (such as **James Gordon Bennett's** *New York Herald*) made brief stops at Herald Square in the nineties on their way north—leaving behind the square with a newspaper's name.

In 1904 the Pennsylvania Railroad **opened its tunnel** under the Hudson and cut a broad swath to its monumental two-block-square station (opened 1910), erasing some of the **Hell's Kitchen tenements.** (In the 1930s, Lincoln Tunnel approaches cut down more of the slums.) The **new station** quickly attracted the equally monumental General Post Office, some major hotels, and a cluster of middle-class department stores, which found the square an ideally convenient goal for **their march up Sixth Avenue** from 14th Street. By the 1920s, garment manufacturing had moved from the Lower East Side into the streets surrounding these pivot points. Today's garment industry is concentrated in the 30s and 40s between Sixth and Eighth Avenues, with suppliers of fabrics, trimmings, and such located to the east as far as Madison Avenue.

Herald Square Walking Tour: Broadway and 34th Street (BMT and IND Sixth Avenue Lines, 34th Street Station) to Fifth Avenue and 38th Street.

[1.] Herald Square, intersection of Sixth Ave. and Broadway bet. W. 34th and W. 35th Sts. *Minerva, the Bellringers, and Owl,* 1895. Antonin Jean Carles, sculptor. Plaza, 1940. Aymar Embury II.

This small triangular park, namesake of the *New York Herald's* two-story palazzo (1895. McKim, Mead & White. Demolished, 1921.) just to the north, is dominated by the newspaper's once crowning clock. Every hour **Stuff and Guff,** the two bronze mannequins, pretend to strike the big bell as **Minerva** supervises from above. At noon they make an especially joyful sound. **Don't confuse** this square with **Greeley Square** to the south [11.].

[2.] Greenwich Savings Bank, Broadway, NE cor. W. 36th St. 1924. York & Sawyer.

Giant Corinthian columns **march around three sides** of this temple-like bank, interrupted only by columnar signs on two facades that almost undo the effect. Inside, more columns define a **grand oval rotunda** with central skylight.

Keen's English Chop House, 72 West 36th Street, just east of Sixth Avenue. Founded 1878, known for fine mutton chops and thousands of clay pipes, signed by satisfied customers, on the ceiling. *Out of business, 1977.*

[3.] Macy's Department Store, W. 34th to W. 35th St., Broadway to Seventh Ave. Original (Broadway) building, 1901. DeLemos & Cordes. New (Seventh Avenue) building, 1931. Robert D. Kohn.

The older eastern half of **"the world's largest store"** is sheathed in a dignified **Palladian facade.** The newer, western half is **Art Deco.** In the southeast corner there appears to be the **world's busiest hot dog stand** with a "Macy's" sign on top. It's actually a five-story 19th-century house bought at the outrageous price of $375,000 (ca. 1900) by Robert S. Smith, Macy's next door neighbor and bitter rival at their old 14th Street location. Smith's store has long since folded, but his heirs annually collect a fortune from Macy's for the sign.

The Broadway entrance and show windows have been remodeled, but the 34th Street side shows the handsome original details; *note* the **canopy, clock,** and the **hefty turn-of-the-century lettering.**

[3.] Macy's Dept. Store (1967 photo)

[7.] New York's General Post Office

[4a.] Former Manhattan Center/originally **Manhattan Opera House,** 311 W. 34th St., bet. Eighth and Ninth Aves. 1906. Altered since.

Traditional gathering place for union contract debate and votes. Proposed as a ballet theater, it is now a facility of the **Unification Church** (the Rev. Sun Myung Moon).

[4b.] Midtown South Station House, N.Y.C. Police Department, 357 W. 35th St., bet. Eighth and Ninth Aves. 1970. Frost Assocs.

A freestanding temple to incarceration; its dark brown brick adds to the gloom of this loft-shadowed side street.

[5.] Statler-Hilton Hotel/formerly **Hotel Pennsylvania,** Seventh Ave., SE cor. W. 33rd St. 1918. McKim, Mead & White.

Like its neighbor to the south, the former **Equitable Building,** this Classical block is set back 15 feet from the building line in response to the *old* **Pennsylvania Station** colonnade that faced it. It was a center for the big bands of the 1930s, and Glenn Miller wrote a tune called *PE 6-5000,* still the hotel's number.

[6.] Madison Square Garden Center, W. 31st to W. 33rd St., Seventh to Eighth Aves. 1968. Charles Luckman Assocs.

Anybody who remembers the **vast** Roman Revival **waiting room** and **even vaster iron and glass train shed** of McKim, Mead & White's 1910 station **will feel bereaved** here.

The **replacement entertainment and office complex** covering two blocks includes a 20,000-seat "garden," a 1,000-seat "forum," a 500-seat cinema, a 48-lane bowling center, a 29-story office building, an exposition "rotunda," an art gallery, and the usual dining, drinking, and shopping areas—all above the railroad station, which was underground to begin with, but used to have a ceiling 150 feet high. The new "garden," the third one, and closer to Madison Square than the second—is housed in **a precast-concrete-clad cylinder** and roofed by a 425-foot-diameter cable structure which **only physically replaces** its grand and beautiful noble predecessor.

[7.] General Post Office, Eighth Ave., bet. W. 31st and W. 33rd Sts. W side. 1913. McKim, Mead & White. ★

The two-block row of tall Corinthian columns, and what is probably **the world's longest inscription,** once faced the equally long, stubbier row of Doric columns of Penn Station.

Detours to the west:

[8a.] Westyard Distribution Center, Tenth Ave., bet. W. 31st and W. 32nd Sts. E side. 1970. Davis, Brody & Assocs.

A gutsy concrete structure that spans the Penn-Central tracks below. Its penthouse shelters an ice skating place, **Sky Rink:** crowded, with *no windows*—and *no views.*

[8b.] Spearin Preston & Burrows, Inc. (office building), 446 W. 34th St., bet. Ninth and Tenth Aves. 1967. Edelman & Salzman.

A neat little office block occupying a sliver of land left over after the approaches to the third tube of the Lincoln Tunnel were cut through.

[9a.] St. John the Baptist Church (Roman Catholic), 211 W. 30th St., bet. Seventh and Eighth Aves. 1872. Napoleon LeBrun. **[9b.] Capuchin-Franciscan Friary,** 210 W. 31st St. 1975. Genovese & Maddalene.

Lost in the Fur District is this **exquisite** single-spired brownstone church, a **Roman Catholic** midtown **Trinity.** The interior, of white marble, radiates light. Worth a special visit. The friary is a properly modest new work on the opposite block front.

[10a.] Originally **23rd Precinct Station House, N.Y.C. Police Department/**now **Manhattan Traffic Unit B,** 134 W. 30th St., bet. Sixth and Seventh Aves. 1905.

Battlements, merlons, embrasures, crenellations—**a fortress out of place** among loft buildings but serving the area by the contribution of its wit to a midtown canyon.

[10b.] The S.J.M. Building (lofts), 130 W. 30th St., bet. Sixth and Seventh Aves. 1927. Cass Gilbert, Inc.

Assyrian Revival. An early bronze and glass curtain wall embraced by a pair of masonry elevator towers. Figures in **Mesopotamian friezes** race around the walls of the building at each setback. And over the two entrances stylized lions glare at each other in polychromed terra-cotta low-relief.

[11.] Greeley Square, intersection of Sixth Ave. and Broadway, bet. W. 32nd and W. 33rd Sts.

Horace Greeley (1811–1872), founder of the *New York Tribune,* is remembered by this park and a statue (1890. Alexander Doyle).

[12.] Hotel Martinique, W. 32nd St., NE cor. Broadway. 1897. Henry J. Hardenbergh. Alterations since.

An **opulent French Renaissance pile,** topped with several stories of mansards; the south facade is the real front.

[13a.] Hotel Clinton/originally **Life Building,** 19 W. 31st St., bet. Broadway and Fifth Ave. 1894. Carrère & Hastings.

This ornate Classical facade once enclosed the offices of the very literate humor magazine *Life* (from which the present Time-Life organization bought the name in 1936). Visible mementos include the inscriptions **"wit"** and **"humor"** and a pattern of *L*'s back-to-back on handsome iron balconies.

[13b.] Wolcott Hotel, 4–10 W. 31st St., bet. Broadway and Fifth Ave.

An **extravagant** French Empire bay-windowed facade, carved, corniced and mansard-roofed; the style conceals middle-class seediness behind.

[14.] Bank of Tokyo Trust Co., 320 Fifth Ave., NW cor. W. 32nd St. 1962. Carl J. Petrilli & Assocs.

An **exquisite insertion** at ground level of a branch bank with oriental echoes into a Beaux Arts office block. Within are rock gardens and wood sculpture *redolent* of Japan.

[15.] Empire State Building, 350 Fifth Ave., bet. W. 33rd and W. 34th Sts. 1931. Shreve, Lamb & Harmon.

Once the world's tallest building, originally 1,250 feet high to the top of its mooring mast for apocryphal dirigibles. That height remained unequalled until completion of the **World Trade Center** towers, a record since surpassed. Planned during the booming twenties, it went up during the Depression. Largely vacant in its early years, it was said that the building relied on the stream of sightseers to the observation decks to pay its taxes.

The monumental Fifth Avenue entrance is not as interesting as the modernistic stainless steel canopies of the two street entrances. All of them lead to two-story-high corridors around the elevator core (with 67 elevators in it), which is crossed here and there by stainless steel and glass-enclosed bridges. The observation deck's telephone is 736-3100.

Empire State site: This pivotal spot has been occupied by two previous sets of landmarks. From 1857 to 1893 it was the site of two mansions belonging to the Astor family. Mrs. William Astor's place, on the corner of 34th Street, was for years the undisputed center of New York social life, and the capacity of her ballroom gave the name "The 400" to the city's elite. But in the early 1890s a feud developed between Mrs. Astor and her nephew, William Waldorf Astor, who had the house across the garden on 33rd Street. He and his wife moved to Europe and had a 13-story hotel built on his property, naming it the *Waldorf* (the name of the first John Jacob Astor's native village in Germany). Within a year after it opened in 1893, Mrs. Astor wisely decided to move out of its ominous shadow (up to 65th Street and Fifth Avenue) and put a connecting hotel, the *Astoria,* on her property. When the 17-story structure was completed in 1897, the hyphenated hotel immediately became a social mecca. The requirement of full formal dress (tails) in the Palm Room created a sensation even then, but made it the place to be seen. Successful as it was, the old Waldorf-Astoria operated under a curious agreement that the elder Mrs. Astor could have all connections between the buildings walled up at any time on demand.

[16.] B. Altman & Company (department store), Fifth Ave., bet. E. 34th and E. 35th Sts. E side. 1906, extended 1914. Trowbridge & Livingston.

Even after the Waldorf-Astoria opened in the nineties, Fifth Avenue from the 30s north remained **solidly residential.** Benjamin Altman made a prophetic breach by **moving his department store** from Sixth Avenue and 18th Street to this corner. To make the change less painful, it was designed as a dignified eight-story Renaissance Revival block. The Fifth Avenue entrance shows the **atmosphere** Altman was trying for. Altman's set off a rush of fashionable stores to Fifth Avenue above 34th Street. Many of them made a second jump from the upper 30s to the 50s, leaving Altman's ironically isolated.

[17.] 390 Fifth Avenue/formerly **Russek's**/originally **Gorham Building,** SW cor. W. 36th St. 1906. McKim, Mead & White. Alterations.

When Altman's opened at 34th Street, Gorham's, **the famous jewelers,** had just completed its Italian Renaissance **palace.** Russek's kept the fine architecture largely intact. The lower floors have been inappropriately altered, but the original columns and arches are visible on the 36th Street side.

[18.] 409 Fifth Avenue/originally **Tiffany's,** SE cor. E. 37th St. 1906. McKim, Mead & White. Alterations.

Finished only a year after the Gorham Building by the same architects, this more massive structure was modeled after the **Palazzo Grimani** in Venice. The 37th Street side retains the original motif of three ranks of giant columns shouldering a broad cornice.

[19a.] W. & J. Sloane/formerly **Franklin Simon & Co.**, Fifth Ave., SW cor. W. 38th St. 1922. **[19b.] Lord & Taylor,** Fifth Ave., NW cor. W. 38th St. 1914. Starrett & Van Vleck.

These two buildings were the first along the avenue to dispense with colonnades and look frankly commercial. They are **pleasantly uncomplicated** in the middle floors but have vestiges of the palazzo at top and bottom.

[13b.] Wolcott Hotel: side street gem   **[17.]** Orig. Gorham Bldg., 390 Fifth

---

A Few Notions: The side streets between Fifth and Sixth Avenues in the upper 30s are full of suppliers of trimmings for garments and millinery, and their windows are a great show. Beads, rhinestones, spangles, and laces predominate on West 37th Street, milliners' flowers and feathers on West 38th.

End of Herald Square Walking Tour. Fifth Avenue buses downtown, Sixth and Madison Avenue buses uptown. Subways along 42nd Street.

MURRAY HILL

The country home of **Robert Murray** once stood near where East 37th Street now crosses Park Avenue; it was here that **Murray's wife** is said to have **served tea to General Howe** and his staff while the Revolutionary troops escaped to the northwest. In the late 19th century, social status on the fashionable hill was highest near the great mansions of Fifth Avenue, dropping off toward the east, where carriage houses gave way to tenements at **"el"-shaded** Third Avenue. When commerce moved up Fifth Avenue in the early 1900s, Murray Hill became an isolated but **vigorous patch of elegance,** centered about Park Avenue, where through traffic (first horsecars, then trolleys, now cars) was diverted into the old railroad tunnel from 33rd to 40th Streets. Fashionable Murray Hill has gradually **shifted to the east,** where carriage houses have become residences, and **commerce** has made **slow but steady inroads** on the other three sides.

Murray Hill Walking Tour: Park Avenue and East 33rd Street (IRT Lexington Avenue line, 33rd Street station) to Park Avenue and East 42nd Street.

[1.] 3 Park Avenue (office building) and **Norman Thomas High School,** bet. E. 33rd and E. 34th Sts. E side. 1976. Shreve, Lamb & Harmon Assocs., architects. *Obelisk for Peace.* Irving Marantz, sculptor.

An **architectural and fiscal amalgam** developed by the Educational Construction Fund. The 42-story sorrel brick tower, turned **diagonally to** school and street grid below, springs above its neighbors and is further accentuated at night when its top is bathed in orange light.

In Memory of an Armory: Though the picturesque **71st Regiment Armory** (1905. Clinton & Russell) was demolished to build 3 Park Avenue, its bronze plaque, polished up, graces the terrace wall at East 33rd Street.

 [2a.] 475 Park Avenue South (office building), SE cor. E. 32nd St. 1970. Shreve, Lamb & Harmon Assocs., architects. *Triad.* Irving Marantz, sculptor.

Prismatic forms associated with 1960s skyscrapers here have cut corners—intricately detailed in brick, dark metal, and glass to produce a refreshing form.

[2b.] 2 Park Avenue, bet. E. 32nd and E. 33rd Sts., W side. 1927. Ely Jacques Kahn.

A very neat pier-and-spandrel pattern on the walls of this office block bursts into Art Deco **angular terra-cotta decoration** in primary colors at the top.

[3.] Gilbert Kiamie Residence/formerly **Grolier Club,** 29 E. 32nd St., bet. Madison and Fifth Aves. 1889. Charles W. Romeyn & Co. ★

Superb Richardsonian Romanesque with brownstone—smooth, rough, and carved. Unlikely specimen in a street of loft buildings.

[1.] 3 Park Ave./Norman Thomas H.S.   **[3.]** Originally The Grolier Club

[4a.] Church of the Incarnation (Protestant Episcopal), 205 Madison Ave., NE cor. E. 35th St. 1864. Emlen T. Littel. Enlarged, 1882. **[4b.] The H. Percy Silver Parish House,** 209 Madison Ave., bet. E. 35th and E. 36th Sts. E side. 1868. Robert Mook. Altered, ca. 1905. Edward P. Casey. **[4c.] Anthroposophical Society in America**/originally **J.P. Morgan carriage house,** 211 Madison Ave., bet. E. 35th and E. 36th Sts.

Three **orphans** from Madison Avenue's **earlier elite years:** a dour Gothic church, a Renaissance Revival town house named for a rector of the adjacent church, and a millionaire's stable.

[5a.] Morgan Library, 33 E. 36th St., bet. Madison and Park Aves. 1906. McKim, Mead & White. Addition at 29 E. 36th St., NE cor. Madison Ave. 1928. Benjamin W. Morris. ★

Brunelleschi would be pleased by this, his offspring. The addition, built on the site of the J. Pierpont Morgan, Sr., mansion after his death, modestly defers to the older part. The **interior is notable** not only for its exhibits of rare prints and manuscripts, but for Morgan's **opulent** private library, maintained just as he left it. Open to the public. Telephone: 685-0008.

[5b.] Lutheran Church in America/formerly **J. P. Morgan, Jr., Residence,** 231 Madison Ave., SE cor. E. 37th St.

A Classical block that has suffered from additions to and restoration of its brownstone. The iron balustrades on the first-floor windows are outstanding. The church **successfully contested** its official landmark designation in the courts: *money* is more important than *history*, even to Luther's heirs, who foresaw commercial development possibilities on this prime site.

[6a.] Consulate General of the Polish People/originally **DeLamar Mansion,** 233 Madison Ave., NE cor. E. 37th St. 1905. C. P. H. Gilbert. ★

The interiors of this **Dutch sea captain's mansion** are as opulent as the exterior, and largely intact.

[4b.] H. Percy Silver Parish House   **[6a.]** Originally The DeLamar Mansion

[6b.] 19 and 21 East 37th Street, bet. Madison and Park Aves. ca. 1900.

Exceptionally fine town houses. Note the Corinthian porch of No. 19, the doorway and iron balustrades of No. 21.

Union League Club: The effete neo-Georgian pile at the southwest corner of East 38th Street and Park Avenue (1931. Morris & O'Connor) is the red brick home of a club founded by Republicans who left the Union Club [see Upper East Side 13c.] in 1863, incensed by its failure to expel Confederate sympathizers.

[7.] Church of Our Saviour (Roman Catholic), 59 Park Ave., SE cor. E. 38th St. 1959. Paul C. Reilly.

Apparently correct **Gothic Romanesque** archeology. Among its inconsistencies, however, is *air conditioning equipment* where, in a true Romanesque church, a *carillon* would be.

[8a.] Advertising Club of New York/originally **J. Hampton Robb Residence,** 23 Park Ave., NE cor. E. 35th St. 1898. McKim, Mead & White.

A brown brick and brownstone Italian Renaissance **"palazzo."** Stately.

[8b.] Hotel Ten Park Avenue, NW cor. E. 34th St. ca. 1930.

The massing of this apartment hotel resembles a larger-than-life **crystalline outcropping** of some exotic mineral. Its golden-hued brick and the expansive windows divided into tiny panes set an appropriate domestic scale. *Terrific.*

[9a.] The New Church (Swedenborgian), 112 E. 35th St., bet. Park and Lexington Aves. 1858.

A small-scaled whitewashed Italianate structure that adds a bit of open space to a block of good town houses.

[9b.] J.F.D. Lanier Residence, 123 E. 35th St., bet. Lexington and Park Aves. 1903. Hoppin & Koen.

All intact, inside and out, this Corinthian pilastered Beaux Arts town house is the tiara on this block of brownstones.

[10.] 157 and 159 East 35th Street (carriage houses), bet. Third and Lexington Aves. ca. 1890.

Two conversions to modern use. No. 157 is restrained and successful. No. 159, which *was* the more ebullient architectural statement (note the terra-cotta garlands at the cornice), suffers from a stuffy ground floor reconstruction.

[11.] Sniffen Court Historic District, 150–158 E. 36th St., bet. Third and Lexington Aves. ca. 1850–1860. District designated, 1966. ★

Ten Romanesque Revival brick carriage houses make a mews, **a tasteful oasis.**

[9a.] The New Church (Swedenborgian)

[11.] Sniffen Court Historic District

[12.] 130 East 37th Street, SW cor. Lexington Ave.

Colorful example of 1920s-style remodeled house, Latin variety.

[13a.] 152 East 38th Street, bet. Lexington and Third Aves. 1858. Remodeled, 1935. Robertson Ward. ★

The front garden is a happy urban design gift for this block.

[13b.] 149 East 38th Street, bet. Lexington and Third Aves. 1902.

A **Dutch Renaissance** carriage house with carved heads of animals.

[14.] 125 East 38th Street, NW cor. Lexington Ave.

A large house redone in **Old Charleston** style.

La Maison Japonaise (restaurant), 334 Lexington Ave. cor. E. 39th St. Telephone: MU 2-7375.

"French cooking with an oriental accent," the menu says, or to put it another way, *sukiyaki bourguignon.* Lunch and dinner. Wines by carafe. Moderate.

[15.] 148 East 40th Street, bet. Third and Lexington Aves. ca. 1875.

A lonely, lovely carriage house, complete with center doors, now languishing amidst characterless high rises on all sides. **Outstanding Second Empire detailing.**

[16.] Chess and Athletic Club/originally **Ernest Flagg Residence,** 109 E. 40th St., bet. Lexington and Park Aves. 1905. Ernest Flagg.

The **palatial city house** architect Flagg built for himself has an intriguing tiled entrance (for his auto, **lowered to the garage** below by **a built-in elevator).** The elaborate entrance opens onto an opulent multi-level interior. [For Flagg's country house, see Staten Island 10b.]

[17.] Architects Building, 101 Park Ave., NE cor. E. 40th St. 1912. Ewing & Chappell and LaFarge & Morris.

Scores of architects' offices fill the office floors above the **Architects' Samples Corporation** on the first floor. A semipermanent exhibit of building materials, fixtures, and equipment is open to the public. Telephone: 683-1400.

[18.] Originally **Airlines Building,** 80 E. 42nd St., SW cor. Park Ave. 1940. John B. Peterkin.

Limestone Art Moderne long since **abandoned by the airlines.** Originally, before air traffic expanded (and Manhattan's streets choked with traffic), airport buses left from the basement.

End of Murray Hill Tour: Grand Central offers a variety of rapid transit and commuter connections.

Miscellany

[19.] Originally **Kips Bay Brewery,** 660 First Ave., bet. E. 37th and E. 38th Sts., E side. ca. 1898. Additions.

Lager beer, ales, and porter, its colorful posters once boasted. They also featured this fortress of a building with curious mansarded cupolas at opposite corners of the roof. Brewing has disappeared here; substantial floors once meant for **mash cookers** and **brew kettles** now serve the needs of picture services, relief organizations, and an architect whose rear wall picture window enjoys **East River** views.

BRYANT PARK AREA

The land where **Bryant Park** and the **Public Library** now are was set aside in **1822** by the city as a potter's field. The Egyptian style **Croton Reservoir,** with walls 50 feet high and 25 feet thick around a four-acre lake, was completed on the Fifth Avenue side (site of the New York Public Library) in 1842. The locale was still at the northern fringe of the city in 1853 when New York's imitation of London's *Crystal Palace* was put up on the park site; it burned down in 1858. In 1884 the park was named for **William Cullen Bryant** (1794–1878), well-known poet and journalist; in 1900 the reservoir was razed to make way for the library.

Bryant Park Area Walking Tour: West 42nd Street between Fifth and Sixth Avenues (IRT Flushing Line, Fifth Avenue Station; IND Sixth Avenue Line, 42nd Street Station) to Fifth Avenue and 46th Street. The tour passes through one building open during weekday business hours: the Bar Association Building (37 West 43rd Street; 42 West 44th Street).

[1.] Bryant Park, Sixth Ave., bet. W. 40th and W. 42nd Sts. E side. Present design, 1930s. Scenic landmark. ★

A serene and formal garden filled with statues of **William Cullen Bryant** (1911. Herbert Adams), Phelps-Dodge copper magnate **William E. Dodge** (1885. J. Q. A. Ward), **Goethe** (1932. Karl Fischer), and **José de Andrada,** father of Brazil's independence (1954. José Lima), and a convention of drug pushers.

[2.] City University Graduate Center, C.U.N.Y./originally **Aeolian Hall,** 33 W. 42nd St., bet. Fifth and Sixth Aves. 1912. Remodeled, 1970. Carl J. Petrilli & Assocs.

What was once a concert hall and then a five-and-ten is now a bluestone-floored pedestrian arcade forming an **elegant shortcut** between 42nd and 43rd Streets. It also acts as access to the graduate school's spaces above and library and auditorium below, as well as a pass-through gallery for changing exhibitions of art and design. The top floor is an equally inviting "buffeteria" *open to all* (nonuniversity people must pay a minimum). Telephone: 790-4395.

[3.] W.R. Grace Building, 1114 Ave. of the Americas, SE cor. W. 43rd St., alternately known as 41 W. 42nd St. 1974. Skidmore, Owings & Merrill.

An insult to the street, its swooping form nominally bows to zoning requirements for setbacks but was, in fact, an opportunity for some flashy architectural ego. The plaza behind is a bore.

Subway passage: Connecting the 42nd Street Station of the Sixth Avenue IND Subway and the Fifth Avenue Station of the IRT Flushing line is an underground passageway (1975) which is rare for the city: It is well lighted, lined with dapper, leather-colored structural tile blocks, and enhanced by a group of bold photographic enlargements of nearby street scenes, old and new, transferred to porcelain enamel panels. Among the views are those of today's Bryant Park when it was the site of New York's Crystal Palace, the Latting Observatory tower, and the old Croton Reservoir.

[4.] Originally **Bush Terminal Building,** 132 W. 42nd St., bet. Sixth and Seventh Aves. 1918. Helmle & Corbett.

This building rises **480** feet from a base only **50** by **200** feet, built by the developers of Brooklyn's vast industrial complex [see WC Brooklyn/Sunset Park 5.].

[5a.] Bryant Park Studios, 80 W. 40th St., SE cor. Sixth Ave. ca. 1900. Charles A. Rich.

A Beaux Arts extravaganza whose double-height studios gather north light from across Bryant Park via double-height windows.

[5b.] American Radiator Building, 40 W. 40th St., bet. Fifth and Sixth Aves. 1924. Hood & Fouilhoux.

Centerpiece in a row of **Renaissance** club facades is designer Hood's black brick and gold terra-cotta Gothic-inspired tower. The first-floor facade, of bronze and polished black granite, and the black-marble-and-mirror-clad lobby are worth a close look. The plumbing fixture showroom is a later addition.

[5c.] Wendell L. Willkie Building of Freedom House/originally **The New York Club,** 20 W. 40th St., bet. Fifth and Sixth Aves. ca. 1885. Henry J. Hardenbergh.

A one-time gentlemen's club—note the terra-cotta seal up high in the colossal brick gable—and today an office building for a variety of organizations. The **New York Chapter of the American Institute of Architects** is headquartered here.

[6.] Republic National Bank/originally **Knox Building,** 452 Fifth Ave., SW cor. W. 40th St. 1902. John H. Duncan. Remodeled, 1965. Kahn & Jacobs.

This *exuberant* **Classical** showcase was built for **Col. Edward Knox,** hatter to presidents.

[7.] The New York Public Library, Fifth Ave., bet. W. 40th and W. 42nd Sts. W side. 1911. Carrère & Hastings. Lions, E. C. Potter, sculptor. Figures over fountains, Frederick MacMonnies, sculptor. ★

The **apogee of Beaux Arts** for New York, a white marble "temple" magnificently detailed inside and out, entered over extravagant terraces and imposing stairs. Here knowledge is stored in a place worthy of aspiration—a far cry from one's local library-supermarket.

The Roman Renaissance detailing **is breathtaking.**

[8a.] 500 Fifth Avenue (office tower), NW cor. 42nd St. 1931. Shreve, Lamb & Harmon.

A 699-foot-high phallic pivot balancing a great tin can marked "500."

[8b.] Manufacturers Hanover Trust Co./formerly **Manufacturers Trust Co.,** 510 Fifth Ave., SW cor. W. 43rd St. 1954. Skidmore, Owings & Merrill.

This building led the banking profession out of the cellar and onto the street; a glass-sheathed **supermarket of dollars.**

[8c.] Israel Discount Bank/formerly **Manufacturers Trust Company,** 511 Fifth Ave., SE cor. E. 43rd St. Remodeled, 1962. Luss, Kaplan & Assocs. Ltd.

Superb renovation of a Renaissance bank interior. All old fittings that could be kept have been; everything added is clearly *new.*

[9.] Century Association, 7 W. 43rd St., bet. Fifth and Sixth Aves. 1889–1891. McKim, Mead & White. ★

A **delicate Palladian facade** for an intellectuals' club. The large window above the entrance was originally an open loggia.

[10a.] The Association of the Bar of the City of New York, 37 W. 43rd St., and 42 W. 44th St., bet. Fifth and Sixth Aves. 1895. Cyrus L. W. Eidlitz. ★

A Classical limestone structure with the **massive sobriety** of the law.

The Algonquin: The hotel and restaurant at 59 West 44th Street has a 1902 Renaissance facade like many others, but it has been a rendezvous for theater and literary figures for over 50 years. In the 1920s, its Oak Room housed America's most famous luncheon club, the *Round Table,* at which **F. P. Adams, Robert Benchley, Harold Ross, Dorothy Parker,** and others sat. Stop for refreshment in the closet-sized Blue Bar or on one of the easy chairs in the lobby. Telephone: MU 7-4400.

[10b.] New York Yacht Club, 37 W. 44th St., bet. Fifth and Sixth Aves. 1899. Warren & Wetmore.

A fanciful example of Beaux Arts design with windows that look like the sterns of old ships worked in among the columns.

[7.] N.Y. Public Library Central Bldg.   **[10b.]** New York Yacht Club (detail)

[10c.] Harvard Club, 27 W. 44th St., bet. Fifth and Sixth Aves. 1894. Major additions, 1905, 1915. All by McKim, Mead & White. ★

A modest Georgian exterior housing some imposing spaces; their large scale can be seen in the 45th Street rear facade.

[10d.] Mechanics' and Tradesmen's Institute Building/originally **Berkeley Preparatory School,** 20 W. 44th St., bet. Fifth and Sixth Aves. 1891. Lamb & Rich.

A free, evening technical school founded in 1820 is housed in this dour Classical structure. The interior is a surprise: **a three-story gallery-ringed drill hall** housing a library and exhibits of old locks, the **John H. Mossmann Collection.** Savor particularly "A Very Complicated Lock." Open to the public. Telephone: MU 7-4279.

[11.] 1166 Avenue of the Americas (office tower), bet. W. 45th and W. 46th Sts. E side. 1973. Skidmore, Owings & Merrill.

A black **Saran Wrap** lemon, but only fiscally so—the bottom dropped out of the city's office rental market just as it was completed. Finally converted into a commercial condominium in 1977. Sleek and restrained.

 [12.] 1180 Avenue of the Americas/originally **Phoenix Building,** NE cor. W. 46th St. 1963. Emery Roth & Sons.

Perhaps the **finest** handling of an office tower within the maximum envelope of the old Zoning Resolution. The syncopated setbacks and the carefully studied detailing of the strip windows and tiers of continuous brick spandrels make this a fine work. The attempt to be "pretty" at street level is the building's major failing.

End of Bryant Park Area Walking Tour: Most convenient subways are at Rockefeller Center (IND), a few blocks north at 47th through 50th Streets.

TIMES SQUARE AREA

Up to the 1890s, all of the 40s and 50s west of Seventh Avenue were written off as **Hell's Kitchen,** a seething mixture of factories and tenements where **even the cops moved in pairs.** The rich ventured in only as far as Broadway in the upper 40s, an area of carriage shops for the horsey set called **Long Acre,** after a **similar district** in London.

Then big things happened quickly. **Charles Frohman** ventured to open a theater at 40th Street and Broadway just north of the then-new Metropolitan Opera, in 1893; **Oscar Hammerstein I** did him one better in 1895 by opening the Olympia, a block-long palace on Broadway between 44th and 45th Streets (then a muddy stretch) with a concert hall, a music hall, and a theater. Soon lavish restaurants like Rector's and Café de l'Opéra were dispensing lobster and champagne to **Diamond Jim Brady, George M. Cohan,** and the rest of the turn-of-the-century theater and sporting world. When the city decided to route its first subway west from Grand Central along 42nd Street, then north on Broadway, *New York Times* publisher **Adolph Ochs** saw a chance to outdo his competitors by erecting an imposing tower at Broadway and 42nd. He got the station there officially named "Times Square" on April 19, 1904.

By then the area was established as the theater district, and the evening crowds and broad vistas attracted **the early electric sign makers;** the 1916 Zoning Resolution made specific allowances for vast signs in the area. In the 1920s, **neon and movies** took over. In Hollywood's heyday, movie-and-variety palaces preempted the valuable Broadway frontier, and legitimate theater retreated to the side streets. The signs got bigger as the crowds got bigger, and began to feature things like **moving waterfalls** and **real smoke rings.** As big-time movies waned in the 1950s and 1960s, most of the palatial movie theaters were razed, and Times Square was **on the verge** of an office building boom.

In the 1970s some glassy office blocks arrived, and so did an enormous **explosion in pornography** and the sale of live sex on the streets and in "massage" parlors.

Eighth Avenue and west:

[1.] Port Authority Bus Terminal, W. 40th to W. 41st Sts., bet. Eighth and Ninth Aves. 1950. Decks added, 1963. Expansion to W. 42nd St. 1978. All by Port Authority design staff.

Glorious Pennsylvania Station **is only a memory;** Grand Central Terminal **is endangered.** But the Port Authority Bus Terminal **grows in popularity** as the city's vomitory for commuter and long-distance buses. *Glorious it's not.*

[2.] Franklin Savings Bank, 661 Eighth Ave., NW cor. W. 42nd St. 1974. Poor, Swanke, Hayden & Connell.

A one-story orange brick and concrete bank that is a far cry from its Beaux Arts predecessor, once diagonally across the intersection. (For one thing **it lacks the spinning clock** that once hung out over the sidewalk.) Nevertheless, the brick and concrete interior is **a refuge** from the *flesh circus* constantly underway outside. The zebra stripes painted on the reentrant walls of the bank's L-shaped high-rise neighbor fail to control the chaotic scene.

[3.] GHI Building (Group Health Insurance)/originally **McGraw-Hill Building,** 330 W. 42nd St., bet. Eighth and Ninth Aves. Raymond Hood, Godley & Fouilhoux.

Hood designed this tower with continuous horizontal bands of blue-green terra cotta at the time his vertically striped **Daily News Building** [see Turtle Bay-U.N. 4.] was going up at the other end of 42nd Street. The lobby carries out the visual theme. This was the *only* **New York** building shown in Johnson and Hitchcock's epoch-making book *The International Style* in 1932. However, the detail is Art Deco.

[4a.] Holy Cross Church (Roman Catholic), 333 W. 42nd St., bet. Eighth and Ninth Aves. 1870. Henry Engelbert. **[4b.] Holy Cross School,** 332 W. 43rd St. 1890. L.J. O'Connor.

Identified as being in **"the Byzantine style"** when built, the brick facade conceals the verdigris construction over the crossing, octagonal drum, dome, lantern, and crucifix (148 feet to the top). This was the parish church of **Father Duffy** of World War I fame [see his statue at Duffy Square]. The school, on West 43rd Street, has a rich **Romanesque Revival** facade of red brick and matching terra cotta.

Paddy's Market: A stretch of Ninth Avenue, between 36th and 42nd Streets, was once full of pushcart food venders, banished in the 1930s. The market soon revived, however, as shops with big outdoor displays featuring fresh fruit and vegetables, Italian, Greek, Polish, Spanish and Philippine products.

[5.] Manhattan Community Rehabilitation Center, N.Y.S. Office of Drug Abuse Services, 460 W. 41st St., bet. Ninth and Tenth Aves. and 550 Tenth Ave. NE cor. W. 40th St. 1970. Gueron, Lepp & Assocs.

A west-of-Times-Square-motel and a public library branch, both emptied by changing patterns of city living, converted to a drug addicts' rehabilitation center by adding a **handsome new board-framed concrete and brown brick reception center** whose appearance is crushed by its neighbors. (The removal of the window mullions on the library regrettably gives its facade the look of a blank stare.)

[6.] Model Tenements for N.Y. Fireproof Tenement Association, 500–506 W. 42nd St., SW cor. Tenth Ave. and 569 Tenth Ave., bet. W. 41st and W. 42nd Sts. ca. 1900. Ernest Flagg.

Their fireproof qualities may have been a step forward for tenements, but having lost their ironwork embellishments, they are today *grim,* very grim, in appearance.

[7.] Originally **Charles Scribner's Sons Printing Plant,** 311 W. 43rd St., bet. Eighth and Ninth Aves. ca. 1908. Ernest Flagg.

Flagg, architect of Scribner's headquarters, stores, and town house [see index] was, predictably, also architect for this straightforward industrial facility, whose iron curtain wall is marred by a thoughtless ground floor "improvement." See faded sign on west wall.

East of Eighth Avenue:

[8.] Candler Building, 220 W. 42nd St., bet. Seventh and Eighth Aves. 1914. Willauer, Shape & Bready.

The nationwide success of *Coca Cola* persuaded **Asa Candler,** its supersalesman, to build this gleaming white terra-cotta-clad tower off Times Square. Its skin, like that of those around it, is begrimed.

World's First "Moving" Sign: First to electrify passers-by along the Great White Way were the election returns of 1928 delivered along the Motogram, a 5-foot-high, 360-foot-long sign flasher that wrapped around the Times Tower's four sides and utilized 14,800 lamps to convey its constantly changing messages. The tower has changed its face; the Motogram remains.

[9.] One Times Square/formerly **Allied Chemical Tower**/originally **Times Tower,** W. 42nd St., Broadway, and Seventh Avenue. 1904.

Eidlitz & MacKenzie. Remodeled, 1966. Smith, Smith, Haines, Lundberg & Waehler.

The New York Times moved into its 25-story tower with **dramatic timing** on December 31, 1904, marking the occasion with a fireworks display at midnight that made Times Square **the place to see the New Year in** ever since. The paper moved out in a couple of decades to larger quarters on West 43rd Street, but the name remained until the original Italian Renaissance terra-cotta skin was stripped off and replaced with **Miami Beach marble.** Act One Restaurant on the top floor. Telephone: 695-1880.

[10.] 142 W. 42nd St. (1907 postcard)   **[11b.]** 1-2-3 Hotel, 123 W. 44th Street

[10.] 142 W. 42nd Street/formerly **Newsweek Building**/originally **Knickerbocker Hotel,** SE cor. Broadway. 1902. Marvin & Vavis, architects. Bruce Price, consultant.

An office building now fills the Classical, mansard-topped shell of a hotel—originally commissioned by **Col. John Jacob Astor**—where **Enrico Caruso** and **George M. Cohan** once lived. It had a $10,000 gold service for sixty and a bar so fashionable in the 1890s that it was known as the "42nd Street Country Club." A mural from this bar now sets the theme for the **King Cole Bar** at the **St. Regis-Sheraton Hotel** [see Fifth Avenue 16a.].

[11a.] Originally **The Lambs Club**/now **Manhattan Church of the Nazarene,** 130 W. 44th St., bet. Sixth Ave. and Broadway. 1904. McKim, Mead & White. ★

A **neo-Federal style** clubhouse built for a still-lively actors' group. The group has moved elsewhere.

[11b.] 1-2-3 Hotel/originally **Hotel Girard,** 123 W. 44th St., bet. Broadway and Sixth Ave.

A tan and limestone pile—one of many which once filled Times Square's side streets—**extravagantly decked out** with German Renaissance gables and dormers. *Endangered.*

[12.] Astor Plaza, 1515 Broadway, bet. W. 44th and W. 45th Sts. W. side. 1969. Kahn & Jacobs.

A 50-story office tower that **replaced** one of Times Square's long-time landmarks, **the Astor Hotel.** From afar its finial fins look like the tail of an impaled spaceship.

This was the first building to exploit the special *Times Square Theater District* zoning bonuses that allowed the developer to build more than normal bulk in return for the construction of a new legitimate theater.

[12a.]. Shubert Alley, from W. 44th St. to W. 45th St., bet. Seventh and Eighth Aves.

Now a convenience for theatergoers, this private alley was once where aspiring actors gathered in front of the offices of **J. J.** and **Lee Shubert** when plays were being cast.

[12b.] Ma Bell's Restaurant, 218 W. 45th St., at Shubert Alley. 111 Astor Plaza. Telephone: 869-0110.

A spot for pre-theater drinks and after-theater supper. Moderate prices. Telephones on every table allow table-talking without table-hopping.

Sardi's: The restaurant at 234 West 44th Street, strategically located among theaters and at the back door to *The New York Times,* has for decades been the place for actors to be seen—except during performance hours. Fine Italian food. Telephone: 221-8440.

[13a.] Lyceum Theater, 149 W. 45th St., bet. Sixth Ave. and Broadway. 1903. Herts & Tallant. ★

Powerful neo-Baroque columns predominate. Saved from demolition in 1939, it survived to be **the oldest New York theater** still used for legitimate productions and **the first to be landmarked.**

[13b.] Church of St. Mary the Virgin (Protestant Episcopal), 145 W. 46th St., bet. Sixth Ave. and Broadway.

A rich liturgical oasis in this precinct of **Mammon, booze,** and **pornography**—incense and liturgy here exceed that of the Catholic counter-Reformation.

[14.] Helen Hayes Theater/originally **Folies Bergère Theater/**later **Fulton Theater,** 210 W. 46th St., bet. Broadway and Eighth Ave. 1911. Herts & Tallant. Canopy, 1955.

A terra-cotta facade **worked by a crochet hook:** cream with blue highlights. The original had no canopy, just three tall arched openings.

Great women of the theater are honored in sculpture on the facade of the I. Miller Building (West 46th Street, NE corner of Seventh Avenue). Mary Pickford, Rosa Ponselle, Ethel Barrymore, and Marilyn Miller; all by A. Stirling Calder, father of the late, famed inventor of mobiles, Alexander Calder.

[13a.] The Lyceum Theater: ornate   The statue of Father Francis P. Duffy

Duffy Square: The northern triangle of Times Square is dedicated to **Father Francis P. Duffy** (1871–1932), a national hero in World War I as "Fighting Chaplain" of New York's 69th Regiment, later a friend of actors, writers, and mayors as pastor of **Holy Cross Church** on West 42nd Street. His statue (1937. Charles Keck) faces the back of one representing **George M. Cohan** (1878–1942), another Times Square hero (1959. George Lober).

[15a.] Tkts, W. 47th St., bet. Seventh Ave. and Broadway. 1973. Mayers & Schiff.

The uptown half of Duffy Square is occupied by the Times Square Theater Center **[tkts],** an elegant pipe and canvas structure, where **half-price ducats** are available *just before showtime.* Telephone: 354-5800.

[15b.] Forty-Ninth Street Subway Station, BMT, beneath Seventh Ave., bet. W. 47th and W. 49th Sts. 1973. Johnson-Burgee.

Brilliant glazed vermillion brick sets the tone for a reconstructed subway station, the *only one* in the entire city that can be called a fully satisfying environment. All surfaces, as well as lighting and graphics, were redone. Even the sound level from passing express trains was reduced by the provision of welded track and half-height, sound-absorbing hollow masonry walls. Now for the Transit Authority to redo all the remaining stations . . .

[15a.] Times Square Theater Center   **[20a.]** Clinton Youth and Family Cen.

[22.] The Hearst Magazine Building: plinth for an office tower never built

[16.] Engine Company 54, Ladder Company 4, Battalion 9, N.Y.C. Fire Department, 782 Eighth Ave., SE cor. W. 48th St. 1974. Department of Public Works.

Even the city's avenue of streetwalkers needs fire protection. This muted brown brick cubist exercise provides it. Congratulations.

[17.] Originally **Earl Carroll's Theater**/later **Casa Mañana,** W. 50th St., SE cor. Seventh Ave. 1931. George Keister, architect. Joseph J. Babolnay, designer. Lower facade altered, 1977.

This Art Deco polychromed-brick showplace (now sadly desecrated by bronze anodized aluminum and lots of signs) gave rise to showman Earl Carroll's boast, **"Through these portals pass the most beautiful girls in the world."** After Carroll vacated, Billy Rose opened another lavish nightclub, Casa Mañana.

[18.] Americana Hotel, Seventh Ave., bet. W. 52nd and W. 53rd Sts. E side. 1962. Morris Lapidus & Assocs.

A sleek supermotel that offers characterless but efficient quarters for the traveler. For character and class go to the Plaza or St. Regis.

Dining and Dancing, Times Square style: With venerable Lindy's gone from Times Square, **Jewish-American** delicatessen style food, long-favored by entertainers, reaches its peak at the **Stage Delicatessen,** a small, crowded place at 834 Seventh Avenue between West 53rd and West 54th Streets. (Telephone: 245-7850.) Big dance halls, once common around the square, survive only in the sedate **Roseland,** in a former ice skating palace at 239 West 52nd Street (between Broadway and Eighth Avenue).

[19.] Al and Dick's Steak House, 151 W. 54th St., bet. Sixth and Seventh Aves. 1948. Nemeny & Geller.

Sound architecture—rare in popular restaurants. A plain wood front leads to a masculine interior of stone, brick, brass, and wood. The elegant original canopy is gone.

Fifty-fourth Street west of Eighth Avenue:

[20a.] Clinton Youth and Family Center, Y.M.C.A./originally **Eleventh Judicial District Court,** 314 W. 54th St., bet. Eighth and Ninth Aves. Altered, 1970. James Stewart Polshek & Assocs.

Archways, entrance doors, and ventilators painted primary red, yellow, and blue **announce arrival at** this limestone Beaux Arts courthouse, now converted into a recreation center. Next door, the Depression-era police station continues to perform.

[20b.] Midtown North Precinct House, N.Y.C. Police Department/originally **18th Precinct,** 306 W. 54th St. 1939. Department of Public Works.

A serene limestone cube contrasts with the chaos of entertainment-district police business flowing into and out of its doors. Note the free-standing **Art Moderne lanterns** of stainless steel that flank the entrances.

[20c.] St. George Tropeforos Hellenic Orthodox Church/formerly **New Amsterdam Building,** 307 W. 54th St. 1886.

This **Romanesque Revival** building began as a small office building and now, painted the colors of Greece—blue and white—serves as a church. The joyous ornament is still evident.

[21.] St. Benedict's Church (Roman Catholic)/formerly **Church of St. Benedict, the Moor,** 342 W. 53rd St., bet. Eighth and Ninth Aves. ca. 1877.

This church for **black Catholics** was founded in 1883 at 210 Bleecker Street. In the mid-1890s the congregation moved to this **Italianate** building at the edge of what was then a **middle class** black community.

[22.] Originally **International Magazine Building/now **Hearst Magazine Building,** 959 Eighth Ave., bet. W. 56th and W. 57th Sts., W side. 1928. Joseph Urban.

Shades of the Austrian **Secession movement,** this sculptured extravaganza was commissioned by the William Randolph Hearst publishing empire.

CLINTON

From Ninth Avenue westward to the Hudson, roughly **opposite the Times Square theater district,** lies the area known today as Clinton, after the park of the same name at its western edge between West 52nd and West 54th Streets. From the Civil War to World War II the area down to about

West 30th Street was better known as **Hell's Kitchen,** one of the city's **most notorious precincts.** Gangster rule in its early years and the frequency of slaughterhouses, freight yards, factories, and tenements (to house those whose meager livings these industries provided) established the physical character the area has today. It is a quality the current inhabitants **wish to upgrade,** and the area boasts a number of improvements toward that end. But they are few in number and the ubiquitous lofts, repair shops, and taxi garages and the disappearance of pier activity (as well as piers) have made this stretch one that is unfamiliar to all except those who live or work here. It remains **an enigma** why Clinton, **so close to the heart** of Manhattan's central business district, **remains a backwater.**

Another festive activity of the district was once **the sailing of ocean liners.** Most of the big ones docked along the Hudson between 42nd and 52nd Streets; now all but extinct, their cruise ship successors stop at the new three-fingered passenger ship terminal between 48th and 52nd Streets.

[3c.] St. Clement's Episcopal Church   **[8.]** Sacred Heart of Jesus R.C. Church

[1.] Manhattan Plaza (apartment complex), W. 42nd to W. 43rd Sts., Ninth to Tenth Aves. 1977. David Todd & Assocs.

Two 45-story red brick balconied towers anchor this block-square amalgam intended to **spur redevelopment** of the Clinton community. Between the towers, on the garage deck, are all sorts of recreational activities for the residents of the 1,688 apartments.

[2.] Film Center Building, 630 Ninth Ave., bet. W. 44th and W. 45th Sts. E side. 1929. Buchman & Kahn.

Typical of 1920s' Art Deco-influenced loft buildings whose designs are just skin deep. This one, however, has **a gem** of a **polychromed elevator lobby** (and an asymmetric, moderne bronze tenants' directory).

[3a.] Playground, N.Y.C. Department of Parks & Recreation, W. 45th to W. 46th Sts., midblock, bet. Ninth and Tenth Aves. Reconstructed, 1977. Michael J. Altschuler, architect. Outdoor mural, 1973. Arnold Belkin, Cityarts Workshop. Mosaics, 1974. Philip Danzig, with community participants.

An **unusual reconstruction** of the ubiquitous city playground: community-crafted mosaics on the walls, reflections and distortions from polished stainless steel mirrors, weight-lifting devices and gymnastic equipment for macho users, all beneath a Mexican-inspired outdoor mural of social commentary. No picturesque charmer this but **a response to diverse user needs.**

[3b.] Clinton Court, 420 W. 46th St., bet. Ninth and Tenth Aves.

A charming backwater only partially visible through a locked gate.

[3c.] St. Clement's Church (Protestant Episcopal)/formerly **St. Cornelius Church,** 423 W. 46th St., bet. Ninth and Tenth Aves. ca. 1870.

A most **unusual and picturesque** parish church. Victorian brickwork, fish-scale slate shingles, and very pointed Gothic Revival arched windows. For years the church has also served as the home of the **American Place Theater** and for many noteworthy dance and dramatic productions.

[3d.] Originally **Wessell, Nickel & Gross Co.,** 452–458 W. 46th St., bet. Ninth and Tenth Aves. 1888.

A **New England-style mill** building (complete with mill yard entered through robust iron arched openings) squeezed onto an urban site. The factory made the *innards* for pianos.

Landmark Tavern, 626 Eleventh Ave., SE cor. W. 46th St. Telephone: 757-8595.

It dates from 1868 and looks every year of its **hundred-plus** years: dark wood, dusty mirrors, floors of two-bit-sized round white tiles, and Franklin stoves for heat on cold days. There's even a **panelled** and **stained glass** "gentlemen's" off the bar. Go for the atmosphere—the pub food is just okay. Moderate.

[4.] Salvation Army Thrift Store/originally **Acker, Merrall & Condit Company,** 536 W. 46th St., bet. Tenth and Eleventh Aves. ca. 1910.

A stately baronial factory of tapestry brick and expansive neo-Roman arches.

[5.] N.Y.C. Passenger Ship Terminal, Port Authority of New York and New Jersey, Hudson River at W. 48th, W. 50th, and W. 52nd Sts. along Twelfth Ave. W side. 1976. The Port Authority design section.

When the *Liberté, Queen Mary, United States,* or *Rafaello* were still plying the oceans, it was said that what New York City needed to dignify transatlantic arrivals and departures were modern superliner piers. The **piers were finally built;** the **superliners,** however, **were scrapped.**

[6a.] Park West High School, W. 50th to W. 51st Sts., bet. Tenth and Eleventh Aves. 1977. **[6b.] 747 Tenth Avenue (apartment complex),** SW cor. 1976. Both by Max O. Urbahn Assocs.

The school's West 50th Street facade's powerful forms, raw concrete and striated block, evoke a landlubber's image of a World War II aircraft carrier. The West 51st Street facade, on the other hand, is disconcertingly placid. The high-rise apartment tower at the corner is less impressive. A joint UDC-ECF venture.

[7.] N.Y. Telephone Company (office building), 425–437 W. 50th St., bet. Tenth and Eleventh Aves. 1930. Voorhees, Gmelin & Walker.

A telephone building from the era when *people* were still needed to complete your phone call (thus requiring windows) and the **image of a building** in the community **was a high priority** (thus justifying the willow leaf Art Deco ornament).

[8.] Sacred Heart of Jesus Church (Roman Catholic), 457 W. 51st St., bet. Ninth and Tenth Aves. ca. 1901. Napoleon LeBrun & Sons.

A **symmetric confection** of deep red brick and matching terra cotta frosted with light-colored stone arches, band courses, and copings.

[9.] Switching Center, N.Y. Telephone Company/American Telephone & Telegraph Company, 811 Eleventh Ave., bet. W. 53rd and W. 54th Sts. W side. 1964. Exterior, Kahn & Jacobs. Interior, Smith, Smith, Haines, Lundberg & Waehler.

A tall windowless monster which looks, from a distance, as though it's covered with glistening mattress ticking.

[10a.] Harbor View Terrace, N.Y.C. Housing Authority, W. 54th and W. 55th, and W. 55th and W. 56th Sts., bet. Tenth and Eleventh Aves. 1977. Herbert L. Mandel.

The height of midblock housing is limited by zoning, which explains why these are **in scale** with the adjacent mixed usage community. The combination of cast-in-place concrete and deep-terra-cotta-colored giant brick for walls and bronze anodized aluminum for balcony railings **furthers the domesticity** of the design. (The project is built over the air rights of the depressed West Side freight line.)

[10b.] Clinton Tower (apartments), 790 Eleventh Ave., NE cor. W. 54th St., and 590 W. 55th St., SE cor. Eleventh Ave. 1975. Hoberman & Wasserman.

The high-rise tower and its low-rise leg on West 55th Street are clad in a combination of smooth and striated pink concrete block. They embrace a courtyard and play area that gather the noonday sun.

[15.] Haaren High School (entrance)

[16.] IRT Powerhouse/now Con Edison

Brittany du Soir (restaurant), 800 Ninth Ave., at W. 53rd St. Telephone: CO 5-4820.

An authentic touch of France, once one of a pair—but Café Brittany, across the avenue, has closed. Despite its name, lunch is served as well as dinner. Moderate; no credit cards.

San Juan Hill: The rise in topography near Ninth Avenue and West 57th Street was, at the turn of the century, a black community dubbed San Juan Hill after the heroic exploits of a black unit in the Spanish American War. This stretch of West 57th Street between Eighth and Ninth Avenues bears a curiously Parisian look.

[11.] Henry Hudson Hotel/originally **Clubhouse, American Women's Association,** 353 W. 57th St., bet. Eighth and Ninth Aves. 1929. Benjamin Wistar Morris.

A landmark on San Juan Hill, it began as **a club for young women,** served as bachelor officers' quarters in World War II, and since 1975 has housed WNET, the city's public television outlet. Note **the bridge in the sky** connecting the roof gardens of the two wings.

[12.] Catholic Apostolic Church, 417 W. 57th St., bet. Ninth and Tenth Aves. 1885. F. H. Kimball.

A **superior work** of urban architecture, **three-dimensional**—not merely a facade—now almost forgotten because of bulky nonentities that squeeze against but fail to conceal it. Its **restrained coloring** of russet brick and terra cotta add to its power.

[13.] William J. Syms Operating Theater, Roosevelt Hospital, SW cor., W. 59th St. and Ninth Ave. 1892. W. Wheeler Smith.

The *oldest* member of this constantly regrowing complex: **a teaching amphitheater.**

[14.] Church of St. Paul the Apostle (Roman Catholic), Columbus Ave., SW cor. W. 60th St. 1876, 1885. Jeremiah O'Rourke. Altar and ciborium, 1890. Stanford White. Ceiling and windows, John La Farge.

An unadorned fort on the outside, except for one inexplicable mural over the entrance, it turns into **a Roman basilica** inside, embellished with the works of such as **Augustus Saint-Gaudens, Frederick MacMonnies,** and **John La Farge,** with the advice of **Stanford White** and **Bertram Goodhue.** All of their efforts are lost in the thick atmosphere. The largest un-cathedral in America.

[15.] Haaren High School/originally **DeWitt Clinton High School,** 899 Tenth Ave., bet. W. 58th and W. 59th Sts. 1906. C. B. J. Snyder.

Flemish Renaissance Revival **encrustations** enliven the facades of this old high school.

[16.] Originally **Interborough Rapid Transit Company (IRT) Power-house**/now **Consolidated Edison,** W. 58th to W. 59th Sts., bet. Eleventh and Twelfth Aves. 1904. McKim, Mead & White.

A brick and terra-cotta temple to power that **once boasted** six tall smokestacks **belching smoke** from enormous coal furnaces. The coal was received at an adjacent dock on the Hudson and transported to bunkers in electric conveyor belts; ashes were removed the same way. All the electricity for the original IRT subway, opened in 1904, was generated here.

[17.] Gardner Warehouse Co./originally **Rossiter Stores, New York Central and Hudson River Railroad Company,** Twelfth Ave., NE cor. W. 59th St. 1889. Walter Katté, chief engineer.

A blockful of solid, masonry warehouses, their walls patterned with **tiers of arched openings** each protected by steel shutters, these being more recent efforts in the style of the city's 19th-century "stores" [see WC Brooklyn/Fulton Ferry 6b.].

PARK AVENUE: 42ND–59TH STREETS

The one-mile stretch from Grand Central Terminal to East 59th Street— the busiest portion of Park Avenue—is **a uniquely successful integration** of railroad and city. The avenue itself is built over the old New York Central lines (also used by the New Haven division), and, up to 50th Street, the buildings along it are built over the fan-shaped yards.

Open New York Central Railroad yards behind Snook and Hatfield's old station

By 1913, Park Avenue, side streets, and buildings jointly covered the old yards

The railroad's **right of way,** down what was originally Fourth Avenue, dates back to 1832 when the **New York and Harlem Railroad** terminated at Chambers Street. The **smoke and noise** of locomotives were later banned below 23rd Street, then 42nd Street, as the **socially prominent** residential areas **moved north.** At 42nd Street the original, cupolaed **Grand Central Depot,** with **a vast iron and glass train shed,** was opened in 1871 (J. B. Snook, architect; R. G. Hatfield, shed engineer. Remodeled, 1898, Bradford L. Gilbert).

In the early 1900s, when electric locomotives were introduced, the railroad took **audacious steps** that **increased the value of its property** many times over and gave the city a three-dimensional composition that was one of the major achievements of **the City Beautiful era.** The terminal itself was made more efficient—and compact—by dividing its 67 tracks between *two* subterranean levels. The portions of Park Avenue north and south of the terminal were joined together for the first time, by a system of automobile viaducts wrapping around the station.

New engineering techniques for isolating tall buildings from railroad vibrations made possible **a complex of offices and hotels** around the station and extending north above the yards and tracks. By the onset of the Great Depression the avenue north through the 50s was lined with **remarkably uniform rows** of apartments and hotels, all solid blocks about 12 to 16 stories high, punctuated here and there by the divergent form of a church or club. Although some of the buildings had **handsome central courtyards,** their dense ground coverage must have made **summer living unbearable** in pre-airconditioning times—but then people who lived here **never summered in the city.**

Firm as these palaces appeared, most of them lasted only a few decades. Their loss, as a result of the office building boom of the 1950s and 1960s (convenient to Grand Central) eliminates the air of elegance that once was here. Today *only one* apartment building survives below 50th Street, No. 417 Park Avenue.

Park Avenue Walking Tour: Park Avenue and East 42nd Street (IRT Lexington Avenue, Times Square shuttle, and Flushing Line, Grand Central Station) to Park Avenue and East 59th Street.

[1.] Grand Central Terminal, 42nd St. at Park Ave. N. side. 1903–1913 (viaducts completed 1919). Reed & Stem and Warren & Wetmore. ★ Painted ceiling over main concourse, Whitney Warren with Paul Helleu and Charles Basing.

The remarkably functional scheme of the terminal and its approaches is housed in an imposing Beaux Arts Classical structure. The main facade, facing down Park Avenue, is a fine symmetrical composition of triumphal arches, filled in with steel and glass, surmounted by **a colossal clock and sculpture group** (by Jules Coutan) in which **Roman deities fraternize** with an American eagle—confusing symbolism perhaps, but of **very imposing** scale and composition.

The main room inside is unexpectedly spare in detail, a virtue now obscured by an **Off Track Betting** installation and by advertising displays. The simple ceiling vault, 125 feet across, and decorated with the **constellations** of the zodiac, is actually hung from steel trusses. Smaller spaces are structurally spanned by **Guastavino tile vaulting,** left exposed, with handsome effect, in parts of the lower level.

Grand Central Oyster Bar: This restaurant is world-renowned for its shellfish stews and pan roasts. The oyster bar and its equipment are worth seeing under exposed tan tile vaulting low enough to touch. Telephone: 532-3888.

[2a.] Pan Am Building, 200 Park Ave. 1963. Emery Roth & Sons, Pietro Belluschi, and Walter Gropius.

This **latter-day addition** to the Grand Central complex was purely a speculative venture. The building **aroused protest** both for its enormous volume of office space—2,400,000 square feet, **the most** in any single commercial office building at the time—and for **blocking the vista** up and down Park Avenue, previously **punctuated, but not stopped,** by the New York General Building tower [see 3.]. The precast concrete curtain wall was one of the first in New York.

The busy Pan Am lobby is accessible from the terminal, street level, and viaduct level, and is **"enriched"** by art works, including a vast **Josef Albers** mural, a **Richard Lippold** space sculpture, and screen-like metal works by **Gyorgy Kepes,** in the north lobby.

Note the staid Classical buildings across Vanderbilt Avenue from Pan Am at East 44th Street: the **Yale Club** (NW corner), identified in letters only one inch high, and the **Hotel Biltmore** (SW corner), noted for the clock in its elegant lobby where college students traditionally meet, and for its also traditionally clubby Bar, formerly Men's Bar, now sexually integrated.

Pan Am restaurants: The east side of the Pan Am lobby, at street level, has a row of three eateries with lively decoration representing three nations: **Charlie Brown's** (Edwardian English Club), the **Trattoria** (jet-age Italian), and **Zum Zum** (Wursthaus German). At the very top of the building, just below what was once the helicopter port, is the **Sky Club**—great for views and drinks. Telephone: 867-9550.

[2b.] Zum Zum, Pan Am Building lobby (the original unit of the chain). 1964. George Thiele, designer.

The **prototype** Zum Zum from which all the others descended. Yum yum.

[2c.] Pan American World Airways Ticket Office, Vanderbilt Ave., SE cor. E. 45th St. 1963. Edward Larrabee Barnes and Charles Forberg.

The major tenants gave the Pan Am Building its **most noteworthy** public space. The arrangement of freestanding curvilinear elements against a brightly lit undulating white wall is especially effective seen from outside.

[2a.] The Pan Am Building, a behemoth   [3.] Old New York Central Building

[3.] Originally **New York Central Building**/now **New York General Building,** 230 Park Ave., bet. E. 45th and E. 46th Sts. 1929. Warren & Wetmore.

This office tower, **symbol** of the then-prosperous railroad, was once **visible for miles** north and south along Park Avenue. Its fanciful cupola and opulent but impeccably detailed lobby **departed from the sobriety** of the terminal and the surrounding buildings.

The north facade, once a remarkably successful molding of urban space, maintained the cornice line of buildings flanking the avenue to the north, carrying it around **in small curves** to create **an apse of grand proportions,** crowned by the tower. Only a fragment of the original composition now remains, in the relation of the building to 240 Park Avenue. Carved into this north facade are two **tall portals for automobile traffic,** clearly differentiated from the central lobby entrance and the open pedestrian passages to the east and west. The **renaming** from **Central to General** required only the filling and recutting of *two* letters over the auto portals.

[4.] Union Carbide Building, 270 Park Ave., bet. E. 47th and E. 48th Sts. W side. 1960. Skidmore, Owings & Merrill.

The 53-story **sheer** tower is **articulated** with bright stainless steel mullions against a background of gray glass and black matte-finished steel panels. The thirteen-story wing to the rear (well related in scale to Madison Avenue) is linked to the tower by a **narrow transparent bridge,** dramatically placed at the north end of Vanderbilt Avenue. The site of the building over railroad yards made it necessary to start elevators at the *second* floor, reached by escalators.

[5.] Bankers Trust Building, 280 Park Ave., bet. E. 48th and E. 49th Sts. W side. 1963. Emery Roth & Sons; Henry Dreyfuss, designer. Addition behind, 1971. Emery Roth & Sons. Oppenheimer, Brady & Lehrecke, associated architects.

A rare example of an industrial designer (Dreyfuss) playing a major role in the design of a large building, most obvious in the very neat concrete curtain wall. The effort to fit into the old Zoning Resolution envelope without producing the stepped back wedding-cake silhouette has produced two rectangular masses that simply coexist.

[6.] Barclay Hotel, 111 E. 48th St., NW cor. Lexington Ave. 1927. Cross & Cross.

An elegant survivor of the Park Avenue development of the 1920s. Cocktails are served on the terrace overlooking the lobby, the centerpiece of which is a large gilded bird cage.

[7.] Waldorf-Astoria Hotel, 301 Park Ave., bet. E. 49th and E. 50th Sts. E side. 1931. Schultze & Weaver.

When this **world-famous institution** moved from its original site, where the Empire State Building now rises, it chose to build in **a sedate version** of the Art Deco style. The facades and lobbies once were a picture of 1930s chic, but in the early 1960s the management tried to turn back the clock to the Edwardian period; whatever couldn't be replaced was gilded. The 625-foot towers, which have a separate entrance on East 50th Street, have been home to such notables as **President Hoover, General MacArthur,** the **Duke of Windsor,** and **Secretary of State Henry Kissinger.**

[8a.] St. Bartholomew's Church (Protestant Episcopal), Park Ave., bet. E. 50th and E. 51st Sts. E side. 1919. Bertram G. Goodhue. Entrances relocated from old St. Bartholomew's, Madison Ave. SE cor. E. 24th St., 1902. ★ McKim, Mead & White. **Community House,** 1927. Bertram G. Goodhue Assocs., and Mayers, Murray & Philip. ★ Sallie Franklin Cheatham Memorial Garden, 1971. Hamby, Kennerly, Slomanson & Smith.

[8b.] General Electric Building/originally **RCA Victor Building,** 570 Lexington Ave., SW cor. E. 51st St. 1931. Cross & Cross.

St. Bartholomew's and the buildings behind it gave the old Park Avenue what it desperately needed: open space, color, variety of form and detail. Around its open terrace at the 50th Street corner are arrayed picturesque polychrome forms that rise to the **ample dome** of the church, dip, then soar to the **570-foot pinnacles** of the General Electric tower. Supporting roles in the related composition are played by the **old Cathedral High School,** just south of G.E., and the turrets of the **Beverly Hotel,** on the far side of Lexington Avenue.

[9a.] Seagram Building, 375 Park Ave., bet. E. 52nd and E. 53rd Sts. E side. 1958. Ludwig Mies van der Rohe and Philip Johnson; Kahn & Jacobs.

The bronze and bronze-glass tower that **re-introduced the idea of plaza** to New York. **Mies van der Rohe** brought here and to reality the **fantasies he proposed for Berlin** in the twenties; **Philip Johnson,** his biographer and acolyte (then, not now) designed its interiors. **Phyllis Lambert,** daughter of Seagram board chairman, the late Samuel Bronfman, was the *catalyst* for it all, bringing architectural standards learned at Vassar to her father. Love and respect for his daughter here allowed **a modern monument.**

The plaza, daring in that it was proposed at all (considering real estate values) is a bit of a bore; but at Christmastime the trees and lights are like a great piling of bridal veil—a delight.

[9b.] The Four Seasons (restaurant), 99 E. 52nd St., bet. Park and Lexington Aves. 1959. Philip Johnson & Assocs. Telephone: PL 1-4300.

An entrance dominated by a Picasso stage backdrop for *Le Tricorne* (1929) leads from the Seagram lobby into the restaurant to the north and the bar to the south. The walnut-paneled dining room is laid out around a square pool, the other room around the square bar, over which is a quivering brass rod sculpture by **Richard Lippold.** Both rooms are impeccably designed to the last napkin, tableware by **L. Garth Huxtable.** A stair connects the bar with the East 52nd Street lobby, one floor below, adorned with modern paintings. At this entrance, planting boxes and doormen's uniforms **are changed quarterly to mark the seasons.**

Dining at the Four Seasons is elegant and expensive. Sightseers are not generally welcome, but during the afternoon lull (around 4 P.M.) the management may be more permissive.

[5.] The Bankers Trust Co. Building   **[9a.]** The Seagram Building and Plaza

[8a.] The Romanesque portal of St. Bartholomew's Church. McKim, Mead & White

---

Brasserie: The Seagram Building's second restaurant, less lavish but well designed, is entered at 100 East 53rd Street. Its menu is basically Alsatian (quiche, choucroute), but you can have anything from a beer or a sundae to a full-course dinner. The Brasserie also makes up picnic baskets, with wine if you wish. Open 24 hours a day. Telephone: PL 1-4840.

[10.] Racquet and Tennis Club, 370 Park Ave., bet. E. 52nd and E. 53rd Sts. W side. 1918. McKim, Mead & White.

An **elegant Brunelleschian foil** for the Seagram's plaza, this "Florentine Renaissance palazzo" is a wealthy male chauvinist's club housing **squash** (both lemon and racquets) and one of the few extant "court tennis" courts (the game of *Louis Quatorze*).

[11.] Lever House, 390 Park Ave., bet. E. 53rd and E. 54th Sts. W side. 1952. Skidmore, Owings & Merrill.

These prismatic forms, now small-scaled for Park Avenue, **were the avant-garde** of the metal and glass curtain wall, first receiving the reflections of ornate neo-Renaissance stonework from the Racquet Club to the south, and assorted classy apartments to the north and east.

[10.] The Racquet and Tennis Club   **[11.]** Lever House in a 1952 photo

[12a.] Citicorp Center, Lexington Ave., bet. E. 53rd and E. 54th Sts. E side. 1978. Hugh Stubbins & Assocs. **[12b.] St. Peter's Church (Lutheran).** 1977. Hugh Stubbins & Assocs. Erol Beker Chapel of the Good Shepherd. Louise Nevelson, designer-sculptor.

A **tour-de-force** for the skyline as a stylish silhouette; and for the pedestrian a hovering cantilevered hulk under which **nests** the new St. Peter's Church. The **smooth aluminum facade** lacks the rich austerity of 140 Broadway (its flush, but black, predecessor).

The raked profile at its crest was a gesture to the idea of a sloping sun collector—but now is just a vestigial form, as is the Mercedes-Benz radiator cap and symbol (the radiator is elsewhere under the hood these days).

[13.] Chase Manhattan Bank Branch, 410 Park Ave., SW cor. E. 55th St. 1959. Skidmore, Owings & Merrill (bank). Emery Roth & Sons (building).

A building of wedding cake form, common in its time, with a **better than usual** metal and glass curtain wall, designed to meet the needs of the bank on the lower two floors. The bank interior has unusually refined details. The high second-floor banking room is an impressive setting for an **Alexander Calder** mobile.

[14.] East 55th Street, bet. Park and Lexington Aves. **[14a.] Community Building, Central Synagogue,** 121 E. 55th St. 1967. Kahn & Jacobs.

Just off Park Avenue is **a remnant** of what many streets in the East 50s once were like. For most of the block it is shaded by trees and not by high buildings. The fine old houses along it shelter many enterprises, including fashionable wig-makers. The tall, polished granite facade of the synagogue community building has destroyed the scale of the street. An unhappy intrusion.

[15.] Central Synagogue (Congregation Ahawath Chesed Shaar Hasho-mayim), 652 Lexington Ave., SW cor. E. 55th St. 1872. Henry Fernbach. ★

The oldest building **in continuous use** as a synagogue in New York, this one represents the rough-hewn Moorish style considered appropriate in the late 1800s. Although dour on the exterior, except for the **star-studded** bronze cupolas, the synagogue has an interior **gaily stenciled** with rich blues, earthy reds, ochre, and gilt—Moorish but distinctly American 19th century.

[16.] Mercedes-Benz Showroom, 430 Park Ave., SW cor. E. 56th St. 1955. Frank Lloyd Wright.

In the master's first New York City work, his creativity seems to have been smothered by the cramped space. More notable in that *he* did it, rather than for *what* he did.

[17.] Universal Pictures Building, 445 Park Ave., bet. E. 56th and E. 57th Sts. E side. 1947. Kahn & Jacobs.

The first office building built on this once-residential portion of Park Avenue, it achieved **a prismatic distinction** as the first evenly stepped back "wedding cake" form—precisely prescribed by the zoning law.

End of Park Avenue Tour: BMT at Fifth Avenue and 60th Street or IRT/BMT at Lexington.

DRY DOCK COUNTRY

Rarely has commerce marked a section of the city so effectively as the Dry Dock Savings Bank, through its stakeout of "Dry Dock Country." Its edges are ill-defined, but its kernel contains the action center of Bloomingdale's and Alexanders (and of course, the Dry Dock itself). For purposes of this guide, we will bound it by Lexington and First Avenues, 57th and 62nd Streets.

[1.] Alexander's (store): the foil to Bloomingdale's here in Dry Dock Country

[1.] Alexander's, Lexington to Third Aves., most of E. 58th to E. 59th Sts. 1965. Emery Roth & Sons.

The modestly designed, and modestly priced, contents are what is important here. The container is innocuous commercial modern pretending to be more.

[2.] Decoration and Design Building, 979 Third Ave., NE cor. 58th St. 1965. David & Earl Levy.

The zigguratted New York *zoning envelope* is capitalized into a positive architectural statement (if you **look** skyward).

[3.] Bloomingdale's, 59th to 60th Sts., Lexington to Third Aves.

An aggregation of **Victorian** and Art Deco (740 Lexington Ave. building. 1930, Starrett & Van Vleck) structures completely interlocking on the interior. One of the most comprehensive and sophisticated stores in the country. Good taste is prevalent, but not infallible. Nevertheless it has been accepted as a place and arbiter for the young "upper middle class": expensive.

La Bonne Soupe East, 987 Third Ave., bet. E. 58th and E. 59th Sts. 1975. Telephone: 759-2500.

Modest menu of soup, quiche, croque monsieur or madame, and fondue in an elegance of wood and glass. The slender neon sign is the way neon should be used.

Bookmasters, 999 Third Ave., bet. E. 59th and E. 60th Sts. Telephone: 355-8117.

A spacious, eclectic store, displaying mostly paperbacks. Subjects (including art and architecture) are arranged by clearly visible general headings.

[4.] Cinema I and Cinema II, 1001 Third Ave., bet. E. 59th and E. 60th Sts. 1962. Abraham W. Geller & Assocs. PL3-6022/PL3-0774.

Another piggyback pair, of great architectural **quality. Abe Geller** and his wife, who did the interiors, have produced a simple elegance with counterpoints of rich paintings and graphics. Instead of escapist entertainment in escapist environments (as in a 1920s movie "palace"), movies here are serious business.

[4.] Cinema I and Cinema II: a piggyback pair of great architectural quality

[5.] Alvin Ailey Dance School/originally the **Henry Keep Flower Memorial** and **Halsey Day Nursery, St. Thomas' Parish,** 229 E. 59th St. bet. Second and Third Aves. 1896. Wolfgang Partridge.

This Gothic Revival holdout was built by Governor Roswell P. Flower (of Flower Fifth Avenue Hospital fame) in memory of his son.

Yellowfingers, 1009 Third Ave., SE cor. 60th St. Telephone: 751-8615.

A place for *aspiring* swingers. Short order food, beer, and wine.

Serendipity 3, 225 E. 60th St., bet. Second and Third Aves.

A boutique upstairs, and mostly trivia below in this former shop with restaurant that has become restaurant with shop.

[6.] 400 East 57th Street (apartments), First Ave. bet. E. 56th and E. 57th Sts. E side. 1931. Roger H. Bullard, Philip L. Goodwin, and Kenneth Franzheim.

An Art Deco multistory apartment building in the style of Central Park West's **Century** and **Majestic.**

[7.] Roosevelt Island Tramway Station, SW cor. Second Ave. and E. 60th St. 1976. Prentice & Chan, Ohlhausen.

This aluminum and concrete construction houses many-colored machinery: fantasies inspired by **Charlie Chaplin's** *Modern Times:* and it all actually works to propel passengers. The ride to **Roosevelt Island** is a silent, bird's-eye view of city and river—a moving observation deck. **[Other Islands 4.–6.]** The fare is one subway token each way. Buy the tokens at a subway station; they are not for sale at the Tramway terminal.

[8.] Trinity Baptist Church, 250 E. 61st St., bet. Second and Third Aves. 1930. Martin Hedberg.

An early modern building with **Art Nouveau** moments: total architecture from concept to the smallest detail, this was, perhaps, the swan song (for New York) of creative craftsmanship complementing architecture. The yellow-brick facade uses the *idea* of brick to a maximum: **corbeled, arched, stepped, pierced, grilled:** it's a mason's wall. (But, in fact, it is a false front almost twice the size of the actual space behind.)

Daly's Dandelion/formerly **Daly's Bar,** 1029 Third Ave., SE cor. E. 61st St. and Third Ave. 838-0780.

A venerable bar now usurped by chic (with prices adjusted accordingly). Note the glass: stained, cut, and frosted.

[9.] Weyhe's Bookstore and Gallery, 794 Lexington Ave., bet. E. 61st and E. 62nd Sts. ca. 1920. Henry Churchill.

A non-American experience of great charm is in store here. One of five basic sources of new and old art and architecture books (**Wittenborn, Hacker, Jaap Rietman,** and the **Architectural Book Publishing Co.** are the other four), this delightful shop is packed with books of all vintages. Upstairs (by a flight immediately inside the shop door) is a small gallery of etchings, engravings, silk screens, and lithographs.

[10.] Treadwell Farm Historic District, generally both sides of the midblocks of E. 61st and E. 62nd Sts. bet. Second and Third Aves. District designated, 1967. ★

Two streets of brownstone houses: uniform rows of human scale sought by the affluent among surrounding commercial blocks. See Astor Place/East Village [18a.] for another Tredwell memory (they spelled it both with and without the extra **a**).

Gino's Restaurant, 780 Lexington Ave., bet. E. 60th and E. 61st Sts. Telephone: TE 8-9827.

A good Italian restaurant of the pasta-is-only-one-aspect-of-Italy variety. Moderate in price.

Colonial Nut Shoppe, 782 Lexington Ave., bet. E. 60th and E. 61st Sts. Telephone: TE 8-6056.

Lozenges, drops, nuts, bars, displayed as your **Victorian grandfather** would have: but not for a penny. A refreshing throwback.

Le Veau d'Or Restaurant, 129 E. 60th St., bet. Park and Lexington Aves. TE 8-8133.

Excellent. Certainly the best food (basically French) for its moderate price in Manhattan. Crowded in two ways: the tables are small and close together, and deserved popularity brings customers in droves. Phone first.

TURTLE BAY–UNITED NATIONS

The tract known by the mid-18th century as **Turtle Bay Farm** extended roughly from East 40th to East 49th Streets, from Third Avenue to the East River. The **little cove** that gave it its name is now covered by the gardens on the northern half of the United Nations grounds. **Bucolic** in the early 19th century, the area was **invaded** around 1850 **by riverfront industry,** with shantytowns inland that were replaced by tenements. By 1880, "el" trains were rumbling along both Second and Third Avenues. Town houses on the Beekman tract along the river around East 50th Street remained respectable (due to deed restrictions against industry) until about 1900 and were among the first in the area to be rehabilitated.

There was much **ambitious building and renovation** in the 1920s, but it was not until six city blocks of slaughterhouses along the river were razed in 1946 for the United Nations and the Third Avenue el (the last one to operate in Manhattan) closed down in 1955 that Turtle Bay was ready for thorough rehabilitation.

Turtle Bay Walking Tour: East 42nd Street between Park and Lexington Avenues (IRT Grand Central Station) to Lexington Avenue and East 49th Street. The entire tour is about two miles long.

[1a.] Bowery Savings Bank, 110 E. 42nd St., bet. Park and Lexington Aves. 1923. York & Sawyer.

Monumental in its arched entrance; even more so in its great and richly detailed banking room.

[1b.] Chanin Building, 122 E. 42nd St., SE cor. Lexington Ave. 1929. Sloan and Robertson. Lobby, Jacques Delamarre.

Surprising combinations of angular and floral decoration—even Gothic buttresses—sprout on this **exuberant** office tower. See the lobby, especially the extraordinary convector grilles.

[1b.] Bas reliefs on Chanin Building   **[2.]** The Art Deco Chrysler Building

[2.] Chrysler Building, 405 Lexington Ave., NE cor. E. 42nd St. 1930. William Van Alen.

Tallest building in the world **for a few months,** before the completion of the Empire State Building [see Herald Square 15.], 1,048 feet to the top of its spire. One of the first uses of stainless steel over a large exposed building surface. The decorative treatment of the masonry walls below changes with every setback and includes story-high **basket-weave** designs, gargantuan **radiator-cap gargoyles,** and a band of **abstract automobiles.** The lobby is an Art Deco composition of African marble and chrome steel.

[3.] Mobil Building/originally **Socony Mobil Building,** 150 E. 42nd St., bet. Lexington and Third Aves. 1955. Harrison & Abramovitz.

A 1,600,000-square-foot building sheathed with embossed stainless steel panels. A clever bore.

Bus shelters: Patterned after Parisian bus shelters (the Gallic versions have three legs, not four, and other differences) are a host of elegant brown-painted steel and tempered glass pergolas which began to proliferate on the city's street corners in 1975. Even the full-color advertising which supplies light (and income to the entrepreneurs) is good looking. Architects: Holden, Yang, Raemsch & Terjesen.

[4.] Daily News Building, 220 E. 42nd St., bet. Third and Second Aves. 1930. Howells & Hood. Addition, SW cor. Second Ave. 1958. Harrison & Abramovitz.

Howells and Hood abandoned the Gothic sources with which they won the *Chicago Tribune* tower competition in 1922, and here used **a bold, striped verticality:** patterned red and black brick spandrels and russet window shades alternating with white brick piers, the whole effect to minimize the appearance of windows in the prism. The 1958 addition **wisely repeated** the same stripes, but in different proportions to yield wider windows. The street floor, outside and in, is ornamented in Art Deco abstractions. See the **enormous revolving globe** and **weather instruments** in the (mostly) original old lobby.

[4.] Bas relief, The New York Daily News Building, Howells & Hood, architects

[5.] The Ford Foundation Building

[5.] Ford Foundation's indoor garden

[5.] Ford Foundation Building, E. 42nd St., bet. First and Second Aves. 1967. Kevin Roche, John Dinkeloo & Assocs.

People and plants here share a world **worthy of Kew,** elegantly contained in masses of brick and stretches of glass.

[6.] Tudor City, E. 40th St. to E. 43rd St., bet. First and Second Aves. 1925–1928. Fred F. French Co., H. Douglas Ives.

An **ambitious private renewal effort** that included 12 buildings, with 3,000 apartments and 600 hotel rooms **along its own street** (Tudor City Place), hovering on abutments over First Avenue. Restaurants, private parks, shops, and a post office round out the little city, all in Tudor style. Everything faced in toward the private open space, away from the surrounding tenements, slaughterhouses, and generating plants. As a result, **almost windowless walls** now face the United Nations.

La Bibliothèque (restaurant), 341 E. 43rd St., E of Tudor City Place. Telephone: 689-5444.

At the head of a monumental stair overlooking the United Nations, this pleasant restaurant offers an overseeing outdoor cafe. Expensive.

[7.] The United Nations Headquarters buildings viewed across the East River

[8.] 1 United Nations Plaza building

[12.] The Beekman Tower Apartments

[7.] United Nations Headquarters, United Nations Plaza (First Ave.), bet. E. 42nd and E. 48th Sts. E side. 1947–1953. International Committee of Architects, Wallace K. Harrison, chairman. **[7a.] Library addition,** NE cor. E. 42nd St. 1963. Harrison, Abramovitz & Harris.

John D. Rockefeller Jr.'s donation of the $8,500,000 site, already assembled by **real estate tyro William Zeckendorf** for a private development, decided the location of the headquarters. The team of architects included **LeCorbusier** of France, **Oscar Niemeyer** of Brazil, and **Sven Markelius** of Sweden, and representatives from ten other countries. The whole scheme is clearly a LeCorbusier concept (seconded by Niemeyer), but the details are largely Harrison's.

The 544-foot-high slab of the Secretariat (only 72 feet thick) dominates the group, with the Library to the south, the General Assembly to the north—its form played against the Secretariat's size—and the Conference Building extending to the east over Franklin D. Roosevelt Drive, out of sight from U.N. Plaza. Every major nation **has donated some work of art** to the headquarters. Immediately noticeable is England's gift, a **Barbara Hepworth** sculpture standing in the pool (a gift from U.S. schoolchildren) in front of the Secretariat. Probably the most interesting are the **three Council Chambers** donated by three Scandinavian countries.

The city, under **Robert Moses'** direction, made way for the U.N. by diverting First Avenue's through traffic into a tunnel under United Nations Plaza and opening up a half-block-wide landscaped park, Dag Hammarskjold Plaza, along East 47th Street—**a meager space** in the shadow of tall buildings, with no view at all of the U.N. Headquarters. The General Assembly lobby and gardens are open to the public. Enter at East 46th Street.

Guided tours of U.N. Headquarters: Telephone 754-7765.

Dining: At the coffee shop, lower level (ordinary), or lunch weekdays at the Delegate's Dining Room (elegant)—call 754-7625 for reservations.

[8.] One United Nations Plaza (offices/hotel), NW cor. E. 44th St. 1976. Kevin Roche, John Dinkeloo & Assocs.

Folded graph paper—an elegant scaleless envelope of aluminum and glass, its form sliced at its corner and sheltering the pedestrian at the street with an overhead glass apron. The public spaces within are some of the best in New York's modern architecture.

The building is more notorious than distinguished: **a passing bit of superstyle.**

Try the **Ambassador Grill's** mirrored-ceiling bar, whose optical illusions tend to intensify the alcohol's proof. Telephone: 355-3400.

[9a.] Originally **Beaux Arts Institute of Design/**now **Reeves Sound Studios,** 304 E. 44th St. 1928. Dennison & Hirons.

The fantasies of Beaux Arts architectural education in this country (heavily influenced by the techniques of the École des Beaux Arts in Paris) are incorporated in this structure, built when the system was already on the wane. The style is, of course, Art Deco.

[9b.] Beaux Arts Apartment Hotel, 307 and 310 E. 44th St. 1930. Kenneth Murchison and Raymond Hood, Godley & Fouilhoux.

Named for the adjacent Beaux Arts Institute building, this pair of **cubistic compositions** in light and dark tan brick face each other across the side street.

United Nations Plaza (First Avenue between East 42nd and East 49th Streets)

[10a.] United States Mission to the United Nations, 799 United Nations Plaza, W side. 1961. Kelly & Gruzen and Kahn & Jacobs. **[10b.] Institute of International Education,** 809 United Nations Plaza, W side. 1964. Harrison, Abramovitz & Harris.

The penthouse Edgar J. Kaufmann Conference Rooms suite is one of the two U.S. works of Alvar Aalto.

[10c.] Carnegie Endowment International Center, 345 E. 46th St., NW cor. United Nations Plaza. 1953. Harrison & Abramovitz. **[10d.] United Engineering Center,** 345 E. 47th St., NW cor. United Nations Plaza. 1961. Shreve, Lamb & Harmon.

A row of institutional offices not quite equal to their setting.

[11.] 860/870 United Nations Plaza (apartments), bet. E. 48th and E. 49th Sts. E side. 1966. Harrison, Abramovitz & Harris.

Desirable for views and social location, not architecture.

[12.] Beekman Tower Apartments/originally **Panhellenic Hotel,** First Ave. NE cor. Mitchell Place (E. 49th St.). 1928. John Mead Howells.

A miniature reprise to Eliel Saarinen's second-prize **"styleless"** design in the 1922 *Chicago Tribune* tower competition. Howells (with Raymond Hood as partner) took first prize with a free neo-Gothic entry. Originally a hotel for women members of **Greek letter societies.**

A walk along FDR Drive: At the east end of East 51st Street, steps lead down to a small park and a footbridge over the Franklin D. Roosevelt Drive. **Cross the bridge** for a back view of Beekman Place and a view of the drive disappearing at East 52nd Street under a Sutton Place South apartment house. A few rocks in the river off 52nd Street mark what was **Cannon Point** before the drive was built. From the walk along the river there is a good view of:

[13.] River House, 435 E. 52nd St., E of First Ave. 1931. Bottomley, Wagner & White.

A palatial 26-story cooperative apartment house. The River Club, on its lower floors, includes squash and tennis courts, a swimming pool, a ballroom, and had, prior to the construction of the FDR Drive, **a private dock** on the river **where the best yachts tied up.**

 [14.] Greenacre Park, 217–221 E. 51st St., bet. Second and Third Aves. 1971. Sasaki, Dawson, DeMay Assocs., landscape architects. Goldstone, Dearborn & Hinz, consulting architects.

A gift to the city by the daughter of John D. Rockefeller, Jr., Mrs. Jean Mauzé. It is larger and fussier than its predecessor, Paley Park [see Fifth Avenue 11a.].

[15a.] 2 Dag Hammarskjold Plaza (office building), NE cor. Second Ave. 1971. Raymond & Rado.

A **demure** curtain-walled office tower set on an elevated terrace designed to display outdoor sculpture. **Changing exhibits** all year round just a few steps up from Second Avenue.

 [15b.] Japan House, 333 E. 47th St., bet. First and Second Aves. 1971. Junzo Yoshimura and Gruzen & Partners.

Japan's **public architectural emissary** to the City of New York. Delicately detailed, inside and out, it stages cultural exhibitions open to the public. Information: 832-1155.

[16.] Turtle Bay Gardens Historic District, 226–246 E. 49th St., bet. Second and Third Aves. (also 227–247 E. 48th St.). Remodeled, 1920. Clarence Dean. District designated, 1966. ★

Two rows of ten houses each, back to back, assembled by Mrs. Walton Martin. A six-foot strip was taken from the backyard of each house to form **a common path and garden.** Near a very old willow tree at the center of the group is a fountain copied from the **Villa Medici.** Low walls and planting mark off the private yards. House interiors were remodeled with living rooms opening to the yard, lowered front doors in pastel-painted stucco fronts. Such notables as **Katharine Hepburn, Leopold Stokowski, E. B. White,** and **Tyrone Power** have lived here.

[14.] The entrance to Greenacre Park, larger and fussier than Paley Park

[17a.] 219 East 49th Street (residence), between Second and Third Aves. 1935. Morris Sanders.

A ground floor office and two duplexes, all clearly expressed on the facade in the **moderne style** of the thirties. Dark glazed brick was used to fend off soot, balconies to control sunlight.

[17b.] Amster Yard, 211–215 E. 49th St., bet. Second and Third Aves. 1870. Remodeled, 1945. Harold Sterner. ★

The vagaries of **early property transfers** created this inside-the-block space. A passage with a slate floor and iron settees leads into a garden, from which the office of **James Amster Associates,** other interior designers, and a few shops can be reached. Look carefully for the mirror at the end of the garden vista. Sculptor **Isamu Noguchi** once did his work in this yard.

[18.] Originally **William Lescaze Residence,** 211 E. 48th St., bet. Second and Third Aves. 1934. William Lescaze. ★

A **pioneering modern town house,** protected from city atmosphere by glass block and air conditioning. The office is at the bottom, house above, with a living room occupying the whole top floor.

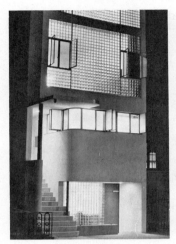

[18.] Lescaze House, 1934 photograph   **[22.]** Modern Museum's Guest House

[19.] Harcourt Brace Jovanovich (HBJ) Building/originally **Harcourt Brace & World Building,** 757 Third Ave., NE cor. 47th St. 1964. Emery Roth & Sons. Book store by Cloethiel W. Smith & Assocs.

The recessed loggia (with benches) behind the red granite columns leads to **the unusual store** by America's best-known woman architect.

[20.] Streetscape, around 747 Third Avenue Building, SE cor. E. 47th St. 1971. Pamela Waters, designer.

While the aluminum and glass, curtain-walled office tower at 747 is more of the same, the sidewalk treatment is certainly unusual, its **convoluted surface** resembling the aftereffects of an earthquake without the earthquake. Developer **Mel Kaufman** commissioned it as he did at his Lower Manhattan efforts, 77 Water Street and 127 John Street [L Manhattan/Financial District 30. and 32., respectively].

[21.] Shelton Towers Hotel, Lexington Ave., bet. E. 48th and E. 49th Sts. 1924. Arthur Loomis Harmon.

One of the first tall buildings (34 stories) to use the setback requirements of the 1916 Zoning Resolution creatively, **it made a great impression** on architects and artists of the 1920s. Brick masses accented with sparse, vaguely Romanesque, details.

End of Turtle Bay Walking Tour: The closest subway is the IRT Lexington Avenue at East 51st Street. The IND is at East 53rd at either Lexington or Third Avenues.

Miscellany:

[22.] Originally **Museum of Modern Art Guest House**/now **Philip Johnson Residence,** 242 E. 52nd St., bet. Second and Third Aves. 1950. Philip Johnson.

Roman brick and painted steel front a house built for guests of the Rockefeller Brothers (John D., Jr., David, Nelson, and Winthrop), who later gave it for similar guest purposes to the Museum of Modern Art. Now Johnson, its architect, has bought it for his house in town.

The Bridge Company (kitchenware), 212 E. 52nd St., E of Third Ave. Telephone: 688-4220.

Chic and functional kitchenware for reverse snobs. Browse among the pots, mugs, knives, and various fiendish parers, scallopers, corers, and what-have-yous. Julia Child does.

[23.] 312 and 314 East 53rd Street, bet. First and Second Aves. 1866. ★

A pair of wood town houses of Second Empire inspiration with interesting **corbeled** entrance hoods and **round-topped** dormers.

[24.] Recreation Center and Indoor Pool, N.Y.C. Department of Parks and Recreation/originally **Fifty-fourth Street Public Bath and Gymnasium,** 348 E. 54th St., bet. First and Second Aves. 1906. Werner & Windolph.

A *minor* building with a *major* facade. For once the screened roof space is part of the overall design, heralded by four **super monumental** Classical columns.

[25.] 909 Third Avenue (office building), and **Franklin D. Roosevelt Station, U.S. Post Office.** 1967. Max O. Urbahn & Assocs.

The tower's **deeply coffered** cast concrete **window walls** prove that three-dimensionality *per se* does not necessarily make a building gutsy. The podium is **New York 10022's** mail-handling factory.

[26.] 919 Third Avenue (office building), bet. E. 55th and E. 56th Sts. E side. 1970. Skidmore, Owings & Merrill.

Another [see L Manhattan/Financial District 65.] smooth black metal and glass monumental curtain wall that has P. J. Clarke's as a foil.

P. J.'s: This characteristic 19th-century relic (at 915 Third Avenue, northeast corner of East 55th Street) with a dining room in the rear has always been known officially as Clarke's Bar, but to generations of collegians it has been "P. J.'s" and it is partly responsible for the rash of other places called P. J. "Something." Seen by millions as the set for the movie *Lost Weekend,* it has lots of real cut glass and mahogany, and one of the most lavish old-fashioned men's rooms in the city. Clarke's is so economically successful that everything on the block except its first two floors was demolished for 919. Telephone: PL 9-1650.

FIFTH AVENUE: 45TH–57TH STREETS

This stretch of the avenue, where fashionable shops **have been concentrated** since the 1920s, was a solid line of mansions, churches, and clubs at the turn of the century. **Two factors** maintained the elegance of Fifth Avenue as the stores moved north along it: the **Fifth Avenue Association** (whose members have fought off billboards, bootblacks, parking lots, projecting signs—even funeral parlors) and **the lack of "els" or subways.** To provide **a genteel alternative** for rapid transit, the Fifth Avenue Transportation Company was established in 1885, using horse-drawn omnibuses until 1907, followed by the fondly remembered open-top (until 1936) double-deck buses, and closed-top double-deckers until 1953. Despite a fight by the association, all traffic on today's avenue runs only south-ward. Beginning in 1976, **double-decker buses returned,** this time handsome British Leylands.

Double-Decker Tour: If you are patient (not too many are scheduled) you can take a self-guided tour of Manhattan on the upper level of a 1976-vintage double-decker bus, all for the price of a Transit Authority token (half-price Sundays and holidays), one way. For first chance at upper-deck seats, the best place to wait: On West 32nd Street east of Seventh Avenue for the No. 4 to the Cloisters [see U Manhattan 31.]; at Houston Street and West Broadway for No. 5 to Broadway and West 157th Street, Audubon Terrace [U Manhattan 3.]. No. 4 goes uptown on Madison; No. 5 on Sixth. Each returns downtown via Fifth. Both use Riverside Drive thus providing great views of the Hudson.

[1.] Fred F. French Building, 551 Fifth Ave., NE cor. 45th St. 1927. Fred F. French Co., H. Douglas Ives.

The headquarters of the prosperous designer-builder company has **strange multicolored faience** at the upper floor setbacks and a well-preserved ornate lobby.

[2.] La Potagerie (soup restaurant), 554 Fifth Ave., bet. W. 46th and W. 47th Sts. W side. 1971. George Nelson & Co.

A variety of soups and desserts, cafeteria style, in a **warm and inviting** carefully designed (down to the napkin) setting. Reasonably priced. Wine available. [Also see nearby Pot Au Feu, Rockefeller Center 3.]. Telephone: 586-7790.

Gotham Book Mart, at W. 47th Street, in the heart of the city's jewelry district, is a great, though cramped and cluttered, bookshop. Its strengths are literature, poetry, dance, and esoterica. Its loyal customers are the literati of the city and the world. Upstairs, in the gallery (clubhouse for the James Joyce Society), are changing exhibitions including those on postcards, its owner's passion.

[3a.] Brentano's (bookstore), 586 Fifth Ave., bet. W. 47th and W. 48th Sts. W side. Alterations, 1965. Warner, Burns, Toan & Lunde.

Three narrow passages lead from the avenue and two streets into a multilevel central space full of books, jewelry, ceramics, etc.

[3b.] National Bank of North America, 592 Fifth Ave., SW cor. W. 48th St. 1964. Hausman & Rosenberg.

Elongated **black portholes** serve as windows for this stark white-marble-veneered prism. Once the jewelry firm of Black Starr & Frost (1912. Carrère & Hastings) until "modernized."

[4a.] Charles Scribner's Sons (bookstore), 597 Fifth Ave., bet. E. 48th and E. 49th Sts. E side. 1913. Ernest Flagg.

An ornate black iron and glass storefront opening to a grand, two-story, plaster-vaulted mezzanined space: an almost-basilica.

[4a.] Charles Scribner's Sons (store)   **[4b.]** The cubistic Goelet Building

[4b.] Goelet Building, 608 Fifth Ave., SW cor. W. 49th St. 1932. E. H. Faile & Co. Lower floors altered, 1966. Lester Tichy & Assocs.

Above the new base, the crisp original cubist office building with rich geometry of contrasting materials.

[4c.] Swiss Center Restaurants: Swiss Pavilion, Fondue Pot, 4 W. 49th St., bet. Fifth Ave. and Rockefeller Plaza. 1969. Interior Concepts, Inc., designers.

Understated stucco walls contrasted with a vermillion enameled cylinder on the outside; equally elegant detailing inside. Pavilion on the ground floor (expensive), fondue in the basement (moderate). The kitschy canopy is a later addition which should be removed.

The Rockefeller Center area is covered in a separate section beginning on page 169.

[5a.] St. Patrick's Cathedral (Roman Catholic), E. 50th to E. 51st Sts., bet. Fifth and Madison Aves. 1879. Towers, 1888. James Renwick, Jr., and William Rodrigue. ★ **[5b.] Archbishop's (Cardinal's) Residence,** 452 Madison Ave., NW cor. E. 50th St. and **Rectory,** 460 Madison Ave., SW cor. E. 51st St. 1880. James Renwick, Jr. ★ **Lady Chapel,** 1906. Charles T. Mathews. ★

Renwick's adaptation of French Gothic was weakened by his use of unyielding granite and his deletion of the flying buttresses (without deleting their pinnacle counterweights). But the cathedral, with its twin 330-foot towers, is **a richly carved counterfoil** to Rockefeller Center, across Fifth Avenue. Go in. The **Lady Chapel,** added behind the altar, is in **more academically correct** French Gothic.

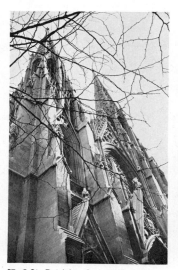

[5a.] St. Patrick's Cathedral (R.C.)   **[6.]** Originally the Villard Houses

[6.] Originally **Villard Houses,** 451–455 Madison Ave., bet. E. 50th and E. 51st Sts. 1884. McKim, Mead & White. **24 East 51st Street.** 1886. Babb, Cook & Willard. **29½ East 50th Street.** 1909. McKim, Mead & White. ★

Three brownstone mansions form a chaste early Italian Renaissance **palazzo,** its courtyard separated from Madison Avenue's traffic by elaborate ironwork. The original trio, the conception of newspaper publisher **Henry Villard,** was expanded along the side streets by the addition of two harmonious wings. Although the complex has seen a variety of nonresidential uses, many of its **great interior spaces** remain in pristine condition.

[7.] Olympic Tower, 645 Fifth Avenue, NE cor. 51st St. 1976. Skidmore, Owings & Merrill. **Olympic Place,** from E. 51st to E. 52nd Streets. 1977. Chermayeff, Geismar & Assocs.; Zion & Breen, designers. Levien, Deliso & White, architects. Abel, Bainsson, landscape architects.

An **elegant urban idea** for multi-uses (apartments over offices over shops) in a sleek, but dull, skin. To the pedestrian its graces are its elegant shops, but especially the arcade—Olympic Place—that **penetrates the building midblock,** from St. Patrick's to 52nd Street, with a skylit, treed, and waterfalled public space of gray granite. Its dedication to public use allowed the owner to build a bigger building than normally permitted.

[8a.] Cartier, Inc./originally **Morton F. Plant Residence,** 651 Fifth Ave., SE cor. E. 52nd St. 1905. Robert W. Gibson. Remodeled as shop, 1917. William Welles Bosworth. **[8b.] Extension at 4 East 52nd Street/** originally **private residence.** 1905. C. P. H. Gilbert. ★

Two fine mansions well adapted to the needs of a fine jewelry shop. The **Plant mansion** is the sole remnant of the period when this stretch of Fifth Avenue housed Astors, Goulds, Belmonts, and Vanderbilts.

[9.] 650 Fifth Avenue Building, SW cor. W. 52nd St. 1978. John Carl Warnecke & Assocs.

Horizontal bands of strip windows alternate with spandrels of reddish brown granite. The setback and public mall are a result of the **Fifth Avenue Special Zoning District** requirements. Sponsored by the **Pahlavi Foundation,** a work of the Shah of Iran.

Twenty-one Club: Jack and Charlie's place, at 21 West 52nd Street, was only one of several Prohibition-era clubs on its block to become fashionable in the 1930s but it alone remains, having become successor to Delmonico's and Sherry's as café society's dining room. Telephone: 582-7200.

[10.] 666 Fifth Avenue, bet. W. 52nd and W. 53rd Sts. W side. 1957. Carson & Lundin.

A million square feet of office space wrapped in embossed aluminum. Note the sculpted waterfall and ceiling by sculptor **Isamu Noguchi** in the arcade.

[11a.] Samuel Paley Plaza, 3 E. 53rd St., bet. Fifth and Madison Aves. 1967. Zion & Breen, landscape architects. Albert Preston Moore, consulting architect.

A parklet contributed by William S. Paley, founder of CBS, and named for his father. A **great oasis** in good weather **to refresh** in the spray of the waterfall, and **to lightly snack.**

[11b.] Harper & Row Bookstore, 10 E. 53rd St., bet. Fifth and Madison Aves. 1973. Smotrich & Platt, architects. Chermayeff & Geismar, designers.

The midblock headquarters of the publishing firm is announced by **mirror-finished cylinders** at the sidewalk. The reflective surfaces are echoed in the **high-style bookshop** on four double-height display columns on which are displayed eye-catching multiples of new editions' dust jackets. **Don't miss the exhibition** on the history of Harper's—on the mezzanine up the stair to the left.

[8a.] Orig. Morton Plant Residence   **[12.]** St. Thomas' Episcopal Church

[12.] St. Thomas' Church and Parish House (Protestant Episcopal), 1 W. 53rd St., NW cor. Fifth Ave. 1914. Cram, Goodhue & Ferguson. Reredos. Bertram G. Goodhue and Lee Lawrie. ★

One of Goodhue's **finest essays** in picturesque massing and detail, built on a constricted corner. Note the play of dense detail against big plain surfaces. The powerful French Gothic interior **culminates** in the shimmering white, richly carved reredos behind the altar.

[13a.] Museum of Modern Art, 11 W. 53rd St., bet. Fifth and Sixth Aves. 1939. Philip L. Goodwin and Edward Durell Stone. Additions and alterations, 1951 and 1964. Philip Johnson & Assocs.

The *history* of modern art, rather than its *current events,* is here **enshrined.** The original (1939) building was **a catechism** of the International Style (so dubbed by MOMA's 1932 exhibition, presented by Henry Russell Hitchcock and Philip Johnson): an austere streetfront of marble veneer, tile, both opaque and transparent glass, with a pleasant roofgarden worthy of a Le Corbusier acolyte. **It survives now** in the upper floor facades of the central building, the basement lounge and auditorium, and the main stairwell. The greatly enlarged lobby and most of the exhibition spaces are by Johnson. Its 1951 west wing and 1964 east wing **depart progressively farther** from the original flat International Style surfaces, ending on the east with **deeply three-dimensional** grids of painted steel standing free of the wall.

His **finest contribution** is the garden, an expansion and remodeling of his own earlier one. Here elegant stone, plantings, pools, and fountains have been composed into a serene and urbane oasis, perhaps the **greatest urban garden ever built.** From its upper level, there are excellent views of the garden and museum, some surrounding towers, and a remarkable row of buildings on the north side of West 54th Street.

Don't miss the Philip Goodwin Gallery for displays of architecture, furniture, and industrial design.

For hours, film and exhibit programs, and entrance fee information, call 956-6100.

[13b.] Museum of Modern Art Bookstore II, 1973, 1975. Abraham Rothenberg Assocs. and Thomas Lowrie. Located in **[13c.]** Formerly **The Theatre Guild**/now **Museum of Modern Art offices,** 23 W. 53rd St., bet. Fifth and Sixth Aves. 1901. Joseph Howland Hunt and Richard Howland Hunt.

Leaving the **marvelous exterior** essentially untouched, the ground floor of this superb town house was **rearranged to make** a showplace for the MOMA's books, notepaper, and adult games/toys. Great for gifts.

[13d.] Museum of Contemporary Crafts, 29 W. 53rd St., bet. Fifth and Sixth Aves. 1956. David Campbell.

Diverse exhibit spaces on many levels **carved out of** an old row house. The exhibits are often staged with great sophistication. For current exhibit and admission fee information: 977-8989.

[13e.] American Crafts Council/originally **America House,** 44 W. 53rd St., bet. Fifth and Sixth Aves. 1961. David Campbell.

The parent organization of the museum is **headquartered** here. By the same architect.

Early American Folk Arts: A small museum on this very pleasant subject can be found upstairs in an old house at 49 West 53rd Street. For program information and admission fee call 581-2474.

[14a.] America-Israel Cultural Foundation/formerly **William H. Moore Residence,** 4 E. 54th St., bet. Fifth and Madison Aves. 1900. McKim, Mead & White. ★

When Fifth Avenue's flanks were lined with residential palaces, fortresses, and châteaux, the side streets were lined with such as this.

[14b.] Alpha Garage, 15 W. 54th St., bet. Fifth and Madison Aves. 1965. Parking Plans, Inc.

The white cast-in-place concrete frames (*can you believe it?*) which comprise its wall to the street make this garage **a welcome neighbor.** (The original developer was in the concrete business and considered this project to be **free advertising.**)

[15a.] University Club, 1 W. 54th St., NW cor. Fifth Ave. 1899. McKim, Mead & White. ★

A super palazzo **beyond** the Medici's wildest dreams.

[15b.] Philip Lehman Residence, 7 W. 54th St., bet. Fifth and Sixth Aves. 1900. John H. Duncan.

Not only has Robert Lehman's fine private collection of paintings been removed to the Metropolitan's **Lehman Wing,** so have this town house's original interiors. [See Upper East Side 25a.]

[15c.] Rockefeller Apartments, 17 W. 54th St., bet. Fifth and Sixth Aves. 1936. Harrison & Fouilhoux.

Elegant **cylindrical bay windows** overview the Museum of Modern Art Garden—on part of a midblock strip of land **acquired by the Rockefellers** when their Center was assembled. The leftovers include the **Donnell Library** on West 53rd Street, the **Museum of Modern Art,** and **this urbane place.** The garden within is a pleasant *private* oasis.

[13a.] Original Museum of Modern Art   **[15c.]** The Rockefeller Apartments

[15a.] McKim, Mead & White's University Club, a super Italian "palazzo"

[16a.] St. Regis-Sheraton Hotel, 2 E. 55th St., SE cor. Fifth Ave. 1904. Trowbridge & Livingston. Addition to east, 1925.

A richly decorated Beaux Arts mass that gets **better toward the top.** Second only to the Plaza in number of prominent guests, the hotel is especially popular with foreign diplomats. **The Maisonette** in winter and the **St. Regis Roof** in summer have long attracted **high society** for dining and dancing. The King Cole Bar is designed around a **Maxfield Parrish** mural that once graced the Knickerbocker Hotel bar [see Times Square 10.]. The brass-and-glass porter's **sidewalk kiosk** is a **gem.**

[16b.] Mario Buccellati (jewelers), 703 Fifth Ave., SE cor. E. 55th St. Remodeling, 1964. Fleishman & Sedlis.

An elegant shop where the St. Regis dining room used to be.

[17.] Gotham Hotel, 2 W. 55th St. SW cor. Fifth Ave. 1905. Hiss & Weeks.

The **mate of the St. Regis** across the street, a little more angular, but just as ornate—and almost as fashionable, mainly with movie stars. All control over Fifth Avenue shopfronts was lost here.

[17.] The Gotham (apartment) Hotel

[20b.] The I. Miller Shoe Salon

[18.] Sona the Golden One, 7 E. 55th St., bet. Fifth and Madison Aves. 1965. Richard Meier and Elaine Lustig Cohen Assocs.

An oriental **bazaar.**

[19.] Rizzoli International Bookstore/formerly **Cartier Building,** 712 Fifth Ave., bet. W. 55th and W. 56th Sts. W side. 1907. A. S. Gottlieb. Altered.

A street-floor front of Neapolitan opulence leads into **a treasury** of fine books and magazines, open to browsers until midnight. Books on **architecture** and **New York City** are well represented. Elsewhere in the building the Rizzoli publishing empire pursues its various ventures.

Eat Street: That's columnist Earl Wilson's name for West 56th Street between Fifth and Sixth Avenues. It holds a record for a single block, with about two dozen restaurants—from French and Italian to Japanese and Korean. Above the close ranks of canopies are some interesting old house fronts.

[20a.] Genesco Building/originally **Heckscher Building,** 730 Fifth Ave., SW cor. W. 57th St. 1921. Warren & Wetmore.

The first office building erected after passage of the city's 1916 Zoning Resolution. Surprisingly, because of eclectic detailing (such as the rooster that once topped its water tank enclosure), it reveals no radical departure from old ways. The Museum of Modern Art's **first gallery** opened here on an upper floor in 1929.

[20b.] I. Miller Shoe Salon, 730 Fifth Ave., SW cor. W. 57th St. 1961. Victor Lundy.

Treelike wood-clad columns in the two-story space spread at the ceiling with **cathedral-like effect.** The original muted colors have been livened up by the owners. Washing the inside of the plate glass windows, screened by the wood, seems a perpetual problem.

Tiffany's: One of the oldest and most famous jewelers in the world came to the corner of Fifth Avenue and 57th Street in 1940. The show windows in its massive polished granite facade (727 Fifth Avenue) are famous for their miniature stage-setting displays.

ROCKEFELLER CENTER AREA

The waves of elegant construction that rolled up Fifth Avenue never reached as far west as Sixth. Rockefeller Center was expected **to trigger renewal** in the 1930s, but the Sixth Avenue "el," running up to 53rd Street until 1940, was too grim an obstacle. It was not until an enormous new **Time-Life Building** went up at West 50th Street in 1960 that a Sixth Avenue building boom started.

[1.] Rockefeller Center, W. 48th to W. 51st Sts., Fifth to Sixth Aves. 1931–1940. Reinhard & Hofmeister; Corbett, Harrison & Macmurray; Raymond Hood, Godley & Fouilhoux. **[1a.] Warner Communications Building**/originally **Esso Building,** 15 W. 51st St., at Rockefeller Plaza. 1947. Carson & Lundin. **[1b.] Radio City Music Hall.** 1932.

An island of **architectural excellence,** this is the greatest urban complex of the 20th century: an understated and urbane place that has become a classic lesson in the point and counterpoint of space, form, and circulation. Its **campanile** is the **RCA Building,** a slender, stepped slab **rising precipitously** from Rockefeller Plaza proper, that **many-leveled** pedestrian space surrounding and overlooking the **ice skating rink** in winter, outdoor cafes in summer, all overseen by *Prometheus* (1934. Paul Manship). Opposite, **Channel Gardens** rises on a flower-boxed slope to Fifth Avenue between the low-scaled French and British Pavilions: the foliage here an elegance changed with the seasons.

[1.] Rockefeller Center, the greatest urban complex of the twentieth century

Limestone, now grayed cast-aluminum, and glass clad these towers and their low-scaled neighbors: a straightforward, modern skin, **unencumbered by the need for stylishness,** but nevertheless **of great style;** elegant, and perhaps the most undated modern monument that New York enjoys.

The **assorted annexes** to the Center along the Avenue of the Americas (Sixth Avenue) **are of lesser stuff,** posturing, bulbous boxes built in the sixties and seventies, grabbing onto the Rockefeller Center name, organization, and underground passages, but sorry neighbors to their parent buildings. Included here are the **Time-Life, Sperry-Rand, McGraw Hill, Exxon, Celanese** buildings and others. They, in concert with the Zoning Resolution of 1961, brought **barren plazas** to the Avenue of the Americas: good intentions misdirected that present lifeless places without people, windswept and dull. The midblock **open air arcades to the west** of the three southernmost towers fail equally to become animated.

The Channel Gardens: The gently sloped and fountained space which takes you from Fifth Avenue to the stairway leading into the sunken plaza is called Channel Gardens since it is, like the **English Channel,** the *separation* between France (**La Maison Française** to the south) and the United Kingdom (the **British Empire** Building to the north). Among the shops that line its shores:

Librairie de France, Libreria Hispanica, La Maison Française.

A funky bookshop featuring French language books and books about France in English, as well as a smaller selection of Spanish works. This is the place to buy Michelin Guides in all their varieties.

[3.] Pot Au Feu (soup restaurant)

[5.] Eero Saarinen's CBS Building

[1b.] EL-AL Israel Airlines, La Maison Française. 1964. Samton Assocs., architects. Wall relief, Glen Michaels.

A neat airline office.

[1c.] Singer Showroom, La Maison Française at Rockefeller Plaza. 1965. Victor Lundy.

An opulent display area for sewing machines, fabrics, and notions. Its atmosphere is *hardly* one of domesticity.

Places designed to dine in:

[2.] Pearl's (Chinese restaurant), 38 W. 48th St., bet. Fifth and Sixth Aves. 1973. Gwathmey Siegel. Telephone: JU 6-1060.

Across from Rockefeller Center, a subdued design **unlike any other** Chinese restaurant. **Elegant and sophisticated,** as is the food, and the prices.

[3.] Pot Au Feu (soup restaurant), in the Exxon Building, 123 W. 49th St., bet. Sixth and Seventh Aves. 1973. Charles Mount and Judith Kovis Stockman.

If you **sense a similarity** in style then you've guessed that this soup and stew eatery was designed by the two who earlier collaborated on **La Potagerie** [see Fifth Avenue 2.]. Colorful, reasonably priced, fun. There's a dimly lit bar in back. Telephone: 765-4840.

[4a.] United States Steakhouse Company (restaurant), 120 W. 51st St., in Time-Life Building. 1975. Gwathmey Siegel, architects. George Lois, graphic designer. Altered, 1976. Stockman & Manners.

An American steakhouse in a dark, elegant **high-style** setting. Moderate to expensive. Have a drink at the handsome bar. Telephone: 757-8800.

[4b.] Seamen's Bank for Savings, 127 W. 50th St. in Time-Life Building. 1971. Carson, Lundin & Shaw.

A ribbon of veined, dark green polished marble forms a sinuous wall, into which are cut elongated portholes that contain masterpieces of sailing ship modeling (and, incidentally, the bank's tellers). The bank is a masterpiece, too.

[5.] CBS Building (Columbia Broadcasting System), 51 W. 52nd St., NE cor. Sixth Ave. 1965. Eero Saarinen & Assocs. Interior architects, office floors: Carson, Lundin & Shaw. Interior designers, office floors: Knoll Planning Unit.

Saarinen's **only high-rise building** is a sheer, freestanding 38-story, concrete-framed tower clad in dark gray honed granite; a **somber** and **striking** understatement.

One of several buildings of its time to depart from established post-and-beam framing. CBS supports its floors instead on its central core and a dense grid—in effect a bearing wall—at the exterior.

The **Ground Floor,** an elegant restaurant, whose name gently spoofs the many top-floor restaurants, was designed down to table settings by the Saarinen office. Telephone: 751-5152.

[6.] New York Hilton, 1335 Avenue of the Americas (Sixth Ave.), bet. W. 53rd and W. 54th Sts. 1963. William B. Tabler.

Clearly designed for conventions, this 2,200-room hotel has a **low, horizontal box** of public spaces hovering above deeply recessed entrances; rising from it is **a thin vertical slab** of guest rooms. The **rick-rack blue glass walls** of the slab give each room a bay window and have a pleasing crystalline look when seen at an angle. The clarity of the exterior volumes is not reflected in the interior.

[7.] The Mill at Burlington House, 1345 Avenue of the Americas, NW cor. W. 54th St. 1970. Chermayeff & Geismar, designers.

An 8½-minute **endless carpet** past a colorful multimedia presentation **on the nature of textiles** (by Burlington Industries, of course) **and American life.** Well worth a visit. **Free.** For hours, call: 333-3622.

CENTRAL PARK SOUTH

The neighborhood stretching between the south side of the park and the parallel West 57th Street corridor has **a sense of unity** generated by these strong lines and the cultural institutions at Columbus Circle and nearby in the Carnegie Hall area. It is a transition, a zone between Times Square **honky-tonk** and Central Park **gentility,** with Fifth Avenue's **elegance percolating west** through it into Clinton, just **starting to emerge** from years of shabbiness.

[1.] Columbus Circle, Broadway at W. 59th St.

This focal point, where Broadway glances the corner of Central Park, was the **obvious** place for **monumental treatment,** but it turned out to be a

few sculptures in a **tangle of traffic.** Gaetano Russo's statue of *Columbus* (1892) is at the hub; architect H. Van Buren Magonigle's *Maine Memorial* (1913) wallows in from the park corner, with a boatload of figures by sculptor Attilio Piccirilli.

[2a.] N.Y.C. Department of Cultural Affairs/formerly **New York Cultural Center**/originally **Gallery of Modern Art,** 2 Columbus Circle, bet. Eighth Ave. and Broadway. S side. 1965. Edward Durell Stone.

A compact white marble confection with vaguely Middle Eastern motifs, commissioned by A & P's **Huntington Hartford** and shaped to the constricted site. It shows off well when seen from the north, on Broadway, gleaming among larger, darker structures. This may have persuaded **Gulf + Western,** its neighbor across Columbus Circle, to purchase it and present it to the city as headquarters for the **Department of Cultural Affairs.**

[1.] *Maine* Memorial, Columbus Circle   **[2a.]** Orig. The Gallery of Modern Art

[2b.] 240 Central Park South (apts.)   **[3.]** Old American Fine Arts Society

 [2b.] 240 Central Park South, SE cor. Broadway. 1941. Mayer & Whittlesey.

Two apartment towers rising from a one-story, **garden-topped podium** give all the big windows and balconies a good view. There are some problems of form in the ziggurat top, but the detailing is fine. Note the **zigzag storefronts** on Broadway.

Central Park South east of No. 240 is an impressive cliff, including luxury hotels and apartments, but there is little, except for the careful decoration on the old **Gainsborough Studios,** No. 222, that calls for a close look. (1908. C.W. Buckham, architect. Frieze, Isidore Konti.)

[3.] Arts Students League/originally **American Fine Arts Society,** 215 W. 57th St., bet. Seventh Ave. and Broadway: 1892. Henry J. Hardenbergh. ★

A stately French Renaissance structure, originally built for an organization that included the **Architectural League,** is now an art school.

[4.] The Osborne Apartments, 205 W. 57th St., NW cor. Seventh Ave. 1885. James E. Ware.

The **crazy-quilt** exterior of Classical and Chicago School stonework and glassy storefronts hides elegant interiors, hinted at in the marble vestibule and lobby.

[5.] Alwyn Court Apartments, 180 W. 58th St., SE cor. Seventh Ave. 1909. Harde & Short. ★

A French Renaissance exterior, every square foot of which is **literally encrusted** with terra-cotta decoration. The ground floor has been altered to glean retail rents. Too bad.

[6.] Carnegie Hall, W. 57th St., SE cor. Seventh Ave. 1891. William B. Tuthill; William Morris Hunt, Dankmar Adler, consultants. ★

The caramel block of the hall itself is **engulfed** in the **bristling** offices and studios above and around it. The hall, **noted more for its sound** than its appearance, was **almost lost** in the early 1960s when Philharmonic Hall went up, but is now constantly booked. The building also houses a fine recital hall and a cinema.

[5.] Alwyn Court (apartment house)   **[6.]** Carnegie Hall and adjacent studios

[7.] Manhattan Life Insurance Building/originally **Steinway Hall,** 111 W. 57th St., bet. Sixth and Seventh Aves. 1925. Warren & Wetmore.

A sober Classical tower built by one of the many music concerns clustered around Carnegie Hall. The change of ownership has not changed the colorful street-floor piano showroom.

[8.] 125 West 55th Street (carriage house), bet. Sixth and Seventh Aves. ca. 1885.

A particularly **robust** stable which survived over the years as a restaurant and jazz museum.

[9.] City Center of Music and Drama/originally **Mecca Temple (Masonic),** 135 W. 55th St., bet. Sixth and Seventh Aves. 1924. H. P. Knowles.

Saved from destruction by **Mayor LaGuardia,** this **Spanish-tile-domed** multitiered theater has served for decades as a performing arts center for the city. The architecture is delightfully absurd, to be expected from members of the **Ancient and Accepted Order of the Mystic Shrine,** its original builders.

Fun Furs and Fun Food: Among West 57th Street's motley wares are off-beat furs—second-hand in shops between Sixth and Seventh Avenues, brand-new between Fifth and Sixth. For a more elegant (and expensive) selection, try the smorgasbord at the Copenhagen, 68 West 58th Street (MU 8-3690). The St. Moritz Hotel, at Sixth Avenue and 59th Street, offers a real sidewalk Café de la Paix and Rumpelmayer's lavish ice cream and confections (PL 5-5800).

UPPER WEST SIDE

A great deal of whatever it is that is New York is concentrated in the Upper West Side. Between Central Park and the Hudson River, from 60th Street north to Cathedral Parkway, this area has been defamed as both **an airtight cage** and **a gilded ghetto.** But it is neither. Despite massive problems, it is an area of **liveliness and hope** and contains a diversity of people, buildings, stores, and institutions rubbing shoulders with one another. Sandwiched between the **green oases** of Central Park on the east and Riverside Park on (most of) the west, the Upper West Side is one of the city's **densest population centers**—it should be no surprise that it is also **a treasure chest** of buildings, spaces, and amenities.

For the purposes of this guide we have divided the Upper West Side's three square miles into precincts: **Lincoln Center, Riverside Drive, Central Park West, the West Side Urban Renewal Area, and Manhattan Valley.** The remaining one, the vital center, is loosely termed **Broadway and Environs.** This area surrounds the all-important diagonal thoroughfare whose dual necklaces of shops along its broad sidewalks is (perhaps stretching a point) the closest thing we have in New York to **the boulevards of Paris.** With but one exception, the renewal area, the sequence within a precinct is in an uptown direction, away from the central business district. The renewal area is just the reverse since it was staged, sequentially, from north to south.

LINCOLN CENTER

The southern part of the Upper West Side developed quickly in the 1880s along Columbus Avenue, the route of **the Ninth Avenue "el,"** which intersected Lincoln Square at Broadway and 65th Street. The area was never fashionable except along Central Park. By the late 1940s the part west of Broadway was **a slum,** fostered by its **proximity to** the New York Central **railroad yards** lying between West End Avenue and the river. This area was the subject first of low-rent subsidized apartments and then of a twelve-block **urban renewal project** that cleared the tenements and is the site now of Lincoln Center, Lincoln Towers apartments, and Fordham University's in-town campus as well as many other public and institutional buildings.

The area described below lies between 60th and 70th Streets from Broadway to the Hudson.

[1.] Gulf + Western Plaza (office building), Columbus Circle bet. Central Park West, Broadway, and W. 61st St. 1969. Thomas E. Stanley.

This **flatiron-shaped site** did not produce a flatiron-shaped building, just a **rectangular slab** plus the bronze-anodized aluminum and glass Paramount Theater "hat box" which fills the space left over on the Broadway side. The movie theater—not to be confused with the grandiose but now-removed Paramount in Times Square—lies below the podium.

[2.] American Bible Society Building, 1865 Broadway, NW cor. W. 61st St. 1966. Skidmore, Owings & Merrill.

The precast concrete of this burly building is exposed; its bridge-sized beams make **a giant ladder** of the Broadway end.

[3.] Fordham University, Lincoln Center Campus, W. 60th St. NW cor. Columbus Ave. **[3a.] Fordham Law School (south building),** 1962. Voorhees, Walker, Smith, Smith & Haines. **[3b.] Leon Lowenstein Center (north building),** 1969. Slingerland & Booss.

Part of the same urban renewal package as Lincoln Center's performing arts spaces, these buildings fortunately don't attempt to join the overuse of travertine. Nevertheless their **bleached surfaces** are very white and very monotonous.

[4a.] Sofia Brothers, Inc. (storage warehouse)/originally **Kent Columbus Circle Garage,** 47 Columbus Ave., bet. W. 61st and W. 62nd Sts. E side. 1930. Jardine, Hill & Murdock.

A midblock **Art Deco delight.** All walls, even those on lot lines that might one day have been masked by tall neighbors (such as Lincoln Plaza Tower, for example), were embellished with some (two-dimensional) ornament. Curiously enough, this structure was built as **an early "automatic" (meaning elevatored) garage.** Today's storefront blocks the earlier wide entry for the now all-but-forgotten LaSalles, Packards, and Pierce-Arrows.

[4b.] Lincoln Plaza Tower (apartments), 44 W. 62nd St., SE cor. Columbus Ave. 1973. Horace Ginsbern & Assocs.

A pleasing 30-story stack of **bay windows** and **dish-shaped balconies** caught in an embrace of cylindrical columns.

[2.] American Bible Society Building   **[4b.]** Lincoln Plaza Tower (apartments)

[5.] Lincoln Center for the Performing Arts, W. 62nd to W. 66th Sts. Columbus to Amsterdam Aves. 1962–1968. Wallace K. Harrison, director of board of architects (composed of architects of individual buildings).

This **travertine acropolis** of music and theater represents an initial investment of more than $165 million of early 1960s dollars—mostly in private contributions—along with federal aid in acquiring the site and a state contribution to the New York State Theater.

The project **aroused dissent** on both urbanistic and architectural grounds. The congestion caused by the location of so many large theaters in one cluster (with only meager public transportation) has been an obvious problem, left unsolved by the vast underground garage beneath the project. Making **a single impressive group** out of structures with such demanding interior requirements has **imposed inhibitions** on the individual buildings. As a result, *New York Times* critic Ada Louise Huxtable wrote, "Philharmonic Hall, the State Theater, and the Metropolitan Opera are lushly decorated, conservative structures that the public finds pleasing and most professionals consider a failure of nerve, imagination and talent."

"Fortunately," she continued, "the scale and relationship of the plazas are good, and they can be enjoyed as pedestrian open spaces."

[5a.] New York State Theater, SE cor. Lincoln Center, Columbus Ave., bet. W. 62nd and W. 63rd Sts. W side. 1964. Philip C. Johnson and Richard Foster.

This 2,800-seat theater, designed mainly for ballet and musical theater, also includes a vast four-story foyer suitable for receptions and balls. It is the **most frankly Classical building** in the group. The plaza-level lobby is a Baroque space that seems to have been carved from the enveloping travertine. The **grand foyer** above it, by contrast, is bounded by tiers of busy metal balcony railings, gold-colored chain drapery, and a gold velvet ceiling. It is dominated by two **wonderful white marble sculptures,** enlargements of earlier **Elie Nadelman** works. The "Delancey Street rhinestone" lights and chandeliers, inside and out, are a false note.

[5.] Lincoln Center for the Performing Arts: a night view from Columbus Ave.

[5b.] Damrosch Park, [5c.] Guggenheim Bandshell, SW cor. Lincoln Center, W. 62nd St., NE cor. Amsterdam Ave. 1969. Eggers & Higgins.

Planned as a space for free outdoor concerts, this park surrounds a flat, **intricately paved** center section with an edge of verdant formal landscaping. The bandshell, hugging Amsterdam Avenue on the west, seems to derive its form from **Middle Eastern antecedents,** thus adding yet another curious dimension to the already **eclectic** Lincoln Center scene.

Eating near Lincoln Center

O'Neal's Baloon, 48 W. 63rd St. at Columbus Ave. Telephone: 765-5577.

Dating from the Lincoln Center era, this pub-cum-enclosed-sidewalk-café was to be called O'Neal's Saloon. But saloons are a holdover **temperance union no-no;** hence, Baloon—the story goes—which meant changing only one letter in the sign. Draws a big crowd at performance times.

Liberty Café, 43 W. 64th St. E of Columbus Ave. Telephone: 877-1119.

A 55-foot-high replica of the **Statue of Liberty** has **crowned the storage warehouse** of the same name since 1902—she lost the torch in a windstorm long ago. The ground floor of the warehouse (and a mezzanine) have, as a result of Lincoln Center, seen some successful **adaptive reuse** as a chic before- and after-performance café.

Fiorello's, 1900 Broadway, bet. W. 63rd and W. 64th Sts. Telephone: 595-5330.

Looking for an off-the-beaten-track candle-lit Italian café with checkered tablecloths? This isn't it. It's on Lincoln Center's doorstep, brightly lit, well designed, and good for a quick Italian meal. An al fresco sidewalk café operates in warm weather.

Columbus Avenue north of Lincoln Square also has many places to eat, snack, and nosh.

[5d.] Metropolitan Opera House, W side of Lincoln Center, bet. W. 63rd and W. 64th Sts. 1966. Wallace K. Harrison. Lobby paintings facing the plaza, Marc Chagall.

After years of trying to remove itself from its garment center location on Broadway between 39th and 40th Streets—negotiating at one point to occupy what eventually became the site of Rockefeller Center's RCA Building—the Met finally came here, to Lincoln Center. It is the **focal building** of the complex and its largest hall. It is also **a schmaltzy pastiche of forms,** materials (mostly travertine), and effects beginning with self-consciously **sensuous red-carpeted stairs** (which wind around themselves at the entrance) and ending with **brilliant Austrian crystal chandeliers** (which hang in the tall lobby space, as they do in the hall itself until, at the start of a performance, they silently rise to the gold-leafed ceiling). The café at the top of the lobby offers a **dazzling view down** into the entry area and out across the plaza.

[5g.] Avery Fisher Hall, Lincoln Cen.   **[10.]** Columbia College of Pharmacy

[5e.] Vivian Beaumont Theater, NW cor. Lincoln Center, Amsterdam Ave., SE cor. W. 65th St. Eero Saarinen & Assocs. **[5f.] Library and Museum of the Performing Arts, N.Y. Public Library,** 111 Amsterdam Ave. 1965, Skidmore, Owings & Merrill. Pool sculpture in plaza, *Reclining Figure,* Henry Moore.

An **unusual collaboration** of both **architects and architecture.** The library fills the massive, travertine-clad attic story which cantilevers over the 1,100-seat repertory drama theater at plaza level. The building forms a **handsome backdrop** for the **reflecting pool** and its **modern sculpture,** especially when the glass-enclosed, split-level lobby is lighted and populated. In the main theater—there is a smaller one below—neutral, dark interior surfaces do not compete with the **colorful tiered seating** or the action on the **highly flexible stage.**

The library-museum, best entered through the link connecting it to the opera house, has typically meticulous SOM details, **a fun-to-shop-in boutique** specializing in performing arts books and memorabilia and always some lively exhibits arranged by its **Shelby Collum Davis Museum.** The lowest entrance from Amsterdam Avenue opens upon both a small lecture hall and a charming exhibit space given over to theater-related shows. For exhibit and program information, call 799-2200.

[5g.] Avery Fisher Hall/originally **Philharmonic Hall,** NE cor. Lincoln Center, Columbus Ave. bet. 64th and 65th Sts. W side. 1962. Max Abramovitz. Reconstructed, 1976. Johnson-Burgee, architects. Cyril Harris, acoustical engineer. Stabile suspended from lobby ceiling, 1962, Richard Lippold, sculptor.

The many-tiered lobby of this concert hall has a clear glass enclosure set inside an arcade defined by tall, crisply tapered travertine columns. The most controversial of the performing arts center's buildings, its hall has been **rebuilt a number of times** in attempts to solve its well-publicized acoustical deficiencies. The most elaborate change, in 1976, converted the hall into **a classic European rectangle** (and redesigned the public lobby spaces as well) to **wide acclaim** from both acoustical and architectural critics.

[5h.] Juilliard School of Music, Broadway bet. W. 65th and W. 66th Sts. W side. 1968. Pietro Belluschi, with Eduardo Catalano and Westermann & Miller.

Connected to the superblock of Lincoln Center proper by a bridge over West 65th Street, this is the youngest of the center's buildings. **Monolithic in appearance,** it is as if carved from travertine. It makes the best of an irregular site caused by Broadway's diagonal slash.

Lincoln Center Mall: Late in 1966 an ill-advised plan was announced to create a landscaped mall that would link Lincoln Center's Plaza with Central Park, a long city block away. The plan called for the demolition of the West Side YMCA (1930. Dwight James Baum) and the meeting house of the New York Society for Ethical Culture along with other structures between West 63rd and West 64th Streets—the Broadway frontage was, by that time, already vacant, an enormous parking lot. Additionally, an enormous block-sized underground parking area was envisioned beneath the proposed greenery. The plan lost and the threatened institutions remain. From the parking lot, however, grew the ASCAP Building, a spastic work that seems unable to respect either the rectangular street grid or Broadway's diagonal. Some decades everything goes wrong.

[6.] Broadway Mall Improvements, Dante Park, Lincoln Square, W. 72nd to W. 74th Sts., W. 95th to W. 96th Sts., 1972. Glasser & Ohlhausen.

Cylindrical concrete kiosks, their **royal blue "kepis"** announcing the intersecting cross streets, identify the sites of the first stage of **upgrading the sitting spaces** along Broadway's center islands. Long favored as resting places by older West Siders, many have taken in the sun (and exhaust fumes) behind what one wag characterized as **"the ramparts we watched."**

[7.] 2 Lincoln Square, and **Church of Christ of Latter-Day Saints,** Columbus Ave., bet. W. 65th and W. 66th Sts. E side. 1975. Schuman, Lichtenstein & Claman.

Responding, no doubt, to the expectations set by Lincoln Center, the front is **pompous.** But hidden in the depths of the public arcade are some tall, surprisingly **poetic** spaces.

[8.] Gutterman's Funeral Chapel/formerly **Campbell Funeral Church,** 1970 Broadway, bet. W. 66th and W. 67th Sts. E side. 1892. McKim, Mead & White. Considerably altered.

The warm orange brick laid in tall deep arches and the Mission Style cornice reveal more about this building's original appearance than do its lower floors. It was here, in 1926, that all New York mourned the passing of movie idol **Rudolph Valentino.**

[9.] Columbia Fireproof Storage Warehouse, 149 Columbus Ave., bet. W. 66th and W. 67th Sts. E side. 1893. G.A. Schellenger.

Light, ventilation, and views are largely unnecessary in a warehouse. In lesser hands those utilitarian exemptions could lead to a tedious facade. Fortunately, architects of the late 19th century were challenged by the simplicity of the problem, this ornate example being **one of a diminishing number** extant in the city. [See WC Brooklyn/Fulton Ferry 2., Bedford-Stuyvesant 16., and H Manhattan/Harlem 11.]

[10.] College of Pharmaceutical Science, Columbia University/originally **College of Pharmacy of the City of New York,** 115 W. 68th St., bet. Columbus Ave. and Broadway. 1894. Little & O'Connor.

A **fuddy-duddy** old building which seems, nevertheless, to scoff at its lesser neighbors.

[11a.] Genghiz Khan's Bicycle (restaurant), 197 Columbus Ave., SE cor. W. 69th St. 1974. Gamal El Zoghby.

The architectural equivalent of a carefully tailored suit. All the white formica parts fit together perfectly. Turkish cooking. Telephone: 595-2138.

[11b.] Christ and St. Stephen's Church (Protestant Episcopal)/originally **St. Stephen's Church,** 120 W. 69th St., bet. Columbus Ave. and Broadway. 1880. Altered, 1897.

Predating the Dakota and, therefore, left over from when the West Side was among the city's **great open spaces.** Its green front yard is **a small-scaled oasis** in this dense precinct.

 [12.] Originally **Pythian Temple/**now **Building M, Borough of Manhattan Community College, CUNY,** 135 W. 70th St., bet. Columbus Ave. and Broadway. 1927. Thomas W. Lamb.

Hollywood may have its Grauman's Chinese, New York has its Pythian Temple! Hidden on an anonymous side street, this **opium-smoker's dream** is best seen from across the street—or better still, from someone's upper-floor apartment to the south. Is the rumor correct that this is slated to be the next home of the Iranian Mission to the UN?

Eating on Columbus: Columbus Avenue and surroundings have attracted a wide and refreshing range of restaurants. As you travel uptown: No. 198, **Sakura Chaya;** No. 202, **Lenge;** No. 210, **Rikyu** (all Japanese); No. 201, **Red Baron** (continental); No. 220, **India Cafe** (Indian); No. 240, **Victor's** (Cuban); No. 323, **Ruskay's** (continental. . .open 24 hours. . .try breakfast). Also, at Amsterdam Avenue and West 77th, **P.S. 77,** not a school but a French restaurant.

West of Lincoln Center

[13.] Former **Phipps Houses (apartments),** 235, 239, 243, 247 W. 63rd St., E of West End Ave. (cul-de-sac). 1907. 236, 240, 244, 248 W. 64th St., bet. Amsterdam and West End Aves. 1911. Both by Whitfield & King.

Slum clearance efforts west of Lincoln Center made a thorough sweep between the late forties (Amsterdam Houses) and the urban renewal projects of the sixties. The only residential buildings which remain from the early 20th century are these, billed as **"model tenement houses"** by Henry Phipps' pioneering housing society. They offer **little as urban design** but their interior planning was **an esteemed prototype** for future efforts to improve housing for the **laboring classes.**

Outdoor mural: The east wall of 236 West 64th Street overlooks the open space of a humdrum city playground. Until 1970 it stood unadorned—until City Walls, Inc., arranged to make it a bigger-than-life "canvas" for an Allan D'Arcangelo painting. There are more than 70 such outdoor murals by a variety of sponsors sprinkled throughout the city.

[14a.] Amsterdam Houses Addition, N.Y.C. Housing Authority, 240 W. 65th St., bet. Amsterdam and West End Aves. 1974. Oppenheimer, Brady & Lehrecke.

Change does not come easily. Overly self-conscious concern for design, to achieve a break with the dead-public-housing-hand of the past, can be forgiven in this structure. Its designers' **expressionistic use of angles** and exposed concrete **give character** (and triangular bay windows) to the project.

[14b.] Lincoln-Amsterdam House, 110 West End Ave., bet. W. 64th and W. 65th Sts. E side. 1976. David Todd & Assocs.

Multistory housing is treated here almost as **heroic,** nonrepresentational **sculpture-in-the-round.** The arrangement of apartments insures different plastic qualities for each of the facades within a strong, unified composition of cast concrete and large orange brick. The **views across the Hudson** understandably draw out the richest qualities in the design, the west facade.

The "back lot": Exterior scenes in Hollywood productions are often filmed in studio "back lots," expansive outdoor spaces in which mock-ups of the necessary scenery are concocted at considerable expense. For the filming of Leonard Bernstein's musical saga *West Side Story,* what better (and cheaper) substitute for Hollywood artifice than the streets of the West Side itself? The vacating of the Lincoln Square Urban Renewal Area in the late fifties provided just such an opportunity for its tenements to have their day on film before they came crashing down.

[15.] Martin Luther King, Jr., High School, 122 Amsterdam Ave., bet. W. 65th and W. 66th Sts. W side. 1975. Frost Assocs., architects. William Tarr, sculptor.

A glass box of enormous size and scale sits proudly on the busy avenue. A **self-weathering steel,** Mayari R, was employed in both the school's carefully detailed curtain wall and in the **boldly fashioned memorial sculpture** to the slain civil rights leader, which towers over the sidewalk.

[16.] American Red Cross Building, 150 Amsterdam Ave., bet. W. 66th and W. 67th Sts. W side. 1964. Skidmore, Owings & Merrill.

A "temple" built with a firm but perhaps **naive commitment** to the **"less is more"** principle. Surveying traffic-choked Amsterdam Avenue, its low podium is hardly an acropolis.

[17.] Lincoln Square Center for the Arts/originally **26th Precinct Station House, N.Y.C. Police Department/**later **20th Precinct,** 150 W. 68th St., bet. Broadway and Amsterdam Ave. ca. 1889. N.D. Bush.

A dignified composition: segmental and semicircular arched openings linteled in neatly carved stone and set into a russet brick field. Lucky for us that it has found another use.

[18.] The Lincoln Square Synagogue: house of worship clad in travertine veneer

[18.] Lincoln Square Synagogue, 200 Amsterdam Ave., NW cor. W. 69th St. 1970. Hausman & Rosenberg.

The theaters of nearby Lincoln Center set the travertine tone for the area, and this mannered, curvy, articulated synagogue picks up the cue. The travertine bank to the north actually came first but the two together seem to be making an **inadvertent comment** about moneychangers at the temple.

[19.] Public School 199 Manhattan, 270 W. 70th St., SE cor. West End Ave. 1963. Edward Durell Stone & Assocs.

Notable mostly for its being an **early example** of a city public school designed by a prominent architect. It was built in connection with the **red brick megaslabs** of the 2,000-odd-unit Lincoln Towers urban renewal project around it.

Terrain that slopes steeply west to the banks of the river, **a roller coaster** of north-south gradients, **the water level route** of the smoke-belching New York Central and Hudson River Railroad, and the Palisades **across the flowing Hudson River** currents—contrasts that made the planning of "the Riverside Park and Avenue" a **powerful challenge** to landscape architect Frederick Law Olmsted. Between 1873 and 1910, Olmsted, and his associates and successors, developed **a great green waterside edge** for the West Side as he and Calvert Vaux had earlier created "the Central Park" on the inland site. The style was in the tradition of English landscape architecture, **naturalistic and picturesque.** Development along Riverside Drive (and straight-as-an-arrow West End Avenue behind it) resulted **from the magnetism** of this great urban design.

In the 1930s the Henry Hudson Parkway Authority, using WPA funds, added a four-lane highway to the park area (since expanded to six) and a host of recreational amenities—essentially the **amalgam of asphalt and greenery** we see today. This change accomplished two other important results: it **covered** the now-electrified freight line, and it **built** the highway in part on filled land both contributing **to additional (if noxious)** recreation space.

[1a.] Originally **Lydia S. Prentiss Residence,** 1 Riverside Dr., NE cor. W. 72nd St. 1901. C.P.H. Gilbert. **[1b.] Residence,** 311 West 72nd St., NE cor. Riverside Dr. 1902. C.P.H. Gilbert.

Two **self-satisfied** town houses that herald the start of Riverside Drive's côte du limestone.

[1c.] The Chatsworth (apartments), 346 W. 72nd St., SE cor. Henry Hudson Pkwy. and 353 W. 71st St., W end of W. 71st St. 1904. Annex, 340 W. 72nd St. 1906. Both by John E. Schlarsmith.

The Chatsworth is actually **three towers.** The **two main buildings** are on West 72nd and West 71st Streets, gracious russet colored brick apartment blocks embellished with lavish limestone trim—**the annex** to the east on West 72nd is lower and all limestone. The main towers are in the West Side tradition of the Kenilworth and Rossleigh Court/Orwell House. [See Central Park West 20a., 27b., and 27c.]

[1d.] Originally **Spencer Aldrich Residence,** 271 W. 72nd St., NE cor. West End Ave. 1897. Gilbert A. Schellenger. Altered.

The mercantile uses to which the lower floors have **thoughtlessly been converted** serve only to point up the richness of what remains, the sprightly forms of the upper floors and roof.

Schwab House: A rare Gallic composition of pinnacles, spires, chimneys, and steeply sloping roofs once embellished the Drive's skyline between West 73rd and West 74th Streets. Consciously seeking to bring the joys of the French château to the banks of the Hudson, architect Maurice Hebert adapted the facades of three—Blois, Chenonceaux, and Azay-le-Rideau—to the needs of Andrew Carnegie's associate, Charles M. Schwab. The enormous Schwab residence was not only freestanding, but it occupied, with its surrounding gardens, an entire city block (it had formerly been the New York Orphan Asylum). Schwab could afford it since he was reputed to earn, in the days before income taxes, an annual salary of $1,000,000 a year. Unfortunately the mansion was not to survive New York's post–World War II building boom. Completed in 1906, it was demolished in 1948 and replaced by another Schwab House, this time a 16-story red brick human hive of a type more familiar to New Yorkers.

[2.] Row houses, 301–305 W. 76th St., 343–357 West End Ave., W side, and 302–306 W. 77th St. 1891. Lamb & Rich.

A varied and witty row which enlivens a whole blockfront of West End Avenue. Long may they reign.

Clarence F. True

Lower Riverside Drive, as the earliest area opened to improvement, was **slated to be filled with flats,** according to an 1899 account by a local architect and land developer, Clarence F. True. It was he, he stated, who recognized **the higher potential** of the area by **buying up** all available Driveside parcels below West 84th Street and **covering them** "with beautiful dwellings" of his own design. **Hardly typical** row houses (though built speculatively and employing party walls), **many** of these elegant mansion-residences **have survived.** Highly idiosyncratic in appearance, they are readily identified as being in **the True style** (characterized at the time as Elizabethan Renaissance): ornate roof lines, crow-stepped gables, bay, bow, and three-quarter-round oriels, and so on. Most are concentrated in these groupings:

[3.] True houses: [3a.] 40–46 Riverside Drive, 337 W. 75th St., 334–338 W. 77th St. **[3b.]** 74–77 Riverside Drive, 320–326 W. 80th St. **[3c.]** 81–89 Riverside Drive, 307–323 W. 80th St., 316–320 W. 81st St. **[3d.]** 105–107 Riverside Drive, 332 W. 83rd St. All 1890s. All by Clarence F. True.

[2.] Row house: 301 West 76th Street   **[4c.]** Row house: 307 W. 78th Street

[4a.] West End Collegiate Church and School, West End Ave., NE cor. W. 77th St. 1893. Robert W. Gibson. ★

It's easy to understand the generous use of **Dutch stepped gables** on this church's facade since the **roots of** the Reformed Church in America **lie in the Netherlands.** But don't draw hasty conclusions about the reintroduction of a style missing since the days of New Amsterdam. Here, along West End Avenue, McKim, Mead & White **had already built** such a Dutch-inspired house **as early as 1885** (demolished) and another one predating the church (not by McK, M & W) **still remains** at the northwest corner of West 78th Street.

Entered from the next block north is a new addition to the old school building:

[4b.] The Collegiate School (annex), 260 W. 78th St., bet. Broadway and West End Ave. 1968. Ballard, Todd & Assocs.

A **highly disciplined facade** that, because it faces north, rarely receives the sunlight necessary to show it off to best advantage. The student-designed mural that later **superimposed a sunrise** over the ground floor limestone wall also fails to provide the needed light.

[4c.] Row houses, 301–307 W. 78th St., and 383–389 West End Ave. 1886. Fredrick B. White.

Individualistic houses by an architect who died, shortly after their completion, at the untimely age of twenty-four.

[5.] Riverside Park, Riverside Dr. to the Hudson River bet. W. 72nd and W. 145th Sts. 1873–1910. Original design, Frederick Law Olmsted. New work, 1888. Calvert Vaux and Samuel Parsons, Jr. Completion, Frederick Law Olmsted, Jr. Reconstruction for Henry Hudson Parkway, 1937. Clinton F. Lloyd.

To the endless relief of stifled West Siders, this green ribbon of hills and hollows, monuments, playgrounds, and sports facilities **fringes some 50 blocks** of winding Riverside Drive, all the while **covering the now-freight-only rail line** in a tunnel below. One of its most complex parts is the **three-level structure** at West 79th Street: traffic circle at the top, masonry arcade and pedestrian paths surrounding a splendid, circular, single-jet fountain at the middle level, and, at the bottom, parking space for frequenters of the **79th Street Boat Basin.**

[6a.] 411 West End Avenue (apartments), SW cor. W. 80th St. 1936. George F. Pelham II.

Art Deco with touches of Corbusier-inspired ships' railings on the balconies and terraces near the top. Note how "drapes" of ornament cascade from some of the parapets (in stainless steel) and over the entrance (in cut stone).

[6b.] 307–317 West 80th Street (row houses), bet. West End Ave. and Riverside Dr. ca. 1890.

Gothickesque—not the Gothic Revival of earlier years nor the Collegiate Gothic of the 1920s—and **picturesque,** too. Note the stained glass over the doors and windows (except for No. 317, which has also been painted). These houses are in handsome company on both sides of the street.

[9a.] The Red House (apartment block)   [10b.] Church of SS Paul and Andrew

[7a.] All Angels' Episcopal Church, West End Ave., SE cor. W. 81st St. 1890. Samuel B. Snook of J. B. Snook & Sons. Altered, 1896. Karl Bitter Studio.

Turning the axis of this church **diagonally to the street grid** was a brilliant if subtle design decision which gave character to the intersection (at least until a less-subtle design decision gave it a superhuman television set as competitor across the way—see below). There is an intimate garden adjacent, created by the church's geometry, reached from West 81st Street.

[7b.] The Calhoun School Learning Center, 433 West End Ave., SW cor. W. 81st St. 1975. Costas Machlouzarides.

A **modern-day Gulliver** must have been here and left behind his giant-sized TV. And if one picture tube (along West End Avenue) isn't enough, another (along West 81st Street) has been provided **as a spare.** A more unsubtle and out-of-scale response to this urban-design challenge is hard to imagine. Fortunately (in the warm-weather months at least) maples provide **a green screen.**

[8.] 309–315 and 317–325 West 82nd Street (row houses), bet. West End Ave. and Riverside Dr. ca. 1892.

Two groups of Roman-brick-plus-brownstone-trimmed residences, **the first rich** in intricately formed roofs, dormers, chimney pots, finials, colonnettes; **the second more restrained** with handsome verdigris-colored cornices.

Mount Tom: Not in Massachusetts but along the Drive, a rocky protuberance in Riverside Park at West 84th Street. Edgar Allen Poe, who lived at 84th and Broadway in the summers of 1843 and 1844, found the height a special place from which to contemplate the Hudson.

[9a.] The Red House (apartments), 350 W. 85th St., bet. West End Ave. and Riverside Dr. 1904. Harde & Short.

A romantic 6-story masterpiece. Note the **dragon and crown** cartouche set up high into the brickwork. These talented architects **also designed** the **Studio Building** on West 77th Street and the **Alwyn Court Apartments** on West 58th Street.

[9b.] 316–326 West 85th Street (row houses), bet. West End Ave. and Riverside Dr. ca. 1895.

This group of six was designed as a unit. The stoop railings are only **one voluptuous example** of fine stone carving **everywhere abundant.**

[10a.] 530 West End Avenue (apartments), SE cor. W. 86th St. 1912. Mulliken & Moeller.

A representative West End Avenue example of the Renaissance palazzo adapted to high-rise living. **Fine masonry craftsmanship** in the early tradition.

[10b.] Church of St. Paul and St. Andrew (United Methodist)/originally **Church of St. Paul (Methodist Episcopal),** West End Ave. NE cor. W. 86th St. 1897. R. H. Robertson.

A **startling work** for the West Side or for the rest of the city for that matter. While other architects (including Robertson himself) were pursuing more-or-less faithful revival-styled churches, this work is in the imaginative vein of the French neo-Classicist architects **Claude Nicholas Ledoux** or **Étienne-Louis Boullée.** The octagonal corner tower is reminiscent of the fire tower which was once part of the **Jefferson Market** [see photograph, V Manhattan/Greenwich Village 28a]. St. Andrew's Church was on West 76th Street until 1937, when it merged with St. Paul's [see Broadway 13b.]

[10c.] St. Ignatius Church (Protestant Episcopal), 552 West End Ave., SE cor. W. 87th St. 1902. Charles C. Haight. Shrine (inside), 1926. Cram & Ferguson.

One of Haight's less-inspired works. Perhaps he decided that this site, adjacent to its already completed West 86th Street neighbor [see above] demanded a piece of background architecture. Thankfully these **churches and the row houses** that remain in the vicinity **combine** to keep West End Avenue from being **a monotonous apartment house canyon.**

[10d.] Cathedral Preparatory Seminary (Roman Catholic)/formerly **McCaddin-McQuick Memorial, Cathedral College**/originally **St. Agatha's School,** 555 West End Ave., SW cor. W. 87th St. 1908. Boring & Tilton.

Dignity personified in red brick and limestone.

[11a.] 560 West End Avenue (town house), NE cor. W. 87th St. 1890. Joseph H. Taft.

The pair of **bulbous protuberances** (like fleshy ears) are a curiosity in this house which once had **five similar neighbors** to the north. These were among the many West Side projects of W. E. D. Stokes, developer of the Ansonia Hotel.

[11b.] 565 West End Avenue (apartments), NW cor. W. 87th St. 1937. H. I. Feldman.

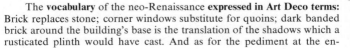

The **vocabulary** of the neo-Renaissance **expressed in Art Deco terms:** Brick replaces stone; corner windows substitute for quoins; dark banded brick around the building's base is the translation of the shadows which a rusticated plinth would have cast. And as for the pediment at the entrance, its 1930s stand-in is a small, streamlined, stainless steel cornice. The canvas and pipe canopy in this apartment, as in too many others, is a practical but unrelated afterthought.

[11c.] 562 West End Avenue (apartments), bet. W. 87th and W. 88th Sts. E side. 1913. Walter Haefli.

An effective use (or reuse) of Doric columns to flank the entrance.

[12a.] Congregation B'nai Jeshurun, 257 W. 88th St., bet. Broadway and West End Ave. 1918. Henry B. Herts and Walter Schneider. **[12b.] Community Center,** 270 W. 89th St. 1928. Henry B. Herts. Louis Allan Abramson, associate.

The synagogue's facade is **a Moorish fantasy** from the waning days of an era when important Jewish houses of worship were designed in an exotic Byzantine/Romanesque mode. The community center one block north is considerably more restrained.

[13b.] Soldiers' and Sailors' Monmt.   **[15.]** The Cliff Dwellers' Apartments

[13a.] Yeshiva Chofetz Chaim/originally **Isaac L. Rice Residence, "Villa Julia"/**then **S. Schinasi Residence,** 346 W. 89th St., SE cor. Riverside Drive. 1901. Herts & Tallant. Additions and alterations, 1906–1948.

Though at one time the Drive was lined with **numerous freestanding mansions,** today only this maroon brick villa and one other survive. Isaac L. Rice, a successful **industrial pioneer** in the field of electric storage batteries [see E Bronx 27.] commissioned this residence and named it Villa Julia **for his wife,** the prescient founder of the Society for the Suppression of Unnecessary Noise. In 1908 the building was sold to **S. Schinasi,** a member of the well-known **cigarette manufacturing firm** of Schinasi Brothers. That same year Schinasi's brother, Morris, was awaiting completion of *his* freestanding mansion on the Drive, at West 107th Street. Curiously **it is these two** Schinasi mansions **that survive** [see 22.].

[13b.] Soldiers' and Sailors' Monument, in Riverside Park, Riverside Dr. at W. 89th St. 1902. Stoughton & Stoughton and Paul E. M. Duboy.

A marble monument to the Civil War dead modeled on the **Choragic Monument of Lysicrates** in Athens (a favorite history of architecture quiz question). Duboy was the architect of that other West Side monument, the Ansonia Hotel [see Broadway 8a.].

[14.] Joan of Arc Statue, in Joan of Arc Park, Riverside Dr. at W. 93rd St. 1915. Anna Vaughn Hyatt Huntington, sculptor. John V. Van Pelt, architect.

The Maid of Orleans, **in full armor,** stands in her marching steed's stirrups, looking heavenward **with sword held high.** The bronze equestrian sculpture sits atop a granite pedestal containing **stones from Reims Cathedral** and from the old tower at Rouen in which Joan was imprisoned and tried. The space between the two-way portion of the Drive and the one-way part is officially Joan of Arc Park (1.578 acres).

No doubt this statue and its park influenced the naming of the junior high school built a quarter of a century later, to the west [see Broadway 31b.].

[15.] Cliff Dwellers' Apartments, Riverside Dr., NE cor. W. 96th St. 1914. Herman Lee Meader.

An **odd building** predating the **Art Deco interest in Mayan motifs.** It is known primarily for the **naturalistic frieze** of mountain lions, rattlesnakes, and buffalo skulls. They symbolize the life of the Arizona cliff dwellers but serve to tie these prehistoric people to **Manhattan's modern cliff dwellers.** All in all, **an underrated facade.**

Woodman, Spare That Tree: In 1837 an old elm on the property of the Stryker's Bay Mansion—which then stood on a hill northeast of the 96th Street viaduct—was to be cut down. George Pope Morris, journalist and poet (1802–1864) was inspired to pen the poetic exhortation which saved the tree.

[17.] 838 West End Avenue (apts.)   **[18.]** Master Apartments, W. 103rd St.

[16a.] Carrère Memorial, Riverside Park at W. 99th St. 1916. Thomas Hastings.

A small granite-balustered terrace at a lower level of the park entrance contains a graffitied, **barely noticeable** memorial tablet to one of New York's **great architects,** John Merven Carrère (of Carrère & Hastings) who was killed in an automobile accident in 1911.

[16b.] Firemen's Memorial, Riverside Dr. at W. 100th St. 1913. Attilio Piccirilli, sculptor. H. Van Buren Magonigle, architect.

Courage and *Duty* guard this large pink marble monument to **"soldiers in a war that never ends."** Embedded in the plaza is a bronze tablet to the fire horses who also served in that "war."

[17.] 838 West End Avenue (apartments), SE cor. W. 101st St. 1914. George & Edward Blum.

Intricate vinelike forms make large terra-cotta tiles into damask, thus embellishing this building and recalling a **Sullivanesque** approach to ornament.

[18.] Master Apartments/formerly **Master Institute of United Arts and Riverside Museum/**formerly **Roerich Museum,** 310 Riverside Dr., NE cor. W. 103rd St. 1929. Helmle, Corbett & Harrison and Sugarman & Berger.

Built to house a school, museum, auditorium, and restaurant in a residential hotel. Artist **Nicholas Roerich,** whose museum was once located within the building [see 21, its current location], seems to have been responsible for the idea of **shading the building's brickwork** from a purpled base to a pale yellow top. Wind-borne soot has all but eradicated the color change—but a similar color palette is still visible elsewhere on the West Side [see Central Park West 5.].

Book browsing: The Upper West Side is book lover's country—not chain bookshops, you understand, but the personal kind run for an involved clientele, repeat customers who can be expected to drop in often. Browsing is encouraged at each. Listed in an uptown direction:

Radius, 240 W. 72nd St. W of Broadway. Telephone: 874-0670. Hardback and softcover with emphasis on newly published books, art and architecture, and service to the customer. You will find hot coffee in the back.

Big Apple, 282 Columbus Ave., bet. W. 73rd and W. 74th Sts. Telephone: 874-1568. Specializes in poetry and such small presses as Paddington, Swallow, and Grey Fox.

Eeyore's, 230 W. 82nd St. E of Broadway. Telephone: 362-0634. A small shop with a consuming passion for children's books, a wide range of which are stocked.

Murder Ink, 271 W. 87th St. W of Broadway. Telephone: 362-8905. A specialty shop for intrepid mystery fans where the owner's cats are draped languidly over the merchandise. The shop sponsors evenings of sherry and discussion with fellow buffs and authors.

Barqu, 216 W. 89th St. E of Broadway. Telephone: 362-0706. Used books from a wide range of subject areas.

New Yorker, 250 W. 89th St. W of Broadway. Telephone: 799-2050. Around the corner from the theater of the same name and upstairs through the minuscule newspaper and magazine shop street level entry. Little magazines and periodical esoterica downstairs; a wide selection of largely soft-cover books upstairs.

Woman Books, 201 W. 92nd St. at Amsterdam Ave. Telephone: 873-4121. As the name indicates, a bookshop for those with a feminist inclination.

Dolphin, 2743 Broadway bet. W. 105th and W. 106th Sts. Telephone: 866-8454. An honest-to-goodness used book store displaying a knowledgeable and selective taste: books on New York City have an honored place.

[19.] Riverside-West 105th Street Historic District, generally along Riverside Dr. bet. W. 105th and W. 106th Sts., plus some of both sides of W. 105th St. bet. West End Ave. and Riverside Dr. District designated, 1973. ★

Paris o'er the Hudson. Enjoying a magnificent setting overlooking the city's great river is this **enclave** of French Beaux Arts town houses. Executed between 1899 and 1902 the houses were designed by four different architectural firms: Janes & Leo, Mowbray & Uffinger, Hoppin & Koen, and Robert D. Kohn. Of special interest is

[19a.] New York Buddhist Church and American Buddhist Academy, 331–332 Riverside Dr., bet. W. 105th and W. 106th Sts. No. 331, formerly **Marion Davies Residence,** 1902. Janes & Leo. No. 332, 1963. Kelly & Gruzen. Included within the historic district. ★

The heroic-size bronze statue of **Shinran-Shonin** (1173–1262), founder of a Buddhist sect, became a *local* landmark before the official designation of the area by the city. A church and social center occupy the two buildings.

[20.] Statue of Franz Sigel, Riverside Dr. at W. 106th St. 1907. Karl Bitter, sculptor. W. Welles Bosworth, architect of base.

A placid equestrian statue of a commander of the Union Army during the Civil War. In the **iconography of equestrian sculpture** the steed's four legs touching terra firma mean the hero died a peaceful death: in the case of Sigel (1824–1902) he resigned his military commission in 1865 and then published and edited a German language newspaper.

[21.] Nicholas Roerich Museum, 319 W. 107th St., bet. Riverside Dr. and Broadway. Telephone: UN 4-7752.

Permanent collection of the work of Nicholas Roerich, prolific artist, designer, explorer, and philosopher. Architectural landmarks of his native

Russia were the subjects of many of Roerich's early paintings, and he contributed to the design of 310 Riverside Drive [see 18.].

[22.] The Children's Mansion (school)/originally **Morris Schinasi Residence,** 351 Riverside Dr., NE cor. W. 107th St. 1909. William B. Tuthill. ★

A marble freestanding château by **the architect of Carnegie Hall.** See the other remaining freestanding mansion on the Drive, also once owned by a Schinasi [13a.].

[23.] Assumptionist Provincial House/formerly **America Press Building,** 329 W. 108th St., bet. Broadway and Riverside Drive. ca. 1900. Thomas Graham. Altered, 1902. Horgan & Slattery.

Actually two double-width row houses joined to form one, internally interlocked residence for a Roman Catholic order. **Spiffy from bottom to top:** ornate limestone carving, a fine cool-red brick, and verdigris copper detail in the dormers of the mansard roof.

BROADWAY AND ENVIRONS

From 70th Street to Cathedral Parkway (110th Street)

Broadway's route in this area dates from the laying out, in 1703, of the **Bloomingdale Road,** named for the hamlet of **Bloemendael** located around today's West 105th Street. At first the road measured only about 33 feet across but, as its popularity as a route increased, so did its width. In 1849 it was widened to 75 feet and for the first time given the name **Broadway.** By 1868, its width was 150 feet, its course was straightened between 59th and 155th Streets, and it was renamed **The Boulevard,** by which it was known until 1899 when its earlier name was once again bestowed: **Broadway.**

[1a.] The Dorilton (apartments), 171 W. 71st St., NE cor. Broadway. 1900. Janes & Leo. ★

If you are walking uptown along Broadway this robust mansarded Beaux Arts masterpiece **will begin to prepare you** for the even greater Ansonia a few blocks north.

[1b.] Blessed Sacrament Church (Roman Catholic), 152 W. 71st St., bet. Columbus Ave. and Broadway. 1921. Gustave Steinback.

The facades of sanctuary and rectory are brilliantly modeled to exploit this **difficult midblock site** into which the church **has been squeezed.** Though the stonework is **not heavily tooled** there is a **vigorous interplay** of volume, void, and silhouette which is just enough for the **shallow viewing space** of a typically narrow 60-foot-wide side street. The rose window is in striking reds and blues. See Steinback's other churches, too.

[2a.] Christ Church (Protestant Episcopal), 211 W. 71st St., bet. Broadway and West End Ave. 1890. Charles C. Haight. Addition, 1925. **[2a.] Rectory.** 1893. Rose & Stone.

This Romanesque Revival church of orange brick with terra-cotta trim is unusual in that its nave runs **parallel to West 71st Street.** Actually the church was once entered from Broadway—but in 1925 the congregation **sold that valuable frontage** and **demolished the east end** of the church (including a glorious octagonal bell tower) thus confining its activities to the remaining **Greek Cross portion.** The eight-story office building visible at the corner has occupied the site since.

[2b.] Originally **The Godmothers League/**now **The Children's Day Treatment Center and School,** 255 W. 71st St., bet. Amsterdam and West End Aves. 1950. Sylvan Bien.

Architects had come to realize that the **International Style was victor** in the post–World War II **battle of styles** but for some it was difficult to adjust to that new vision. This modest work **reflects the struggle.** The Godmothers League began around World War I as an agency helping to save abandoned babies—today its efforts are directed to the needs of emotionally disturbed children.

[2c.] 274, 276 West 71st Street, bet. Amsterdam and West End Aves.

Shades of Philadelphia architect **Frank Furness' excesses** are visible in the window projected over the entrance of this **Queen Anne maverick.**

[3.] 232 West End Avenue (residence), bet. W. 70th and W. 71st Sts. 1887. E. L. Angell. New facade, 1904. Herts & Tallant.

The lack of a projecting stoop on West End Avenue's narrow sidewalk failed, in this unusual case, to cheat the residents of the **ceremony of ascending** its steps to wave a parting greeting. The unusual facade results from a turn-of-the-century alteration **stylistically reminiscent** of other Herts & Tallant efforts of the period such as the Aguilar Branch Library [H Manhattan/East Harlem 14.].

Harsenville: Named for the family which settled it, this hamlet was one of a number strung along what is today Broadway. Its rustic charm attracted a number of French émigrés fleeing their Revolution's Reign of Terror. Louis Philippe (later king of France) lived near here, as did statesman Charles Maurice de Talleyrand-Périgord.

Noto (jewelry and objects), 245 W. 72nd St. W of Broadway. Telephone: 877-7562.

Wit, taste, and an appreciation of the unusual are the hallmarks of this **eclectic shop** uprooted from an earlier midtown location. Great for gifts.

[4a.] Sherman Sq. kiosk (1907 photo)   **[8a.]** Ansonia Hotel: enduring delight

[4a.] Sherman Square IRT Subway Entrance, Broadway and Amsterdam Ave. S of W. 72nd St. 1904. Heins & La Farge.

Although their black-painted cast-iron and glass **subway kiosks are all gone,** this and a few **other masonry structures** by these architects **still remain** [see WC Brooklyn/Boerum Hill 9a., for example]. Clearly the number of subway riders who use this entrance today exceeds its designers' modest expectations. As a result, **its future is clouded.**

[4b.] Verdi Square and Giuseppe Verdi Statue, Broadway, Amsterdam Ave., and W. 73rd St. 1906. Pasquale Civiletti, sculptor. Scenic landmark. ★

This small green honors the great Italian composer. At the base of the marble statue are **life-size figures** of four characters from Verdi's operas, *Aïda, Falstaff, Otello,* and *La Forza del Destino.*

Spaced Gallery, 165 W. 72nd St. E of Broadway. Telephone: 787-6350.

An art gallery devoted to displaying the *graphic* talents of architects as well as of those whose subject is architecture. One flight up and invariably worth a visit.

[5.] Formerly **The Earlton (studios),** 118 W. 72nd St., bet. Columbus and Amsterdam Aves. 1915. Buchman & Fox.

A West Side phenomenon, **one of a group of studios** developed by builder Edward W. Browning. [See 6a. and Central Park West 12b. and 14.].

[6a.] **126 West 73rd Street (studios),** bet. Columbus and Amsterdam Aves. 1915. Buchman & Fox.

Déjà vu? No, this is **another** of those slender white West Side ghosts [see 5., and Central Park West 12b. and 14.].

[6b.] **Sherman Square Studios,** 160 W. 73rd St., bet. Columbus and Amsterdam Aves. 1929. Tillion & Tillion.

Casement-windowed apartments specially soundproofed for the needs of professional musicians, and long before Lincoln Center became a neighbor. Though weathered by time, the architects' names can be found **on the cornerstone** to the west.

[7.] **Central Savings Bank,** 2100 Broadway, NE cor. 73rd St. 1928. York & Sawyer, architects. Decorative iron work, Samuel Yellin Studio. ★

Founded in 1859 as the "German Savings Bank in the City of New York," a name dispensed with during the anti-German period of World War I, the banks' board members **chose the architects of the Federal Reserve Bank** [see Financial District 74.] to create its new West Side office. They chose well, for this is **a miniature Federal Reserve,** one of the West Side's **noblest and most imposing** edifices.

[8a.] **Ansonia Hotel,** 2108 Broadway, bet. W. 73rd and W. 74th Sts. W side. 1904. Graves & Duboy. ★

In the words of the city's Landmarks Commission, the Ansonia's effect is one of **"joyous exuberance profiled against the sky."** The collaboration between a demanding developer, **W. E. D. Stokes**—he was descended from **Phelps Dodge** on his paternal side and **Ansonia Brass & Copper** on his maternal—and an architect steeped in the forms of Parisian apartment buildings, Paul E. M. Duboy, seems to have had **a magic result.** The Ansonia is one of New York's architectural gems. Judging from the "guest list" of this apartment hotel, a **galaxy of important figures** thought so too: Enrico Caruso, Arturo Toscanini, Lily Pons, Florenz Ziegfeld, Theodore Dreiser, Sol Hurok, and Igor Stravinsky, to name but a few.

[8b.] Originally **The Level Club (of the Masonic order)/**then **Hotel Riverside Plaza,** 253 W. 73rd St., bet. Broadway and West End Ave. 1926. Clinton & Russell.

This neo-Romanesque verging upon Art Deco facade retains the **secret signs and symbols** required by the original client, a **Masonic** organization.

[9a.] **161–169 West 74th Street** and **301–309 Amsterdam Avenue,** NE cor. W. 74th St. 1886. Lamb & Rich.

Early West Side row housing which, though altered at the corner, still conveys a clear sense of the area's initial development. **No. 161** has been **least touched** by change.

[9b.] **153, 155, 157, 159 West 74th Street,** bet. Columbus and Amsterdam Aves. 1887. James Brown Lord.

More early development. No. 153 has been **surgically separated** from its **Siamese twin**—note the half remainder of its foliate cartouche. No. 159 winds up, after alteration, with two stoops: the original used as a planting bed, and a new one which makes **a floral semicircle** out of the original wall ornament.

[10a.] **Beacon Theater,** 2124 Broadway, bet. W. 74th and W. 75th Sts. E side. 1928. Walter Ahlschlager.

Skip the exterior. It's the **opulent interior,** second only to that of Radio City Music Hall, that counts. **Go in,** even if you must attend a Miss Bare America contest.

[10b.] Astor Apartments, 2141–2157 Broadway, bet. W. 74th and W. 75th Sts. W side. ca. 1905. Clinton & Russell.

One of William Waldorf Astor's apartment developments. He was a major landowner in this community.

[11.] 254 West 75th Street, bet. Broadway and West End Ave. ca. 1885.

Three arches make this an extra special row house with great brick-, stone-, and ironwork. The blocks between Broadway and West End in the 70s hold **many row house surprises.** Take a stroll and keep your eyes peeled.

[12.] Berkley Garage/originally **The New York Cab Co. (stables),** 201 W. 75th St., NW cor. Amsterdam Ave. ca. 1889.

Three great Romanesque Revival half-round arches on 75th Street **trumpeted entrance** to the horses and drivers using this onetime multistory stable. Its visual links to the Marshall Field Wholesale Store (1887. H. H. Richardson) in Chicago are clear.

[13a.] Riverside Memorial Chapel (funeral home), 331 Amsterdam Ave., SE cor. W. 76th St. 1925. Joseph J. Furman and Ralph Segal.

Designed using a **limited palette** of browns and dull reds. It is **a soothing result,** executed in tapestry brick, matte terra cotta, stucco, and a gray slate roof.

[13b.] West Side Institutional Synagogue/originally **St. Andrew's Methodist Episcopal Church,** 120 W. 76th St., bet. Columbus and Amsterdam Aves. 1889. Altered, 1958.

One approach to converting a church to a new use following a severe fire. The only part recommended is **what remains of the original.** St. Andrew's merged with St. Paul's on West 86th and West End in 1937 [see Riverside Drive 10b.].

[14a.] The Evelyn (apartments), 101 W. 78th St., NW cor. Columbus Ave. 1886. Emile Gruwé.

A big, bold symphony in reds: brick with all kinds of wonderful unglazed terra-cotta flourishes.

[14b.] West 78th Street, bet. Columbus and Amsterdam Aves. ca. 1885–1890.

A modern public school and other regrettable "improvements" have emasculated what was once **one of the wittiest streetscapes** of the Upper West Side. The wit was due, in part, to the works of **Rafael Guastavino** [of arch vaulting fame—see H Manhattan/Morningside Heights 3a.] who designed the **fun-filled** red and white quintet, Nos. 121–131, and Nos. 118–134 across the way (all completed in 1886). The client for these rows, Bernard S. Levy, allowed Guastavino, then a recent emigrant from Catalonia, to introduce his system of **"cohesive construction"** in No. 122 making it an entirely fireproof row house. (Levy himself lived at No. 121 between 1886 and 1904.) Don't fail to look at the **curious stepped balusters** along the stoops in front of Nos. 157–167. Their unusual forms and shadows are a favorite among architectural photography buffs.

[15.] The Apthorp Apartments, 2101–2119 Broadway to West End Ave., W. 78th to W. 79th Sts. 1908. Clinton & Russell. ★

This unusually grand, handsome, richly ornamented limestone Renaissance Revival building occupies an entire block. The individual entrances are reached through **high vaulted tunnels** and **a large interior court** with a fountain in its center. Probably the best of the surviving Astor apartments in New York.

[16.] Mt. Neboh Congregation, 130 West 79th St., bet. Columbus and Amsterdam Aves. 1928.

Another West Side synagogue which has **borrowed heavily from the Byzantine style** with one special distinction: the facade is intentionally roughened so as to call special attention to its seeming antiquity.

[17.] Hotel Lucerne, 201 W. 79th St., NW cor. Amsterdam Ave. 1904. Harry B. Mulliken.

Distinguished detailing in **plum-colored brownstone** and brick. The deeply modeled, banded entrance columns, adopted from the Baroque, are great.

[18.] First Baptist Church, Broadway, NW cor. W. 79th St. 1892. George Keisler.

Resembling the life that swirls past it on this busy Broadway corner, this church's eclectic facade too is **busy, restless,** and **polyglot.**

[14a.] The Evelyn (apartments) (detail)   **[19.]** West 80th St. Community Center

[15.] The Apthorp Apartments: elegant ironwork enhances the arched entrance

[19.] West Eightieth Street Community Child Day Care Center, 223 W. 80th St., bet. Amsterdam Ave. and Broadway. 1972. Kaminsky & Shiffer.

The hoped-for **creative plaything** on the scale of side street architecture didn't make it despite good intentions.

Zabar's (gourmet foods), 2245 Broadway, bet. W. 80th and W. 81st Sts. Telephone: 787-2000.

Larger-than-life horn of plenty: wall-to-wall food—and on weekends, wall-to-wall people, as well. What makes Zabar's remarkable is its phenomenal variety of foodstuffs from all over the world. It combines the delights of the Jewish "appetizing store" with charcuterie, salumeria, and Wurstgeschäft, adds an array of cheeses, coffees, and breads, and offers a selection of cooking utensils and cookbooks, too. Quintessential New York.

[20a.] Hotel Endicott, Columbus Ave., bet. W. 81st and W. 82nd Sts. W side. ca. 1889. Edward L. Angell.

The durability of red brick and matching terra-cotta ornament still preserves **a sense** of what this hotel once was—both a fashionable and a comfortable place to stay. Since World War II it has fallen into **a state of disrepair, architecturally** and **socially.**

[20b.] West 81st Street, bet. Columbus and Amsterdam Aves. ca. 1888–1892.

Not the most stylish of West Side side streets any more but filled with **a rich assortment** of facade detail that will reward those who crane their necks. **Blast those landlords** who think a coat of grey deck paint can erase the excesses of another era. It merely **dulls the delight.**

[26a.] The Sudeley (apts.), 76 W. 85 St.   **[28.]** The Belnord Apartments: entry

[21.] Marvin Gardens (restaurant), 2274 Broadway, bet. W. 81st and W. 82nd Sts. 1975. Haroutiun Derderian.

A crisply designed restaurant with a popular bar. Though the name derives from the game of **Monopoly,** the design is too cool to carry the connection any further. Telephone: 799-0578.

[22.] Holy Trinity Roman Catholic Church, 213 W. 82nd St., bet. Amsterdam Ave. and Broadway. ca. 1900.

Drawing upon many stylistic influences and bearing a dome upon a band of **clerestory oculi windows,** this modestly located church—it doesn't occupy a corner site—has intricate brickwork and white-glazed terra cotta.

Information Kiosk: On West 83rd Street just west of Broadway is a freestanding community-sponsored information kiosk located along the edge of the sidewalk. It's not exactly Parisian but it's good news.

[23.] Engine Company 74, N.Y.C. Fire Department, 120 W. 83rd St., bet. Columbus and Amsterdam Aves. 1888. Napoleon LeBrun & Sons.

Can't you see the horses **charging out of the doorway** pulling a bright red and polished brass fire engine **billowing white clouds** of water vapor? The horses and steam engine are gone but the iron jib **for hoisting hay** is very much in evidence overhead.

[24.] Louis D. Brandeis High School, 151 W. 84th St., bet. Amsterdam and Columbus Aves. 1965. Charles Luckman Assocs.

Compared with nearby postwar public and junior high schools, this was an improvement. But compared with the West Side's ebullient row housing it's a bore.

[25.] Broadway Fashion Building, 2315 Broadway, SW cor. W. 84th St. 1931. Sugarman & Berger.

Long before the curtain walls of metal and glass descended upon midtown, this curtain wall of metal and glass *and* **glazed terra cotta** came to grace Broadway. The retail signs at street level, however, are a disgrace.

[26a.] Apartments, 74, 76, and 78 W. 85th St., SE cor. Columbus Ave. 1895.

The facades of this trio are ordinary for this period. But the foliate carving in the entrances—particularly SUDELEY at No. 76—is exquisite and intact. **Try to make out the letters** incised over No. 74. Are they a Roman numeral? Do they spell CLIIION? Is the word CLIRION? Or is this a rare example of **the inadequate speller** turned stone carver?

[26b.] The Brockholst (apartments), 101 W. 85th St., NW cor. Columbus Ave. 1890. John G. Prague.

Endearingly dark and craggy for rockface stone and brick, this behemoth is **laced with delicate ironwork** fire escapes. It announces its name in floral terra-cotta relief.

[27.] West-Park Presbyterian Church, Amsterdam Ave., NE cor. W. 86th St. 1890. Henry F. Kilburn.

A fine Romanesque Revival edifice in brownstone. Were it and its tall tower not overwhelmed by the grim apartment building to the north, it would be one of the West Side's loveliest landmarks.

[28.] Belnord Apartments, Amsterdam Ave. to Broadway, W. 86th to W. 87th Sts. 1908. H. Hobart Weekes. ★

Like its smaller cousin the Apthorp [see 15.] this massive Renaissance Revival structure is built around a garden court.

Items [29.–31c.] lie within the **West Side Urban Renewal Area,** treated separately on pages 205–208.

[29.] West 87th Street, bet. Columbus and Amsterdam Aves.

Some **fine row houses** in this block: Nos. 133 and 147 look as though different architects designed the successive tiers; Nos. 137 and 139 make an intriguing combination; No. 159 has a black, weathered cornice that might **almost be a Louise Nevelson** sculpture.

[30a.] Playground, Public School 166 Manhattan, E of school, 132 W. 89th St., bet. Columbus and Amsterdam Aves. 1967. M. Paul Friedberg & Assocs., landscape architects.

A playground jointly operated by the Board of Education and the city's Department of Parks and Recreation, it was commissioned by the **Vincent Astor Foundation** as a radical departure in playground design.

[30b.] Claremont Stables, 175 W. 89th St., bet. Columbus and Amsterdam Aves. ca. 1889.

These **high-rise stables** owe their survival to their use as domicile for horses used on **Central Park's bridle paths.** Riding a steed from here to the park offers a special architectural experience: **looking** at the row house facades **from a horse's back,** a vantage point more commonly available to 19th-century viewers. We're told **it makes a difference.**

In the late 1960s it was proposed that the stable be removed to make way for urban renewal, a replacement to be made available as part of **an enormous new mounted police complex** to be built within Central Park. Park preservationists **raised an outcry** against tampering with the park; others pointed out that horses had always been a **part of that scene.** The preservationists prevailed, thus canceling the park project; the forces of urban renewal ran out of money, thus extending the life of these stables. Rent a horse. Telephone: SC 4-5100.

St. Gregory the Great: The east lot line wall of the Church of St. Gregory the Great, 144 West 90th Street, is the surface upon which sculptor Earl Nieman developed a heroic relief of the saint, visible some distance away.

Souen Macrobiotic (restaurant), 2444 Broadway, bet. W. 90th and W. 91st Sts. Telephone: 787-1110.

An inexpensive Japanese restaurant (no liquor) which dotes on the minimal.

The Library (restaurant), 2475 Broadway, at W. 92nd St. Telephone: 799-4860.

The books are real and in abundance but hardly worth filching. The atmosphere they create, however, is friendly. Omelettes and other light dishes are available from a wide menu as are drinks from the sometimes overly boisterous bar. Moderate prices.

[31a.] 125–139 and 151–159 West 93rd Street (row houses), bet. Columbus and Amsterdam Aves. ca. 1895.

Two groups of Queen Anne facades in red and gray. Curiously restrained for this style.

[31b.] Junior High School 118 Manhattan, Joan of Arc Junior High School, 154 W. 93rd St., bet. Columbus and Amsterdam Aves. 1941. Eric Kebbon.

Reflecting relatively high land values, this school was built upward rather than laterally. Almost mimicking in limestone relief the high-rise character of the building is **a luxuriant mythic beanstalk** emerging from an urn; it "grows" between the entrance doors.

[31c.] Iglesia Adventista Del Septimo Dia/originally **The Nippon Club,** 161 W. 93rd St., bet. Columbus and Amsterdam Aves. 1912. John Van Pelt.

A **serene facade** in a curiously different style, perhaps influenced by the work of the Chicago School. The deep overhanging cornice on crisply modeled console brackets gives the facade **a convincing terminus** against the sky.

 [32.] At Our Place (restaurant)/originally **Cleopatra,** 2527 Broadway, near W. 95th St. 1970. Gamal El Zoghby.

An ultra-sophisticated earth-colored and dark blue exterior is left behind as you enter a stepped, mirrored, carefully modulated (and somewhat claustrophobic) interior full of architectural and culinary surprises. When the restaurant changed names it was decided to reuse as many as possible of the bold sans-serif sign letters in the new name, hence the one chosen—it required only the fabrication of a new "U."

[33.] Pomander Walk, 261–267 W. 94th St. and 260–266 W. 95th St. bet. Broadway and West End Ave. 1922. King & Campbell.

Pomander Walk is a tiny street in the **London suburb of Chiswick.** It first came to New York as the name of a stage play. This charming **double row** of small town houses arrayed along a north-south pedestrian byway is **modeled after the stage sets** used in the New York production. Note the metalwork over the entrance.

 [34.] East River Savings Bank, 743 Amsterdam Ave., NE cor. W. 96th St. 1927. Walker & Gillette.

A Classical temple inscribed with **exhortations to the thrifty.** Note how the fluted columns come right down to the sidewalk rather than observing the tradition of terminating on a stepped base.

[35.] Holy Name of Jesus Church (Roman Catholic), Amsterdam Ave., NW cor. W. 96th St. 1891. T. H. Poole.

This **tight-chested ungiving German-Gothic-influenced facade** is forbidding. **Enter** for a more pleasing architectural experience—particularly the beamed ceiling.

[36.] St. Michael's Church (Protestant Episcopal), 225 W. 99th St., NW cor. Amsterdam Ave. 1891. Robert W. Gibson.

A church complex: tall tower, rounded apse, arcades, parish house, rectory, and a quiet garden, all darkened by years of soot. Inside are mosaics and Tiffany glass.

[37.] Midtown Theater, 2626 Broadway, bet. W. 99th and W. 100th Sts. 1933. Boak & Paris.

A design **more appropriate to a 1930s interior** made into a weatherproof facade through the imperviousness of glazed terra cotta. Art Deco.

[38.] 2641 Broadway and 225 West 100th Street, NW corner. 1870s.

Amidst the masonry canyons of Broadway, West End Avenue, and the side streets stands this **wood frame holdout** from the West Side's **"frontier days."**

[39.] Straus Park and Memorial Fountain/originally **Bloomingdale Square,** Broadway and West End Ave., at W. 106th St. 1914. H. Augustus Lukeman, sculptor. Evarts Tracy, architect.

Named Bloomingdale in 1907 not for the midtown department store (pure coincidence) but for the old settlement here of **Bloemendael** (flower dell in Dutch). The *Titanic* disaster, in 1912, claimed the lives of **Macy's owners** Isidor and Ida Straus who had lived overlooking the triangle on the northwest corner of West 106th Street. The park was **renamed in their honor** and the monument completed two years later.

[31c.] Seventh Day Adventist Church   **[1.]** Century Apartments: Art Deco

[40.] The Manhasset (apartments), 301 W. 108th St. and 300 W. 109th St. along Broadway, W. side. 1904. Janes & Leo.

Crass commercialism has **concealed the elegance** of the original stores but up above, **oh what attention to detail!** As if unable to control their creativity the architects topped their building off with a story-high banded brick ribbon, then a **hefty cornice,** and above that a smooth light-colored brick expanse with a two-story mansard above that! Imagine Broadway's appearance **if it had more** of these flanking it.

CENTRAL PARK WEST/THE "PARK BLOCKS"

While the Upper West Side is a place of contrasts and **one in constant flux,** Central Park West, if not the so-called "park blocks," has generally maintained **an unflagging fashionable quality**—at least up through 96th Street. The park blocks began to be converted into rooming houses following World War II, a pattern turned around somewhat by **the rising desirability of brownstone living** among upwardly mobile middle-class families and by the "singles" of the West Side. In the northern stretch the Urban Renewal Act **helped save its row house stock** on the park blocks above 86th Street—their health can be seen to fall off the greater their distance from Central Park. Olmsted and Vaux's **great green space,** one of the **major attractions** in the settlement of the West Side, still acts as an important **touchstone** to the community's health.

This precinct begins above Columbus Circle and includes Central Park West up to 96th Street and the park block corridor up to 86th Street. North of 86th Street lies the West Side Urban Renewal Area [which see].

[1.] Century Apartments, 25 Central Park West, bet. W. 62nd and W. 63rd Sts. 1931. Office of Irwin S. Chanin; Jacques Delamarre, architectural director.

Like the Majestic [see 13.] by the same architects, it makes some **pleasant gestures toward modern style.** The name recalls a lavish and unprofitable **Century Theater,** designed by Carrère & Hastings, which stood on the site from 1909 until razed for the apartments.

[2.] New York Society for Ethical Culture, 2 W. 64th St., SW cor. Central Park West. 1910. Robert D. Kohn, architect. Estelle Rumbold Kohn, sculptor. ★

Considered in the architectural press of its time to be quite the best piece of Art Nouveau architecture yet designed in this century, it has lost prestige since then. **Warning:** It is not as exuberant as Hector Guimard's Parisian efforts nor those in Brussels by Victor Horta, nor does it match the quality of Otto Wagner's or Josef Hoffmann's Viennese works. It is, however, **a clear departure** from the Beaux Arts.

[3.] The Prasada (apartments), 50 Central Park West, SW cor. W. 65 St. 1907. Charles W. Romeyn and Henry R. Wynne.

Banded limestone columns, monumental in scale, and other freely interpreted Classical ornaments **embellish but do not quite animate** this bulky apartment facade.

 [4a.] Holy Trinity Lutheran Church, Central Park West, NW cor. W. 65th St. 1903.

A **refreshing break** in Central Park West's phalanx of boxy apartment blocks. The kaleidoscope-like rose window and the **delicate flèche** over the crossing are notable.

[4b.] Estelle R. Newman City Center, Jewish Guild for the Blind, 15 W. 65th St., bet. Central Park West and Columbus Ave. 1971. Matthew J. Warshauer.

A **horizontally striped box** (dark glass and metal strip windows alternating with cream-colored precast concrete spandrels) projects from an orange salt-and-pepper glazed brick utility core.

[5.] 55 Central Park West (apartments), SW cor. W. 66th St. 1930. Schwartz & Gross.

Art Deco evolved through a carefully studied **modulation of brick planes** and boldly fluted ornament. If the sun seems brighter at top than at bottom, look more carefully at the brick color. It changes subtly.

[6a.] Congregation Habonim (synagogue), 44 W. 66th St., bet. Central Park West and Columbus Ave. 1957. Stanley Prowler and Frank Faillance.

A stained-glass cube set forty-five degrees to itself and its neighbors along the street. Its setback permits a better understanding of the old armory next door.

[6b.] Originally **First Battery Armory, New York National Guard**/then **102nd Medical Battalion Armory**/now **American Broadcasting Companies (television studios),** 56 W. 66th St., bet. Central Park West and Columbus Ave. 1901. Horgan & Slattery. Altered, 1978. Kohn Pederson Fox.

Lots of **stylistic bravado** here but only **in the front ranks** (as a sidelong glance from the east will reveal). The reserves are utilitarian and dull (never having been meant to be seen), in contrast with the **elegantly attired architectural forces** leading the march: a fun-filled facade which might as well be one of those intricate European cardboard scale models. Nevertheless, a delight!

[6c.] Originally **St. Nicholas Skating Rink**/then **St. Nicholas Arena**/now **American Broadcasting Companies Broadcast Operations and Engineering,** 57 W. 66th St., bet. Central Park West and Columbus Ave. 1896. Ernest Flagg and Walter B. Chambers.

All those layers of stucco and two tones of battleship gray try, but fail, to hide this onetime pleasure palace's post–Chicago World's Fair ornament. Though the row of wood flag poles has been **snipped off** at the roof line, the bases of their shafts are still visible, embraced by **charming swirls** of masonry and wrought iron.

Studio Street: The park block of West 67th Street is a haven for those who like either studio living or vicariously experiencing the arts by living amongst artists: there are no fewer than six studio buildings on the block. Among them:

[7.] Hotel des Artistes (apartments), 1 W. 67th St., bet. Central Park West and Columbus Ave. 1918. George Mort Pollard.

The **fanciful facade** clearly shows the balconied studios behind it. An early tenant, Howard Chandler Christy, painted a pin-up girl (his specialty) to decorate the cozy **Café des Artistes** on the first floor. An **all-time roster** of tenants of the elaborate (and lavish) spaces would also include Isadora Duncan, Norman Rockwell, Alexander Woolcott, Noel Coward, Fannie Hurst, and former mayor John V. Lindsay.

[8a.] Swiss Home of the Swiss Benevolent Society, 35 W. 67th St., bet. Central Park West and Columbus Ave. 1905. John E. Schlarsmith.

The scale of the red and white parts and the whole are harmonious. The forms **calm your anxiety** about being a stranger in a far-off land.

[8b.] 39–41 West 67th Street (studios), bet. Central Park West and Columbus Ave. 1907. Pollard & Steinam.

Four stacks of bay windows **zip up the street facade** of this tall narrow studio building: kind of an early curtain wall, they are of sheet metal, not masonry.

Tavern-on-the-Green: The entrance to this once-again remodeled eating-drinking-dancing spot, built around Central Park's 1870 sheepfold, is at 67th Street and Central Park West. Expensive. Telephone: 873-3200.

[6b.] Orig. 1st Battery Armory NYNG   **[10a.]** Hebrew Union College/J.I.R.

[9a.] Second Church of Christ, Scientist, Central Park West, SW cor. W. 68th St. 1900. Frederick R. Comstock.

Boring save for its difficult-to-see **green domes**—best seen from the edge of the park.

[9b.] 14 West 68th Street (town house converted to apartments), bet. Central Park West and Columbus Ave. 1895. Louis Thouvard.

A **somber brownstone box** whose entrance is from an adjacent and **compensating green space** open to the street. Imagine when the house had a view clear into Central Park. . . .

[10a.] Hebrew Union College–Jewish Institute of Religion/originally **The Free Synagogue,** 40 W. 68th St., bet. Central Park West and Columbus Ave. 1923. S. B. Eisendrath & B. Horowitz. **[10b.] Stephen Wise Free Synagogue,** 30 W. 68th St. 1941. Bloch & Hesse.

Somber and unobtrusive. Today's college building was the sanctuary until the new one was begotten in 1941. An **important center** of the Reform Jewish movement.

[11.] Congregation Shearith Israel (synagogue), 99 Central Park West, SW cor. W. 70th St. 1897. Brunner & Tryon. ★

The newest home of New York's **oldest Jewish congregation,** founded downtown in what was then New Amsterdam by Spanish and Portuguese immigrants in 1655. A connected **"Little Synagogue"** reproduces the Georgian style of the congregation's first real synagogue, built in 1730; it contains many furnishings used in that building.

It is unclear why the congregation settled for this stuffy design back in 1897. Perhaps it was **a compromise** between the **glitter of "White City"** architecture of the 1893 Chicago World's Fair and the **dignified needs** of a religious building. The three venerable Shearith Israel cemeteries which resist the march of progress in Manhattan belong to this congregation [see index for locations].

[15.] Dakota Apartments (1920's)   **[20a.]** The Kenilworth (apts.) entry

[12a.] Row houses, W. 71st St., bet. Central Park West and Columbus Ave. 1890s.

What a **terrific selection!** No. 24 is especially fine with its unusual stoop, cupids at its cornice, concave shell-molded lintels over the topmost windows. Nos. 26, 28, and 30 show that handsome houses **come in threes:** an elegant russet color scheme (brick, stone, terra cotta, and the cartouches) and wide doors that must certainly have invited the purchase of expansive furnishings. Note how the imitation cement plaster "stonework" **has been tooled to disguise** the removal of No. 30's stoop. On the stoops of Nos. 32–40 a gentle separation of the balusters as they reach the sidewalk **subtly signals you** to enter. Across the street Nos. 33–39 offer both **hungry** and **satiated** lions' heads to decorate the doorway keystones. An architectural feast.

[12b.] Formerly **The Bromley (studios),** 31 W. 71st St., bet. Central Park West and Columbus Ave. 1916. Robert L. Lyons.

A tall studio building faced on its narrow street frontage by white glazed terra cotta. One of a West Side breed [see 14. and Broadway 5. and 6a.].

 [13.] Majestic Apartments, 115 Central Park West, W. 71st to W. 72nd Sts. 1930. Office of Irwin S. Chanin; Jacques Delamarre, director of architecture.

One of four twin-towered apartment buildings that make the skyline along Central Park West a unique visual treat. This **streamlined building** has wide banks of windows that extend around its sides. The much-copied brickwork patterns and futurist forms were designed by **sculptor René Chanbellan.**

[14.] 42 West 72nd Street (studios), bet. Central Park West and Columbus Ave. 1915. Buchman & Fox.

Another lanky white studio tower [see 12b.].

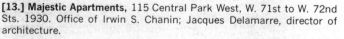

[15.] Dakota Apartments, 1 W. 72nd St., NW cor. Central Park West. 1884. Henry J. Hardenbergh. ★

The city's first luxury apartment house. Designed for **Singer Sewing Machine's heir** Edward S. Clark, it dominated Central Park before the park drives were paved. **A prestige address,** particularly for those in the arts, since the days when this part of the city was thought to be out in the Dakota Territory.

[16a.] 15A–19 and 41–65 **West 73rd Street (row houses),** bet. Central Park West and Columbus Ave. 1885. **[16b.]** 101 and 103 **West 73rd Street (apartments and row house),** NW cor. Columbus Ave. 1879. All by Henry J. Hardenbergh.

These houses are a product of **another collaboration** of the client and architect of the Dakota Apartments, Clark and Hardenbergh. (Regrettably their **delicate beauty** is **overwhelmed** by midblock apartment houses.) Originally there were two long rows bracketing Columbus Avenue with larger flats' houses at the corners. Only the one to the west remains, from an era prior to the Dakota's construction.

[17.] The Langham (apartments), 135 Central Park West, W. 73rd to W. 74th Sts. 1905. Clinton & Russell.

A **ponderous prism** till you look at the roof line where a simple cornice has been so elaborated with ornament and ornate dormers that **it sparkles with light.**

[18.] 18–52 West 74th Street (row houses), bet. Central Park West and Columbus Ave. 1904. Percy Griffin.

A **phalanx of eighteen** neo-Georgian row houses fills the block's south side and bears such names as Park Terrace, Riverside, and Hayden Manor. **Built to compete with apartment buildings** of the time, which were growing in popularity, these 25-foot-wide, 17- to 19-room houses **each boasted** four or **five bathrooms** and an electric elevator. It is easy to understand their conversion to school and nursing home uses.

[19.] San Remo Apartments, 145–146 Central Park West, W. 74th to W. 75th Sts. 1930. Emery Roth.

The twin-towered silhouette shows **finialed Roman temples against the sky**—the giant building is the home of many well-known New Yorkers.

[20.] Central Park West–76th Street Historic District, Central Park West bet. W. 75th and W. 77th Sts., including W. 76th St. W to Nos. 51 and 56, and 44 W. 77th St. District designated, 1973. ★

In addition to the buildings on Central Park West and West 77th Street, covered below, the historic district encompasses a **variety of row housing** along West 76th Street dating between 1889 and 1900. The earliest, Nos. 21–31, is by architect **George M. Walgrove** in which he uses neo-Grec trim and a newly fashionable rock-faced surface treatment. The most recent, Nos. 8–10, is Upper East Side-like in its neo-Baroque **town house flamboyance** by John H. Duncan, designer of Grant's Tomb and Brooklyn's Soldiers' and Sailors' Memorial Arch at the entrance to Prospect Park. Works by other architects fill in both sides of the block: **G. A. Schellenger, Schickel & Ditmars,** and **Cleverdon & Putzel.** The architecture is decorative, the designation abounding with references to garlanded brackets, Herculean heads, elegant cartouches, and spiral colonnettes.

[20a.] The Kenilworth (apartments), 151 Central Park West, NW cor. W. 75th St. 1908. Townsend, Steinle & Haskell. Included within the historic district. ★

A cubical russet brick **wedding cake** topped by a grand convex mansard roof. The pastry chef's whipped-cream efforts are executed in limestone in the interests of posterity.

[20b.] Universalist Church of New York and Parish House/formerly **Church of the Divine Paternity/**originally **Fourth Universalist Society,** Central Park West, SW cor. W. 76th St. 1898. William A. Potter. Included within the historic district. ★

Oxford University on Central Park West: this church sports a neo-Gothic tower reminiscent of **Oxford's Magdalen College.** In its early years **Andrew Carnegie** could be seen attending church here, along with other prominent New Yorkers.

 [20c.] New-York Historical Society, 170 Central Park West, bet. W. 76th and W. 77th Sts. Central portion, 1908. York & Sawyer. North and south wings, 1938. Walker & Gillette. ★ Included within historic district. ★

Resembling a Parisian bibliothèque, this is both an **important museum** and **a research library for American and local history.** It is almost certain that **a witty and informative exhibition** on some aspect of the city's history will be on display when you visit. Call 873-3400 for hours and exhibit information. Among the library's vast holdings are the McKim, Mead & White files and the 432 original watercolors of Audubon's *Birds of America.*

[20d.] The Studio Building, 44 W. 77th St., bet. Central Park West and Columbus Ave. 1909. Harde & Short. Included within the historic district. ★

The sites for this and adjacent apartments along West 77th Street were already built upon with row housing when the **abundant north light** provided by the openness of Manhattan Square across the street encouraged redevelopment. Though a great deal of terra cotta was removed in 1944, the **lacy tapestry** of the neo-Gothic facade is still **breathtaking.**

Hungry? During the 1970s, Columbus Avenue's many empty storefronts were rescued from oblivion by a serendipitous group of enterprising restaurateurs. Between Manhattan Square and Lincoln Center is arrayed a wide variety of eateries on both sides of the avenue. Enjoy.

[21a.] American Museum of Natural History, Manhattan Square, Central Park West to Columbus Ave., W. 77th to W. 81st St. General plan and first wing, 1872–1877. Calvert Vaux and J. Wrey Mould. West 77th Street wings, 1892–1898. J. C. Cady & Co., and 1899. Cady, Berg & See. Columbus Avenue wing and powerhouse, 1908. Charles Volz. Additions, 1924, 1926, 1933. Trowbridge & Livingston. Theodore Roosevelt Memorial, Central Park West, 1936. John Russell Pope, architect. Roosevelt statue and heroic figures on attic. James Earle Fraser, sculptor. Animal relief, James L. Clark, sculptor. ★

Conceived by Vaux and Mould, "Architects of the Department of Public Parks," to be **the largest building on the continent.** The museum trustees had other thoughts and V&M's wing, the first, is now **only barely visible** from Columbus Avenue. The best parts of the building are Cady's Romanesque Revival efforts on West 77th Street, though Pope's pompous Central Park West facade, the Roosevelt Memorial, is the one that gets the publicity photos and therefore **seems to be** the important one. Exhibits within range from ponderous to exhilarating. See the **Hall of Minerals and Gems,** 1976, and **The People Center,** 1973. For hours, programs, and admission contributions, call 873-4225.

[21b.] Hayden Planetarium, American Museum of Natural History, W. 81st St., bet. Central Park West and Columbus Ave. 1935. Trowbridge & Livingston.

This verdigris-copper dome perched on a brick box combines a clear expression of the **astonomical sky theater** inside with **an ambiguity of forms** which have come to be associated with **the mysteries of Middle Eastern theology.** For program title, performance times, ticket prices, call 873-8828.

[22.] The Beresford (apartments), 1 and 7 W. 81st St. and 211 Central Park West, NW cor. 1929. Emery Roth.

Named for the hotel it replaced, the Beresford is another of Central Park West's twin-towered luxury apartment buildings **but with a plus:** it has a twin-towered silhouette not only from the lawns of Central Park to the east but from those of Manhattan Square directly to the south, a result of **three** Baroquoid projections above its roof.

[23a.] Congregation Rodeph Sholom (synagogue), 7 W. 83rd St., bet. Central Park West and Columbus Ave. 1930. Charles B. Meyers. **[23b.] Day School,** 12 W. 84th St. 1976. Michael Rabin Assocs.

The synagogue is an inflated but restrained facade in the neo-Romanesque style. The school, reflecting a seventies fad of deeply recessed windows and sloped brick reveals, is a reconstruction of an earlier group of row houses.

[24.] 65, 67, and 69 West 83rd Street (row houses), and **71 West 83rd Street (apartments),** bet. Central Park West and Columbus Ave.

These row houses are exuberant Queen Anne in style, planned so that No. 69 carries their recessed facades out to the building line where **the group curtsies** to No. 71, a restrained **exquisitely detailed** apartment house. Note the bronze balcony railings and the curious angle the west wall makes with the street—the result of **a rambling property line** from the West Side's earliest farming era.

[25.] Church of St. Matthew and St. Timothy (Protestant Episcopal), 26 W. 84th St., bet. Central Park West and Columbus Ave. 1970. Victor Christ-Janer.

Following a disastrous fire in the late 1960s, this **radical, cast-in-place concrete edifice** was substituted. The bold simplicity of the exterior does not prepare you for **the carefully modulated circumlocutory entry** and what you find within: a rich combination of white (plaster) and gray (concrete) surfaces set off by warm natural wood pews, metallic organ pipes, and a richly colored mosaic crucifix and fabric hangings. **A fine work.**

[26.] 241 Central Park West (apartments), NW cor., W. 84th St. 1930. Schwartz & Gross.

Subtly colored glazed terra cotta **sprouts** (literally) from the brickwork of this Art Deco structure. The West 84th Street side is beautifully modeled at street level.

[27a.] 53–75 West 85th Street (row houses), bet. Central Park West and Columbus Ave. ca. 1885.

This long row conceals none of its charming red and white Queen Anne style excesses, except for Nos. 69 and 71, which were covered over by a nine-foot-deep olive green glazed brick addition which is **truly an affront** to all sensibilities.

[27b.] Rossleigh Court, 1 W. 85th St., NW cor. Central Park West. 1906. **[27c.] Orwell House**/formerly **Hotel Peter Stuyvesant**/originally **Central Park View,** 257 Central Park West, SW cor. W. 86th St. 1905. Both by Mulliken & Moeller.

Twin apartment buildings occupying the full Central Park West blockfront. They are of **a disarming and cheery purple brick** set off to advantage by limestone trim.

Renewal Area: Central Park West's frontages between West 87th and 97th Streets and the park blocks in that stretch all lie within the official boundaries of the West Side Urban Renewal Area. CPW's apartment buildings (with the exception of No. 325) did not directly benefit from the designation, but many of the side street brownstones, converted into single-room-occupancies and rooming houses, did. (No. 235, scheduled to be demolished, was saved, upgraded, and turned into a co-op.) [For the side streets, therefore, see the precinct called West Side Urban Renewal Area; for the continuation of CPW's buildings uptown to West 97th, see below.]

[28a.] The Walden School /originally **The Progress Club,** 1 W. 88th St., NW cor. Central Park West. 1904. Louis Korn. Story added. Holden McLaughlin & Assocs. **[28b.] Andrew Goodman Building (addition to west).** 1974. Edgar Tafel & Assocs.

The **desire to relate** the addition's facade to that of the now-cornice-less Classical Revival style original building **is commendable.** The result, on the other hand, misses the mark.

[29.] The St. Urban (apartments), 285 Central Park West, SW cor. W. 89th St. 1904. Robert L. Lyons.

CPW's only *single-towered* apartment building. Its tower is splendidly crowned by dome and cupola, gray shingles and verdigris trim.

[30.] The Eldorado (apartments), 300 Central Park West, W. 90th to W. 91st Sts. 1931. Margon & Holder.

The northernmost of the twin-towered apartment houses along Central Park West. Art Deco metalwork embellishes **the base** (subtle bronze reliefs) and **the towers** (Flash Gordon finials).

[31.] The Ardsley (apartments), 320 Central Park West, SW cor. W. 92nd St. 1931. Emery Roth.

Mayan influences appear in this Art Deco apartment building, particularly in the modeling of the upper stories. In addition, there is a quality almost like that of **inlaid furniture** in the ribbons of contrasting brick which enrich the surfaces of the upper facades. And at the street level, closest to the eye, are precast exposed aggregate terrazzo reliefs in subtle colors and forms. Compare this with the San Remo [see 19.] completed by the same firm the previous year.

[32.] Columbia Grammar and Preparatory School, 5 W. 93rd St., bet. Central Park West and Columbus Ave. 1907.

What's interesting here is the neo-Classical frieze adorning this building below its **surprisingly modern-looking** deep, flat cornice.

[33.] 336 Central Park West (apts.)   **[34.]** 1st Church of Christ, Scientist

[33.] 336 Central Park West (apartments), SW cor. W. 94th St. 1929. Schwartz & Gross.

This 16-story apartment is **crowned with terra-cotta reminiscences** of Egyptian-styled **papyrus stalks**—not to be confused with the 19th-century Egyptian Revival style of which very few examples remain in the city. The tapestry brick enriches the viewer's experience closer to eye level.

[**The West 95th Street park block,** a diverting detour, is described in West Side Urban Renewal Area 4a.]

[34.] First Church of Christ, Scientist, 1 W. 96th St., NW cor. Central Park West. 1903. Carrère & Hastings. ★

The architects of the Beaux-Arts-styled New York Public Library at Fifth Avenue and 42nd Street here flirt with the forms of **Nicholas Hawksmoor's** great Baroque churches in London. **Exciting.**

WEST SIDE URBAN RENEWAL AREA

The blocks between West 87th and West 97th Streets, from Amsterdam Avenue to Central Park West, sheltered 40,000 residents in 1956 when this area's **acute social and physical decline** indicated **a need for public action.** In a series of moves the district, one of the **most densely populated** in the country, was designated the West Side Urban Renewal Area and plans were drawn for change.

The concepts that emerged were **radically different** from those of earlier renewal efforts. Exploitation of the highest possible rental scales was abandoned. **Clearance and rebuilding** from scratch, once the *only* redevelopment tools, were combined with **rehabilitation and renovation,** particularly of the basically sound side street brownstone row houses. Steps were taken to insure an economic and social mix within the district by providing both **separate** low-rent projects and also low-rent families **within** middle-income developments. And, finally, the plan called for **phased development** from West 97th Street south to encourage the relocation of on-site tenants. The final plan as amended called for 2,500 low-income units, 5,421 middle-income units, and 151 luxury units. In addition, 485 **brownstones were to be saved** and renovated.

The results are most visible architecturally along Columbus Avenue, along both sides of which stand the new high-rise construction. The side streets have been **more subtly upgraded,** largely behind the facades, in backyards and in added street trees or street embellishment, as on West 94th Street.

One thing is clear. The renewal effort, **though not without its critics,** has done much **to turn around the decline** of this part of the West Side.

Unlike the manner in which we have pursued the other West Side precincts in this guide, this one proceeds from north to south to reflect the north to south phasing of the redevelopment plan. The first project, Park West Village, actually **predates** these plans (it is within another urban renewal area, West Park) but is included first, both as **a logical part** of the urban renewal story and as an example of the techniques **which had been abandoned.** Start at West 96th Street and Amsterdam and then continue over to Columbus and proceed south. [Also see Broadway 29.–31c. for other entries which lie within the official urban renewal area.]

[1.] Park West Village, Amsterdam Ave. to Central Park West, W. 97th to W. 100th Sts.

This large and banal housing development was built in the aftermath of the 1957 Manhattantown **urban renewal scandal.** Developers had acquired six blocks of tenements at **a reduced price** from the city under the federal urban renewal program. Instead of developing the site they sat tight for five years collecting rents, neglecting repairs, and inventing ingenious schemes **to exploit their unhappy tenants.** Some say these disclosures marked the beginning of N.Y.C. construction czar Robert Moses' loss of power.

West Side Urban Renewal Area.

[2a.] New Amsterdam (apartments), 733 Amsterdam Ave., bet. W. 95th and W. 96th Sts. E side. 1971. Gruzen & Partners.

Buff brick, which this building uses in profusion, seems always to be an architectural bugaboo—very difficult, because of its blandness, to use well. This is **a striking exception.** The concrete balconies, made private by tall side walls, exposed concrete floor slabs, and floor-to-floor window modules, make for a strongly designed tower. Unfortunately, too much is going on at street level.

[2b.] RNA House, 150 W. 96th St., bet. Columbus and Amsterdam Aves. 1967. Edelbaum & Webster.

A concrete beehive of a facade.

[3.] Columbus House, 95 W. 95th St., along Columbus Ave. bet. W. 95th and W. 96th Sts. E side. 1970. Horace Ginsbern & Assocs.

A **highly articulated** concrete structure with expansive balconies sandwiched between deep protruding columns. (Note that the balconies don't begin until the ninth floor.) The sidewalk level detailing—standing-seam sloped metal roofs for both the tower and the adjacent one-story shops—is **the best** of any of the renewal area's new works.

[4a.] West 95th Street, bet. Central Park West and Columbus Ave.

Diversely styled row houses, luxuriant trees, and lots of care make this **one of the loveliest** of the "park blocks." A leisurely walk will reveal delightful touches: sculpted griffins and cherubs, fine lanterns, recently added but simply designed metal guards around the street tree pits, **a magnificent twisted vine** against No. 27's bow window, the fussy concern (competition?) with appliqué house numbers. The **rhapsodic** architectural **exercise in circles and arcs** at the entrances, balconies, and stoops of Nos. 6 and 8 is a small delight. The quality of this block is attributable in many respects to the influence of the West Side Urban Renewal Area in which it is included.

[4b.] West 95th Street, bet. Columbus and Amsterdam Aves.

Potentially one of the West Side's finest streets, certainly from an urban design viewpoint. It is good to see evidence of **restoration underway and completed;** less so that which seems temporarily halted. Of particular interest is No. 143, a wider-than-usual single house ornamented in the Gothic mode but with neo-Renaissance proportions.

[4c.] Congregation Ohab Zedek (synagogue), 118 W. 95th St., bet. Columbus and Amsterdam Aves. 1926. Charles B. Meyers.

Intricate terra-cotta ornament enriches the tall Byzantine arch which **sums up** this synagogue's facade.

[4d.] West Side Manor, 70 W. 95th St., along Columbus Ave., bet. W. 94th and W. 95th Sts. E side. 1968. Gruzen & Partners.

A long prism perpendicular to Columbus Avenue. The avenue side is buff brick and bland; both side street facades are recessed balconies and bland. Bland.

[4e.] Jefferson Towers, 700 Columbus Ave., bet. W. 94th and W. 95th Sts. W side. 1968. Horace Ginsbern & Assocs.

Alternating the arrangement of balconies—separated on odd floors and joined on even floors—creates **a powerful rhythm** in the facade, **too powerful.**

Experimental street improvements: The two blocks of West 94th Street between Central Park West and Amsterdam Avenue are the site of an early 1970s experiment in modulating the width of city side streets by interrupting the endless rows of parked cars with brick paved projections, suitably greened with trees or shrubs, that neck the asphalt roadway width appreciably.

[5.] Gottesman Playground, W. 94th St., bet. Columbus and Amsterdam Aves. N side. 1970. M. Paul Friedberg & Assocs., landscape architects.

Imaginative design is only one of many ingredients for the success of an urban playground. **Time weighs heavily on teen-agers' lives** and translates into destructive behavior in an unsupervised outdoor space like this—unsupervised because, as a privately sponsored facility, it was to have been the ward of the adjacent cooperative apartment corporation. Maintenance and supervision proved to be too expensive, hence a bombed-out playground.

[6a.] Strykers Bay Houses (apartments), 689 Columbus Ave., bet. W. 93rd and W. 94th Sts. E side. 1967. Holden, Egan, Wilson & Corser.

Red brick, corner windows, and rounded brick penthouses enclosing elevator machinery and a water tank: it resembles the best of public housing of the forties and fifties rather than urban design of the seventies. Low-key and comfortable, nevertheless. The smaller building on West 94th Street, almost square in plan, has more satisfying proportions.

[6b.] Columbus Park Towers, 100 W. 94th St., along Columbus Ave. bet. W. 93rd and W. 94th Sts. W side. 1967. Ballard, Todd & Snibbe.

Rough-board-formed concrete balcony balustrades add what design distinguishes this brownish brick slab.

[7a.] Columbus Manor (apartments), 70 W. 93rd St., along Columbus Ave. bet. W. 92nd and W. 93rd Sts. E side. 1971. Liebman & Liebman.

A tall "Buffter" Keaton, pork pie hat and all.

[7b.] Leader House (apartments), 100 W. 93rd St., along Columbus Ave., bet. W. 92nd and W. 93rd Sts. W side. 1972. Dominick Salvati.

This tower appears severe to the eye, as though its sponsors believed that **severity in appearance** would automatically **lead to economical monthly rents.** It doesn't. This is a buff brick and reinforced concrete building which looks as if the brick walls hold up the exposed concrete—actually **it's just the other way.**

[8.] 74 West 92nd Street (apartments), N.Y.C Housing Authority, and Goddard Riverside (New) Community Center, 647 Columbus Ave., bet. W. 91st and W. 92nd Sts. E side. 1965.

A lackluster Housing Authority building in an out-of-the-ordinary (but thankfully not buff) dark brown brick.

[9.] 5 West 91st Street (apartments), bet. Central Park West and Columbus Ave. 1972. Horace Ginsbern & Assocs.

A modest six-story work which evidences in the development of its facade a clear desire **to enrich the streetscape without heroic efforts** or **lavish budget.** It does.

[10.] Trinity School, 139 W. 91st St., bet. Columbus and Amsterdam Aves. **[10a.] Main Building.** 1894. Charles C. Haight. **[10b.] East Building**/originally **Parish House, St. Agnes Chapel (Protestant Episcopal).** 1892. William A. Potter.

Founded in 1709. Among the many interlocked buildings this school occupies are the Anglo-Italianate brownstone Main Building, the **wonderful Romanesque Revival remnant** of an otherwise demolished Trinity Parish outpost (St. Agnes Chapel), and the podium of Trinity House.

[10c.] Trinity House (apartments) and Trinity School addition, 100 W. 92nd St., along Columbus Ave., bet. W. 91st and W. 92nd Sts. W side. 1969. Brown, Guenther, Battaglia, Seckler.

At grade an extension of adjacent Trinity School; neatly stacked apartments in a tower above. An intricately fashioned facade which reminds you of a **Chinese wood block puzzle:** pull out the magic piece and the whole thing will come apart.

[11.] Play area, Stephen Wise Towers, N.Y.C. Housing Authority, W. 90th to W. 91st Sts., midblock bet. Columbus and Amsterdam Aves. Play area only. Richard G. Stein & Assocs., architects. Constantino Nivola, sculptor.

A modern horse fair for West Side cowboys and cowgirls is the feature of the play area subsidized by the J.M. Kaplan Fund to enliven this otherwise pedestrian public housing. It sees some heavy use, but, alas, there is no ASPCA to protect horses cast in concrete.

 [12.] St. Martin's Tower (apartments), 65 W. 90th St., along Columbus Ave. bet. W. 90th and W. 91st Sts. E side. 1971. Ifill Johnson Hanchard.

Design through the arrangement of balconies, this time in repetitive groups of four: two pairs, one above the other, and then a space—a kind of **architectural square dance.** The facade details are well handled, but the massing of the building is clunky. The sculptural concrete element at the West 90th Street corner is refreshing until you realize it conceals (not too well) a ventilation grille from the cellar.

[13.] Turin House Apartments, 609 Columbus Ave., bet. W. 89th and W. 90th Sts. E side. 1972. Holden, Yang, Raemsch & Corser.

Pink concrete block walls (the construction dollar bought less in the '70s than in the '60s) instead of brick give this spartan building a deceiving scale. So do the two-story-high fenced-in "sky lobbies" on the side street facades. The barred cages on the avenue facade are fire exits between adjacent duplex apartments, the new building code's substitute for the more traditional fire escape.

[14.] Heywood Tower (apartments)/originally **Heywood Broun Plaza,** 175 W. 90th St., along Amsterdam Ave., bet. W. 90th and W. 91st Sts. E side. 1974. Gerald Karlan.

Monotonous.

[15.] Glenn Gardens (apartments), 175 W. 87th St., NE cor. Amsterdam Ave. 1975. Seymour Joseph.

Two wings form this **housing complex.** The tall one on the avenue is banal but the lower slab on West 88th Street is interesting.

Now that you've reached the south edge of the renewal area you've noticed boarded-up buildings and numerous rubble-strewn lots. These are the price of renewal, particularly in the context of bureaucratic city, state, and federal agencies pitted against demanding and outspoken local community groups. Eventually the debates may conclude and the renewal effort can be carried through to completion.

MANHATTAN VALLEY

A new event in Manhattan's **usually predictable** gridiron plan occurs at West 100th Street. It is here, between Central Park West and Columbus Avenue, that a new north-south thoroughfare is born, **Manhattan Avenue,** which strikes out northward across Cathedral Parkway into Harlem. As it moves north, the topography it covers **begins to drop** (as does the economic level of the community), and this falling off of the terrain has given rise to the **unofficial naming** of the area as Manhattan Valley. For the purposes of the guide we have defined it as being bordered by West 100th Street and Cathedral Parkway (West 110th Street) and by Central Park West and Amsterdam Avenue.

[1.] Association Residence for Women/originally **Home for Respectable Indigent Females,** 891 Amsterdam Ave., bet. W. 103rd and W. 104th Sts. 1881. Richard Morris Hunt.

Vacated in 1975, this institution, once open only to women who had not "lived as servants," **may be demolished** if an alternate use (and budget) is not found. Its red brick forms and its busy, dormered and gabled roof lines are **a visual asset** to the neighborhood.

[2.] Grace United Methodist Church/originally **Grace Methodist Episcopal Church,** 131 W. 104th St., bet. Columbus and Amsterdam Aves. 1905. Cady, Berg & See.

The corner sites were taken by the time this **midblock church** was built. The housing project's green space across the way gives it air and the light necessary **to illuminate** its orange Roman brick.

[3a.] West End Presbyterian Church, 325 Amsterdam Ave., NE cor. W. 105th St. 1891. Henry Kilburn.

Romanesque Revival but restrained—not Richardsonian at all. The tall delicately striped brick corner tower marks the intersection well. Note the **refined ornament** to which terra cotta lent itself—almost damask, but of a scale demanded of architecture.

[3b.] Public School 145 Manhattan, The Bloomingdale School, 150 W. 105th St., bet. Columbus and Amsterdam Aves. 1961. Unger & Unger.

Bright vermillion column caps and a concrete entrance canopy reminiscent of **an angel's wings** highlight this school's facade.

[3c.] St. Gerasimos Greek Orthodox Church, 155 W. 105th St., bet. Columbus and Amsterdam Aves. 1951. Kokkins & Lyons.

A design which **refuses to abandon old traditions** but arrives nevertheless at a strong composition in limestone and orange brick.

[4.] Manhattan Avenue (row houses), bet. W. 104th and W. 106th Sts. ca. 1888.

The row houses along both sides of most of this two-block stretch **are quite charming** and somewhat reminiscent of the much finer group along Convent Avenue in the Hamilton Heights Historic District.

[5.] Towers Nursing Home/originally **New York Cancer Hospital,** 2 W. 106th St., SW cor. Central Park West. 1887. Charles C. Haight. ★

A **castellated palace** with **squat circular towers,** a tall chapel and a handsome arcaded porch facing the park. This was the first hospital in the nation devoted exclusively to the care of cancer patients. In recent years it has seen service as a nursing home, but **its future is clouded.**

[5.] Orig. New York Cancer Hospital   **[6.]** Cathedral Parkway Houses (apts.)

[6.] Cathedral Parkway Houses (apartments), 125 W. 109th St., bet. Columbus and Amsterdam Aves., through to Cathedral Pkwy. 1975. Davis, Brody & Assocs. and Roger Glasgow.

Two enormous **zig zag shaped** towers occupy opposite corners of this midblock, hilly site; between them courses a private, terraced, open space which leaps from level to level, street to street. The towers, **cousins** to Davis, Brody's **Waterside, Yorkville and Ruppert, and Riverpark** in the Bronx, are here more self-consciously articulated in plan and in massing to **minimize the impact** of their massiveness **upon the smaller scale** of the adjacent community. The site was formerly occupied by **Woman's Hospital.**

CP

CENTRAL PARK

This great work of art, the *granddaddy* of American landscaped parks, was named a **National Historic Landmark** in **1965.** Better still, for the sake of its eternal preservation, it is now a "scenic landmark," so designated by the **New York City Landmarks Preservation Commission.** This latter designation, happily, has *teeth* (whereas the national one is largely honorific and hopeful). Many believe that *this* park and the **Brooklyn Bridge** are the two greatest man-made contributions to New York City.

But who made this 840-acre (larger than Monaco) masterpiece possible in the center of New York City? One of the first was poet **William Cullen Bryant,** who, in **1844,** called for a large, public pleasure ground (at that time, Washington Square was considered uptown). After landscape architect **Andrew Jackson Downing** appealed for a park the idea caught on and both mayoralty contestants made it a promise in the **1850** campaign. The winner, Ambrose C. Kingsland, kept his word, and the Common Council took action.

The site was then physically unprepossessing: *"A pestilential spot where miasmic odors taint every breath of air,"* one report concluded. But it was available. Land was acquired (1856) for $5,500,000, and surveyed by **Egbert L. Viele.** Clearing began the next year: squatters and hogs were forcibly removed, often with the aid of the police; bone-boiling works and swill mills were torn down, swamps were drained, and the omnipresent Manhattan schist was blasted.

Venerable trees, planted at Olmsted & Vaux's direction, shade wooded paths

The first Board of Park Commissioners, helped by a committee including poet **William Cullen Bryant** and writer **Washington Irving,** decided in **1857** that an open competition should determine the park's design.

Greensward, so named by winners **Frederick Law Olmsted** and **Calvert Vaux,** won out among the **33** designs submitted. It was a simple, uncluttered plan, calling for a picturesque landscape: glade, copse, water, and rock outcroppings. Bridges (each individually designed by **Vaux**) separated footpaths, bridle paths, and the carriage drives (which were curved to prevent racing). The four sunken transverse roads for crosstown traffic were revolutionary.

Ten million horse cartloads of stone, earth, and topsoil were moved in or out of the site as *Greensward* became an actuality. It took nearly **20** years (the time it took to build most of a French cathedral in the Middle

Ages), but, long before completion, the park became the place for the rich and poor to promenade, to see and be seen. Today it is even more the playground for New Yorkers; for some a place to enjoy nature, for many the only country they have ever seen, for others a magnificently designed **Garden of Eden** to ease the strains of city living; and most recently a place of amateur gambling, gamboling, and beer-drinking for citizenry from all boroughs.

Central Park is the forecourt and front garden to the residential slabs and towers of Central Park **South,** Central Park **West,** newly named Central Park **North,** and **Fifth Avenue** (otherwise Central Park East). At the southeast or Plaza corner the surrounding towers make romantic reflections in its waters (for the postcard maker), and enjoy its great space, a happy symbiosis for both.

Invasions

Despite continuing threats of preposterous intrusions, the original plan was closely followed until the age of the automobile and active sports. In 1912 the gravel drives became asphalt, and two new entrances were cut through on Central Park South. Permanent tennis courts were then constructed. The *first* paved playground, the **Heckscher,** appeared in **1926;** others followed. By the 1950s large structures had sprung up, all partially financed by philanthropists: The **Wollman Memorial Rinks,** the **Delacorte Theater,** the **Children's Zoo,** and the **Lasker Pool-Rink:** some worthy additions, others vulgar and ugly intruders.

SOUTH AND NORTH

By topography and design the park falls into two sections. The large "pastoral" south is by far the more familiar, but the north, mostly neglected, is well worth a visit in its contrasting wild picturesqueness: a worthiness best savored in groups by day (avoided totally by dusk or dark) for personal security. The following two tours are meant to serve only as an introduction to these sections.

Walking Tour A: Conservatory Water (at East 72nd Street and Fifth Avenue) to Grand Army Plaza (59th Street and Fifth Avenue) or the Zoo. Arrive via 68th Street Station of the Lexington Avenue IRT Subway; Madison or Fifth Avenue buses.

Enter at Fifth Avenue and 72nd Street (this is **Inventors' Gate,** one of Vaux's eighteen named gates piercing the park's wall). Detour to the south to view the delightful **East 72nd Street Playground** (1970. Richard Dattner & Assocs.) [1.]. Turn back north, crossing the park drive, and bear left past the **Pilgrim Memorial** (1885. John Quincy Adams Ward, sculptor) [2.]. Note the pilgrim's spectacular bronze boots. Descend **Pilgrim Hill** to the **Conservatory Water [3.],** a formal neo-Renaissance concrete basin, named for the conservatory (greenhouse) promised but unbuilt on its eastern shore. Model boats for rent at the **Alice H. and Edward A. Kerbs Memorial Boathouse** (1954) [4.] are usually sailing here (races April through October mornings). Two statues overlook this water: **Alice-in-Wonderland** (Margarita Delacorte Memorial. Jose de Creeft, sculptor) and **Hans Christian Andersen** (George J. Lober, sculptor. Otto F. Langmann, architect. 1956). Neither is of any great artistic merit, but both are loved and beloved by swarming children (storytelling at Andersen, May–September, Saturdays, 11 A.M.). From here look across the water to enjoy a view of Fifth Avenue through a filigree of branches and/or leaves.

Continue around the western shore to the path leading west to **Trefoil Arch,** a brownstone tunnel with a wood ceiling, and pass under the **East Drive** to reach the shore of the **Lake [5.],** where a gondola and a circuiting public launch once accompanied the flotilla of rowboats. The **72nd Street Boathouse** (1954) [6.] is in the brick neo-Victorian style favored by Parks Commissioner **Robert Moses.** Note the rowboat sculpture, from a fudgy clay, cast into bronze, in the front court (Irwin Glusker, sculptor. 1967). The boathouse has a snackbar, and a pleasant terrace overlooking the Lake. The bicycle concession to the right is jammed, particularly on those days and evenings when the park drives, closed to traffic, become the cyclists' province.

The path along the south shore reaches the **Terrace [7.],** the only formal architectural element of the *Greensward* plan. Jacob Wrey Mould detailed the stonework, but Vaux was the conceptual designer. **Bethesda Fountain** (1870. Emma Stebbins, sculptor. Calvert Vaux, architect) is the centerpiece, with a bronze out-winged **Angel of the Waters** crowning vigorous chubby cherubs (Purity, Health, Peace, and Temperance). The terrace is a faded elegance of brick paving, sandstone bordered, walled and crowned. Unhappily, noise, gambling, beer-drinking—a general visual and aural cacophony—dominate this once gracious place.

Side Trip: Southwest of the **Terrace** stands the **Bow Bridge** (1879. Calvert Vaux. Restored, 1974), a cast-iron elegance spanning the Lake to the **Ramble.** The bosky Ramble [8.], where even vigilant bird-watchers have been known to lose their way on the mazelike paths, contains meandering streams, exotic trees and shrubs, and small, hidden lawns. At its north the **Ramble** ascends to **Vista Rock,** topped by **Belvedere Castle [9.],** former home of the city's weather station (about to be restored. 1978. James Lamantia). Below the Castle is **Belvedere Lake,** last vestige of the old reservoir drained in 1929. The reservoir's dry bed was used by squatters during the Depression, then filled in, becoming the **Great Lawn [10.],** today's favored spot for touch-football, soccer, and softball matches. The **Delacorte Theater [11.]** (remodeled 1976. Giorgio Cavaglieri), with summer Shakespeare, hovers over the New Lake's western flank. The **22nd Precinct, N.Y.C. Police Department [12.] ★,** on Transverse Road Number 3, is another Calvert Vaux building (1871). East, behind the Metropolitan Museum of Art [see UES 25a.] rises the **Obelisk [13.]** from the reign of Thutmose III in 1600 B.C. A gift from the Khedive of Egypt, it was erected in the park in 1881. Resume tour.

Another Side Trip: The **Ladies Pavilion [14.]** (Vaux & Mould. 1871) now rests on a promontory on the west side of the Lake (near the W. 72nd St. entrance), purportedly moved there from its original location at Columbus Circle (used for ladies awaiting streetcars, and bumped by the erection of the *Maine* Monument). Here vandalized and ruined, it was reincarnated by the efforts of Parks Department Monuments Officer **Joseph Bresnan:** a lacy cast-iron Victorian place.

The Mall [15.], the Park's grand promenade, lies south of the Terrace Arcade. Pass through, noting the glazed and decorated tile ceiling. The Mall's axis points to the Belvedere Castle, deliberately kept small by architect Vaux to lengthen the perspective. Now full-grown trees have almost obliterated the vista. Behind the limestone half-hemispherical vaulted bandshell is the **Pergola [16.],** a low, light-filtered wood trellis, one of the park's few remaining wisteria-covered arbors. The **Mall,** in recent years, has been a place for action, rather than strolling: juggling, banjo-playing, drug-dealing, beer-drinking, gambling, hamburger-eating, and so forth.

On the **Mall** are several statues: **Fitzgreene Halleck** (J. Wilson Mac-Donald. 1877). A prissy and pretentious bronze of a self-styled poet. **Walter Scott** (1872. John Steell). The 100th anniversary of Scott's birth is memorialized by this dour bronze, a copy of Steell's original in the Scott Memorial in Edinburgh. **Robert Burns** (1880. John Steell) is represented as a faraway and saccharin romantic. **Columbus** (1894. Jeronimo Suñol). An entranced religious maniac. **Shakespeare** (1870. John Quincy Adams Ward). The thoughtful bard in pantaloons.

Side Trip: West of the Mall, past the closed Center Drive, stretches the **Sheep Meadow [17.],** a sweeping lawn where sheep grazed until banished in 1934 (they lived in what is now the Tavern-on-the-Green). From the north end is a splendid view of skyscrapers. To the southwest, along Central Park West, stands the **Tavern [18.],** newly renovated elegantly once more for greenhouse and terrace dining. Nearby is Central Park's first **Adventure Playground** (1966. Richard Dattner and Associates).

At the southern end of the **Mall** cross the drive, and don't blame Olmsted for not providing an underground passage here: the Marble Arch, the park's most famous bridge, was here until the 1930s. Take the southeast path along the drive, and, while crossing over the 65th Street transverse road, notice how little the sunken road intrudes into the park. To the right, a path leads past the **Dairy [19.],** a sturdy Gothic Revival building now shorn of its original porch. Note Manhattan schist, and sandstone neo-Gothic colonnettes. **Vaux designed it.**

Another Side Trip: Head west, to the north of the hillsite of the **Kinderberg,** once a large arbor. It's now replaced by the squat **Chess and Checkers House [20.],** a gift of Bernard Baruch, a red and beige brick neo-Ruskinian cum Moses (Robert, that is) octagonal lump. Continue west, under Playmates Arch beneath the drive to the **Michael Friedsam Memorial Carousel** (1951), another beige and red brick octagon replacing an earlier one, destroyed by fire. Resume tour.

From the **Dairy,** after dropping down to the left, the path passes east of the Chess and Checkers site. Skirt southeast around the **Wollman Memorial Rink [21.]** and go up the hill along the fence enclosing the **Bird Sanctuary [22.]. Gapstow Bridge,** crossing the Pond [23.], is a good place to admire the reflections of the city's towers in the water below. A few swans and many ducks are usually swimming around. Swanboats, the same as those still in the Boston Gardens, sailed here until 1924. Leave the park by the gate across from Sherman's statue, or, if you want to feed the animals, go, via **Inscope Arch [24.]** under the East Drive, northeast of the Pond.

End of Tour: Nearest transit is the BMT line at the Plaza or Fifth Avenue buses.

Side Trip: The **Zoo [25.],** off Fifth Avenue at 64th Street, is a favorite haunt of New Yorkers. It is a formal plaza contained by simple arched brick buildings, and a handsome place for the sauntering pedestrian. The caged animals are less lucky, although the centrally placed sea lions are usually exuberant. Try a beer and a hot dog on the terrace overlooking it all. The Arsenal **[26.]** [see UES 8a.] is a participant in the Zoo plaza by default.

The view across the Lake and Ramble   Abraham & Joseph Spector Playground

Walking Tour B: The Pool to Conservatory Garden. (Arrive via IND 8th Avenue Subway to 96th Street Station.) Begin at Central Park West and 100th Street.

The Boy's Gate gives access to a path descending to the **Pool [27.].** It is the start of the waterway which flows east to Harlem Meer, and was once the course of Montayne's Rivulet that led to the East River.

Side Trip: North of the Pool is the **Great Hill [28.],** where picnickers once enjoyed an unobstructed view of the Hudson and East Rivers. Perched on a cliff to the northeast is a lonely **Blockhouse [29.],** a remnant of the fortifications built during the War of 1812 when the British threatened the city. Resume Tour.

At the eastern end of the **Pool,** the **Glen Span** carries the West Drive over the Ravine. On the other side flows **the Loch,** formerly a healthy sized body of water, now a trickle. This is very picturesque and completely cut off from the city.

Side Trip: To the south, behind the slope, is the North Meadow [30a.], scene of hotly contested baseball games: to get there, take **Springbanks Arch [30b.].** Resume Tour.

In wet weather the Loch cascades down before disappearing under the East Drive at **Huddlestone Bridge.** Through the arch in front of Harlem Meer [31.] you can see the park's most disastrous "improvement," the **Loula D. Lasker Pool-Rink [31a.].** New Yorkers have always tried to give things—especially buildings—to their park. Few succeeded until recent years when park administrators misguidedly encouraged philanthropic bequests.

To the right of the Loch find **Lamppost No. 0554.** (All the older lampposts were designed by Henry Bacon in 1907, and all bear a street-designating plaque; here, the first two digits indicate that this one stands at 105th Street.) A path goes sharply uphill and then turns east, crossing the East Drive below **McGown's Pass,** which was fortified by the British during the Revolutionary War. The **Mount [32.],** to the right, was for many years the site of a tavern; its chief ornament today is the park's mulch pile.

The path descends to **Conservatory Garden [33.],** designed by Thomas D. Price in 1936. The "Greensward" Plan called for a large arboretum of native trees and shrubs to be planted here. Instead, a conservatory was built at the turn of the century but torn down in 1934. On the east side the **Vanderbilt Gate** opens on Fifth Avenue. Nearby is the **Museum of the City of New York,** where historical material of the park is on display. [See UES 42b.]

Special events: All sorts take place in the park, with each Park Commissioner choosing his own brand. Daily information on what's doing may be had by calling the special recorded announcement: 755-4100

End of Tour: Transportation: IRT Lexington Avenue Subway Stations at 96th or 103rd Streets, and via Fifth or Madison Avenue buses.

Other delightful Playgrounds include the Ancient Play Garden between the 85th and 86th Street drives into the Park (1972. Richard Dattner and Associates); the Water Playground section of the Heckscher Playground toward Central Park South and Seventh Avenue (1972. Richard Dattner and Associates); and the Spector Playground near Central Park West and 86th Street (1976. Abraham Rothenberg Associates).

All are places of the adventurous, exploratory child, leaving the hard predictability of New York streets for a **place of fantasy and physical challenge:** incidentally handsome, sculptural places with rich materials and textures.

UPPER EAST SIDE

[1a.] The Plaza, Fifth Ave., W. 58th to W. 60th Sts. SE cor. Central Park.

The **Plaza,** formally called **Grand Army Plaza,** is *The* Plaza to New Yorkers, and New York's first (and, until 1973, only) public urban plaza for people. The Police Plaza [Civic Center/Chinatown 23.] is number two (chronologically). Plazas at Rockefeller and Lincoln Centers and at the World Trade Center are parts of private building complexes; but here, in the European tradition, is an outdoor room contained by buildings of varied architecture and function, an island of urbane repose. The more significant half (the area is bisected by 59th Street) to the south is centered on the **Plaza Hotel** on the west and the **General Motors Building** across Fifth Avenue.

UPPER EAST SIDE

E. 110 St.

T IRT

E. 108 St.

E. 106 St.

44

43

42b

42a

41 Mt. Sinai Hospital

T IRT

E. 104 St.

E. 102 St.

E. 100 St.

East Harlem

E. 98 St.

40
39a

38a,b   39b   38d
38c   **T** IRT
37   E. 96 St.

36a,b   36c,d   36e   1

35c,d
35a,b   34c   35e
34b
34a   33g,h 34e 34d
33b-e   12
33a 33f
32b,c
32a
31b

31c   31d
31a

30a,b   30c,d   14

29 28a
      28b   28c
27a 26a 27c
25 27b 26b
     25c
24a
24b   23

22b   22c,d

22a
21a,b

E. 94 St.

E. 92 St.

E. 90 St.

2

3

11b 13 11a   10

Yorkville   8   7

E. 88 St.

E. 86 St.

UES

E. 84 St.

20

E. 82 St.

E. 80 St.

21 24
23 23

4 Carl
Schurz
Pk.
5

6

9

19

17 16

31b,c

**Metropolitan
Museum of Art**   25

5b

**Upper
East
Side**

T IRT

22
20c

20d

E. 78 St.

E. 76 St.

18

East River

**The
Far
East**

20a 20b
19b,d 19f
19c 19e
19a 18b
18a   19g
17a,b 18c
17c 17d,e
16a,b,c 16e
     16d 16f
     15f

15a

15b-e
14a,c 14d
13a
13b
12a,e 12d-m
12b
11c,d 12e,f
11b,e 11f
10a-d 11i 11h
       10e 10f

9a,b   9c,d,e

8c,d

8b

7a,b,c
6b,c
6a
5b
5a
4b

4a 3b
3a

**Manhattan
House to
Tower
East**

15h

15g
14e-k
13c
12n,o
      T IRT
      6
      5 4 3

10h,i

1 2

13

11

9

10

8

7

2

1

E. 74 St.

E. 72 St.

E. 70 St.

E. 68 St.

E. 66 St.

E. 64 St.

Central Park

The Zoo   8a

14a

11a

8a

8e   7d,e
     7d,e
6d

9

4c 4d

8f,g,h
7d,e

IRT/BMT

T

3e,f
3c
3d

1

2a   2b

2c-f   2g-i

Midtown

**Cornell-
New York
Hospital**   6

**Rockefeller
Univ.**   8

9

12

11   10

Queensboro Bridge

E. 62 St.

E. 60 St.

E. 58 St.

12

5 4 3

7

1

5

7

8

19

4

3

Roosevelt Island

Wards Is.

N

0   1000   2000   3000 feet

The **Plaza** is ornamented by varied paving and trees enclosing the **Pulitzer Fountain,** surmounted by *Pomona,* a lithe lady by **Karl Bitter** on a cascade of pools by Carrère and Hastings.

South are the buildings of **Bergdorf Goodman** (*1928. Buchman & Kahn.*) and the **Paris Theatre** (*1948. Emery Roth & Sons, with interiors by Warner-Leeds Assocs.*). Looming high in the local skyline is **9 West 57th Street,** a black and white swooping form, its windbracing displayed like proud suspenders (*1974. Skidmore, Owings & Merrill.*).

General Sherman occupies the **Plaza's** northern half: more of a traffic turnaround than a pedestrian enclave. **The General (William Tecumseh)** is here marching, not through **Georgia,** but rather in allegory. **Augustus Saint-Gaudens** (*saynt gawdens*) presented this casting at the **Paris Exposition** of **1900,** and the good General mounted his present pedestal in **1903.** Now the oldest resident of this place, he antedates the **Plaza Hotel** by four years.

[1b.] The Edwardian Plaza Hotel. 1907   **[1d.]** The General Motors Building

[2f.] D/R (Design Research, a store)   **[2g.]** Ritz Tower (apartment hotel)

[1b.] The Plaza Hotel, W. 58th to W. 59th Sts., facing the Plaza. 1907. Henry J. Hardenbergh.

A vestige of **Edwardian** elegance. **Hardenbergh,** its designer, graced **New York** with another, and equal, social and architectural monument: **The Dakota** (apartment house). The white glazed brick and green-copper-and-slate mansard roof have been returned to their pristine splendor in a recent cleaning. One of the most exciting views of **New York** (Eloise-style) is from any room on the north side, from the third to the fifth floors. From there eyes can skim the trees in a dramatic perspective of **Central Park** and **Fifth Avenue. Frank Lloyd Wright** was a devotee of the **Plaza:** he used it as his New York headquarters.

[1c.] Shezan (Indian Restaurant), 8 W. 58th St. 1976. Gwathmey Siegel. Telephone: 371-1414.

An elegant place of *light and illusion* (Gwathmey's words). **Expensive.**

[1d.] General Motors Building, E. 58th to E. 59th Sts., Fifth to Madison Aves. 1968. Edward Durell Stone, Emery Roth & Sons, Associated Architects.

Here once lay the **Savoy Plaza** (Hotel) and a miscellany of others, none particularly distinguished. The hue and cry over the new **tower** was based not on architecture but on the loss of elegant shopping amenities in favor of automobile salesmanship (an auto showroom is particularly galling at the spot in New York that most honors the pedestrian). But, most of all, who needs a plaza on a plaza?

In the sunken central space Vidal Sassoon's shop is a lurking star (1976. Gwathmey Siegel).

F. A. O. Schwartz, 745 Fifth Ave., SE cor. E. 58th Street.

Toy store to the world. The second floor contains every gadget a parent would care to buy for him- or herself (in the name of his or her child).

[1e.] Sherry-Netherland Hotel, Fifth Ave., NE cor. E. 59th St. 1927. Schultze & Weaver.

A tower fit for a *muezzin* crowns its peaked and finialed roof. The bar along **Fifth Avenue** is one of **New York's** greatest: venerable elegance. **A la Vieille Russie** vends wares of **Czarist** opulence, in keeping with the high style of its landlord.

[2a.] Manufacturers Hanover Trust Company, 1 E. 57th St. NE cor. Fifth Ave. 1966. Skidmore, Owings & Merrill.

A subtle and elegant update of the first two floors of a **neo-Classic** building.

[2b.] IBM Showroom, 590 Madison Ave., SW cor. E. 57th St. Altered, 1959, Eliot Noyes.

The architecture of display.

[2c.] Georg Jensen, 601 Madison Ave., bet. E. 57th and E. 58th Sts. 1974. James Stewart Polshek & Assocs.

Mirror-letters form an elegant *graphic* facade to this emporium of Scandinavian glass, dishes, flatware, and gifts.

[2d.] Georg Jensen Specials/formerly Bonniers, 605 Madison Ave. bet. E. 57th and E. 58th Sts. 1949. Warner-Leeds Assocs.

Originally commissioned as a bookstore for the Swedish publishing house **Bonniers,** it is elegant, understated, and without stylistic mannerisms. The *gangplank stair* in a two-story stairwell became one of the source materials of modern design.

[2e.] Fuller Building, 45 E. 57th St., NE cor. Madison Ave. 1929. Walker & Gillette, architects. Elie Nadelman, sculptor.

The Brooks Brothers of Art Deco: black, gray and white.

[2f.] D/R (Design Research)/formerly the Galerie Norval, 53 E. 57th St., bet. Madison and Fifth Aves. 1965. Alteration by Benjamin Thompson.

A modern architect's dream. Collected in one four-storied store are furniture, kitchen equipment, cutlery, dresses—in fact, everything that is portable and has been touched by the wand of good design. It could well be an exhibition from the **Museum of Modern Art;** but fear not, the exhibits are for sale. **Benjamin Thompson,** an architect from Boston, started **D/R** on Brattle Street in Cambridge. Expensive.

[2g.] Ritz Tower, Park Ave., NE cor. E. 57th St. 1925. Emery Roth and Carrère & Hastings.

A 42-story tower, a stepped obelisk, **conspicuous on the skyline.** Rich details around the street-level walls are matched only by the opulent enterprises behind them, such as Charles of the Ritz.

At **111 East 57th Street** (in the sideflank of the Ritz Tower) stood France's greatest restaurant in America, Le Pavillon, founded by Henri Soulé at the New York World's Fair of 1939, then moved here to fulfill the wildest dreams of both gourmands and gourmets—unhappily it is defunct (Soulé died in 1966) and currently the home of the First Women's Bank (1975. Stockman & Manners Assocs., designers).

[2h.] The Galleria, 119 E. 57th St. bet. Park and Lexington Aves. 1975. David Kenneth Specter, Philip Birnbaum, Associated Architects.

Luxury apartments stacked over offices and a club, embracing a balconied seven-story public galleria (cf. **The Galleria, Milan**): skylit balconied space that penetrates the block to **58th** Street allowing pedestrian delight in passing through the block. Pretentious, but it has some grounds to be so.

[2h.] The Galleria (mixed use bldg.)   **[3b.]** The C.I.T. Financial Building

[2i.] 137 East 57th Street, NW cor. Lexington Ave. 1930. Thompson & Churchill.

A pioneering piece of structural virtuosity: the columns are recessed **9** feet from the skin. Steel tensile straps hang the perimeter floors and walls from roof girders. **Churchill's** talented answer kept the columns out of the stream bed that passed under the building's corner.

[2j.] La Cabaña, 146 E. 57th St., bet. Lexington and Third Aves.

Bizarre bazaar? A delightful **Victorian** restaurant. Expensive for both lunch and dinner. Note the deeply articulated tile floor. Telephone: 758-3242.

[3a.] The Playboy Club, 5 E. 59th St., bet. Fifth and Madison Aves. Remodeled, 1962, Oppenheimer, Brady & Lehrecke. Altered, 1976, Paul K. Y. Chen.

This building is the key link in an international **bacchanal.** The matter-of-fact facade belies the multi-leveled stack of balconies, mezzanines, and intertwining spaces behind. The lettering-cornice is the real giveaway: it has no real desire to be an exclusive club.

[3b.] C.I.T. Building, 650 Madison Ave., bet. E. 59th and E. 60th Sts. 1957. Harrison & Abramovitz.

A wraparound from the **Playboy Club** to the **Copacabana,** it nestles between the new and the old high life. Black granite and stainless steel; victimized by its tenancy on the ground floor: life insurance, banking, brokerage, do little to enliven the active pedestrian street. *Oh, for an elegant bar or shop!* (Its predecessor, an elegant Art Moderne two-story taxpayer by Lamb & Rich, was filled with life: a sad reprise.)

[3c.] Olivetti Building/originally **Pepsi-Cola Building,** 500 Park Ave., SW cor. E. 59th St. Skidmore, Owings & Merrill.

An **understated elegance** that bows to the scale of its Park Avenue neighbors rather than advertising itself as the newest (of its time) local modern monument. Large bays of glass are enlivened by the seemingly random arrangements of partitions (that **kiss the glass** with rubber gaskets) and vertical blinds.

Built for Pepsi-Cola (who withdrew to the suburbs) it was happily bought by **Olivetti,** the **world's foremost patron** of architecture, planning, and good design.

[3d.] Argosy Print and Book Store, 115 E. 59th St., bet. Park and Lexington Aves. 1966. Kramer & Kramer.

An elegant shop that replaces the streetstands of thirty years ago along this block: used books, maps, and prints filled the sidewalk to the delight of browsers, as on the **Left Bank** of the **Seine.** Upstairs (by elevator) are floors devoted to old prints, painting, and specialized books. Perhaps too elegant, too stylish, too neat for such a bookstore, **Argosy** is the current uptown outpost of a trade that still flourishes on the flanks of Fourth Avenue, in dusty storefronts between **Astor Place** and **14th Street.**

[3e.] The Lighthouse: N.Y. Association for the Blind, 111 E. 59th St. bet. Park and Lexington Aves. 1964. Kahn & Jacobs.

A simple limestone facade with tall, color-anodized, aluminum-framed windows. Its placement forms a tiny plaza with the wall of the corner building. The four stacks release air conditioning exhaust without subjecting pedestrian passersby to the usual blasts of warm, stale "air." Patronize the handcrafted delights of the ground-floor shop.

[3c.] The elegant Olivetti Building   **[3e.]** N.Y. Association for the Blind

[3f.] 110 East 59th Street, bet. Park and Lexington Aves. 1973.

A notch above its speculative competition. A simple, understated, unpretentious tower. The sculpture (1973. Tony Rosenthal.) in the south plaza **(on 58th Street)** is a rich, carved piece of a bronze cylinder.

Copacabana, 10 E. 60th Street (in the Hotel Fourteen).

A huge nightclub by contemporary standards, from the era of big bands and big shows, **à la Ziegfeld.** Now a double-deck discothèque.

[4a.] The Harmonie Club, 4 E. 60th St., bet. Fifth and Madison Aves. 1905. McKim, Mead & White.

A high-rise **Renaissance** palace for a men's club.

[4b.] The Metropolitan Club, 1 E. 60th St. NE cor. Fifth Ave. 1893. McKim, Mead & White. Wing to the east, 1912, Ogden Codman.

J. P. Morgan organized this club, primarily for friends who were not accepted in others. An **Italian** palazzo is crossed with a proper **English** carriage entrance and courtyard. The interior is an *extravaganza* of space, marble, coffers, and gilt: Corinthian columns, velvet ropes, and scarlet carpeting.

The eastern wing houses the **Canadian Club.**

[4c.] The Grolier Club, 47 E. 60th St. bet. Madison and Park Aves. 1917. Bertram G. Goodhue.

Named for the (16th-century) French bibliophile **Jean Grolier,** this club is for those devoted to the bookmaking crafts. Poor **Grolier's** name was taken in vain for another building, the "gold skyscraper" at **Lexington Avenue** and **51st Street.**

[4d.] Christ Church (Methodist), 520 Park Ave. NW cor. E. 60th St. 1932. Ralph Adams Cram.

A church designed to *appear* aged: the random limestone and brick is intended to look like a sophisticated patch job, centuries old. Similarly, the marble and granite columns appear to be, in the **Romanesque** and **Byzantine** manner, pillage from **Roman** temples. Handsome, and of impeccable taste, it is an archeological and eclectic stage set for well-to-do parishioners.

[5a.] Hotel Pierre, 2 E. 61st St. SE cor. Fifth Ave. 1928. Schultze & Weaver.

A romantic, towered hotel, with a mansard roof silhouette.

[5b.] 800 Fifth Avenue, NE cor. 61st St. 1978. Ulrich Franzen & Assocs.

Here, until 1977, was the Mrs. Marcellus Hartley Dodge house—the seldom used, seemingly abandoned town house of a Rockefeller kin. A blockbuster of an apartment house, set back from the avenue, with a plaza between itself and a false facade matching the Knickerbocker Club to the north.

Madame Romaine de Lyon (restaurant), 32 E. 61st St., bet. Madison and Park Aves. Telephone: 758-2422.

A superb idea for lunch. Extraordinary, formidable—its menu offers 538 varieties of omelettes. Bring your own wine, if necessary, for no such beverages are available here. Depending upon ingredients, omelette prices vary. Expensive.

[6a.] The Knickerbocker Club, 2 E. 62nd St. SE cor. Fifth Ave. 1914. Delano & Aldrich.

An elegant **neo-Georgian** limestone and brick mansion. Classy detailing.

[6b.] The Fifth Avenue Synagogue, 5 E. 62nd St. bet. Fifth and Madison Aves. 1959. Percival Goodman.

An *urban temple,* occupying a typical mansion site of the 60s. Limestone, with sharply incised, oval-pointed windows, filled with stained glass; as with all buildings where stained glass is a major design element, these read as black voids from without, save after sunset (when the interior is illuminated).

[6c.] Johnson O'Connor Research Foundation/formerly **Charles Steele House,** 11 E. 62nd St., bet. Fifth and Madison Aves. ca. 1900.

Extravagant brick and limestone house inspired by the French Second Empire.

Le Provençal (Restaurant), 21 E. 62nd St., bet. Fifth and Madison Aves.

Popular, crowded, a good solid French kitchen. Table d'hôte dinners: expensive. A neighborhood restaurant that has acquired a place on the edge of haute cuisine but still retains neighborhood scale and flavor. Credit cards accepted.

[6d.] The Colony Club, 564 Park Ave., NW cor. E. 62nd St. 1924. Delano & Aldrich.

Female social leadership is split between the **Colony** and the **Cosmopolitan,** the former more oriented to grandes dames, the latter to the activists. The **Colony** was founded in **1903** by the wives of those who mattered.

A neo-Georgian red brick and limestone town "palace."

[7a.] 817 and 820 Fifth Avenue, NE and SE cors. of E. 63rd St. 1916. Starrett & Van Vleck.

A pair of high-rise palazzos of limestone, copper-corniced, these are two of the great **eclectic** apartment houses of New York: magnificent relics of the **irrational Twenties.**

[7b.] The New York Academy of Sciences/ originally the **Gladys Watson Ziegler Residence,** 2 E. 63rd St. bet. Fifth and Madison Aves. 1920. Sterner & Wolfe.

A pasty palace, large without elegance.

[7c.] 14, 16, and 18 East 63rd Street. ca. 1875.

The **"brownstone"** is here elevated to mansion status, unlike the endless rows to the east of **Park Avenue.** The composite-columned porches on Nos. **16** and **18** are grand for their time; Nos. **15** and **17** are the more pretentious *nouveau riche* neighbors across the street. (Nouveau riche in the time of **14, 16,** and **18;** today old money to us!)

[7d.] Third Church of Christ, Scientist, 585 Park Ave., NE cor. E. 63rd St. 1923. Delano & Aldrich.

Lantern over a flat dome: **neo-Georgian.**

[7e.] Originally **Hirsch Residence,** 101 E. 63rd St., bet. Park and Lexington Aves. 1970. Paul Rudolph.

Somber brown steel and glass construction gives an understated face to a **grand** set of private house spaces behind.

[8a.] The Arsenal, in Central Park facing Fifth Ave. at E. 64th St. 1848. Martin E. Thompson. ★

The **fortified retreat** of **New York's** park commissioners and their staffs. Originally the central cache of military explosives in the state, it became city property only **nine** years after completion. The **Zoo** was at first in its basement. Now the **Arsenal** participates in the design of the **Zoo's** plaza as an object but has little to do with its zoo workings.

[8b.] The Institute of Aeronautical Sciences/formerly **Edward Berwind House,** 2 E. 64th St. SE cor. Fifth Ave. 1896. N. C. Mellon.

Edward Berwind built this Romanesque-Renaissance house for "town" and "The Elms" in Newport for "country." **Berwind,** then the largest owner of coal mines in the world, fueled the **U.S. Navy** through the **First World War.** Note the rich verdigris (brass or copper oxidation) on the ornamental railings that surround the "moat."

[8c.] New India House/formerly **Mrs. Marshall Orme Wilson House,** 3 E. 64th St. bet. Fifth and Madison Aves. 1903. Warren & Wetmore.

Powerful, molded limestone; slate and copper mansarded attic with grand dormers and oval windows. **The guts are at the sky.** This is **Warren & Wetmore's** only "modest" remnant (they were the architects of **Grand Central Station**). It is now owned by the Indian government, a happy fate which preserves this ex-private palace, like others in similar straits, for a little while, if not forever.

[8d.] Wildenstein & Company, 19 E. 64th St. bet. Fifth and Madison Aves. 1932. Horace Trumbauer.

Travertine in and travertine out: an art palace (never a house) that marked, with a bow, the end of **Trumbauer's** rich, eclectic career. Beautiful in proportion and patina. Note the two-story **Ionic** pilasters.

[8e.] The Verona, 32 E. 64th St. SE cor. Madison Ave. ca. 1900.

Names were once as important as numbers. The entrance to this **Edwardian** high-rise **Italian** palazzo is elegantly flanked by bronze lamp standards.

[8f.] Central Presbyterian Church/formerly the **Fifth Avenue Baptist Church,** 593 Park Ave. SE cor. E. 64th St. 1922. Pelton, Allen & Collens.

The original Baptist congregation left here to build their monument, **Riverside Church,** with the same architects and **John D. Rockefeller's** money.

[8g.] Asia House, 112 E. 64th St., bet. Park and Madison Aves. 1959. Philip Johnson & Assocs. Open to the public. Telephone: PL 1-4210.

The **Asia Society** maintains a small gallery here in the space of a double-width brownstone; tinted glass and white-painted steel are composed into a delicate street-wall. The opacity of the glass is sometimes disturbing, causing the building to appear solid, a mirror of the opposite side of the street. *Only at night* is the volume of interior space apparent.

[8g.] Asia House (gallery & offices)   [8h.] The Edward Durell Stone House

[8h.] Edward Durell Stone House, 130 E. 64th St., bet. Park and Madison Aves. 1959. Edward Durell Stone.

The original body, before remodeling, was similar to the two **"brownstones"** to the east and one to the west. The facade, and hence space, of the structure was extended to the permissible building line and clad with the same terrazzo grillage **Stone** had used so successfully at the **American Embassy, New Delhi, India.**

[9a.] Temple Emanu-El, 1 E. 65th St., NE cor. Fifth Ave. 1929. Robert D. Kohn, Charles Butler and Clarence Stein; with Mayers, Murray & Philip, consultants.

Occupying the site of Mrs. (Caroline Schermerhorn) Astor's mansion, this is one of the largest bearing-wall halls extant: that is, the east-west walls are solid masonry, supporting transverse steel beams for the roof. A huge hall (for **2,500**) seats more worshippers than **St. Patrick's Cathedral!** A monumental monolith.

[9b.] 17 East 65th Street/formerly **Sherman M. Fairchild House,** bet. Fifth and Madison Aves. 1941. George Nelson and William Hamby.

A new concept in the relation of building and urban lot, continued by **Philip Johnson** in his 1951 **Museum of Modern Art** guest house [see Turtle Bay–UN **22.**]. Two separate functional elements, one at the street (living room, dining room, kitchen), and one at the rear lot line (bedrooms), are joined by a court, within which ramps of glass form flying bridges over the garden below. The facade **belies** what it shields. Above, the overhanging second and third floors are screened by continuous, power-driven wood louvers. Sadly, the new brick-red paint job demeans it: it should be returned to its pristine condition.

[9c.] The American Federation of the Arts/formerly **Benson Bennett Sloan House,** 41 E. 65th St., bet. Madison and Park Aves. 1910. Trowbridge & Livingston. Interior remodeling, 1960. Edward Durell Stone.

The galleries within **(open to the public)** shelter traveling exhibitions gathered and circulated by the Federation. Telephone: YU 8-7700.

[9d.] 45–47 East 65th Street/formerly the **Sara Delano and Franklin Delano Roosevelt Houses.** 1910. Charles A. Platt. ★

Twin brick and limestone houses commissioned by **F.D.R.'s** mother for herself **(45)** and the future president **(47)**. It was here, in the fourth-floor front bedroom of No. **47**, that **F.D.R.** began his recovery from polio. Now No. **45** is the **Institute for Rational Living,** No. **47** the **Sara Delano Roosevelt Memorial House.**

[9e.] 55 East 65th Street, bet. Madison and Park Aves. 1893. Thom & Wilson.

An *early* apartment of brick and brownstone, now happily saved by remodeling into cooperatives.

[10a.] Yugoslav Mission to the U.N./formerly **R. Livingston Beeckman House,** 854 Fifth Ave., bet. E. 66th and E. 67th Sts. 1905. Warren & Wetmore. ★

Communists savor splendor as much as do **Capitalists.**

[10b.] Lotus Club/formerly **William J. Schiefflin Residence,** 5 E. 66th St. bet. Fifth and Madison Aves. 1900. Richard Howland Hunt.

A French **Second Empire** limestone and brick extravaganza, with ebullient limestone and cast iron detailing. Hunt designed the *Great Hall* of the **Metropolitan Museum.**

[10b.] Former W.J. Schiefflin House   **[10d.]** Philippine Mission to the U.N.

[10c.] Polish Delegation to the U.N./formerly **Charles Scribner Residence,** 9 E. 66th St. bet. Fifth and Madison Aves. 1912. Ernest Flagg.

Flagg's greater work was **Scribner's** store. This is *dull* **Flagg.**

[10d.] Philippine Mission to the U.N./originally **Harris Fahnestock Residence,** 15 E. 66th St., bet. Fifth and Madison Aves. 1918. Hoppin & Koen.

Their **chef d'oeuvre** was the *old* **Police Headquarters** [Little Italy **4.**].

[10e.] 45 East 66th Street, NE cor. Madison Ave. ca. 1900. Harde & Short.

They hoped for perpendicular Gothic. A *glassy* facade of **12** over **12** double-hung windows.

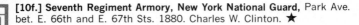

[10f.] Seventh Regiment Armory, New York National Guard, Park Ave. bet. E. 66th and E. 67th Sts. 1880. Charles W. Clinton. ★

A *friendly* brick fort. **New York** armories were composed of two distinct elements: a three- or four-story collection of office, meeting, and social spaces, and a vast drill hall. The latter is, in this instance, **187** by **290** feet of clear space, sufficient for maneuvering modern military vehicles.

The Armory was, in large part, furnished and detailed on the interior by **Louis Comfort Tiffany,** son of **Charles,** founder and owner of Fifth Avenue's Tiffany & Co. **Louis** rejected the business world for that of the applied arts. His studios eventually specialized in decorative crafts ranging from the stained glass for which he is best remembered today to stonecarving, metalworking, casting of bronze: all crafts complementing the ornate Late Victorian architecture of his architect-clients. In *this* case some tables were turned: **Stanford White** worked under **Tiffany's** direction on this interior work, rather than the later, and more obvious, reversed relationship.

[10g.] The Cosmopolitan Club, 122 E. 66th St., bet. Park and Madison Aves. 1932. Thomas Harlan Elett.

The northern outpost of **"New Orleans"** cast iron. A club for women professionals and semi-professionals. Its male counterpart is the Century Association [Bryant Park Area **9.**].

[10f.] Seventh Regiment Armory, New York National Guard: a friendly fort

[10h.] John Hay Whitney Garage/formerly **Horace Havemeyer Garage,** 126 E. 66th St., bet. Park and Lexington Aves. 1895. W. J. Wallace & S. E. Sage.

A handsome brick arch is portal for nine Whitney cars: rarely does even consciously monumental architecture achieve such power. The archivolt (decorative band around the arch) is **breathtaking.**

[10i.] Church of St. Vincent Ferrer (Roman Catholic), SE cor. E. 66th St. and Lexington Ave. 1923. Bertram Grosvenor Goodhue. ★

A *fashionable* parish church built during the post-World War I boom; rockface granite with limestone trim, detailing, and sculpture. Academically **correct and precise.** The uniformity of materials and details gives a somewhat manufactured quality: the **"rockface"** is self-conscious.

[10j.] 131–135 East 66th Street and 130–134 East 67th Street along Lexington Ave. E. side. 1905. Charles A. Platt. ★

Twin residential "palaces," ranking with **The Dakota** [Central Park West **15.**] in architectural distinction. The **Doric** porticos are elegant. Note the duplex windows on the side street facades.

[11a.] Seventh Regiment Monument, Fifth Ave. W. side. on axis with E. 67th St. at Central Park. 1927. Karl Illava, sculptor.

Dynamic bronze. *Seething* bayonets.

[11b.] Residence, Consul General of Japan, 4 E. 67th St., bet. Fifth and Madison Aves. 1909. Attributed to Carrère & Hastings.

Brick and limestone mansion.

[11c.] 13 East 67th Street/formerly **Martin Beck House,** bet. Fifth and Madison Aves. 1921. Henry Allan Jacobs.

A **Serlian** arch at the second floor (the Italian architect-author Serlio recorded this form, as developed by Palladio).

[10j.] 131–135 East 66th St. (apts.)   **[11d.]** The Regency Whist Clubhouse

[11a.] The Seventh Regiment Monument, dynamic bronze, with seething bayonets

[11d.] Regency Whist Club/originally **Cortlandt Field Bishop House,** 15 E. 67th St., bet. Fifth and Madison Aves. 1904. Ernest Flagg.

A turn-of-the-century Paris town house by the architect of Scribner's Bookstore and the Singer Building [Fifth Avenue **4a.** and SoHo **17.**] respectively. Note the "French" balconies for security (mostly psychological) at the casement windows.

[11e.] 16 E. 67th St./formerly **Jeremiah Milbank House,** bet. Fifth and Madison Aves. 1906. John H. Duncan.

A **double**-width limestone house.

[11f.] Pierre Balmain, 795 Madison Ave., bet. E. 67th and E. 68th Sts. 1974.

A chic, streamlined, stainless-steel shopfront.

[11g.] Histadrut Foundation for Educational Travel, 33 E. 67th St., bet. Madison and Park Aves. 1903. Robertson & Potter.

[11h.] Egyptian Mission to the U.N., 36 E. 67th St., bet. Madison and Park Aves. 1906. Henry Bacon.

Bacon designed the **Lincoln Memorial** in Washington.

[11i.] 51–53 East 67th Street, bet. Madison and Park Aves. ca. 1880.

Long before the rise of **Park** and **Fifth** Avenues these were the town houses of the well-to-do. Now they seem dull ancestors to the grandeur surrounding them.

[12a.] Indonesian Delegation to the U.N./formerly **J. J. Emery House,** 5 E. 68th St., bet. Fifth and Madison Aves. 1894. Peabody & Stearns.

A mansion, but without good proportions, scale, or style. Study it!

[12b.] 8 East 68th Street/first **Otto Kahn House,** bet. Madison and Fifth Aves. 1900. John H. Duncan.

One of a classy trio with Nos. 6 and 10: French mansarded limestone town houses.

 **[12c.] Center for Marital and Family Therapy/**formerly **George T. Bliss House,** 9 E. 68th St., bet. Fifth and Madison Aves. 1906. Heins & La Farge.

Sir John Soane, revived, 100 years later. (He was the precocious designer of the now-demolished Bank of England and of his own *bizarre* house: now the Soane Museum.) The great Ionic columns are *appliqué* (they support the sky). Warm salmon brickwork. **Smashing.**

Halston, the high-fashion designer, holds court in a shop at the northeast corner of Madison Avenue and 68th Street. The battered (i.e., sloped as in an earth mound) glass and stucco facade looks strangely Mexican.

[12d.] 35 East 68th Street, bet. Madison and Park Aves. 1900. Carrère & Hastings.

The ornament is extravagant on this cut-rate Carrère & Hastings palace.

[12e.] 40 East 68th Street, bet. Madison and Park Avenues. ca. 1898. Attributed to Flagg & Chambers.

Monumental bay window and a bold mansard roof.

[12f.] Dominican Academy/formerly **Michael Friedsam House,** 44 E. 68th St., bet. Madison and Park Aves. 1921. Frederick G. Frost.

[12g.] National Municipal League, 47 E. 68th St., bet. Madison and Park Aves. 1906. Adams & Warren.

Good but **not** great. Bold Renaissance detail.

[12h.] Automation House, 49 E. 68th St., bet. Madison and Park Aves. 1914. Trowbridge & Livingston. Remodeled 1970. Oppenheimer, Brady & Lehrecke.

The sheer glass without subdivisions gives this remodeled **neo-Georgian** house an *eerie* scale.

[12i.] Council on Foreign Relations/formerly **Harold I. Pratt House,** 58 E. 68th St., SW cor. Park Ave. 1920. Delano & Aldrich.

Harold was the youngest son of **Brooklyn's 19th-**century industrialist, **Charles Pratt,** kerosene magnate and later a major shareholder with **John D. Rockefeller** in *the* Standard Oil Company. Each son built a minor palace, the first three along **Clinton Avenue** in **Brooklyn** [see WC Brooklyn/Clinton Hill **5a., b., and c.**], opposite their father's mansion. When **Harold's** turn came, due to the changing fashions of **New York** (Manhattan) *vis-à-vis* Brooklyn, he chose **Park Avenue** for this English Renaissance limestone "palace."

[12j.] Center for Inter-American Relations/formerly **Soviet Delegation to the U.N./**originally **Percy Pyne House,** 680 Park Ave., NW cor. 68th St. 1909. McKim, Mead & White. ★

The **Marquesa de Cuevas** (a Rockefeller gone Spanish) saved this *grand* **neo-Georgian** house by purchasing it and presenting it to the Center.

The parts of **680–690 Park Avenue** are far less important than the whole: Georgian architecture's greatest contribution to remember today is not the style of individual buildings but an attitude toward urban design. Buildings of character, quality, and refinement were subordinated to a larger system of designing cities: the whole is greater than the sum of its parts.

These move up Park Avenue toward 69th Street but are numbered (as entries) as parts of [12.] to include this inseparable group as a unit.

[12i.] The Council on Foreign Relations/formerly the Harold I. Pratt House

[12j.,k.,l.,m.] The parts are far less important than the neo-Georgian whole

[12k.] Spanish Institute/formerly **Oliver D. Filey House,** 684 Park Ave., bet. E. 68th and E. 69th Sts. 1926. McKim, Mead & White. ★

Pyne's son-in-law built in the space of **Pyne's** onetime garden.

[12l.] Istituto Italiano di Cultura/formerly **William Sloane House,** 686 Park Ave., bet. E. 68th and E. 69th Sts. 1918. Delano & Aldrich. ★

Sloane's family gave their name to **W. & J. Sloane,** the great New York furniture store.

[12m.] Italian Consulate/formerly **Henry P. Davison House,** 690 Park Ave., SW cor. E. 69th St., and **52 E. 69th St.,** adjacent. 1917. ★ Walker & Gillette.

Built for the founder of the Bankers Trust Company. Crisp Georgian, delicately detailed.

[12n.] Hunter College, Park Ave., bet. E. 68th and E. 69th Sts. 1940. Shreve, Lamb & Harmon, Harrison & Fouilhoux, Associated Architects. New buildings at E. 68th St. and Lexington Ave. halted in beginning construction, 1977, Ulrich Franzen & Assoc.

An interruption in the pace of **Park Avenue. Hunter** is not only modern and glistening with glass, but it is also set back 10 feet from the lot line. The new buildings adjacent are, to date, abandoned foundations, waiting for New York's fiscal crisis to abate and allow them to rise.

[12o.] Old Buildings, Hunter College/briefly **Hunter High School,** 930 Lexington Ave., bet. E. 68th and E. 69th Sts. 1913. C. B. J. Snyder.

The last gasp of John Ruskin here caused quality education to be housed in an "English Gothic" shell. It first housed the prestigious Hunter High, part of the city public school system, enrolling talented girls from throughout the city through a competitive examination program. Hunter High (now co-ed) has now moved to the fortlike former I. S. 29 building. [See this section: **36d.**]

[12o.] Old buildings, Hunter College   **[14f.]** Visiting Nurse Service of N.Y.

[13a.] East 69th Street, Fifth to Madison Aves.

Roll Call: No. 9 East (*1915, Grosvenor Atterbury.*), **11** East (*1924, Delano & Aldrich.*), **12** East (*1914, William Welles Bosworth.*) are interesting solely as lesser comparative works of good architects. No. **16** East (*1929,* **English-Speaking Union.**) is in proper fancy dress for these hands-across-the-sea: crisp red brick, white-trimmed **Georgian Revival,** with supporting brass knocker and wrought iron.

[13b.] East 69th Street, Madison to Park Aves.

This block is of human scale, rich and changing, of varied architectural style that produces, with more than usual emphasis, a whole greater than the sum of its parts. **Roll Call: No. 27** East (*1922, York & Sawyer.*) charming stone (ashlar) neo-Gothic; **31** East (*1917, C. P. H. Gilbert.*) **neo-Georgian** for the **Consulate-General of Austria; 33** East (*1910, Howells & Stokes.*); **35** East (*1910. Walker & Gillette.*); **36** East (*1923, Carrère & Hastings; Shreve, Lamb & Blake.*). Lesser works by name architects: **42** East (*1930, Edward S. Hewitt.*), a **Gothic Revival** house now occupied by the **Jewish National Fund;** and **50** East (*1918, Henry C. Pelton.*) a grand house.

[13c.] Union Club, 101 E. 69th St., NE cor. Park Ave. 1932. Delano & Aldrich.

The **oldest** club in **New York** is housed here in the style of the English **18th** century. Limestone and granite with a slate mansard roof.

[14a.] Frick Collection/formerly **Henry Clay Frick Residence,** 1 E. 70th St., facing Fifth Ave. 1914. Carrère & Hastings. Renovated as a public museum. 1935. John Russell Pope. ★ Addition to the east. 1977. Harry

Van Dyke and John Barrington Bayley. Russell Page, Landscape architect. Open to the public. Telephone: 288-0700.

The garden is a pleasant break in the almost continuous east wall of Fifth Avenue.

Bland, sometimes fussy, frequently indecisive, the exterior belies a rich interior, both in architecture and contents. The glass-roofed courtyard, entered almost directly, is a *delightful* transition from the noisy, bustling street: damp, still, except for what seems, in contrast, to be the *rich noise of water* from a central fountain, this is a place for pause, utterly relaxing—not surprising in the work of the same architect who created similar islands of light, sound, and repose at the **Mellon Gallery** in **Washington.**

The eastern addition is an anacronism for these times: a **Beaux Arts Revival** garden court atop a world of underground services.

[14b.] Richard Morris Hunt Memorial, E. 70th St. and Fifth Ave., fronting Central Park. 1898. Bruce Price, architect. Daniel Chester French, sculptor.

Hunt was founding president of the **American Institute of Architects** and architect of **Beaux Arts** monuments: *cf.* the central portion of the **Metropolitan Museum of Art, 12** blocks to the north.

[14c.] East 70th Street, Fifth to Madison Aves.

Roll Call: No. 11 East (*1909. C. P. H. Gilbert.* ★.), **15** East (*1907. Charles I. Berg.* ★.), **17** East (*1909. Heins & La Farge and A. L. Jackson.* ★.) are interesting more for their survival as a group than for special merits separately. However, **19** East (*1909. Thornton Chard.* ★.) and **21** East (*1918. William J. Rogers.* ★.) are now jointly the **Knoedler Gallery,** where, in **19,** three elegant arches spring from **Tuscan** columns.

Fraser Morris, at the southeast corner of 74th Street and Madison Avenue, is a venerable source of elegant specialty groceries and gift baskets. Even though only the rich can use it daily, consider its displays for your own special gourmet events, or that once-in-a-lifetime gift basket.

[14d.] East 70th Street, Madison to Park Aves.

Roll Call: No. 32 East (*1910. Taylor & Levi.*). Note the piers and urns: Renaissance Revival. **No. 36** East (*1884, Remodeled 1919, Louis S. Weeks.*). Romanesque detail, light and dark sandstone (brownstone), eclectic with a very human scale. **No. 43** East (*1929, Mott Schmidt.*). The warm pocked texture of travertine. **No. 45** East (*1929, Aymar Embury II*). An unusual grey travertine with the subtlest possible relief of ornamentation. **No. 46** East (**Lowell Thomas Building, Explorers' Club/***formerly* **Stephen C. Clark House,** *1912, Frederick J. Sterner.*). A glassy **Gothic Revival** place; a charming garden pergola tops its neo-Georgian garage.

[14e.] 723 Park Avenue/formerly **Milliken House,** NE cor. E. 70th St. and Park Ave. ca. 1870.

The spiral fire stair at the rear (off 70th Street) is an *unconscious architectural highlight* of this somber, conservative, brownstone town house, which is to be demolished to provide space for a new facility of Asia House.

[14f.] The Visiting Nurse Service of New York/formerly **Thomas W. Lamont Residence,** 107 E. 70th St., bet. Park and Lexington Aves. 1921. Walker & Gillette.

"English Gothic" for the taste of the country parson's son who became head of **J. P. Morgan & Son.** Ashlar with cut limestone; gabled shingle roofs: unexpected in the continuous facade architecture of these blocks—a welcome break in rhythm.

[14g.] 115 East 70th Street, bet. Park and Lexington Avenues.

Bold **neo-Georgian** at the larger scale of an **Italian Renaissance** palace.

[14h.] 117 East 70th Street, bet. Park and Lexington Aves. 1932. Frederick Rhinelander King.

A grand limestone mansarded house.

[14i.] 124 East 70th Street, bet. Park and Lexington Aves. 1941. William Lescaze.

A *dated* modern house that seems to say **"look at me."** See Lescaze's own house at **211 East 48th Street** [Turtle Bay/United Nations **18.**].

[14j.] Paul Mellon House, 125 E. 70th St., bet. Park and Lexington Aves. 1965. H. Page Cross.

One of the few town houses built in Manhattan since the **Second World War.** Anachronistic; a charming confection signalling a stuccoed "French Provincial" that France never experienced.

[14k.] 131 East 70th Street, NW cor. Lexington Ave. ca. 1895.

Bays and bumps. Projections and recessions. Stained glass, copper, leaded windows: a **picturesque extravaganza.**

[15a.] Birch Wathen School/formerly **Herbert N. Straus House,** 9 E. 71st St. bet. Fifth and Madison Aves. 1932. Horace Trumbauer.

Travertine palace of *great* elegance [see 21a. below].

[15b.] Frick Art Reference Library, 10 E. 71st St., bet. Fifth and Madison Aves. John Russell Pope. Open by appointment. Telephone: 288-8700.

The *verbal* annex to the Frick Collection adjacent.

[15c.] Wenner-Gren Foundation for Anthropological Research, 14 E. 71st St., bet. Fifth and Madison Aves. 1913. York & Sawyer.

Magnificent bronze gates. A great overhanging cornice shelters a **Guastavino-**vaulted penthouse balcony.

[15d.] 18 East 71st Street, bet. Fifth and Madison Aves. 1911. John H. Duncan.

Duncan also designed Grant's Tomb [Morningside Heights **20.**].

[15e.] Catholic Center for the Blind, 22 E. 71st St., bet. Fifth and Madison Aves. 1923. C. P. H. Gilbert.

Smashing. Wide house with grand proportions in limestone.

[15f.] St. James Protestant Episcopal Church, NE cor. Madison Ave. and 71st St. 1884. R. H. Robertson. Rebuilt 1924. Ralph Adams Cram. Replacement (by a smaller spire) of collapsed tower, 1950. Richard Kimball.

Crisp brownstone and steel produce modern overtones on this **neo-Gothic** body.

[15g.] New York Society for the Prevention of Cruelty to Children, 110 E. 71st St., bet. Park and Lexington Aves. ca. 1920.

Paired **Tuscan** columns carry the facade to the street, allowing a lusty, deep-revealed entrance porch.

[15h.] 131 East 71st Street/formerly **Elsie de Wolfe House,** bet. Park and Lexington Aves. Remodeled 1910. Ogden Codman, Jr., and Elsie de Wolfe.

The *original* de-stooped house. **Miss de Wolfe,** the original "lady decorator" (later, as **Lady Mendl,** the almost original party-giver), set the pace for brownstone conversions throughout Manhattan's **Upper East Side.** The few remaining stoops are, in reaction, nostalgically protected and preserved.

[16a.] Lycée Français/formerly **Oliver Gould Jennings House,** 7 E. 72nd St., bet. Fifth and Madison Aves. 1899. Flagg & Chambers. ★

Rich opulence of the Paris of Napoleon III. Vermiculated stonework.

[16b.] Lycée Français/formerly **Henry T. Sloane House,** 9 E. 72nd St., bet. Fifth and Madison Aves. 1896. Carrère & Hastings. ★

The **French** have occupied their own image: an *architectural home* away from home.

[16c.] 19 East 72nd Street, NW cor. Madison Ave. 1936. Rosario Candela and Mott B. Schmidt.

A timid "moderne" apartment house. The site was that of Charles Tiffany's grand Romanesque Revival mansion (an early McKim, Mead & White masterpiece), later decorated and occupied by his son, Louis Comfort Tiffany.

[16d.] 867 Madison Avenue/formerly **Olivotti Building**/originally **Gertrude Rhinelander Waldo House**, SE cor. E. 72nd St. 1898. Kimball & Thompson. ★

Every part of this building exudes personality. Now used principally as a commercial structure, housing galleries and interior decorators (the most celebrated being **Christie's of London**, who use the original salon and conservatory for exhibition galleries), each space has a strong external character, the antithesis of the flexible, universal, modern office building.

[16e.] Manufacturers Hanover Trust Company, 35 E. 72nd St., bet. Madison and Park Aves. 1931. Cross & Cross.

A bank, of all things, in the manner of the **Brothers Adam** (who worked in **18th**-century **London** and **Edinburgh**). Painted a light gray.

[16f.] 54 East 72nd Street. ca. 1950.

Glass is used here for *natural* light, not sight, except for a random glimpse through the louvers or draperies. A simple, background modern building.

[16g.] 750 Park Avenue, SW cor. E. 72nd St. and Park Ave. 1951. Horace Ginsbern & Assocs.

A strong statement of white balconies and red brick in the relatively *bland* wall of **Park Avenue.**

[14j.] The Paul Mellon Town House

[16g.] 750 Park Avenue (apartments)

[17a.] 5 East 73rd Street, bet. Fifth and Madison Aves. 1902. Buchman & Fox.

Made grander by **No. 11's** garden that "sets it off."

[17b.] 11 East 73rd Street/formerly **Joseph Pulitzer Residence.** 1903. McKim, Mead & White.

It would be happy on the **Grand Canal** in **Venice:** paired Ionic composite columns frame a *glassy body*. Note the marshmallow rustications at the ground floor. The **Pulitzer Prize** (for architecture, a sad omission from that set of annual awards) should be given, retroactively, to this great building.

[17c.] 20 East 73rd Street, bet. Fifth and Madison Aves. 1896. Alexander M. Welch.

This is the best in its row (12 to 38 inclusive).

[17d.] Madison Avenue Presbyterian Church, NE cor. E. 73rd St. and Madison Ave. 1899. Altered 1960. Adams & Woodbridge.

Sheer walls contrast sharply with ornate detail, to the end that what is normal **neo-Gothic** carving seems more ornate and complex in contrast.

[17e.] James Lenox House/site of the former **Presbyterian Home** (1869–1974, Joseph Esterbrook), 49 E. 73rd St., bet. Madison and Park Aves. 1976. Rogers, Butler, Burgun, & Bradbury.

A spare and inelegant replacement to a marvelous Victorian monstrosity. Social values prevailed, without architecture in concert.

[17f.] The Buckley School (Addition), 113 E. 73rd St., bet. Park and Lexington Aves. 1962. Brown, Lawford & Forbes.

A simple, well-scaled facade for an extension through the block from **74th** Street for a *venerable* boys' private primary school.

[18a.] 927 Fifth Avenue, SE cor. 74th Street. 1917. Warren & Wetmore.

A modest (in *facade,* not rent) neo-Renaissance limestone apartment house.

[18b.] East 74th Street, Fifth to Madison Aves.

Modest houses of *pallid* architecture, pleasant as a group, but insignificant as individuals.

[18c.] 32 East 74th Street, bet. Madison and Park Aves. 1935. William Lescaze.

A handcrafted vision of the machine esthetic (common to most **Bauhaus**-inspired design and architecture: the *idea* of the machine or machine-made product is more important than the fact that it is made by a machine). Designed in white, it has recently been painted battleship gray. **Too bad.**

[17f.] Addition, the Buckley School   **[19e.]** Whitney Museum of Amer. Art

[19a.] French Consulate, 934 Fifth Ave., bet. E. 74th and E. 75th Sts. 1926. Walker & Gillette.

A *timidly* scaled neo-**Renaissance** building.

[19b.] The Commonwealth Fund/formerly **Edward S. Harkness House,** 1 E. 75th St., NE cor. Fifth Ave. 1905. Hale & Rogers. ★

A *classy* palace guarded by an intricate wrought iron fence.

[19c.] Harkness House for Ballet Arts/formerly **Thomas J. Watson House,** 4 E. 75th St., bet. Fifth and Madison Aves. 1896. Carrère & Hastings. Renovated 1965. Rogers, Butler & Burgun.

[19d.] 5 and 7 East 75th Street, bet. Fifth and Madison Aves. 1902. Welch, Smith & Provot.

Tooled and rusticated limestone.

[19e.] Whitney Museum of American Art, Madison Ave. SE cor. E. 75th St. 1966. Marcel Breuer and Hamilton Smith.

Almost as startling on the city street as the **Guggenheim,** it vends its wares with a vengeance. Reinforced concrete clad in granite, moated, bridged, cantilevered in progressive steps overshadowing the mere patron, it is a forceful place and series of spaces. The cantilevered floors recall the machicolations (stepped, overhanging battlements) of **Carcassonne.** Beware of boiling oil! The Whitney, nevertheless, is at the top of the list of *must-be-seen* modern objects in New York.

[19f.] Miss Hewitt's Classes/formerly **Dr. Ernest Stillman House,** 45 E. 75th St., bet. Madison and Park Aves. 1925. Cross & Cross.

A late neo-Georgian town house. **Dr. Stillman** was an amateur fire buff (as was Mayor LaGuardia), and had installed an alarm system that would tell him where any current fire was located. He often attended, and served as unpaid physician to those needing care.

[19g.] Temple Israel, 112 E. 75th St., bet. Park and Lexington Aves. 1966. Schuman & Lichtenstein.

Overpowering and austere synagogue.

[20a.] Sotheby, Parke-Bernet Galleries, 980 Madison Ave., bet. 75th and 76th Sts. 1950. Walker & Poor, architects. Wheeler Williams, sculptor.

Parke-Bernet has understood and catered to America's cultural starvation: buy history or at least live vicariously with the remnants of history. Unfortunately, Parke-Bernet's "house" is an insipid box unrelated to any cultural values. The Wheeler Williams sculpture pinned on the facade is a dreary gatekeeper: meaningless art at the portal of "art is money."

[20b.] Hotel Carlyle, 35 E. 76th St., facing Madison Ave. 1929. Bien & Prince.

One of the last gasps of the **Great Boom,** this became, in its latter years, **New York** headquarters for *both* the **Truman** and **Kennedy** administrations. Both presidents usually stayed here when visiting the city. **Ludwig Bemelmans** was unleashed with delightful success in the bar; even the ceiling was not spared his whimsical brush: airplanes and birds float overhead.

[20c.] Percy and Harold D. Uris Pavilion, Lenox Hill Hospital, NE cor. Park Ave. and 76th St. 1975. Rogers, Butler, Burgun & Bradbury.

A handsome carved-brick monolith, a *stylish* contrast to the same firm's banal pink metal and glass curtain wall next door.

[20d.] St. Jean Baptiste Church (Roman Catholic), Lexington Ave., SE cor. 76th St. 1913. Nicholas Serracino. ★

Pomp, but *not pompous.* Various **Roman** parts are clustered about a nave and transepts, unfortunately with a pasty result. It seems more stage architecture than the stuff of which cities are made, but has a picturesque silhouette. The congregation was originally **French Canadian.**

[21a.] New York University Institute of Fine Arts/formerly **James B. Duke House,** 1 E. 78th St., NE cor. Fifth Ave. 1912. Horace Trumbauer. Interior remodelled, 1958, Robert Venturi, Cope & Lippincott. ★.

Reputedly a push here and a pull there made a **Bordeaux** house into this austere and elegant town house, originally built for the **Dukes,** whose resources were those of the **American Tobacco Company.** Now it serves New York University graciously.

[21b.] Cultural Services, French Embassy/formerly **Payne Whitney House,** 972 Fifth Ave., bet. E. 78th and E. 79th Sts. 1906. McKim, Mead & White. ★

A **pale** neighbor to the grand Dukes adjacent.

[22a.] Ukrainian Institute of America/formerly **Augustus van Horn Stuyvesant House,** 2 E. 79th St., SE cor. Fifth Ave. 1899. C. P. H. Gilbert.

A French **Gothic** palace. The precedents are limited: few in the Middle Ages ever achieved commercial wealth. The classic comparison is the house of **Jacques Coeur** at Bourges (France).

[22b.] Hanae Mori/formerly **Richard Feigen Gallery,** 27 E. 79th St. bet. Fifth and Madison Aves. Altered, 1969. Hans Hollein and Baker & Blake.

A chromium cylinder dominates this cubistic stucco entrance.

[22c.] New York Society Library/formerly **John S. Rogers House,** 53 E. 79th St., bet. Madison and Park Aves. 1917. Trowbridge & Livingston. ★

The library of the **New York Society** (rather than a library for members of *society*). Anyone may join for a yearly membership fee: **150,000** volumes and a quiet reading room. Telephone: 288-6900.

[22d.] Greek Consulate/originally **George L. Rives House,** 69 E. 79th St., bet. Madison and Park Aves. 1908. Carrère and Hastings. Remodeled 1962. Pierre Zannettos.

Another handsome facade after the **English** architects and brothers, **Robert and James Adam.**

[23a.] Lewis S. Morris House, 116 E. 80th St., bet. Park and Lexington Aves. 1920. Cross & Cross. ★

[23b.] George Whitney House, 120 E. 80th St., bet. Park and Lexington Aves. 1920. Cross & Cross. ★

[23c.] Clarence Dillon House/formerly **Edward H. Bigelow House,** 124 E. 80th St., bet. Park and Lexington Aves. 1930. ★

[23d.] Junior League of the City of New York/formerly **Vincent Astor House,** 130 E. 80th St., bet. Park and Lexington Aves. 1928. Mott Schmidt. ★

These four houses form a grand grouping of wide neo-**Georgian Regency** town houses, a quartet of the last to be built in this grand scale in New York. Number **130** rises above its neighbors, a grand travertine facade in the manner of the **English Brothers Adam.**

[24a.] 998 Fifth Avenue, NE cor. E. 81st St. 1910. McKim, Mead & White. ★

A *pacesetter* in the design of **Fifth Avenue.** Peek at the Japanese garden trellis over the wall behind (along 81st Street).

[24b.] Café du Parc, Stanhope Hotel, 997 Fifth Ave. SE cor. 81st St. 1965. (Hotel, 1926, Rosario Candela.)

A pleasurable addition to an old and elegant hotel. The sights are equal to those offered café-sitters worldwide: girls, the Metropolitan Museum, tottering dowagers, Rolls-Royces, and the near-jet-set.

[25a.] Metropolitan Museum of Art, in Central Park facing Fifth Ave. bet. 80th and 84th Sts. **Rear facade** (now visible only within Lehman Wing), 1880. Calvert Vaux & J. Wrey Mould. **SW wing and facade,** 1888, Theodore Weston. **Central Fifth Avenue facade,** 1895–1902, Richard Morris Hunt and Richard Howland Hunt. **Side wings along Fifth Ave.,** 1906, McKim, Mead & White. **Thomas J. Watson Library,** 1965, Brown, Lawford & Forbes. **Front stairs, pools, Lehman Wing, and Great Hall renovations,** 1975, Roche, Dinkeloo & Assocs. **Various other additions,** 1975–1978, Roche, Dinkeloo & Assocs. ★ Telephone: 736-2211.

The **Columbian Exposition** (Chicago World's Fair) of **1893** was the neo-Renaissance design example for this elegant warehouse of art. The opposing **Romanesque Revival** lost the battle at that fair, now the grounds of Chicago's **Jackson Park.**

Vaux's earlier Ruskinian Gothic kernel is now largely encased: the Fifth Avenue frontage filled in with a **City Beautiful palace** in the manner of **Versailles,** the behind encased and devoured by the Lehman Wing, a flashy glass pyramid flanked by walls designed to screen what Roche and Co. thought to be the vulgar excesses of Vaux. It is a rich and confusing mélange; exciting, grand, controversial, often elegant, sometimes banal. The main hall is still one of the great spaces of New York: our only New York suggestion of the great visionary neo-**Roman** spaces of the **17th-**century **Italian** draftsman, **Piranesi.**

The wares within are without peer. Savor them moment by moment, year by year. Mandatory contribution on entry.

[25b.] Cleopatra's Needle, behind the Metropolitan Museum, ca. 1600 B. C. (reign of Thutmose III).

A gift of the Khedive of Egypt in 1880, it was rolled over tortuous topography from the Hudson River on cannonballs to the "worst place within the city for getting an obelisk to." William H. Vanderbilt paid for its carriage.

[25c.] East 82nd Street, Fifth to Madison Aves., on axis of the main entrance of the Metropolitan Museum.

Rich facades as a group frame the main entrance of the Met, as if houses for the court of **the** palace of art.

[26a.] 25 East 83rd Street, NW cor. Madison Ave. 1938. Frederick L. Ackerman, Ramsey & Sleeper.

A modern monument, not in its external elegance, but in its pacesetting technology: the first centrally air-conditioned building in the city (note that there are no grilles penetrating the walls—air is drawn in at the roof and distributed by interior ductwork). Now aging a bit, one needs a secure ego to live here: it is not in the "modern" *flash and lobby* style. It has more **guts** than skin.

[26b.] 130 East 83rd St. bet. Lexington and Park Aves. 1923. Thomas Paterson, Jr.

In a glass case outside this doorway there is always a small show of photographs of New York City; the exhibit at the 24 Hour Gallery changes at the full moon.

[27a.] Marymount School/formerly **Burden House/**originally **Mrs. Harriet V. S. Thorne House,** 1028 Fifth Ave., SE cor. 84th St. 1902. C. P. H. Gilbert.

Praise to the **Church** for preserving this handsome mansion by default.

[27b.] Church of St. Ignatius Loyola (Roman Catholic), SW cor. Park Ave. and E. 84th St. 1898. Ditmars & Schickel. ★

Vignola (Baroque Italian architect) in the American manner, with a **German** accent. Limestone, superscaled, air conditioned; grim, proper, and **Park Avenue-ish.** The chapel downstairs is an ethnic balancer, dedicated to **St. Laurence O'Toole.**

[27b.] Church of Saint Ignatius Loyola, grim, proper, and Park Avenue-ish

[27c.] Regis High School, 55 E. 84th St., bet. Madison and Park Aves. 1917. Maginnis & Walsh. ★

Eight grand **Ionic** columns are the armature of this facade.

[28a.] 21 East 85th Street and 1132, 1134, 1136, 1138, and 1140 Madison Avenue. ca. 1892. Sacheverell Mongoose.

A brick and terra-cotta terrace (English grouping of jointly designed town houses), now sullied by *unhappy* storefronts on the avenue.

[30d.] The Milton Steinberg House   **[32a.]** Church of the Heavenly Rest

[31a.] Frank Lloyd Wright's Solomon R. Guggenheim Museum (photograph 1966)

[28b.] Park Avenue Christian Church/formerly **South Reformed Church,** SW cor. Park Ave. and E. 85th St. 1909–1911. Cram, Goodhue & Ferguson.

Native materials, here Manhattan schist, were assembled with inspiration from the **Sainte Chapelle** in Paris. Such were the words of **Cram,** but the inspiration seems to have been effective largely for the *flèche* (**Sainte Chapelle** is a glass box with incidental stone supports; this is a stone box with incidental glass).

[28c.] New World Foundation/formerly **Lewis G. Morris House,** 100 E. 85th St., SE cor. Park Ave. ca. 1910. ★

The English 19th-century radical **Richard Norman Shaw** converted Georgian fantasies into such rich and complex places as this. Galleries, bays, bumps, in and out.

[29.] Yivo Institute/formerly **Mrs. Cornelius Vanderbilt House**/originally **William Starr Miller House,** SE cor. Fifth Ave. and E. 86th St. 1914. Carrère & Hastings.

An elegant émigré—from the **Place des Vosges** without the **Place**; a town palace of limestone and brick, encrusted with Ionic pilasters, crowned with a slate mansard roof.

[30a.] Liederkranz Hall, 6 E. 87th St., bet. Fifth and Madison Aves.

The adjacent sculptured remnant from the hall's former building (on **East 58th** Street between Park and Lexington: now demolished) gives this site especial charm (*1896, G. Moretti, sculptor.*). Nice academic **Beaux Arts.**

[30b.] Phelps-Stokes Fund/formerly **Buttinger House,** 10 E. 87th St., bet. Fifth and Madison Aves. 1958. Felix Augenfeld & Jan Pokorny.

Built as a residence around a private library, which occupies a handsome, two-story glass-walled place.

[30c.] Park Avenue Synagogue (addition), SE cor. Madison Ave. and E. 87th St. (197?).

This addition will absorb the Steinberg House next door, veneering it with its own new and stylish heavy concrete facade.

[30d.] Milton Steinberg House, Park Avenue Synagogue, 50 E. 87th St., bet. Madison and Park Aves. 1955. Kelly & Gruzen. Stained glass, Adolf Gottlieb.

A sleek stained-glass facade forms a rich nighttime tapestry in front of this activities-and-office building. Friday night (time of Jewish Sabbath-eve services) is the best time to savor it.

[31a.] Solomon R. Guggenheim Museum, Fifth Ave. bet. E. 88th and E. 89th Sts. 1959. Frank Lloyd Wright. Addition along E boundary facing E. 89th St. Taliesin Associated Architects.

The **Guggenheim's** central space is one of the greatest modern interiors in the world: a museum **more important as architecture** than for the contents it displays. To appreciate it, take the elevator (half round) and meander, literally, between the structural baffles, down the ramp. The painted exterior concrete has not aged happily. And the side-street addition is a labored affair, a decorative *parody* of **Wright** by son-in-law **William Wesley Peters.**

[31b.] St. David's School/formerly the **Cutting Houses,** 12, 14, and 16 E. 89th St., bet. Fifth and Madison Aves. 1919. Delano & Aldrich.

Johnjohn Kennedy brought notoriety to this school by his attendance in these handsome neo-Georgian town houses.

[31c.] National Academy of Design, 3 and 5 E. 89th St., bet. Fifth and Madison Aves. and 1083 Fifth Ave. No. 3, 1914. Ogden Codman, Jr. No. 5, 1958, William and Geoffrey Platt. No. 1083, remodeled 1915, Ogden Codman, Jr.

A center of *conservatism* in the arts. Founded in **1825,** it includes architects, painters, graphic designers.

[31d.] 45 East 89th Street, facing Madison Ave., bet. E. 89th and E. 90th Sts. 1973. Philip Birnbaum; Oppenheimer, Brady & Lehrecke, Associated Architects.

A notch above its competition, its handsome brown brickwork, particularly at the lower levels, was designed by **Thomas Lehrecke** around a basic body by **Philip Birnbaum.** The body is a blockbuster, a state of affairs that can't be condoned, regardless of other virtues.

[32a.] Church of the Heavenly Rest (Protestant Episcopal), SE cor. Fifth Ave. and E. 90th St. 1927–9. Hardie Philip of Mayers, Murray & Philip, architects. Pulpit Madonna, Malvina Hoffman, sculptor. Exterior sculpture, Ulrich Ellerhausen.

Stripped Gothic, this has some of the strong, but austere, massing that prefigures modern as a style if not a fact.

[32b.] 17 East 90th Street, bet. Fifth and Madison Aves. 1917. F. Burrall Hoffman, Jr. ★

A very classy base, rusticated and arched, supports simple **neo-Georgian** above.

[32c.] 15 East 90th Street, bet. Fifth and Madison Aves. 1927. Mott B. Schmidt. ★

Bland neo-Georgian neighbor to **No. 17,** above.

 [33a.] Cooper-Hewitt Museum, the Smithsonian Institution's National Museum of Design/formerly the **Columbia School of Social Work**/ originally **Andrew Carnegie House,** 2 E. 91st St., along Fifth Ave. bet. E. 90th and E. 91st Sts. 1901. Babb, Cook & Willard. ★ Museum alterations. 1977. Hardy Holzman Pfeiffer Assocs.

When **Carnegie** built this "chateau," squatters were his neighbors. **Louise** and **Andrew Carnegie** lived here from **1901** until the surviving Louise's death in **1949.** Its new life is as houser and exhibitor of the great collection originally assembled for the **Cooper Union** by the Cooper and Hewitt families: the decorative arts, from wallpaper to furniture. A modest renovation visually.

[33a.] The Cooper-Hewitt Museum/formerly the Andrew Carnegie House & Garden

[33b.] Convent of the Sacred Heart/formerly **Otto Kahn House,** 1 E. 91st St. NE cor. Fifth Ave. 1918. C. P. H. Gilbert & J. Armstrong Stenhouse. ★

A huge house: an American version of an English version of an Italian Renaissance palazzo (cf. **Papal Chancellery** in Rome). It is rich, but *subdued,* as expected in **Boston** or **Florence.**

[33c.] Duchesne Residence School/formerly **James A. Burden House,** 7 E. 91st St., bet. Fifth and Madison Aves. 1902. Warren & Wetmore. ★

Built by the industrialized ironmonger from **Troy** whose commercial legacy is the **American Machine and Foundry Company** (AMF). A freestanding palazzo with a side court.

[33d.] Consulate of the U.S.S.R./originally **John H. Hammond House,** 9 E. 91st St., bet. Fifth and Madison Aves. 1909. Carrère & Hastings. ★ Alterations 1976. William B. Gleckman.

Hammond's world was recorded in *popular* history when Benny Goodman became his son-in-law.
The **Soviet** government appreciates *style* and bought it for their first **New York** consulate since **1942.** A "palace" worthy of anybody.

[33e.] John B. Trevor House, 11 E. 91st St., bet. Fifth and Madison Aves. 1921. Trowbridge & Livingston. ★

A pale neighbor of the magnificence to the west.

[33f.] The Spence School, 22 E. 91st St., bet. Fifth and Madison Aves. 1929. John Russell Pope.

A high-rise, watery neo-Georgian by someone who should have known better: John Russell Pope, whose Mellon Gallery is one of Washington's most elegant oases.

[33g.] The Dalton School, the First Program, 61 E. 91st St., bet. Park and Madison Aves. ca. 1925.

A large neo-Georgian town house of good scale.

[33h.] Brick Presbyterian Church, NW cor. Park Ave. and E. 91st St. 1938. York & Sawyer; Lewis Ayres, Designer. Chapel of the Reformed Faith. 1952. Adams & Woodbridge.

The safe bumpety-brick and limestone-lanterned **neo-Georgian** of the Thirties.

[34.] Carnegie Hill Historic District. Two separate midblock areas: E. 92nd, E. 93rd and E. 94th Sts., bet. Fifth and Madison Aves.; E. 90th, E. 91st and E. 92nd Sts., bet. Madison and Park Aves. District designated 1974. ★

A landmark district created more to preserve the handsome local midblock *scale* than any pervasive and consistent architectural quality.

[34a.] 1107 Fifth Avenue, SE cor. E. 92nd St. 1925. Rouse & Goldstone.

Mrs. Marjorie Meriwether **Post** (*Toasties*) commissioned this vertically stacked town palace to allow herself a superb **54**-room triplex vantage point in space. Note the elegant auto entrance on **92nd** Street.

[34b.] The Jewish Museum/formerly **Felix M. Warburg House,** 1109 Fifth Ave., NE cor. E. 92nd St. 1908. C. P. H. Gilbert. New building, 1963, Samuel Glazer.

A Gothic chateau with a **Miami Beach** annex.

[34c.] Sculpture, on the Island in Park Avenue, N of E. 92nd St. 1972. Louise Nevelson, sculptor.

A purposely rusty (self-weathering) steel construction: a forlorn modern loner in these **neo-Renaissance** precincts.

[33b.] Convent of the Sacred Heart

[33c.] The Duchesne Residence School

[34d.] Young Men's Hebrew Association, SE cor. Lexington Ave. and 92nd St. 1928. Gehron and Ross.

A city-wide center for cultural affairs, the **YMHA's** Kaufmann auditorium holds readings from the resident **Poetry Center** in addition to concerts and lectures of more general interest.

[34e.] 120 and 122 East 92nd Street, bet. Park and Lexington Aves. 1871 and 1859 respectively. ★

Wooden houses from more rural times, although they, in their then isolation, had to conform to the Commissioners' (grid) plan of **1811.** They have a homely scale.

[35a.] Smithers Alcoholism Center, the Roosevelt Hospital/formerly **Billy Rose House**/originally **William G. Loew House,** 56 E. 93rd St. bet. Madison and Park Aves. 1932. Walker & Gillette. ★

The *last* great mansion, it has the manners of **John Soane,** the avant-garde Regency architect who used classic parts with a fresh attitude to form and space.

[35b.] Permanent Mission of Romania to the U.N./formerly **Virginia Graham Fair Vanderbilt House,** 60 E. 93rd St., bet. Madison and Park Aves. 1930. John Russell Pope. ★

Look at the voussoirs: each has the face of a different woman.

[35c.] 67 and 69 East 93rd Street. 1927. Delano & Aldrich. ★

The garage and a guest house: companions to **No. 75,** below.

[35d.] Synod of Bishops of the Russian Orthodox Church outside Russia/formerly **George F. Baker, Jr., House**/originally **Francis F. Palmer House,** 75 E. 93rd St., NW cor. Park Ave. 1917–1928. Delano & Aldrich. ★

A lesson in town design in itself, and how to respect and reinforce the form of street and avenue while creating both private garden space and richness and variety of architectural form. The "French" courtyard is worthy of an *Hôtel de Ville.* **Baker's** private railroad car could pull in, under his house, from the **New York Central** line passing under **Park Avenue.**

[36c.] Facade of Squadron A Armory

[38d.] The Florence Nightingale Home

[35e.] 176 East 93rd Street, bet. Lexington and Third Aves. 1973. Gueron & Lepp.

A brick *tour de force:* apartments for three families. Arched, and arch.

[36a.] International Center of Photography/formerly **National Audubon Society**/originally **Willard Straight House,** 1130 Fifth Ave., NE cor. E. 94th St. 1914. Delano & Aldrich. ★ Remodeled, 1974, Robert Simpson.

Elegant, distilled, refined; a sharp, precise, intellectually studied **American neo-Georgian** house with a homely residential scale. The **Center** is a pleasant, low-keyed use of its original rooms.
Open to the public. Telephone: 860-1777.

[36b.] 5–25 East 94th Street, bet. Fifth and Madison Aves. ca. 1885.

A speculator's row of brownstone, whitestone, and rockface ashlar **Romanesque Revival** houses with a variety of detail for "individuality." **Numbers 15, 17, 21, and 25** are the most vigorous of the lot.

[36c.] Facade of Squadron A Armory, New York National Guard, Madison Ave., bet. E. 94th and E. 95th Sts. 1895. John Rochester Thomas. ★

A fantasy of brickmason's virtuosity: arches, corbels, machicolations, crenellations; plastic, neomedieval modeling. Now a **play-castle,** a backdrop for the open space of **Hunter High School** to the east.

[36d.] Hunter High School/formerly **I.S. 29,** Park to Madison Aves., E. 94th to E. 95th Sts. 1969. Morris Ketchum, Jr. & Assocs.

Castellated brick complementing its old machicolated neighbor, the west facade of which is preserved as a monument along Madison Avenue. But why didn't they use the same elegant colored mortar?

[37.] Lycée Français de New York/formerly **Mrs. Amory S. Carhart House,** 3 E. 95th St., bet. Fifth and Madison Aves. 1913. Horace Trumbauer. ★

A French school in a **Francophile** town palace. The carriage (garage) doors with a people-door inset are a typical French division between the public world and the private house and garden.

[37a.] Edith Fabbri House/now **The House of the Redeemer,** 7 E. 95th St., bet. Fifth and Madison Aves. 1916. Grosvenor Atterbury.

A limestone palazzo with iron gates and a pillared entrance. This is a special place amidst the middle class.

[38a.] Manhattan Country School/originally **Ogden Codman, Jr., House,** 7 E. 96th St., bet. Fifth and Madison Aves. 1915. Ogden Codman, Jr. ★

Painted limestone, a shuttered *cartoon* of the **Renaissance** from a talented amateur night.

[38b.] St. Francis de Sales Convent/originally **Pierre Cartier House,** 15 East 96th Street, bet. Fifth and Madison Aves. 1915. Ogden Codman, Jr.

The doors are **Parisian** and for carriages; the small and inset door within a pedestrian porthole. Note the great knocker and carved wood swags.

[38c.] The Emerson School, 12 E. 96th St., bet. Fifth and Madison Aves. ca. 1915. Attributed to Ogden Codman, Jr.

Note the garlanded swags.

[38d.] Florence Nightingale Nursing Home, 175 E. 96th St., bet. Lexington and Third Aves. 1967. William N. Breger Assocs.

A penthouse provides a giant, hovering "cornice" over an open roof deck [also see **Long-Term Care Facility,** E. Harlem **2.**].

[39a.] Russian Orthodox Cathedral of Saint Nicholas, 15 E. 97th St., bet. Fifth and Madison Aves. 1901–1902. ★

An *exotic* form amongst the dour surroundings created by predominantly rich northern European Protestants. One of two onion-domed churches in **Manhattan** (this one has five!); the other is at St. George's on 7th Street. High **Victorian, Ruskinian,** polychromatic (red brick, blue and yellow tile), crosses, arches, ornations.

[39b.] Baum-Rothschild Staff Pavilion, Mt. Sinai Hospital, 1249 Park Ave., SE cor. Park Ave. and E. 97th St. 1968. Pomerance & Breines.

Seventeen stories of exposed concrete and brick for a better-than-average apartment house.

[40.] St. Bernard's School, 4 E. 98th St., bet. Fifth and Madison Aves. 1918. Delano & Aldrich.

For boys, *not* the dogs of monks. An awkward **neo-Georgian.**

[41.] Mt. Sinai Hospital, E. 98th to E. 101st Sts., Fifth to Madison Aves. Original buildings, 1904, Arnold W. Brunner. **[41a.] Klingenstein Pavilion,** 1952, Kahn & Jacobs. **[41b.] Annenberg Building,** 1976, Skidmore, Owings & Merrill.

Like **Topsy,** it tried to grow within the grid (absorbing two cross streets), rebuilding itself in the same manner as Roosevelt and Lenox Hill Hospitals; the body remains and gradually changes its appearance.

The **Annenberg** Building at center block, surrounded by a plaza space, is a great, rusty, cadaverous *blockbuster* of a building, an incursive hulk that dominates the skyline of **East Harlem** (to its east).

Sphere (1967, Arnaldo Pomodoro.) is a sophisticated punctuation to the plaza space.

The **Metzger Pavilion** (by Brunner) faces Annenberg at midblock, a French Baroque-Revival *delight.*

[42a.] New York Academy of Medicine, 2 E. 103rd St., SE cor. Fifth Ave. 1926. York & Sawyer. Library open to the public.

Literal eclecticism: a little bit of **Byzantine** detail and mannerism; a pinch of northern Italian **Lombardian** Romanesque: monolithic and massive, windows and doors are tiny apertures.

What may be the world's largest collection of cookbooks is surprisingly housed here, the gift of Dr. Margaret Barclay Wilson. She (if not all physicians) believed that the enlightened, disciplined and/or enriched palate led to well-being of the mind and/or body.

[42b.] Museum of the City of New York, 1220 Fifth Ave., bet. E. 103rd and E. 104th Sts. 1932. Joseph H. Freedlander. ★ Telephone: 534-1672.

The product of a competition between five invited firms, this is a bland neo-Georgian building. The contents *try* to make up for any architectural deficiencies: "dioramas" demonstrate the physical form and history of **New York** to children (both old and young). Savor **Indians,** maps, **Dutch** and **English** colonists, antique toys, **Rockefeller** rooms, period rooms, ship models, portraits, a mishmosh.

Seek out the model (on the first floor) of the **Castello** plan of **New Amsterdam:** the best visualization available of that **Dutch** beaver-trading town.

Alexander Hamilton and DeWitt Clinton face Central Park from niches in the facade (Adolph A. Weinman, sculptor).

[43.] Flower & Fifth Avenue Hospitals/New York Medical College, E. 104th to 105th Sts., along Fifth Ave. 1921. York & Sawyer.

A *homeopathic* medical school (see your doctor for an explanation). This is one of York & Sawyer's lesser works.

[44.] Fifth Avenue Lakeview Apartments, E. side of Fifth Ave., E. 106th to E. 107th Sts. 1976. Gruzen & Partners; Castro-Blanco, Piscioneri & Feder.

Exposed concrete with nougat-colored brick. The buildings surround useable midblock plaza space. *Pleasant, but dull.* See the same firm's vigorous **Schomburg Plaza,** three blocks north.

YORKVILLE

This northeastern quadrant of the **Upper East Side** is named for the village originally centered along the spine of **86th Street** that became the **German** *main street* of **New York.** For purposes of this guide we will bound it by **77th** Street, **Lexington** Avenue, **96th** Street, and the **East River.** Architectural interest is scattered: the wealthy latecomers having migrated only to the riverside (Gracie Square, East End Avenue), the bulk of the area's building is housing for the lower middle class. There is a punctuation of new towers for the *nouveau riche,* and that occasional monument, or just special place, that we list below.

[1.] Stanley Isaacs Houses, N.Y.C. Housing Authority, First Ave., bet E. 93rd and E. 95th Sts. E side. 1966. Frederick G. Frost, Jr. & Assocs.

The poor have the best views, and breezes, in New York. Open-access corridors modulate the standard brick and aluminum windows of this small (*coat,* not vest pocket) housing project. The **barrel-vaulted** community center is another architectural and social step to give place for participation in the community to project residents.

[2.] Former **Municipal Asphalt Plant,** York Ave. to the Franklin D. Roosevelt Drive, E. 90th to E. 91st Sts. 1944. Kahn & Jacobs. ★

New York's most **modern** landmark. Exposed concrete over an arched steel frame, this bold work of *industrial architecture* has not been matched in New York for bald functional and esthetic logic. It was scheduled to be a gymnasium for a proposed school and housing complex, now tabled (Davis, Brody & Associates).

[3.] Gracie Square Gardens, through the center of the block, E. 89th to E. 90th Sts. bet. York and East End Aves.

An unpretentious group of six-story brick apartment buildings whose principal charm is their common central garden.

[4.] Gracie Mansion, official residence of New York's mayor/originally **Archibald Gracie House,** in Carl Schurz Park opposite E. 88th St. 1799. ★ Public spaces wing added, 1966. Mott B. Schmidt.

A remote country residence in its day, Gracie's house has been through the mill of reconstruction and restoration. The 1966 addition permits the mayor to use the house while others think *they* are using it. Its country peers from the same era include the Hamilton Grange (1802), Abigail Adams Smith House (1799), Jumel Mansion (1765), and Van Cortlandt Mansion (1748).

[2.] Former Municipal Asphalt Plant   **[4.]** Orig. Archibald Gracie's house

[5.] Carl Schurz Park and John Finley Walk, East End Ave. to the East River, E. 81st to E. 90th Sts. Remodeled (for the F.D.R. Drive). 1938. Harvey Stevenson and Cameron Clark.

Carl Schurz: general, minister, senator, secretary of the interior, editor; the most prominent German immigrant of the 19th century. He lived in **Yorkville** near this park.

The construction of the **Franklin D. Roosevelt Drive** brought the park its greatest glory: the edge of the city is enjoyed in common by motorists below at the water's edge, and by pedestrians above.

From the edge, view:

Triborough Bridge, opened **1936:** an elevated viaduct on Wards and Randalls Islands connected by four over-water bridges—one between the two islands, and three to the three boroughs. The views from automobiles are handsome, particularly approaching Manhattan from Queens; even better from the same route on foot.

Hell Gate Bridge (*1917. Gustav Lindenthal, engineer.*) is the reason Pennsylvania Station is a *station* rather than a **terminal.** Traffic brought under the Hudson River from the old terminal point in **Jersey City** can continue underground and under-river to **Queens,** thence over the **Hell Gate** and **Little Hell Gate** (now filled in) to the **Bronx, Westchester,** and **Boston.** The bowstring trusses (both upright and inverted) are handsome engineering.

Randalls Island became a park and headquarters of the **Triborough Bridge and Tunnel Authority** when the new **Triborough Bridge** made it accessible—the stadium is a center of **European** football-soccer matches and *super summer concerts.*

Wards Island: the Ward brothers farmed here in the **1780s.** Now it's occupied by a sewage disposal plant (to the east of the Triborough's roadway), **Manhattan State Hospital,** and a small but lovely and very *rural* park connected to **Manhattan** by an ungainly footbridge with spectacular views. The bridge was predicated on the development of the whole island as a park, but the hospital, originally scheduled to be demolished, was reincarnated in a vigorous program of mental health facilities. The local result is not happy: the three tall slabs of tan brick are of an overpowering and oppressive scale, unrelated to the bridge or the balance of the Island.

[6.] 91 East End Avenue, bet. E. 83rd St. and Gracie Square.

A black stucco, stylish exterior.

[7.] Henderson Place Historic District, N side of E. 86th St., bet. York and East End Aves. Lamb & Rich. 1882. District designated 1969. ★

A charming cul-de-sac overpowered and vulgarized by the monster apartment building flanking its west.

[11a.] 245 East 87th Street (apts.)   **[17.]** The Cherokee Apartment House

[8.] 435 East 86th Street, bet. First and York Aves. 1973. William B. Gleckman.

An artful and over-designed building attempting an aggressive modern image. External *styling* here does not bring with it any guarantees of well-designed modern guts.

 [9.] 525 East 85th Street, between York and East End Aves. 1958. Paul Mitarachi.

Two storied house, glass-sheathed: gardens in both front and rear, allowing the raised living room to overview its own garden to the south.

Le Boeuf à la Mode, 539 E. 81st St., bet. York and East End Aves. Telephone: *RH 4-9232.*

Pot roast, French style; an eastern oasis in a **desert of restaurants.** Dinner only. *Closed Mondays.* Moderate priced complete (table d'hôte dinners).

[10a.] Church of the Holy Trinity (Protestant Episcopal), 316 E. 88th St., bet. First and Second Aves. 1897. Barney & Chapman. ★

A little bit of the **Loire Valley** (laced with bits of French Gothic) plus a great deal of imagination produced this urban complex that respects its neighbors and creates, within its own embrace, a *garden oasis* (note the sassafras tree) for this park-poor and plazaless precinct.

(Filigreed clay, brick and terra cotta, weathered copper, red shingles: the main church has dark, rich, Victorian stained glass over squat neo-Gothic aisles.) Modern glass in the cloister chapel is by **Robert Sowers.**

[10b.] Rhinelander Children's Center, Children's Aid Society, 350 E. 88th St. bet. First and Second Aves. 1890. Vaux & Radford.

Another beneficence, like the Church of the Holy Trinity, of the Rhinelander sisters. Unfortunately the facade has been slushed with mortar.

[11a.] 245 East 87th Street, NW cor. Second Ave. 1966. Paul & Jarmul.

The same economics, the same materials the same zoning and building laws as its speculative apartment-house peers, here in the hands of someone who cares: the bold massing of the balconies reads with great richness on the avenue.

[11b.] Group Residence for Young Adults, Jewish Board of Guardians, 217 E. 87th St., bet. Third and Second Aves. 1968. Horace Ginsbern & Assocs.

Bold, plastic, concrete "brutalist" (but not brutal). Classy, personal, distinguished: a modern monument.

Jacob Ruppert's Brewery occupied the multiblocks between **90th** and **93rd** Streets, **Second** and **Third Avenues** for the glory of the German beer hall (this is **Yorkville**). Thirty-four buildings gradually accrued over three-quarters of a century. Where there were originally almost a hundred breweries (i.e., in New York), now there are **none:** the beermaking removed to automated stainless steel factories in places like **Wichita, Kansas,** and **Cranston, R. I.**

[12.] Yorkville Towers and Ruppert Towers/originally site of most of the **Ruppert Brewery,** Second to Third Aves., E. 90th to E. 92nd Streets. 1976. Davis, Brody & Assocs.

Bulky modeled form. Notches, slots, cut corners from the vocabulary initiated by this firm at **Waterside** [Four Squares **73.**]. The density is immense, overwhelming. Given that millstone, the architects have handled an unfortunate program in a sophisticated manner. Talent can't save us from behemoths.

[13.] 230 East 88th Street, bet. Second and Third Aves. 1968. David Todd & Assocs.

The access to apartments is via open, grilled galleries, allowing "floorthrough" apartments throughout.

[14.] Uptown Racquet Club, 151 E. 86th St. bet. Lexington and Third Aves. 1976. Copelin, Lee & Chen.

A *stylish* form in ribbed concrete block crowns an older women's specialty shop.

Cafe Hindenburg, 220 E. 86th St., Second and Third Aves.
A landmark in **German** pastry and "continental" lunch or dinner. It is the best remnant from Yorkville's original and almost monolithic German population.

[15.] New York Turnverein, SE cor. E. 85th St. and Lexington Ave. ca. 1900.

A Germanic Renaissance Revival in granite, brick, and limestone, for a German sports club.

[16.] John Jay Park, Cherokee Place (E of York Ave.) to the Franklin D. Roosevelt Drive, E. 77th to E. 78th Sts.

A small neighborhood park with swimming pools and playgrounds; intensively used. It carries a lush parasol of trees.

[17.] Cherokee Apartments, E. 77th to E. 78th Sts., on Cherokee Place. ca. 1900. Henry Atterbury Smith.

A *second* glance here is well-deserved. These simple buildings are *rich* in new architectural thoughts for their time: the triple-hung windows allow a tenant to step onto a narrow French balcony and view the river; and even if one doesn't make the step, one has a dramatic sense of space and view. The units are entered through **Guastavino** tile-vaulted tunnels opening into central courtyards, from which, at each corner, stairs rise five flights. Note the wrought iron seats and iron and glass canopies sheltering the stair climber from the rain.

[18a.] The Town School, 540 E. 76th St., SW cor. Franklin D. Roosevelt Drive. 1973. Armand Bartos & Assocs.

Stylish brickwork with incised and splayed windows and entry.

[18b.] 430 East 77th Street, bet. First and York Aves. 1971.

A conversion from tenement to luxury apartments with *style*. Brick piers and arches and iron railings give this a **rich order** unmatched by the marble-framed and plastic-plant-festooned lobbies of its vulgar competitors.

[19.] City and Suburban Homes, York Ave. to Franklin D. Roosevelt Drive, E. 78th to E. 79th Sts. 1900. Ernest Flagg.

Experimental housing by Flagg, without the charm of the neighboring Cherokee.

[23.] Row houses, 157–165 E. 78th St.   **[3.]** Congregation Zichron Ephraim

[1.] Manhattan House/1952 photograph/site of the old Third Avenue car barns

[20.] Hungarian Baptist Church, 225 E. 80th St., bet. Second and Third Aves. ca. 1890.

An *exotic* brick and terra-cotta takeoff on an Italian palazzo.

[21.] Yorkville Branch, New York Public Library, 222 E. 79th St. bet. Second and Third Aves. 1915. James Brown Lord. ★

Another **Palladian,** neo-Renaissance **London** club, but here for the masses, not the classes.

[22.] 180 East 78th Street. 1938. E. H. Faile, engineer. Adjacent caretaker's cottage. 1939. Richard B. Thomas.

A bland exterior hides one of the cleverest urban ideas in Manhattan: row houses piggybacked over shopping. When the **"el"** was still up, the small windows facing the avenue (and the el's noise and grime) provided minimum vision and air required by the city building code.

[23.] 157–165 East 78th Street, Lexington to Second Aves. ★

A variety of architecture: **Georgian** rows, **Victorian** terraces, and even a sleek modern alteration. The quality of this pair of blocks is first-rate urban architecture; note particularly Nos. **153** to **165, 208** to **218, 233** to **241,** and **255** to **261.**

[24.] 235 East 78th Street. 1964. Bruce Campbell Graham.

A 14-foot house, handsomely remodeled for separate use of upper and lower duplexes. The brick walls and black wrought iron fences are strong, simple, and appropriate to the Victorian facade behind.

Rappaport's Toy Bazaar, 1381 Third Ave., bet. E. 78th and E. 79th Sts.
A neighborhood institution for more than two generations: a department store of toys.

MANHATTAN HOUSE TO TOWER EAST

This unnamed hillcrest runs from **66th** to **72nd** Streets, falling away toward the north, the south, and Second Avenue. Before the 1950s, its spine was the clanking steel and wood-grilled elevated trestle along Third Avenue, an economic and social wall limiting migration to its east. When the **el** was scrapped (reducing the convenience of rapid transit for this neighborhood) the eastern blocks blossomed with high-rise luxury, the first, and most distinguished, example being Manhattan House.

[1.] Manhattan House, 200 E. 66th St., bet. Third and Second Aves. 1950. Skidmore, Owings & Merrill and Mayer & Whittlesey.

This is the closest **Manhattan** offers, philosophically, to the "blocks" of **Le Corbusier,** his "machines for living" (misinterpreted by many as implying a mechanistic way of life).

The subtle esthetic decision to choose pale gray glazed brick and white-painted steel windows by itself raised this block above its coarse new neighbors (white-glazed brick + aluminum sash = pasty). The balconies become the principal ornament, but unfortunately they are small and precarious for those with any trace of vertigo.

The block was occupied from **1896** to **1949** by the **Third Avenue Car Barns** where first horse cars and then electric streetcars were housed. It was an elaborate French Second Empire mansarded "palace" (*1896. Henry J. Hardenbergh.*).

[2.] Sign of the Dove Restaurant, 1110 Third Ave., NW cor. E. 65th St.

Two hundred years ago there was a **Dove Tavern** near this spot. The present **Dove** is an elegant **neo-Victorian** bar cum hothouse, the product and property of a talented amateur (dentist). It is, however, overpriced and pretentious.

It is said that Nathan Hale was hanged near the *old* **Dove.**

[3.] Park East Synagogue/Congregation Zichron Ephraim, 163 E. 67th St., bet. Lexington and Third Aves. 1890. Schneider & Herter.

Inside, a **Victorian** preaching space, nominally made Jewish through **Saracenic** detail. Stripped to its essentials it could be **Civil War** period Catholic or Congregational. Outside, it is a confection that might have been conceived in a Moorish trip on **LSD:** a *wild,* vigorous extravaganza.

[4.] Engine Co. 39, Ladder 15 N.Y.C. Fire Department/originally Old Fire Department Headquarters, 157 E. 67th St., bet. Lexington and Third Aves. 1886. Napoleon Le Brun & Sons.

Brownstone and brick Romanesque.

[5.] 19th Precinct Station House, N.Y.C. Police Department, 153 E. 67th St., bet. Lexington and Third Aves. ca. 1890.

Limestone "Florentine palace" architecture. Rusticated (stone blocks cut with deep reveals) base supports a turgid **Victorian** body.

[6.] Sam and Esther Minskoff Cultural Center, Park East Day School, S side, E. 68th St., bet. Lexington and Third Aves. 1974. John Carl Warnecke & Assocs.

Yellow brick articulated with granite. A throwback to the curvilinear streamlined architecture of the early thirties.

[7.] Oscar's Salt of the Sea Restaurant, 1155 Third Ave., bet. E. 68th and E. 69th Sts.

Bright, clean, packed with people, this restaurant caters mostly to the local trade. It has a simple, natural, unselfconscious interior and serves well-prepared seafood in a like manner. If you are alone, sit at the counter. Note the elegant **"P. T. Barnum"** gilt lettering.

[8.] N.Y.C. Headquarters, Federal Bureau of Investigation, 201 E. 69th St., NE cor. Third Ave.

The **FBI** here are concealing themselves with vinyl planting and a cheap, decorative entrance frame appropriate to a *schlock* apartment house.

[9.] 163 and 165 East 70th Street, bet. Lexington and Third Aves. 1901. Mainzer, Gilbert & Gilbert.

Supergrand carriage houses with mansard roofs: 163 was John D. Rockefeller, Jr.'s, and **165,** Stephen C. Clark's (Singer Sewing Machine Co.).

[10.] The Lenox School, 154 E. 70th St., bet. Lexington and Third Aves.

A large neo-Gothic house. An annex to the neo-Renaissance main school building at No. 170.

[11.] 251 East 71st Street, bet. Second and Third Aves.

Star Trek? Elliptical bubbles in aluminum frames punctuate a stucco facade.

[9.] 163 and 165 East 70th Street   **[12.]** Tower East (apartment house)

[12.] Tower East, 190 E. 72nd St., along Third Ave., bet. E. 72nd and E. 71st Sts. 1962. Emery Roth & Sons.

A sheer, freestanding tower; four apartments per floor, with magnificent views. If economics had not forced a ground floor of shops in whole or in part, a local plaza could have been gained for the neighborhood. A pleasant neighborhood "art" movie theater occupies the 71st Street corner: **Tower East Cinema.**

[13.] 235 East 72nd Street, between Second and Third Aves. 1947. Lewis J. Ordwein.

A simple, modern facade replaces a "brownstone."

THE FAR EAST

Here is the land of the tenement, and, at the river edge, facilities for health care and research (**Second Avenue** to the **East River**, the **Queensboro Bridge** to **75th Street**). Memories of the **18th** century include the simple but handsome **Smith House [11.],** and the land where the **Rockefeller University** is now located: originally the **Schermerhorn** summer farm! The **Far East** has now gained a neighbor still further east—**Roosevelt Island**—accessible through these precincts via the **Tramway** [Dry Dock Country **6.**].

[1.] 310 East 75th Street, bet. Second and First Aves. ca. 1930.

Art Moderne apartment house of graded colors of brick. The corner windows were not only stylish but an exciting spatial event for the tenants.

[2.] 225 East 74th Street, bet. Second and Third Aves. ca. 1930.

Rounded brick forms: Art Moderne.

[7.] The Premier (apartment house), a simple, crisp, but forceful facade

[3.] Institute for Muscle Diseases, 515 E. 71st St., bet. York Ave. and the Franklin D. Roosevelt Drive. 1961. Skidmore, Owings & Merrill.

Neat, well-designed, and dull.

[4.] Payson House, 435 E. 70th St., on York Ave. bet. E. 70th and E. 71st Sts. 1966. Frederick G. Frost, Jr. & Assocs.

Three staggered slabs straddle two service corridors: a dramatic freestanding form for a New York Hospital staff residence.

[5.] Jacob S. Lasdon House (Residence), Cornell University Medical College, 420 E. 70th St., bet. First and York Avenues. 1975. Conklin & Rossant.

Concrete and glass, elegant and crisp; a friendly, cool, and handsome neighbor.

[6.] New York Hospital/Cornell University Medical College, York Ave. to the Franklin D. Roosevelt Drive, E. 68th to E. 70th Sts. 1933. Coolidge, Shepley, Bulfinch and Abbott.

The word **massing** could have been invented to describe this great medical complex. It will grow, extend, and replace itself on a platform over the **East River Drive** (to the **river's** edge, as **Carl Schurz Park** covers the drive in the Eighties, or as do apartment buildings at 53rd Street).

[7.] The Premier, 333 E. 69th St., bet. First and Second Aves. 1963. Mayer, Whittlesey & Glass; William J. Conklin, designer.

A simple, crisp, but forceful facade of exposed concrete and brick. The contained balconies are far more **useable** and **weatherproof** than those toothy ones punctuating innumerable lesser buildings.

[8.] The Rockefeller University/formerly the **Rockefeller Institute for Medical Research,** E of York Ave., E. 64th to E. 68th Sts. Site acquired 1901.

A campus for research and advanced education occupies a high bluff overlooking the **East River,** once the summer estate of the **Schermerhorn** family of **Lafayette Street.** The first building opened in **1903.**

Caspary Auditorium (*1957. Harrison & Abramovitz.*) is the gloomy dome adjacent to York Ave. It once sparkled with blue tile, but weather problems caused its re-roofing with what might whimsically be thought of as gutta-percha.

The **President's House** (*1958. Harrison & Abramovitz.*) is a limestone and glass country house tucked in a corner at the bluff's edge.

Ask the guard for permission to look around.

[9.] Nurses' Residence, Cornell University–New York Hospital School of Nursing, 1320 York Ave., bet. E. 66th and E. 67th Sts. 1965. Harrison & Abramovitz.

A freestanding glass tower opposite the **Caspary Auditorium.**

 [10.] Rockefeller University Staff Housing, SE cor. E. 62nd St. and York Ave. 1975. Horace Ginsbern & Assocs.

A superior, **designed,** apartment house.

[11.] Colonial Dames of America/originally **Abigail Adams Smith House,** 421 E. 61st St., bet. First and York Aves. 1799. ★

A modest, but real, **Federal** ashlar stone building. Built as a stable by the son-in-law of **President John Adams,** it served a never-completed manor house that burned to the ground in **1826.** Subsequently the stable was promoted in status and served as a hotel, until in turn converted to use as a private house in **1833.**

[12.] Wall in front of former Chermayeff House, 347 E. 62nd St. bet. Second and First Aves. Ivan Chermayeff, designer.

A simple remodeling is enhanced by the playful graffiti of a bicycle.

H

THE HEIGHTS AND THE HARLEMS

North of Cathedral Parkway, Central Park North, and 110th Street, for the most part, lie the areas of Morningside and Hamilton Heights, Harlem, and East Harlem, the last extending southward to 97th Street east of Park Avenue. **The Heights precincts** are known for their **college complexes**—Columbia, Barnard, Teachers—the **seminaries** below the 125th Street valley, and CCNY above it; the **Harlems** are the city's best-known **black and Hispanic ghettos.** All four areas offer relics of the past, signs of **revitalization, as well as of decay,** and a display of **diverse life-styles** which reflect their **varied populations.** There is much to tempt the eye . . . and the mind.

MORNINGSIDE HEIGHTS

From Cathedral Parkway north to West 125th Street, the western hilly side of Manhattan Island is Morningside Heights. Between **the steep escarpment** of Morningside Park on the east and the more **gentle slopes** along the Hudson lie many of Manhattan's **most impressive** visual, architectural, and cultural delights. The site of a 1776 Revolutionary War skirmish, Morningside Heights became in the 19th century the site of the Bloomingdale Insane Asylum and the Leake and Watts Orphan Asylum. The opening of Morningside Park in 1887, Riverside Drive four years later, and the simultaneous settlement here of major cultural institutions permitted the development of **several magnificent groups** of buildings, each in a **well-designed** setting. High-density housing along Riverside and Morningside Drives provided **people-power** for the institutions and for an active community life.

Tips for touring: In general, Morningside Heights is a walker's area. Landmarks are densely spaced; college students and the more permanent population populate the streets. The same can't be said for the other three precincts, where a car is the best means of locomotion and also the best guarantee of security. A word to the wise: stay out of Morningside, Colonial, and St. Nicholas Parks. They are not policed and are avoided by local residents, sensitized to the danger of assault that empty paths and heavy greenery imply.

West of Broadway

[1.] The Hendrik Hudson (apartments), 380 Riverside Dr. bet. Cathedral Pkwy. and W. 111th St. 1907. **Broadway addition** (now **College Residence Hotel),** 601 Cathedral Pkwy., NW cor. Broadway, 1908. Both by William L. Rouse.

Originally the Hendrik Hudson was a grandiose apartment building in a Tuscan villa style jacked up in scale to fit its Riverside Drive site: projected balconies, bracketed Spanish tile cornices, and two Palladian-styled towers capped with overhanging hipped roofs. These **embellishments** and both interior and exterior elegance **have been reduced** by time, economics, and the elements. What remains largely undiminished is the **bold, expressive ornament,** particularly on the Broadway addition (and also **on a relative** at the northeast corner of Broadway and West 111th Street).

[2.] Bank Street College of Education, 610 W. 112th St. bet. Broadway and Riverside Dr. 1970. Harry Weese & Assocs.

A **tall, distinguished, reserved** composition. A suave sliver of mirrored glass chamfers the corners of the **muted brick prism.** This teachers' training school had its beginnings on Bank Street, in Greenwich Village, hence its name.

St. John the Divine to Carl Schurz's statue:

[3a.] Cathedral Church of St. John the Divine (Protestant Episcopal), Amsterdam Ave. at W. 112th St. E side. 1892–1911. Heins & La Farge. Work continued, 1911–1942. Cram & Ferguson. **[3b.] St. Faith's House (Deaconess School).** 1912. Heins & La Farge. **[3c.] Synod House.** 1913. Cram & Ferguson. **[3d.] Choir School.** 1913. Cook & Welch. **[3e.] Bishop's Home and Deanery.** 1914. Cram & Ferguson. **[3f.] Open Air Pulpit.** 1916. Howells & Stokes.

Bishop Henry Codman Potter (1834–1908) was responsible for initiating this enormous **architectural coronet** to crown the Morningside Heights. In 1891 he arranged to purchase the site of the Leake and Watts Orphan Asylum (whose romantic Greek Revival building still remains) and, after **an architectural competition,** commissioned architects **Heins and La Farge** to design the church. The apse, choir, and crossing bear their **Byzantine-Romanesque influence.** By 1911 the bishop and both architects had died (Potter's tomb is in the church's St. James Chapel) and a new **architectural figure** came upon the scene, **Ralph Adams Cram** of Cram & Ferguson. Cram's style was **the French Gothic,** though over the years other versions of Gothic (and other architects: Thomas Nash, Henry Vaughan, Carrère & Hastings) were employed, all **working within Cram's grand scheme.** By 1941, our entry into World War II and the year of Cram's death, only his great nave and the west front (minus its towers) were complete. There **the work stopped.** Though a number of **plans for completion have been proposed** in the intervening years, none has been adopted.

One of the more visible exterior elements is the 105-foot-diameter black asphalt-covered dome over the incomplete crossing. Built of Guastavino vaulting, a process developed by Spanish architect Rafael Guastavino, **it required no interior support** during the course of construction, craftsmen working from the completed vault (of three staggered laminations) as they laid the remaining swirls of tile **using a special adhesive mortar.** The resulting underside, handsomely patterned, is **visible**

THE HEIGHTS/THE HARLEMS

from within, although the original church plans had called for concealing it with mosaics.

Despite its incompleteness and mix of styles it is **an impressive interior,** enormous not only in plan but in volume, its side aisles being built as high as the nave. Do **visit the baptistry and ambulatory chapels** radiating from the apse.

On the landscaped grounds are a number of **ancillary buildings,** among them the Synod House on Cathedral Parkway, whose Amsterdam Avenue portal is embellished with sculpture **from Alexis to Zinzendorf.**

Were St. John the Divine to be completed it would be the world's largest cathedral, though not as large as St. Peter's in Rome. St. Peter's, large as it is, is not a cathedral. The Pope, as bishop of Rome, maintains his seat (his "cathedra") at the Church of St. John, the Lateran, actually outside the Vatican's walls. Size does not a cathedral make.

[3.] Cathedral of St. John the Divine: looking north in a 1917 postcard view

[4a.] Amsterdam House (nursing home), 1060 Amsterdam Ave., NW cor. W. 112th St. 1976. Kennerley, Slomanson & Smith.

An elegantly designed multistory slab for the care of the elderly. The use of naturally finished wood-framed windows is **a masterful touch.**

[4b.] 113th Street Gatehouse, New Croton Aqueduct, W. 113th St., SW cor. Amsterdam Ave. ca. 1890. **[4c.] 119th Street Gatehouse,** W. 119th St., SE cor. Amsterdam Ave. ca. 1890.

Construction **labor was cheap** in the 1880s when the New Croton Aqueduct was built, and a manufactured item, such as **cast-iron pipe, was expensive.** It was more economical, therefore, to minimize the use of pipe when water pressures were minimal and to use **masonry aqueduct** instead. Between 119th and 113th Streets such a masonry aqueduct, **horseshoe-shaped in cross section,** runs under the center line of Amsterdam Avenue. These **extraordinarily finely crafted** stone gatehouses stand above the shafts at both ends of the aqueduct portion where pipes join it from the north and continue to the south.

[5a.] St. Luke's Hospital, Morningside Dr., bet. W. 113th and W. 114th Sts. W side. Original building, 1896. Ernest Flagg.

The western pavilions have been replaced, and the handsome baroque drum and dome are **in danger** of being lost; but the high mansard roofs and the profusion of Classical detail give the original buildings their **dignity and charm.**

[5b.] Église de Notre Dame (Roman Catholic), Morningside Dr., NW cor. W. 114th St. Apse, 1910. Dans & Otto. Remainder, 1915, 1928. Cross & Cross. ★

Like the nearby cathedral, **this church is also unfinished.** The interior must be lighted artificially because the oversized drum and dome, designed to bring skylight into the church, were never built. For a sense of what completion would bring, **visit nearby St. Paul's Chapel** at Columbia [see **8d.**] whose drum and dome **are in place.**

A **surprising contrast** to the smooth pale stone interior of the church is the rough dark stone replica behind the altar of the **grotto at Lourdes.**

[6.] 44–47, 50, and 65 Morningside Drive (apartments), bet. W. 114th and W. 116th Sts. ca. 1910.

Among the most sought-after housing on Morningside Heights. They look comfortable from the outside, and just imagine the views. Many on the Columbia faculty call these home.

[7.] Statue of Carl Schurz, Morningside Dr. at W. 116th St., E. side. 1913. Karl Bitter, sculptor. Henry Bacon, architect.

This is an excellent place from which to view Harlem from afar. Rising from the patchwork quilt roofscape below is a tall white building to the north, the Harlem State Office Building [see Harlem **40.**]. Schurz (1829–1906) was a reformer, an avid conservationist, and editor of the *New York Evening Post* and the *Nation.*

Eats and Drinks: The acclaimed watering place of Morningside Heights is the dark, cavernous, and notorious **West End Cafe,** 2911 Broadway, between 113th and 114th (telephone: 864-8817), a bar which has attracted the locals for decades and in the forties was where Beat writers William Burroughs, Jack Kerouac, and Allen Ginsberg hung out. For pastry and coffee, try **The Hungarian Pastry Shop,** 1030 Amsterdam Avenue near 111th (telephone: 866-4230). For heavier dining there's **The Symposium** (Greek), 544 W. 113th, midblock between Broadway and Amsterdam (telephone: 749-9327); **The Green Tree (Hungarian),** 1034 Amsterdam, corner of 111th (telephone: 864-9106); and **V&T (Italian),** 1024 Amsterdam near 110th (telephone: 663-1708).

Columbia and Barnard:

[8.] Columbia University Campus, W. 114th to W. 120th Sts., bet. Broadway and Amsterdam Aves. Original design and buildings, McKim, Mead & White. Construction begun, 1897. Additions and changes by others.

Columbia is one of the nation's **oldest, largest, and wealthiest** institutions. Prior to relocating here on the Heights, Columbia **occupied two other campuses,** the first southwest of the current City Hall and later a site east of Rockefeller Center's buildings. (The university still owns Rockefeller Center real estate, from which it derives **a substantial income.**) Today's main campus occupies land bought from the **Bloomingdale Insane Asylum.**

The original campus buildings, north of 116th Street (now a pedestrian walkway), are situated **on a high terrace,** two flights of stairs above surrounding streets and separated from them by high, forbidding granite basements. The south campus, **a late addition** south of West 116th street, is terraced below the level of the 116th Street pedestrian way.

Arranged along Classical lines, the campus is **dominated** by the great, domed, limestone Low Library. The Italian Renaissance style **instructional buildings,** of red brick, limestone trim, and copper-green roofs, are **arranged around the periphery** of the campus and are **augmented** by planting, tasteful paving, statues, plaques, fountains, and a variety of Classical ornament and detail. All of this, however, **fails to animate the campus** into either a dramatic or picturesque composition. The old buildings, except for Low Library and St. Paul's Chapel, and the new, except for Fairchild, are lifeless.

It must be said that McKim, Mead & White's **original concept** of a densely built-up campus, with a narrow central quadrangle and six intimate and sheltered side courts, **was never followed.** Only the court between Avery and Fayerweather Halls was completed, and this is now changed by the subterranean extension of Avery Library. The alternative to the compact plan, plus an **explosive growth** in the university, resulted in the **spread of university buildings** to the remainder of Morningside Heights, with even **an ill-fated attempt** to build a gymnasium in Morningside Park.

[8a.] Low Memorial Library. 1897. McKim, Mead & White. ★

Columbia University's most noteworthy visual symbol, familiar to millions of Americans via the news media as the backdrop for the 1968

student riots, is the **monumental, domed, and colonnaded** Low Library, named not for its size but for its donor, **Seth Low** (1850–1916), class of 1870, mayor of Brooklyn, president of Columbia, mayor of New York. Set at the top of three tiers of graciously proportioned steps, this **dignified centerpiece** for the campus so **dominates its open space** that for many years a small sign cautioned the unfamiliar with the words, "THIS IS NOT BUTLER LIBRARY." The reference is to the fact that Low is no longer the university library, its interior spaces being more **suited to ceremonial and administrative uses** than to shelf space and reading rooms. Off the rotunda to the east is a small **library of Columbiana** with items of interest to those who wish to trace the university's march northward through Manhattan from its 18th-century beginnings downtown as King's College.

[8a.] Low Memorial Library, Columbia University, and statue of Alma Mater

[8d.] St. Paul's Episcopal Chapel

[8i.] Fairchild Life Sciences Center

[8b.] Alma Mater. 1903. Daniel Chester French, sculptor.

Centered on the formal stair one tier below Low is **the personification of Columbia,** *Alma Mater,* the once-gilded bronze statue which forms the background of nearly every university graduation ceremony. An **evocative sculpture,** the enthroned figure extends her hand in welcome as she looks up from the mighty tome of knowledge lying open in her lap. Meanwhile, secreted in the shadows of her robes on her left side is her *familiar,* an owl. **As a symbol,** *Alma Mater* has understandably **elicited both love** (a protest in 1962 which caused a newly applied gilding to be removed in favor of the more familiar green patina) **and hate** (in 1968 she survived a bomb blast during that period of student unrest).

Charles Follen McKim: Despite the commonly held belief to the contrary, *not* all buildings produced by the architectural firm of McKim, Mead & White were by its most famous partner, Stanford White. Chief architect for the Columbia campus was Charles Follen McKim (1847–1909), commemorated in a bronze plaque set into the pavement in front of *Alma Mater*. The Latin inscription can be translated as "The monuments [of an artist] look down upon us throughout the ages."

[8c.] Butler Library/originally **South Hall.** 1934. James Gamble Rogers.

This is Columbia's **major library.** Its collections are notable but it is overshadowed architecturally by Low at the north end of the campus lawn. Named for **Nicholas Murray Butler** (1862–1947), who was Columbia's president between 1902 and 1945, the period of the university's enormous growth.

[8d.] St. Paul's Chapel (Protestant Episcopal). 1907. Howells & Stokes. ★

In the **initial period of development** of the Morningside Heights campus, general planning and design were **almost entirely a McKim, Mead & White monopoly.** One of two exceptions (the other was Arnold W. Brunner's School of Mines) is this especially fine chapel, **the best of all Columbia's buildings.** It is a gift of sisters Olivia Egleston Phelps Stokes and Caroline Phelps Stokes, daughters of wealthy financier and philanthropist Anson Phelps Stokes (1838–1913). The beautifully executed work was the design of Howells & Stokes, one of whose partners, Isaac Newton Phelps Stokes (author of *The Iconography of Manhattan Island*) was their brother. The interior is filled with **exquisite Guastavino vaulting** and **magnificent light,** which pours down from above. A visit during a performance of antique works by one of Columbia's musical groups will also reveal its sonorous acoustics.

The last surviving building of the Bloomingdale Insane Asylum, on whose site the original Morningside Heights campus of Columbia was built, is East Hall, just south of St. Paul's. As part of the asylum it was called the Macy Villa. It has since served the university as its Alumni House and is currently the Foreign Student Center.

Behind Philosophy Hall, an extension to the east of the upper campus; access over Amsterdam Avenue:

[8e.] Law School, Amsterdam Ave., NE cor. W. 116th St. 1963. **[8f.] School of International Affairs,** Amsterdam Ave., SE cor. W. 118th St. 1971. Both by Harrison & Abramovitz.

The block-long bridge that links this pair of **whiter-than-white** highrise extensions to the campus makes a **gloomy tunnel** of Amsterdam Avenue below. Looking up at Law's south facade from the terrace you almost expect a dictator **to strut out** onto the cantilevered box **to harangue the multitudes.** An enormous sculpture by **Jacques Lipchitz** was a 1977 addition to the west facade.

[8g.] Avery Hall. 1912. McKim, Mead & White. Underground addition and courtyard to east, 1977. Alexander Kouzmanoff & Assocs.

One of nine similar instructional buildings, Avery Hall houses the School of Architecture and **Avery Library,** the **largest architectural library** in the nation.

[8h.] Marcellus Hartley Dodge Physical Fitness Center. 1974. The Eggers Partnership.

This fancily named gym addition eventually replaced the **abortive project** that was to occupy a site off Morningside Drive in the park, opposition to which sparked the student riots of the late 1960s.

[8i.] Sherman Fairchild Center for the Life Sciences. 1977. Mitchell/Giurgola Assocs.

A radically designed building which **shields the campus** from the banal facade of Seeley W. Mudd Hall, behind. Fairchild is clad with a screen that seems a **vertical extension** of the **red tile pavers** that cover Columbia's terraces.

West of the Columbia Campus:

[9a.] Colosseum (apartments), 435 Riverside Dr., SE cor. W. 116th St. 1910. Schwartz & Gross.

Like a heavily embroidered tapestry, this unusual curved facade, together with its opposite-handed sibling across West 116th Street (3 Claremont Avenue), forms a gateway from Riverside Drive up to the main entrance of the Columbia campus at the Broadway crest of the hill—best seen from the Drive.

[9b.] Originally **Eton Hall** and **Rugby Hall (apartments),** 29 and 35 Claremont Ave. **[9c.] Peter Minuit Hall (apartments),** 25 Claremont Ave. All bet. W. 116th and W. 119th Sts. W Side. 1910. Gaetan Ajello.

Eton and Rugby comprise one opulent facade of white-glazed brick embellished with bold, white-glazed terra-cotta ornament. Minuit is a slightly lesser relative to the south. All are by the unsung architectural hero of Morningside Heights and the Upper West Side, Gaetan Ajello. Between 1910 and 1930 he designed some fifty apartment buildings in these areas for the Paterno and Campagna real estate interests—the "C" emblazoned on the terra-cotta shields here stands for Campagna [see NW Bronx **13.**]. Neatly incised on all three cornerstones of these apartments (as on many of his other works) can be found his architectural calling card: GAETAN AJELLO, ARCHITECT.

[10.] Barnard College, W. 116th to W. 120th Sts., bet. Broadway and Claremont Ave. **[10a.] Millbank, Brinkerhoff and Fiske Halls,** N end of campus. 1890, 1896, 1897. Lamb & Rich. **[10b.] Barnard Hall.** 1917. Arnold W. Brunner. **[10c.] Lehman Library.** 1959. O'Connor & Kilham. **[10d.] Milicent McIntosh Center.** 1969. Vincent G. Kling & Assocs. **[10e.] Helen Goodhart Altschul Hall.** 1969. Vincent G. Kling & Assocs.

The **newest buildings,** the low McIntosh student center and the 14-story Altschul science tower—both made of white limestone—are **the most striking and successful** on the campus. The earlier red brick groups seem to reflect **a desire to bow** to Columbia's early structures across Broadway. Barnard was established to be the undergraduate women's equivalent of Columbia College for men by **Frederick A. Barnard** (1809–1889), the Columbia president who, in the 19th century, **championed the cause of equal rights for women** in higher education.

Terrace Restaurant Atop Butler Hall, 400 W. 119th St., SW cor. Morningside Dr. Telephone: MO 6-9490.

The **highest** public restaurant in upper Manhattan. Continental cuisine and atmosphere; superb views of the city. (To get equally good views without food or drink, visit the upper-floor lounge of the School of International Affairs [see **8f.**].)

Aki Dining Room (Japanese), 420 W. 119th St., E of Amsterdam Ave. Telephone: UN 4-5970.

Down the block from Butler Hall in a converted ground floor apartment. Very unpretentious atmosphere. Try your Japanese here—it's often the only language spoken by the waiters.

North of the Columbia Campus:

[11.] Teachers College, Columbia University, 525 W. 120th St., bet. Amsterdam Ave. and Broadway. **[11a.] Main Hall.** 1892. William A. Potter. **[11b.] Macy Hall/**originally **Macy Manual Arts Building,** N of Main Hall. 1894. William A. Potter. **[11c.] Frederick Ferris Thompson Memorial Hall,** W of Main Hall. 1904. Parish & Schroeder. **[11d.] Russell Hall,** E of Main Hall. 1923. Allen & Collens. **[11e.] Thorndike Hall,** NW of Main Hall. 1973. Hugh Stubbins & Assocs. **[11f.] Whittier Hall (dormitories),** Amsterdam Ave. bet. W. 120th and W. 121st Sts. W side. 1901. Bruce Price.

Tightly squeezed into a full city block, this semi-autonomous branch of Columbia offers **a rich range of red brick architecture** largely from the turn of the century. Peeking above the composition from West 121st Street—it is entered through a court from West 120th Street—is **a sleek new high-rise addition,** 81 years removed from the earliest building.

[11g.] Originally **Horace Mann School**/now **Horace Mann Hall, Teachers College,** Broadway, bet. W. 120th and W. 121st Sts. E side. 1901. Howells & Stokes and Edgar H. Josselyn.

Horace Mann School was founded in 1887 as the laboratory school for Teachers College, but those activities are now conducted in the more suburban Riverdale campus [see NW Bronx **3.**]. Its charming forms, however, continue to **enliven the Broadway blockfront** it commands, as it now serves TC in other capacities.

[12.] **Bancroft Hall (apartments), Teachers College,** 509 W. 121st St., bet. Amsterdam Ave. and Broadway. 1911. Emery Roth.

Tucked away on a dark side street in the shadow of Teachers College is this **ebullient eclectic warhorse** of a facade: aggressive, bold, charming, mysterious. An altogether wonderful discovery.

[10e.] Altschul Hall, Barnard College   **[13.]** Public School 36 Manhattan

[11a.] Main Hall, Teachers College: first building on campus (photo ca. 1893)

[13.] **Public School 36 Manhattan, The Morningside School,** 123 Morningside Dr., NE cor. Amsterdam Ave. 1967. Frederick G. Frost, Jr. & Assocs., architects. William Tarr, sculptor.

This school is actually a group of separate buildings situated on top of rock outcroppings on a **site demapped from Morningside Park.** Simple brick stair towers, cast concrete construction, and large rectangular windows mark the earliest arrival of the **New Brutalism** in upper Manhattan. The **self-weathering steel** sculpture is a particularly **harmonious element** in the overall design.

[14.] Jewish Theological Seminary, 3080 Broadway, NE cor. W. 122nd St. 1930. Gehron, Ross, Alley. David Levy, associated architect.

A **clunky,** oversized neo-Georgian building houses the **central institution** of the Conservative movement in American Judaism. The tower, used as library stacks, was the scene of a tragic fire in 1966.

[15.] Union Theological Seminary, W. 120th to W. 122nd Sts., bet. Broadway and Claremont Aves. 1910. Allen & Collens. Altered, 1952. Collens, Willis & Beckonert. ★

A stronghold of **theological modernism** and **social consciousness** is housed in a Collegiate Gothic quadrangle of rockface granite with limestone trim. Two handsome perpendicular towers, an exquisite chapel, library, refectory, and dormitories **recall medieval Oxbridge.**

[16.] Interchurch Center, 475 Riverside Dr., bet. W. 119th and W. 120th Sts. 1958. Voorhees, Walker, Smith, Smith & Haines.

A bulky work that attempts to harmonize with, but only detracts from, lyrical Riverside Church to the north.

[17.] Riverside Church (Baptist), Riverside Dr., bet. W. 120th and W. 122nd Sts. 1930. Allen & Collens and Henry C. Pelton. Burnham Hoyt, designer. South wing, 1960. Collens, Willis & Beckonert.

The **ornament of Chartres** adapted to a 21-story high-rise **steel-framed church.** Funded by John D. Rockefeller, Jr., this church enjoys the finest in available materials, stone carving, and stained glass of its era. Its 392-foot-high tower (largely an office building disguised as a place of bells) is surmounted by the 74-bell **Laura Spelman Rockefeller Memorial Carillon,** with its 20-ton tuned bass bell. Both carillon and bell are **the largest in the world.** Commanding an imposing site along Riverside Drive, its opulence was criticized upon its completion as "a late example of bewildered eclecticism." Nevertheless, despite problems of scale which seem to make it smaller than it is, particularly when up close, the church is easily **the most prominent architectural work** along the Hudson from Midtown to the George Washington Bridge.

Take an elevator to the carillon and climb the open stairway past the bells to **a lofty windblown observation deck.** For information regarding the modest fee and for bell ringing schedules, call 749-7000.

[18.] Manhattan School of Music/originally **Juilliard School of Music/Institute of Musical Art,** 120 Claremont Ave., NE cor. W. 122nd St. 1910. Donn Barber. Additions, 1931. Shreve, Lamb & Harmon. **[18a.] Mitzi Newhouse Pavilion.** 1970. MacFadyen & Knowles.

Innocuous limestone with a neat concrete and glass cafeteria pavilion.

[19.] International House, 500 Riverside Dr. N of Sakura Park, N of W. 122nd St. 1924. Lindsay & Warren, Louis Jallade, partner-in-charge.

The multistory residence for the **numerous foreign** (and other) **students** who attend the nearby centers of higher learning. A structure made important by its setting—the formal plantings of **Sakura Park**—rather than by any particular architectural merit of its own.

[20.] Grant's Tomb/General Grant National Memorial, National Park Service, Riverside Dr. at W. 122nd St. 1897. John H. Duncan. Mosaic benches, 1973. Pedro Silva, Cityarts Workshop.

The contributions of 90,000 subscribers paid for this **pompous sepulcher,** the design of which was chosen via an architectural competition. (It is a free copy of **Governor Mausoleus' tomb** at Halicarnassus—present-day Turkey—of 300 B.C.: hence a **"mausoleum."**) As attention-getting as this pile of granite is from Riverside Drive, here parted to create its spacious lawned site, it is **a far better work inside.** There, through the massive bronze doors in a great solemn white marble setting, lie President and Mrs. Grant in identical **polished black sarcophagi,** resting side by side for eternity.

The sinuous, colorful, amusing mosaic-ed bench which rings the tomb's plaza (and, curiously, doesn't compete with the tomb itself) is a "beautification effort" which involved community residents in this monument on their doorstep. Shades of **Gaudí** and his **Parque Güell—the mosaics are wonderful.**

To the memory of an amiable child: Almost lost at the edge of the great space commanded by the monumentality of Grant's Tomb is a tiny fenced area (across and down a few steps from the west driveway) in which stands a modest stone urn "Erected to the Memory of an Amiable Child." The urn marks the grave of a five-year-old who fell to his death from these rocks on July 15, 1797. When the property was sold the child's uncle asked that the grave remain inviolate, a request which, despite the bureaucratic problems involved, has been observed through the years. The views of the Hudson Valley are particularly beautiful from this tranquil spot.

[21a.] 560 Riverside Drive (apartments), N of Tiemann Place. 1964.
[21b.] 2 St. Clair Place (offices), W of W. 125th St. 1969. Columbia University facilities. Brown, Guenther, Battaglia, Seckler.

An enormous apartment complex for individuals and families connected with Columbia and its sister institutions on the Heights. Gleaming white, beveled, concrete picture-framed windows repeat and repeat and repeat in the low office wing.

HAMILTON HEIGHTS

This precinct, west of St. Nicholas and Colonial Parks from 125th Street north to Trinity Cemetery, includes the old **village of Manhattanville,** the once-famous **"Sugar Hill,"** and **the City College campuses.** The precinct takes its name from the country estate of Alexander Hamilton. Hamilton's home and other 19th-century houses, churches, and institutional buildings survive, but most of the existing buildings here date from the construction of the Broadway IRT subway, which opened in 1904.

[1.] St. Joseph's Church (Roman Catholic), 401 W. 125th St., NW cor. Morningside Ave. 1889. Herter Brothers.

An unpretentious church of **modest scale and detail.** The north end features an interesting intersection of four roof gables. Note the blind oculi about the rear doors.

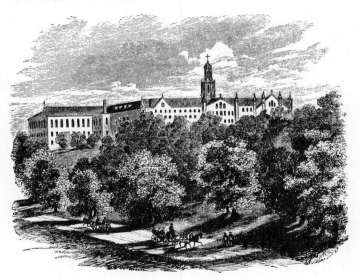

𝔄𝔠𝔞𝔡𝔢𝔪𝔶 𝔬𝔣 𝔱𝔥𝔢 𝔖𝔞𝔠𝔯𝔢𝔡 𝔥𝔢𝔞𝔯𝔱,
Manhattanville, New York.

Manhattanville: Along the west end of the valley which **cleaves** Morningside Heights (on the south) and Hamilton Heights (on the north) grew the village of Manhattanville on both sides of today's West 125th Street, which leads to the former landing of the ferry across the Hudson to Fort Lee, New Jersey. A **bustling village** more in the **New England mill town tradition** than in that of New York City, the settlement supported **a pigment factory,** D. F. Tiemann & Co. (below 125th Street), **a worsted mill** (on 129th Street west of Broadway), **Yuengling Brewery** (128th Street east of Amsterdam), as well as a grammar school, post office, and a sprinkling of churches. **Manhattan College began** in 1853 along Broadway at 131st Street before relocating to Riverdale. The area still retains in its structures vestiges of its **19th-century industrial beginnings.** At Broadway and 125th Street are two worthy restaurants:

Tien Tsin Restaurant, 569 W. 125th St., E of Broadway. Telephone: MO 6-5710.

Northern Chinese cooking is and has always been this restaurant's forte. Beer and booze.

The Shanghai Cafe, 3217 Broadway, N of W. 125th St. Telephone: MO 2-1990.

The **elder statesman** of northern Chinese cooking, a landmark for two generations and showing its age. Less spicy than the Tien Tsin around the corner across Broadway. Beer but no booze.

Where 125th Street turns today it once did not. The diagonal street in the valley between Morningside and Hamilton Heights was called Manhattan Street and ran obliquely to the street grid only because the topography made the valley between Morningside and Hamilton Heights the natural route for a wide thoroughfare—along it ran the streetcars to the Fort Lee Ferry. In 1920, however, it was decided that Manhattan Street should be renamed West 125th Street, and the old part of the original West 125th Street, west of Morningside Avenue, was renamed LaSalle Place. The city fathers also bestowed other new names: Moylan Place for West 126th Street (now eradicated by General Grant Houses), Tiemann Place (after the old color works) for 127th Street, and St. Clair Place for 129th Street. Incidentally, the oblique route of 125th follows a geological fault line, similar to California's San Andreas, but not nearly so active.

[2a.] IRT Broadway Line Viaduct, Broadway and W. 125th St. 1904.

The sweeping latticed arch and its abutments are **worthy of Eiffel.** Best seen from the west where the Transit Authority's gross billboard is less evident.

[2b.] Prentis Hall (Department of Chemical Engineering), Columbia University/originally **Sheffield Farms Milk Company,** 632 W. 125th St., bet. Broadway and St. Clair Place. 1906. Edgar J. Moeller.

Milky white glazed terra cotta, now somewhat yellowed and begrimed, is this **ex-dairy's face to the world.** How appropriate (poetically, at least) that it is now a chemical engineering laboratory.

[3.] Riverside Drive Viaduct, bet. W. 124th and W. 135th Sts. 1901.

From Morningside Heights to Hamilton Heights this lacy (from below) steel viaduct steps off 26 bays of **filigreed steel arches** across the 125th Street valley.

[4a.] Originally **Engine Company 37, N.Y.C. Fire Department,** 503 W. 126th St., bet. Amsterdam Ave. and Old Broadway. ca. 1892.

Old fire houses are sturdy and readily reusable—this a case in point. The structure stands on a block originally devoted to **a sprawling charitable institution** called **Sheltering Arms,** today a city park and swimming pool. West on West 126th Street are other community oriented buildings.

[4b.] Manhattanville Neighborhood Center/originally **The Speyer School,** 514 W. 126th St., bet. Amsterdam Ave. and Old Broadway. 1902. Edgar H. Josselyn.

Built as a **demonstration school** for Teachers College and as a neighborhood settlement. It continues to perform only the latter function. Note the **Flemish Renaissance** silhouette of its parapet.

[4c.] St. Mary's Church-Manhattanville (Protestant Episcopal), 521 W. 126th St., bet. Amsterdam Ave. and Old Broadway. 1909. Carrère & Hastings and T. E. Blake. **[4d.] Rectory.** ca. 1850.

Its name cut into stone in Old English characters and its archaic forms try to hold onto the image of Manhattanville as **a remote 19th-century village.** The mid-19th century white frame rectory, set back from the street to the west of the church, is a delightful surprise.

[4e.] Originally **Bernheimer and Schwartz Pilsener Brewing Company,** W. end of block bounded by W. 128th and W. 126th Sts. E side of Amsterdam Ave. ca. 1885.

A phalanx of 19th-century red brick brewery buildings (a descendent of the even earlier occupant of this site, Yuengling Brewery), now applied to a variety of 20th-century uses. The most charming is the one (a stable?) at 454–458 West 128th, almost at the end of the dead-end street.

The Met's tin shed: The corrugated-iron-sheathed grimy shed occupying some two-thirds of an acre at 495 West 129th Street east of Amsterdam Avenue shelters all manner of bulky sets for the Metropolitan Opera House in Lincoln Center. It was built before the turn of the century as a storage shed for Amsterdam Avenue streetcars. The expanse of sloping roof, unusual for Manhat'an, is best seen from the hill behind, along 130th Street.

[5a.] Riverside Park Community Apartments, 3333 Broadway, bet. W. 133rd and W. 135th Sts. W side. 1976. **[5b.] Intermediate School 195 Manhattan, The Roberto Clemente School,** 625 W. 133rd St. 1976. Both by Richard Dattner & Assocs., Henri A. LeGendre & Assocs., and Max Wechsler Assocs.

The local leviathan: a great slab-sided half octagon that embraces river views and the sun. A NYC Educational Construction Fund project, this oyster has as its pearl the new local school.

[6.] Broadway Mall Improvements, bet. W. 135th and W. 137th, W. 144th and W. 146th Sts. 1972. Glasser & Ohlhausen.

The northernmost group of a redesign (first stage) of the center malls along upper Broadway. [See UWS Manhattan/Lincoln Center **6.**] The **neglected condition** of the malls, old and newly rebuilt, is **deplorable.**

𝕹𝖆𝖙𝖎𝖔𝖓𝖆𝖑 𝕬𝖈𝖆𝖉𝖊𝖒𝖞 𝖔𝖋 𝕯𝖊𝖘𝖎𝖌𝖓

[7.] Our Lady of Lourdes Church (Roman Catholic), 467 W. 142nd St., bet. Convent and Amsterdam Aves. 1904. O'Reilly Bros.

A **bizarre reincarnation** made from parts of three important buildings. The gray-and-white marble and bluestone facade on West 142nd Street includes elements salvaged from the Ruskinian-Gothic-influenced **National Academy of Design** (1865. Peter B. Wight), which once stood at what is today the northwest corner of East 23rd Street and Park Avenue South. The apse of the church and parts of its east wall are built from the architectural elements of the **Madison Avenue end of St. Patrick's Cathedral,** removed to build the Lady Chapel that is there today. And the elaborate pedestals flanking the steps which lead up to the church are relics of department store magnate A. T. Stewart's residence, **"Marble Palace"** (ca. 1867. John Kellum), which stood on the northwest corner of 34th Street and Fifth Avenue until 1901.

North River Pollution Control: Projecting out into the Hudson River (also called the North) between West 133rd and West 145th Streets is an enormous water pollution control plant whose equally enormous roof deck is destined to become a park to serve the adjacent congested community. Between 1969 and 1975 at least three designs for the park were developed, but no decision seems in the offing.

[8a.] Originally **Academy of the Holy Child (Roman Catholic)**/then **St. Walburgas Academy,** 630 Riverside Dr., NE cor. W. 140th St. ca. 1910.
[8b.] Country villa, 625–627 W. 140th St., bet. Broadway and Riverside Dr. ca. 1865.

The Riverside Drive building is **forbidding** in its dark gray rockface stone raiment. But set back in an overgrown green space off West 140th Street is a surprisingly tranquil-looking **wood frame villa** which has, at least temporarily, escaped this culture's hunger for the destruction of old masterworks.

City College's Campuses:

[9.] City College, C.U.N.Y./originally **City College of New York. North Campus,** W. 138th to W. 140th Sts., Amsterdam Ave. to St. Nicholas Terrace. 1905. George B. Post.

This, the original campus of what was once endearingly referred to as CCNY, is a **by-product** of the city's transit system. It is **built of Manhattan schist** (excavated during the construction of the IRT Broadway Subway) trimmed with white-glazed terra cotta. Its **"cathedral"** is Shepard Hall, a towered, skewed neo-Gothic hulk encrusted with terra-cotta detail. Its **satellites** across Convent Avenue, also in Gothic fancy dress, are party, however, to **a formal neo-Renaissance** plan and courtyard.

[9.] City College, C.U.N.Y.: Shepard Archway to North Campus (photo ca. 1960)

[9a.] Steinman Hall (Engineering), Convent Ave., bet. St. Nicholas Terrace and W. 141st St. E side. 1962. Lorimer & Rose.

Glass block modern. Heavy-handed. [Also see **10c.**]

[9b.] Mahoney Hall (Science and Physical Education), Convent Ave., S. of W. 138th St. E side. 1971. Skidmore, Owings & Merrill.

Exposed concrete grillage on a battered precast rocky concrete base. An **unfriendly place** to the passing pedestrian.

[9c.] North Academic Complex, W. 135th to W. 138th Sts., bet. Convent and Amsterdam Aves. Under construction (halted, 1976). John Carl Warnecke & Assocs.

A giant gray **megastructure** whose **skewed geometry** is motivated (justified?) by old Shepard Hall's 45-degree angle to the city's grid. It sits on the site of what was **once Lewisohn Stadium,** a mecca for **outdoor**

concertgoers. Intended as a link between the two campuses, city fiscal problems may dictate that it will never be completed.

[10.] South Campus/formerly **Manhattanville College of the Sacred Heart**/originally **Academy and Convent of the Sacred Heart,** W. 130th to W. 135th Sts. bet. Convent Ave. and St. Nicholas Terrace. **[10a.] President's House**/formerly **Gatehouse, Manhattanville College,** Convent Ave., NE cor. W. 133rd St. 1912. **[10b.] Finley Student Center and Goldmark Hall**/formerly **Main Building and Chapel, Manhattanville College.** 1847–1890.

The Roman Catholic **academy** and the **convent** for its teachers, the Ladies of the Sacred Heart, for which bordering Convent Avenue is named, were **established here** in 1841. In 1952 the college and the sisters moved to Westchester and the city bought the complex and turned it over to City College. The oldest buildings on this campus are brownstone Romanesque. The newest buildings are:

[10c.] Morris Raphael Cohen Library, in South Campus, Convent Ave., SE cor. W. 135th St. 1957. Lorimer & Rose.

Glass block modern. Heavy-handed. [Also see **9a.**]

[10d.] Aaron Davis Hall (Performing Arts), in South Campus, Convent Ave., SE cor. W. 135th St. 1978. Abraham W. Geller & Assocs. and Ezra D. Ehrenkranz & Assocs.

An expression of complexity: this intricate building designed to house three theaters within and to serve one without, an open air amphitheater.

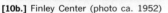

[10b.] Finley Center (photo ca. 1952)   **[11.]** 135 St. Gatehouse, Croton Aq.

Near the City College campuses:

[11.] 135th Street Gatehouse, Croton Aqueduct, W. 135th St., SW cor. Convent Ave. 1890.

A rockface brownstone (top) and granite (bottom) fort. This is the end of the 12-foot-diameter **masonry aqueduct** from High Bridge [see U Manhattan **10.**]. Here the water is distributed into a **network of pipery** whose next stop is the 119th Street Gatehouse [Morningside Heights **4c.**].

[12.] Hamilton Heights Historic District, generally along Convent Ave. bet. W. 141st and W. 145 Sts., including parts of Hamilton Terrace, W. 140th, W. 141st, W. 142nd, W. 143rd, W. 144th, and W. 145th Sts. Designated, 1974. ★

Until the extension of the elevated rapid transit up the West Side in 1879, this was a rural area **dotted with the country houses** of the affluent. Among them was Alexander Hamilton's "Grange" on a site that is today the south side of West 143rd Street between Amsterdam and Convent Avenues.

The advent of the "el" brought a period of **speculative expansion** in the 1880s. Since Convent Avenue ended at West 145th Street and Hamilton Terrace formed **a closed loop** denying access to through traffic, this area became a protected enclave, ideally suited to **high-quality residential**

development. The results of that flurry of construction, dating from 1886 to 1906, comprise the **picturesque row houses** which are the richness of these blocks, houses designed by architects William E. Mowbray, Adolph Hoak, William Ström, Robert Kelly, George Ebert, Henri Foucheaux, John Hauser, and the firm of Neville & Bagge. **Punctuating the horizontality** of these groups of three- and four-story houses **are three churches** marking gateways to the district: Convent Avenue Baptist, St. James Presbyterian, and St. Luke's. It was St. Luke's purchase of Hamilton's Grange that caused the Grange to be moved, in 1889, to its current site within the district where it served as the congregation's chapel during the construction of the adjacent church between 1892 and 1895.

The **romantic appearance** of the district and its varied row houses exerted **a special appeal** upon professors and staff from neighboring City College who, after the campus opened in 1907, began to take up residence here. In recent years the area's popularity waned, but it is **once again on the upswing** as a result of the **brownstone revival movements** of the 1960s and 1970s.

[12a.] 280–298 Convent Avenue (row houses), bet. W. 141st and W. 142nd Sts. W side. 1899–1902. Henri Foucheaux. **320–336 Convent Avenue (row houses),** bet. W. 143rd and W. 144th Sts. W side. 1890–1892. **311–339 Convent Avenue (row houses),** bet. W. 142nd and W. 144th Sts. E side. 1887–1890. Adolph Hoak. All included within the historic district. ★

Picturesque houses all, with a profusion of ornament and roots in a variety (and intermix) of ancient styles: Flemish, Tudor, and Romanesque. Those at the north end further enhance the streetscape by being set back behind gently raised frontyards.

[12b.] St. Luke's Church (Protestant Episcopal), Convent Ave., NE cor. W. 141st St. 1892. R. H. Robertson. Included within the historic district. ★

A brownstone Romanesque Revival structure, massive in scale and volume, making the most of **contrasts in texture** in the working of the stone surfaces. It is unfortunate that the **monumental tower** above the arched corner doorway, which would have completed the composition, **was never finished.** Note the **stately arcade** of half-round arches across the Convent Avenue front.

[12c.] Hamilton Grange National Monument, National Park Service, 287 Convent Ave., bet. W. 141st and W. 142nd Sts. E side. 1802. John McComb, Jr. ★ Included within the historic district. ★

This, the **country home** of Alexander Hamilton (1757–1804), has been stored here for more than 75 years awaiting the choice of a suitable permanent site.

A **frame house** in the Federal style now bearing the cream-colored paint of the Park Service, it stands **squeezed** between St. Luke's and a group of apartment buildings, a **discomfiting posture** for so historic a structure. The interior has not been refitted for public visitation either, beyond the bland installation of some furnishings in the parlor floor rooms, a disappointment. Telephone: 283-5154.

[12d.] Convent Avenue Baptist Church/originally **Washington Heights Baptist Church,** 351 Convent Ave., SE cor. W. 145th St. 1899. Lamb & Rich. Included within the historic district. ★

This Gothic Revival church has a **checkerboard** stone facade usually associated with Romanesque Revival buildings. Squat and ungainly.

Aunt Len's Doll and Toy Museum, 6 Hamilton Terrace, N of W. 141st St.

A former schoolteacher, Mrs. Lennon Holder Hoyte (known to everyone in the community as Aunt Len), has over her many years collected an **astounding range of dolls and toys** which cheerfully clutters every **nook and cranny** of a typical Hamilton Terrace row house. Open to the public. Call before coming: 281-4143.

[12e.] St. James Presbyterian Church and Community House/formerly **St. Nicholas Avenue Presbyterian Church,** St. Nicholas Ave., NW cor. W. 141st St. 1904. Ludlow & Valentine. Included within the historic district. ★

As the century turned, the competence and richness of Revival styled church architecture ebbed. This bland work's urban design value is **to mark entry** to the district to those approaching from the east, the Harlem Valley.

Vintage street lamp: The lazily wandering route of Old Bloomingdale Road across northern Manhattan is marked today by the diagonal of Hamilton Place. Where this street meets Amsterdam Avenue, creating the triangle of space known officially as Alexander Hamilton Square, stands an early cast-iron street lamp. It is not of the bishop's crook variety but a more monumental version with a baronial base and two lamps rather than one. These relics of the turn of the century can still be found infrequently throughout Manhattan. Long may they shine.

[13a.] Lower Washington Heights Neighborhood Family Care Center, 1727 Amsterdam Ave., NE cor. W. 145th St. 1975. Abraham W. Geller & Assocs.

A corner plaza is the main contribution of this over-scaled salmon brick structure.

[13b.] Hamilton Grange Branch, N.Y. Public Library, 503 W. 145th St., bet. Amsterdam Ave. and Broadway. 1906. McKim, Mead & White. ★

All the **ruffles and flourishes** of a Florentine palazzo transferred to a New York street. The same architects' later 115th Street Branch is far superior. [See Harlem **5.**]

[14.] Public School 153 Manhattan, The Adam Clayton Powell, Jr., School, 1750 Amsterdam Ave., bet. W. 146th and W. 147th Sts. W side. 1975. Bureau of Design, N.Y.C. Board of Education.

Simple massing and neat brick details mark this work, **appropriately restrained:** this community is already **busy with street life** and the **ornate relics** of earlier architects.

[15.] Row houses, W. 147th St., bet. Broadway and Riverside Dr. S side. ca. 1900–1905.

Though these houses are not extraordinary, their sitting **on this steep hill** makes this a special street.

[16.] Temple B'nai Israel (synagogue), 610 W. 149th St., bet. Broadway and Riverside Dr. 1920.

Limestone facade, battered walls, and a handsome verdigris-copper high dome.

[17.] Church of the Crucifixion (Anglican), Convent Ave., NW cor. W. 149th St. 1967. Costas Machlouzarides.

An airfoil roof is the hat on these curved concrete forms. One can only wish the luxuriant ivy well as it encloses this over-designed **tour-de-force.**

[18.] City Temple, Seventh Day Adventists' Church/originally **Mt. Neboh Temple (synagogue),** 564 W. 150th St., bet. Amsterdam Ave. and Broadway. 1917.

From temple (Jewish) to temple (Christian), in a half-century. A Spanish tile roof tops this **adventure** in clinker brick masonry and intricate dark brown terra cotta. Sober but proud.

[19a.] Dawn Hotel (former residence), 6 St. Nicholas Place. ca. 1888.
[19b.] 8 St. Nicholas Place (former residence), SE cor. W. 150th St. 1885.

A neglected row house (No. 6) adjoined by the shingle style **extravaganza** on the corner (No. 8) sporting a griffin on its pinnacle. All in all a curious enclave left over from the early days of urbanization. Most notable of the group is across West 150th Street:

[19c.] Originally **James Anthony Bailey Residence/**now **M. Marshall Blake Funeral Home,** 10 St. Nicholas Place, NE cor. W. 150th St. 1888. Samuel B. Reed. ★

Rockface limestone, **stylishly Dutch-gabled,** corner towered. A once-major mansion owned by **circus entrepreneur** Anthony Bailey—he had joined with showman **Phineas T. Barnum** in 1881 to form the Barnum & Bailey circus.

[19d.] 14 St. Nicholas Place (residence), bet. W. 150th and W. 151st Sts. ca. 1890.

Another of these exuberant houses.

[20.] Originally **Joseph Loth & Co. "Fair and Square" Ribbon Factory,** 1828 Amsterdam Ave., bet. W. 150th and W. 151st Sts. W side. 1886.

In 1893, *King's Handbook of New York* praised this local version of **a New England textile mill:** "Good taste and a degree of public spirit were shown by the Firm in so designing the outward aspect of their establishment to avoid the prosiness of business and to keep in harmony with the surroundings." Six hundred workers once produced the ribbons **known to seamstresses across the country** in 15 widths, 200 colors, and up to 90 styles. Note the radiating wings visible from the side streets. (**"This Label is on the Best Ribbon Made"** is the motto painted across the factory's end wall on West 150th Street, still legible after all those years.)

[21.] Originally **32nd Precinct Station House, N.Y.C. Police Department/**now **S.S. & D. Wham, Inc.,** 1854 Amsterdam Ave., SW cor. W. 152nd St. 1872. N.D. Bush.

A wonderful **Victorian relic**—long may it serve! Brick with brownstone graining and a dignified mansard roof trimmed with cast-iron cresting against the sky.

[22a.] Upper Manhattan Medical Group, 1865 Amsterdam Ave., NE cor. W. 152nd St. 1953. Nemeny, Geller & Yurchenko.

Red brick within a white-painted concrete grid: windows **happen where needed** rather than as part of an abstract composition. The central courtyard is an intimate sun-swept delight.

[22a.] Upper Manhattan Medical Group: reveals thoughtful window placement

[22b.] Residence, on Old Croton Aqueduct right-of-way, 473 W. 152nd St., bet. St. Nicholas and Amsterdam Aves. Residence, ca. 1870.

A scene out of Tennessee Williams. Set way back from the street—actually behind a diagonal swath through the street grid **reserved for the Old Croton Aqueduct**—is a sagging but symmetrical clapboard villa.

Milestone: Remarkably preserved in the underbrush in front of the villa on West 152nd Street **[22b.]** is one of Manhattan's ancient milestones, marked 1769. It reads "9 MILES FROM N. YORK." For a display of other milestones, visit the New-York Historical Society [UWS Manhattan/Central Park West **20c.**].

[22c.] Dance Theatre of Harlem/formerly **a garage,** 466 W. 152nd St., bet. St. Nicholas and Amsterdam Aves. ca. 1920. Altered, 1971. Hardy Holzman Pfeiffer Assocs.

An early adaptive reuse effort by a firm of architects who **champion the ordinary:** both in what they begin with and what they add. Pipes, ducts, bare lighting fixtures, old walls—all get used and, **miraculously,** become much more in the process.

[22d.] 456, 458, and 460 West 152nd Street (row houses), bet. St. Nicholas and Amsterdam Aves. ca. 1890.

A trio framed by bay-windowed projections: half-cylindrical on the west; half-hexagonal on the east.

[22e.] Wilson Major Morris Community Center of St. John's Baptist Church, 459 W. 152nd St., bet. St. Nicholas and Amsterdam Aves. 1970. Ifill & Johnson.

Before being shuttered in steel to resist the wear and tear of vandalism, this was a **modest study** in beige brick, precast exposed aggregate, and glass with a particularly neat parapet treatment. Morris was founder of **St. John's Church** across the street at No. 448.

[23a.] St. Luke A.M.E. Church (African Methodist Episcopal)/originally **Washington Heights Methodist Episcopal Church,** 1872 Amsterdam Ave., SE cor. W. 153rd St.

Both the **barn-red-painted church,** both of whose symmetrical spires have disappeared, and its adjacent **barn-red-painted rectory** are bright spots in the community. This is **one of four churches** along this block of West 153rd Street across from the stillness of Trinity Cemetery. The other three:

[23b.] Church of St. Catherine of Genoa (Roman Catholic) and Rectory, 504–506 W. 153rd St., bet. Amsterdam Ave. and Broadway. 1890. **[23c.] Russian Holy Fathers Church (Russian Orthodox),** 526 W. 153rd St. ca. 1925. **[23d.] Christ Evangelical Lutheran Church/**originally **Washington Heights German Evangelical Lutheran Church,** 544 W. 153rd St. 1896. Altered, 1921.

Across from Trinity Cemetery, it seems, is a particularly suitable place for building churches. St. Catherine's is of golden-hued brick with **a stepped gable.** Its rectory is an interesting asymmetrical study. The Russian Church, **set back** some ten feet from the adjacent housing, seems reticent to reveal its **lovely blue onion dome** surmounted by a golden, three-armed cross. The Evangelical Church has, regrettably, **seen better days.**

[24a.] 411–423 West 154th Street (row houses), bet. St. Nicholas and Amsterdam Aves. **[24b.] 883–887 St. Nicholas Avenue,** bet. W. 154th and W. 155th Sts. W side. ca. 1890.

Despite the **all-too-visible results** of permastone veneer hucksters, these mansard-roofed row houses in a high-above-the-side-street setting make them **a robust addition** to the community. The magnificent elms on West 154th Street help too. The south side's row houses are newer, more reminiscent of Central Park West's park blocks.

HARLEM

> ". . . there is so much to see in Harlem."
> —Langston Hughes

To those who haven't been above 110th Street, Harlem means the black ghetto, wherever it may be. But **New York is different** from all other cities, and **its Harlem is different** from all other ghettos. This Harlem consists of a variety of contrasting little Harlems, some distinct, some overlapping. Saturday night Harlem is one place. It is a very different place on Sunday morning. Then you have literary Harlem, political Harlem, religious Harlem, West Indian Harlem, black nationalist Harlem, and philanthropic Harlem.

In other cities the ghettos either radiate from the oldest and most dilapidated neighborhoods or are relegated to the wrong side of town, where they sorely lack transporation and social facilities. But Harlem became New York's black ghetto when its housing was relatively new. Here we find **churches and institutions** set on **wide boulevards** or facing **well-designed parks and plazas.** Three major subway lines give Harlem access to other parts of the city. The stores, restaurants, and hotels of 125th Street maintained their largely white clientele long after the departure of the area's white population.

The old village of **Nieuw Haarlem** was established by Peter Stuyvesant in 1658 in what is now East Harlem and connected with New Amsterdam, ten miles to the south, by a road built by the Dutch West India Company's black slaves. Eight years later the British Governor **drew a diagonal** across Manhattan, from the East River at 74th Street to the

Hudson River at 129th Street, to separate New York from Harlem. Early in the 19th century **James Roosevelt** cultivated a large estate along the East River before moving to Hyde Park. A country village existed at 125th Street and First Avenue.

The **opening** of the Harlem River Railroad in 1837 marks the beginning of Harlem's development **as a suburb for the well-to-do.** Many of the handsome brick and brownstone rows of this era still survive. The **extension of the elevated** to Harlem in 1879 was **followed by the construction** of tenement houses along the routes of the "els" and apartment houses—**some on a lavish scale**—along the better avenues. These were augmented by schools, clubs, theaters, and commercial buildings.

The building of the IRT Lenox Avenue Subway in 1901 encouraged **a real estate boom** in Harlem; many more apartments were built than could be rented. Entire buildings adjacent to Lenox Avenue near 135th Street were unoccupied. Just at this time **the Tenderloin,** west of Herald Square, where a large part of the city's black population was living, **was being redeveloped.** The construction of Pennsylvania Station, Macy's Department Store, large hotels, offices, and loft buildings was forcing them **to seek living space** elsewhere. But in no other parts of the city were blacks welcome.

The Negro settlement in the high-prestige neighborhood of Harlem was made possible by **Philip A. Payton,** a remarkable black realtor. Alert to both the **opportunity in Harlem** and the **desperate housing situation** in the Tenderloin, he was able to open Harlem's many vacant apartment buildings to blacks by **assuming the management** of individual buildings and **guaranteeing premium rents** to their landlords. The availability of good housing for Negroes was unprecedented; the **hard-pressed Negro community flocked** to Payton's buildings, often paying **exorbitant rents** but, for a short while at least, **enjoying good housing.**

Seventh Avenue: In the olden days, surnames of dignitaries became the official titles of city thoroughfares. In this fashion Sixth Avenue above Central Park became Lenox Avenue—after James Lenox, philanthropist and bibliophile, founder of what became the New York Public Library's Lenox Collection. In recent years, however, the style has been to include longer names. That same Sixth Avenue below Central Park is officially Avenue of the Americas, though few use that title. To honor Harlem civil rights champion, provocative preacher, and flamboyant congressman Adam Clayton Powell, Jr., Seventh Avenue north of Central Park was officially proclaimed a boulevard and redubbed with *all* of Powell's names, thus creating an unwieldy mouthful for addresses or directions. In the interests of simplicity, the guide uses Seventh Avenue; no offense intended.

Since Payton's day, Harlem's troubles have been due not to the area's physical shortcomings but to the **abuse and exploitation** that our society visits upon its black members. The great black immigration of the twenties, instead of being allowed to spread, **was bottled up** in this one area. The **privations** of the Great Depression, the **inadequacy** of public and private measures to deal with poverty, and the **failures** of urban renewal have further burdened Harlem and its people.

In spite of exploitation, neglect, and the passing of time, **Harlem has survived** as one of New York's places of interest. Fine **patrician rows** of private houses, and **excellent** churches, communal buildings, and commercial blocks, which **progress has erased** from more fashionable neighborhoods, **survive, neglected, in Harlem.**

Northwest of Central Park: St. Nicholas to Morningside Avenues

[1.] Semiramis (apartments), 137 Central Park North, bet. St. Nicholas and Seventh Aves. ca. 1905.

Rough cut stone and maroon brick were combined here to produce a facade which lives up to its name; **Semiramis** was **a mythical Assyrian queen** known for her beauty (and to whom is ascribed the building of Babylon). Unfortunately the cornice is no more.

[2.] Elevator Entrance and Electrical Substation/originally for **Manhattan Railway Company,** 311–313 Cathedral Parkway, bet. Manhattan and Eighth Aves. 1903. George H. Pegram, engineer.

At street level the **raucous entreaties** of the automobile age—*Flats Fixed, Radiators, Auto Glass*—may conceal the original building, but a look upward will reveal the **villa style** Roman brick remnants of an earlier era. The building dates from the time when a new station was added to the Ninth Avenue elevated, which **turned north** here from Cathedral Parkway as it made its one block shift from Ninth Avenue (Columbus) to Eighth. Since the station was a **considerable height** above the street, elevators were installed.

[3.] Morningside Park, bet. Cathedral Pkwy. and W. 123rd St., Manhattan and Morningside Aves. and Morningside Dr. Preliminary plan, 1873. Revised plan, 1887. Both by Frederick Law Olmsted and Calvert Vaux. Western retaining wall and bays, 1882. J. Wrey Mould.

This narrow strip of park land contains **the high and rocky cliff** that **separates Harlem,** below and to the east, **from Morningside Heights,** above and to the west. It preserves a bit of **primeval Manhattan** as a dramatic foreground to the Cathedral of St. John the Divine, visible at its crest. Proposals of the mid-sixties aimed at solving both the social problems of Harlem and the space problems of the institutions on the Heights by cluttering the park with buildings. Public School 36 [see Morningside Heights 13.] **ate away** the northwest corner of the park, and a proposed Columbia University gymnasium **was to usurp** two additional acres of public park. The scar visible in the park is what remains of that abortive plan, cancelled by the student riots of 1968.

[4.] Junior High School 88 Manhattan/originally **Wadleigh High School for Girls,** 215 W. 114th St., bet. Seventh and Eighth Aves. 1905. C.B.J. Snyder.

This red brick school is embellished with stained glass, installed when it was built as a prestige high school for girls. Later it became dense Harlem's *only* high school—this time coed.

[5.] 115th Street Branch, N.Y. Public Library, 203 W. 115th St., bet. Seventh and Eighth Aves. 1908. McKim, Mead & White. ★

Rusticated limestone, arched windows, and a carved seal of the city, guarded by a pair of angels, recall the **Pitti Palace** in Florence. One of **the most handsome** branch libraries in the entire city.

[6.] Originally **Regent Theater,** 1910 Seventh Ave., SW cor. W. 116th St. 1913. Thomas W. Lamb.

Venice's **Doge's Palace** adapted to the needs of the early motion picture. **S. L. Rothafel** (1882–1936), later to become famous across the nation as **"Roxy,"** began his career here as a picture palace impresario successfully steering the theater out of its initial, catastrophic management failings.

[7.] Graham Court Apartments, Seventh Ave., NE cor. W. 116th St. 1901. Clinton & Russell.

Built for the Astor Estate, this, the most luxurious apartment house in Harlem, contains **eight elevators.** Surrounding a court, it is entered through **a splendid arched passageway,** two stories high. Later in the decade these architects designed the Apthorp, another courtyarded apartment [see UWS Manhattan/Broadway **15.**].

[8.] St. Thomas the Apostle Church (Roman Catholic), 260 W. 118th St., SW cor. St. Nicholas Ave. 1907.

No name is to be found on this church, but its finely detailed neo-Gothic facade, prominently entered via a stairway and an arcaded porch, demands attention.

[9.] Originally **Schinasi Brothers Cigarette Company**/now **Champ Morningside Children's Center,** 311 West 120th St., bet. Eighth and Manhattan Aves. ca. 1905.

Two **mysterious medallions** adorn this otherwise plain facade: one bears a crowned and pyramided seal of **"Egyptian Prettiest";** the other displays a bas-relief bust of one Eliel Constan Tiusperpavov. The plaques relate to the original use of the structure, the sale of **expensive Turkish cigarettes** popular in this country at the turn of the century. The purveyors were the **Schinasi Brothers,** two of whose freestanding mansions overlook the Hudson River on the Upper West Side [see UWS Manhattan/Riverside Drive **13a.** and **22.**].

[10a.] Church of the Master (United Presbyterian), 86 Morningside Ave., bet. W. 121st and W. 122nd Sts. 1972. Victor Christ-Janer and Roger Glasgow. **[10b.]** Originally **Morningside Avenue Presbyterian Church,** 360 W. 122nd St., SE cor. Morningside Avenue. 1904.

The new building, built of vertically arranged gray concrete block resembling **masonry shingling,** overshadows (stylistically) the traditional orange brick church building to the north.

[11.] Former **Dwyer Warehouse**/originally **O'Reilly Storage Warehouse,** 258–264 St. Nicholas Ave., NE cor. W. 123rd St. 1892. Cornelius O'Reilly.

In 1915, three storage warehouses occupied this block of St. Nicholas Avenue; today only the orange brick shell of this one, and its annex on West 124th Street, do. Note the flush quoins in contrasting red brick.

[12.] 28th Precinct Station House, N.Y.C. Police Department, 2271 Eighth Ave., bet. W. 122nd and W. 123rd Sts. and St. Nicholas Ave. 1974. Lehrecke & Tonetti.

Set in a triangular space left over after the chaotically arranged streets have taken their share, this carefully designed two-story police station is **a superb architectural work** that observes a subtle and witty respect for materials not unlike that of **Louis Kahn's** late efforts.

Between Lenox and St. Nicholas Avenues: To the 125th Street Corridor.

[13a.] Public School 208 Manhattan, The Alain L. Locke School, 21 West 111th St., bet. Fifth and Lenox Aves. **[13b.] Public School 185 Manhattan, The John Mercer Langston School,** 20 W. 112th St. Both, 1968. Katz, Waisman, Weber.

A modest pair of schools in brick and exposed aggregate trim set back to back on the through-block site. The schools are identified in **elegantly fashioned** bronze and colored-porcelain enamel letters.

[14.] Memorial Baptist Church/originally **Northminster Presbyterian Church,** 141 W. 115th St., bet. Lenox and St. Nicholas Aves. 1905.

Powerful circular and arched **openings framed in limestone** set into a field of dark red and black tapestry brickwork. A **robust** facade.

[15.] Malcolm Shabazz Mosque No. 7/formerly **Muhammad's Temple of Islam**/originally **Lenox Casino,** 102 W. 116th St., SW cor. Lenox Ave. Converted to temple, 1965. Sabbath Brown.

An innocent translation of the forms of a Middle Eastern mosque into the vernacular materials of 20th-century shopping centers. The aluminum pumpkin-shaped dome is surmounted by a forever-spinning golden crescent.

[16.] Refuge Temple/formerly **Harlem Casino,** 2081 Seventh Ave., NE cor. W. 124th St. Interior renovated, 1966. Costas Machlouzarides.

The Refuge Temple was founded in 1919 by the Rev. R. C. Lawson, who **criticized the lack of emotionalism** in Harlem's more established churches and offered recent migrants the **fire, brimstone, and personal Christianity** with which they were familiar down South.

Frawley Circle to Mount Morris

[17.] Arthur A. Schomburg Plaza (apartment complex), E. 110th to E. 111th Sts., bet. Fifth and Madison Aves. 1975. Gruzen & Partners and Castro-Blanco, Piscioneri & Feder.

Two **handsome,** 35-story-high **octagonal prisms** mark the northeast corner of Central Park—Frawley Plaza—intended to be an elegant traffic circle but long a backwater of greasy gas stations and other blight. Sharing the site with these prominent apartment towers are an 11-story rectangle along Madison Avenue and a one-story-high garage podium that occupies the mid-block and provides for varied outdoor activities on its **inviting wood-trellised deck.** A project of the state's UDC.

[17.] The Schomburg Plaza apts.: visual highlights at Central Park's NE corner

[18.] Originally The Brewster (apartments)/then The State Bank, 1400 Fifth Ave., NW cor. W. 115th St. ca. 1897.

Furnished rooms now occupy this distinguished Renaissance Revival limestone structure. It must once have been an experience **worthy of the Medicis** to enter this banking palace.

[19.] Originally Engine Company 58, N.Y.C Fire Department, 81 W. 115th St., bet. Fifth and Lenox Aves. 1892. Napoleon LeBrun & Sons.

Another former firehouse of the many designed by **the architects of the Metropolitan Life tower.** They gave an appropriate amount of attention to each.

[20.] Originally The Avon (apartments)/then The Public Bank/now Bankers' Trust Co., 1770 Madison Ave., NW cor. E. 116th St. ca. 1896.

A sea of closely spaced, freely interpreted Doric columns. The upper floors are gone.

[21.] Bethel Way of the Cross Church of Christ/originally **Congregation Shaari Zadek of Harlem,** 25 W. 118th St., bet. Fifth and Lenox Aves. 1900. Michael Bernstein.

Fanciful forms borrowed from Islamic architecture grace the facade of what, in another culture, might have been **a harem.** Here its beginnings were as a synagogue later converted to church uses as demographic tides shifted.

[21.] Bethel Church/orig. synagogue   **[22a.]** Fire Watchtower, Garvey Park

[25.] Row houses along Lenox Avenue continue to reflect Victorian charm

The Mount Morris Area west to Lenox:

[22.] Marcus Garvey Memorial Park/formerly **Mount Morris Park**/originally **Mount Morris Square,** interrupting Fifth Ave. bet. 120th and 124th Sts., Madison Ave. to Mount Morris Park W. Land purchased by the city, 1839.

Truly a mount springing out of the flat plain of central Harlem, a logical platform for a fire watchtower which still remains. The park's **unruly rocky terrain** caused it to be largely left alone by park planners until the 1960s, when two major buildings were inserted. In 1973 the **park was renamed** in honor of black leader **Marcus Garvey** (1887–1940).

[22a.] Fire Watchtower, in park SW of Madison Ave. and E. 121st St. 1856. Julius Kroehl, engineer. ★

The **lone survivor** of many fire towers that once surveyed New York for signs of conflagration. The structure employs a post-and-lintel cast-iron frame similar to that used by **John Bogardus** in his warehouses.

 [22b.] Mount Morris Recreation Center and Amphitheater, N.Y.C. Department of Parks and Recreation, in park, along Mount Morris Park W. opp. W. 122nd St. E side. 1969. Lundquist & Stonehill.

Despite the ill-advised community-painted murals added later, this intrusion into the park is, at least, **a dignified one.**

[22c.] Mount Morris Park Swimming Pool and Bathhouse, N.Y.C. Department of Parks and Recreation, in park, SW of Madison Ave. and W. 124th St. 1969. Ifill & Johnson.

This intrusion, in contrast to **[22b.]**, is crude.

[23.] Mount Morris Park Historic District, Mount Morris Park W. to W of Lenox Ave., bet. W. 119th and W. 124th Sts. District designated, 1971. ★

Stately residences along the west flank of the hilly picturesque park and others along the side streets reflecting the **varied Victorian styles** of the late 19th century characterize the fabric of this small district. Interrupting the **warp and woof** are a sprinkling of fine churches and other institutional buildings which date from the area's urbanization as a fashionable and highly desirable community. Fortunately the area has **maintained its architectural character** over the decades. Among the architectural firms whose works are represented in the district, in addition to those responsible for the buildings listed below, are Thom & Wilson, James E. Ware, and George F. Pelham.

[26.] The Mt. Olivet Baptist Church   **[27.]** St. Martin's Episcopal Church

[24.] Mount Morris Presbyterian Church/originally **Harlem Presbyterian Church,** Mount Morris Park W., SW cor. W. 122nd St. 1905. T. H. Poole. Included within the historic district. ★

By the time this Classically inspired church was built, the effects of the Chicago World's Fair's **"White City"** were being felt.

[25.] Row houses, Lenox Ave., bet. W. 120th and W. 121st Sts. E. side. 1888. Demeuron & Smith. Included within the historic district. ★

A Victorian row of ten with distinctive mansard roofs.

[26.] Mount Olivet Baptist Church/originally **Temple Israel,** 201 Lenox Ave., NW cor. W. 120th St. 1907. Arnold W. Brunner. Included within the historic district. ★

Once one of the most prestigious synagogues in the city, this neo-Roman structure dates from the period **after** the turn of the century when a number of **German Jewish** families **took up residence** in the town houses that had earlier been occupied by families of Dutch, English, and Irish descent. Except for the installation of a baptismal pool, the **lavish marble interior** of the synagogue **remains intact.**

[27.] St. Martin's Episcopal Church and Rectory/originally **Holy Trinity Episcopal Church,** W. 122nd St., SE cor. Lenox Ave. 1888. William A. Potter. ★ Included within the historic district. ★

In the spirit of Richardsonian Romanesque but not of the quality of the style's originator. The bulky tower houses **one of the finest carillons** in the entire country, a group of 40 bells which places it **second in size** in the city to the 74 at Riverside Church [see Morningside Heights **17.**].

[28.] Ephesus Seventh Day Adventist Church/formerly **Second Collegiate Church**/originally **Reformed Low Dutch Church of Harlem,** 267 Lenox Ave., NW cor. W. 123rd St. 1887. J. R. Thomas. Included within the historic district. ★

A lofty spire makes this edifice an important Lenox Avenue landmark.

[29a.] Bethel Gospel Pentecostal Assembly/originally **Harlem Club,** 36 W. 123rd St., SE cor. Lenox Ave. 1889. Lamb & Rich. Included within the historic district. ★

When this splendid Romanesque Revival brick club opened it served the local elite. Today its handsome forms serve the local community as a church.

[31.] Orig. The Morris (apartments)　　[35.] Intermediate School 201 Man.

[29b.] Greater Bethel A.M.E. Church (African Methodist Episcopal)/originally **Harlem Free Library.** 1892. Lamb & Rich. Included within the historic district. ★

This present-day religious building adjacent to the old Harlem Club was originally built to serve as one of the city's many free libraries. In 1904 it joined the New York Public Library system, and a new branch building for the area was built in 1909 at 9 West 124th Street, with **Carnegie funds.**

[30.] Ethiopian Hebrew Congregation/originally **Dwight Residence,** 1 W. 123rd St., NW cor. Mt. Morris Park W. 1890. Frank H. Smith. Included within the historic district. ★

A mansion in the neo-Renaissance style, first introduced into these parts by architects McKim, Mead & White. Now occupied by **a congregation of black Jews.**

[31.] Originally The Morris (apartments)/then **Mount Morris Bank and Safety Deposit Vaults,** 81–85 E. 125th St., NW cor. Park Ave. 1889. Lamb & Rich.

Begrimed by the incessant passage of commuter trains rattling by on the adjacent Park Avenue viaduct, this once elegant address is now **almost "invisible."** Look carefully—its Richardsonian Romanesque arches and stained glass are there!

Northern Fifth and Madison Avenues: Above 125th Street

Studio Museum in Harlem, 2033 Fifth Ave., at E. 125th St.

Museum and cultural center for local and national black art. Telephone: 427-5959. RELOCATED

[32.] Mount Moriah Baptist Church/originally **Mount Morris Baptist Church,** 2050 Fifth Ave., bet. E. 126th and E. 127th Sts. W side. 1888. Henry F. Kilburn.

Gone are the brownstone mansions, the **gently pitched stoops** spilling out onto the **wide sidewalks,** and the **generous trees.** What remains, among other relics of Fifth Avenue above 125th Street, is this **green-gray stone** church, now even more morose in appearance than when new.

[33.] Metropolitan Community Methodist Church/originally **St. James Methodist Episcopal Church,** Madison Ave., NE cor. E. 126th St. 1871. **[33a.] Rectory,** 1981 Fifth Ave. N of church. 1871.

Very proper and somber Victorian brownstone clads this Gothic Revival edifice. In **charming contrast** is the **prim,** mansarded minister's house to the north, whose **cast-iron cresting** still remains.

[34.] St. Andrew's Church (Protestant Episcopal), 2067 Fifth Ave., NE cor. E. 127th St. 1891. Henry M. Congdon. ★

A rugged rockface church whose tall clock tower is not set at the corner of the intersection but, rather, **in a more modest location,** against the south transept along East 127th Street. The corner, therefore, is available for a picturesque, south-facing side entrance.

[35.] Intermediate School 201 Manhattan, The Arthur A. Schomburg School, 2005 Madison Ave., bet. W. 127th and W. 128th Sts. 1966. Curtis & Davis.

A rectangular windowless masonry doughnut raised on concrete stilts offers **no glassy temptations** along the street for vandals to vandalize. Despite the rich brick and concrete textures with which the architects adorned the school's exterior, the local community used the **absence of windows** as a **rallying cry** during the period of racial unrest **to force decentralization** of schools which coincided with I.S. 201's opening. Though a pleasing composition in the abstract, the public space under the building is dark, oppressive, and uninviting.

[36.] 17, 19, 21, 23, and 25 West 129th Street (row houses), bet. Fifth and Lenox Aves. ca. 1890.

An unusual row because of its **Tudor Gothic details** executed in red brick and red unglazed terra cotta. No. 17 is closest to mint condition.

[37a.] All Saints' Church (Roman Catholic), E. 129th St., NE cor. Madison Ave. 1894. Renwick, Aspinwall & Russell. **[37b.] Rectory,** 47 E. 129th St. 1889. Renwick, Aspinwall & Russell. **[37c.] School,** 52 E. 130th St. 1904. W.W. Renwick.

The best of Harlem's ecclesiastical groupings. The Gothic tracery and terra-cotta ribboning of the buff, honey-colored, and brown brick wall surfaces make **a confection** of these related buildings designed by the successor firms to that of James Renwick, Jr.

[38.] St. Ambrose Church (Protestant Episcopal)/originally **Church of the Puritans (Presbyterian),** 15 W. 130th St., bet. Fifth and Lenox Aves. 1875.

The original name of this rockface Gothic Revival structure came **as the price** of its construction: **a gift was proferred** with the condition that the congregation (then the Second Presbyterian Church of Harlem) **take on the name** of the Church of the Puritans which had just sold its lease on Union Square. The gift—and name—were accepted.

The 125th Street Corridor: Lenox to Eighth Avenues

[39.] 125th Street Medical Building/originally **H.C.F. Koch & Co. (dry goods store),** 132–140 W. 125th St. bet. Lenox and Seventh Aves. 1893. William H. Hume & Son. Altered.

This was the first of the old established **dry goods merchants** of lower Sixth Avenue [see M Manhattan/Chelsea **12.–19.**] to move northward. It moved **too far;** its success as Harlem's chief department store lasted **only some 30 years.** Its name remains in the building's pediment.

[40.] Harlem State Office Building, 163 W. 125th St., NE cor. Seventh Ave. 1973. Ifill Johnson Hanchard.

Built to provide a state resource and symbol within the Harlem community, this monumental work set in a monumental plaza was a tangible outgrowth of the 1960s' racial unrest. It is a second cousin to Albany's Empire State Plaza **edifice-complex**—both architecturally and politically.

[41.] Theresa Towers (office building)/originally **Hotel Theresa,** 2090 Seventh Ave., bet. W. 124th and W. 125th Sts. W side. ca. 1910. Altered, 1971.

Long **a favored meeting spot** in Harlem, the Theresa attracted Cuba's Prime Minister **Fidel Castro** as his New York hotel when he visited the U.N. in 1960. It has since been converted to office use.

[42.] M. W. King Solomon Grand Lodge, A.F. & A.M. and **Star of Hope Grand Chapel, D.E.S. (Masonic temple)/**originally **Alhambra Theater,** 2114 Seventh Ave., SW cor. W. 126th St. 1905. J. B. McElfatrick & Co. Altered, 1976.

A Beaux-Arts tour-de-force in Flemish bond brick and fancifully mixed terra-cotta ornaments by a firm of well-known theater architects. Now adapted for use by the Ancient Free & Accepted Masons and the Daughters of the Eastern Star.

[43.] Commonwealth Building, 215 W. 125th St., bet. Seventh and Eighth Aves. 1971. Hausman & Rosenberg.

Developed jointly by a local community group (black and Puerto Rican) and a suburban real estate company (white), this crisp, white concrete, precast facade is a happy addition to West 125th Street. The rear facade, on West 126th, is less pretentious but equally handsome.

The Apollo Theater: Although it dates from 1913, the Apollo, at 253 West 125th Street, became one of Harlem's high spots beginning only in 1934. That year the old Hurtig and Seaman Theater, with a white-only admissions policy, was taken over by Leo Brecher and Frank Schiffman, who renamed it the Apollo and opened its doors to the black community. Since then it has been known as *the* Harlem showplace for black entertainers. For years it was the attraction that drew white audiences to Harlem. Bessie Smith, America's "Empress of the Blues," appeared that first year, followed by other blues singers such as Billie Holiday and Dinah Washington. Huddie (Leadbelly) Ledbetter sang from its stage in the thirties shortly after doing time for murder. Duke Ellington's sophisticated style and Count Basie's raw-edged rhythms filled the house later. Following World War II "bebop" had its fling: Charlie (Bird) Parker, Dizzie Gillespie, Thelonius Monk, and more recently the names of such entertainers as Gladys Knight and Aretha Franklin have glittered on its marquee. Beginning in the mid-seventies, however, the Apollo, in response to falling audiences, ended its live presentations in favor of a film-only policy. Too bad.

[44.] Originally **Pabst Concert Hall,** 243–251 W. 124th St., bet. Seventh and Eighth Aves. (Entrance originally on W. 125th St.) ca. 1900.

Though the entrance to this concert hall was on bustling 125th Street, the **fantastic arched roof** is best seen from the rear on 124th. Note how the curve of the roof is expressed by the brick facade.

North of 125th Street: Tree of Hope, The Schomburg Center, Striver's Row, Sugar Hill

[45.] Originally **Methodist Third Church of Christ/**now **Baptist House of Prayer,** 80 W. 126th St.; bet. Fifth and Lenox Aves. ca. 1890.

This converted building and its neighbors at Nos. 82 and 84 (originally **Ellerslie Rooms**) make a fine Romanesque Revival combination.

Mural: Enlivening the upper facade of rebuilt 159 West 127th Street is a bold mural embodying monumental scale and forms. Credits: Norman Messiah, James Buckley, Thierey Kuhn.

[46.] Metropolitan Baptist Church/originally **New York Presbyterian Church,** 151 W. 128th St., NE cor. Seventh Ave. 1884.

A rockface white stone edifice **enlivened at the entrance** by polished orange granite columns bearing amusing Romanesque **"afro" capitals,** and over the side chapel by a majestic half-cone of a roof.

[47.] Salem United Methodist Church/originally **Calvary Methodist Episcopal Church,** Seventh Ave., NW cor. W. 129th St. 1887. Enlarged, 1890.

This church once had the largest Protestant church auditorium and membership in the city. The simple brick structure is embellished by a **carefully detailed** bell tower and **splendid arched paneled** doors.

[48.] The Astor Block, W. 130th St., bet. Fifth and Lenox Aves. S side.

Three-story brick, single-family row houses with wooden porches and large front and side yards. A **restrained beauty** which has been tarnished by years of economic distress.

[49.] Row houses, W. 130th St., bet. Lenox and Seventh Aves. N and S sides. ca. 1885–1890.

Two wonderful rows of houses flank this street, many displaying their original stoops and original cast-iron balustrades once painted to simulate brownstone. Large trees, too, contribute to the street's **enviable** environmental qualities.

[40.] Harlem State Office Building   **[46.]** Metropolitan Baptist Church

[50.] Lionel Hampton Houses (apartments), 273 W. 131st St., NE cor. Eighth Ave.; 201 W. 130th St., NW cor. Eighth Ave.; 410 St. Nicholas Ave., bet. W. 130th and W. 131st Sts. 1974. Bond Ryder Assocs.

One tall and two low apartment buildings, as well as a two-story retail/office structure, comprise this **appealing** masonry composition which straddles an irregular site on both sides of St. Nicholas Avenue. Note the way in which the L-shaped window openings and the through-wall air conditioners develop a pattern, which then becomes the **dominant theme** of the facades.

Liberation Bookstore, Lenox Ave., NW cor. W. 131st St. Telephone: 281-4615.

A bookshop that prides itself, rightfully, for its stock of books related to black history and black studies.

[51a.] Williams Christian Methodist Episcopal Church/formerly **Lafayette Theater,** 2225 Seventh Ave., bet. W. 131st St. and W. 132nd St. E side. ca. 1910.

Since 1951 this church has occupied this complex of three buildings, **originally designed** as a complete **neighborhood entertainment center,** with a large theater, ballroom, restaurant, tavern, public meeting rooms, and offices. For three decades the Lafayette was the nation's leading black theater. The 1913 production of *Darktown Follies* drew so much critical applause that it is credited with having started the vogue of outsiders' coming to Harlem for entertainment.

[51b.] Site of the Tree of Hope, center island of Seventh Ave. at W. 131st St. N side.

The tree which once grew in the middle of the avenue across from what was once the Lafayette Theater is gone, as is its replacement contributed by dancer **Bill "Bojangles" Robinson** (1878–1949)—see his bronze plaque set into the pavement. What remains to mark the spot where out-of-work black entertainers **traded gossip and leads on jobs** is a decorative sculpture (1972. Algernon Miller). It is hoped this metal tree will withstand the abuse of automotive exhaust fumes. A poor substitute.

[52.] St. Aloysius' Roman Catholic Church, 209 W. 132nd St., bet. Seventh and Eighth Aves. 1904. W. W. Renwick.

Deep purple brickwork and pale green glazed brick trim harmonize with terra cotta that **resembles Belgian lace.** All together they produce an evocative and delicate facade.

[53.] Engine Company 59, Ladder Company 30, N.Y.C. Fire Department, 111 W. 133rd St., bet. Lenox and Seventh Aves. 1962. Giorgio Cavaglieri.

Perhaps fashionable in its time, this bright red-glazed brick-plus-black-metal-trimmed firehouse completely negates the more enduring architectural values of its older tenement neighbors, with their richly worked twisted steel fire escape railings and intricate cut-stone plinths.

Beale Street: Life among blacks in Harlem stimulated the curiosity of outsiders for the forbidden, particularly during the Roaring Twenties. Exploiters arranged specially trumped-up visits (for those who could pay) to see "the primitive essence of Harlem Life." The nightspots along West 133rd Street between Lenox and Seventh Avenues, with such names as Dickie Wells', Mexico's, Pod's and Jerry's, and the Nest, were in the center of such activity. Its similarity to Beale Street in Memphis caused the name to be popularly applied to the street in Harlem. The Great Depression called a halt to such goings-on.

[54a.] St. Philip's Church (Protestant Episcopal), 214 W. 134th St., bet. Seventh and Eighth Aves. 1911. Vertner W. Tandy and George W. Foster.

This spare, Gothic style brick church was founded in the notorious **"Five Points"** section of the Lower East Side in 1809. A century later it was able to sell its properties in the Tenderloin for almost $600,000. With this **windfall** the church **purchased its present site,** as well as a row of ten apartment houses on West 135th Street previously restricted to whites. When the congregation began its move to Harlem, white tenants living in the apartment houses were evicted, and their places were made available to blacks.

The church design was a collaborative effort of **two black architects;** Vertner W. Tandy was **the first black** to be granted an **architectural registration** in New York State.

[54b.] Public School 92 Manhattan, The Mary McCleod Bethune School, 222 W. 134th St., bet. Seventh and Eighth Aves. 1965. Percival Goodman.

A **gentle blend** of creamy cast-in-place concrete framing, Hudson River red brick, and yellow-ochre exposed aggregate precast spandrels make for **a thoughtful design** with **no architectural fireworks** employed. Why aren't more city schools as good?

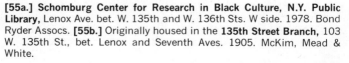

[55a.] Schomburg Center for Research in Black Culture, N.Y. Public Library, Lenox Ave. bet. W. 135th and W. 136th Sts. W side. 1978. Bond Ryder Assocs. **[55b.]** Originally housed in the **135th Street Branch,** 103 W. 135th St., bet. Lenox and Seventh Aves. 1905. McKim, Mead & White.

The 135th Street library was the **unofficial headquarters** of the **black literary renaissance** of the twenties. Arthur A. Schomburg (1874–1938) was a Puerto Rican black who privately undertook the task of **collecting the raw materials of black American history,** which were then in danger of loss through neglect by the academic community. In 1926 the **Carnegie Corporation** of New York **purchased the collection** and had it deposited here with **Schomburg** himself **as its curator.** In 1972 the Schomburg Collection was formally renamed as a research center.

By 1978 the long awaited blockfront-long new Schomburg Center will open with proper facilities for the storage, conservation, and dissemination of the written, aural, and visual materials which comprise the archive's treasures. Telephone: 862-4000.

[55c.] Countee Cullen Branch, N.Y. Public Library, 104 W. 136th St., bet. Lenox and Seventh Aves. 1942. Louis Allen Abramson.

This Art Moderne library, named for a poet of the Harlem renaissance, **Countee Cullen** (1903–1946), was built as an extension to the former 135th Street Branch, the original home of the Schomburg Center [see 55a and 55b.].

[54b.] Public School 92 Manhattan, the Mary McCleod Bethune School: a gem

---

Madame C. J. Walker: Born to freed slaves shortly after the Civil War, this enterprising promoter became a millionaire through the development and sale of hair-straightening products. Her home and adjacent hair parlor occupied the site on which Countee Cullen Branch Library was built. She died in 1919 in Irvington, N.Y., where she had earlier bought a home on the main street, to the consternation of her white neighbors.

[56.] Harlem Branch, Y.M.C.A., 180 W. 135th St., bet. Lenox and Seventh Aves. 1932. James C. Mackenzie, Jr.

A stately red-brown brick Y not to be confused with its 1919 vintage predecessor across the street. Note the pair of **broken-pediment** entranceways built from the same brick.

[57.] Row houses, W. 136th and W. 137th Sts., bet. Seventh and Eighth Aves. ca. 1895.

A row house flock the equal of any within the Upper West Side's park blocks, except that these are in Harlem.

[58.] Row houses, 26–46 Edgecombe Ave., bet. W. 136th and W. 137th Sts. E side, and 321 W. 136th St., bet. Edgecombe and Eighth Aves. ca. 1885.

Victoriana set along a triangular intersection (Dorrence Brooks Square), the backdrop for which is St. Nicholas Park. Before the greenery of the park was cut back to provide mediocre recreation space, the contrast between nature and architecture must have been vivid. No. 26 at the corner of West 136th Street, though down at the heels, is particularly noteworthy.

[62.] St. Nicholas Historic District (King Model Houses): West 139th St.

[59a.] Union Congregational Church/originally **Rush Memorial A.M.E. Zion Church (African Methodist Episcopal),** 60 W. 138th St., bet. Fifth and Lenox Aves. ca. 1910. **[59b.] St. Mark's Roman Catholic Church**/originally **Church of St. Mark the Evangelist,** 65 W. 138th St. 1908.

A curious juxtaposition on opposite sides of the street: two small pinkish-red-painted brick churches trimmed with Gothic style light-colored stone, each with a pair of ornately fashioned wood entrance doors.

[60.] Abyssinian Baptist Church, 132 W. 138th St., bet. Lenox and Seventh Aves. 1923. Charles W. Bolton.

An **uninteresting** building architecturally **but a landmark** in Harlem due to the charisma, power, and notoriety of its spellbinding preacher, **Adam Clayton Powell, Jr.** (1908–1972). Powell's **reform accomplishments** while a member of the House of Representatives, **and his flamboyance,** were known throughout the community and across the country as well. The church has established **a memorial room,** open to the public, containing artifacts from his life. Call AU 6-2626 before paying a visit.

[61.] Casino Renaissance, 2351 Seventh Ave., SE cor. W. 138th St. ca. 1925.

The casino and adjacent theater constitute a commercial community center, combining a great variety of entertainments.

[62.] St. Nicholas Historic District (The King Model Houses), generally W. 138th to W. 139th Sts., bet. Seventh and Eighth Aves., including 202–250 W. 138th St. and 2350–2354 Seventh Ave. 1891. James Brown Lord. 203–271 W. 138th St., 202–272 W. 139th St., and 2360–2378 Seventh Ave. 1891. Bruce Price and Clarence S. Luce. 203–267 W. 139th St. and 2380–2390 Seventh Ave. 1891. McKim, Mead & White. District designated, 1967. ★

By the time David H. King, Jr., built these **distinguished row houses and apartments** he had already been widely **recognized as the builder** responsible for the old **Times Building** of 1889, Stanford White's **Madison**

Square Garden, and the base of the **Statue of Liberty.** Displaying rare vision, King commissioned the services of three different architects at one time to develop this group of **contiguous blocks** for the well-to-do. The results are **an urbane grouping** reflecting the differing tastes of the architects: all with similar scale, varied but harmonious materials, and related styles—Georgian-inspired in the two southern blocks, neo-Italian Renaissance in McKim, Mead & White's northern group. In addition, they share **the amenity of rear alleys** with entrances from the side streets. No wonder they were so prized by their original, white, occupants.

After the turn of the century, as Harlem became **first a refuge for blacks** and **then a ghetto,** the homes and apartments **retained their prestige** and attracted (by 1919) many ambitious as well as successful blacks—people in medicine, dentistry, law, and the arts (such as W. T. Handy, Noble Sissle, and Eubie Blake). As a result, the name **"Striver's Row"** became a popular term for the district in the twenties and thirties.

[62a.] Victory Tabernacle Seventh Day Christian Church/originally **Equitable Life Assurance Company,** 252 W. 138th St., bet. Seventh and Eighth Aves. 1895. Jardine, Kent & Jardine.

Ill-advised signs and signboards fail to conceal this **Moorish temple** built **to sell life insurance** to New Yorkers drawn to the newly opened "suburb" of Harlem, and particularly **to its immediate neighbors,** the residents of the King Model Houses.

[63.] West 139th Street Playground, N.Y.C. Department of Parks and Recreation, Lenox Ave., bet. W. 139th and W. 140th Sts. W side. 1971. Coffey, Levine & Blumberg, architects and landscape architects. Henri A. LeGendre, consultant. Mural, 1971. Children's Art Carnival. Mural repainted, 1976.

One of **the most successful reconstructions** of an existing city playground. The space has been modulated, the levels altered, and play equipment introduced in a confident way which responds to the needs of a typically diverse community. Missing, thankfully, are cutesy-pie forms or bomb shelter boldness. **A model for the future.** Thanks go to the *Reader's Digest* people for their funding.

[64.] St. Charles Borromeo Church (Roman Catholic), 211 W. 141st St., bet. Seventh and Eighth Aves. 1888. Altered, 1973, L.E. Tuckett & Thompson.

The destruction of the nave of this church by fire provided the opportunity for contemporary reuse by building a **modern miniature sanctuary** within the walls of the original.

[65.] Harlem School of the Arts, 645 St. Nicholas Ave. N of W. 141st St. W side. 1977. Ulrich Franzen & Assocs.

A distinguished Harlem institution, once housed next door at St. James' Presbyterian Church Community House. It now occupies its own **intricately programmed building,** nuzzled against the **craggy hillside** of Hamilton Terrace's backyards. [For St. James see Hamilton Heights **12e.**]

[66.] Row houses, Bradhurst Ave., bet. W. 143rd and W. 145th Sts. W side. ca. 1885.

Stoop removal and general lack of maintenance have hurt this **inventive row** of Victorian houses. Nevertheless their wit prevails.

[67.] Colonial Play Center (swimming pool and bathhouse), in Colonial Park, Bradhurst Ave., bet. W. 145th and W. 147th Sts. W side. 1936. N.Y.C. Parks Department. Aymar Embury II, consulting architect.

The **most dramatic** of the city's WPA-built pools. Cylindrical volumes squeeze the abutting sidewalk and alternate with an assortment of half-round arches. These spring from varied Romanesque-inspired capitals to create **a powerful statement** in bold, red brick masonry worthy of its Roman aqueduct (hence "Romanesque") forbears. The **confident design** of this outdoor natatorium **overcomes the shortcomings** of its unskilled masons: bricks in some archways bunch up as they reach their crests, giving them almost the shape of a pointed arch. This free diversity of embellishment and unevenness in craftsmanship appropriately echoes the Romanesque style.

Sugar Hill: The model of the sweet life in Harlem was identified, between the 1920s and 1950s, with a stretch of Edgecombe Avenue west of (and overlooking) the escarpment of Colonial Park and the Harlem Valley below. The multiple dwellings which line Edgecombe above West 145th Street as it ascends Coogan's Bluff were the accommodations to which upwardly mobile blacks aspired and in which those who had achieved fame lived: Cab Calloway, Duke Ellington, Walter White, Roy Wilkins, Thurgood Marshall, W. E. B. DuBois, Langston Hughes.

Riverbend, Dunbar, and Harlem Houses:

[68.] Riverbend Houses (apartments), Fifth Ave., bet. E. 138th and E. 142nd Sts. E. side. 1967. Davis, Brody & Assocs.

Social and aesthetic concerns are here melded into a single, eminently successful apartment development **respectful of street lines** along Fifth Avenue. Dense, compact, of vernacular materials imaginatively used, it has 625 apartments in the sky for moderate-income families. The tall end towers consist of flats; the 8- and 10-story structures in between contain duplexes reached by outdoor passages which provide tenants with **semiprivate terraces** overlooking the Harlem River. **A monumental breakthrough** in urban, publicly subsidized housing.

[68.] Riverbend Houses (apartments): a seminal design in subsidized housing

The giant brick: A revolution in brick began at Riverbend Houses. As the costs of laying brick skyrocketed in the decades following World War II, the standard brick ($2\frac{1}{2}''$ high × 8″ wide) was frequently replaced by the newly developed jumbo ($3\frac{1}{2}''$ high × 8″ wide). This resulted in an economy but introduced a subtle but insidious change of scale where the eye was fooled into thinking the standard, more delicately sized and proportioned brick was being used. To achieve yet a greater economy and to introduce a new scale in exterior masonry units, architects Davis, Brody & Associates developed the giant brick ($5\frac{1}{2}''$ high × 8″ wide) working with manufacturers, masonry contractors, and the trade unions. The giant, used first at Riverbend, reduced handling costs, lessened the number of mortar joints, and changed the aesthetics of brick construction.

[69.] 369th Regiment Armory, N.Y. National Guard, 2366 Fifth Ave., bet. W. 142nd and W. 143rd Sts. W side. 1932. Van Wart & Wein.

A superb example of the art of bricklaying. In the case of this armory the mason's efforts are in **deep purpley-red** and exhibit a moderne style rather than an attempt to reconstruct a medieval fortress.

[70.] Dunbar Apartments, bet. W. 149th and W. 150th Sts., Seventh to Eighth Aves. 1928. Andrew J. Thomas. ★

Named for black poet **Paul Lawrence Dunbar** (1862–1966) these six apartment buildings, grouped around a landscaped inner court, have been the **home of such notables as** Countee Cullen, W. E. B. DuBois, A. Philip Randolph, Bill (Bojangles) Robinson, and Matt Henson, who, as part of the Perry expedition, was the first westerner to set foot upon the North Pole. Financier John D. Rockefeller, Jr., conceived the project **to be a model for solving Harlem's housing problem;** under the pressures of the Great Depression, however, he finally foreclosed his mortgages and sold the property. It has been a rental development ever since.

[71.] Harlem River Houses, N.Y.C. Housing Authority, bet. W. 151st and W. 153rd Sts., Macombs Place and Harlem River Dr. 1937. Archibald Manning Brown, chief architect in association with Charles F. Fuller, Horace Ginsbern, Frank J. Forster, Will Rice Amon, Richard W. Buckley, John L. Wilson. Michael Rapuano, landscape architect. Heinz Warnecke, assisted by T. Barbarossa, R. Barthé, F. Steinberger, sculptors. ★

Riots in Harlem in 1935 precipitated the planning and design of this, **the first** federally funded, federally owned, and federally built housing project in the city. Writing in 1938 of the four-story apartment buildings grouped around open landscaped courts embellished with sculpture, **Lewis Mumford** exuberantly stated that the project offers "the equipment for decent living that every modern neighborhood needs: sunlight, air, safety, play space, meeting space, and living space. The families in the Harlem Houses have higher standards of housing, measured in tangible benefits, than most of those on Park Avenue." Perhaps he was being too exuberant.

EAST HARLEM

East Harlem, once **Italian Harlem,** is today **Spanish Harlem.** It was **never** the **prestigious** residential district that Central Harlem originally was. The remaining older housing stock of East Harlem **reveals** its **working-class beginnings.** For a century it has been the home of laborer immigrants and their families, including large German, Irish, Jewish, and Scandinavian populations. The once particularly sizable Italian community, now reduced markedly, sank its roots here prior to 1890. Today, East Harlem is **El Barrio,** Spanish for "the district," overwhelmingly Puerto Rican in population, heritage, and culture, whose first settlers came here around the time of **World War I.**

From the ubiquitous, family-owned *bodegas,* or grocery stores, to be found on practically every street, to El Museo del Barrio, the sophisticated local museum on Fifth Avenue, East Harlem is **an important link** to the unique traditions of a significant and growing number of New York City's Hispanic residents.

We have included within East Harlem the area lying north of East 97th Street and east of Park Avenue.

[1.] Staff Residence, Mount Sinai Hospital, 1240 Park Ave., SE cor. E. 97th St. 1967. Pomerance & Breines.

A snappy, slender tower with balconies that presides over the portal of the Park Avenue tunnel into Grand Central Terminal.

[2.] Long-Term Care Facility, Florence Nightingale Nursing Home, 1760 First Ave., bet. E. 97th and E. 98th Sts. 1974. William N. Breger Assocs.

A **confident sculptural handling** of the oversize-brick massing. A physical asset to the streetscape in this part of town.

[3.] Electrical Substation, N.Y.C. Transit Authority/originally **Manhattan Railway Co.,** Third Ave., SW cor. E. 99th St. ca. 1902.

The two blocks between East 98th and 99th Streets stretching from Third Avenue west to Park are today the host for the apartment towers of Lexington Houses. In 1879 they were the site of the **newly built 99th Street yard** of the Manhattan Railway Company's **Third Avenue "el."** It was **not until 1900** that **electric-powered** elevated trains were first tested—until then the trains were pulled by **smoke-belching miniature steam locomotives.** With the successful test, the elevated systems were soon all electrified, creating **the need for substations** such as this. **All that remains** of the elevated railway empire in this vicinity is this grimy but handsome orange brick structure and a stretch of rough stone retaining wall on East 98th Street.

[4.] MaBSTOA Bus Garage/once **Metropolitan Street Railway Company (trolley barn),** E. 99th to E. 100th Sts., Lexington to Park Aves. ca. 1885.

Try to imagine this building in 1907, perhaps the heyday of trolley transportation in Manhattan, when its owner, Metropolitan Street Railway Company, controlled a total of **47 streetcar lines** and **300 miles of track.** That year its 3,280 cars handled 571 million passengers—not all from this barn, thank goodness, which limited its activities only to the Lexington Avenue and the Lexington-Lenox Avenue lines. Today the brick structure, minus tracks, serves as a **considerably less colorful** diesel bus garage. The **acronym** is for **M**anhattan **a**nd **B**ronx **S**urface **T**ransit **O**perating **A**uthority.

[5.] Church of the Resurrection, East Harlem Protestant Parish, 325 E. 101st St., bet. First and Second Aves. 1965. Victor A. Lundy.

A windowless red brick pillbox, falling somewhere between a fallout shelter and a Maginot Line fortress. Designed for a setting among grimy tenements, most of which have since been demolished, **its starkness was meant as a bold and powerful contrast.** Today it seems contrived, sitting among vacant lots. Economy dictated substitution of a built-up roof for the planned-for brick pavers. The interior is more inviting.

 [6a.] Metro North Plaza/Riverview Apartments, bet. E. 100th and E. 102nd Sts., First Ave. and Franklin D. Roosevelt Dr. 1976. **[6b.] Public School 50 Manhattan, The Vito Marcantonio School.** 1975. Both by Conklin & Rossant.

Exposed cast concrete frames with ribbed-block infill make **high-rise and low-rise** housing here arranged in **a chaste, symmetrical pattern.** The school, approached on a ramp at the far east end of the complex, makes a **dramatic statement** within the discipline of the same materials. A combined effort of the state Urban Development Corporation and the city Educational Construction Fund.

The painted bridge: All structural steel bridges must be painted regularly to protect their vulnerable surfaces against corrosion. It is rare, however, that the colors chosen vary much from gun-metal gray or bureaucratic green. Fortunately for all of us the idea that bridges could be painted richer, happier colors struck architects William Conklin and James Rossant [see **6a.** and **6b.**] just as the Wards Island Pedestrian Bridge—over the East River above Metro North—was up for its periodic rehueing. This time, in 1976, the bridge came out blue-violet (towers), cadmium yellow (walkway), and vermillion (trim), making it urban sculpture of the finest sort. A spectacular improvement!

[7.] 23rd Precinct Station House, N.Y.C. Police Department, and Engine Company 53, Ladder Company 43, 4th Division, N.Y.C. Fire Department, Third Ave. SW cor. E. 102nd St. 1974. Milton F. Kirchman.

A sloping site and a combination of clients—the Police Department, the Fire Department, and the city's coordinating agency, the Department of Public Works—give rise to this **three-dimensional cubist composition.**

[8.] Exodus House, 309 E. 103rd St., bet. First and Second Aves. 1968. Smotrich & Platt.

A **spartan work** in the style of the New Brutalism. No fancy materials or details in this nonprofit drug treatment center, no sanctimonious messages in its simple forms. **Gutsy.**

[9a.] The Church of the Living Hope, 161 E. 104th St., bet. Lexington and Third Aves. Altered, ca. 1969. **[9b.]** Originally **Engine Company 53, N.Y.C. Fire Department,** 179 E. 104th St. ca. 1898. **[9c.] Hope Community Hall**/originally **29th Precinct Station House, N.Y.C. Police Department,** 177 E. 104th St. ca. 1898.

A **curious trio** of buildings, two of which began as the fire and police outposts for this area. The **explosive expansion** of the city's construction program in the 1960s and 1970s replaced them [see **7.**] and **enabled reuse** as a community amenity. The ogee curves in the wrought iron balconies on the police station are lovely.

[10.] Park East High School (temporary location)/originally **Manhattan School of Music,** 230–240 E. 105th St., bet. Second and Third Aves. 1928. Donn Barber. Additions, Francis L. Mayer.

A **refined set of facades** as befits an institution dedicated to bringing refinement to the huddled masses, the Manhattan School of Music. That institution has moved to Morningside Heights **in a game of musical chairs** with the Juilliard School of Music, which moved to Lincoln Center.

[11a.] St. Cecilia's Church (Roman Catholic), 120 E. 106th St., bet. Park and Lexington Aves. 1887. Napoleon LeBrun & Sons.

This ornately embellished facade is one of East Harlem's **special treasures.** The material of the facade is primarily glazed terra cotta **worked with great skill and imagination.** The facade is enhanced by a huge bas-relief of St. Cecelia as a youthful organist.

[8.] Exodus House treatment center   **[11b.]** Originally P.S. 72 Manhattan

[11b.] Massive Economic Neighborhood Development (MEND)/originally **Public School 72 Manhattan**/then **Public School 107,** 1680 Lexington Ave., bet. E. 105th and E. 106th Sts. W side. ca. 1892.

Patterned brickwork and a handsome tower give **solidity and authority** to this venerable one-time schoolhouse, while ivory paint hides its age. Its days **may be numbered.**

[12.] Franklin Plaza Cooperative/originally **Franklin Houses, N.Y.C. Housing Authority,** bet. E. 106th St. and E. 108th St., First and Third Aves. 1959. Holden, Egan, Wilson & Corser. Plaza and play areas altered, 1961, Mayer & Whittlesey.

One of **the most graceful groups** of residential towers of its period and patrimony in Manhattan. First intended as subsidized public housing, this development became a cooperative under the auspices of community groups. The gardens and play areas were redesigned later in an early attempt to enrich the ground plane.

El Museo del Barrio, 1935 Third Ave., bet. E. 106th and E. 107th Sts.

Occupying part of the Franklin Plaza Cooperative's Third Avenue retail space is a museum directed to serving the needs of the local Spanish-speaking population. A gallery with changing exhibits is open to the public from time to time. Call 369-6010.

 [13.] 1199 Plaza (apartment complex), bet. E. 107th and E. 110th Sts., First Ave. and Franklin D. Roosevelt Dr., plus extension to E. 111th St. along the Drive. 1975. The Hodne/Stageberg Partners, architects. Herb Baldwin, landscape architect.

Four U-shaped red brick configurations each step down from 32-story towers of flats to ten-, eight-, and six-story wings of duplexes to house humanely a high density of residents, 450 persons to the acre. And, as an added extra, the complex achieves **an effective though not impolite** separation between public entry and shopping space along First Avenue and the varied outdoor spaces overlooking the East River that the cooperator-tenants and their guests may enjoy in comparative privacy and safety. Curiously enough this **very handsome project**—make sure to see it both from First Avenue and from FDR Drive—was designed by a Minneapolis architectural firm on the basis of its winning entry (not used) in a 1963 architectural competition to develop the site. Twelve years of redesign, red tape, and construction resulted in one of the city's **most impressive and most livable** works of multifamily housing. Incidentally, 1199 is not an address but the name of the project's sponsors, **District 1199** of the National Union of Hospital and Health Care Employees, AFL-CIO.

[14.] Aguilar Branch, N.Y. Public Library, 174 E. 110th St., bet. Third and Lexington Aves. 1899. Expanded and new facade added, 1905. Both by Herts & Tallant.

A **triumphal gateway to knowledge,** three stories high, replaces an earlier, even better one, half as wide, by the same architects. Comprised of **two monumentally scaled Classical columns** and a cornice framing a 20th-century cast-iron multistory facade within. Originally founded in 1886 as an independent library to serve immigrant Jews (**Grace Aguilar** was a British novelist of Sephardic descent), it was brought into the N.Y. Public Library system and expanded by a Carnegie gift. It now serves a newer, Hispanic population.

[15.] Park Avenue Enclosed Market, La Marqueta, "The Market," Park Ave. bet. E. 111th and E. 115th Sts., under the railroad viaduct.

A **hothouse of small merchants.** Sheltered by the elevated viaduct on which rumble the commuter trains in and out of Grand Central Terminal is one of the most **colorful, fast-moving, fragrant, and boisterous** of New York's **commercial pageants.** A mecca for both bargain hunters and those who love to bargain.

[16a.] James Weldon Johnson Houses, N.Y.C. Housing Authority, bet. E. 112th and E. 115th Sts., Third to Park Aves. 1948. Julian Whittlesey, Harry M. Prince, and Robert J. Reiley.

Within the genre of publicly assisted housing projects of the 1940s and 1950s (of which a swath can be seen all the way between First and Lenox Avenues) this is **one of the best.** Well-proportioned buildings of varying heights and a large plaza, small courts, and sculpture all contribute to the quality.

[16b.] Public School 57 Manhattan, The James Weldon Johnson School, 176 E. 115th St., SW cor. Third Ave. 1964. Ballard, Todd & Snibbe.

An overhanging cornice, generous windows divided into small panes, and molded bricks make this school a warm, safe, and friendly place. The scale of this building **would enhance and respect** a block of row houses; in its setting amidst large housing projects, its attention to scale is, unfortunately, largely unnoticed.

[17a.] St. Paul's Church (Roman Catholic), 121 E. 117th St., bet. Park and Lexington Aves. **[17b.] Rectory,** 113 E. 117th St. Both 1908. Neville & Bagge.

The handsome towers contribute to making this an especially fine church, a very late Romanesque Revival design.

[13.] 1199 Plaza (apartment complex): a visual treat from within and without

[18.] Assemblea de Iglesia Pentecostal de Jesucristo/originally **First German Baptist Church of Harlem,** 220 E. 118th St., bet. Second and Third Aves. ca. 1895.

An **ebullient** facade with a wide, inviting half-round arch entrance now painted in cream and tan.

[19a.] Iglesia Luterana Sion/originally **St. Johannes Kirche U.A.L.,** 217 E. 119th St., bet. Second and Third Aves. 1873.

An early masonry church for this community, then remote from the center of the city much further downtown. The church began as a home for a German-speaking congregation—today it serves those who speak Spanish.

[19b.] Originally **Engine Company 35, N.Y.C. Fire Department,** 223 E. 119th St., bet. Second and Third Aves. 1890. Napoleon LeBrun & Sons. ca. 1892.

LeBrun's firm practically **held a monopoly** on city firehouses at the start of the Gay Nineties. This one, as many others, credits the firm's efforts on a brownstone plaque over the apparatus door.

[20.] Public School 7 Manhattan, The M. Samuel Stern School, 160 E. 120th St., SE cor. Lexington Ave. 1958. Perkins & Will.

Three glass and paneled cubelike pavilions connected by glass-enclosed ramps house the classrooms of this school. Unfortunately, the building is now covered with steel mesh screening **to curtail rock-throwing vandals.** An alternate, if no more satisfying, solution to rock throwing in these parts is to build without windows on the street [see Intermediate School 201, Harlem **35.**].

[21a.] Harlem Courthouse, 170 E. 121st St., SE cor. Sylvan Place. 1893. Thom & Wilson. ★

This handsome brick and stone courthouse is **a model governmental palace** of the 1890s, now used for far more humble governmental functions. A rich array of forms (gables, archways, the imposing corner tower) and materials (water-struck red brick, bluestone, granite, terra cotta, and copper) make this fine work **both a Landmark and a landmark.**

[21b.] Sylvan Court, E. 121st St., N of Sylvan Place. ca. 1885.

Seven brick town houses grouped around a pedestrian off-street walkway that suffers from a regrettable lack of care.

[21c.] Elmendorf Reformed Church, 171 E. 121st St., bet. Sylvan Pl. and Third Ave. ca. 1910.

A small church with an unusual, but undistinguished, limestone facade is the **oldest congregation in Harlem** and the successor to the Dutch church founded here in 1660.

[22.] Chambers Memorial Baptist Church/originally **Carmel Baptist Church**/then **Harlem Baptist Church,** 219 E. 123rd St., bet. Second and Third Aves. 1891.

The gabled brick front wall of this church is modulated with **a witty array** of windows and doors.

[23.] Iglesia Adventista Del Septimo Dia/originally **Our Saviour (Norwegian) Lutheran Church,** 237 E. 123rd St., bet. Second and Third Aves. ca. 1912.

A humble facade enriched by an arched entryway and Spanish tile cladding on its gently pitched gable roof.

[24.] Taino Towers (apartment complex), bet. E. 122nd and E. 123rd Sts., Second and Third Aves. 1977. Silverman & Cika.

Unlike most governmentally subsidized housing for the poor, this project was **not** conceived of, designed through, or financed by the local housing authority. It was sponsored by **a persistent coalition** of local residents and community leaders together with the project's architects. As a result it is no predictable masonry fortress; it reminds you more of the **hotel architecture of Miami Beach.** Its crisp, 35-story towers reflect the sky in enormous picture windows of tautly stretched glass set in articulately framed white concrete. The towers **contrast** not only **with the mundane** red brick forms of typical low-rent, high-rise housing for the poor but even more with the **easy-going squalor** of adjacent El Barrio.

The financing scheme, dependent upon leasing a quarter of a million square feet of commercial space on the first six stories to rent-paying community services, **ran into trouble** with the **1975–1976 recession** and New York City's fiscal crisis. The large glass areas, designed before the energy crunch of 1974, may prove to be yet **another serious headache.** Meanwhile the towers give a gleaming new face to the drabness of East Harlem.

[25.] East Harlem Triangle Community Service Building, 2322 Third Ave., NW cor. E. 126th St. 1974. Herbert Tannenbaum.

A structure built to serve the community's organizational needs (early childhood center, social services, meeting rooms, etc.). It has **the look of Olivetti's social service buildings** in Italy back in the fifties.

UPPER MANHATTAN

Upper Manhattan is that fingerlike peninsula reaching to the north from Manhattan's bulkier body below, its southern bound here marked by **Trinity Cemetery.**

Indian cave dwellers once lived in **Inwood Park.** The father of our country not only gave part of this area its name, **Washington Heights,** but he slept and headquartered here (Morris-Jumel Mansion). This district was once a country preserve of the wealthy, and some of their estates have remained intact in a variety of forms, even though very rich people no longer live here. Museums, parks, a medical center, a bus terminal, and a university occupy sites here; and an assortment of other sacred and secular institutions are ornaments to this urban district. But mainly it is filled with apartment houses, making it one of the **most densely populated parts** of the city, while its parks, institutions, and dramatic river views make it one of the most liveable. The **Broadway** Subway reached **Dyckman Street** and **St. Nicholas Avenue** in the spring of **1906** and was the major impetus for the development of the eastern section. The **Eighth Avenue Subway** opened in the fall of **1932,** encouraging still more apartment house construction.

Within **Upper Manhattan,** and particularly in the subdivision called **Washington Heights,** is a maze of ethnic subcommunities. The once-predominant **Irish,** mostly departed, now share this district with more recent newcomers to the city: **Blacks, Puerto Ricans,** and many other **Latin Americans.** The **Greek** and **Armenian** colonies here are large. In the thirties, after the rise of **Hitler,** so many German refugees settled here that the area became known, cynically, as the *Fourth* Reich.

[1.] Gatehouse, Trinity Cemetery   [2.] The Chapel of the Intercession

[1.] Trinity Cemetery, Riverside Dr. to Amsterdam Ave., W. 153rd to W. 155th Sts. Open only by special permission from Trinity Parish. Boundary wall and gates, 1876. Gatehouse and Keeper's Lodge, 1883. Vaux & Radford. Grounds, 1881. Vaux & Co., landscape architects.

Bucolic topography. The cemetery climbs the hill from a spot near the river to its crest at Amsterdam Avenue, affording some idea of the topography of Upper Manhattan before man cut, molded, and veneered it with brick, concrete, and asphalt. This was once a part of the farm of **J. J. Audubon,** the great artist-naturalist, whose home was near the river at 155th Street, and who is buried here (directly behind the church along 155th Street). Every Christmas Eve carolers visit the grave of **Clement Clarke Moore,** author of *Visit from St. Nicholas.* This was the rural cemetery of Wall Street's **Trinity Church.**

Sadly missing today is the suspension bridge over Broadway (Vaux, Withers & Co., architects; George K. Radford, engineer) which linked the cemetery's two halves. It was demolished in 1911 to build:

[2.] Chapel of the Intercession (Protestant Episcopal) and Rectory, Broadway, SE cor. W. 155th St. 1914. Cram, Goodhue & Ferguson. ★ ▥

Set in **Trinity Cemetery,** this was the largest chapel of Trinity Parish (now an independent church). Here is the dream of the Gothic Revivalist come true: a **large country church, tower, cloister, parish house,** and **vicarage,** all set on a bucolic hillside overlooking the Hudson. Inside stone piers support a wooden hammer-beam roof, washed in light from neo-French 13th-century glass. Loose chairs, rather than pews, make it seem all the more a church of the Île de France. See the charming cloister off the 155th Street entrance.

[3.] Audubon Terrace, Broadway bet. W. 155th and W. 156th Sts. W. side. Master plan, 1908, Charles Pratt Huntington.

Four small museums and the **National Institute of Arts and Letters** face on an awkward court, intended to be Classical, but poorly proportioned. **A vacuous and pallid Beaux Arts exercise.**

[3a.] Museum of the American Indian, Heye Foundation, Audubon Terrace, Broadway, NW cor. W. 155th St. 1916. Charles Pratt Huntington. Telephone: AU 3-2420.

Originally the private collection of **George G. Heye,** this is now a comprehensive museum concerned with the prehistoric Western Hemisphere and the contemporary American (north, central, and southern) Indian. All clad in **miniature Ionic** limestone Renaissance Revival.

[3.] Audubon Terrace (4 museums): a vacuous and pallid Beaux Arts exercise

[3b.] American Geographical Society   **[3c.]** Hispanic Society's Courtyard

[3b.] Originally **American Geographical Society Building,** Audubon Terrace, Broadway, SW cor. W. 156th St. 1916. Charles Pratt Huntington.

The largest geographical library and map collection in the Western Hemisphere was housed in this building, relocated to the **University of Wisconsin at Milwaukee** for financial reasons.

[3c.] Hispanic Society of America, Audubon Terrace. West Building, 1908. Charles Pratt Huntington. East Building and additions to West Building, 1910–1926. Charles Pratt Huntington, Erik Strindberg and H. Brooks Price. Telephone: 690-0743.

This is a richly appointed storehouse of Hispanic painting, sculpture, and the decorative arts. The sunken court opposite is a **pompous neo-Baroque place** filled with dull and academic bronze sculpture.

[3d.] American Numismatic Society, Audubon Terrace, S side. 1908. Charles Pratt Huntington. Telephone: AU 6-3030.

A museum devoted entirely to coins, medals, decorations, and paper money. It contains the most comprehensive numismatic library in the country.

[3e.] National Institute of Arts and Letters/American Academy of Arts and Letters, Audubon Terrace. **Administration Building,** 633 W. 155th St. 1923. William M. Kendall. **Auditorium and Gallery,** 632 W. 156th St. 1930. Cass Gilbert. Telephone: AU 6-1480.

The institute and academy were founded to honor distinguished persons in literature and the fine arts. The administration building contains a permanent exhibition of the works of the American Impressionist **Childe Hassam,** a library, and a museum of manuscripts by past and present members.

[4.] Church of Our Lady of Esperanza (Roman Catholic), 624 W. 156th St., bet. Broadway and Riverside Dr. 1912. Charles Pratt Huntington. Remodeled, 1925. Lawrence G. White.

The green and gold interior of this church adjoining Audubon Terrace contains stained-glass windows, skylight and a lamp, all given by the King of Spain at its opening in 1912.

[5a.] The Morris-Jumel Mansion: in the Tuscan-columned Georgian-Federal style

---

IRT's Hoosick: Named after the Hoosick Tunnel near North Adams, Massachusetts, which holds the record as the longest two-track tunnel in the U.S. The tunnel, for the IRT Broadway-Seventh Avenue Line, is cut through solid rock under Broadway and St. Nicholas Avenue between W. 157th Street and Fort George.

[5.] Jumel Terrace Historic District, around Jumel Terrace, bet. W. 160th and W. 162nd Sts., Edgecombe Ave. and St. Nicholas Ave. District Designated 1970. ★

[5a.] Morris-Jumel Mansion, Edgecombe Ave., NW cor. W. 160th St. ca. 1765. Remodeled, 1810. ★ Included within the historic district. ★

Built by **Roger Morris** as a summer residence for his family, it served for a time during the Revolution as Washington's headquarters. But for most of that war the house was in British hands (as was all of Manhattan, and, therefore, all of New York of that day). After the war it served as a roadside tavern until 1810, when Stephen Jumel purchased it and completely renovated the house in the then-modern **Federal** style. The **finest view in Manhattan** is blocked by bulky apartment buildings to the south.

In **Tuscan-columned Georgian-Federal style,** with a facade of wood boards and quoins simulating stone, a shingled behind. The hipped roofs to balustraded captain's walks are admirable cornices to this classic square linked to an octagon. Open to the public.

[6.] Columbia-Presbyterian Medical Center, W. 165th to W. 168th Sts., Broadway to Riverside Dr. 1928–1947. James Gamble Rogers, Inc. 1947–1964. Rogers & Butler. 1964–1974. Rogers, Butler & Burgun.

A **bulky set** of medical facilities at cliff edge on the Hudson. No special architecture here, just very special medical care.

[7.] Augustus Long Library and Health Sciences Center, College of Physicians and Surgeons, W. 168th to W. 169th Sts., Ft. Washington Ave. 1976. Warner, Burns, Toan & Lunde.

Another solemn and somber brick and self-weathering steel giant [see the **Annenberg Building** at Mt. Sinai: Upper East Side **41.**].

[8.] Bard-Haven Towers, (staff housing) 100 Haven Ave., bet. W. 169th and W. 171st Sts., W side overlooking Henry Hudson Pkwy. 1971. Brown, Guenther, Battaglia & Galvin.

Tall cliffhangers (literally) that cling to the escarpment and enjoy wonderful Hudson views. The corbeled lower stories are a dramatic event to the thousands of drivers who approach the George Washington Bridge every day.

Freud's Library: In the Freud Memorial Room of the Neurological and Psychiatric Institutes is shelved part of Sigmund Freud's personal library.

[9.] Highbridge Park, W. 155th to Dyckman Sts., Edgecombe and Amsterdam Aves. to the Harlem River Dr. 1888. Calvert Vaux and Samuel Parsons, Jr. Altered.

Once the site of an amusement park, marina, and promenade, this park gains its beauty from a steep slope and rugged topography; an excellent vantage point to survey the **Harlem River Valley.**

[9a.] Adventure Playground, in Highbridge Park, Edgecombe Ave., bet. W. 163rd and W. 165th Sts. E side.

Tunnels, mountains, slides produce an **imaginative world** for child's play.

[10.] High Bridge/originally **Aqueduct Bridge,** Highbridge Park at W. 174th St. 1839–1848. New central span, 1923. ★

This is the **oldest remaining bridge** connecting Manhattan to the mainland. It was built to carry Croton water to Manhattan. Originally the bridge consisted of closely spaced masonry piers and arches. The central group, however, was replaced by the present cast-iron arch at the time of construction of the **Harlem River Ship Canal.** The pedestrian walk has been closed for many years.

[11.] Highbridge Tower, Highbridge Park at W. 173rd St. Completed 1872. Attributed to John B. Jervis. ★

This landmark tower, originally used to equalize pressure in the **Croton Aqueduct,** now simply marks the Manhattan end of **High Bridge.** Adjacent is the site of a large (and well-used) public outdoor swimming pool.

[12.] Henry Hudson Parkway.

Driving south into Manhattan on this parkway, hugging the Hudson, is one of New York's **great gateway experiences.** From **Riverdale** (the affluent West Bronx) one passes over the **Henry Hudson Bridge** (a dramatic object from the distance, but a bore at first hand), then descends to the banks of the **Hudson.** Then past the Cloisters, romantically surmounting a hilltop, lonely and wondrous; through a wooded area; then under the majestic **George Washington Bridge.** All of a sudden the skyline of Manhattan materializes, and the **rural-urban transition** is complete.

[13.] Fort Washington Presbyterian Church, 21 Wadsworth Ave., NW cor. W. 174th St. 1914. Carrère & Hastings.

Brick and limestone English Baroque: its **Tuscan** columns and pilasters, broken pediments, and console-bracketed tower bring us back to **Christopher Wren's** 17th-century reconstruction of London.

[14.] United Church/originally **Loew's 175th Street Theater,** Broadway, NE cor. W. 175th St. 1930. Thomas W. Lamb.

The **Reverend Ike** now holds forth here in Nouveau Riche splendor reminiscent of *archaic Miami.* This terra-cotta place was once at the apogee of movie palace splendor, when Hollywood ruled the world, and **everyone** went to the movies on Saturday and other nights.

[14.] The United Church/originally Loew's 175th Street Theater. 1930. T.W. Lamb

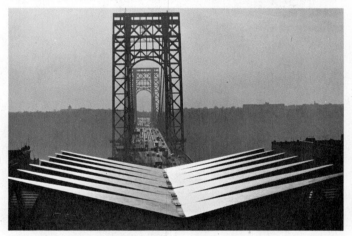

[15.] and **[17.]** George Washington Bridge and Bus Station, a "seat of grace"

[15.] George Washington Bridge, Hudson River at W. 178th St. 1931. O. H. Ammann & Cass Gilbert.

"The **George Washington Bridge** over the **Hudson** is the most beautiful bridge in the world. Made of cables and steel beams, it gleams in the sky like a reversed arch. It is blessed. It is the only seat of grace in the disordered city. It is painted an aluminum color, and, between water and sky, you see nothing but the bent cord supported by two steel towers. When your car moves up the ramp the two towers rise so high that it brings you happiness; their structure is so pure, so resolute, so regular that here, finally, steel architecture seems to laugh. The car reaches an unexpectedly wide apron; the second tower is very far away; innumerable vertical cables, gleaming against the sky, are suspended from the magisterial curve which swings down and then up. The rose-colored towers of New York appear, a vision whose harshness is mitigated by distance."

—**Charles Edouard Jeanneret (Le Corbusier)**
from *When the Cathedrals Were White,*
Reynal and Hitchcock, 1947.

The lower level, added in **1962,** has markedly changed the proportions of the bridge, not to speak of perverting the original intentions: the lower level was to be a transit connection, rather than another vomitory for cars.

[16.] The Little Red Lighthouse, Ft. Washington Park below the George Washington Bridge. 1921.

Directly under the east tower of the George Washington Bridge, the lighthouse was built to steer grain barges away from the shoals of Jeffrey's Hook. When navigational lights were mounted on the bridge, it was no longer used and was put up for auction in 1951. A barrage of letters from children who had read *The Little Red Lighthouse and the Great Gray Bridge,* by **Hildegarde Hoyt Swift,** saved the lighthouse: now maintained by the Department of Parks.

[17.] George Washington Bridge Bus Station, E of the bridge bet. Ft. Washington and Wadsworth Aves. 1963. Port of New York Authority and Pier Luigi Nervi.

A **concrete butterfly** shelters a bus terminal at the end of the bridge, interlocking with the IND Eighth Avenue Subway. The shape is excused as a form for natural ventilation for the noxious buses; it also provides the opportunity for a formal *tour de force* for **Dr. Nervi,** an engineer more comfortable with *Italian* economics, where his skills provide the cheapest, as well as the most exciting, forms. Here, with the millstone of the Port Authority engineering staff, his forms were labored and the economics absent.

[22.] Main Building, Yeshiva University, with Middle Eastern eclectic detail

[18.] Bridge Apartments, bet. W. 178th and W. 179th Sts., Wadsworth and Audubon Aves. 1964. Brown & Guenther.

An early experiment in residential air rights over a highway: but fumes, dirt, and noise rise to the unfortunate dweller above. At best the depressed bridge approaches should have been decked over to provide artificial ground for the residents resident, and the fumes mechanically exhausted. The curtain wall buildings are, therefore, ensmogged, and, incidentally, fussily detailed.

[19.] Washington Bridge, W. 181st St. and Amsterdam Ave. to the Bronx. 1888.

A magnificent arch bridge not to be confused with the *George* Washington. Great steel filigree for the **Major Deegan** or **Harlem River** driver; a flat plane to those who cross on top.

[20.] Alexander Hamilton Bridge, W. 178th to W. 179th Sts. to the Bronx, 1964.

The bridge bringing the Cross Bronx Expressway to the George Washington Bridge approaches in Manhattan: serviceable, but dull to look at.

[21.] Yeshiva University Campus, W. 183rd to W. 187th Sts., along Amsterdam Ave.

A mixed bag of architectural tricks, more a collection of separate opportunities, successes, and failures than an integrated whole or sum.

[22.] Main Building, Yeshiva University, Amsterdam Ave., SW cor. W. 186th St. 1928. Charles B. Meyers Assocs.

This is one of the great romantic structures of its time. Domes, towers, and turrets can be seen miles away, and the architect's lavish use of orange stone, copper and brass, ceramic tile, and **Middle Eastern eclectic** architectural detail makes a visual treat.

[23.] Central Library, Yeshiva University, 1967. Armand Bartos & Associates

[23.] Central Library, Yeshiva University, Amsterdam Ave., bet. W. 185th and W. 186th Sts. W side. 1967. Armand Bartos & Assocs.

A rich composition of brick, terra cotta and glass **highly articulated** to make the best of sun, shadow, and view: super-bay windows.

[24.] Science Center, Belfer Graduate School of Science, Yeshiva University, 2495 Amsterdam Ave., at W. 184th St. E side. 1968. Armand Bartos & Assocs.

Bulky brick piers for a warehouse of science.

[25.] Isabella Neimath Home and Geriatric Center, 525 Ft. Washington Ave. 1965. Joseph D. Weiss.

A home for the elderly, providing small apartments designed to meet their special needs. The pitched and folded roof was designed ostensibly in deference to its older neighbor (the original home) which no longer exists: replaced by an addition to this addition. Oh well.

[26.] Fort Washington Collegiate Church, Ft. Washington Ave., NE cor. W. 181st St. 1907.

This small "country" church dates from the time Washington Heights was really country: brick and timber Gothic Revival.

The Highest Point: In **Bennett Park,** along the west side of Fort Washington Avenue between 183rd and 185th Streets, is a rock outcropping that is the highest point in Manhattan, 267.75 feet above sea level. An added bonus is the outline of Revolutionary War **Fort Washington,** marked by stone pavers.

[27.] Hudson View Gardens, 116 Pinehurst Ave., bet. W. 183rd and W. 185th Sts. 1925. George F. Pelham.

"Collegiate Gothic" encrusted with Virginia creeper, of brick with simulated half-timbering, this **romantic and urbane cluster** of multiple dwellings embraces private gardens and enjoys, from many parts, romantic river views.

[28.] Castle Village, 120–200 Cabrini Blvd., bet. W. 181st and W. 186th Sts. 1938. George F. Pelham II.

At **Hudson View,** Pelham embraced his public space; at **Castle Village** he planted himself in it. Each floor of these cruciform buildings contains nine apartments, eight of which have river views. The site was formerly occupied by the Paterno estate: its massive retaining walls still retaining the present building site.

[29.] 16 Chittenden Avenue, at W. 186th St.

The guest house of the former **Paterno** estate perches on a great pier that drops to the parkway's edge below.

[30.] Fort Tryon Park, W. 192nd to Dyckman Sts., Broadway to Riverside Dr. Frederick Law Olmsted, Jr.

A gift of the Rockefeller family to New York City, this site was formerly the **C. K. G. Billings estate** (the triple-arched driveway from Riverside Drive was its entrance). The park is famous for its flower gardens.

The fort's grand site still remains; a plaque states: "The northern outwork of Fort Washington, its gallant defense against the Hessian Troops by the Maryland and Virginia Regiment, 16 November 1776, was shared by Margaret Corbin, the first American woman to take a soldier's part in the War for Liberty."

[31.] The Cloisters, Metropolitan Museum of Art. 1934–1938. Charles Collens

[31.] The Cloisters, Metropolitan Museum of Art, Fort Tryon Park. 1934–1938. Charles Collens of Allen, Collens & Willis. Alterations to receive the Fuentadueña Chapel, 1961, Brown, Lawford & Forbes. Telephone: 923-3700.

Named for the French and Spanish monastic cloisters imported and reassembled here in concert with a **twelfth-century chapter house,** the **Fuentadueña Chapel,** and a **Gothic and a Romanesque chapel.** The concept and the reality are both very romantic; the siting at this river-viewing crest is an overwhelming confrontation between the city and a Hudson River School painter's view of, not surprisingly, the Hudson River.

Contents are the majority of the medieval art collection of the Metropolitan Museum of Art. Most impressive are the **Unicorn tapestries.** Check with the Cloisters for exact times of concerts of Medieval and Renaissance music held there from time to time.

Into the depths: The two deepest subway stations in the City are near here (why deepest? the land merely gets higher and the tracks get—at least relatively—lower!): the IRT Seventh Avenue-Broadway Line at 191st Street and Saint Nicholas Avenue (180 feet below the street, or the street is 180 feet above the subway); and the IND station at 190th Street and Fort Washington Avenue (165 feet down; we're 165 feet up). In both cases elevators whisk passengers up and down: level-equalizers.

[32.] Dyckman House, Broadway, NW cor. W. 204th St. 1783. Telephone: 755-4100. ★

The site is monumental, the porch lovely. Rebuilt by **William Dyckman** after the destruction of the previous building by the British, this is the **only 18th-century farmhouse** remaining in Manhattan. With its gambrel roof and brick and fieldstone lower walls, the house shows a strong Dutch influence. The interior, with random-width chestnut floors and original family furnishings, is well worth a visit.

THE OTHER ISLANDS

In addition to Manhattan and Staten, islands unto themselves, and Long, the western part of which island the city's two largest boroughs (Queens and Brooklyn) occupy, the city is infested with yet **other islands.** Some are so **small or low-lying** that the tides keep them under water most if not all of the time. Others appear in official documents but are in fact **submerged** by the city's offal in numerous landfill projects. Yet others are **joined,** either to each other or to some "mainland," so that they are no longer *truly* islands. Jamaica Bay, within the jurisdiction of both Brooklyn and Queens, has bits of mucky land which fall into all of the above categories. Luckily for municipal officials already overwhelmed by less arcane issues, the **National Park Service** now worries about most of Jamaica Bay's islands, pols, marshes, and hassocks as part of its **Gateway National Recreation Area.**

Among the larger, inhabited or once inhabited islands within the city's waterways—in some cases not normally open to the public—are

Liberty Island
Formerly known as Bedloes Island.

[1.] Statue of Liberty (National Monument), National Park Service, built atop Fort Wood. 1886. Frédéric Auguste Bartholdi, sculptor; Alexandre Gustave Eiffel, engineer; Richard Morris Hunt, architect of the base. Additions to the base, 1972.

Conceived as a memorial to French-American friendship, Bartholdi's colossal sculpture *Liberty Enlightening the World* is indeed colossal: she stands 151 feet high, the tip of the flaming torch in her upraised hand rises some 395 feet above the harbor's waters, her index finger is 8 feet long, her eyes each $2\frac{1}{2}$ feet wide. Journey to Liberty Island via the privately operated, regularly scheduled ferry (telephone: BO 9-5755 for schedule and fare) and ascend the 168-step helical stair through the verdigrised sheets of thin ($\frac{3}{32}$-inch-thick) copper to the observation platform in the seven-spiked crown. There (if the crowd behind allows you enough time to gaze) you will see the city's great harbor spread all around.

The statue, the **Museum of Immigration** in its now expanded base, and the lawns and walkways are open to the public and are under the jurisdiction of the National Park Service. Telephone: 732-1286.

The New Colossus: The symbolic relationship between Liberty's welcoming form and the millions of immigrants arriving in steerage in New York harbor was not established formally until 1903. It was then that a plaque was affixed to the statue bearing the lines of a poem written in 1883 by Emma Lazarus as part of a fund-raising effort for the statue. Its last lines capture the cry of Liberty's silent lips:

> *"Give me your tired, your poor,*
> *Your huddled masses yearning to breathe free,*
> *The wretched refuse of your teeming shore.*
> *Send these, the homeless, the tempest-tost to me,*
> *I lift my lamp beside the golden door."*

To the disappointment of many who climb the stair to the top, the poem is not inscribed on the tablet grasped in Liberty's left hand—that inscription reads JULY IV MDCCLXXVI.

Ellis Island

[2.] Originally **United States Immigration Station**/now **Ellis Island National Monument, National Park Service.** 1898. Boring & Tilton.

Fanciful **bulbous turrets** proclaim the now unused buildings of Ellis Island where the majority of European immigrants landed on these shores following the turn of the century (1,285,239 entered the U.S. in 1907 alone, the peak year). Philip Johnson's **monument to immigration** (which would have displayed **the names of all who passed through** Ellis's portals) suffered the fate of other monumental proposals in the **anti-hero seventies.** To open the island to limited visitation, the Park Service now permits **seasonal visits** to the buildings via the Liberty Island ferry. For information and transportation costs, telephone: 732-1286 or BO 9-5755.

Governors Island

Its name derives from an act of the New York Assembly in 1698 which set the land aside **"for the benefit and accommodation of His Majesty's governors."** In the interim it has not only served to house the colony's governors but also for such sundry uses as a sheep farm, quarantine station, racetrack, and game preserve. It is best known, of course, as **a military fortification,** a use which remained until 1966 when the U.S. Coast Guard took command. Public visitation to the island is **strictly limited** to special **open-house weekends** in the warm weather months, when the forts, green spaces, and a Coast Guard cutter or two are available for inspection. Bring a picnic lunch. The ferryboat leaves from the Battery and is free—no visitors' cars are allowed. Information: 264-4996 or 264-8733.

[2.] U.S. Immigration Sta., Ellis Is.   **[3b.]** Castle Williams, Governors Is.

[3a.] Fort Jay/also known as **Fort Columbus** (1808–1904), entrance to east of ferry landing on Andes Rd. 1798. Rebuilt, 1806. ★

The officers' dwellings set within the walls of the fort add a note of domesticity **that diminishes the fearsomeness** of this now **dry-moated fortress,** built in a pentagonal, star-shaped plan. The brownstone Federal entranceway is a felicitous effort bearing a **handsome sculptural composition.**

[3b.] Castle Williams, Andes Rd., W cor. Hay Rd., W of ferry landing. 1811. Lt. Col. Jonathan Williams, chief engineer, U.S. Army. Converted to military prison, 1912. ★

Appearing from the harbor to be fully circular in shape (hence its one-time nickname, **"The Cheesebox"**) this 200-foot-diameter red sandstone fortification **is actually chevron-shaped** in plan on its inland side. It, together with Castle Clinton at the Battery [see L Manhattan/Financial District **1.**], was built to crisscross with cannon balls the waterway between them during the War of 1812. They were never used.

Williams, its designer, was Benjamin Franklin's nephew and the individual for whom Williamsburg, Brooklyn, was named.

[3c.] Originally **The South Battery**/now incorporated into **Officers' Club,** Comfort Rd., W cor. Barry Rd., SE of ferry landing. 1812.

This fort, built to command Buttermilk Channel, the harbor's waterway between Governors Island and Brooklyn, is now largely hidden by additions made to accommodate its later use as the island's officers' club.

[3d.] Chapel of St. Cornelius the Centurion (Protestant Episcopal), Barry Rd., W cor. Evans Rd., SE of ferry landing. 1905. Charles C. Haight.

Built by **Trinity Parish** during the period (1863–1924) when the War Department did not see fit to assign an official Army chaplain to the military reservation. **Inside** the Gothic Revival chapel hang **87 battle flags and regimental colors** from all periods of American history.

[3e.] The Blockhouse, Bldg. 9, Barry Rd., SE of ferry landing. 1843. Martin E. Thompson. Altered. ★

Spare Greek Revival now minus its entrance steps.

[3f.] The Admiral's House/originally **Commanding General's Quarters, Bldg. 1,** Barry Rd., S of Andes Rd., SE of ferry landing. 1840. ★

This imposing brick manor house, porticoed front and rear with slender white two-story-high Doric colonnades, served such illustrious generals as Winfield Scott, John J. Pershing, Omar N. Bradley, and Walter Bedell Smith.

[3g.] The Dutch House, Bldg. 3, Barry Rd., S of Andes Rd., SE of ferry landing. 1845.

Built to resemble the typical house of a New Amsterdam settler but used initially as a commissary storehouse. Now officers' quarters.

[3h.] The Governor's House, Bldg. 2, W cor. Andes and Barry Rds., SE of ferry landing. ca. 1708. Altered 1740 and since. ★

The oldest structure remaining on the island, **truly Georgian** in style since its official use as residence for the British governors required **textbook adherence** to the style of the motherland. An unpretentious yet dignified Flemish-bonded brick manor house.

[3i.] Brooklyn-Battery Tunnel Ventilator Building, Triborough Bridge and Tunnel Authority, off Governors Island, SE of ferry landing. 1950.

The prominent white octagonal prism which contributes little to the harbor panorama but subtracts a lot via its bulk and unfriendly scale.

Erosion and landfill: Governors Island, called *Nooten Eylandt* (or Nutten Island) in the Dutch period (1625–1664), then encompassed 170 acres. But by the early 1900s the action of the harbor's tides had washed away the southwestern portion, reducing the acreage to a mere 70. At that point the south seawall ran roughly between Castle Williams and the South Battery along today's Hay, Clayton, and Comfort Roads. During the 20th century the placement of material dredged from the harbor's channels and rock excavated from subway construction extended the island to its present 173 acres.

Roosevelt Island

"Instant City" is what some people call Roosevelt Island but "New Town in Town" was the catch phrase preferred by the state's Urban Development Corporation. Back in 1971, UDC won the opportunity to create a high-density residential community in the center of the 2½-mile-long, 800-foot-wide sliver of land in the East River then known as Welfare Island, a cordon sanitaire for the city's poor, destitute, and chronically ill. An **ambitious master plan by Philip Johnson and John Burgee** evoked **a community for pedestrians** arranged along a network of streets which flowed north from the island's proposed subway stop on the 63rd Street Crosstown Line, then under construction. Residents' and visitors' **cars were to be stored in a megagarage** at the foot of the small lift bridge to Long Island City, and **a minibus system** would link the garage at the south with the subway at the north. In addition, **parks would be created** at both tips of the island and in the middle as well, focused upon architectural landmarks which remained from the island's previous uses.

Changes in thinking about the number of people, the height of buildings (the 8 to 10 stories in the master plan being increased to 20 along the main street), the need to coordinate construction with the removal of existing buildings, delays in the completion of the subway link, double digit inflation, and finally UDC's fiscal collapse, all **contributed to departures** from the master plan. The most significant consequence of the changes was the reduction (forced by UDC's collapse) of population from the minimum **"critical mass"** of 18,000 persons needed to sustain healthy shopping, a hotel, restaurants, and entertainment. As a result only Southtown, with 2,138 units, less than half of the number originally contemplated, was built. Northtown, in the space between today's residential enclave and the planned subway station, is only a hope for the future. But the unexpected gave rise to at least **one positive development,** the crash-program construction of a romantic aerial tramway from Manhattan. It would substitute for the lack of subway service, whose inauguration was years away, in the mid-1980s.

The silent but **exhilarating aerial voyage** via overhead tramcar (a subway token's fare each way) is an appropriate way to reach Roosevelt Island. (Cars must enter via the bridge from Queens and park in the Motorgate parking garage.) The **silent ride** is echoed by **the curious silence** one finds on the island, **a stone's throw** from Manhattan's elegant east shore. The quiet is broken only by the **buzz of auto tires** along FDR Drive across the channel to the west and **the hum of Big Allis,** Con Edison's turbine generator, on the opposite shore. Infrequently, the eerie stillness is interrupted by the **staccato beat of rotors** overhead from aircraft using the Sixtieth Street Heliport. Beyond these sounds are only the gentle noises of harbor craft and the splash of the East River waters along the seawalls which gird the island.

Rechargeable battery-powered electric buses whirr you from the tramway station along the length of the **gently zigzagged** residential spine called, naturally, **Main Street,** as far as Motorgate, which contains not only the parking garage but the community's only supermarket, too. On both sides of Main Street are arranged the apartment blocks, each a variation on a **U-shaped plan,** the open sides of the U's facing the river, the highest sections making **a not-displeasing canyon** of Main Street, the lower tiers of apartments stepping down toward the island's east and west promenades.

A walk through the community should include a saunter along Main Street as well as along the two perimeter walks whose views are entrancing.

The Central Part

[4a.] Aerial Tramway Station, N of Queensboro Bridge. 1976. Prentice & Chan, Ohlhausen.

Main point of pedestrian arrival at Roosevelt Island until completion of the subway (which will never compete successfully with the **sensuous delights** of this aerial voyage). The form of this tramway station conjures up **images of Switzerland,** its steep skislope roof being very different from its Manhattan mate [See M Manhattan/Dry Dock Country **7.**].

[4b.] Old Welfare Island Service Building, N of Aerial Tramway Station, 1942. Moore & Hutchins and Percival Goodman.

Combined in a structure reminiscent of **constructivist architecture** are an enormous central laundry, service vehicle garage, and fire station for the island hospital's needs. Scheduled for demolition.

[4c.] Sports Park, S of Queensboro Bridge. 1977. Prentice & Chan, Ohlhausen.

A long, earth-colored, ground-hugging gymnasium building, plus outdoor accoutrements.

[4d.] Blackwell Farm House, in Blackwell Park, E side of Main St., S of Eastwood. 1796–1804. Restored, 1973. Giorgio Cavaglieri. ★ **[4e.] Blackwell Park.** 1973. Dan Kiley & Partners, landscape architects.

This modest clapboard dwelling is the rebuilt home of the Blackwells who owned and farmed this island, once named for the family, between the late 1600s and 1828 when it was purchased by the city. With the construction of a penitentiary the following year, the house became the residence for the first of the many island institutions' administrators.

[4f.] Eastwood (apartments), 510, 516, 536, 546, 556, 566, 576, and 580 Main St., E side, opp. "Big Allis," generator of Consolidated Edison. 1976. Sert, Jackson & Assocs.

The crisp, undulating accretion of buildings whose **unifying arcades** line the east side of Main Street. The occupants of its thousand units are **low, middle, and moderate income** tenants. Their windows face the **candy-cane-striped smokestacks** of Con Ed's erratic electric generator, "Big Allis" (for Allis Chalmers, its manufacturer), and the **industrial dreariness** of that part of Long Island City. (The wealthier live on the west side of Main Street.) **Bright red accents** on the brown ribbed-block facades are **a trademark** of the architects; they have become **the theme color** for the whole development as well.

Schools: A radical innovation in the city's public education policy places divisions of the Roosevelt Island community's public school system into five separate minischools built in conjunction with each of the apartment towers. Blackwell Primary School (grades K-2) just north of the farmhouse, and Island House Middle School (3-4), Westview Upper School (5-6), Rivercross Intermediate School (7-8), and Eastwood Arts School (shared facilities) comprise Public School/Intermediate School 217 Manhattan. Athletics for all are centralized at Sports Park **[4c.].**

[4g.] Rivercross (apartments), 505, 513, and 541 Main St. W side opp. Rockefeller University. 1975. Johansen & Bhavnani, architects. Dan Kiley & Partners, landscape architects.

Brightly painted **nautical ventilating funnels** announce the southernmost of the island's three luxury buildings, this one a cooperative. This and its neighbor to the north [4j.] rely on dun-colored cement asbestos panels as cladding for much of their exteriors, a material which imparts a sober, urbane look from afar (good), but a thin, expressionless surface up close (bad).

[4h.] Originally **Chapel of the Good Shepherd (Protestant Episcopal)**/now **Good Shepherd Community Ecumenical Center,** 543 Main St. 1889. Frederick Clarke Withers. Restored, 1975, Giorgio Cavaglieri. ★ Plaza, Johansen & Bhavnani, architects. Lawrence Halprin Assocs., landscape architects.

A **stroke of genius** to have preserved—and handsomely restored—this **vigorously designed** 19th-century country chapel for 20th (and 21st) century use. The old bronze bell (cast in 1888 by Mencely & Co., West Troy, N.Y.) has been placed on the plaza as **a charming sculptural note.**

Eats: Light meals are available along the Eastwood arcade at La Piccola Mela, The *Little* Apple (telephone: 688-4702). But good weather and the wondrous river views suggest a picnic: fixins available at either the Roosevelt Island Delicatessen (579 Main Street in Island House) or at Sloan's supermarket (in Motorgate).

[4i.] East and West Promenades. 1975. Zion & Breen, landscape architects.

Both beautifully detailed: the west promenade, facing Manhattan, is the more complex of the two, utilizing multilevels; the east promenade is modest, more subtle, equally enjoyable.

[4j.] Island House (apartments), 551, 555, 575 and 595 Main St. W side, opp. Cornell-New York Medical Center. 1975. Johansen & Bhavnani, architects; Lawrence Halprin Assocs., landscape architects.

More housing for the wealthier. Island House is entered, **as an ocean liner,** via gangplanks, brightly painted in orange and yellow. As in Rivercross to the south **[4g.],** there is a prominent skylight-enclosed year-round indoor pool on the river frontage.

[4k.] Westview (apartments), 595 and 625 Main St., W side, opp. Hospital for Special Surgery. 1976. Sert, Jackson & Assocs.

Dark gray-brown brick plus the **idiosyncratic bright red accents** mark Sert's Manhattan-facing effort for the wealthier, as contrasted with his more extensive project across Main Street for the less well-do-do, built of masonry block.

[4l.] Roosevelt Island Bridge/originally **Welfare Island Bridge,** over East Channel, East River, connecting 36th Ave., Queens, with Motorgate garage and the Roosevelt Island street system. 1955. Repainted in new colors, 1971.

It's **amazing** what a carefully chosen color scheme can do to **revitalize an existing bridge** and its environs: a blue-violet superstructure (suspending lavender counterweights in its two towers) and trimmed in crimson, it set the tone for (and was outdone by) the repainting of the Ward's Island Pedestrian Bridge upriver [see H Manhattan/East Harlem **6c.**].

[4m.] Motorgate (garage complex), N of Roosevelt Island Bridge. 1974. Kallmann & McKinnell.

A parking garage with initial capacity for 1,000 cars and expansion capability for 1,500 more. The dramatic, glass-enclosed entrance structure for pedestrians is a structural *tour-de-force.*

[4n.] Service Complex/Fire Station, N of Motorgate. 1975. Kallmann & McKinnell.

Where the fire engines are housed and the terminal of the **Disney World-proven** refuse collection system, a giant underground vacuum collector connected to the rubbish chutes of all the new buildings.

The Southern Part

[5a.] Goldwater Memorial Hospital/originally called **Welfare Hospital for Chronic Diseases,** S of Sports Park. 1939. Isadore Rosenfield, senior architect, N.Y.C. Department of Hospitals; Butler & Kohn; York & Sawyer. Addition to S, 1971.

Low-rise chevron-shaped balconied wings extend from a central north-south spine giving patients confronted with long confinements **a maximum** of sunlight and river views.

[5b.] City Hospital/originally **Island Hospital/**then **Charity Hospital,** in proposed Landmark Park, S of Goldwater Memorial Hospital. 1859.

A grim reminder of the 19th-century medical ministrations to the needy. Built of stone quarried on the island by **convicts** from the adjacent penetentiary.

[5c.] Strecker Memorial Laboratory, in proposed Landmark Park, SE of City Hospital overlooking E channel of the East River. 1892. Withers & Dickson. Third story added, 1905. ★

A neo-Renaissance work which contrasts in both scale and style with its 19th-century neighbors to the north and south. In its day the city's **most sophisticated** medical research facility.

[5d.] Smallpox Hospital, in proposed Landmark Park, SW of Strecker Memorial Laboratory. 1856. James Renwick, Jr. S wing, 1904. York & Sawyer. N wing, 1905, Renwick, Aspinwall & Owen. ★

Years of **disuse and exposure** to the elements have made this into **a natural "Gothick" ruin.** Its official landmark designation further encourages such a role in quoting architectural historian **Paul Zucker** on the subject of ruins: ". . . an expression of an eerie romantic mood . . . a palpable documentation of a period in the past . . . something which recalls a specific concept of architectural space and proportion." The designation suggests the structure possesses all of these. It does.

[5e.] Proposed **Franklin D. Roosevelt Memorial,** in proposed FDR Memorial Park, S tip of island. Design, 1974. Louis I. Kahn.

A romantic but probably ill-fated design proposal for an understated monument to the American president for whom the island was renamed in 1973. It would have been the **only work** in New York City of Louis Kahn (1901-1974), one of this country's greatest architects.

[5f.] Delacorte Fountain, S tip of island. 1969. Pomerance & Breines, architects.

An artificial geyser of prechlorinated river water which, despite the 250-foot maximum height of its **white plume,** fails to carry the day against the vast panorama of the city.

[4k.] Westview (l) **[4f.]** Eastwood (r)   **[4m.]** The Motorgate (garage complex)

The Northern Part

[6a.] Originally **Octagon Tower, N.Y.C. Lunatic Asylum/**later **Metropolitan Hospital,** in proposed Octagon Park, N of Northtown. 1839. Alexander Jackson Davis. Mansard roof and entry stair added, ca. 1880, Joseph M. Dunn. Temporary preservation measures, 1970, Giorgio Cavaglieri. ★

A romantic tower surmounted by a later convex mansard "dome" sans the two wings which once extended from it, those demolished in 1970. UDC's fiscal problems prevented its intended total restoration as a *folie* in as-yet-unbuilt Octagon Park.

[6b.] Bird S. Coler Hospital, N end of island. 1952. Addition to S, 1954.

An undistinguished design left over from the late 1930s whose construction was delayed by World War II and was finally begun in 1949.

[6c.] Lighthouse, in proposed Lighthouse Park, N tip of island. 1872. James Renwick, Jr., supervising architect, Commission of Charities and Correction. ★

Built on a tiny island just off the tip of today's Roosevelt Island (and since joined to it) under the direction of the Board of Governors of the city's Commission of Charities and Correction, whose supervising architect at the time was Renwick. The lamps for this "private" lighthouse were later furnished by the U.S. Lighthouse Service.

The legend of John McCarthy: An inscription carved on the local gray gneiss ashlar of the Roosevelt Island Lighthouse adds credence (of a sort) to the old legend that a 19th-century patient at the nearby lunatic asylum was permitted to build this structure. It reads:

THIS IS THE WORK/WAS DONE BY/JOHN MCCARTHY/WHO BUILT THE LIGHT/HOUSE FROM THE BOTTOM TO THE/TOP ALL YE WHO DO PASS BY MAY/PRAY FOR HIS SOUL WHEN HE DIES

Official records are vague but indicate there may be some truth to the tale.

Wards Island/Randalls Island

Located in the vicinity of the turbulent Hell Gate at the junction of the East and Harlem Rivers; at one time separate islands but today joined as a result of landfill operations. **Randalls,** the northernmost of the two, is the home of the Triborough Bridge interchange as well as the administrative headquarters of the Triborough Bridge and Tunnel Authority. In Downing Stadium are held a variety of entertainment and sporting events as well as the Festival of San Juan, the patron saint of Puerto Rico.

Wards Island is a recreation area joined to Manhattan by a pedestrian bridge [see H Manhattan/East Harlem **6c.**] at East 103rd Street and is the site of a number of city and state facilities. Among them are

[7a.] Firemen's Training Center, Wards Island, NE part of island opp. Astoria Park, Queens. 1975. Hardy Holzman Pfeiffer Assocs.

This state Urban Development Corporation project, to substitute for the old firemen's training center demolished on Roosevelt Island, is **a confident work** of architecture and **a witty one,** too—shades of those wonderfully exuberant Napoleon LeBrun & Sons' firehouses of the 1890s! To the left of the entrance road sits a great shed-roofed space rising from **a berm of earth** (which seems to throw off water too quickly to support vegetation) entered through corrugated steel **culverts.** To the right lies a **mock city** (built of brown vitrified tile block) meant to be set afire and extinguished as part of the firemen's training. Unfortunately for visitors, the complex is fenced in and guarded by a gatehouse (though sometimes not by a gatekeeper).

[7b.] Rehabilitation Building, Manhattan Psychiatric Center/formerly known as **Manhattan State Hospital,** Wards Island, S of hospital buildings. 1970. Caudill Rowlett Scott.

A two-story "halfway house" in the stern shadow of an earlier generation's high-rise mental hospital.

[7c.] Manhattan Children's Treatment Center, N.Y. State Department of Mental Hygiene, Wards Island, opp. E. 107th St. recreation pier. 1972. Richard G. Stein & Assocs.

Campus style low-rise residence, teaching, and treatment facilities for mentally retarded and emotionally disturbed children. Vitreous block in variegated tones of brown enrich the appearance of this handsome grouping.

The other Other Islands: The city is filled with islands, many of them not accessible to the public either because of official edict or simple geography. In the first category are such city-owned (and guarded) examples as Rikers Island, in the East River just north of LaGuardia Airport (reached by a bridge from Hazen Street in Queens but under the jurisdiction of the Bronx), the home of many city penal institutions; North Brother Island, just adjacent to Rikers, site of now-abandoned Riverside Hospital— "Typhoid Mary" Mallon was its best-known resident—and Hart Island, east of City Island, where the city's potter's field is located. Quite visible but inaccessible because of geography (the currents of the East River) are tiny bits of land such as Belmont Island, south of Roosevelt opposite the United Nations, and Mill Rock, just east of 96th Street. But the richest assortment of islands, the nesting ground of thousands upon thousands of birds who migrate along the Atlantic Flyway, is the myriad group which comprises the semi-aquatic wonderland of Jamaica Bay, now part of the National Park Service's Gateway National Recreation Area.

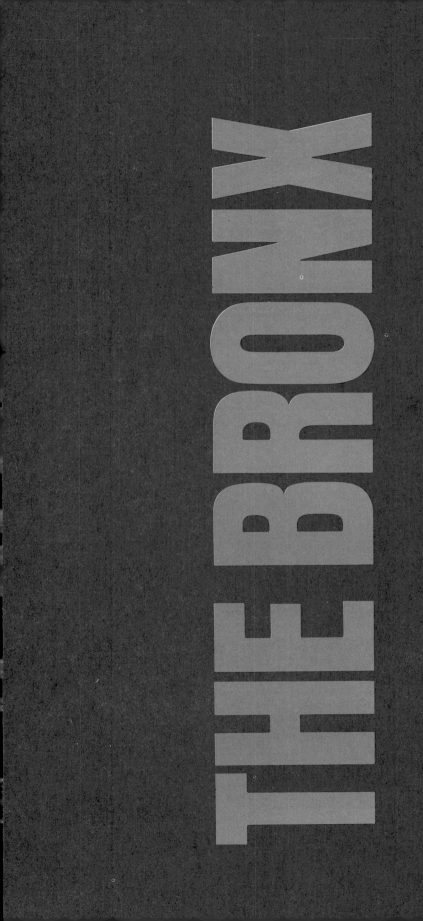

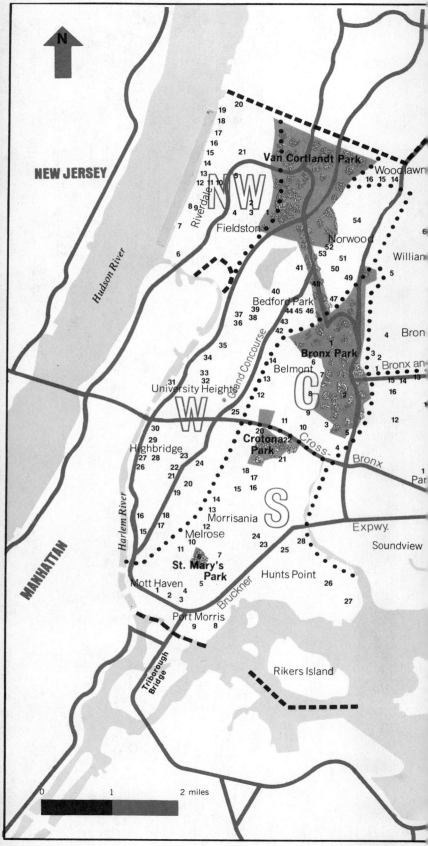

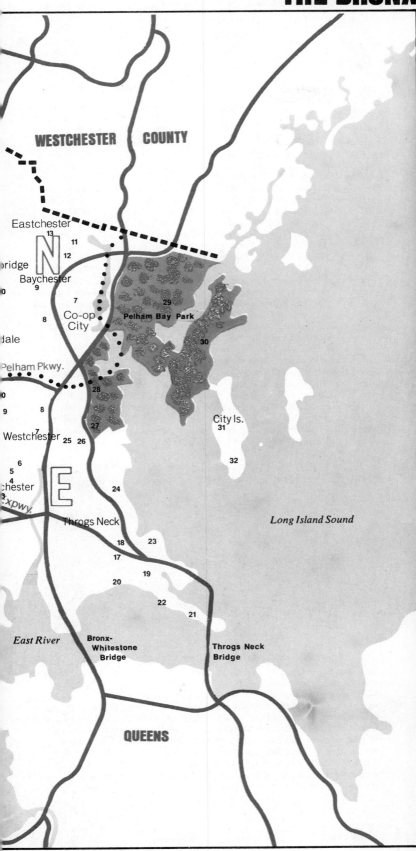

WESTCHESTER COUNTY

Eastchester
13
11
bridge
12
Baychester
9

7
29
8
Co-op
City
Pelham Bay Park

dale
30

Pelham Pkwy.

0
28
9   8

City Is.
27
31

Westchester   25   26
32

6
5
4
chester
xpwy.
24

Long Island Sound

Throgs Neck

18   23

17

20   19

22

21

East River   Bronx-
Whitestone
Bridge

Throgs Neck
Bridge

QUEENS

2

THE BRONX

Borough of The Bronx/Bronx County

The northernmost of New York City's five boroughs, this is the only one which is physically joined to the North American mainland—the others are (or once were) either islands by themselves or parts of another, Long Island. The only wrinkle is the *borough* of Manhattan, which is no longer quite the equivalent of the *island* of Manhattan, not since the straightening out of the Harlem River in 1895. This major **earth-moving effort** severed the community of Marble Hill from the northern tip of Manhattan Island and joined it instead, some years later, to the Bronx, using as fill the earth dug out of the **excavations for Grand Central Terminal.**

Like the County of Westchester, of which it was a part for some 200 years, Bronx County's topography consists of **hills and valleys** in the west end and what was originally a **marshy plain** to the east. To this day are visible the rocky outcroppings and streets of steps which characterize many areas of the West Bronx. The east is, as a result of **nonstop landfill** and a recent **population explosion** in red brick housing, less identifiable as a marsh. But a drive or walk through Pelham Bay Park will reveal some of the borough's **sylvan, preurbanized reeded landscapes** along the peninsulas which extend into Long Island Sound.

In the 19th century the Bronx was covered with farms, market villages, embryo commuter towns, country estates, and a number of rambling charitable institutions. It was then a place of **rural delights.** In 1874 the western portion of the Bronx (designated Western, Northwestern, Central, and Southern Bronx in this guide) was annexed to the city. Bridge-building and the extension of elevated rapid transit lines from Manhattan, and then a growth of population, industry, and schools followed **political union.** The eastern Bronx (designated as Eastern and Northern Bronx in this guide) became part of New York City in 1895.

BOSTON ROAD FROM 168 ST. LOOKING EAST, BRONX, NEW YORK CITY.

Except for some parts of Riverdale, the westernmost, hilliest, and least accessible part of the borough, the physical vestiges of the old villages with such names as West Farms, Morrisania, Kingsbridge, and Middletown were submerged by 20th-century development. At first the **extension of the rapid transit lines** along Jerome Avenue, Boston Road and White Plains Road, Westchester Avenue, and finally along Grand Concourse made the Bronx the next step in **upward mobility** for hundreds of thousands of families of average but improving means. But the post–World War II suburban exodus drained away many of their offspring. And governmental housing policy relocated many of the older generation who remained, eastward to Co-op City, a huge development of thirty-five-story apartment towers, bedding down, in aggregate, some 55,000 people.

Three quarters of the way through the 20th century the Bronx has become home to a population that is predominantly nonwhite, and to an inordinate number of poor. Though stable communities continue to flourish with populations drawn from all racial and economic backgrounds, much of the South, Central, and West Bronx carries the appellation **"Fort Apache,"** with areas approaching the appearance of a burnt-out wilderness, scenes not unlike those in **war-ravaged** cities.

In contrast to the visible decay of many of its communities, however, is the **green leafy** camouflage of the borough's larger **parks,** and the **parkways** which link them. They are the result of a plan by local visionaries devised back in 1883 and largely executed in the two decades that followed. Though the parks and parkways show the scars of economic deprivation and personal as well as municipal poverty—broken benches, broken glass, broken tree limbs—they continue to comprise the **most generous park system** in the city. The ability of nature to rejuvenate itself (fully one fifth of the Bronx's area—5,861 acres—is park land, although admittedly large amounts are not yet developed) coupled with the foresight of the borough's early planners may offer guidelines for the future.

Prospect Theatre, Bronx, New York City.

Tips on Touring: The Bronx, the smallest of New York's outer boroughs, is still quite large. Its southwestern quadrant—south of Fordham Road and west of the Bronx River (except for some notably healthy parts such as Belmont) is a large area beset by economic and social problems. The northwest, Riverdale, is picturesque, convoluted, and very hilly. The Bronx east of the Bronx River is simply vast. All this adds up to a recommendation that **touring be best done by car** with enough stop-offs to stretch your legs and to permit looking with greater care—so much can be missed, even when driving at a crawl. A car can provide a needed sense of protection in a devastated area but don't forget to be prepared to **roll up your windows** in hot weather when approaching a fire hydrant being used to provide relief from the heat. Otherwise some playful kids will cup their hands around the spray and inundate you. It's nothing personal on their part, but it's no fun driving with a puddle in your lap. Get a **street map** before embarking. The pocket atlases of the city are large enough to read but small enough to maneuver in the confines of a car.

For those **intrepid pedestrian wanderers** a good option is a mix of Bronx Park (zoo and botanical garden), Fordham University's Gothic-styled campus, and (except on Sundays) the nearby Italian community of Belmont and its wonderful European shopping street, Arthur Avenue. [See **Central Bronx** for the details.] **Mass transit** to a good starting point: Take the subway (IND D train or IRT Jerome Avenue Line No. 4 train) to the station marked Fordham Road. Then change (another fare—exact change, please) for Bus BX 12 or BX 24 eastbound to Southern Boulevard and Fordham Road, where you will find the zoo on the south side of the street; the garden on the north.

Remember there is **safety in numbers.** Don't walk in desolate areas. Don't tour at night. Do take a friend along—it's more fun that way.

Meanwhile, there is much to see:

S

SOUTHERN BRONX

The South Bronx

Though their names persist into the present, the country villages that once existed in the South Bronx have long disappeared. Soon after the **Civil War** the farms that existed here from colonial days began to give way to private homes and tenement rows. In more recent days these have given way to **arterial highways** and **public housing** developments. The rapid growth of other parts of the Bronx in the 20th century eclipsed the South Bronx and shifted the focus of commerce, entertainment, and government to other parts of the borough. Successive waves of immigrants and industries have passed in and out of the South Bronx, but their **footprints** are hard to find. Without money, power, or prestige, the South Bronx has been unable to cultivate its ornaments. **Landmarks** venerated in other places are overlooked in this area. Some have completely disappeared; others are marked for demolition. Many have been burned down, but some survive and wait to be rediscovered.

MOTT HAVEN

Site of Jordan Mott Iron Works, 1828–1906.

Mott, inventor of a coal-burning stove, established a factory west of Third Avenue, between East 134th Street and the Harlem River in 1828. The venture prospered and grew. Some buildings of the iron works can still be seen from the western walkway of the Third Avenue Bridge. It was Mott who founded the village of Mott Haven, whose monogram "MH" persists in the mosaics of the 138th and 149th Street stations of the IRT Jerome Avenue Line.

The Broncks: The first European settlers of this area were Jonas Bronck, a Dane from Amsterdam, and his family, whose farmhouse is believed to have been located east of the Third Avenue Bridge. Though some say the borough's **official** name, *The* Bronx, owes its initial article to friends of the settlers saying "Let's pay a visit to the Broncks," the less romantic but more accurate explanation lies elsewhere. As it was common to speak of the **Army of the Potomac** or the **valley of the Hudson,** each taking their names from rivers, so it was with the lands along the banks of the local river here, the Bronx River.

[1.] Mott Haven Historic District, generally along both sides of Alexander Ave. bet. E. 137th and E. 141st Sts. including **[1a.] St. Jerome's Roman Catholic Church.** 1898. Dehli & Howard. **[1b.] 40th Precinct Police Station.** 1924. Thomas E. O'Brien. **[1c.] Mott Haven Branch, New York Public Library.** 1905. Babb, Cook & Willard. **[1d.] Tercera Iglesia Bautista (Third Baptist Church)**/originally **Alexander Avenue Baptist Church.** 1902. Ward & Davis. District designated, 1969. ★

This is the old Bronx at its best. Not only are there well-designed row houses and apartments here but four fine institutional buildings as well, two of which, the churches, handsomely define the district at its south and north ends. No. 280 Alexander Avenue was the home of **Edward Willis,** a local land developer for whom nearby Willis Avenue is named.

[2.] The Bertine Block, 414–432 E. 136th St. bet. Willis Ave. and Brown Place. S side. ca. 1890.

A decorative grouping of low-stooped houses bearing diverse ornament, intricate rooflines, and even some stained glass, all unified through use of a pale yellow face brick.

[3.] Plaza Borinquen, 3 sites: 1) E. 137th St. bet. Willis Ave. and Brown Place. 2) E. 137th St. NW cor. Brown Place. 3) E. 138th St. to E. 139th St. bet. Willis and Brook Aves. 1974. Ciardullo-Ehmann.

Eighty-eight triplex apartments contained in groups of row houses thoughtfully planned to fill three different kinds of **scattered sites** within the existing housing fabric. The red-brown masonry, with similarly toned mortar and bright highlights in the orange and red air conditioner covers, heralds a new look for the South Bronx. [Also see WC Brooklyn/Red Hook 2.] **Borinquen** is the name given the island of Puerto Rico by its original settlers, the **Taino people.**

[3.] Plaza Borinquen: a view from the courtyard of the low-rise housing

[4a.] St. Ann's Church (Protestant Episcopal) and Graveyard, 295 St. Ann's Ave. bet. E. 139th and E. 141st Sts. W side. 1841. ★

An old stone-walled church turned slightly askew to the street grid and facing a space that is neither street nor true oasis, St. Ann's is an echo from the Bronx's dim past. Mysterious hummocks in front of the edifice mark burial vaults in which early parishioners' remains are entombed. Adjacent is the weathered wood of play equipment installed as a 1960s' social response to the neighborhood's deprived children. Memories of those once-hopeful days swirl around you along with the dust at your feet.

[4b.] Centro de Salud Segundo Ruiz Belvis, (neighborhood family care center) E. 142nd St. NW cor. St. Ann's Ave. 1972. Frost Assocs., architects; William Tarr, sculptor.

An important step forward: not just a needed community health center but a physical symbol of hope in the cityscape.

[4c.] José de Diego-Beekman Houses, 346 St. Ann's Ave. bet. E. 141st and St. Mary's Sts. E side. ca. 1901. Rehabilitation and redesign, 1975, Beyer-Blinder-Belle.

Some early-20th-century tenements are being turned around into late-20th-century housing resources. This is but one of a number of examples in the South Bronx. It is believed by some that the renewal of existing housing stock is the **more realistic** (if not the most glamorous) solution to a pressing human need for urban shelter.

[5.] St. Mary's Park, St. Ann's to Jackson Aves., St. Mary's to E. 149th Sts. Reconstructed, 1936.

This park is named for St. Mary's Church, a wooden country church that stood on Alexander Avenue and East 142nd Street until its demolition in 1959. The crest of the hill at the north end of the park is a good place from which to survey this neighborhood. It was once known as **Janes' Hill** and belonged to Adrian Janes, whose family's **famous iron works** was located nearby.

The Capitol Dome: On the south side of Westchester Avenue between Brook and St. Ann's Avenues is the site of what was once the **Janes, Kirtland & Co. Iron Works.** It was here, in one of America's largest foundries of its time, that were cast such lowly devices as iron furnaces and such elegant items of architectural ironwork as **Central Park's Bow Bridge.** But literally crowning partners Janes' and Kirtland's many achievements was the casting and erection (using horsepower) of the **8,909,200 pounds** of iron which became the Capital Dome in Washington, D.C., completed in 1863.

[6.] Intermediate School 162 Bronx, The Lola Rodriguez de Tio School, 600 St. Ann's Ave. NE cor. E. 149th St. 1970. Lathrop Douglass.

Cream-colored precast concrete and brown brick: a large, rambling work occupying much of the block. Neat but indecisive—the precast grid appears and disappears for no apparent reason. Compare with the Art Deco former **N.Y.C. Child Health Station** across 149th Street, a minor but totally coherent (though much-vandalized) statement.

[7a.] St. Anselm's Church (Roman Catholic), 673 Tinton Ave. bet. E. 152nd St. and Westchester Ave. W side. 1918. Gustave Steinback.

This church's exterior is bare-bones-brick practically everywhere except around the entrance, where some poetically illustrated glazed tile plaques and neo-Romanesque ornament soften the bluntness of the masonry. But as the exterior is **bold and forceful,** the interior is **soft and supple,** its details a combination of Byzantine and Romanesque motifs created by brothers of the Benedictine order who came here from Germany in the 1920s. A **blue-green light** floats down upon the sanctuary from a circular, stained glass clerestory as though lighting a grotto. The walls **shimmer** with the brothers' ceramic tile **tesserae.** It is both a surprising and moving experience.

[7a.] St. Anselm's RC Church: its rich volumes are best seen from the rear

[7b.] Hunts Point Multi-Service Center, 630 Jackson Ave. NE cor. E. 151st St. 1974. Bond Ryder Assocs.

One of a number of new institutions which grew out of the Model Cities Program in the South Bronx, this radical building, turned diagonally to its old tenement neighbors, seems out of place with its rich, yellow ochre block and almost opaque-seeming, dark-tinted sheets of glass.

PORT MORRIS

East of the Bruckner Expressway and the Bronx approaches to the Triborough Bridge and south of East 141st Street lies a peninsula of industry **largely forgotten** by the wheels of progress: Port Morris. It was developed as a **deep-water port** by the Morris family during the mid-19th century, in the hope of rivaling New York. The Hell Gate Plant of the

Consolidated Edison Company and Richard Hoe & Company, manufacturers of printing press machinery, are located here.

[8.] Richard Hoe & Company, Printing Machinery and Saws/formerly **DeLavergne Refrigerating Machine Company,** 910 E. 138th St. from Locust Ave. to W of Walnut Ave. S side. ca. 1875.

Robust brick industrial sheds of the 19th century and a more ornate office building in the same style at the southwest corner of Walnut Avenue and East 138th Street. The Hoe Company found a use for DeLavergne's buildings after it vacated its own 19th-century complex on Manhattan's Lower East Side to make way for the Amalgamated Housing along Grand Street. Colonel Richard M. Hoe **invented the rotary printing press** in 1846.

[8.] Richard Hoe & Co./DeLavergne Co.   [10a.] Immaculate Conception Church

Schlitz Inn, 737 E. 137th St. NW cor. Willow Ave. Telephone: 669-8770.

The last of many restaurants that once served the German community of the South Bronx. Today its fare consists of simple dishes and, naturally, Schlitz beer.

[9.] Bronx Grit Chamber of Wards Island Water Pollution Control Plant, City of New York, 158 Bruckner Blvd. bet. St. Ann's and Cypress Aves. S side. 1936. McKim, Mead & White.

An impressive exercise in the neo-Baroque but a little late in this century for such antics.

MELROSE

Dominating this community is the traditional business and entertainment center of the borough, called the Hub, the intersection of five busy streets: East 149th Street, Third, Willis, Melrose, and Westchester Avenues. Old-timers can recall the area as a **bustling entertainment center** with fare ranging from silent flicks and burlesque to operatic performances, and trolley lines converging from every direction. The Bronx stretch of the Third Avenue "el," which once clattered overhead, was removed in the 1970s but the pace on the street remains **furious and chaotic,** an expression of the coming together of the many Hispanic and black communities, of which Melrose and the rest of the South Bronx is today comprised. If there is a word to sum up the Hub's purpose it is **"buy!"** Alexander's first store at 2952 Third Avenue and a one-time branch of Fourteenth Street's Hearns', which still bears the name, are the flagships for hundreds of smaller merchants.

[10a.] Immaculate Conception Church of the Blessed Virgin Mary (Roman Catholic), 389 E. 150th St. NW cor. Melrose Ave. 1887.

This austere yet handsome brick Romanesque Revival church boasts the highest steeple in the borough. It recalls the days when the Germans were the most populous ethnic group in the Bronx and their prominence in the building trades, brewing, and in the manufacture of musical instruments was of central importance to the borough's prosperity. The facades of the rectory on the west, the church in the center, and the Redemptorist Fathers home on the east make a handsome composition of brick detail and arched windows. A later auditorium on the southwest corner of 151st Street and Melrose Avenue is a reserved Beaux Arts composition.

[10b.] 361 East 151st Street and **614 Courtlandt Avenue (apartments).**

In a neighborhood where the tides of change are everywhere apparent, here is a miraculously intact three-story-high town house complete with intricate detailing on a mansard roof.

[11a.] Lincoln Hospital Center, N.Y.C. Health and Hospitals Corporation, Morris Ave. SW cor. E. 149th St. 1976. Max O. Urbahn Assocs. Brick bas-relief mural, Aleksandra Kasuba.

The brickwork of this up-to-date health care facility is just too much of a good thing. Of an indescribably strident earth color, it aggressively grabs your attention as does what must be the largest bronze anodized-aluminum identification sign in the world. On the other hand, the swirled brick **bas-relief** on the 149th Street side is a handsome addition to the streetscape.

[11a.] The Lincoln Hospital Center   **[13.]** Old Bronx Borough Courthouse

[11b.] Michelangelo Apartments, E. 149th to E. 150th Sts. bet. Morris and Park Aves. 1976. Weiner & Gran and Jarmul & Brizee.

If this project's flat, uninteresting facade on 149th Street was meant as a foil to the more colorful, more three-dimensional one of Lincoln Hospital Center across the street, it succeeds. But there must have been a better way. A project of the state Urban Development Corporation.

MORRISANIA

[12a.] Former **Ebling Brewery,** St. Ann's to Eagle Aves. N of E. 156th St. **[12b.]** Former **Hupfel Brewery,** St. Ann's to Eagle Aves. bet. E. 159th and E. 161st Sts. Both late 19th century.

The South Bronx being a German neighborhood in the 19th century, there was a continuing demand for **lager beer.** Before the advent of refrigeration, the brewing of lager (from the German *liegen,* to lie still) required a **chilled place to age.** Caves cut into hillsides made it possible to pack the beer kegs with naturally cut ice and then to seal the openings temporarily until the beer had aged. No surprise then that these former breweries backed up to the Eagle Avenue **escarpment** (it is **so steep** that Eagle Avenue negotiates East 161st Street over a high bridge). The caves still exist but are used today for less romantic manufacturing purposes. During Prohibition, both caves and breweries were converted into **indoor mushroom farms.** Incidentally, those handsome row houses at **709–727 Eagle Avenue,** below East 161st Street, are said to have been built as residences for key individuals in the brewing process.

[13.] Old **Bronx Borough Courthouse**/now **Criminal Court of the City of New York, Bronx County Branch,** E. 161st St., Brook Ave., and Third Ave. 1906. Michael J. Garvin.

Strong vertical forms set against the fine horizontal lines cut into its base make this Beaux Arts structure a monument as well as a building. In spite of more than seven decades of smoke, grime, neglect, and the rattling of the now-gone Third Avenue "el," it remains grand, even though its metalwork is tarnished and its walls are covered with soot. The leaf-crowned statue of **Justice by G. E. Roine** which peered into every passing train for so many years from the south facade may not be there much longer . . . a replacement courthouse is scheduled to open nearby [see W Bronx 20.].

[14.] Former **Sheffield Farms Company (Milk) Bottling Plant,** 1051 Webster Ave. bet. E. 165th and E. 166th Sts. W side. 1914.

Though milk is no longer pasteurized and bottled behind this glazed terra-cotta facade, the cows and milk bottles are still visible—in the ornament. Note also, **on Clay Avenue** behind the bottling plant, the pairs of red brick/gray stone-trimmed residences.

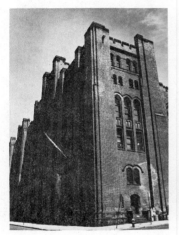 

[15a.] 105th Artillery Armory, N.Y.N.G.   **[15b.]** St. Augustine's Catholic Church

[15a.] 105th Artillery Armory, N.Y. National Guard, 1122 Franklin Ave. NE cor. E. 166th St. 1910. Charles C. Haight.

A dark, red brick fortress with slit-like windows looks down on a steep street of stairs. Together with **Hines Park** and the facade of St. Augustine's Church, the armory provides the backdrop for an exciting but forgotten urban space. It is the perfect stage for a **medieval melodrama** or a childhood game of **knights-in-armor.**

[15b.] St. Augustine's Church, 1183 Franklin Ave. NW cor. E. 167th St. 1894. **[15c.] St. Augustine's School,** 1176 Franklin Ave. bet. E. 167th and E. 168th St. E side. 1904.

Renaissance and Baroque elements are combined in the somber but imposing facade of the church. The parish school up the block to the north is distinguished by a sculpture group projecting from the tympanum of its classical pediment.

[16a.] Morris High School, E. 166th St. NE cor. Boston Road, 1901. C.B.J. Snyder.

A powerful, turreted central tower, gabled green copper roof, buff brick, and terra-cotta trim make this a model of Public School Gothic.

[16b.] 1074 Cauldwell Avenue/1076 Cauldwell Avenue (residences), SE cor. Boston Rd. S of E. 166th St.

Two gleaming, well-cared-for, expansive Victorian frame houses which preside over a dusty intersection that has seen better days.

[17.] 1266 Boston Road/1270 Boston Road (residences), bet. E. 168th and E. 169th Sts. E side of McKinley Sq.

Somewhat narrower structures than those three blocks away on Cauldwell Avenue, these are in the **Grant Wood-American Gothic mode.** Perhaps it is no accident that they survive: one is surrounded by a high, chain-link fence; the other is cheek-by-jowl with a firehouse.

[18a.] Former Eichler Mansion/now Department of Mental Health, Bronx-Lebanon Hospital Center, Fulton Division, 1285 Fulton Ave. SW cor. E. 169th St. 1890. De Lemos & Cordes.

A plethora of riches: yet *another* residential relic of the 19th century, this time of red brick and terra cotta. Eichler was a **beer magnate** and his mansion sat on the hill looking west to his **brewery** once located at Third Avenue south of East 169th Street.

[18b.] Originally Temple Adath Israel   [24.] Orig. Montefiore Congregation

[18b.] Former Temple Adath Israel, 551 E. 169th St. bet. Fulton and Third Aves. 1889?

This modest edifice is considered by some to be the first Jewish synagogue to be built in the Bronx. It has since served the Puerto Rican community as a Baptist church.

[19a.] Lewis S. Davidson, Sr., Houses, N.Y.C. Housing Authority, 810 Home St. S side. 1150, 1152 Union Ave. E side. 1221 Prospect Ave. W side. 1973. Paul Rudolph.

Exposed cast-in-place concrete frames with dark gray ribbed block infill, these eight-story low-rent apartment buildings are a refreshing change from the years of monotonous red brick towers previously bestowed upon the city's neighborhoods by the Authority. [See E Bronx 25. for a more dramatic version designed at the same time.]

[19b.] Engine Company 82, Ladder Company 31, N.Y.C. Fire Department, 1213 Intervale Ave. NW cor. E. 169th St.

This Beaux Arts firehouse figures heavily in the 1972 bestseller about fire fighting in the South Bronx, Dennis Smith's *Report From Engine Co. 82.*

[19c.] Walls AME Zion Church (African Methodist Episcopal)/formerly Holy Trinity Lutheran Church, 891–895 Home St. NE cor. Intervale Ave.

A charmingly conceived yellow brick church which effectively makes use of a triangular plot of land just across from Engine Co. 82.

[20.] Crotona Park, Fulton, Third, Tremont, and Arthur Aves., Crotona Park North, East, and South, and a small jog to Southern Blvd. and E. 175th St. Reconstructed, 1936. **[20a.] Crotona Play Center,** in Crotona Park, Fulton Ave. at E. 175th St. E side. 1936. N.Y.C. Park Department and Aymar Embury II.

Formerly the estate of the Bathgate family (for whom the nearby avenue was named), Crotona Park is one of six sites for parks selected by a citizens' committee in 1883. Named for **Croton,** an **ancient Greek city** renowned as the home of many **Olympic champions,** the park contains a vast array of sports facilities which are in sad disarray today. The best and, at least to the eye, the most enduring, the play center (actually a bathhouse and swimming pool) is one of the **great red brick WPA structures** built in the 1930s.

[21.] Junior High School 98 Bronx, The Herman Ridder Junior High School, 1619 Boston Rd. SW cor. E. 173rd St. ca. 1940. Eric Kebbon.

Named for the philanthropist who was publisher of the *New York Staats-Zeitung.* On a difficult irregular site the architect has employed a handsome multifaceted tower as a point of focus for the limestone-clad building. The design is a **late-blooming** combination of Beaux Arts and Art Deco classicism.

[22.] Former **Biograph Company Studios,** 807 E. 175th St. and 790 E. 176th St. bet. Marmion and Prospect Aves. ca. 1905.

Before the movie moguls folded their tents and stole away to Hollywood, New York City was the center of early motion picture production. These studios were used by **Thomas A. Edison** (1847–1931) for his later work in film.

HUNTS POINT

[23.] Patrolman Edward P. Lynch Center, Police Athletic League/formerly **The Martinique Club,** the **Longwood Club/**originally **The White Mansion,** 974 E. 156th St. SW cor. Beck St. ca. 1870.

Turned at an angle to today's street grid this venerable country house has seen a long series of adaptive reuses. Despite its down-at-the-heels look, it is a welcome sight in this besieged community.

A bouquet of houses: Early-20th-century row houses are not what you imagine when the name Hunts Point is mentioned. But such rows (actually 2½-story semi-detached pairs) do exist and are as fresh a visual bouquet as one could wish: Beck Street between Longwood and Leggett Avenues, Kelly Street between Longwood Avenue and East 156th Street, and East 156th Street between Beck and Dawson Streets. Mature street trees help, too.

[24.] United Church/originally **Montefiore Congregation,** 764 Hewitt Place, bet. E. 156th St. and Longwood Ave. E side. ca. 1900.

This lyrical, pastel-painted, white-trimmed edifice smiles **beamingly** down its one block axis, Macy Place, toward busy, noisy Prospect Avenue, one of Hunts Point's main drags. Originally a Jewish synagogue patterned after the Eastern European model, it nevertheless was crowned with twin onion domes! Today, reflecting ethnic and religious shifts in the community, a crucifix occupies the space between the domes.

[25a.] American Bank Note Company, Lafayette Ave. NE cor. Tiffany St. 1911.

The **peninsular portion** of the Hunts Point community is separated from the rest of the South Bronx not by a waterway but by a deep railroad cut, once the tracks of the **NYNH&H,** and the massive elevated **Bruckner Expressway.** Guarding a main entry to the "peninsula" is this dark and spare masonry fortress which serves to guard its valuable contents as well. Printed within are **billions** of pesos, cruzeiros, colons, sucres, and gourdes for Mexico, Brazil, Costa Rica, Ecuador, and Haiti (respectively), stock certificates, travellers' checks, and even lottery tickets.

[25b.] Corpus Christi Monastery, 1230 Lafayette Ave. at Baretto St. E side. 1899.

The best time to visit this cloistered community of Dominican nuns is on Sunday afternoon, when they sing their office. The church, with its beautiful polished mosaic floor, bare walls, and scores of candles, is then fully lighted.

[25c.] Spofford Juvenile Detention Center, N.Y.C. Department of Social Services/originally **Bronx Youth House for Boys,** 1221 Spofford Ave. NE cor. Tiffany St. 1958. Kahn & Jacobs. **[25d.]** Originally **Sevilla Home for Children/**more recently **Bronx Youth House for Girls,** Lafayette Ave. SW cor. Manida St. ca. 1900.

These two institutions share a superblock with the Corpus Christi Monastery. The Sevilla Home, originally a nonsectarian home for destitute girls, is no longer in use, its pale-yellow-stuccoed walls in the Spanish Renaissance Revival style falling into ruin. The Spofford Center, sterile in appearance (its white brick walls help), continues to attract headlines not for its architecture but for the notoriety associated with the quality of its social services.

Drake Park: In the center of this forgotten plot of land at Hunts Point and Oak Point Avenues stands an iron fence enclosing the graves of many early settlers of the area including members of the Hunt family itself, for which the point is named. Poet Joseph Rodman Drake (1795–1820) is also buried here, hence the name of the park and nearby Drake Street. Other poets honored by streets in the surrounding, ill-kempt industrial area: Halleck, Whittier, Longfellow, and Bryant.

[26.] New York City Terminal Market, along Halleck St. bet. Lafayette and East Bay Aves. 1965. Skidmore, Owings & Merrill.

Spacious facilities for trailer trucks and railroad cars are provided in this decentralized wholesale fruit and vegetable market (the Hunts Point markets were a keystone in the city's planning strategies of the sixties and seventies). A model of SOM efficiency, enhanced by black-painted steel, blue-tinted glass, and occasional walls of carmine red brick. A Les Halles, however, it isn't.

[27.] Hunts Point Cooperative Meat Market, Hunts Point Ave. S of East Bay St. 1976. Brand & Moore.

Most dramatic of the facilities which comprise the **second stage** of the Hunts Point Market, these three long, low yellow-ochre masonry blocks capture the spirit of the wholesale market very well. Their smaller Stage II neighbors, by other architects, do considerably less well.

[28.] Bright Temple AME Church/formerly **Temple Beth Elohim/**originally **"Brightside,"** 812 Faile St. NE cor. Lafayette St. ca. 1860.

This handsome Gothic Revival stone mansion, like the White Mansion [see S Bronx 23.], is turned to its original view and not to the street pattern imposed later.

ⓒ

CENTRAL BRONX

The Central Bronx includes the Bronx Zoo, the New York Botanical Garden, Fordham University, and the district encompassing the Webster Avenue corridor on the west and the Bronx River area on the east. Its south boundary is the **gash** of the Cross-Bronx Expressway. Within this area can be found a **great variety** of flora, fauna, land uses, housing types, and building conditions. Institutions of **world prominence** are within sight of **humble** and **exotic** neighborhood establishments. Long-forgotten landmarks lie close to excellent new community structures that may one day become landmarks for future generations.

[1a.] Conservatory Range: the glass houses at the N.Y. Botanical Garden

BRONX PARK AND WEST FARMS

[1.] New York Botanical Garden, Bronx Park, N of E. Fordham Rd. site, 1895. Calvert Vaux and Samuel Parsons, Jr. Information, hours, programs: 220-8777.

The Botanical Garden, incorporated in 1891 and patterned after the **Royal Botanical Gardens** at Kew, England, is one of the leading institutions of its kind in the world. Its scientific facilities include a conservatory, museum, library, herbarium (a collection of dried plants), research laboratory, and a variety of groves and gardens. The selection of this site within Bronx Park, as recommended by **Vaux and Parsons,** enables the garden to perform a second valuable function: it contains and preserves the **beautiful gorge** of the Bronx River, a **virgin hemlock forest,** and some of the **historic buildings** which were here before the park was created. It occupies 240 acres of city park land at the northern extreme of Bronx Park.

[1a.] Conservatory Range. 1902. William R. Cobb for Lord & Burnham, greenhouse manufacturers. Altered 1938, 1953. Restoration, 1978. Edward Larrabee Barnes & Assocs. ★

A great group of greenhouses in the tradition of Decimus Burton's Great Palm House at Kew, and Paxton's Crystal Palace. Many years of deterioration threatened the glass fairyland and its wide-ranging plant species, but at the last minute, restoration rather than replacement won out—a victory for plants and people alike.

[1b.] Museum Building. 1902. Robert W. Gibson. Addition, 1973. **[1c.] Laboratory Building.** 1957. Brown, Lawford & Forbes.

Two contrasting works in purpose, scale, design, and age which share a common formal axis near the original main entrance to the garden.

[1d.] Old Lorillard Snuff Mill. ca. 1840. Restored, 1954. ★

This building, together with a later gatehouse and stables, are all the improvements that remain from the extensive local land holdings of **the Lorillards,** a family whose name is still associated with the **tobacco industry.** Built of local fieldstone, the mill once used the adjacent waters as power **to grind snuff,** a more popular tobacco product in the 19th century than it is today. Fortunately, the mill building, a fine example of **local industrial architecture,** was adapted into a public snack bar (open summer months only), and its new terrace is a lovely place to snack to the bubbly sounds of the adjacent river.

The Bronx River Gorge: Just north of the snuff mill is an arched stone footbridge, a great spot from which to view the gorge of the Bronx River and the turbulent waters that carved it over the millennia. It is yet one other surprising event in a city filled with them. Another, the nearby hemlock forest, is the last remaining part of a stand of trees that once covered much of New York City.

[2.] The Bronx Zoo/officially **New York Zoological Park,** Bronx Park, S of E. Fordham Rd. Opened in 1899. Original architects, Heins & La Farge. Hours, admission charges, information: 933-1759.

At the Bronx Zoo's opening ceremonies, visitors were officially welcomed not to one of the "small closed zoological gardens of Europe" but to "a free Park, projected upon a scale larger than has ever been attempted before." By today's standards the 252 acres of the Bronx Zoo are cramped in comparison to more modern and expansive zoos in other cities. And though the zoo is "free" in the sense of large rambling meadows, pastures, and dusty plains, rising costs have severely limited the times when admission is gratis.

Nevertheless, the Bronx Zoo is the **largest** of the city's five zoos—though privately run it occupies city park land and receives a city subsidy—and is **the most ambitious,** in both **concept** and **execution.** The area is divided into basically two parts. At the north end is **Baird Court,** a large space around whose grassy plots and sea lion pool are formally arrayed many of the zoo's original buildings. This part is more like a zoological garden, with indoor and outdoor caged species and a pavilion housing **animal heads and horns,** trophies of some of the naturalist-hunter founders. The remainder of the zoo's acreage is devoted, more or less, to a more naturalistic zoological *park,* culminating in **moated exhibitions,** the African Plains of 1941, and the **forest** along the Bronx River to be devoted to displaying the wildlife of Asia. To shorten walking distances between all these places the management has introduced an aerial **"Skyfari"** and will add a monorail people-mover in the Asian area.

[2a.] Paul J. Rainey Memorial Gate. 1934. Paul Manship, sculptor; Charles A. Platt, architect of gate lodges and gateposts. ★ **[2b.] Rockefeller Fountain.** 1910. ★ Both at E. Fordham Rd. entrance.

Manship's beautifully scaled Art Deco-inspired bronze gates, a gift of **Grace Rainey Rogers**—they are dedicated to her brother—open upon an earlier, handsomely detailed Italian garden. In the center of the driveway's turnaround is an early-18th-century Italian fountain picked up near **Lake Como** by benefactor **William Rockefeller.**

[2a.] Paul J. Rainey Memorial Gate, Bronx Zoo, Pelham Pkwy. Entrance

[2c.] Lion House. 1903. **[2d.] Primate House.** 1901. **[2e.] Administration Building.** 1910. **[2f.] Main Bird House.** 1905. **[2g.] Elephant House.** 1911. Heins & La Farge. **[2h.] Heads and Horns Building.** 1922. All surround Baird Court, H. A. Caparn, landscape architect.

The zoo's formal Baird Court was a direct outgrowth of the **city-beautiful** precepts of the **World's Columbian Exposition** of 1893. It was a controversial afterthought to what had been an initial desire to treat the zoo grounds as **a naturalistic park.** The elephant house, a classical palace with a Byzantine interior, a high dome, and terra-cotta decoration, could serve as **capitol of a banana republic.**

[2i.] The African Plains, near the Boston Rd. zoo entrance. 1941. Harrison & Foulhoux.

Moats rather than bars protect the public from the lions, while other moats protect the other animals of the savannah from both lions and visitors. Full-size replicas of indigenous buildings attempt to recreate an African landscape in the Bronx.

[2l.] The World of Birds, Bronx Zoo   **[3a.]** The Lambert Houses apartments

[2j.] Aquatic Bird House. 1964. Goldstone & Dearborn. **[2k.] The World of Darkness.** 1969. Morris Ketchum, Jr. & Assocs. **[2l.] The World of Birds.** 1972. Morris Ketchum, Jr. & Assocs.

Three modern works of architecture can be found in the zoo: The Aquatic Bird House; the World of Darkness, a windowless building that reverses day and night for the visitor in order to display cave-dwelling and nocturnal animals; and the World of Birds, the most effective of the three. This display of some 550 birds in 25 different habitats is a plastic, flowing composition of rounded, rough-faced concrete block forms dramatically illuminated within by skylights. Visitors here walk in rooms *with* birds, not on the other side of grilles from them—it makes a lot of difference.

[3a.] Lambert Houses (apartments), Shopping Plaza, and Parking Garage, along Boston Rd. bet. Bronx Park South and E. Tremont Ave. 1973. Davis, Brody & Assocs., architects; A.E. Bye Assocs., landscape architects.

These distinctive sawtooth-plan apartment, shopping, and parking structures south of Bronx Park were commissioned by **Phipps Houses,** a nonprofit foundation concerned with building **better housing** in the city. They utilize a special 8″-thick single-wythe bearing wall of special rich red-clay bricks as a unifying construction material in all the buildings. In the six-story residential buildings, wood joists bear on the walls to form floors and roofs. The south end of the shopping plaza bounds **old West Farms Square,** once a **trolley car hub** and a secondary commercial center for the entire borough.

[3b.] Former **Peabody Home**/now **Circle Missions, Inc.,** 2064 Boston Rd. NE cor. E. 179th St. 1901.

Now contained within the Lambert Houses properties and in the shadow of the IRT elevated lumbering overhead, this fine red brick building in a Tudor Gothic style adds a **syncopated note** to the area's ambience. It was once a home for the aged; it is now occupied by the followers of the late **Father Divine.**

[3c.] Old West Farms Soldier Cemetery, E. 180th St. NE cor. Bryant Ave. (now a pedestrian walk).1815. ★

Forty veterans of four wars lie in repose here amidst trees and shrubs in this **oasis of calm** adjacent to the west edge of Lambert Houses:

tombstones of soldiers from the War of 1812, the Civil War, the Spanish-American War, and World War I may be seen through the fence surrounding this two-thirds-acre site. After many years of neglect and desecration, the locally organized **Civil War Memorial Committee,** reconstituted about 1950, came to the rescue, restored the site and memorial statue, and achieved its recognition as an official landmark.

[3d.] Intermediate School 167 Bronx, The Lorraine Hansberry School, 1970 West Farms Rd. SE cor. E. Tremont Ave. 1973. Max O. Urbahn Assocs., Inc.

Defining part of the south edge of old West Farms Square [see 3a.] is this **crisply designed** city school, **a far cry** from most of its predecessors of the 1940s and 1950s. It uses a cast-concrete structural frame and dark, rough-ribbed concrete block infill to achieve its neat and dramatic geometry. The site it occupies was once that of the **Bronx Bleachery,** a well-remembered industry probably because of the **negative impact** it had upon the purity of the adjacent Bronx River.

[4.] Originally **New York Coliseum**/now **N.Y.C. Transit MaBSTOA Bus Repair Facility (Manhattan and Bronx Surface Transit Operating Authority),** E. 177th St. bet. Devoe and Bronx Park Aves. S side. 1927.

Built originally for the **Sesquicentennial Exposition** of 1926 in Philadelphia and subsequently dismantled and reerected here. Prior to World War II the bulky bowstring arched structure was the site of indoor **automobile races** and **boxing matches**—it seated 15,000 people. During the war it was commandeered as an army ordnance repair facility, which is not too different from its use today. To its west was once the **amusement park** and **swimming center** called **Starlight Park** on the east bank of the Bronx River.

[5.] Former **New York, Westchester & Boston Railway Company Administration Building**/now **Entrance to E. 180th Station of the IRT Dyre Avenue Subway,** 481 Morris Park Ave. NW cor. E. 180th St. 1912. Fellheimer & Long, Allen H. Stem, associated. ★

Twin towers capped with red tile roofs and walls of warm-hued, bush-hammered concrete identify this headquarters building in the **Italian Villa style** for a railroad **that never made it.** The NYW & B was to be a suburban line that would glamorously and swiftly transport commuters to the suburbs developing around White Plains and Port Chester prior to World War I. The architecture, **picturesque in appearance,** was to set the tone. The enterprise, having never made a profit, finally **failed in 1937.** The N.Y.C. Transit Authority's IRT Dyre Avenue line still uses some of the city route [see E Bronx 16.].

FORDHAM/BELMONT

[6.] Fordham University, Rose Hill Campus, generally E of Webster Ave., N of E. Fordham Rd., S and W of Southern Blvd. **[6a.] Administration Building**/central part formerly **Rose Hill Manor House.** 1838. ★ **[6b.] University Church**/officially **Our Lady, Mediatrix of All Graces,** 1845, William Rodrigue. Transept, chancel, crossing and lantern added, 1929. ★ **[6c.] St. John's Residence Hall,** 1845, William Rodrigue. ★ **[6d.] Thebaud Hall**/originally **Science Hall,** 1886, Eugene Kelly. **[6e.] Keating Hall,** 1936, Robert J. Reiley.

A Jesuit institution since 1846, the university began as St. John's College in 1841, founded by the **Right Reverend John Hughes** (later New York's first Catholic archbishop) and guided initially by its first president, **John McCloskey** (later America's first cardinal). Hughes commissioned his brother-in-law, **John Rodrigue,** to design a residence hall and church for the fledgling institution to accompany the already existing Rose Hill Manor House—for which this campus is named. Later Rodrigue associated with **James Renwick, Jr.,** in the design of the new St. Patrick's Cathedral [see M Manhattan/Fifth Avenue 5a.] which upon completion was dedicated by then-**Cardinal McCloskey.** (Detect a closeness here?)

Fordham derived its present name in 1905 from that of the old manor, later village, of Fordham—**not the other way around,** as some well-meaning community people will have you believe. The campus's physical presence, along heavily traveled East Fordham Road, is very strong. Mature trees, dense shrubs, green lawns, and a group of harmonious gray stone **Collegiate Gothic** buildings (built mostly from designs by architect Emile G. Perrot between 1911 and 1930) offer a distinguished contrast to the tacky commercial architecture of the Bronx's automobile row adjacent to the campus. The best of Fordham's buildings, save the early **Manor House,** a rough-stone, country-style **Greek Revival masterpiece,** is the last in the Collegiate Gothic style, Keating Hall. A picturesque work carefully sited, it is diminished in quality only by the steel transmitting antenna of the university FM station, WFUV.

Two literary tales relate to the campus. It is said that the 98-acre Fordham campus was the setting for James Fenimore Cooper's novel, *The Spy.* And it is also said that the bell in the University Church (appropriately dubbed "Old Edgar") was the inspiration for Poe's poem, *The Bells.* [He lived nearby—see W Bronx 43.].

[6e.] Keating Hall at Fordham University: most imposing building on campus

The Bronx's Little Italy: The fork in the street grid where Crescent Avenue diverges from East 187th Street (just a few blocks southeast of Fordham University) provides a space which, straight out of the Mediterranean tradition, has fostered a great marketplace for the cohesive Italian–American community of Belmont. Along East 187th Street, past Belmont Avenue and the area's religious and social rallying point, Our Lady of Mt. Carmel Roman Catholic Church, and into busy, colorful Arthur Avenue, you will find arranged a multitude of small retail shops which resemble those which were once the mainstay of New York's streets. Long may they prosper here! Freshly baked Italian breads, salami, and olive oil. *Latticini freschi,* fresh fish, and clams on the half shell from a common plate served on a wooden sidewalk stand (with unlimited lemons). Drop into the European-feeling New York City Retail Market, a Fiorello LaGuardia morality gesture of 1940 that removed Arthur Avenue's pushcast peddlers but, thankfully, not the street life. It's all worth an extra-special good weather visit . . . every day but Sunday, of course.

Dominick's Restaurant, 2335 Arthur Ave. bet. E. 186th St. and Crescent Ave. Telephone: 733-2807.

A restaurant without a menu. Small. Hearty. Delicious. Reasonably priced. Try it at lunchtime when the neighborhood regulars drop in.

White Castle (eatery), 552 E. Fordham Rd. SE cor. Lorillard Place.

This is not a recommendation for food (what can a 20¢ hamburger be made of?) nor for atmosphere—it's all rather utilitarian: stainless steel and aluminum, cramped, and dingy. Rather this purveying machine for fast food, open twenty-four hours a day, is a lesson in how unresponsive a 20th-century structure can be to basic human environmental requirements. Free parking.

The **twin parks** referred to in the urban renewal catch phrase are Bronx and Crotona which very roughly bracket, on the north and south, this geographic area of the Bronx. In 1966–1967, when renovation of existing housing stock was unfashionable and building economics had not made arson and abandonment the way of life in multistory communities such as this, a **scattered site, infill-housing** location study was financed by the **J. M. Kaplan Fund.** The results, translated into architecture by talented and mostly young architects, form more than twenty projects scattered along the east and west flanks of a mile-square area. They are a **model** of governmentally influenced **urban design** and **notable** low- and moderate-income **high-rise apartment architecture** as well. Sponsors included the N.Y.C. Educational Construction Fund (ECF), the N.Y.C. Housing Authority (NYCHA), and most significant and influential of all, the N.Y. State Urban Development Corporation (UDC). While Twin Parks projects were on their way up, however, much of the rest of Tremont and East Tremont went down.

[7a.] Keith Plaza (apartments)/P.S. 205A Bronx (grades 1–4), 2475 Southern Blvd. bet. E. Fordham Rd. and E. 187th St. W side. **[7b.] Kelly Towers North Apartments,** 2405 Southern Blvd. NW cor. E. 187th St. **[7c.] Kelly Towers South Apartments/P.S. 205B Bronx (early childhood center),** 2375 Southern Blvd. SW cor. E. 187th St. (Twin Parks projects.) 1975. Giovanni Pasanella.

Pasanella, the architect of these three apartment blocks, was the most prolific of those associated with the Twin Parks renewal effort [see C Bronx 12a, b, c, d, and 13a.]. Though the apartment plans used here are the most conventional of any of those projects, the resulting buildings, in subtle shades of tan, are among his most convincing when seen as elements in the cityscape. Keith Plaza, the graceful, 30-story tower at the north end of the trio, acts as a **pylon** to mark an **important gateway** into the community—it is located close to the point where busy East Fordham Road (U.S. 1) crosses Southern Boulevard. Unfortunately, the actual corner site could not be used; it had long been occupied by a unit of a nationwide **orange-roofed ice cream** and **fried clam chain,** a **somewhat older** local landmark.

[7a.] Keith Plaza apts./P.S. 205A Bx.   [8b.] Twin Parks apts./Crotona Ave.

[7d.] 2841 Crotona Avenue (former residence), NW cor. E. 189th St. ca. 1900.

Hidden behind Keith Plaza is this **old residence,** a stalwart stone symbol of wealth antedating Twin Parks and now partly concealed by a humdrum hamburger stand.

[8a.] 2311 Southern Boulevard, 760 East 183rd Street (apartments), SW cor. **[8b.] 2260 Crotona Avenue (apartments),** bet. E. 183rd and Grote Sts. E side. **[8c.] 725, 735 Garden Street (apartments)** bet. Prospect and Crotona Aves. N side. (Twin Parks projects.) Richard Meier & Assocs.

These three dark-red, oversized-brick-clad UDC-sponsored buildings are the **most successful** in all of Twin Parks in graciously recognizing the adjacent neighborhood without pandering to existing materials, building heights, or details. Through careful volumetric, spatial, and materials choices, the simple, stepped-brick masses **add to,** rather than fight with, **the neighborhood's fabric.** They also offer the extra plus of making the existing even more visible and, therefore, more interesting, as well. The design has so many **good things** about it that you tend to miss the out-of-place *Titanic* ship railings and the bland treatment of the ground plane. The chain link fencing added later under the buildings is, on the other hand, hard to miss . . . and regrettable.

[9a.] 2111 Southern Boulevard (apartments), NW cor. E. 180th St. **[9b.] 800, 820 East 180th Street (apartments),** SW cor. Southern Blvd. (Twin Parks projects.) 1973. James Stewart Polshek & Assocs.

Sponsored by UDC, these [and not Keith Plaza, see 7a.] were intended to be the urban design gateway to Twin Parks from the east. They fail to live up to the intention despite the brash two-dimensional black-on-tan striping of the brickwork on both the 31-story tower and its 9-story neighbor to the south. A satisfying note: the inclusion of retail stores at the base of both buildings **attracts street life** to "the project."

[9c.] Ella Rivers Memorial Swimming Pool and Bathhouse, N.Y.C. Parks and Recreation Department, E. 180th St. bet. Prospect and Mapes Ave. S side. (Twin Parks project.) 1971. Heery & Heery.

Theoretically, good-looking outdoor swimming pools are a political asset. In addition to providing **warm weather diversions,** they don't cost the city too much to operate since 9 out of every 12 months they lie dormant. Judging from the hostile graffiti on this one, some of the locals must have caught on to this callous game.

[10a.] 730 Oakland Place (apartments). [10b.] 750 East 179th Street (apartments). [10c.] 740 East 178th Street (apartments), all bet. Prospect and Clinton Aves. All S side. (Twin Parks projects.) 1974. Skidmore, Owings & Merrill.

Crisp, modular, precast concrete 16-story rectangular prisms with crisp, modular, precast concrete balconies. **Veddy, veddy spiffy**—but what have these to do with life in the Bronx, or anywhere for that matter? The buildings were precast in sections a few miles away and erected here as one of UDC's experimental HUD-aided Operation Breakthrough projects.

[11a.] Atkin, Bassolino & Gibson (architects' office building), 1989 Belmont Ave. bet. E. Tremont Ave. and E. 179th St. W side. 1964. Atkin Assocs.

A curious personal architectural statement in corbeled brick designed and used by an architectural firm which serves the greater local community.

[11b.] Former **Bronx Masonic Temple,** 1933 Washington Ave. bet. E. Tremont Ave. and E. 178th St. W side. 1905.

Having seen better days, this fraternal meeting place, through its overblown Classical details, adds one more unexpected visual event to an already surrealistic landscape of a community in decay. Note the lodge name and number woven into the tesseraed floor of the entrance.

[12a.] 1880 Valentine Avenue (apartments), bet. Webster Ave. and E. 178th St. E side. (Twin Parks project.) 1973. Giovanni Pasanella.

On an almost unbuildable narrow triangle commanding the undisciplined open space of a complicated street intersection and a **hilly green ether** that was once called Echo Park is this brilliant solution to a difficult problem. Stepping its way **hither and yon** and **up, up, up** is this dark-red, oversized-brick-clad UDC building for elderly tenants. It's perfect.

[12b.] 1985 Webster Avenue (apartments), bet. E. 178th and E. 180th Sts. W side. **[12c.] 2000 Valentine Avenue Apartments,** bet. E. 178th and E. 180th Sts. E side. **[12d.] 2100 Tiebout Avenue Apartments,** NE cor. E. 180th St. (Twin Parks project.) 1973. Giovanni Pasanella.

The most controversial buildings in Twin Parks: 1) Elevators stop every $2\frac{1}{2}$ floors, thus eliminating 60% of the normal corridors and creating very liveable apartments—but at the same time irritating the buildings' contractors who were out for profits, not challenges. 2) The buildings are powerful sculptural statements, vaguely reminiscent of Le Corbusier's **Unité d'Habitation** in Marseilles; their dark red brick walls add to their assertiveness. 3) A number of details were overlooked. The most glaring: a meaningful handling of the open space between the Webster and Valentine Avenue buildings.

[12.] Twin Parks apts./Valentine Ave.   **[13b.]** Giannone-Webster PAL Center

[14b.] Intermediate School 137 Bx.   **[14c.]** Twin Parks apts./E. 184 St.

[13a.] Twin Parks West Sites 1 & 2 Apartments, N.Y.C. Housing Authority, 353, 355, 360, 365 Ford St., 355, 365 E. 183rd St. W of Webster Ave. 1974. Giovanni Pasanella.

Though these low-income projects utilize the same skip-stop elevator concept as the Pasanella-designed UDC apartment buildings a few blocks to the south [12b., 12c., 12d.], they are less self-assertive. Differing-height wings (rather than a bold rectangular ground plan), the elimination of cantilevered projections at the elevator-served floors, and the introduction of small fire exit projections which add punctuation to the facades make this housing a bit more conventional in appearance.

[13b.] Patrolman Andrew F. Giannone-Webster Community Center, Police Athletic League, 2255 Webster Ave. NW cor. Ford St. (Twin Parks project.) 1974. Smotrich & Platt.

With a name that is almost longer than the building, this is a refreshingly disarming small-scale community amenity built by UDC.

[14a.] 333 East 181st Street (apartments), at Crane Sq., Tiebout Ave., and Folin St. E side. (Twin Parks project.) 1973. Prentice & Chan, Ohlhausen, architects. R.T. Schnadelbach, landscape architect.

Given a complex program of zero- to 5-bedroom apartments by their client, UDC, and a cliffside site that had always served as a **natural line of demarcation** between two neighborhoods, these architects tackled both problems head on. Elimination of an elevator corridor on every third floor and the use of duplex apartments (resulting in **lyrical window patterns** on the two main facades) were the responses to the problems posed by the program. Construction of a **long ramped stairway** along the face of the cliff resolved the problem of access. An exceptionally satisfying statement—as though this building was always meant to occupy this site.

[14b.] Intermediate School 137 Bronx, The Angelo Patri School, 2225 Webster Ave. bet. Folin St. and E. 181st St. W side. (Twin Parks project.) 1975. The Architects Collaborative.

Named for educational philosopher Angelo Patri, a hero in the nearby Italian-American community (he was principal of P. S. 45 Bronx), this **exuberant colorful design** makes one wonder what was ever wrong with public school. If the education that goes on within matches the **verve** and **imagination** of the architecture a victory will have been achieved. Another UDC project.

[14c.] 355, 365 East 184th Street (apartments), bet. Marion and Webster Aves. N side. 1973. Prentice & Chan, Ohlhausen, architects. R.T. Schnadelbach, landscape architect.

Tackling another rough site [see 14a.] this architect/landscape architect team began at the beginning, with a strong site plan. The result is a **sunken courtyard** embraced on $3\frac{1}{2}$ sides by a set of continuous brick-walled apartment blocks, this time with a smooth, serene window pattern. Note the neat **diagonal recesses** at the block's **reentrant corners:** they solve an old bugaboo—how to light a room in such a location without having windows wind up at one end or the other. Here those spaces are living rooms and the windows are in the very center but on the bias. **Consummate artistry** is evident here. Unfortunately the power of water to erode is all too evident from the scars in the courtyard's landscaping.

W

WESTERN BRONX

THE WEST BRONX

The West Bronx is known as a place of wholesome blandness. The pairs of diminutive cast-stone lions that guard the entrances to so many of the area's apartment houses are an attempt at **elegance** but result in a **dreary sameness.** But a closer look at this area will yield some surprises. It is the spot in America, second to none, to see the largest single array of Art Deco-inspired ornament—on apartments built between 1927 and 1942. An array of housing, schools, parks, hospitals, industries, and public works of social and architectural interest are all located here. This, too, though you may not believe it at first, is a place of urban diversity.

[15.] Former **Cashman Laundry,** Gerard Ave. NE cor. E. 140th St. 1932. R.G. and W.M. Cory.

A stylistic little brother to the same architects'/engineers' Starett-Lehigh Building. [See M Manhattan/Chelsea 22.]

[16.] Bronx Terminal Market, City of New York, Exterior St., Cromwell Ave., and E. 151st St. (entrance at W. 149th St.). North buildings, 1925. South buildings, 1935.

Originally, these 37 acres of land, the multistory yellow brick fortress/refrigerated warehouse, and the four-towered "castle" west of the Deegan Expressway were developed by Mayor John Hylan (1918–1925) to remove the city's fruit and vegetable markets from **downtown congestion.** His seventeen-million-dollar effort failed. Wishing, a decade later, to transform **"Hylan's Folly"** into **a LaGuardia success,** that reform mayor invested another $1.7 million to build the ten low, white brick buildings over the remainder of the site plus a curvilinear-steel-arcaded "farmers' square." Though successful, it failed also to unseat Manhattan's centrally located, if inefficient, wholesale markets.

In the sixties and seventies, **Hunts Point** became the city's policy commitment for food wholesaling [see S Bronx 26., 27.] and the future of the old Bronx Terminal Market became clouded. As one wag said at the time, "If you ever defrost it, the whole thing would collapse!" It still stands.

The Grand Concourse: The Grand Concourse, one of the grand boulevards of New York, was designed in 1892 by Louis Risse as the **"Speedway Concourse"** to provide access from Manhattan to the large parks of the Bronx. The original design provided **separate paths** for horse-drawn vehicles, cyclists, and pedestrians, and for grade separation through bridges at all major intersections.

[17a.] Security Mutual Insurance Company, 500 Grand Concourse, SE cor. E. 149th St. 1965. Horace Ginsbern & Assocs.

The first office building in the Bronx in 25 years. Precast concrete panels give a sculptured texture to this handsome structure.

[17b.] IRT Subway Junction, beneath E. 149th St. and Grand Concourse. Lower level, 1904. Upper level, 1917.

Here two subway stations have been built one above the other, separated by a mezzanine. (The trains on the upper level are marked "Woodlawn Road," a **nonexistent destination.**) The lower station, in the Parisian manner, is one large **barrel vault.** Despite uninspired decoration, poor lighting, and minimal maintenance, this station is one of the **exciting** spaces of the subway system. On the southwest corner of the intersection above is a former entrance to the station which bears the name **Mott Avenue,** the thoroughfare which preceded Grand Concourse in these parts.

[17c.] General Post Office, The Bronx/originally **Bronx Central Annex, U.S. Post Office Department,** 558 Grand Concourse, NE cor. E. 149th St. 1935. Thomas Harlan Ellett, architect; Louis A. Simon, supervising architect.

The chaste gray brick walls and windows set in tall arches fail to achieve the dignity they seek. The best to be said for the building is that it has WPA murals by **Ben Shahn** in the public lobby.

[18a.] Cardinal Hayes High School (Roman Catholic), 650 Grand Concourse, SE cor. E. 153rd St. 1941. Eggers & Higgins.

Made reticent by its uninspired buff brick, the school's plan in the form of a quarter circle effectively creates an inviting green forecourt. Building embellishments are also reticent but in the Art Deco mode.

[18b.] Former **Morgan Steam Laundry Company,** 700 Grand Concourse, bet E. 153rd and E. 156th Sts. E side. ca. 1920.

An intriguing octagonal smokestack together with flatroofed, precociously modern boxy forms distinguish this maroon brick industrial structure. It serves other purposes today: Bed City, a furniture emporium.

Franz Sigel Park: Named for a Civil War general, this craggy park, on the west side of Grand Concourse north of East 153rd Street, is now the repository of graffitied concrete "park furniture" installed by overzealous governmental bureaucrats in the early seventies in the mistaken belief that physical amenities, any amenities, will cure acute social and economic ills.

[19a.] Thomas Garden Apartments, 840 Grand Concourse, bet. E. 158th and E. 159th Sts. 1928. Andrew J. Thomas.

A block-square development of five-story walk-up buildings grouped about a westernized **Japanese garden** in a sunken central court. All of the units are reached through the court by walking past concrete lanterns, a water course (now dry), and charming bridges. The short flights of steps leading down into the court effectively **separate the building** entrances from the busy Concourse traffic outside. This project, **named for its architect,** is one of two [see H Manhattan/Harlem 70.] designed by him for John D. Rockefeller, Jr., who hoped to solve the problems of the slums by investing in middle-income housing.

[19b.] The Bronx County Building, 851 Grand Concourse, SW cor. E. 161st St. 1934. Joseph H. Freedlander and Max Hausle, architects. Sculpture at four entrances: Adolph A. Weinman, sculptor; Edward F. Sanford, George Snowden, Joseph Kisselewski, associates. Frieze, Charles Keck.

An enormous, 10-story-high mostly limestone pile whose ponderous form is, luckily, relieved by sleek modern sculpture, both in the round and on friezes which beribbon its walls. In addition to courts and borough offices, it houses the **Bronx Museum of the Arts** within its main floor elevator lobby. The museum is a modest community museum with frequently changing travelling exhibits and examples of the work of local artists and craftspeople. Hours and program information: 681-6000.

[19c.] 888 Grand Concourse (apartment house), SE cor. E. 161st St. 1927. Emery Roth.

An Art Deco apartment building occupying what was once a chic Bronx location. Note the carved out cylindrical entrance space polychromed in terrazzo, tesseraed walls, and mirrored ceiling. Proceed through the revolving door for a glimpse of the moderne lobby.

[20.] New Family and Criminal Courts Building, City of New York, E. 161st St. bet. Sheridan and Sherman Aves. N side. 1977. Harrison & Abramovitz.

If architecture is expressive of the social order, then this bulky structure tells us that justice must be ponderous, rigid, and self-righteous.

[21.] Yankee Stadium, E. 161st St., SW cor. River Ave. Osborn Engineering Co. 1923. Rebuilt, 1976. Praeger-Kavanagh-Waterbury.

Built by brewery magnate Colonel Jacob Ruppert for the team he owned and for its most valuable player, Babe Ruth (the short right field helped him to set his home run record). In the early 1970s someone got the idea that the New York Yankees were the key to the neighborhood's, the Bronx's, and New York City's economic salvation and so the whole stadium—as well as acres of adjacent fallow land—were rebuilt at a cost of some $100 million, a sum the city will probably never stop paying interest upon. There are fewer columns to obstruct vision and many, many more parking spaces but the adjacent community seems, if anything, to have increased its rate of decay.

Alex and Henry's Restaurant, 862 Courtlandt Ave. near E. 161st St. Telephone: 585-3290.

Serving American and Italian food, this is where the local politicians eat. It's four blocks from the Bronx County Building.

GRAND CONCOURSE AND EAST

[22.] The Lorelei Fountain, Joyce Kilmer Park, Grand Concourse, SW cor. E. 164th St. 1899. Ernst Herter, sculptor.

The fountain honors the author of *Die Lorelei,* Heinrich Heine, whose bas-relief portrait is on the south side of the base. The statue was presented to the city by a group of New Yorkers of German ancestry in 1893 after the sculptor's gift had been rejected by Düsseldorf, Heine's birthplace. The donors wanted it placed at Manhattan's Grand Army Plaza, where the Sherman statue now stands. But Heine's ethnic background—he was both a German and a Jew—together with the statue's questionable artistic merits, made that site unavailable. After six years of debate the statue was placed in its present location. But even here its troubles continued. After its unveiling the fountain was vandalized, restored, and then for a time put under constant police protection. Judging from the graffiti which covers it again today, protection is once again required.

[23.] Andrew Freedman Home, 1025 Grand Concourse, SW cor. McClellan St. 1924. Wings, 1928. Joseph H. Freedlander and Harry Allan Jacobs.

This subdued gray-and-yellow limestone palace is French-inspired, but its setting in a garden gives it the air of a large English country house. It is a home for the aged endowed by Freedman, a leading **subway contractor** and owner of the baseball team which became the **N.Y. Giants.** The panic of 1907 made him fearful of losing the comforts to which he had become accustomed, and he established this home for **aged indigents** who could show that they had once enjoyed affluence. (A retired **czarist general** was a guest here for a time.)

[24.] Daughters of Jacob Geriatric Center: Main Building/formerly **Home and Hospital of the Daughters of Jacob,** 321 E. 167th St. bet. Findlay and Teller Aves. N side. 1920. Louis Allen Abramson. **[24a.] Findlay House/Weinstein-Ratner Pavilion,** 1175 Findlay Ave. W side. 1971. Louis Allen Abramson. **[24b.] Geriatric Center,** 1160 Teller Ave. E side. 1973. Blumenkranz & Bernhard.

Another, this time less fashionable-looking, home for the aged: the ungainly, **tall Roman colonnade** and pediment which leans against the entrance to the original building was supposed to give it a dignified appearance. It is that building, built as eight **radiating spoked wings** set at the end of a generous **Italian garden,** that is of interest. The radiating plan was a common one for hospitals (and penitentiaries) always seeking more efficient centralized control.

[25.] Originally **Elizabeth M. Shuttleworth Residence,** 1857 Anthony Ave. SW cor. Mt. Hope Pl. 1896. Neville & Bagge.

A private residence in the form of a miniature chateau of rock-faced gray stone with finely carved limestone trim. Note particularly the modelling of the faces within the **circular medallions** near the roof. A mimosa tree and other verdant vegetation almost conceal this welcome relic of the past in an otherwise drab area.

Self Expression: The urge to create is not limited to credentialed professionals. Harold Swain, an attorney by trade, had such a desire to build. And build he did, between 1908 and 1955, on the north side of East 172nd Street just west of the Concourse. Parked cars and weeds conceal what remains today of his little house, garage, indoor swimming pool, and the other structures, but it's still possible to spy them, built of crazily patterned bricks, stones, tiles, and discarded bottles and scraps of glass.

HIGHBRIDGE/MORRIS HEIGHTS/UNIVERSITY HEIGHTS

These neighborhoods lie west of Grand Concourse and follow the University Avenue ridge and the Harlem River from Macombs Dam Park below West 161st Street northward to the vicinity of Kingsbridge Road. They contain hundreds of the **familiar** Bronx apartment houses, older one-family wooden homes, and a **variety** of institutions, public works, and landmarks, many of **national fame** and importance. Highbridge, the area south of the Cross-Bronx Expressway, was settled in the 1830s by Irish workers who built the Old Croton Aqueduct and High Bridge as well as the railroad which soon appeared on the banks of the Harlem River.

[26.] Unused IRT Subway Tunnel, bet. Jerome Ave. at Anderson Ave. W side, to Major Deegan Expwy. below W. 161st St. E side. 1918.

The **steep ridge** which forms this part of the West Bronx has barely begun before it is penetrated by this now-abandoned subway tunnel. Barely three blocks long, it was built to connect the Ninth Avenue "el" at the old site of the Polo Grounds baseball stadium in Manhattan with the IRT Jerome Avenue elevated line—some of the structural steel for the connecting shuttle can still be seen nearby at River Avenue and East 162nd Street. Neither tunnel portal is particularly visible; the west one can be glimpsed fleetingly from the Major Deegan Expressway. Once there were plans to use the tunnel, following its closing in 1955, for a trolley museum.

[27.] American Female Guardian Soc.   [28.] Park Plaza Apartments (detail)

[27.] Muhammad's Mosque of Islam/originally **American Female Guardian Society and Home for the Friendless,** 936 Woodycrest Ave. NE cor. Jerome Ave. ca. 1901. William B. Tuthill.

This institution was built as an eclectically styled mansion and sits on a commanding precipice overlooking the valley of Macombs Dam Park and Yankee Stadium. Never as elegant as its Park Avenue (Manhattan) counterparts, it nevertheless adds a needed note of grandeur to this community.

Macombs Dam Park: This park, at Jerome Avenue and West 161st Street, together with the Macombs Dam Bridge into Manhattan, recalls the nearby site of Robert Macomb's 1813 dam across the Harlem River which used the waterway's tidal flow to operate a mill until his neighbors demolished it, in 1838, in order to open the river to shipping. Considering the *river's* later success as a vital ship canal, the park and bridge should perhaps have been renamed for Macomb's prophetic neighbors.

[28.] Park Plaza Apartments, 1005 Jerome Ave. bet. Anderson Ave. and E. 165th St. 1928. Horace Ginsbern.

One of the earliest (and one of the best) Art Deco-inspired apartment buildings in the Bronx. Influenced both by the 1925 *Exposition Internationale des Arts Décoratifs et Industriels Modernes* in Paris, and motifs from **Mayan architecture** then fashionable. Note the elaborate polychromed terra-cotta ornament.

[29a.] Noonan Plaza (apartments), 105–145 W. 168th St. NW cor. Nelson Ave. 1931. Horace Ginsbern.

These seven-story apartments are arranged to form a quadrangle and are entered diagonally through a highly decorative masonry arcade which leads to a central court, the original splendors of which can only be guessed at today. Art Deco–cum–Mayan is the idiosyncratic style of the Ginsbern firm at the time. One of the West Bronx's key Depression monuments.

[29b.] Union Reformed Church of Highbridge, 1272 Ogden Ave. bet. W. 168th and W. 169th Sts. E side. 1889.

A quaint stone church which contrasts beautifully with the moderne decor of Noonan Plaza immediately adjacent.

[29c.] Public School 11 Bronx/formerly **Grammar School No. 91,** 1257 Ogden Ave. bet. W. 168th and W. 169th Sts. W side. 1889.

A picturesque gem of an old multistory school building. Note the carving of its original designation right into the stonework. A lot was lost architecturally when the late Victorian love of decoration disappeared—fortunately remnants such as this remain.

[29c.] Orig. Grammar School No. 91   [31b.] River Park Towers apartments

[30.] Carmelite Monastery, 1381 University Ave. opp. W. 170th St. W side. Maginnis & Walsh. 1940.

When the walkway of adjacent High Bridge was open to pedestrians the house of this **cloistered community** was best seen from there, from the riverside. Hugging the steep slope of the hill which tumbles down to the Harlem River valley, the elements of this latter-day, **medieval-style** building—its tower, cells, chapel, cloister, and gardens—all became visible without revealing the life of contemplation within its walls. Today only its carefully crafted University Avenue facade is readily available to visitors.

[31.] Former **Harlem River State Park and Harlem River Housing,** W of Major Deegan Expwy. at W. Tremont Ave.

Once this was decaying riverside frontage. It had been the site of miscellaneous coal docks and the Consolidated Ship Building Corporation and was **cut off** from the adjacent residential community by the tracks of the Penn Central Railroad and the Deegan Expressway. Beginning in the late 1960s these valuable land resources were **returned to public use** by the combined efforts of the City of New York, the New York State Park Commission for New York City, and the New York State Urban Development Corporation. As the projects were completed, the state park was renamed for Roberto Clemente, a local **baseball hero** killed in a plane crash, and the housing was renamed, naturally, River Park Towers, to reflect their setting.

[31a.] Roberto Clemente State Park/originally **Harlem River Bronx State Park,** Matthewson Rd. off W. Tremont Ave. Bridge along Harlem River. 1973. M. Paul Friedberg & Assocs., landscape architects; Dean McClure, architect for recreation building.

The first of what is planned to be a series of state parks in the city, this intricately designed **recreation playland** offers swimming, diving, gymnasium events, and a **wonderful stroll** along the seawall of the adjacent Harlem River. It may not have the verdancy of an upstate park but its **lively forms** animate an otherwise isolated urban setting.

[31b.] River Park Towers (apartments), 10, 20, 30, 40 Richman Plaza off Cedar Ave. Bridge along Harlem River. 1975. Davis, Brody & Assocs., architects; M. Paul Friedberg & Assocs., landscape architects.

A variation of the earlier Waterside project [see M Manhattan/Four Squares 73.], these two intricate and tall brick apartment towers (actually two pairs of buildings joined) form a **dramatic landmark** from both sides of the river and to the millions of motorists who pass by them every year at highway speed. To those who live in the towers (and those who visit) they are **equally satisfying** up close—particularly the combination **pedestrian and vehicular plaza** on which the apartment towers, parking garage, and retail stores front and from whose edges the tall shafts rise seemingly **to infinity.**

[31c.] Public School/Intermediate School 229 Bronx, Cedar Ave. Bridge, NE cor. Richman Plaza. 1977. Caudill Rowlett Scott.

Utilizing the air rights over the railroad tracks, this is a most unorthodox school in appearance, having only the bare minimum of windows but a very dramatic exterior appearance.

Old Croton Aqueduct: Completed in 1842, the old Croton Aqueduct was the first dependable source of drinking water for the growing city. It runs a 32-mile downhill course from Croton Reservoir in Westchester County to High Bridge. In this area of the West Bronx it is particularly apparent since much of its course is topped by a green walkway and sitting areas. Its most visible part is its southern edge along University Avenue just above West Tremont Avenue, but the green ribbon is available for public use for some fifteen blocks along a route which parallels University Avenue some 30 yards to the east. Take a stroll.

[32.] Calvary Methodist Church, 1885 University Ave. bet. W. Tremont and W. Burnside Aves. W side. 1924.

This church's rough stone walls contrast with its refined stained glass windows. The small but strongly composed building appears as a bastion against the changes which are sweeping the area. Built and physically endowed by a moneyed community in the 1920s it now serves a congregation which must struggle to maintain the fine qualities of the edifice.

[33.] Gatehouse, New Croton Aqueduct, W. Burnside Ave. SW cor. Phelan Place. ca. 1890. Benjamin S. Church, engineer.

One of a **series** of stone buildings to be found in the Bronx and Manhattan built to service the city's second water supply system, the New Croton Aqueduct (1885–1893). The gray stone structure is detailed to **reflect pride** not only in the **reliability** and **pureness** of the drinking water but the **skills** of the stonecutters who crafted it.

The Old N.Y.U. Uptown Campus

[34.] Bronx Community College, C.U.N.Y./formerly **New York University, University Heights Campus,** University Ave. bet. W. 180th St. and Hall of Fame Terrace, W side, to Sedgwick Ave. and vicinity. Original grounds and Ohio Field, 1894. Vaux & Co., landscape architects.

Begun in the 1890s, this 50-plus-acre campus was until 1973 the uptown campus of New York University. In that year the **properties were sold** to the city of New York for use as a campus for Bronx Community College, and the N.Y.U. College of Engineering was absorbed into a newly renamed Polytechnic Institute of New York, in downtown Brooklyn.

Today's campus seems overpopulated by buildings placed in a disturbingly **helter-skelter**—as opposed to charmingly picturesque or Classically formal—fashion. Its planning has been criticized almost from the beginning for not taking advantage of the views down into the **still-beautiful gorge** of the Harlem River. (To make the best of a campus tour, obtain a small map in Philosophy Hall near the entrance to the Hall of Fame.)

[34a.] The Hall of Fame for Great Americans, entrance on Hall of Fame Terrace. 1901, 1914. McKim, Mead & White. ★ Telephone: 220-1330 or 553-4450.

Not a hall at all but a roughly semicircular **Classical arcade** between whose columns are arrayed bronze busts of great Americans. They are picked by a college of more than **100 electors** chosen from the fields of higher education, science, jurisprudence, and business, and from among others in public life. The colonnade was conceived of by N.Y.U. **Chancellor MacCracken** to camouflage, from Sedgwick Avenue below, the unsightly high foundation walls underpinning **Stanford White's** Library, Philosophy Hall, and Language Hall.

[34b.] Gould Memorial Library ★, Cornelius Baker Hall of Philosophy ★, Hall of Languages ★, 1900. All by McKim, Mead & White.

These three buildings—Gould is the domed one in the center—together with the Hall of Fame Arcade are the *pièce de résistance* of this campus and their design is attributed to architect Stanford White himself. Looked at in terms of their **exquisitely detailed** stone exteriors they achieve a grand Classical Revival composition. Unfortunately, the spaces within the halls lack that grandeur.

[34c.] Gould Hall of Technology/Begrisch Lecture Hall. 1964. Marcel Breuer & Assocs. **[34d.] Julius Silver Residence Center and Cafeteria.** 1964. Marcel Breuer & Assocs. **[34e.] Technology Two.** 1972. Marcel Breuer and Hamilton Smith.

Three additions to the campus before the N.Y.U. administration got its signals straight about the future. Both technology halls suffer from a concrete pomposity.

[34f.] South Hall/formerly **Justus H. Schwab Residence.** 1857. **[34g.] Butler Hall**/formerly **William Henry W. T. Mali Residence.** ca. 1859. **[34h.] MacCracken Hall**/formerly **Henry Mitchell MacCracken Residence**/originally **Loring Andrews Residence.** ca. 1880. Hall of Fame Terrace bet. Loring Place and Sedgwick Ave. N side.

Three mansions that predate the campus. Schwab was New York representative for the North German Lloyd Steamship Company. Mali was the Belgian Consul General in New York. MacCracken was chancellor of N.Y.U. and founder of the Heights campus. Loring Andrews was owner of much of the land that formed the campus.

[34i.]. Sedgwick Residence Hall, W. 183rd St. bet. Loring Place and Sedgwick Ave. N side. 1969. La Pierre, Litchfield & Partners.

Before leaving its uptown campus, N.Y.U. succeeded in integrating this large new building in a community of small old ones. No longer in use since Bronx Community College doesn't need dorms.

Beyond the old N.Y.U. Campus:

[35.] St. Nicholas of Tolentine Church (Roman Catholic), University Ave. SW cor. Fordham Rd. 1928. O'Connor & Delaney.

Using a design vocabulary derived from Gothic antecedents, this gray stone church heralds the important event of the intersection of two broad thoroughfares.

KINGSBRIDGE HEIGHTS

[36.] U.S. Veterans' Hospital, 130 W. Kingsbridge Rd. bet. Webb and Sedgwick Aves. S side. 1922. Replacement hospital, 1979, Max O. Urbahn Assocs., Inc.

This commanding green hillside site with spectacular views, across the Harlem Valley, of upper Manhattan has provided for the needs of a number of diverse occupants over the years. During the British occupation of New York it was a site for one of their forts. Later it was a private estate and served as the Catholic Orphan Asylum before becoming a veterans' hospital in the twenties. The 1979 all aluminum-clad replacement will call even more attention to itself than its immense neo-Georgian predecessor.

[37.] 2744 Kingsbridge Terrace (residence), N of W. Kingsbridge Rd. E side.

Close by the vast veterans' hospital is this tiny monument, a stucco castle with numerous gables, balconies, crenelated turrets, a weather vane, a TV antenna, and a tunnel leading from "the dungeon" to the street.

[38.] The Jewish Home and Hospital for the Aged. [38a.] Salzman Pavilion, 100 W. Kingsbridge Rd. bet. Webb and University Aves. S side. 1975. **[38b.] Greenwall Pavilion,** 2545 University Ave. at W. 192nd St. W side. 1972. Both buildings by Weiss Whelan Edelbaum Webster.

On what was once the site of the Hebrew Infant Asylum are two imposing additions to an institution for the elderly.

[39.] Kingsbridge Armory, 29 W. Kingsbridge Rd. bet. Jerome and Reservoir Aves. 1912. Pilcher & Tachau. ★

Called the largest armory in the world, this picturesque 20th-century fortress, the **Carcassonne of the Bronx,** is probably better-known for peacetime activities such as indoor bicycle races than for the putting down of civil insurrection.

[34a. & b.] Hall of Fame/Gould Lib.   **[39.]** Kingsbridge Armory, N.Y.N.G.

[40.] Herbert H. Lehman College, C.U.N.Y./originally **Hunter College Uptown,** Goulden Ave. SE cor. Bedford Park Blvd. Original buildings, 1932 Thompson, Holmes, & Converse. **[40a.] Library and Shuster Hall,** 1960, Marcel Breuer; Robert F. Gatje, associate. **[40b.] Carman Hall (classrooms and cafeteria),** 1970, DeYoung & Moskowitz. **[40c.] New Library, Speech and Theater, and Auditorium Buildings,** along Paul Ave. 1978? David Todd & Assocs. and Jan Pokorny.

The older buildings never had the architectural glue to pull them together as a composition; the newer ones are more eye-catching but are more prima donnas than anything else. The city's 1975 budget crisis interrupted the construction visible along Paul Avenue.

Jerome Park Reservoir: First filled in 1905, this concrete-lined water storage facility holds 773,000,000 gallons. Goulden Avenue, its eastern boundary, sits atop a combination of the Old Croton Aqueduct and a masonry dividing wall which was to separate it from another part of the reservoir planned as a second stage. The second basin, with a capacity almost twice that of the first, was excavated to the east of the present reservoir extending to Jerome Avenue between West Kingsbridge Road north to Mosholu Parkway. Abandoned in 1912 the pit was filled in and now serves as the site for the Kingsbridge Armory, Lehman College, two subway yards, three high schools, a park, and a couple of publicly aided housing developments!

The reservoir and nearby Jerome Avenue take their name from the Jerome Park Race Track that occupied this site from 1876 until 1890. Leonard W. Jerome, Winston Churchill's grandfather, was a prime mover in the sponsoring American Jockey Club which strived (with success) in elevating horse racing in this country to the status of an aristocratic sport.

[41.] **Tracey Towers,** 20 and 40 W. Mosholu Pkwy. South, SW cor. Jerome Ave. 1974. Paul Rudolph.

The tallest structures in the Bronx, these two apartment buildings (one 41 stories, the other 38) offer their residents phenomenal views in all directions. Similarly, the gray, ribbed-block towers are themselves visible over long distances from which they resemble sand castles with overactive thyroids.

FORDHAM HEIGHTS/BEDFORD PARK/NORWOOD

[42a.] Alexander's (department store)/originally **Wertheimer's,** Fordham Rd. NW cor. Grand Concourse. 1933. Altered into Alexander's, 1938, Starrett & Van Vleck. Additions, 1953–1960, Ketchum, Giná & Sharp, Morris Ketchum, Jr. & Assocs.

Less important for its design, horizontal bands of glass block across its curved but otherwise unadorned facade, Alexander's is a shopping magnet and local landmark of the Fordham Road shopping district. It occupies a dramatic site at the crest of the hill toward which Fordham Road ascends.

[42b.] Creston Avenue Baptist Church, 114 E. 188th St. bet. Creston and Morris Aves. S side. 1905.

Crushed on both sides by retail shops reaching out for customers in this competitive shopping strip, this playful, castlelike church hangs on.

[42c.] Loew's Paradise Theater/now divided into **Paradise Twins 1 and 2,** 2417 Grand Concourse bet. E. 184th and E. 188th Sts. W side. 1929. John Eberson.

Stars and clouds were what made the Paradise special, surely not its reserved terra-cotta facade on the Concourse, a facade minus any projecting marquee (because of the Concourse's special zoning limitations). Inside, this theater was an extravaganza of **ornament, ornament, ornament,** surmounted by a deep blue ceiling over the auditorium, **twinkling stars,** and projected **moving clouds.** Considered by one gourmet of such things the "most beautiful and elaborate" of Eberson's designs.

[43.] Poe Cottage, Poe Park, Grand Concourse, SE cor. E. Kingsbridge Rd. 1816. ★

The cottage was moved into the park from its original site across Kingsbridge Road in 1913. Edgar Allan Poe (1809–1849) lived here from 1846 until a few months before his death. He came here in the hope that the clear country air would aid his ailing young wife. (She died during their first winter in the small house.) Open to the public. For hours and information: 881-8900.

Bedford Park Area:

[44.] St. James Church (Protestant Episcopal), 2500 Jerome Ave. NE cor. E. 190th St. 1865.

A stone Gothic Revival church in the shadow of the Jerome Avenue elevated. The greenery of the churchyard and adjacent St. James Park (1901) seem to block out some of the clatter.

[45.] Bedford Park Presbyterian Church, 2933 Bainbridge Ave. NW cor. Bedford Park Blvd. 1900. R. H. Robertson.

Another stone church which bestows a distinguished tone upon a heavily trafficked street.

[46.] Former **Bedford Park Casino,** 390 Bedford Park Blvd. bet. Decatur and Webster Aves. S side. ca. 1880.

Once a center for neighborhood recreation; today the home of a violin bow manufacturer. Though the ground floor wears a 20th-century look, the upper parts of the wood facade show their 19th-century origins.

[47.] 52nd Precinct Station House/originally **41st Precinct, N.Y.C. Police Department,** 3016 Webster Ave. NE cor. Mosholu Pkwy. 1906. Stoughton & Stoughton. ★

Responding to ambience of a quasi-rural setting at the turn of the century, the architects of Manhattan's Soldiers' and Sailors' Monument [see UWS Manhattan/Riverside Drive 13b.] created a romantic **Tuscan villa-inspired** solution to this precinct house commission. The clock tower bearing polychromed terra-cotta clock faces and deeply projecting eaves is a high point in such romantic design in the city.

Norwood Area:

[48.] Mosholu Parkway, connecting Bronx and Van Cortlandt Parks.

One of the few completed links in the **network of parkways** that was proposed to connect the major parks of the Bronx. At the eastern entrance to the parkway the **Victory Monument** serves to divide traffic.

[49.] St. Brendan's Church (Roman Catholic), Perry Ave. bet. E. 206th and E. 207th Sts. W side. 1966. Belfatto & Pavarini.

St. Brendan is the patron saint of navigators, so it should come as no surprise that this church was built to resemble the **prow of a ship.** There are two churches in this building, and the slope of the site permits us to enter both at ground level. The flat-ceilinged lower church is entered from West 206th Street. The upper church, entered from East 207th Street, is under the **steeply sloped roof.** Near the entrance the ceiling is **low,** and the church **dark,** but as we move toward the altar the **space and light** around us grow. The steeple, part of the upswept roof, forms the prow. The stained glass, **boldly colored,** is particularly beautiful. It is best to visit when the church is in use.

[47.] 52nd Precinct Police Station

[49.] St. Brendan's Catholic Church

[50.] Valentine-Varian House/Museum of Bronx History, 3266 Bainbridge Ave. bet. Van Cortlandt Ave. E. and E. 208th St. E side. 1775. ★

A well-proportioned fieldstone farmhouse moved in the 1960s from its original location across the street on Van Cortlandt Avenue East. Today it is also the home of the **Bronx County Historical Society** and the site of a museum of local history: photos, postcards, old beer bottles, arrowheads and cartridges . . . and topical exhibits. Open to the public. Information, hours, admission charges: 881-8900.

Williamsbridge Oval: The embankment behind the Valentine-Varian House continues to curve around to form an oval which today encloses an elaborate city playground. Between 1888 and 1923 the embankment formed a dam to contain the waters of the Williamsbridge Reservoir, part of the city's water supply system. After its abandonment, tunnels were cut through and play equipment and benches were introduced. Appropriately named, the surrounding streets are called Reservoir Oval East and West.

[51.] Former **Keeper's House, Williamsbridge Reservoir,** Reservoir Oval
E. NE cor. Putnam Pl. ca. 1890. Benjamin S. Church, engineer.

One of the many rock-faced stone buildings built for the city's water
supply system. This one, however, was meant as a residence and office
rather than as a gatehouse or service facility. It has outlived the effective
life of the abandoned reservoir across the street.

[52.] Montefiore Hospital and Medical Center, E. Gun Hill Rd. bet.
Kossuth and Tryon Aves. S side. Original buildings, 1913. Arnold W.
Brunner. **[52a.] Henry L. Moses Research Institute,** E. Gun Hill Rd. SE
cor. Bainbridge Ave. 1966. Philip Johnson & Assocs. **[52b.] Annie
Lichtenhein Pavilion,** Kossuth Ave. bet. E. Gun Hill Rd. and E. 210th St.
E side. 1970. Gruzen & Partners and Westermann/Miller Assocs.
[52c.] Loeb Pavilion, E of Lichtenhein Pavilion. 1966. Kelly & Gruzen
and Helge Westermann. **[52d.] Montefiore Apartments II,** 3450 Wayne
Ave. bet. E. Gun Hill Rd. and E. 210th St. E side. 1972. Schuman,
Lichtenstein & Claman.

Like most hospital campuses nurtured over decades and responding
to growth in population and changes in treatment techniques, this one is
chaotic in appearance. It speaks well for administration and donors that
the newer additions are exemplary in their architecture, beginning with
Philip Johnson's 1966 work. The Montefiore II Apartments is one of the
tallest in the borough; its dark red-brown brick volume is impressive from
both near and far.

[52d.] The Montefiore II Apartments   **[53.]** North Central Bronx Hospital

**[53.] North Central Bronx Hospital, N.Y.C. Health and Hospitals Corpo-
ration,** Kossuth Ave. NE cor. E. 210th St. 1976. Westermann/Miller
Assocs.; Carl Pancaldo; Schuman, Lichtenstein & Claman.

Considering the limitations of the site (space made available from the
existing Montefiore complex), this is a **spectacularly successful** hospital
design when viewed as public architecture. Crisp, neat, bold forms of
brick and precast concrete articulate the street facades and present a
confident and **inviting** appearance.

[54.] Woodlawn Cemetery, entrances at Jerome Ave. N of Bainbridge
Ave. E side and at E. 233rd St. SW cor. Webster Ave.

A lavish array of tombstones, mausoleums, and memorials in a richly
planted setting. Many **wealthy** and **distinguished** people are buried here.
Tombs and mausoleums are replicas and small-size reproductions of
several famous European chapels and monuments. Jay Gould, the
Woolworths, and Mayors John Purroy Mitchel and Fiorello LaGuardia
are among the many famous people interred at Woodlawn.

NW

NORTHWESTERN BRONX

In this precinct, extending from Broadway west to the banks of the Hudson River, can be found **lush estates** and **lavish mansions,** low-rent **subsidized housing,** and block after block of very ordinary, **middle-class apartments.** It differs most from the rest of the Bronx, however, in that some parts—such as the private-streeted community of **Fieldston** and the slopes of the old community of **Riverdale-on-Hudson**—house some of the most affluent and most influential people residing in the borough. **Kingsbridge,** a community which preserves the name of the earliest settlement (which grew up around the first bridge to Manhattan built in 1693), is the flat area along Broadway below West 242nd Street. **Spuyten Duyvil** is the hilly southwestern tip of this precinct from which the graceful arch of the Henry Hudson Bridge springs to its opposite abutment in Manhattan. **Marble Hill** is the area between Spuyten Duyvil and Broadway and is actually a part of Manhattan though separated physically by the channel of the Harlem River Ship Canal. Since it is *not* officially part of the Bronx it will be given short shrift here. Its name describes it well, a steeply sloped mound of Inwood marble (a misnomer for a local limestone) turned upon itself as the result of its old street pattern.

VAN CORTLANDT PARK

[1a.] Van Cortlandt Swimming Pool, Van Cortlandt Park, Broadway at E. 242nd St. E side. 1970. Heery & Heery.

The largest of a series of system-designed, system-built pools completed in a successful crash program intended to break the city's normal, **slow-as-molasses** time schedule for government-financed construction.

[1b.] Van Cortlandt Mansion Museum, Van Cortlandt Park, Broadway bet. W. 242nd and W. 246th Sts. E side. 1748. ★

A carefully preserved fieldstone country house for a wealthy landed family. A simple exterior hides a richly decorated interior (open to the public). It stands south of the area that was once its farm, today an enormous meadow used for a variety of sporting events, particularly cricket (enjoyed by the city's large West Indian population) and model airplane trials. For museum information and hours: KI 6-3323.

Vault Hill, overlooking the Van Cortlandt Mansion, contains the Van Cortlandt family vault. When the British occupied New York in 1776, Augustus Van Cortlandt, the city clerk, hid the municipal records in the vault. In 1781, General Washington had campfires lit here to deceive the British, while he marched to Yorktown for the battle against Cornwallis.

Donaghy Steak House, 5523 Broadway near West 230th St. Telephone: 546-9571, 548-3377.

For meat-and-potato lovers this is a straightforward restaurant with good food and thoughtful service.

Ehring's Tavern, 228 W. 231st St. W of Broadway at Godwin Terrace. Telephone: KI 9-6750, KI 6-9576.

Good food with a German tang . . . and, as a tavern would have it, good drink, too.

FIELDSTON/SPUYTEN DUYVIL/RIVERDALE

Fieldston is the exclusive residential community of lavish private residences which lies north of the Fieldston School and east of the Henry Hudson Parkway. The name originated in 1824 with the founding of the area by early settlers, the Delafields. **Spuyten Duyvil,** an early Dutch name for the region where the Harlem and Hudson Rivers meet, is also the name of the steeply sloped area of the Bronx which overlooks the confluence of the waters. It has been overbuilt with tall undistinguished apartments. **Riverdale,** the northwest strip of this precinct which slopes romantically down to the Hudson's banks, was once a name reserved for the area immediately around the Riverdale station of the New York Central Railroad's Hudson Division. Then it was called Riverdale-on-Hudson. Today, all too many high-rise apartment hulks along Henry Hudson Parkway have **diminished the exclusivity** of both name and community. Fortunately, however, a cadre of tenacious residents, a couple of foreign governments, and some eleemosynary institutions still preserve the mansions, the lovely landscapes, and the tranquil beauty of the older community.

[2.] S.L. Victor Residence, 200 W. 245th St. SW cor. Waldo Ave. 1968. Ferdinand Gottlieb.

A formal, dignified contemporary design in now-grayed redwood siding. Slate-paved stairs ceremoniously lead to a pair of lovely panelled doors which are the formal entry. The street side of the house is discrete with slender windows; the rear, private, opens to the lush backyard. This is a wonderful house.

[3.] Horace Mann High School, 231 W. 246th St. NE cor. Tibbett Ave. **[3a.] Pforzheimer Hall.** 1956. Victor Christ-Janer. **[3b.] Prettyman Gymnasium.** 1968. Charles E. Hughes. **[3c.] Gratwick Science Wing Addition** and **Pforzheimer Hall Renovation.** 1975. Frost Assocs.

Once located next to Teachers College [see H Manhattan/Morningside Heights 11f.], Horace Mann High School (and Horace Mann–Barnard Elementary School south of 246th Street) now occupies this more verdant campus. Pforzheimer, Prettyman, and particularly Gratwick, are interesting newer buildings.

[4.] Fieldston Schools, Manhattan College Pkwy. SW cor. Fieldston Rd. **[4a.] Original buildings.** 1926. Clarence S. Stein and Robert D. Kohn. **[4b.] Tate Library.** 1971. Murphy & Mackey.

A group of private schools, operated by the New York Ethical Culture Society, huddling together on their hilly rise. The early buildings are unassuming in their mixture of traditional materials. The newer Tate Library attempts to bridge the design gulf between then and now.

[4b.] Riverdale-Yonkers Ethical Culture Society, 4550 Fieldston Rd. NE cor. Manhattan College Pkwy. 1965. William N. Breger Assocs.

A simple painted concrete block structure, almost engulfed by the lush landscape.

Fieldston: A community of private streets and romantic, English-inspired homes of the 1920s grouped along the streets north of Manhattan College Parkway—Fieldston Road, with its green central mall, is the quiet main thoroughfare. Among the many charms of the area is the oak tree preserved in the center of the intersection of Delafield and Iselin Avenues. If bicycling or driving, beware of the unkempt condition of the street paving. Potholes are the rule.

[5a.] Conservative Synagogue of Riverdale, Congregation Adath Israel, Henry Hudson Pkwy. NE cor. W. 250th St. 1962. Percival Goodman.

Strong forms in concrete and dark red brick give this synagogue considerable character.

[5b.] Henry Ittleson Center for Child Research, Jewish Board of Guardians, 5050 Iselin Ave. N of W. 250th St. E side. 1967. Abraham W. Geller; M.A. Rubenstein, design associate.

A neatly arranged community of tan block pavilions capped by standing-seam metal roofs. The group, for the treatment of disturbed children, is set well back from the street.

[5c.] Christ Church (Protestant Episcopal), Henry Hudson Pkwy. SE cor. W. 252nd St. 1866. Richard M. Upjohn. ★

A small, picturesque church, of brick and local stone, with a simple pierced-wall belfry. Minimal alterations and careful maintenance have preserved this delightful edifice.

[6.] Henry Hudson Memorial Column, Henry Hudson Park, Kappock St. NW cor. Independence Ave. 1912. Babb, Cook & Welch. Sculpture of Hudson, 1938. Karl Bitter and Karl Gruppe.

The 100-foot Doric column and base were erected on this high bluff by public subscription following the Hudson-Fulton Celebration of 1909. The 16-foot-tall bronze of Hudson gazing out at his river from the top of the column was not installed until long after. It was the work of Karl Gruppe working from a plaster model by his teacher, noted sculptor Karl Bitter.

[2.] S.L. Victor Residence: strict geometry in a rambling green setting

[5a.] Conserv. Synagogue/Riverdale   A scene in the Fieldston community

[7a.] Spuyten Duyvil Branch, N.Y. Public Library, 650 W. 235th St. bet. Independence and Douglas Aves. S side. 1971. Giorgio Cavaglieri.

A dignified building in an area characterized by chaotic and unrelated building development.

[7b.] Park Playground, N.Y.C. Parks and Recreation Department, W. 235th St. SW cor. Douglas Ave. 1975. M. Paul Friedberg & Assocs., landscape architects.

The playground occupies part of the heavily overgrown site of the Seton Hospital for Consumptives, a Roman Catholic institution dating from 1893.

A note of caution: The Riverdale area north of West 240th Street and west of Henry Hudson Parkway is an obstacle course for the unwary. Narrow, winding, hilly streets are commonplace. Without much notice they sometimes narrow first into lanes, then driveways, and then abruptly stop. Street signs are often missing or misleading. Since many of the smaller thoroughfares are not officially mapped and others are private (Fieldston's boundaries, east of the parkway, are comparatively easy to determine from the large private-street signs), maps don't help much. The condition of the streets in the area is frequently abominable, partly a result of the high cost of maintenance and partly because residents wish to discourage idle visiting. Not only do potholes abound but in some areas asphalt bumps have been added to discourage reckless driving since walking and cycling are popular.

All of this has probably contributed to preserving this extra special part of New York. Contributing too are the barking dogs who remain even when the homeowners have taken their cars on an errand. Whether walking, bicycling, or driving, be careful, and beware.

[8.] Eric J. Schmertz Residence, 4550 Palisade Ave. S of W. 247th St. E side. 1971. Vincent A. Claps.

Turned diagonally to the quiet road, this two-story natural-wood-sheathed house is subtly modeled and detailed. One of Riverdale's best contemporary houses.

[9a.] Delafield Botanical Estates, Columbia University/originally **Edward C. Delafield Residence, "Fieldston Hill,"** 680 W. 246th St. SW cor. Hadley Ave. ca. 1865. Altered, 1916. Dwight James Baum.

A large fieldstone house with a stately portico. The Delafields have been associated with the Riverdale area since the early 19th century.

[9b.] Edward A. Ames Residence, 709 W. 246th St. W of Independence Ave. N side. 1971. Hobart Betts & Assocs.

Down a private drive sits this gem of a house, sheathed in natural cedar and glass.

[9c.] Greyston Conference Center, Teachers College/originally **William E. Dodge Residence, "Greyston,"** 690 W. 247th St. SW cor. Independence Ave. 1864. James Renwick, Jr. ★

As Riverdale became a country retreat in the 1860s, this was one of the earliest houses commissioned. Not only was the Dodge family instrumental in the establishment of Teachers College in 1887 but also in the transfer to TC in 1961 of this large, many-gabled, many-chimneyed mansion.

[10.] Riverdale Presbyterian Church and Manse: The Duff House, 4765 Henry Hudson Pkwy. W. at W. 249th St. W side. 1863. James Renwick, Jr. ★

A pair of Renwick designs fortunately framed from distractions on either side by heavy greenery. The Duff House is curious in that its original design called for both a mansard roof and Gothic Revival gables and dormers.

Riverdale's mansions and views: To call attention to every house worth mentioning in this architectural treasure chest of a community would require a tome in itself. Some of its narrow lanes (and the homes that border them) are particularly rewarding. Sycamore Avenue above West 252nd Street has such picturesque buildings you won't believe you're in the city. Try Independence Avenue between West 248th and 254th Streets. The best view of Riverdale and the Hudson beyond is from a point just north of West 252nd Street. And visit Wave Hill, whose entrance is at West 249th Street, for a view Mark Twain and Arturo Toscanini enjoyed.

[11.] "Alderbrook," former Percy Pyne Residence, then **Elie Nadelman Residence,** 4715 Independence Ave. S of W. 248th St. W side. ca. 1880.

An Andrew Jackson Downing-inspired Gothic Revival brick house full of gables and crockets, long the home and studio of sculptor **Elie Nadelman (1885–1946).** Adjacent is a group of houses snugly occupying a private community now called Alderbrook, after the estate whose lands it shares.

[12.] Riverdale Country School, River Campus, W. 248th St. bet. Independence and Palisade Aves. N side. Perkins Study Center, 1967. R. Marshall Christensen. Later additions.

Three wings forming a U-shaped compound create the study center. The roof **design is unusual:** two concave curved planes which never quite meet, leaving a **skylight** along their crest. The study center shares this former property of financier George W. Perkins with two great old Victorian country houses now converted to school use. [For other parts of Perkins' estate, see NW Bronx 14.]

[13.] Former **Count Anthony Campagna Residence,** 640 W. 249th St. bet. Independence and Blackstone Aves. S side. 1922. Dwight James Baum.

Placed exquisitely at the end of a short cobblestoned drive, this stucco-walled and tile-roofed mansion is an **aristocratic building,** somehow more traditionally European in feeling than American.

[8.] The Eric J. Schmertz Residence   **[9c.]** Greyston Conference Center

[14.] Wave Hill Center for Environmental Studies, 675 W. 252nd St. SW cor. Sycamore Ave. Entrance on Independence Ave. at W. 249th St. W side. **[14a.] "Wave Hill," (northern building):** center section, 1844; north wing, late 19th century; armor hall, 1928. Dwight James Baum; south wings, after 1933; general renovation, 1975. Stephen Lepp. ★ **[14b.] "Glyndor II," (southern building)/now C.U.N.Y. Institute of Marine and Atmospheric Sciences at City College,** early 20th century.

Early conservationist and J. P. Morgan partner George Walbridge Perkins bought this estate, and two others which form the adjacent River Campus of the Riverdale Country School [see NW Bronx 12.], in the early 20th century. The neo-Georgian **Glyndor mansion,** which he built soon after, bears his initials on the metal downspouts at the roof. The older **Wave Hill building** he rented out to distinguished individuals, continuing its early role as a residence for the famous, publisher Thomas H. Appleton, Theodore Roosevelt, Mark Twain, and guests such as William Makepeace Thackeray, John Tyndall, T. H. Huxley, and Herbert Spencer. Prior to Perkins' descendants presenting both buildings to the city in 1960, Wave Hill was also the home of Arturo Toscanini and the official residence of the United Kingdom's ambassador to the United Nations. Perhaps Wave Hill's most **intriguing tenant** was **Bashford Dean,** builder of the armor hall. He was curator of arms and armor at the Metropolitan Museum of Art and also curator of reptiles and fishes at the American Museum of Natural History. Between 1906 and 1910 he held both posts **simultaneously!**

Wave Hill Center, its armor hall (now devoid of such things and used for modest exhibits), its exquisite gardens, and its glorious views are open to the public. For information, hours, programs: 549-2055.

John F. Kennedy 1917–1963: While a youngster attending the nearby Riverdale Country School on Fieldston Road, John F. Kennedy lived in the boxy stucco house on West 252nd Street at the southeast corner of Independence Avenue (officially 5040 Independence). That was in the years 1926 through 1928.

[15.] Nicholas de B. Katzenbach Residence/originally **Robert Colgate Residence, "Stonehurst,"** 5225 Sycamore Ave. bet. W. 252nd and W. 254th Sts. W side. 1861. ★

Hidden by newer homes built on Sycamore Avenue and by dense trees is another of the great stone mansions of Riverdale (such as Greyston or Wave Hill) and the Bronx (Van Cortlandt, Bartow). Katzenbach was **U.S. Attorney General** and Undersecretary of State; Colgate an **early entrepreneur** in lead and paint.

[16a.] Salanter Akiba Riverdale Academy, 655 W. 254th St. bet. Independence and Palisade Aves. 1974. Caudill Rowlett Scott Assocs. **[16b.] Administration Building**/originally **Henry W. Boettger Residence.** 1905.

Given a hill which slopes, slopes, slopes, and a need for a structure to join the educational activities of what were once three Hebrew day schools, what better solution than a stepped building? This one is primarily a series of classroom floors and skylighted roof tiers stepping down the slope (providing all with **cross-the-river views**), and unified by a roof structure paralleling the earth's slope. Shades of Harvard's Gund Hall— but here a result of the topography, not whim. The adjacent, expensive, multistory orange-brick **Tudor mansion** left over from the property's original owner was the last of conductor Arturo Toscanini's residences in Riverdale. Note the monogram on the wall: HWB for Henry W. Boettger.

[16a.] Salanter Akiba Riverdale Academy: its classrooms follow the terrain

[17.] Ladd Road, off Palisade Ave. bet. W. 254th St. and Sigma Place. E side. **[17a.] James Strain Residence,** 731 Ladd Rd. E side. 1970. Keith Kroeger Assocs.

A group of houses all built since 1957, clustered along a *cul de sac* around a private swimming pool. The site is the former estate of **Dr. William Sargent Ladd** (hence the name of the road), whose original stone gateposts guard the entrance. The Strain house embodies a geometrical clarity which gives the enclave a center of focus.

[18.] Gethsemane on Hudson Monastery and **Cardinal Spellman Retreat House, Passionist Fathers and Brothers,** 5801 Palisade Ave. opp. Sigma Place. W. side. **[18a.] Riverdale Center of Religious Research**/formerly **Old Residence.** ca. 1895. **[18b.] New Residence and Chapel.** 1967. Brother Cajetan J.B. Baumann, O.F.M.

Neither the old residence, a 3-story shingled Victorian country house, nor the new, an undistinguished orange-brick dorm, are of special interest. It is the new chapel almost hidden from the road that is a dramatic expressionistic architectural/sculptural work.

[19.] The Hebrew Home for the Aged at Riverdale, 5901 Palisade Ave. S of W. 261st St. W side. **Additions: [19a.] Goldfine Pavilion (south building).** 1968. Kelly & Gruzen. **[19b.] Palisade Nursing Home (north building).** 1975. Gruzen & Partners.

This institution awakened early to the benefits and satisfactions of high-**quality architecture for the elderly.** The early work combines exposed concrete and stacked red brick and seems to express in its windows response to the temptations of the spectacular 270° river views. The newer, 7-story all-brick building seems carved from a monumental cube almost as sculptor Gutzon Borglum attacked the Black Hills of South Dakota. Even the utility building off the road shows the architect's care and talent.

[20a.] College of Mount Saint Vincent: the arcades survey the Hudson below

[20.] College of Mount Saint Vincent on Hudson/originally **Convent and Academy of Mount Saint Vincent,** Riverdale Ave. and W. 263rd St. W side. **[20a.] Original College Building,** central section, 1857–1859. Henry Engelbert. Additions: 1865, 1885, 1908, 1952. **[20b.] Library**/formerly **Edwin Forrest Residence, "Fonthill."** 1846. ★ **[20c.] Louise LeGras Hall**/originally **St. Vincent's Free School,** W. 261st St. opp. Netherland Ave. N side. 1875.

The **Sisters of Charity,** who operate the college, purchased this site from actor **Edwin Forrest** (his feud with William Charles Macready in 1840 touched off the **Astor Place Riot**) when their original quarters were to be destroyed by the construction of Central Park. Forrest's house, Fonthill, is as eccentric a building for New York as the **"folly"** it was patterned after was for England, William Beckford's **Fonthill Abbey.** Though this is the best-known building on the campus, the old red brick college itself, four stories high and oh so long, is an unfamiliar and more spectacular sight in the campus. Its 180-foot tall tower rises some 400 feet above the level of the Hudson below. LeGras Hall was, between 1875 and 1910, the sparsely settled Riverdale's only elementary school. It is a charming building, accessible directly from the adjacent 261st Street.

[21.] Diplomatic Residence, Union of Soviet Socialist Republics, Mosholu Ave. NE cor. W 255th St. 1975. Skidmore, Owings & Merrill.

Nineteen stories of apartments built **from the top down** on two cast-in-place concrete masts which form the building's cores. Each floor was fabricated on the ground and **jacked up** to its position in the structure along the masts. The Russians pursued the **patented construction system** after an early conventional design was shelved to save a million dollars in construction.

Barrymore's Inn, 6471 Broadway at Mosholu Ave. Telephone: 549-1500.

Colorful mayor Jimmy Walker is said to have used this out-of-the-way restaurant (when it was still called the Riverdale Inn) to have some privacy (and pleasant repasts) during his amorous adventures with dancer Betty Compton.

Marie's Cookery and Restaurant, 5652 Mosholu Ave. opp. Tyndall Ave. Telephone: 548-0440.

Armenian and continental cooking is how this neighborhood restaurant characterizes its menu. Wines available. Open at 4:30 for dinner only. A pleasant spot.

E

EASTERN BRONX

Until war clouds foreshadowed the start of World War II, this was a **sleepy area** of the Bronx. In its center was a large green space shaded by majestic trees called the **New York Catholic Protectory,** an institute for destitute children. The neighborhoods around it were largely residential with one-, two-, and four-family houses, stray apartment buildings, and all kinds of minor commercial, industrial, and institutional establishments. And **many empty lots.** To the north, along Pelham Parkway, and to the west, down to the Bronx River, were groups of six-story apartment buildings. To the south and east were marshland and peninsulas **jutting out** into the East River and the Long Island Sound: Clasons Point, a **resort** and **amusement center** with a ferry to College Point, Queens; Ferry Point; and Throgs Neck. To the east were the remnants of the old **Village of Westchester,** called Westchester Square, hardly recognizable with the coming of the IRT elevated in 1920. And beyond lay Pelham Bay Park, **the borough's largest,** stretching north to the Westchester County line, and City Island, an oasis in the Sound.

Then the New York Catholic Protectory grounds were purchased by the Metropolitan Life Insurance Company and, in February of 1940, the first tenants of the 40,000 who were to populate **red brick,** high-rise **Parkchester** moved in. **The die was cast.** Empty lots, cattail-filled swamp, even parts of Pelham Bay Park were to be decimated by the **crush** of a new population.

Today, the area south of Bruckner Boulevard is a phalanx of **other red brick housing** projects. Hospital facilities occupy the marshy lands which fed Westchester Creek, now diminished by the construction of a **behemoth high school** only yards from Westchester Square. Two of the peninsulas are springboards for suspension bridges to Long Island. A pleasant stretch of Pelham Bay Park along the banks of Eastchester Bay is now **a projected ski slope,** elevated by countless truckloads of smelly garbage deposited there, politely called landfill. Progress has come to the Eastern Bronx. Its effects are profound.

PARKCHESTER, WESTCHESTER SQUARE AND MORRIS PARK

[1.] Parkchester, E. Tremont Ave., Purdy St., McGraw Ave., White Plains Rd. 1938–1942. Board of Design: Richmond H. Shreve, chairman; Andrew J. Eken, George Gove, Gilmore D. Clarke, Robert W. Dowling, Irwin Clavan, and Henry C. Meyer, Jr.

"A city within a city" was what it was called in its early days. It contained a large movie theater, over 100 stores including Macy's first branch, a local outlet of the N.Y. Public Library, a subway to Manhattan, parking garages for 3,000 cars, and 40,000 residents at a density of 250,000 people per square mile! As planning goes, however, this was an exceptionally thoughtful enterprise. Curving streets, lots of well-kept lawn, shrubbery, and trees, carefully planned pedestrian routes and recreation areas, and playful colored terra-cotta sculpture and face block calculated to inspire and delight whenever visual boredom set in. Metropolitan Life Insurance Company, its sponsor, maintained it for almost 30 years until about the time N.Y.C.'s Human Rights Commission accused it of maintaining a white-only policy. In 1968 Parkchester was sold to real estate giant Helmsley-Spear & Co.

[1.] Parkchester (apartment complex): view of fountain at Metropolitan Oval

[2.] **Boulevard Manor (apartments),** 2001 and 2045 Story Ave. bet. Pugsley and Olmstead Aves. N side. 1974. Gruzen & Partners.

Among the enormous number of multistory housing developments dropped helter-skelter in the area south of Bruckner Expressway in the 1960s and 1970s, these two buildings alone deserve any commendation for their architecture. No unique technology has been employed here, nor any exotic building materials—only a desire to delight the eye of residents and passersby.

[3.] **Westchester-Bronx YMCA,** 2244 Westchester Ave. bet. Castle Hill and Havemeyer Aves. S side. 1971. William A. Hall & Assocs.

This neat juxtaposition of basic geometric volumes is a more utilitarian replacement for the red brick Victorian country house (once the rectory of St. Peter's Church down the street—see below) whose rooms were the previous substitutes for this Y's needs.

Dominick's Restaurant, 2356 Westchester Ave. NE cor. Parker St.

For over a century a good place to eat. Italian food. Down a few steps from the street. Moderate. Telephone: 822-8810.

[4a.] **St. Peter's Church (Protestant Episcopal),** 2500 Westchester Ave. opp. St. Peter's Ave. E side. 1855. Leopold Eidlitz. Clerestory addition and restoration, 1879. Cyrus L.W. Eidlitz. ★ [4b.] **St. Peter's Chapel**/now **Foster Hall.** 1868. Leopold Eidlitz. ★ **Cemetery.** ★

A tribute to the vitality of this picturesque Gothic Revival composition is that it has withstood the vibration and the visual pollution of passing trains on the adjacent Pelham Bay Park elevated structure and has survived to be dubbed an official city landmark.

[5a.] **Ferris Family Cemetery,** Commerce Ave. E of Westchester Sq. bet. Westchester Ave. and Butler Place, S side. 18th century.

As Woodlawn Cemetery is large, Ferris is small . . . but very well kept considering that its once bucolic surroundings are now a grimy industrial area.

Westchester Square: These are the barely recognizable remains of the village green of the ancient town of Westchester, founded in 1653 and known as Oostorp under the Dutch. Under British rule it was the seat of Westchester County from 1683 until 1759. It is now a focus of local shopping and service activities and the terminus of several bus routes.

[5b.] Huntington Free Library and Reading Room/originally **The Van Schaick Free Reading Room,** 9 Westchester Sq. bet. Westchester and Tratman Aves. W side. 1882. Frederick Clarke Withers. Addition to rear, 1891. William Anderson.

When advised of the cost of its upkeep, local taxpayers refused to accept this gift of a fellow resident, **Peter Van Schaick.** It was not until 1891 that it was opened, together with an extension to the rear, through the efforts (and added funding) of railroad magnate **Collis P. Huntington** who maintained a summer residence in nearby Throgs Neck [see E Bronx 20.]. The original library is a modest but joyful red brick creation. Unfortunately the humorless orange brick addition to the south overwhelms Withers' work.

[5b.] The Huntington Free Library   **[6b.]** 1st Presb. Church/Throgs Neck

[7a.] Rehabilitation Center, Bronx State Hospital: it gently hugs its site

[6a.] Herbert H. Lehman High School, E. Tremont Ave. at Hutchinson River Pkwy. S side. 1972. The Eggers Partnership, architects. Roger Bolomey, sculptor.

Built in response to the population explosion of the East Bronx in the 1960s, this school itself explodes over its site. Its gymnasium straddles the adjacent highway; its athletic facilities sit on filled-in Westchester Creek. An angular **rust-brown steel** sculpture boldly marks the entrance to the smooth, precast-concrete-sheathed building.

[6b.] First Presbyterian Church in Throgs Neck, 3051 E. Tremont Ave. bet. Ericson Place and Dudley Ave. N side.

Perched comfortably on a hill above a series of stone retaining walls this red brick, white-trimmed church (and its graveyard to the rear) seem

oblivious to the changes evident along the avenue below. Its steeple is particularly noteworthy.

[7a.] Bronx State Hospital Rehabilitation Center, N.Y.S. Department of Mental Hygiene, 1500 Waters Pl. bet. Eastchester Rd. and Hutchinson River Pkwy. N side. 1971. Gruzen & Partners.

Intricate in plan with many reentrant corners and applied stair towers, yet the forms fall together with an effortlessness that is rare. **A very unassuming** but **very fine** work.

[7b.] Bronx Children's Psychiatric Hospital, N.Y.S. Department of Mental Hygiene, 1000 Waters Pl. bet. Eastchester Rd. and Hutchinson River Pkwy. N side. 1969. The Office of Max O. Urbahn.

An attempt to lessen the oppressive institutional quality of the earliest Bronx State Hospital buildings (by the same firm) through the introduction of a domestically scaled collection of interlinked shed-roofed units.

[8.] Bronx Developmental Center, N.Y.S. Department of Mental Hygiene, Waters Pl. bet. Eastchester Rd. and Hutchinson River Pkwy. N side. 1976. Richard Meier & Assocs.

The advances of 20th-century technology are summed up in the forms and materials of this center for the mentally retarded. Dramatically located on a **spacious and serene** site along the edge of the Hutchinson River Parkway, its long, prismatic forms evoke the majesty of a **rectilinear dirigible.** Clad in a tightly stretched skin of natural anodized-aluminum panels it looks as if it were fabricated by an **aircraft manufacturer,** not by **earth-bound** building contractors. Windows, resembling enormous elongated portholes, add to the machine-age look as does the **proud expression** of the intricate and colorful central mechanical system which controls the building's inner environment. It is a **consummate work** of architecture and is sure to be ranked among the great buildings of its time.

[8.] The Bronx Developmental Center: elegant summation of modern technology

[9.] Albert Einstein College of Medicine, Yeshiva University, 1300 Morris Park Ave. SW cor. Eastchester Rd. **[9a.] Forchheimer Medical Science Building.** 1955. Kelly & Gruzen. **[9b.] Robbins Auditorium, Friedman Lounge, Gottesman Library.** 1958. Kelly & Gruzen. **[9c.] Ullman Research Center for Health Sciences.** 1963. Kiesler & Bartos. **[9d.] Bassine Educational Center for Health Sciences.** 1971. Armand Bartos & Assocs.

Planned for this already crowded and chaotic campus in the future is a cancer research institute. One wonders whether it will be for the human or the architectural variety. Like Topsy (and many other college and hospital campuses) **this place just grew.** Most of the buildings are competent enough but as a group they are a failure. Ullman, the newest, is by far the most distinguished . . . perhaps there is hope.

[9e.] Joe and Evlynne Low Residence Complex, Morris Park Ave. NW cor. Eastchester Rd. 1972. Pomerance & Breines.

An interesting composition of three high-rise apartment towers for the staff of Albert Einstein College and its medical facilities. Across Morris Park Avenue from the main Einstein campus.

[10.] Bronx Municipal Hospital Center, N.Y.C. Health and Hospitals Corporation, Morris Park Ave. to Pelham Pkwy. S., W of Eastchester Rd. Original buildings including Abraham Jacobi Hospital and Nathan B. Van Etten Hospital. 1955. Pomerance & Breines. **[10a.] Rose Fitzgerald Kennedy Center for Research in Mental Retardation and Human Development, Albert Einstein College of Medicine.** 1970. Pomerance & Breines.

The same architectural firm has, over a period of some 15 years, designed buildings for this hospital complex. Note the difference in approach in their most recent structure.

[11.] Physur Professional Building, 1180 Morris Park Ave. NE cor. Hering Ave. 1973. Oppenheimer, Brady & Vogelstein.

An appropriately reserved and dignified building of dark brownish-gray brick with deeply recessed sloped-sill window openings that add interest to the composition.

The world's first air meets: In 1908 and 1909 on a 307-acre site, which lay south of today's Pelham Parkway between Bronxdale Avenue and Williamsbridge Road down to the New Haven right-of-way, were held some of the earliest public trials of powered aircraft. Aviation pioneers Glenn H. Curtiss (and his partner Alexander Graham Bell) and Samuel P. Langley (of the Smithsonian) were drawn to the meets as were as many as 20,000 spectators. The site had earlier been, between 1889 and 1902, the Morris Park Racecourse, replacement for the earlier Jerome Park Race Track whose grounds in the West Bronx had been acquired to build the reservoir bearing the same name. Horse racing moved to Belmont Park in 1903; airplane meets moved, too; and in 1910 a spectacular fire wiped out many of the remaining stables/hangars. Nary a trace of the course remains today save a blocked-up tunnel portal under Bronxdale Avenue which once had allowed crowded railroad coaches to deposit visitors at this one-time recreation mecca in the Bronx.

[12a.] Former **Bronxdale Swimming Pool (abandoned),** Bronxdale Ave. NE cor. Antin Pl. ca. 1928.

Crowds of kids, mommas, and poppas no longer wait to plunge into the cool, chlorinated waters of this answer to the city's **steamy summers.** But the polychromed Art Deco terra-cotta ornament is still there resisting the elements.

[12b.] 2009 Cruger Avenue (apartments), NW cor. Bronxdale Ave. ca. 1930.

It is the West Bronx which is Art Deco heaven but here is a strong work (across the intersection from the Bronxdale Pool) whose **vermillion glazed** terra cotta and extraordinary metalwork single it out.

[13.] Bronx and Pelham Parkway, connecting Bronx Park and Pelham Bay Park.

Rarely referred to by any name other than just Pelham Parkway this **wide** and **luxuriant greenway** has not suffered from the widenings and removal of ancient trees that other thoroughfares in the city have undergone. Prior to World War II the center lanes were closed off on Sunday mornings for bicycle racing.

 [14.] Morningside House, 1000 Pelham Pkwy. S. **[14a.] Reception Building,** SW cor. Lurting Ave. **[14b.] Administration and Medical Services Building,** SE cor. Lurting Ave. 1974. Johnson-Burgee.

A rare architectural **tribute to the dignity** of this culture's aged citizenry. An urbane pair of buildings with a carefully controlled, resort-like exterior.

[15.] Bronx House, The Harris and Sarah Lichtman Building, 990 Pelham Pkwy. S. SW cor. Bogart Ave. 1970. Addition, 1973. Both by Westermann/Miller Assocs.

Whatever architect said "God is in the details" should look at those employed on this building. They are much too fussy and self-conscious.

Kosher pizza, bagels and lox, brisket and flanken: Unassuming Lydig Avenue (a block south of the Pelham Parkway station of the IRT 241st Street-White Plains Road lines), for about five blocks east of White Plains Road, is a busy, happy, prosperous shopping street of a vital Jewish community. How long it will stay this way is anybody's guess but if you're nearby it's worth a visit . . . and a nosh.

[16.] Morris Park Station, of the former New York, Westchester & Boston Railway/now the **Dyre Avenue IRT Line,** Paulding Ave. at the Esplanade. 1912. Fellheimer & Long, Allen H. Stem associated.

This Italian Villa-style station marks the beginning of a **3,940-foot-long subway** by which the defunct NYW & B commuter line bypassed broad tree-lined Pelham Parkway. Over the cut-and-cover construction on both sides of the parkway, property owners constructed an unusually gracious street called the **Esplanade** which cuts diagonally through the street grid. [For the railway's administration building, see C Bronx 5.]

[10a.] Kennedy Retardation Center

[14.] Morningside House: for the aged

THROGS NECK AND ITS WATERSIDE COMMUNITIES

Throgs Neck: Spelled with one or two *g*'s and sometimes with an apostrophe, the name once referred to the outermost peninsula of land beyond East Tremont Avenue's end. Its name is derived from **John Throckmorton** who settled here in 1643, when New York was still under Dutch rule. Until the early part of the 20th century this area was covered with estates. Today its inhabitants are modest, home-owning families.

[17.] Engine Company 72, Ladder Company 55 (deactivated), N.Y.C. Fire Department, 3929 E. Tremont Ave. NE cor. E. 177th St. 1972. Arthur Witthoeft.

Firemen still slide down **brass poles** from their second-floor bunkrooms. In this firehouse the poles are set into tall elegant cylinders at the outside of the building.

[18.] 3077 East 177th Street (apartments), bet. Logan Ave. and Throgs Neck Expwy. N side.

Mixed tones of orange brick, exposed concrete balconies, raked stair tower roofs, and a particularly interesting east facade of this eight-story apartment make it a happy landmark at the confluence of the Cross-Bronx and Throgs Neck Expressways.

[19.] St. Frances De Chantal Church (Roman Catholic), 190 Hollywood Ave. SE cor. Harding Ave. 1971. Paul W. Reilly.

It's hard to miss this church. Perhaps that's one of its faults. No faulting its stained glass, however—**colorful chunks** in the **European style** precast into concrete window panels.

[20.] Preston High School (Roman Catholic)/formerly **"Homestead," Collis P. Huntington (summer) Residence/**originally **H. O. Havemeyer Residence,** 2780 Schurz Ave. SE cor. Brinsmade Ave. ca. 1880.

It is so rare that a summer house with a recorded history survives this long that one is prepared to forgive its lack of architectural distinction. (Huntington and family—whose wealth came from the railroads—contributed to a number of fine buildings in the city [see E Bronx 5b. and U Manhattan 3.]. Original owner Havemeyer was a sugar king.) The newer additions for high school use are unfortunate.

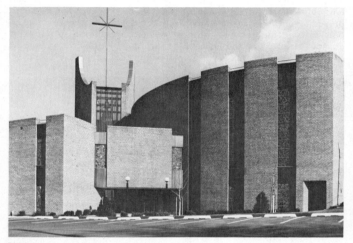

[19.] St. Frances De Chantal RC Church: a curvilinear brick composition

[21.] Fort Schuyler/now **State University of New York Maritime College,** E end of Pennyfield Ave. **[21a.] Fort Schuyler.** 1834–1838. Capt. I. L. Smith. ★ Conversion to **Maritime College,** 1934–1938. Conversion of fort's dining hall to the **Adm. Stephen Bleecker Luce Library,** William A. Hall, 1967. **[21b.] Vander Clute Hall (dormitory, dining).** 1963. **[21c.] Riesenberg Hall (health and physical education).** 1964. **[21d.] Marvin-Tode Hall (science and ocean engineering).** 1967. All by Ballard Todd & Assocs.

A drive along the perimeter road (it changes names a number of times) of this narrow neck of land will reveal views of Long Island Sound that will make looking at the college's architecture difficult. Old Fort Schuyler itself is well worth a stop to visit its interior court, **(called St. Mary's Pentagon),** and for views from its ramparts—another 19th-century fortress (and landmark), Fort Totten, across the sound, is more easily seen from here than from its home borough of Queens. (It's hard to believe that the old fort lay abandoned between 1878 and 1934 when WPA funds enabled restoration for reuse.)

Protecting our sea approaches: America's seacoast fortifications were developed in three stages: The **First System** was started in 1794 when it was feared that we might be drawn into the European wars that followed the French Revolution. The **Second System,** begun in 1807, was motivated by the potential danger from Great Britain—it ended with the War of 1812. The **Third System,** unlike the first two which had been responses to external threats, was initiated in a peaceful era in 1817 and continued until the time of the Civil War. Both Fort Schuyler and Fort Totten (1862–1864) were built as part of this Third System to be able to rake with cannon fire any enemy approaching the Port of New York via the Long Island Sound.

[22.] Silver Beach Gardens Corporation, Pennyfield and Schurz Aves. S to Long Island Sound. (Entrance on Chaffee Ave. at Pennyfield Ave.)
[23.] Edgewater Park, Cross-Bronx Expwy. and Miles Ave. N to Long Island Sound. (Entrance is just W of Miles Ave. at Cross-Bronx Expwy. north service road—a two-way street.)

Two of three **waterside communities** in the Bronx where only the building is owned by the occupant, and ground rent is paid to the owner of the land—the third is Harding Park on Clasons Point. These buildings were originally summer cottages, but they are now winterized. Silver Beach Gardens' Indian Trail affords excellent views of both the Whitestone and Throgs Neck bridges. Also note the bulky community center, once the Hammond-Havemeyer mansion, called the Gibraltar of Long Island Sound.

Both these communities consider their streets private.

[24.] 716 Clarence Avenue (residence), bet. Schley and Philip Aves. ca. 1920.

The views of Long Island Sound make a drive along this part of Clarence Avenue unlike anything else in the city. No. 716 is covered by **mosaic** applied in a **vernacular manner.** So is its garage—and even the birdhouse. Farther west, at 748, is the **clubhouse of the N.Y. Turners,** a group devoted to the adage "Sound body, sound mind."

MIDDLETOWN ROAD, PELHAM BAY PARK, CITY ISLAND

[25.] Middletown Plaza (apartments), N.Y.C. Housing Authority, 3033 Middletown Rd. bet. Hobart and Jarvis Aves. NW side. 1973. Paul Rudolph.

A tall, dramatic cast-concrete frame, gray ribbed block infill, gray window sash, united by architect Rudolph's **limitless imagination,** make this housing for the elderly his best work in the borough and one of the Bronx's most notable architectural works.

[21a.] Luce Library at Ft. Schuyler   **[25.]** Middletown Plaza apartments

[26.] Museum of the American Indian, Heye Foundation Annex, Bruckner Expwy. SW cor. Middletown Rd.

This is a warehouse and research center for the museum whose public galleries are on Audubon Terrace in Manhattan. [See U Manhattan 3a.] Totem poles, Indian houses, and wigwam replicas are displayed on the lawns, but **you can't go inside.**

Pelham Bay Park: The largest of the six parks puchased as a result of the new Bronx parks program of 1883. At that time this one was a distance outside the New York City limits. It contains two golf courses, an archery range, bridle paths, a Police Department firing range (private), and ample facilities for hiking, cycling, and motoring. Shell racing is held in the

North Lagoon. Between 1910 and 1913 a monorail traversed the park from the New Haven Railroad line to City Island.

[27.] Rice Memorial Stadium, Pelham Bay Park, NW of Middletown Rd. and Stadium Ave. ca. 1916. Herts & Robertson.

This concrete stadium is unusual because of the small **Greek temple** atop the bleachers which frames Louis St. Lannes' heroic statue *The American Boy.* The stadium was given to the city by the widow of **Isaac L. Rice** as part of a complex of other athletic facilities including a 330-foot-long swimming pool, bathhouse, bleachers, and a decorative 100-foot-high white marble Doric column. All but the stadium are gone today. The Rices' mansion still stands along Riverside Drive [see UWS Manhattan/Riverside Drive 13a.].

[27.] Rice Stadium, Pelham Bay Park   **[32a.]** Grace Church/City Island

Watt, Ampere, Ohm: In gratitude for Mrs. Rice's gift of athletic facilities in her husband's honor, the city fathers named nearby streets after units of electrical measurement since Rice's name had long been associated with developments in electric storage batteries for automobiles and submarines. Rice was also the inventor of the Rice gambit, a chess opening.

[28.] Pelham Bay Park World War Memorial, Shore Rd. E of Bruckner Expwy. SE side. ca. 1925. John J. Sheridan, architect. Belle Kinney, sculptor.

One of the handsomest and best-maintained monuments (unlike nearby Rice Stadium) in the entire city.

[29.] Bartow-Pell Mansion Museum, Pelham Bay Park, Shore Rd. near Pelham-Split Rock Golf Course, S side. 1675. Alterations, 1836–1845 attributed to Minard Lafever. Restoration, 1914. Delano & Aldrich. ★

Lords of the Manor of Pelham once owned this house which was later enlarged, renovated, and remodeled in the Federal style. The mansion became the home of the International Garden Club in 1914. The Pell family plot, a magnificent formal garden, a view of Long Island Sound from the grounds, and rare and tasteful furnishings within combine to make a visit worthwhile. For information, hours, admission charges: TT5-1461.

[30.] Orchard Beach, East Shore of Pelham Bay Park on Long Island Sound. 1936. N.Y.C. Parks Department, Aymar Embury II.

A large sandy beach reopened in 1936 after extensive remodeling by the WPA and the Department of Parks. The bathhouses are enhanced by a strong set of concrete colonnades, chastely decorated with blue terra-cotta tiles. The beach cafeteria is under the spacious entry terrace. This a good public place, monumental without being overpowering, and efficient without being crowded.

City Island: A tight little island which is part of New York City by law but has scarcely any other connections. Its first industry was the Solar Salt Works, which made salt by evaporating seawater. That was in 1830. Then came oystering and eventually yacht building. (Though this activity has declined, City Island's shipwrights have built a number of our entries in the America's Cup race including the 1968 winner, *Intrepid.*) In the 1900s, filmmaking came to the island and so did D.W. Griffith, Douglas Fairbanks, Sr., and the Keystone Kops, who filmed a scene on Fordham Street. Fish and seafood fanciers are today's most important asset to the island's economy: City Island Avenue is filled with restaurants of every description. As the Hispanic population of the borough burgeons, more and more of City Island's signs seek to cultivate a Spanish-speaking clientele.

[31.] Public School 175 Bronx, 200 City Island Ave. opp. Winters St. NE side. 1975. L. E. Tuckett & Thompson.

The best new building on City Island and one of the best in the borough as well. One problem: can you imagine doing lessons with that distracting blue water view?

[32a.] Grace Church (Protestant Episcopal), City Island Ave. E cor. Pilot St. 1862. **[32b.] Grace Church Rectory,** 104 City Island Ave. bet. Pilot and Marine Sts. NE side. ca. 1862.

A pair of gems that befits an off-the-beaten-track seafaring community. The church is a paragon of Gothic Revival wood craftsmanship. The rectory is a modest wood frame structure which derives from the Italian Villa style.

[32c.] 141 Pilot Street (residence), N cor. City Island Ave. ca. 1862.

More of the same, this house has lathe-turned porch posts and eyebrow windows.

N

NORTHERN BRONX

The Northern Bronx has had some settlement since the 17th century, and for some two months in the 18th century the nation's executive mansion was here, but most of this area's modest homes and scattered groups of apartment houses (as well as gargantuan Co-op City) date from the 20th.

BRONXDALE-WILLIAMSBRIDGE

[1.] New York Institute for The Education of The Blind, 999 Pelham Pkwy. North bet. Bronxwood Ave. and Williamsbridge Rd. 1924. McKim, Mead & White.

An inoffensive campus of neo-Georgian buildings for the elementary and college preparatory education of the blind and visually handicapped.

[2.] Frampton Hall, N.Y. Institute for The Education of The Blind, Astor Ave. NW cor. Paulding Ave. 1971. Eggers & Higgins.

If blindness is not enough of a handicap then mental retardation plus blindness is. This neatly designed facility is for the treatment of just this combination of afflictions.

[3.] 2440 Boston Road (apartments), bet. Waring and Mace Aves. E side. 1972. Davis, Brody & Assocs.

Twenty stories of housing predominantly for the elderly in one tower, count them, two. With a bit of visual **sleight-of-hand,** an otherwise bulky prism is made to look like **two slender shafts** offset slightly from one another. And to top off this architectural **legerdemain** the tower is broader at the top (to accommodate larger apartments) than at the bottom. The adjacent one-story community center is a carefully contrasted foil for the tower.

[4.] Lourdes of America, Bronxwood Ave. NW cor. Mace Ave. 1939.

An amazing sight. Out-of-doors in a stone grotto rising high above the adjacent sidewalks are **hundreds** of **twinkling candles** in tiny red-glass containers, placed there by the devout who have come to share in the many cures claimed for this replica of **the famous French shrine.** On the grounds of St. Lucy's Roman Catholic Church.

[5.] Private Chapel (Roman Catholic), E. 215th St. bet. Holland and Barnes Ave. S side. 1905. Frank Lisanti.

In contrast to the public devotions at Lourdes of America, this is a place for private meditations: a humble chapel transposed from the slopes of southern Italy. Below the bell and the ornate wrought ironwork cross is carved:

F. LISANTI

IN DEVOZIONE

DELL IMMACOLATA

PER SE E FAMIGLIA

ERESSE

1905

[6.] 47th Precinct Station House, N.Y.C. Police Department, 4111 Laconia Ave. bet. E. 229th and E. 230th Sts. W side. 1974. Davis, Brody & Assocs.

It's not unreasonable to conceive of a police station as an updated medieval castle. But when dreams become brick-and-mortar reality, problems can surface. They do here in this overly contrived design.

CO-OP CITY, BAYCHESTER

[7.] Co-op City. Northern section: E of New England Thruway/Baychester Ave. bet. Co-op City Blvd. and Bartow Ave. **Southern section:** E of Hutchinson River Pkwy. E. bet. Bartow and Boller Aves. 1968–1970. Herman J. Jessor, architect. Zion & Breen, landscape architects.

Out in the middle of nowhere, on marshy land that was once the site of an ill-fated amusement park named **Freedomland,** a group of government officials, union representatives, and housing developers **dreamt the impossible dream.** Today the dream may better be described as **a coma.** From out of the **pumped-sand fill** rises a sea of 35-story residential towers, 35 of them, plus 236 clustered two-family houses, and eight multistory parking garages. In addition, there are three shopping centers, a heating plant, a firehouse, and an educational park consisting of two public schools, two intermediate schools, and a high school. In this total **non-environment,** largely designed by bureaucrats with **not a scintilla of wit,** live some 55,000 souls, many of whom vacated sound accommodations in the West Bronx (in many cases Art Deco apartment blocks) to move here. Let's be thankful for the **landscaping**—it's the **best thing** at Co-op City.

[8.] Junior High School 144 Bronx, Michaelangelo School, 2545 Gunther Ave. SW cor. Allerton Ave. 1968. The Office of Max O. Urbahn.

Entirely of cast-in-place concrete, more fashionable as an advanced building material then than now, this well-intentioned design has not aged well. Most regrettable are the later additions of metal mesh screens over the windows to deter stone-throwing vandals.

I Boschetto Restaurant, 1660 E. Gun Hill Rd. cor. Tiemann Ave. Telephone: 379-9335.

Starched tablecloths, gleaming glasses, and hearty Italian food in an out-of-the way place. Moderately expensive.

[9.] Haffen Park Pool, Haffen Park, Burke Ave. S cor. Ely Ave. 1970. Heery & Heery. Adjacent park development, 1971. Coffey, Levine, & Blumberg.

A precast concrete, systems-built pool, constructed as part of a crash program to influence an election campaign (as many public works are intended to do). Neat detailing and early supergraphics commend the design but the lush greenery in Haffen Park, preserved in the park's development, is the most welcome sight.

[3.] 2440 Boston Road apartments

[5.] The Private Chapel of F. Lisanti

[10.] Hillside Homes, five city blocks, W of Boston Rd. bet. Wilson Ave. and Eastchester Rd. 1935. Clarence S. Stein.

Is it high land costs or planning prejudices that seem to make it **impossible to duplicate** this highly successful moderate-rental housing development? Most of the buildings here are only four stories high, and they occupy one-third of the land. A large central playground and community center are provided for school-aged children, while sandboxes and tot lots are placed away from street traffic inside seven large **sunken interior courts** that are reached through tunnel passageways.

EASTCHESTER

When the part of the Bronx lying east of the Bronx River was lopped off Westchester County in 1895, the dividing line ran right through the old Village of Eastchester. As a result, the old village green lies a stone's throw outside city limits. This community of the uppermost northeast Bronx is still referred to, however, by its colonial name. It is largely a wasteland, unfortunately: automobile repair shops, fast food operations, marginal industry and the like. But at its edges and even within are some bright spots.

[11.] Originally **Vincent-Halsey House,** 3701 Provost Ave. bet. Light and Connor Sts. W side. Mid-18th century.

Regrettably this historic house (not open to the public) has been overwhelmed by its ugly industrial neighbors. Today a nondescript old building, it was once a colonial farmhouse set amongst Eastchester's furrowed fields. John Adams moved the presidential mansion here in 1797 to escape a yellow fever epidemic raging in Philadelphia, at that time the national capital. Adams governed the nation from this place for two months, but tragedy did not escape him here. One of his sons drowned while swimming in nearby Eastchester Creek.

[12.] Church of the Nativity of Our Blessed Lady (Roman Catholic), 1510 E. 233rd St. SW cor. Secor Ave. Don Shepherd, designer.

A minor work but one which calls attention to itself because of its location and the rusted structural steel crucifix that dominates the corner of the site.

[13.] Public School 15 Bronx (Annex to P.S. 68 Bronx)/formerly **P.S. 148**/originally a **Village of Eastchester public school,** 4010 Dyre Ave. bet. Dark and Lustre Sts. E side. 1877.

An architectural "pot of gold" at the end of the rainbow-graffitied Dyre Avenue IRT line: a gingerbread brick-and-wood-trimmed schoolhouse which wound up on the New York City side of the boundary when the Village of Eastchester was split in two. Its cheerful forms can't help but bring a smile to your face.

WOODLAWN

Snug against the Yonkers city line, this is the only clearly demarked community in the Northern Bronx—thanks to its neighbors, Van Cortlandt Park on the west, Woodlawn Cemetery on the south, and the Bronx River Parkway and the old railroad right-of-way on the east, the opening of whose commuter route encouraged settlement here in the 19th century.

[13.] Public School 15, The Bronx   **[15.]** The Old 24th Ward School

[14.] Former **Engine Co. 69, N.Y.C. Fire Department,** 243 E. 233rd St. bet. E. 234th St. and Katonah Ave. ca. 1895.

A wood frame firehouse almost across the border into Westchester County. Understandably, it looks more like a barn than a modern fire department facility. **Good carpentry** is everywhere evident.

[15.] Resthaven Nursing Home/formerly **Evander Childs High School Annex**/originally **24th Ward School.** 225 E. 234th St. bet. E. 233rd St. and Katonah Ave. N side. ca. 1890. Altered.

Behind that fake white Colonial portico is a great Romanesque Revival facade—by Lamb & Rich, perhaps?

[16.] 125 East 238th Street (residence), bet. Oneida and Kepler Aves. N side. ca. 1920.

Cream-colored stucco and dark wood trim, styled somewhat in the mode of a bungalow but bearing strong influence of Frank Lloyd Wright's **prairie houses.** Today it is cramped—it once enjoyed a more spacious site.

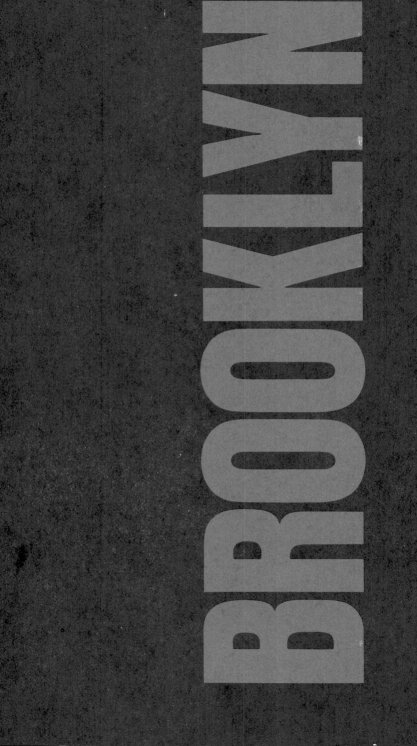

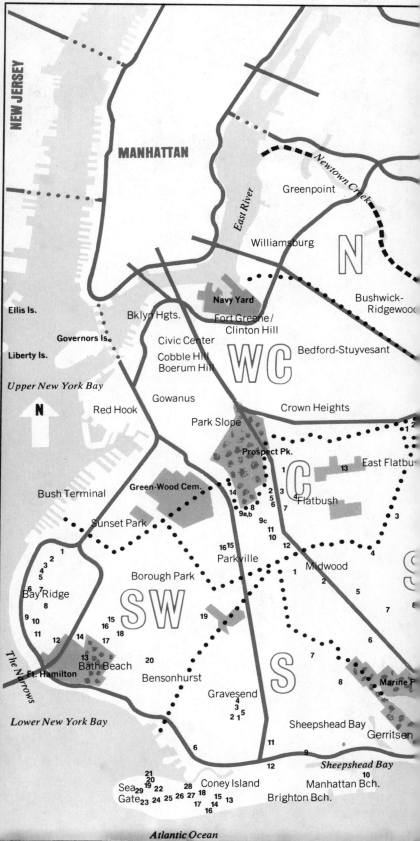

NEW JERSEY

MANHATTAN

East River

Greenpoint

Newtown Creek

Williamsburg

N

Bushwick-
Ridgewood

Ellis Is.

Navy Yard

Bklyn Hgts.

Fort Greene/
Clinton Hill

Governors Is.

Civic Center

Bedford-Stuyvesant

Liberty Is.

Cobble Hill
Boerum Hill

WC

Upper New York Bay

Gowanus

Crown Heights

N

Red Hook

Park Slope

Prospect Pk.

1

C

13 East Flatbu

2

Green-Wood Cem.

14

2
3
4 Flatbush

Bush Terminal

9a,b   8
9c

5
6
7

3

Sunset Park

11
10

12

4

16 15

Parkville

1

Midwood

2

Bay Ridge

1

Borough Park

SW

19

5

7

3
4
5

6 7

8

15
16
18

8

9 10

11   12 14
17

Marine P

13

20

Bath Beach

Bensonhurst

S

7

The Narrows

Ft. Hamilton

Gravesend

8

Marine P

Gerritsen

Lower New York Bay

3
4
2 1 5

Sheepshead Bay

11

9

Sheepshead Bay

6

12

10

21
20
19
Sea 29
Gate 23 24 25 26 27 18 14
22   28 Coney Island
Manhattan Bch.

Brighton Bch.

15 13

16

Atlantic Ocean

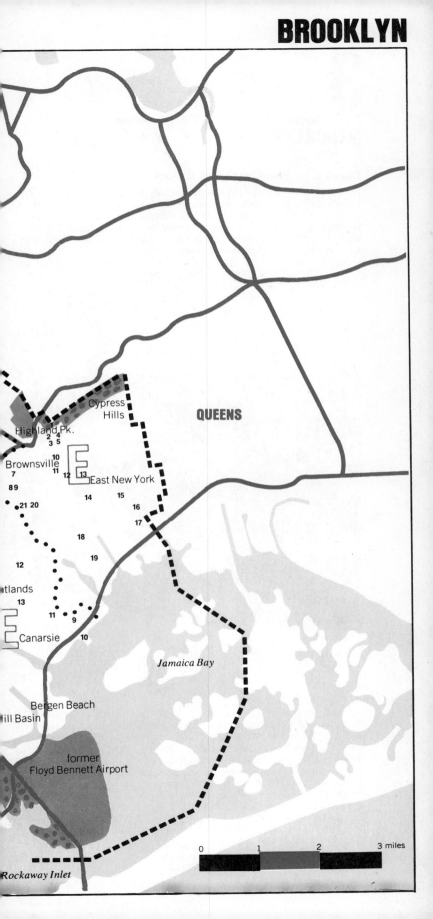

BROOKLYN

QUEENS

Cypress
Hills

Highland Pk.
1
2 4 5
3

10
Brownsville
7
11
8 9
12 13
East New York
14
15
21 20
16
17
18
12
19
tlands
13
11
9
Canarsie
10

Jamaica Bay

Bergen Beach
ill Basin

former
Floyd Bennett Airport

Rockaway Inlet

0   1   2   3 miles

BROOKLYN

Borough of Brooklyn/Kings County

Endless rows of houses—old and new—burned-out apartment buildings bearing the scars of peacetime wars, litter, kids playing stick-ball in the summer, roller-hockey in the winter, steeples silhouetted against the smoggy sky, and the drama of the borrowed skyline across the bay—these are only some of the visual ingredients of Brooklyn's scene. How this scene changes from generation to generation!

The physical objects themselves do not undergo transformation. With certain notable exceptions they seem only to age and get grimier. It is, rather, the way in which we *see* them that changes. Brooklyn today, even to many of its residents, is very often the image of Brooklyn absorbed from driving the limited-access highway: the industry of the north end, the products of American industry awaiting shipment on the docks below Brooklyn Heights, the spin along the Narrows with the Verrazano Bridge punctuating the contrast between people and nature. Motorists also remember the intricate spider web of Coney Island's Wonder Wheel, the endless stretches of swampland at Jamaica Bay, or the 25-mile-an-hour curves in a 50-mile-an-hour car along verdant Interboro Parkway. The placement of our highways and the speed of our cars tend to deemphasize Brooklyn as a residential community and to play up its other attributes.

What a different image Brooklyn must have provided in other periods!

It is amazing that the footprints of civilization have not only been left on Brooklyn's 78.5 square miles, but have in many instances been preserved virtually intact to mark the path of people and culture. They are subtle footprints—after all, time both erodes and covers artifacts of the past. But the sense of Brooklyn as an organism which has grown from a settlement barely 350 years old is concealed from us, not by any lack of evidence, but by the changes in the tempo and focus of our observations. The recent rediscovery of vast stretches of brownstone Brooklyn by a young and sophisticated middle class may mark yet another change in the way we see. Viable and venerable residential communities, backwaters in the mainstream of physical change such as Brooklyn Heights, Park Slope and the Hills—Clinton, Cobble, and Boerum—have once again become desirable neighborhoods. Perhaps the renaissance of these neighborhoods will provide the motivation to explore the rest of the borough. Perhaps that process will provide new opportunities for the renewal and reinterpretation of the lessons and the landmarks of history.

WC

WEST CENTRAL BROOKLYN

Town of Brooklyn/Breukelen

Established as a town before 1658; as a city in 1834. Annexed City of Williamsburgh and Town of Bushwick in 1855, Town of New Lots in 1886, Towns of Flatbush, Gravesend, and New Utrecht in 1894, and Town of Flatlands in 1896. Consolidated into greater New York City in 1898.

The original Town, later City, of Brooklyn encompassed all the brownstone neighborhoods becoming fashionable again today. The residential precincts of Brooklyn Heights, Fort Greene-Clinton Hill, Park Slope, Bedford-Stuyvesant, Crown Heights, and what are now Cobble Hill and Boerum Hill are all within the boundaries of the original town; so is the Brooklyn Civic Center and "department store row" along Fulton Street. In addition, the teeming waterfront facilities from the Manhattan Bridge south to the deactivated Brooklyn Army Terminal lie within the area, as do the backup residential communities of Red Hook, Gowanus, and Sunset Park. And within the old town's boundaries as well are half of both Prospect Park and Green-Wood Cemetery.

Although the extent of the old town can still be accurately charted, it is of little significance as a locality today when compared to the individual communities that comprise it.

CIVIC CENTER/DOWNTOWN BROOKLYN

The independent City of Brooklyn moved quickly to give form to its center of government by building a city hall that still stands as its seat of borough affairs. As the 19th century progressed, Brooklyn's population and wealth grew, and so did the civic center. With city hall as the focal point there soon was built a variety of richly embellished governmental and commercial buildings, hotels, and shopping emporia. But to a visitor to Downtown Brooklyn during this era of physical growth, the most apparent feature was not its richly ornamented buildings but the spindly iron trestles that inundated many of its major streets in zebra-striped shadows. For this part of Brooklyn was to be not only the civic and shopping hub of the city but the transportation hub as well, and the elevateds crisscrossing overhead made their way down Fulton Street and Myrtle Avenue to their connections to Manhattan. It was not till after

World War II that the el structures were removed and today's Cadman Plaza Park was built.

Civic Center/Downtown Brooklyn Walking Tour: From Borough Hall to the Flatbush Avenue-Fulton Street intersection, about a mile away. (Subways to Borough Hall station of the IRT Lexington and Seventh Avenue lines or the BMT Court Street station, Court Street end.)

The first buildings are all gathered around Cadman Plaza. Walk north from Joralemon Street to Tillary Street.

[1a.] Borough Hall/formerly **Brooklyn City Hall,** 209 Joralemon Street at Fulton and Court Sts. N side. 1846–1851. Gamaliel King. Cupola, 1898. Stoughton & Stoughton. ★

A Greek Revival palace, later crowned with a Victorian cupola, it presents a bold face to Cadman Plaza, made particularly monumental by the long, steep mass of steps to its entrance colonnade. First intended to be a lesser copy of New York's City Hall across the river, Borough Hall went through four designs. In the elapsed time, aesthetic moods changed, and the Federal world of 1811, the year of City Hall's completion, became the Greek Revival world of 1830–1860. According to Brooklyn's city directory, King was a grocer until 1830, then a carpenter, not unusual in an era when Thomas Jefferson designed the University of Virginia and the Capitol of the United States was built according to the competition-winning design of a doctor, William Thornton.

[1a.] Borough Hall on ca. 1905 postcard. County Courthouse (demol.) to left

[1b.] Brooklyn Municipal Building, 210 Joralemon St. SE cor. Court St. opposite Borough Hall. 1926. McKenzie, Voorhees & Gmelin.

The background building where much of the municipal bureaucracy functions (as contrasted with the foreground building, Borough Hall, the ceremonial center).

[1c.] Temple Bar Building, 44 Court St., NW cor. Joralemon St. 1901. George L. Morse.

The three unusual ogee-curved cupolas atop this building, Brooklyn's highest at the time, heralded the arrival of the 20th century to the Civic Center.

[2a.] Cadman Plaza (officially S. Parkes Cadman Plaza), bounded by Cadman Plaza W., Court, Joralemon, and Adams Sts. and the Brooklyn Bridge approaches. 1950–1960. Designed by various city and borough agencies. Christopher Columbus monument: statue, 1867, Emma Stebbins, sculptor; base and installation at this site, 1971, A. Ottavino. Senator Robert Francis Kennedy, sculpture, 1972. Anneta Duveen, sculptor.

Scarcely a plaza, this is an amorphous park created by demolition of several blocks east of Brooklyn Heights. A principal goal was the creation of a new setting for Civic Center buildings, to complement Borough Hall. Almost equally important fringe benefits were the elimination of the elevated (rapid transit) tracks that crossed the Brooklyn Bridge and crowded Fulton Street, and the easing of automobile traffic through street-widening. The Stebbins statue of Columbus originally stood in Central Park—it was carved two years after she completed *Angel of the Waters* for the Bethesda Fountain.

[2b.] New York State Supreme Court, 360 Adams St., S part of Cadman Plaza opposite Montague St. 1957. Shreve, Lamb & Harmon.

These architects are best known for the Empire State Building (1933). Note the verdigris lamp standards at the south end, saved from the now-demolished Hall of Records (1905. R. L. Daus).

[2c.] Statue of Henry Ward Beecher, near Johnson St., S part of Cadman Plaza. 1891. John Quincy Adams Ward, sculptor; Richard Morris Hunt, architect of the base.

Mr. Beecher, the preacher and brother of Harriet Beecher Stowe, was relocated from near Borough Hall as part of the new Cadman Plaza. The fence and lawn surrounding the sculpture are unfortunate, for Ward's strong concept needs to give people a chance to come right up to the base.

[2c.] Statue of Henry Ward Beecher   **[3a.]** Brooklyn General Post Office

[3a.] Brooklyn General Post Office, 271 Cadman Plaza E., NE cor. Johnson St. 1885–1891. Mifflin E. Bell (first designs); William A. Freret, successor (successive Supervising Architects, U.S. Treasury Dept.). North half, 1933, James Wetmore, supervising architect. ★

The original building at the south is exuberant granite Romanesque Revival. Deep reveals and strong modeling provide a rich play of light. The taller addition is humorless and barely in the same mold as its forebear.

[3b.] Federal Building and Court House, 275 Washington St., NE cor. Tillary St. on Cadman Plaza. 1961. Carson, Lundin & Shaw.

The embassy to Brooklyn from Washington.

[4.] Brooklyn War Memorial, N part of Cadman Plaza, opposite Orange St. 1951. Eggers & Higgins, architects. Charles Keck, sculptor.

Though its innards contain a large recreation hall, its primary use is as a wall completing the plaza's formal composition of terrace, paths, shrubs, trees, and lawn.

Return to and then follow Tillary Street to the east. Turn left at Jay Street to:

[5.] St. James Cathedral (Roman Catholic)/formerly St. James' Pro Cathedral, Jay St., bet. Cathedral Place and Chapel St. E side. 1903. George H. Streeton.

Georgian, with a handsome verdigris-copper-clad steeple.

The first church on this site (1822) became the cathedral of the Roman Catholic Diocese of Brooklyn in 1853, but around 1896, with the succession of Brooklyn's second bishop, it was officially renamed the pro cathedral. "Pro" in this instance meant "in place of," for that bishop was planning a new, elaborate cathedral of his own, the giant Immaculate Conception Cathedral [see Fort Greene 13.] which never materialized. The pro cathedral became the cathedral once again only in 1972. (Cathedral means, literally, that church which contains the *cathedra,* or chair, of the bishop. Many tourists, particularly in France, are in the habit of elevating all important-looking churches to cathedral status; it bears no relation to size, only to function. And only *one* church in any diocese can hold the cathedra and thereby bear that name.)

Return to Tillary Street and turn left; walk two blocks. Then turn right into Bridge Street.

[6a.] Former **Bridge Street Methodist Church**/now **Polytechnic Institute of New York Annex,** 311 Bridge St., bet. Johnson St. and Myrtle Ave. E side. 1844.

A Greek Revival temple in brick with wood columns and entablature; chaste, excepting the later Victorian stained glass which is exuberant even from the outside.

At Willoughby Street, turn right.

[6b.] New York Telephone Co., Long Island Headquarters, 101 Willoughby St., NE cor. Bridge St. 1931. Voorhees, Gmelin & Walker.

Brick with a graded palette; a delicate aesthetic. Note the equally delicate grillages over the ground floor windows and integrated into the railings of the subway entry at the corner.

[7a.] Former Jay Street Firehouse   Curbside Transit Information Pylon

[6c.] Office Building/originally **New York & New Jersey Telephone Company Building,** 81 Willoughby St., NE cor. Lawrence St. 1898. R. L. Daus.

Brooklyn's first telephone company headquarters. Look closely at the carvings around the entrance: the intertwined TC (for telephone company) over the door; the free use of bells, earpieces, and ancient wall telephones that were worked into the Beaux Arts decoration.

Turn left at Jay Street.

[7a.] Former **City of Brooklyn Fire Headquarters,** 365–367 Jay St., bet. Willoughby St. and Myrtle Ave. E side. 1892. Frank Freeman. ★

This is a building **to write home about.** A powerful Romanesque Revival, brick, granite, and tile structure, it is the New York branch (with Louis Sullivan's Condict Building) of the "Chicago School." Freeman learned much from afar by viewing H.H. Richardson's work, as did Sullivan.

[7b.] Transportation Building, 370 Jay St., NW cor. Willoughby St. 1950. William E. Haugaard & Andrew J. Thomas.

Headquarters of the **New York City Transit Authority.** The two gracious (though dingy) lobbies to the subway, at north and south ends, are fringe benefits gained from a building contiguous to its subway lines. Windows here read as "skin," rather than punctured holes in masonry, by the device of detailing the glass to be flush. Nightly money trains bring the take from all boroughs directly to a spur line in the building's bowels.

[10b.] Dime Savings Bank of Brooklyn: glories of Rome recalled on DeKalb Ave.

Gage & Tollner's (restaurant), 374 Fulton St., bet. Smith St. and Boerum Place. 1889. ★ Telephone: TR 5-5181.

Building and restaurant are (except for ungainly vertical sign on facade) much as they were the day they opened: plush, dark woodwork, mirrors, and gas-lit crystal glitter give a real rather than a decorator's version of the nineties.

Continue on Jay Street across Fulton—at this point its name becomes Smith—to Livingston Street. Here you may take a detour to the west or continue the main part of the tour by turning left on Livingston Street.

Downtown Brooklyn Detour: Nearby, along Schermerhorn and Livingston Streets, are a few interesting structures.

[8a.] N.Y.C. Board of Education Headquarters/originally **Benevolent Protective Order of Elks,** 110 Livingston St., SW cor. Boerum Place. 1926. McKim, Mead & White.

Mention of 110 Livingston (and the activities which go on within) is enough to cause **ennui** in many. The building, a tedious exercise in uninspired stone cutting, is appropriately boring, as well.

Transit Information Pylons, along Livingston St. and other Civic Center/ Downtown thoroughfares. 1975. Samuel Lebowitz Design & Planning, designers.

Locally referred to as **"the hockey sticks,"** these brown, anodized aluminum pylons attempt to make sense of the chaos of the complex municipal transit system.

[8b.] Brooklyn Friends Meeting House and School, 110 Schermerhorn St., SE cor. Boerum Place. ca. 1854. Enoch Straton, builder.

Once a freestanding structure with land and lawns, it is now **sand-wiched** between a widened Boerum Place and the huge volume of the Central Court Building adjacent.

[8c.] Central Court Building, 120 Schermerhorn St., SW cor. Smith St. 1932. Collins & Collins.

Similar in bulk to 110 Livingston Street (see above) but by less-renowned architects, this building **adds to the cityscape** through **the deep entranceway** formed by three tall arches that penetrate its **otherwise formidable facade.**

[8d.] Brooklyn House of Detention (for men), 275 Atlantic Ave., bet. Smith St. and Boerum Place. N side. La Pierre, Litchfield & Partners.

Cheerfully described as the **"Brooklyn Hilton."**

N.Y.C. Transit Authority Museum, Schermerhorn St., NW cor. Boerum Place. Downstairs, in former IND Court Street Subway Station.

A terrific underground museum featuring trains, turnstiles, towers (interlocking), and tesserae (of subway mosaics). Worth a descent. There is a token admission charge.

[8e.] Society for the Prevention of Cruelty to Children/originally **Brooklyn Public Library,** 67 Schermerhorn St., bet. Boerum Place and Court St. N side. ca. 1890. **[8f.] Schermerhorn Street Evangelical Church/**originally **German Evangelical Lutheran Church,** 63 Schermerhorn St., bet. Boerum Place and Court St. N side. ca. 1890.

A handsome pair of buildings done in the last days of the Romanesque Revival style in Brooklyn. Note how the chimney and church belfry are integrated into one form.

End of detour.

The regular tour resumes at Livingston Street and Gallatin Place. Turn left at Gallatin, go a block, and then turn right on Fulton St.

[9a.] A & S Department Store (Abraham & Straus), 420 Fulton St., bet. Gallatin Place and Hoyt St. E side. Main building, 1929, 1935. Starrett & Van Vleck.

Eight assorted buildings are interconnected to form the **great department store of Brooklyn.** Its closest Manhattan counterpart is Bloomingdale's. The section at the northeast corner of Livingston Street and Gallatin Place (1895) has the greatest architectural interest: granite, brownstone, and Roman brick combined with superb **Victorian craftsmanship.** The main building is mild **Art Deco.** And on Fulton Street are chocolate-brown-camouflaged **cast-iron facades** of the original store peeking over later, pompous, street-level alterations.

[9b.] Martin's (department store)/formerly **Offerman Building,** 503 Fulton St., bet. Bridge and Duffield Sts. N. side. 1891. Lauritzen & Voss. Altered.

The Duffield Street side preserves the Romanesque Revival detail in **a great incised sign** and handsome metalwork up high. Not so Fulton Street's face, where an unsympathetic alteration ignores the architecture it might have worked with in concert.

[10a.] Albee Square Mall, DeKalb Ave. NE cor. Albee Sq. W. Gruen Associates.

A glassy indoor shopping mall extending back to Flatbush Avenue Extension. Built on the site of the **old RKO Albee** movie theater, one of Downtown Brooklyn's **last biggies** (demolished 1979). The vaudeville impresario for whom the theater was named. Edward Franklin Albee, was playwright **Edward Albee's grandfather.**

[10b.] The Dime Savings Bank of Brooklyn, off Fulton St., at 9 DeKalb Ave., NE cor. Fleet St. 1907, 1932. Halsey, McCormick & Helmer.

It's the **interior** of this bank that's most remarkable—plan to visit it during bankers' hours. The decor is updated Roman, using gilded, monumental **Liberty-head dimes** as the predominant motif. Money must have been well-managed by those who could afford such splendor.

Follow DeKalb Avenue to the far side of Flatbush Avenue Extension.

[11.] Long Island University, Brooklyn Center, 385 Flatbush Ave. Ext., bet. DeKalb Ave. and Willoughby St. E side.

[11a.] Founder's Hall and Tristram W. Metcalf Hall, L.I.U./originally **Brooklyn Paramount Theater and Offices.** 1928. Altered 1950, 1962.

Brooklyn's **leading movie palace** was converted, in two steps, to university use: the office tower in 1950; the 4,400-seat auditorium, in 1962; the twelve intervening years witnessed the **swan song of popcorn** in these marble halls. A new campus is being given form to the north and features **a few distinguished newcomers:**

[11b.] Humanities Building, L.I.U. 1967. Davis, Brody & Assocs. and Horowitz & Chun.

Strip an existing warehouse to its reinforced concrete frame, provide it with new guts and veneer and, **presto,** a building fit for a university. Fine materials, detailing, and spaces make this **an extraordinary work.**

[11b.] Humanities Bldg., L.I. Univ.

[12b.] Con Edison, Bklyn. Division

[11c.] Library-Learning Center, L.I.U. 1975. **[11d.] Laboratory Building, Arnold and Marie Schwartz College of Pharmacy and Health Sciences, L.I.U.** 1976. Both by Davis, Brody Assocs. and Horowitz & Chun.

Linked to the earlier humanities building by a bright-red-painted **Vierendaal-trussed** glass-enclosed bridge, this crisp complex begins to knit together the disparate older buildings of the reworked Brooklyn Center campus.

Leave the L.I.U. campus and turn left onto Flatbush Avenue Extension.

[12a.] New York Telephone Company Office Building, 395 Flatbush Ave. Ext., bet. DeKalb Ave. and Fulton St. E side. 1976. Skidmore, Owings & Merrill.

[12b.] Consolidated Edison Company, Brooklyn Division, 30 Flatbush Ave., bet. Nevins and Livingston Sts. 1974. Skidmore, Owings & Merrill.

These two buildings form the eastern end of a renewal effort **designed to revitalize an area** which was once the entertainment center of the borough—Con Ed's building occupies the site of the Brooklyn Fox movie/vaudeville showplace, N.Y. Tel's erases the scars of a major re-building of the BMT subway interchange below. Though by the same architectural firm **the two buildings are very different in expression** and in choice of exterior materials. Architecturally, at least, Con Ed seems to have walked off the victor in this battle of the utilities.

[13.] Fulton Street Mall, along Fulton St. and DeKalb Ave. bet. Flatbush Ave. Ext. and Adams St. Seelye, Stevenson, Value & Knecht, engineers. Pomeroy, Lebduska, Assocs., architects.

The magnetism of the Fulton Street shopping area already fills the sidewalks with people. The mall **bestows a blessing upon the commotion** by widening the sidewalks, limiting vehicles to buses, and adding pavilions and lighting.

End of Civic Center/Downtown Brooklyn Walking Tour: The subway station here at Nevins Street and Flatbush offers both IRT Lexington Avenue and Seventh Avenue service. The DeKalb Avenue station, a block back along Flatbush Avenue Extension, provides connections to both BMT and IND subways.

BROOKLYN HEIGHTS

Colonized by well-to-do merchants and bankers from across the river, Brooklyn Heights as we know it today is the **suburban product** of a combined **land** and **"transit"** speculation—in this case the "transit" was the new steam-powered ferry. In 1814 **Robert Fulton's invention,** with financial backing from Hezekiah Pierrepont, first connected the two newly renamed Fulton Streets of Manhattan and Brooklyn by fast boats, giving occasion to Pierrepont and others **(Middagh, Hicks,** et al.) for profitable division and sale of their Heights **"farm land."** With the new ferry it was quicker and easier to go from **Fulton to Fulton** than to cross one of Manhattan's water boundaries farther north. This status continued until the New York and Harlem Railroad provided a connection with suburbs in Westchester County. A **surveyor's grid** marked the Heights into 25- by 100-foot lots as the system for parcel sales; although other subdivisions were made by speculators, the 25-foot dimension is today the **basic module** of the Heights.

That the oldest building still existing was built in 1820 (24 Middagh Street) is not surprising; Pierrepont's lots came on the market in 1819. Prior to this, as late as 1807, there had been **but seven houses on the Heights,** with perhaps 20 more at or near the ferry landing at the river's edge below. By 1890 the infill was **substantially complete,** and the architectural history of the Heights primarily spans those dates. Occasional buildings were built in random locations much later, but the principal pre-1890 urban fabric remained intact when the district was designated an **historic district** by the city, under its **Landmarks Preservation Law,** in 1965. Vacant lots on Willow Place afforded architects Joseph and Mary Merz a chance to add buildings [see 7c.] in serious modern architectural terms, but within the scale of the surrounding environment. These, and Ulrich Franzen's Columbia Heights addition to and adaptive reuse of, under the Landmarks Law, existing row houses [see 34a.], extend **a previously truncated architectural history** to the present.

[1.] Brooklyn Heights Historic District, generally bounded on the W and N by the Brooklyn-Queens Expwy. and Cadman Plaza W., on the S by Atlantic Ave., on the E by Henry St. S to Clark St. and an irregular line to Court St. and Atlantic Ave. District designated, 1965. ★

This was the first district in the city designated under the Landmarks Preservation Law. A good choice.

All the listings in the three walking tours below **lie within** the historic district *except where otherwise noted.*

South Heights Walking Tour: A circuit which begins at Court and Remsen Streets (across from Borough Hall) and ends nearby at Livingston and Clinton Streets. (Subway to Borough Hall station of IRT Lexington and Seventh Avenue lines or Court Street station of BMT local.)

Walk west on Remsen Street from Court Street.

[1a.] Title Guarantee Company/originally **The Franklin Building,** 186 Remsen St., bet. Court and Clinton Sts. S side. ca. 1890. Parfitt Bros. (Not within the historic district.)

One of four Romanesque Revival/Queen Anne red brick extravaganzas in this vicinity by these fraternal architects. [Also see 15a., b., and c.]

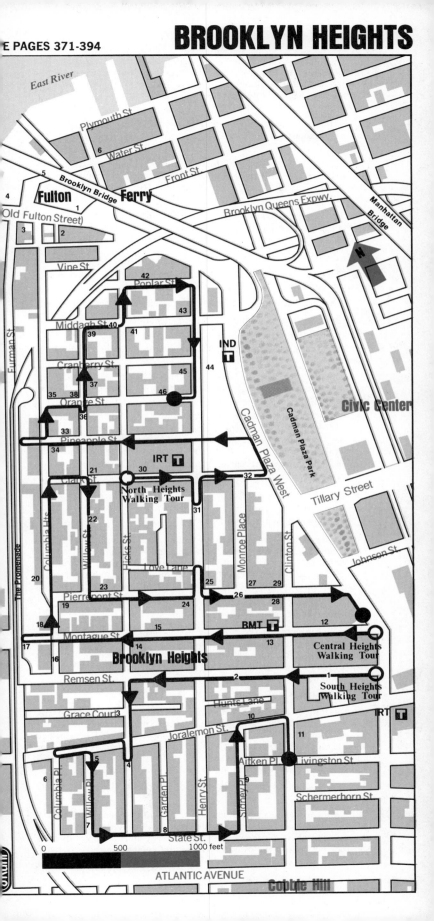

[1b.] Originally **Brooklyn Gas Light Company Headquarters (1857–1895)/**then **Brooklyn Union Gas Company Headquarters (1895–1914)/**now **McGarry Library, St. Francis College (1962),** 180 Remsen St., bet. Court and Clinton Sts. S side. 1857. (Not within the historic district.)

A miraculously saved **"Greek Temple"** which has seen a variety of uses in its more than one hundred years of life. The gas company h.q. moved next door in 1914 to:

[1c.] Originally **Brooklyn Union Gas Company Headquarters (1914–1962)/**now **St. Francis College,** 176 Remsen St., bet. Court and Clinton Sts. S side. 1914. Frank Freeman. (Not within the historic district.)

One of three Downtown Brooklyn buildings with **Classical colonnades** on the upper stories. Compare with 110 Livingston Street and the Central Court Building [Civic Center/Downtown Brooklyn 8a. and 8c.].

At this point you enter the Brooklyn Heights Historic District. ★

[2a.] The Brooklyn Club, 131 Remsen St., bet. Clinton and Henry Sts. N side. ca. 1858.

The paired Corinthian columns and pilasters are strong and elegant.

[2b.] Brooklyn Bar Association/formerly **Charles Condon Residence,** 123 Remsen St., bet. Clinton and Henry Sts. N side. ca. 1875.

Relatively jazzy chromatics of white limestone and dark red brick make this an exuberant note on Remsen Street.

[2c.] Our Lady of Lebanon Roman Catholic Church (Maronite Rite)/originally **Church of the Pilgrims (Congregational),** Remsen St., NE cor. Henry St. 1846. Richard Upjohn.

Certainly Upjohn was **avant-garde** for his time—this has been called the earliest example of Romanesque Revival in this country—a bold massing of ashlar stonework, a solid, carven image. The spire was removed due to deterioration and the high cost of its replacement. The doors at both the west and south portals are **salvage** from the ill-fated liner *Normandie* that burned and sank at its Hudson River berth in 1942.

Turn left on Hicks Street.

[3a.] Grace Church, Hicks St., SW cor. Grace Court. 1847. Richard Upjohn. **Parish House,** to the west, 1931.

Upjohn, after a **radical year** completing the Church of the Pilgrims (Our Lady of Lebanon) went **"straight,"** back to a more academic brownstone Gothic. A recent bit of urban charm is the entrance court, off Hicks Street at the south side, leading to the parish house; a backwater for pedestrians, it is crowned by the **umbrella of a glorious elm** some 80 feet tall. Benches are available.

[3b.] Grace Court. West of Hicks Street.

Its charm once derived from the **juxtaposition** of Grace Church on one side and the deep backyards of Remsen Street's houses on the other. The construction of the **banal** six-story red brick apartment in the 1960s changed that. An enormous elm on its sidewalk helped to mitigate the damage until it toppled in the fall of 1977.

[3c.] Grace Court Alley. E of Hicks St.

A real mews (for Remsen Street and Joralemon Street mansions). A walk to its end and then a turnabout will reveal many charms not visible from Hicks Street: No. 14's **arched bearing wall** of tooled brownstone ashlar is bold, almost industrial. Many of the carriage houses retain their handsome metal **hay cranes,** some used today only for holding potted plants. Note the crisp **contrasting quoins** on Nos. 2 and 4.

[4a.] 262–272 Hicks Street, SW cor. Joralemon St. (No. 272 crudely altered.) ca. 1885.

A **shingle-style** terrace, designed as a group composition. The corbeled brickwork, shingles, and picturesque profiles are romantic: they promised **"identity"** for the separate occupants. Each is different from its neighbor but part of the **overall architectural composition.**

[4b.] Engine Company 224, N.Y.C. Fire Department, 274 Hicks St., bet. Joralemon and State Sts. W side. 1903. Adams & Warren.

A house for fire engines, **in scale** with its house neighbors. A Renaissance Revival building, with copper dormers.

[4c.] 276–284 Hicks Street, bet. Joralemon and State Sts. W side.

Five brick arches (two half-round, three half-elliptical) once swallowed carriages. Note the sculptured **woman's head** on the dormer of No. 276. More across the street at Nos. 291, 293.

[1b.] Bklyn. Union Gas Co. in 1915

[4b.] Engine Co. 224, N.Y.C. Fire Dept.

[2b.] Brooklyn Bar Assoc. (entrance)   **[2c.]** Orig. Church of the Pilgrims

[4d.] Alhambra Center (Catholic Charities)/formerly **St. Charles Orthopaedic Clinic,** 277–283 Hicks St., bet. Joralemon and State Sts. Altered, 1921.

A nonindustrial use of the spiral stair: a handsome, elegant cast-iron form that **enriches** the street.

Double back and return to Joralemon Street; turn left.

[5.] 58 Joralemon Street, bet. Hicks and Willow Sts. S side. ca. 1847.

The world's only Greek Revival subway ventilator. It permits release of **air pressure** built up by the IRT expresses rushing through the East River Tunnel, which lies many feet below Joralemon Street.

[6a.] 29–75 Joralemon Street, bet. Hicks and Furman Sts. N side. 1844–1848.

Twenty-four houses step down Joralemon's hill. Basically Greek Revival, several have been altered. The stepping of the row gives a pleasant rhythm to the group, each pair roughly 30 inches up (or down) from its paired neighbors.

[6b.] Riverside Buildings (apartments), 4–30 Columbia Place, SW cor. Joralemon St. 1890. William Field & Son.

On the river's side they stood, until **truncated** by the Brooklyn-Queens Expressway construction. The original surrounded a central garden, part of which is still contained by the remaining units and the wall of the expressway.

Alfred T. White was a prominent and paternalistic Brooklyn citizen, whose motto **"philanthropy plus 5 percent"** made these, along with the Tower and Home Buildings [see Cobble Hill 4.], the original limited-profit housing: enlightened self-interest in the long term.

Now, back a few steps to Willow Place and turn right.

[7a.] 2–8 Willow Place, bet. Joralemon and State Sts. W side. ca. 1847.

Gothic Revival detail decorates simple brick row houses. In the battle of the Revival styles, the basic plan and spatial arrangement of row houses were almost constant; their cornices, lintels, doorways, and portals are **the variables** that identify the Federal style and the Greek and Gothic Revivals. In many cases, a Federal house was updated to the later fashion of **Greek Revival,** and subsequently from **Greek** to **Gothic.**

[7b.] 43–49 Willow Place. ca. 1846.

This now-bedraggled Greek Revival colonnade comes from a day when **colonnades denoted "class."**

[7b.] 43–49 Willow Place: Brooklyn's last row of colonnaded residences

[7c.] 40, 44, and 48 Willow Place (three separate buildings, one a double house). NW cor. State St. 1966. Joseph & Mary Merz.

These three buildings give new life to Willow Place **while respecting the nature and scale** of the older Heights. Garages occupy ground floor space, and cement block (in a special 8- by 8-inch size), here used sensitively and handsomely, assumes a dignity most thoughtless users miss by a mile. Note the compact integration of garage, rear garden terrace, and handsome wood fence on the State Street side of No. 48.

Turn left on State Street.

[8a.] Garden Place, bet. Joralemon and State Sts.

A handsome urban space, one block long, contained on four sides. Note the terra-cotta, brick, and limestone Queen Anne (No. 26), the **Hansel and Gretel** ex-carriage house (No. 21), and the intruders from

Queens (Nos. 17, 19, 19A). Nos. 40 through 56 form a handsome terrace of row houses.

[8b.] 103–107 State Street, NW cor. Sidney Place. ca. 1848.

A trio, but only No. 107 still has the elegant cast-iron balcony that allows **French doors** to the living room floor.

[7c.] Garment, Clyne, and Merz Residences: 40, 44, 48 Willow Place (r to l)

Turn left onto Sidney Place.

[9a.] Sidney Place, bet. State and Joralemon Sts.

A more varied, more charming version of Garden Place. Its architecture ranges more widely, including all that Garden Place offers but adds a church, St. Charles Borromeo, and such specialties as a 6½-story Greek Revival house! The **front gardens** on the east side between State Street and Aitken Place are unusual [also see 155–159 Willow Street, 22e.]. Nos. 31–49 form a variably altered Greek Revival row (1846–1851).

[9b.] St. Charles Borromeo Church (Roman Catholic), Sidney Place, NE cor. Aitken Place. 1869. P. C. Keely.

A simplified brick Gothic Revival in maroon-painted brick. The plain interior is decorated with wood **"carpenter Gothic"** arches and trim.

[9c.] 18 Sidney Place (apartments), opposite Aitken Place. W side. ca. 1838.

Bold Doric columns and entablature signalled an "important" mansion **(originally three stories and basement);** three more floors were added for its life as a girls' residence. The result is startling at first glance, for it looks no more than a neat, **six-story-plus-basement Greek Revival** house.

Turn right on Joralemon Street.

[10a.] 135 Joralemon Street, bet. Henry and Clinton Sts. N side. ca. 1833.

Opposite-hand plan from **24 Middagh Street** [see 39b.]. Their similarities are concealed by the post–Civil War porch with cast-iron work and the fact that this house is contained between two large buildings.

[10b.] 129 Joralemon Street, bet. Henry and Clinton Sts. N side. 1891. C. P. H. Gilbert.

Squeezed between two undistinguished apartment buildings from two different and later eras, this **grandly scaled dowager** of a house reminds one of a person who has come overdressed to a party.

Turn right on Clinton Street.

[11a.] 138–140 Clinton Street, bet. Joralemon St. and Aitken Place. W side. ca. 1855.

Lintels and cornice lush with volutes and garlands, in cast iron. The detail and profiles survived well in comparison with those carved in brownstone.

[11b.] Packer Collegiate Institute, 170 Joralemon St., bet. Court and Clinton Sts. S side. 1854. Minard Lafever. Addition (Katherine Sloan Pratt House), 1957.

This school is in the style of a brick and brownstone Victorian Gothic **"castle";** its 1957 antiqued addition tries not to detract from the old building's forms.

[11b.] Packer Collegiate Institute   **[12b.]** Orig. National Title Guaranty

[11c.] Originally **St. Ann's Church (Protestant Episcopal)/**now **Auditorium of Packer Collegiate Institute,** Clinton St., NE cor. Livingston St. 1869. James Renwick, Jr.

Brownstone and limestone of different colors and textures make an exuberant and **unrestrained extravaganza.** Renwick produced more academically correct Gothic Revival churches at Manhattan's Grace and St. Patrick's (1846 and 1858–1877, respectively). Perhaps by the time of St. Ann's **his self-confidence had mushroomed.** The copybooks of the Pugins, used at Grace, were discarded in favor of the current events of the architectural scene, particularly the "new" museum at Oxford, by Deane & Woodward, designed and built with the eager assistance of John Ruskin, hence "Ruskinian Gothic."

St. Ann's is **monumental in scale** but **diminutive in size** and therefore doesn't overwhelm its row-house-scaled surroundings.

Home of the Excelsiors: A plaque on the carefully groomed row house at 133 Clinton Street, southeast corner of Livingston Street, identifies this building as once the clubhouse of the Jolly Young Bachelors. By 1854 that social club had evolved into the Excelsiors, an amateur baseball club with the distinction of having as their pitcher James Creighton, credited with having tossed the first curve ball! With the removal from Brooklyn first of the Dodgers and then of their ballpark, Ebbets Field, this brownstone remains one of the last vestiges of organized baseball in the borough.

End of South Heights Walking Tour: To reach the Borough Hall/Court Street subway stations, return to Joralemon Street and walk one block east. If filled with energy, two other Brooklyn Heights walks follow. For a change of pace, a respite, a refreshment, walk south to Atlantic Avenue. [See Cobble Hill.]

Central Heights Walking Tour: Starts and ends at Court and Montague Streets. (Subways to Borough Hall station of IRT Seventh Avenue and Lexington Avenue lines or east (escalator) end of Court Street station of BMT local.)

Montague Street: In Civil War days and later, this was the road to the Wall Street ferry, dipping down (until 1946, the time of the Esplanade) to a water's edge terminal, where Pier 4 is now. A **stone bridge** (1855) by Minard Lafever and a later **passarelle** called the **"Penny Bridge,"** both located west of Pierrepont Place, once carried the brow of the Heights over Montague Street's steep incline, as well as over its **cable car line.**

Walk west on Montague Street.

[12a.] Brooklyn Savings Bank, 205–215 Montague Street, NW cor. Cadman Plaza W. 1962. Carson, Lundin & Shaw. (Not within the historic district.)

In 1963, "urban renewal" swallowed this bank's great Frank Freeman edifice at the northeast corner of Pierrepont and Clinton Streets, his one exercise in revived Roman pomp. In its place we have a neat work which does, at least, hold the street line of Cadman Plaza West—no redundant "plazas" here.

[12b.] Originally **National Title Guaranty Building,** 185 Montague St., bet. Cadman Plaza W. and Clinton St. N side. 1930. Corbett, Harrison & MacMurray. Entrance altered. (Not within the historic district.)

Avant-garde in its time, its Art Deco decor was expressed via **bold three-dimensional massing,** fresh to this day.

[12c.] Citibank, People's Trust Branch/ originally **People's Trust Company,** 183 Montague St., bet. Cadman Plaza W. and Clinton St. N side. 1903. Mowbray & Uffinger. Pierrepont Street rear addition, 1929. Shreve, Lamb & Harmon. (Not within the historic district.)

This is a D. W. Griffith version of a Roman temple. The bank, unfortunately, is neither staffed nor patronized by bacchanalian revelers, so that the total effect is a little wistful, like last year's disused movie set. In marble, not just wire lath and plaster, it states: "more is better." The sculpture in the pediment is Pop Art, particularly when overlaid with anti-pigeon spikes.

[12d.] Manufacturers Hanover Trust Company/formerly **Brooklyn Trust Company,** 177 Montague St., NE cor. Clinton St. 1915. York & Sawyer. (Not within the historic district.)

The bottom is an Italian palace; the top, some Englishman's version of an Italian palace: Corinthian engaged columns rest on rusticated tooled limestone.

[12d.] Manufacturers Hanover Bank **[13b.]** Holy Trinity Episcopal Church

At this point you enter the Brooklyn Heights Historic District.

[13a.] Originally **Franklin Trust Company (office building),** 164 Montague St., SW cor. Clinton St. 1888. George L. Morse.

A granite, rockface base sunk **within a moat** bears limestone arches and, in turn, brick and terra-cotta piers, columns, and arches; capped with a dormered **red tile** roof. A gem.

[13b.] Holy Trinity Protestant Episcopal Church, 157 Montague St., NW cor. Clinton St. 1847. Minard Lafever.

Brownstone, unfortunately, weathers poorly. The interior is cast and painted terra cotta, rather than carved stone. Reredos by **Frank Freeman.**

A bust of its well-known pastor John Howard Melish, by **William Zorach,** is bracketed from the north side of the entrance vestibule.

Montague, the shopping street: Only four blocks long, Montague is a chameleon in that short stretch. It serves residents of the Heights at its west and transient Civic Center frequenters at its east. With rising rents the stores (and their addresses) shift. Among the pluses, three—count 'em—*three* book stores: **Womrath's Books** (with greeting cards), No. 149, **Community Book Store** (new, hard and soft), No. 162, **Boro Book Shop** (used and old), No. 154; for the home: **Summa** (prints of old Brooklyn and elsewhere), No. 152, **Meuniers** (tasteful glassware, china, kitchen utensils), No. 140, **Hudson Bay Leather,** handcrafted hides, No. 91, **Women's Exchange** (precious things), No. 76; a raft of boutiques always in flux such as **Crocus, Zig Zag, Taurus, Off-Price, Takes Two to Tango, and the French Revolution**; food to cook with: **Lassen & Hennig's** (diverse exotica), No. 114, **Leaf & Bean** (tea/coffee), No. 136, **Perelandra** (natural), No. 154, **Cheese Cellar** (what else?), No. 128, and food to eat: Chinese, Mexican, Greek, Italian, Continental, bagels, delicatessen, patisserie, seafood, ice creams, and more. Enjoy!

[14.] Hotel Bossert, 98 Montague St., SE cor. Hicks St. 1909. Matching addition to S, 1912. Both by Helmle & Huberty.

This "modern" hotel was, in the twenties, one of the fashionable centers of Brooklyn social life: the **Marine Roof** (decorated like a yacht by modernist architect Joseph Urban) for dining and dancing offered an unequaled view of the Manhattan skyline and harbor. The home of its founder, Louis Bossert, a millwork manufacturer, still stands. [See N Brooklyn/Bushwick-Ridgewood 12.]

[15a.] The Berkeley-The Grosvenor, 111 and 115 Montague St., bet. Henry and Hicks Sts. N. side. 1885. Parfitt Bros.

Twin Queen Anne brownstone, terra-cotta, and brick apartment houses. **Look up!**

[15b.] The Montague, 105 Montague St., bet. Henry and Hicks Sts. N side. ca. 1885. Parfitt Bros.

Another Queen Anne extravaganza.

[15c.] The Arlington, 62 Montague St., bet. Hicks St. and Montague Terrace. S side. ca. 1900. Parfitt Bros.(?)

And yet another, this one taking frank advantage of the west view to the harbor.

[15d.] The Heights Casino, 75 Montague St., bet. Hicks St. and Pierrepont Place, N side. 1905. Boring & Tilton.

Its founders described this indoor squash and tennis club as a **"country club in the sky."** Handsome brickwork. Note the similarity to the corner apartment building—when the Casino sold its adjacent outdoor tennis courts it extracted certain visual concessions.

[16.] 1–13 Montague Terrace, bet. Remsen and Montague Sts. ca. 1886.

A complete "terrace" (in the English sense of set of row houses) in almost perfect condition.

Take a detour to see the Manhattan skyline.

[17.] The Esplanade, W of Montague Terrace, Pierrepont Place, and Columbia Heights bet. Remsen and Orange Sts. 1951. Andrews & Clark, engineers; Clarke & Rapuano, landscape architects.

The Promenade, as it is known to locals, is a fringe benefit of the construction of this section of the Brooklyn-Queens Expressway, earlier proposed by Robert Moses to bisect the Heights. **Fred Tuemmler** of the City Planning Department created one of the few **brilliant solutions** for the relationship of automobile, pedestrian, and city. A **cantilevered esplanade** was extended out from the level of the Heights to **overlook the harbor** on a fourth level over two levels of traffic and the feeder road for piers below: Furman Street. It is simple and successful: mostly hexagonal asphalt paving block, painted steel railings, hardy shrubbery, and honey locust trees.

Return to the street and turn left onto Pierrepont Place.

[18.] 2 and 3 Pierrepont Place/originally **Alexander M. White and Abiel Abbot Low Houses,** bet. Pierrepont Place and Montague Sts. W side. 1857. Frederick A. Peterson.

The **most elegant** brownstones left in New York. Two of an original row of three, all by the architect of **the Cooper Union:** No. 1, the Henry E. Pierrepont House, was demolished in 1946 in favor of a playground at the time of the esplanade-expressway construction.

Seth Low, **father of Abiel,** was a New Englander who made a "killing" in the China trade. Seth Low, **son of Abiel,** was mayor of Brooklyn, president of Columbia College, then mayor of consolidated New York City.

Alfred Tredway White, Brooklyn **philanthropist** (Brooklyn's Tower, Home, and Riverside Apartments, q.v., Brooklyn Botanic's Japanese Garden, etc.) lived at No. 2 in his youth.

A peek at Pierrepont Street and then back, into Columbia Heights.

[19a.] 6 Pierrepont Street, bet. Pierrepont Place and Willow St. S side. ca. 1890.

Romanesque Revival with a strong, rockface stair, elaborate foliate carved reliefs, and a bay window (overlooking the bay!).

[19b.] 18–14 Pierrepont Street, bet. Pierrepont Place and Hicks St. S side. ca. 1901.

Another "terrace" where the whole is greater than the sum of its parts.

[20a.] 210–220 Columbia Heights: the best remaining brownstone group

[20a.] 210–220 Columbia Heights, NW cor. Pierrepont St. 1852–1860.

Two pairs and two singles, altered, but the best remaining example of group-mansions in brownstone—some have been painted light colors. Note No. 210's rich **Corinthian** capitals.

[20b.] 160 Columbia Heights (apartments), SW cor. Clark St. 1937. A. Rollin Caughey.

An orange brick Art Deco work with corner casement windows and great views of Manhattan.

Turn right into Clark Street.

[21.] Originally **Towers Hotel/**now **Jehovah's Witnesses Residence Hall,** 25 Clark St., NE cor. Willow St. 1928. Starrett & Van Vleck.

Comfortably affluent materials: brick on random ashlar on granite with lots of molded terra-cotta decorations. The four **colonnaded corner towers** (for which the hotel had been named) used to be **spotlighted** after sunset.

Turn right again into Willow Street.

[22a.] Dansk Sømandskirke, 102 Willow St., bet. Clark and Pierrepont Sts. W side.

A brownstone lives again as the Danish Seamen's Church.

[22b.] 109 Willow Street, bet. Clark and Pierrepont Sts. E side, 1905.

This neo-Federal house is gross, with fat columns, ill-proportioned window panes and muntins, crudely cast concrete lintels, and thick joints in the brickwork. People who embrace archeology frequently **miss the point** of the styles they wish to emulate.

[22c.] 108–112 Willow St.: Queen Anne   [22e.] 157 Willow Street (entrance)

[22c.] 108, 110, and 112 Willow Street, bet. Clark and Pierrepont Sts. W side. ca. 1880.

The **"shingle style"** in Brooklyn. Picturesque massing and profiles produce odd internal spaces and balconies, **for our contemporary fun.** Terra-cotta reliefs, elaborate doorways, bay windows, towers, dormers. The English architect **Richard Norman Shaw** was group leader for these fantasies; in his bailiwick he produced what the English called "Queen Anne." The **most successful** grouping of Queen Anne in all of N.Y.C.

Queen Anne: A style of English architecture introduced to this country in the British pavilion at the 1876 Philadelphia Centennial Exposition, it remained popular for some twenty years. Its name is deceiving. Queen Anne of England died in 1714, long before this style was dubbed. But it was in her reign that some of the Gothic and Renaissance elements found in this playful style were earlier revived.

[22d.] 151 Willow Street, bet. Clark and Pierrepont Sts. E side. ca. 1870.

Set back from the adjacent row houses, this carriage house's handsome brick driveway is splayed out away from the street to create the illusion of less depth.

 [22e.] 155–159 Willow Street, bet. Clark and Pierrepont Sts. E side. ca. 1829.

Three charmers (in a league with No. 24 Middagh but in brick) in excellent condition and not too far from their original state. Note **glass pavers** set into sidewalk at No. 157, about which many apocryphal but unsubstantiated stories are told—that they skylight a tunnel leading to the "stable" at No. 151, for instance. The three houses are askew from Willow Street's present line since they were built to the earlier geometry of Love Lane, which once extended this far west.

Take a left onto Pierrepont Street.

[23a.] 35 Pierrepont Street (apartments), bet. Willow and Hicks Sts. N side. 1929. Mortimer E. Freehof.

The roofscape and silhouette of this apartment have every stop pulled out. A pleasantly synthetic "Renaissance" bag of tricks.

[23b.] Hotel Pierrepont, 55 Pierrepont St., bet. Hicks and Henry Sts. N side. 1928. H.I. Feldman.

From the days when even **speculative** hotels had lion finials and griffin gargoyles!

[24.] Orig. Herman Behr Res. (detail)   [25a.] 161 Henry Street (apartments)

[23c.] The Woodhull, 62 Pierrepont St., bet. Hicks and Henry Sts. S side. 1911. George Fred Pelham.

The grundy ground floor belies the extravagant Edwardian French architecture above; neither Edward's England nor his contemporary France had this. A local Heights entrepreneur filled in the sad gap!

[24.] 84 Pierrepont Street/originally **Herman Behr Residence**/later **Palm Hotel**/later **Franciscan House of Studies,** SW cor. Henry St. 1890. Frank Freeman. Addition, 1919.

After Behr, this mansion had a profane, then sacred existence prior to being converted in 1977 to apartments. In the Palm Hotel's declining years it was said to have housed **the local Polly Adler** and her ladies; it then served as a residence for Franciscan brothers. Despite the structure's social vagaries, Freeman's design remains an **important asset** to the Heightscape.

[25a.] 161 Henry Street (apartments), NE cor. Pierrepont St. 1906. Schneider & Herter.

Compare with No. 62 Pierrepont. In the last 30 years, has the external architecture of an apartment building meant anything to an apartment dweller? This strong character shows that *it used to,* bestowing identity to its residents in the process, as does Manhattan's Dakota.

A short one-block detour to the left, to Love Lane.

[25b.] Love Lane and **College Place,** both in the block bet. Henry and Hicks Sts. N of Pierrepont St.

The names of these two **byways** are more charming than the reality, but **the mystery** is worth a detour. Note that Love Lane is skewed from the grid's rectilinear geometry.

[26a.] 104 Pierrepont Street/originally **Thomas Clark Residence,** bet. Henry and Clinton Sts. ca. 1857.

A brownstone row-mansion. Note the ornate console brackets and the verdigris bronze railing atop the majestic stoop.

[26b.] 108 Pierrepont Street/originally **P. C. Cornell House,** at Monroe Place. S side. 1840.

Harried remnants of a great Greek Revival **double house;** the only original part is the **anthemion-ornamented** pediment over the front door. Once two stories and basement, it was made three when No. 114, its adjacent twin, was converted from **mirror-image** into a Romanesque Revival **town castle.**

[27.] Church of the Saviour: Unitarian   **[28.]** Long Island Historical Society

[30a.] St. George Hotel: orig. wing   **[30a.]** St. George Hotel: rear wing

[26c.] The Brooklyn Women's Club/originally **George Cornell House,** 114 Pierrepont St. at Monroe Place. S side. 1840.

Originally the mirror image of 108; altered **(drastically** would be a mild adverb here) in 1887 for publisher **Alfred C. Barnes** [see Fort Greene 6b.]. **A tower for Rapunzel** is available here. Note the single granite column, Romanesque-capped, supporting the "bay."

Monroe Place: A 700-foot-long (80-foot-wide) space, a quiet backwater on axis with Cornell houses described above. The **proportion** of the street and its **containment** at both ends are far more important than the buildings it contains, for this, like Sidney, Garden, and Willow Places, is a product of the **staggered grid** that fortuitously made this area so much richer than most of grid-planned Manhattan or Brooklyn. Do take a look at two houses at the north end: No. 3 (1849) and its later cast-iron planter and goldfish pond, and No. 12 (1847) where shutters have been returned to the facade.

[26d.] Appellate Division, N.Y. State Supreme Court, Monroe Place, NW cor. Pierrepont St. 1938. Slee & Bryson.

A prim and proper Classical Revival monument of the thirties with some Egyptian Revival touches. Not an ugly building, but a boring one.

[27.] First Unitarian Church/properly **Church of the Saviour,** Pierrepont St. NE cor. Monroe Place. 1844. Minard Lafever.

Lafever, a carpenter by training, was a **talented and prolific architect** who practiced in many styles and was, as a result, responsible for a well-known and well-used copybook for builders, *Beauties of Modern Architecture.*

[28.] Long Island Historical Society, 128 Pierrepont St., SW cor. Clinton St. 1878. George B. Post, architect. Olin Levi Warner, facade sculptures.

Post used a bright but narrow range of **"Italian reds,"** in a time when earth colors were popular, from the **polychromy of Ruskin**—see St. Ann's Church [11c.]—to the near **monochromy of Richardsonian Romanesque,** such as the Jay Street Fire House.

High-pitched slate roofs are visible only from abnormal points of view, such as cater-corner across the temporary parking lot from Cadman Plaza. However, the **tower** over the entrance stair, hall, and elevator, bears a very visible **slate-sheathed pyramid.** The monochromatic palette tempers an exuberant range of detail: pilasters, arches, medallions, cornices, sculpture. At the entrance, Viking and Indian flank the doors over Corinthian pilasters.

One of the city's **great architectural treasures,** outside and in. Inside there are always small exhibits to view and a great local history collection. Open to the public; telephone: MA 4-0890.

[29.] St. Ann's Building and Episcopal School/formerly **Crescent Athletic Club,** 129 Pierrepont St., NW cor. Clinton St. 1906. Frank Freeman.

Once the home of one of Brooklyn's most affluent clubs, it boasted a swimming pool, squash courts, a gym, and three grand two-story spaces surrounded by mezzanines. Its life as a club ended in 1940.

End of Central Heights Walking Tour: If hungry, Montague Street's eateries are only one block away, as is the BMT Court Street subway station at Montague and Clinton Streets. The IRT is a block further east at Court.

North Heights Walking Tour: Of the three walks through Brooklyn Heights this offers the greatest contrasts: old and very new, affluent and modest, tiny and large, domestic and institutional; there is even some little industry here. Start on the southwest corner of Clark and Hicks Streets, less than a block west of the IRT Seventh Avenue subway station turnstiles (which are within the St. George Hotel Walk east along Clark Street across from the old hotel, take a brief detour south into Henry Street and then return to Clark and continue east.

[30a.] St. George Hotel, 51 Clark St., bet. Hicks and Henry Sts. N side. Original building, 1885. Augustus Hatfield. Additions, 1890–1923. Some by Montrose W. Morris. Tower, 1930. Emery Roth.

The contrasts of the North Heights are properly introduced by those of the St. George, a set of **architectural accretions** which occupies a **full city block** and which once comprised the **city's largest hotel.** Interior public spaces—not the lobby—such as the ballroom and the mirror-ceilinged pool (closed) reflect **exuberant Art Deco** renovations of the late twenties, the hotel's heyday. Outside, the **oldest portions** are the most fascinating: the mansard-roofed **original** (opposite No. 52 Clark), and the two crusty wings fronting mid-block on Pineapple Street. Also note the crisp white terra-cotta 1913 addition at Henry and Pineapple Streets—there's a colorful **"heraldic shield"** up high, near the corner.

[30b.] Clark Lane (apartments), 52 Clark St. bet. Hicks and Henry Sts. S side. ca. 1927. Slee & Bryson.

Eclectic architects found **a style for every occasion.** These, later the designers of the Appellate Courthouse [26d.], choose Romanesque columns and arches and **grotesque Gothic gargoyles** for this apartment hotel.

[32.] Cadman Towers apartment complex: view from 101 Clark St. onto low roofs

[34a.] Jehovah's Witnesses' Dorm./Library. **[21.]** Orig. Towers Hotel to rear

[31a.] First Presbyterian Church, 124 Henry St. S of Clark St. W side. 1846. W. B. Olmsted. Memorial doorway, 1921. James Gamble Rogers.
[31b.] German Evangelical Lutheran Zion Church, 125 Henry St. S of Clark St. E side. 1888.

These two churches occupy sites almost across from one another. The Presbyterian is solid, stolid, and self-satisfied. The Lutheran is spare and prim (and minus its northern spire). Sometimes a single thistle can be more satisfying than a bouquet of roses.

The route around Cadman Towers and through Pineapple Walk takes you briefly outside the Brooklyn Heights Historic District.

[32.] Cadman Towers, 101 Clark St., bet. Henry St. and Cadman Plaza W. N side., 10 Clinton St. at Cadman Plaza W., W side, plus row housing along Clark St., Monroe Place, and Cadman Plaza W. 1973. Glass & Glass and Conklin & Rossant. (Not within the historic district.)

A **difficult programmatic challenge:** design high-density—therefore high-rise—housing to exploit spectacular views, while respecting the small-scale texture of the surrounding Heights; do so on a constricted site split by a through street; and don't fail to provide for a mix of residential units, shopping, movie theater, house of worship, nursery school, community center, indoor parking, and yes, lots of green space. The result is **one of the city's handsomest** urban renewal projects!

Clad in cool concrete and warm-toned striated block, **two elegant, sawtooth-shaped apartment towers** rise from low parking garages which are, in turn, wrapped with maisonettes whose three stories relate perfectly to the scale of the Heightscape. The remainder of the ground space is used for the shopping area, theater, etc., which leaves no room there for open space so, **ingeniously,** the greenery was placed **on the roof** of the garages for use only by residents and their guests, and connected by a bridge over Clark Street. Regrettably movie, nursery school, and sanctuary (to make up for amenities lost when the site was cleared) remain empty.

Turn left at Cadman Plaza West and left again into the pedestrian mall called Pineapple Walk. Continue west along Pineapple Street itself (back into the historic district), through the dark back side of the St. George Hotel—its rear mysteriously more intriguing than its Clark Street main facade.

[33.] 13 Pineapple Street, bet. Willow St. and Columbia Heights. N side. ca. 1830.

An unusually wide, gray-shingled, white-trimmed single house. Look: the shingles return along both side walls.

[34a.] Jehovah's Witnesses' Dormitory and Library Facility, 119 Columbia Heights, SE cor. Pineapple St. 1970. Ulrich Franzen & Assocs.

An extraordinarily **sensitive response** to new design within the context of the Landmarks Law. The old row house facades to the south of this crisp new building are integrated internally so all function **as one unit.** As a result the stoops are no longer functional but still add to the **visual continuity** of the area. Prior to the official designation of the Heights as a historic district, row houses similar to these were wantonly destroyed by the same organization to build Nos. 124 and 107 further along the street.

If you haven't seen the lower Manhattan skyline from these bluffs, cross Columbia Heights and walk to the right along the Promenade for a block. [For more on this spectacular spot, see 17.] The tour picks up one block north at:

[34b.] Jehovah's Witnesses of Brooklyn Heights Residence, 107 Columbia Heights, SE cor. Orange St. 1960. Frederick G. Frost, Jr. & Assocs.

One of a number of pre-Landmarks Law high-rise dormitories proliferating in the Heights for those who proselytize their faith. New buildings such as this and older ones, rebuilt for this sect's needs, concentrate along Columbia Heights and nearby streets. [For example, see 21.]. Local residents fear that too much Heights land and architecture is being **gobbled up** for the Witnesses' seemingly unending expansionism.

[35.] Hotel Margaret, 97 Columbia Hts., NE cor. Orange St. 1889. Frank Freeman.

Brooklyn here foresaw metal and glass construction of post–World War II. The ornate sheet metal panels have **a nautical look** with their **exposed rivet heads;** appropriate for its harbor-watching tenants. The ranks of fire escapes are not original.

Proceed east along Orange Street and make a short detour to the right along Willow Street to see:

[36.] 70 Willow Street/originally **Adrian van Sinderen House,** bet. Orange and Pineapple Sts. W side. ca. 1839.

A wide Greek Revival house, originally freestanding, now **cheek-by-jowl** with Jehovah's Witnesses to the north. Former owners filled the southern gap with a set-back-from-street stair tower (ca. 1933).

U-turn now on Willow Street and proceed north.

[37a.] 57 Willow Street/originally **Robert White House,** NE cor. Orange St. ca. 1824.

The Orange Street wall is a lusty composition of chimneys, pitched roofs, real and blind windows—but much of it is hidden by dense ivy in the summer.

[37b.] 47–47A Willow Street, bet. Orange and Cranberry Sts. E side. ca. 1860.

When you're **greedy,** divide your property into its smallest salable components. Here, the less-than-12-foot internal dimensions are brilliantly arranged in spite of that greed!

Charlie Brown's Book-Gallerie, 34 Middagh St., near Hicks St. Telephone: 624-1373.

A serious little bookshop (used books only). Great for browsing and buying if you like New Yorkiana, old children's books, first editions, or whatever strikes its owner's fancy (or has come on the market).

[35.] Hotel Margaret (1907 postcard)   **[37a.]** 57 Willow Street residence

Marcolini Wine & Liquor, 66 Hicks St., cor. Cranberry St. Telephone: 875-0590.

If you don't confine browsing to books, sample (off-premises only) the wide selection of wines this warm, friendly shop stocks. Don't good wines go well with good architecture?

[38a.] 11 Cranberry Street/originally **Mott Bedell Residence.** ca. 1840.
[38b.] 13, 15, and 19 Cranberry Street. ca. 1829–1834. NW cor. Willow St.

A fine grouping, the last three being an original matching row (note window lintels and arched entries of Nos. 13 and 19), all altered. Note the **carefully designed** modern fence and gate of No. 19 on Willow Street.

[39a.] 20–26 Willow Street, SW cor. Middagh St. 1846.

No-nonsense Greek Revival, painted brick and brownstone "terrace." Straightforward, austere, yet elegant. Two-story porches **at the rear** look out upon the harbor, their views framed by projecting masonry walls. (No. 22 was the **Henry Ward Beecher** house.)

[39b.] 24 Middagh Street residence: the queen of Brooklyn Heights houses

[39b.] 24 Middagh Street/formerly **Eugene Boisselet House,** SE cor. Willow St. 1824.

The **queen of Brooklyn Heights houses** (Nos. 2 and 3 Pierrepont Place [18.] are the twin-kings). Wood-painted, gambrel-roofed Federal house with a garden cottage connected by a garden wall. **Special notes** are the exquisitely carved Federal doorway and quarter-round attic windows. Throughout, proportion, rhythm, materials, and color **are in concert.**

Having turned the corner onto Middagh Street, continue east.

[40.] Middagh Street, bet. Willow and Hicks Sts. ca. 1817.

One of the **earliest** streets in the Heights, it has most of the remaining wood houses. Aside from the glorious No. 24, they are now a motley lot: **No. 28,** 1829, mutilated beyond recognition; **No. 30,** 1824, Greek Revival entrance and pitched roof still recognizable in spite of the tawdry asphalt shingles; **No. 25,** 1824, mutilated; **No. 27,** 1829, Italianate brownstone in wood shingles with painted trim; **No. 29,** similar to 27; **Nos. 31 and 33,** 1847, mutilated.

From the Middagh St.-Hicks St. corner, before you turn left onto Hicks St., you can see across from the local public school:

[40a.] 56 Middagh Street, bet. Hicks and Henry Sts. 1829. Porch added ca. 1845.

Bold Doric columns give it **guts and style.**

[41a.] Originally **Joseph Bennett Residence,** 38 Hicks St. ca. 1830. Restored, 1976. **[41b.]** Originally **Michael Vanderhoef Residence,** 40 Hicks St. ca. 1831. Restored, 1976. **[41c.] 38A Hicks Street** (behind No. 38). All bet. Middagh and Poplar Sts. W side.

For many years the two multistoried frame buildings which front on Hicks Street were in a sad state of disrepair. Then, **with care and concern,** the current owners removed the composition shingles and frayed clapboards and **restored the facades** to something resembling their original condition. **Hurrah!** Down the alley between can be seen a rare back house on the Heights, a masonry building built with no direct access to the street except via this passageway.

[42.] Originally **Brooklyn Children's Aid Society Orphanage,** 57 Poplar St., bet. Hicks and Henry Sts. N side. 1883.

Built as a home for indigent newsboys, this ornate Victorian institutional building was abandoned during the urban renewal craze of the 1960s—by then it was being used as a machine works—before **adaptive reuse** became the new watchwords. It awaits adoption. **Lost** in the Cadman Plaza Urban Renewal Plan was Rome Brothers Printshop (southwest corner of Cranberry Street and today's Cadman Plaza West), where Walt Whitman himself set the type for his *Leaves of Grass*). **Saved,** however, was an old candy factory—see opposite.

Turn right up the hill on Henry Street—the west side lies within the historic district, the east side lies outside it—as far as Clark Street.

[43.] Henry Street Studios/originally **Mason Au & Magenheimer Candy Company,** 20 Henry St., NW cor. Middagh St. 1885. Theobald Engelhardt. Reconstruction, 1975. Pomeroy, Lebduska Assocs., architects; Martyn and Don Weston, associated architects.

The no-nonsense, **skin-and-bones architecture** of this old factory (brick bearing walls, heavy timber columns and beams, mill flooring, high ceilings) all admirably serve the needs of today's artists for **unencumbered space.** Note the attention given to the north facade and the open space it looks down upon (with a **Louise Nevelson** Cor Ten steel sculpture on loan from the artist). Best of all are the **mouth-watering memories** the repainted lettering on the south facade recall for older candy-freaks: **Peaks,** and **Mason Mints.**

[44a.] Cadman Plaza North (apartments), 140 Cadman Plaza W., N of Middagh St. W side. 1967. **[44b.] Whitman Close (town houses),** 33–43, 47–53, 55–69 Cadman Plaza West, S of Middagh St. W side. **Whitman Close (apartments),** 75 Henry St., at Orange St. E side. **Pineapple Walk (stores),** Pineapple Walk bet. Henry St. and Cadman Plaza W., N side only. 1968. All by Morris Lapidus & Assocs. (All outside the historic district.)

These early, ungainly Cadman Plaza Urban Renewal Area projects, on opposite sides of Middagh Street, attempt to match the scale of Brooklyn Heights by means of **token row** houses in one case (Whitman Close) and a grilled garage matching the height, if not scale, of nearby buildings in the other (Cadman Plaza North). They fail, however, to define the intervening streets as **urban spaces** (rather than simply surfaces on which **autos navigate**), one of the principal values of the Heights. One might as well put a Greek Revival town house from Cranberry Street on an acre in Scarsdale.

[45.] The Cranlyn (apartments), 80 Cranberry St., SW cor. Henry St. 1931. H.I. Feldman.

Art Deco on the Heights. In this building the style manifests itself in glazed terra-cotta reliefs, a bronze-plaque **fantasy** over the entrance, and jazzy brickwork. [Also see 20b.]

Turn right into Orange Street.

[46.] Plymouth Church of the Pilgrims/originally **Plymouth Church,** Orange St., bet. Henry and Hicks Sts. N side. 1849. Joseph C. Wells. **Beecher Memorial Buildings and connecting arcade,** 75 Hicks St., NE cor. Orange St. 1914. Woodruff Leeming.

Henry Ward Beecher was here from 1847 to 1887. Excepting the porch, his church is an **austere box of a barn** in brick, articulated by relieving arches. The Tuscan porch was added long after Beecher left. The church house is "Eclectic" Classic Revival. Its principal virtue is the enclosure, together with the connecting arcade to the church, of a handsome garden court. Here Henry Ward Beecher, as seen through the eyes and hands of **Gutzon Borglum,** sculptor, holds forth (perhaps holds court). Unfortunately, in this era of vandalism, the churchyard, which could be a pleasant place of repose, is locked.

In 1934, the Congregational **Church of the Pilgrims,** which occupied its own church [today Our Lady of Lebanon Church—see 2c.] merged with Plymouth Church, causing its combined renaming.

End of North Heights Walking Tour: The nearest subways are the IRT Seventh Avenue Line in the St. George Hotel or, via the Whitman Close town houses at Cranberry Street, the IND Eighth Avenue Line. If your legs are still nimble you may wish to visit the Fulton Ferry area, the waterfront, and a dramatic view of the Brooklyn Bridge as it leaps across the waters of the East River.

[42.] Orig. Bklyn. Children's Aid Soc. **[43.]** Orig. candy factory/now studios

[46.] Plymouth Church of the Pilgrims: where Henry Ward Beecher preached

FULTON FERRY DISTRICT

Lying north of Brooklyn Heights' **bluffs** and only a short distance across the East River's **rippling tides** from lower Manhattan, this low-lying place offered easy access to the water, a natural spot for **a ferry landing.** At first, in 1642, the site was a muddy flat served by rowboats and sprit-sailed scows. In 1776 it was the port of embarkation for Washington's embattled troops as they **departed Brooklyn** under the cover of **darkness and fog** after their unsuccessful encounter with the British in the Revolution's first major battle after independence was declared. The year 1814 brought the **steam-propelled ferry** and with it an ever-increasing flow of traffic which culminated in the construction of **a large Victorian ferry house** in 1865. But by 1883, the opening of the Brooklyn Bridge (whose colossal granite tower now looms over the area) had already **sealed its doom** as a center of commerce—even though ferry service continued until 1924.

During much of the 19th century, the **downward curving route** to the river of **Fulton Street** (now renamed Cadman Plaza West) was **a bustling**

place lined with all manner of commercial structures, stores, streetcars, and places to eat, drink, and rest one's weary bones. Some of these (though *not* the ferry house) remain today. Remember as you walk the area that Front Street received its name because it was the last thoroughfare above water; **landfill** in the mid-19th century pushed the bulkhead farther west.

[1a.] Originally **Long Island Safe Deposit Company,** 1 Front St., N cor. Cadman Plaza W. (Fulton St.). 1869. William Mundell.

A Renaissance palazzo in cast iron, this **monumentally scaled** bank must have **overshadowed** its older neighbors in the prosperous post–Civil War era during which it opened. Its success was short-lived; by 1891 it had closed as a bank to be used subsequently for more humdrum activities.

[1b.] Originally **Franklin House (hotel),** 1 Cadman Plaza W. (Fulton St.), E cor. Water St. 1830s.

This and the adjacent four-story buildings are among the few remaining hints of the early days of Fulton Ferry when much of the commerce between Long Island and Manhattan Island passed this point.

[2.] Eagle Warehouse & Storage Company of Brooklyn, 28 Cadman Plaza W., SE cor. Elizabeth St. 1893. Additions, 1910. Both by Frank Freeman.

Lettering on buildings is **a lost art.** The enormous alphabet, high on the facade, and the smaller letters ringing the brick arched entrance emphasize the **Victorian roots** of this bulky brick warehouse. The ironwork screens at the arch and over the street-side windows set off the **boldness of the brickwork.** The machicolations (a word every cocktail party one-upsman should know) are equalled locally only in a few remaining armories.

[3.] Originally **Brooklyn City Railroad Company Building,** 8 Cadman Plaza W. (Fulton St.), SE cor. Furman St. 1861. Remodeled, 1975. David Morton. ★

When the **ferryboat was queen,** horse cars would line a row of gleaming tracks set into the cobblestoned space before you waiting to transport commuters deep into the City of Brooklyn. What more appropriate place for the headquarters for that transit combine than here, overlooking the **ebb and flow** of both **tide and passengers?**

[1a.] Orig. Long Island Safe Deposit Co. **[5.]** Brooklyn Bridge in background

Let the Eagle Scream: Hanging forlornly on the vast expanse of brick-work of the Eagle Warehouse is a gilded zinc eagle, somehow unrelated to the mass of the building. Just so. It was placed there to remind us of another incarnation of Aquila, the earliest offices of the Brooklyn newspaper, the *Daily Eagle* (Walt Whitman edited it between 1846 and 1848), which occupied this site long before the warehouse did; actually, part of a pressroom addition has been incorporated in the rear of the warehouse. The eagle dates from a later *Brooklyn Eagle* headquarters, across Johnson Street from the General Post Office, where it surmounted the cupola of the paper's nine-story building. That building is also gone.

[2.] Eagle Warehouse and Storage Co.　Fulton Ferry District (photo 1976)

[4a.] National Maritime Historical Society/originally **Marine Company 7 (fireboat), N.Y.C. Fire Department,** foot of Cadman Plaza W. (Fulton St.). 1926.

This charming vernacular structure *looks* much older than it is. Upon the ending of ferry service and the removal of the grandiose, mansard-roofed Victorian ferry terminal (in 1924—not immediately after the opening of the Brooklyn Bridge at all), this firehouse was built for the crew of a fireboat moored here. It is proposed that a museum or historical society use be found for the building.

[4b.] Fulton Ferry Park, N.Y.C. Department of Ports and Terminals, foot of Cadman Plaza West (Fulton St.), along the banks of the East River. 1976.

The hand of the pier builder is visible in this charming park and bulkhead which has once again made this bit of waterfront accessible to the people. The iron railings along the water's edge are salvage from Park Avenue's center islands, from which they were removed in 1970.

[4c.] Former **Storehouse B-53, N.Y.C. Department of Purchase,** Water St., NW cor. New Dock St. 1936.

Two stories of **Art Moderne** concrete, brick, and large industrial strip windows. The entrance, turned forty-five degrees, carries handsome cast-into-concrete lettering of the period.

[5.] Brooklyn Bridge, East River bet. Adams St., Brooklyn and Park Row, Manhattan. 1883. John A. and Washington Roebling. Reconstruction, 1955. David B. Steinman, consulting engineer. [See Bridges for statistics.] ★

Considered by many to be the **most beautiful** bridge in the world despite Gothic flourishes in the towers. The **spider web** of supporting and bracing cables **richly enmeshes** anyone taking a stroll across the bridge's walkway—**recommended**—the entrance stair is at Cadman Plaza East just south of Prospect Street, about five blocks back along the bridge approaches.

In 1974 the metalwork of the bridge was repainted in the subtle coffee and white colors of the original, rather than Public Works gray. It makes **quite a difference.**

[1a.] Atlantic Avenue Bldg., Long Island College Hospital: carven brick cube

[6a.] Originally **Tobacco Inspection Warehouse,** 25–39 Water St., bet. New Dock and Dock Sts. N side. 1860s.

[6b.] Originally **Empire Stores/**proposed **New York State Maritime Museum,** 53–83 Water St., bet. Dock and Main Sts. N side. Western four-story-high group, 1870. Eastern five-story-high group, 1885. Thomas Stone.

Actually seven brick warehouses built after the end of the Civil War, **forgotten** until **rediscovered** by photographer **Berenice Abbott** for the Federal Art Project of the WPA, then forgotten again until bought by Con Ed as a land bank investment (meaning demolition). Now under consideration as a maritime museum. **They're a natural!**

Corrugated Cardboard Empire: An early entrepreneur in the corrugated box industry, Robert Gair, was responsible for the dozen reinforced concrete loft buildings visible to the east along Water Street from the district (and from other nearby locations and across the river). The structures, designed by William Higginson, cluster around the main building, appropriately located at No. 1 Main Street—that's the one with the cubical tower, semicircular windows, a crested hip roof, and a four-sided (unfortunately nonworking) clock.

COBBLE HILL

South of the Atlantic Avenue, just below fashionable Brooklyn Heights, lies the community of Cobble Hill, filled with row upon row of distinguished housing, a number of institutions, and some fine churches. **Overlooked until the late 1950s,** when an enterprising real estate dealer rediscovered the name **"Cobleshill"** (contained in the Ratzer map of Brooklyn, 1766–1767) and updated its spelling, Cobble Hill has, in the interim, attracted many young couples and families to **brownstone living** in Brooklyn. Cobleshill (or Ponkiesbergh) referred to the steep **conical hill**—since removed—which lay near the intersection of today's Court Street (old Red Hook Lane) with Atlantic Avenue and Pacific Street. Its height, in the colonial period, made it **an important Continental Army fortification** in the Revolutionary War's Battle of Brooklyn.

[1a.] Atlantic Avenue Building, Long Island College Hospital, 70 Atlantic Avenue., SE cor. Hicks St. 1974. Ferrenz & Taylor.

COBBLE HILL—SUNSET PARK

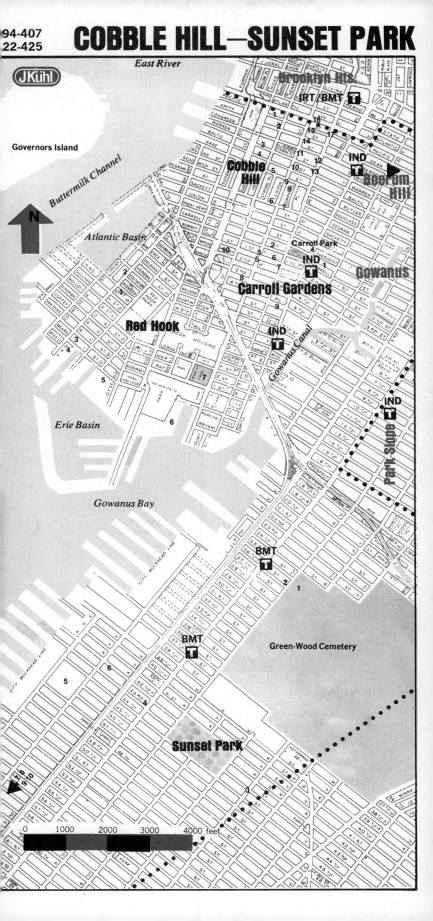

JKühl

East River

Brooklyn Hts.

IRT/BMT

Governors Island

Buttermilk Channel

Cobble Hill

IND

Boerum Hill

N

Atlantic Basin

Carroll Park

IND

Gowanus

Carroll Gardens

Red Hook

IND

Gowanus Canal

IND

Erie Basin

Park Slope

Gowanus Bay

BMT

Green-Wood Cemetery

BMT

Sunset Park

0   1000   2000   3000   4000 feet

Long Island College Hospital is a testament to 19th-century German immigrants who lived here and established this institution to serve the community. Following a decade of no construction and earlier decades where changes were only modest, L.I.C.H. built this large red brick volume which, despite its bulk, is a handsome addition to this end of a revived Atlantic Avenue.

Atlantic Avenue: A Near Eastern bazaar of exotic foods and gifts, particularly on the block between Clinton and Court Streets: halvah, dried fruit, nuts, pastries, dates, olives, copper- and brasswork, goatskin drums, inlaid chests. And Near Eastern restaurants too: hommus, baba ghannouj, kibbee, stuffed squash, cabbage, grape leaves, and wonderful yogurt delicacies as appetizers, entrees, and desserts. In the mid-1970s, Atlantic Avenue became a mile-long magnet for many other shops and services all the way from Hicks Street to Third Avenue in Boerum Hill: art galleries, craft and plant boutiques, antique and collectibles shops, a wide range of restaurants, and many other kinds of constantly changing shops. Worth a leisurely visit.

[1b.] Nurses' Residence, Long Island College Hospital, 349 Henry St., NE cor. Amity St. 1963. Beeston & Patterson.

The next most recent L.I.C.H. building, built eleven years earlier.

[2.] Cobble Hill Historic District, Atlantic Ave. to DeGraw St., Hicks to Court Sts. except for the northwesterly area occupied by Long Island College Hospital. District designated, 1969. ★

Within the district are *all* of the following:

[2a.] The Dudley Memorial, Long Island College Hospital, 110 Amity St., SE cor. Henry St. 1902. William C. Hough.

Richly adorned and in dark red brick, this latter-day miniature French Renaissance palace goes well with its more bourgeois row house neighbors.

[3a.] Originally **St. Peter's Church (Roman Catholic)/**now **St. Paul's, St. Peter's, Our Lady of Pilar Church,** Hicks St., NE cor. Warren St. 1860. P. C. Keely. **[3b.]** Originally **St. Peter's Academy,** 1866. **[3c.]** Originally **St. Peter's Hospital/**now **Congress Nursing Home,** 274 Henry St., bet. Congress and Warren Sts. W side. 1888. William Schickel & Co. Conversion to nursing home, 1963.

Once a full block of ministry to the community's spiritual (church), educational (academy), social (home for working girls at Hicks and Congress Streets), and health (hospital) needs. The red painted brickwork held it all together then. Things have changed.

[4a.] Tower Buildings (apartments), 417–435 Hicks St., 136–142 Warren St., 129–135 Baltic St., E side of Hicks St. 1879. **[4b.] Workingmen's Cottages,** 1–25 and 2–26 Warren Place (bet. Hicks and Henry Sts.). 146, 148, 152, 154 Warren St., S side. 139, 141, 145, 147 Baltic St. N side. 1879. **[4c.] Home Buildings (apartments),** 439–445 Hicks St. and 134–140 Baltic St., SW cor. 1877. All by William Field & Son.

Completion of the **"sun-lighted tenements"** in newly social-conscious Late Victorian London inspired these 226 low-rent apartments and 34 cottages financed by businessman Alfred Tredway White (1846–1924). Innovations such as outside stairs and access corridors achieved **floor-through layouts** and **good ventilation.** Common bathing facilities were provided in the basement. The tiny, $11\frac{1}{2}$-foot-wide cottages line **a private pedestrian way** called Warren Place. None has a back yard, but a rear access space is provided. These six-room dwellings rented for $18 per month (they had cost $1,150 each to build, exclusive of land). Four-room, "high-rise" apartments went for $1.93 a week. The **first low-rent "project"** in New York.

[5.] 412–420 Henry Street (row houses), bet. Kane and Baltic Sts. W side. 1888. George B. Chappell.

After completion, these houses were sold to **F.A.O. Schwarz,** the toy merchant. Only Nos. 412 and 414 retain the original doorways, low stoops, and some of the old ironwork.

Winnie's Mom didn't live here: At 426 Henry Street, just below Kane, a plaque indicates Winston Churchill's mother, Jennie Jerome, was born in that house in 1850. Actually, she was born in 1854 in a house on Amity Street near Court. The confusion results from the fact that Jennie's folks had lived with her uncle, Addison G. Jerome, at No. 292—now No. 426—Henry Street prior to her birth.

[6.] Originally **Strong Place Baptist Church**/then **The Spanish Baptist Church**/now **St. Frances Cabrini Chapel (Roman Catholic),** DeGraw St., NW cor. Strong Place. 1852. Minard Lafever. Originally **Strong Place Baptist Church Chapel**/now **Strong Place Day Care Center,** 56 Strong Place. 1849. Minard Lafever. Renovations of church and chapel, 1969. Louis Bellini.

A stone church with a massive square tower strengthened by large stepped buttresses. On the side is the earlier Gothic chapel.

[7.] **South Brooklyn Seventh Day Adventist Church**/originally **Trinity German Lutheran Church,** 249 DeGraw St., bet. Clinton St. and Tompkins Place. N side. 1905. Theobald Engelhardt.

A late Gothic Revival church in brick.

[8a.] Originally **Dr. Joseph E. Clark Residence,** 340 Clinton St., bet. DeGraw and Kane Sts. W side. Early 1860s.

The widest single house in Cobble Hill, asymmetric, and with a mansard roof: very expansive both laterally and vertically.

[8b.] **334 Clinton Street,** bet. DeGraw and Kane Sts. W side. ca. 1850. Remodeled, 1888. James W. Naughton.

A **kookie** mansard-roofed Queen Anne **miniature,** a result of remodeling by **James W. Naughton,** Superintendent of Buildings for the City of Brooklyn's public schools. A couple of years later, Naughton was architect of that great Brooklyn monument, the old Boys' High School [see Bedford-Stuyvesant 18.].

[4a.] Tower Buildings (left) [4c.] Home Buildings (right): along Hicks Street

[9a.] **Christ Church (Protestant Episcopal),** 320 Clinton St., SW cor. Kane St. 1842. Richard Upjohn. Altar, altar railings, reredos, pulpit, lectern, chairs, 1917. Louis Comfort Tiffany.

Somber random ashlar New Jersey sandstone by the elder of the father and son **architect team,** the Upjohns. The two lived up Clinton Street at No. 296 [see 10a., 10b.].

[9b.] **301–311 Clinton Street, 206–224 Kane Street, and 10–12 Tompkins Place,** 1849–1854.

Nine **classy pairs** of narrow houses in an Italianate mode developed by a New York lawyer, Gerard W. Morris. Very unusual; very lovely.

[9c.] **Kane Street Synagogue, Congregation Baith Israel Anshei Emes**/formerly **Trinity German Lutheran Church**/originally **Middle Dutch Reformed Church,** 236 Kane St., SE cor. Tompkins Place. ca. 1856.

Originally brick with brownstone trim designed in the Norman style; today detailless and smooth-stuccoed resulting in a **bland exterior** (but a more waterproof sanctuary). The congregation is descended from a splinter group of Brooklyn's oldest synagogue, once located at State Street and Boerum Place.

[10a.] Originally **Richard Upjohn Residence,** 296 Clinton St., NW cor. Baltic St. 1843. Richard Upjohn. Fourth story added, bet. 1860 and 1893. Richard Upjohn & Son. **[10b.] Addition to Upjohn Residence,** 203 Baltic St. W of Clinton St. 1893. Richard M. Upjohn.

The saga of the Upjohn residences began with a three-story corner building whose **old brick cornices** are still visible on the Clinton Street side of the **fourth-floor addition.** After the corner house had been converted to multifamily use, Richard M., the son, added the Romanesque Revival addition next door. Note its tall metal bay window and the delicacy of its ironwork at the entrance and on the fire escapes.

[11a.] Verandah Place, S of Congress St., bet. Clinton and Henry Sts. ca. 1850.

A pleasant row of stable buildings, long neglected but now converted into charming residences. **Thomas Wolfe** (1900–1938) lived in one of them. A blandly designed playground and ill-scaled light standards do their best to intrude.

"Church of the Holy Turtle" was the affectionate nickname of the Second Unitarian Church which stood for more than one hundred years on the site of today's Cobble Hill Sitting Park. As built from designs of J. Wrey Mould in 1858, there was no denying the little edifice resembled a tortoise with a high carapace. (Mould's earlier, Manhattan work, the Unitarian Church of the Saviour, boasted a striped facade and was named the "Church of the Holy Zebra"—it too is gone.) With Rev. Samuel Longfellow, the poet's brother, as its first minister the Second Unitarian quickly became known for the cultural interests and abolitionist views of both pastor and his transposed New England flock. By the 1950s, however, the church was abandoned and the site purchased for a new supermarket. Community intervention prevented this and resulted in the creation of the park.

[11b.] 166, 168, and 170 Congress Street (row houses), bet. Clinton and Henry Sts. S side. 1857. **[11c.] 159, 161, 163 Congress Street (row houses),** bet. Clinton and Henry Sts. N side. ca. 1857.

Two trios of Anglo-Italianate dwellings each designed to read as a single unit. The southern group has segmental arched upper-floor windows; the northern group square-headed ones. **Distinguished.**

[12a.] Originally **St. Paul's Church (Roman Catholic)/**now **St. Paul's, St. Peter's, Our Lady of Pilar Church,** Court St., SW cor. Congress St. 1838. Gamaliel King. Steeple, early 1860s. Brownstone veneer, 1888. Additions of new sanctuary and sacristy, 1906. **[12b.] Rectory,** 234 Congress St., bet. Court and Clinton Sts. S side. 1936. Harry McGill.

Its tall, **sculpted verdigris steeple** is **visible for blocks** up and down Court Street. This venerable brick building, the second Catholic church to be built in Brooklyn, was much altered over the years and now barely reveals much of its **original Greek Revival form.** To the west, on Congress Street, where the red brick apartments are today was once St. Paul's Industrial School, and before that the Roman Catholic Female Orphan Asylum.

[12c.] 223 Congress Street (residence), bet. Court and Clinton Sts. N side. 1851. Mansard roof added, late 19th century.

A large Gothic Revival house originally built for use as a combination rectory for St. Paul's across the street and for the **Free School for Boys.** Since 1940 it has been used as a small apartment building. Its earlier dignity is quite evident.

[13a.] 194, 196, 198, and 200 Court Street (apartments), bet. Congress and Warren Sts. W side. 1898. William B. Tubby.

"Foster" is the name this quartet of **turn-of-the-century** apartments bears on its facade. The storefronts are miraculously preserved in almost their original condition.

[13b.] St. Paul's School (Roman Catholic), 203 Warren St., bet. Court and Clinton Sts. 1887.

The property occupied by this large, dignified Victorian school building was once contiguous with the remainder of the St. Paul's complex occupying the entire Congress Street frontage to its rear [12a., 12b.].

[14.] Former **Ralph L. Cutter Residence**/originally **Abraham J. S. DeGraw Residence,** 219 Clinton St., SE cor. Amity St. 1845. Altered, 1891. D'Oench & Simon.

Built as a suburban home for a wealthy commission merchant and his father in the 1840s, the building was expanded to the form visible today. The tower, added for viewing the harbor, became so high that the **first residential elevator in Brooklyn** had to be installed.

[14.] Former R.L. Cutter Residence: an oriel window and Flemish flourishes

Jennie Jerome, b. January 9, 1854: Permastone veneer conceals the original lines of No. 197 Amity Street, the house where a baby girl was born to Mr. and Mrs. Leonard Jerome who were leasing this house (then called No. 8 Amity Street) at the time. Jennie grew up to marry Lord Randolph Henry Spencer Churchill and to give birth, in turn, to a son, Winston.

Dem Bums (restaurant/bar), 160 Court St., at Amity St. Telephone: 624-3800.

Dem Bums (plural) may be gone from Ebbets Field, but Dem Bums (singular, a restaurant reincarnation) isn't. This is the local watering place.

[15.] 214–220 Clinton Street and **147 Pacific Street (apartments),** NW cor. 1892. H. W. Billard.

Transitional style apartment buildings: from Romanesque Revival to neo-Classical. Note the sheet metal bay windows introduced to capture more light and air into the flats.

[16a.] Originally **South Brooklyn Savings Bank,** 160–162 Atlantic Ave., SE cor. Clinton St. 1871. E. L. Roberts.

Despite brutal remodeling of both its lowest stories and its roof balustrade, the **nobility** of this **Tuckahoe marble** bank building **is still evident** to a discerning eye. The bank moved to the east end of the Atlantic Avenue block in 1922 and the decay of this building then began.

Cobble Hill: see map p. 395   **399**

[16b.] 164–168 Atlantic Avenue (lofts), bet. Clinton and Court Sts. S side. Nos. 166–168 completed 1860. No. 164 completed 1864.

Merchant princes of the 19th century (note the stone quoins, the bracketed roof cornices, the dignified pediment framing its vintage) **knew better** how to express quality than those of the 20th (note the storefront).

[17a.] 180 Atlantic Avenue (lofts), bet. Clinton and Court Sts. S side. 1873.

An **original** cast-iron facade including even the frame of the storefront.

[17b.] Main Office, Independence Savings Bank/originally **South Brooklyn Savings Bank,** 130 Court St., SW cor. Atlantic Ave. 1922. McKenzie, Voorhees & Gmelin. Addition, 1936. Charles A. Holmes.

A Florentine Renaissance anchor which marks the northeast corner of this historic district.

End of Cobble Hill Historic District. ★

CARROLL GARDENS

Though the area south of Carroll Park was considered part of Red Hook until a special name was coined in the 1960s, the Carroll Gardens area has been physically distinguishable from surrounding neighborhoods ever since the ideas of **Richard Butts,** a forward-looking land surveyor of the

mid-19th century, were implemented. In his 1846 map he provided for a series of **unusually deep blocks** fronting on what are today First Place through Fourth Place between Henry and Smith Streets. His scheme (which not only allows for **deep frontyards** but standard-sized backyards as well) was then extended eastward to President, Carroll, and Second Streets between Smith and Hoyt—Union Street is wider too but sans the gardens. The result today is **eleven broad allées** lined on both sides with row houses, but paved with only enough asphalt to barely fit three cars abreast. Between row house facade and narrow sidewalk on each side are the **wonderfully lush green front gardens** that gave rise to the area's name, as urbane a sight as any in the city. Too bad that the creativity of Butts has never been publicly honored.

The **best way to know** Carroll Gardens is just to **walk** up and down **its lovely spaces**—comments are not needed.

[1.] Carroll Gardens Historic District, resembling in plan a keystone lying on its side and generally including President and Carroll Sts. bet. Smith and Hoyt Sts. and Hoyt St. bet. President and First Sts. District designated, 1973. ★

It is unclear what real and imaginary fears, what economic, political, and social trade-offs, or administrative vicissitudes caused only *two* of the eleven fine spaces of Carroll Gardens to be officially designated a historic district, but so it is. As a result **much** of Carroll Gardens **lies outside the official boundaries.** Listings below within the historic district are so noted.

[2.] St. Paul's Episcopal Church of Brooklyn, 423 Clinton St., NE cor. Carroll St. 1867–1884. Richard Upjohn & Son. Rectory, 199 Carroll St., bet. Clinton and Court Sts. N side.

Built of dark gray stone with brownstone trim, the church was never completed. Judging from the base of the steeple, visible at the corner, it would have been enormous were it to have been finished.

[3.] Guido & Sons Funeral Home/originally **the Rankin Residence,** 440 Clinton St., SW cor. Carroll St. ca. 1840. ★

Perhaps the finest remaining example of a masonry Greek Revival town house in the city. Note the suave way in which somber gray granite has been used to create a base on which the three stories of brick are built: the plinth; the fence posts (but not the intervening fence); the stoop; and above the plinth the same granite used as ornament: sills, lintels, and capitals for the corner pilasters. Fortunately this treasure is immaculately maintained.

[4a.] South Congregational Church, 336 Court St., NW cor. President St. Mid-19th Century. **[4b.] Ladies Parlor,** to W off President St. 1895. **[4c.] Parsonage,** 255 President St. bet. Court and Clinton Sts. N. side.

The church facade is a series of subtly stepped back planes of brick; a counterpart in masonry of a theater proscenium's **velvety contoured curtain.** Its skyline of verdigris-colored finials sets off the deep red masonry to advantage. To the side are **two wonderful adjuncts** to the church function, the ladies parlor bearing **sprightly** terra-cotta ornament, and the parsonage, a **Gothic Revival delight.**

[5.] Den Norske Sjomannskirke (The Norwegian Seamen's Church)/originally **Westminster Presbyterian Church,** Clinton St., NW cor. First Place. ca. 1865.

Stolid brownstone, eclectic in style: Romanesque Revival, Gothic Revival, Renaissance Revival.

[6a.] Church of the South Brooklyn Christian Assembly/formerly **Norwegian Methodist Episcopal Church/**originally **Carroll Park Methodist Episcopal Church,** 297–299 Carroll St., bet. Smith and Hoyt Sts. 1873. **Parsonage,** 295 Carroll St. 1878. Included within the historic district. ★

Both this church and its neighbor above reflect the **large Scandinavian population** in these parts between the 1890s and 1949, when this Victorian Gothic edifice was sold to its present congregation.

[6b.] 349 Hoyt Street (apartments), bet. Carroll and First Sts. W side. 1884. J. G. Miller, architect-builder. Included within the historic district. ★

Toothed brickwork defines a **vertical groove** at the **apex** of a full, four-story-high **V-shaped bay,** which distinguishes this building built to be a small apartment house.

[7.] 98 First Place, SW cor. Court St. Ca. 1860.

An Italianate villa that is now part of a row house group. The unselfconscious addition of steps to the street floor is somehow not as jarring as it might seem.

[8.] 37–39 Third Place (residence), bet. Henry and Clinton Sts. N side. ca. 1875.

Larger in scale than its neighbors with tall mansard roofs and original cast-iron cresting. The brick corbeling over openings adds a playful note.

[9.] Calvary Baptist Church of Red Hook/originally **South Congregational Chapel,** 118 Fourth Place, bet. Court and Smith Sts. 1890.

This robust rotund chapel is Friar Tuck to its more restrained, heroic Robin Hood, the South Congregational Church at Court and President Streets [See 4a.].

Optical illusions? You can only tell for sure from a land book such as E. Belcher Hyde's of 1912, for example, but it *is* certain that the street facades of the Carroll Gardens row houses framing Carroll and President Streets *are not* parallel with one another. As a matter of fact, the difference is considerable: at the Smith Street end they are 100 feet apart; at Hoyt Street the space between increases to 129 feet. The surveyors' prestidigitation is concealed, however, by the length of these blocks and by the lush greenery.

[10.] Sacred Hearts of Jesus and Mary and St. Stephen's Church (Roman Catholic)/originally **St. Stephen's Church,** Summit St. NE cor. Hicks St. **Rectory,** 108 Carroll St., bet. Henry and Hicks Sts. Both mid-19th century. P. C. Keely.

Another **red-painted brick** ecclesiastical complex of which prolific architect Keely designed many. In all, Keely is believed to have designed **some 700 church** edifices across the country in his professional career.

BOERUM HILL/TIMES PLAZA

As in the case of Cobble Hill and Carroll Gardens, Boerum Hill is a relatively new name for a community trying to **revive** itself **from a neglected past.** Though the area claimed by the neighborhood association is larger, the most intense concern is for streets such as State, Pacific, Dean, and Bergen east of Court and west of Fourth Avenue. In the mid-19th century this was **a fashionable district,** as the fine row housing will itself indicate. Visitors to the area included **Washington Irving, James Fenimore Cooper, and William Cullen Bryant. Sidney Lanier** lived briefly at 195 Dean Street. Today's residents are a **racial and ethnic mix** that contributes **a special flavor** to the community. Times Plaza is the eastern terminus of this area.

[1.] Boerum Hill Historic District, irregular, generally lying bet. the Wyckoff St.-Hoyt St. intersection on the SW and the Pacific St.-Nevins St. intersection on the NE. District designated, 1973. ★

The area chosen for designation includes some of the finest rows of housing and also some of the precinct's **architectural "erratics,"** which add spice to the visual scene. The row houses, single houses, and apartments listed below are among the many **contained within the district's boundaries.**

[2a.] 360 Pacific Street (single house), bet. Hoyt and Bond Sts. S side. ca. 1851.

A particularly fine frame house behind a porch supported by **fluted columns.** The doorway contains later 19th-century doors.

[2b.] 374 Pacific Street (row house), bet. Hoyt and Bond Sts. S side. ca. 1853.

A unique example of Gothic Revival in an otherwise largely homogeneous historic district of Greek Revival **(older houses)** and Italianate **(the newer ones)** styles. Note the Gothic ogee arches in the entrance doors' upper panels. The dragon-headed balcony outside the parlor floor, while amusing, is not original to the house.

[3a.] 245 Dean Street (row house), bet. Bond and Nevins Sts. N side. 1853. John Dougherty and Michael Murray, builders.

This house, one of thirty in this continuous row, remained in the ownership of **one family for many years:** that goes a long way in explaining the **remarkable appearance** of the facade down to the shutters and intricately built-up paired entrance doors.

[3b.] 240, 244 Dean Street (row houses), bet. Bond and Nevins Sts. S side. 1858. Wilson & Thomas, builders.

Two surviving (and refaced) examples of what were, originally, **four** Victorian wood frame cottages.

[4.] Hoyt Street (a group of single houses), bet. Bergen and Wyckoff Sts. E side. **[4a.] 157 Hoyt Street.** ca. 1860. **[4b.] 159, 161, 163 Hoyt Street.** 1871. **[4c.] 163½, 165 Hoyt Street.** ca. 1854.

The north-south streets of the area tend to be the through-traffic arteries and therefore the ones altered at their ground floors into **retail space.** This unusual grouping is an exception. The deep setback of Nos. 163½ and 165 create **an unexpected green oasis** filled with ailanthus and other growing things.

[4d.] 148 Hoyt Street (apartments), SW cor. Bergen St. 1851. Thomas Maynard, builder. Renovation, 1880s.

Three stories of apartments over a tavern. Florid sheet metal work and Queen Anne appearance date from late 19th century changes. **A happy building.**

End of Boerum Hill Historic District. ★ All the Boerum Hill buildings which follow are *outside* the historic district.

[5.] Hospital of the Holy Family (Division of Catholic Medical Center of Brooklyn & Queens), 155 Dean St., bet. Hoyt and Bond Sts. N side. 1888.

The street facade looks more to be a stew than a design since the Queen Anne was more a stew than a style—but a very satisfying one in any case. Note the "1888" interwoven in the unglazed terra-cotta ornament. The old entrance, stuccoed closed (as in "The Cask of Amontillado"), still retains the original steps and railings to nowhere. Weird!

[6a.] Schermerhorn-Pacific Housing, on block bet. State and Schermerhorn Sts., Smith and Hoyt Sts. Scheduled for completion, 1978. J. Sam Unger Assocs., architects. Warren Gran & Assocs., consulting architects.

Originally part of an urban renewal plan which would have resulted in a mix of high- and low-rise housing for a range of income groups. The compromise was a small number of privately financed three-story-plus-basement buildings (no-high-rise) to rent at what-the-market-will-bear prices.

[6b.] "The State Street Houses," 291–299 State St., bet. Smith and Hoyt Sts. N side; 290–324 State St., bet. Smith and Hoyt Sts. S side. Mid-19th century. ★

Located a few blocks away from the official historic district, these groups of row houses, each individually landmarked, are still within the Boerum Hill community. As in other parts of State Street (both on the "Hill" and in Brooklyn Heights to the west), fine examples of 19th-century domestic construction are being sensitively adapted to 20th-century needs.

Other worthy nearby but *unlandmarked* buildings:

[7.] Engine Company 226, N.Y.C. Fire Department, 409 State St., bet. Bond and Nevins Sts. N side. ca. 1880.

Corbeled brick brackets and **perfect cast-iron cresting** at the roof are only two of the special qualities this antique retains for our pleasure. Long may you remain, Injun 226.

[8a.] 492, 494, and 496 State Street (row houses), bet. Nevins St. and Third Ave. S side.

Narrow, elegant, unusual: with rusticated English basements and brick tops. Only two-windows-wide apiece.

[8b.] Originally **Brooklyn Printing Plant of the New York Times,** 59–75 Third Ave. bet. Dean and Pacific Sts. E side. 1929. Albert Kahn, Inc.

This symmetric monumental limestone work **hardly hints** at the straightforward unaffected industrial facilities these architects **would shortly design,** such as the Dodge Half-Ton Truck Plant in Detroit (1938). The **large windows** along Third Avenue permitted the public to **view the printing, collating, and folding** of newspapers by a half-block-long printing press—the papers were then distributed from the through-block alley to the east.

Times Plaza: The five-way intersection of three major routes, Atlantic, Flatbush, and Fourth Avenues—together with two secondary ones, Ashland Place and Hanson Place—forms Times Plaza, named for the *Brooklyn Daily Times,* a newspaper once published nearby, and now dominated by Brooklyn's tallest building, the Williamsburgh Savings Bank Tower. It is at this chaotic coming-together of traffic streams from all directions that the Long Island Rail Road has its Atlantic Avenue Terminal and BAM, the Brooklyn Academy of Music, has one of its two triangular parking areas, the one southeast of the Plaza also serving as a farmers' market in warm weather.

[9a.] Originally **IRT Subway Kiosk,** on triangle formed by Flatbush, Atlantic, and Fourth Aves. 1908. Heins & La Farge. Proposed reconstruction and addition for sidewalk cafe and newsstand, 1977. Stephen Lepp & Assocs.

The extension of the original Manhattan IRT Subway reached Atlantic Avenue in 1908 causing the charming brick and terra-cotta **pavilion** to be built on the central traffic island—probably to give identity to this new-for-its-time mass transit medium. Remember, back in '08 there was an **elevated** along Flatbush Avenue, **trolley cars** moving **helter-skelter** in all directions, **horses and wagons,** and the **new-fangled** automobiles, too. The Kiosk has been defaced over the years since access through it to the subway was long ago discontinued. But there are hopes for an effective substitute use for the island which will restore the structure's appearance.

[9b.] Williamsburgh Sav. Bank Tower   **[11.]** Pacific Branch, Bklyn. Pub. Lib.

[9b.] Williamsburgh Savings Bank Tower, 1 Hanson Place, NE cor. Ashland Place overlooking Times Plaza. 1929. Halsey, McCormick & Helmer.

Byzantine (in design) and proud of it, **Brooklyn's only skyscraper** counts more for its uniqueness in height and ornament. Viewed from Manhattan it (seems to) mark the center of Downtown Brooklyn, but it is actually at its edge, its offices occupied by what seem to be all of Brooklyn's orthodontists. The 26th floor is reserved for public use and includes an outdoor observatory with great views. The space has been known to be used for indoor-outdoor exhibits on such themes as the Revolutionary War's Battle of Brooklyn. Incidentally, as in the World Trade Center, reaching the tower floors requires a change in elevators midway up. Hours and information: 636-7200.

Records set, records broken: While the Williamsburgh Savings Bank Tower is still the tallest office building in Brooklyn (512 feet), it is *not* the tallest structure in the borough. That honor goes to the Board of Education's lacy radio and television transmission tower for WNYE-FM and WNYE-TV atop nearby Brooklyn Technical High School, 29 Fort Greene Place (597 feet). Similarly the Williamsburgh's illuminated clock was the largest four-sided clock in the whole U.S.A. (27 feet in diameter) until the four 40-foot-diameter clocks on the Allen Bradley Building in Milwaukee were finished, in 1962. An up-close look at the grotesquely large hands and illuminated numbers from the tower's observation deck is a worthwhile if surrealistic experience. [See 9b. above.]

[9c.] Hanson Place Central Methodist Church: stores occupy some frontage

[9c.] Hanson Place Central Methodist Church, Hanson Place, NW cor. Saint Felix St. ca. 1930.

Gothic **restyled in modern dress,** an exercise in massing brick and limestone. The street level contains retail stores, a surprising but **intelligent adjunct** to churchly economics. This building replaced an earlier one on the site between 1847 and 1927.

[10.] Church of the Redeemer (Protestant Episcopal), Fourth Ave., NW cor. Pacific St. 1870. P. C. Keely.

Presiding over a chaotic traffic intersection and various (high and low) forms of commerce—for years this corner has been a red-light district—must not make life easy for this church or for its congregation. Too bad, for this muted polychromed edifice has a haunting beauty, often overlooked by passersby.

[11.] Pacific Branch, Brooklyn Public Library, 25 Fourth Ave., SE cor. Pacific St. 1904. Raymond F. Almirall.

If the Church of the Redeemer, across Fourth Avenue, is an architectural symphony, this library branch is **an oompah band:** self-satisfied, robust, and also **unfairly passed over.** (The 1970s' substitution of aluminum window sash is an indignity.)

[12.] Baptist Temple, 306 Schermerhorn St., SW cor. Third Ave. 1894.

This Romanesque Revival **fortress** is a continuing center of **fundamentalist preaching**—the intersection it overlooks is officially Temple Square but acquired the name **"Brimstone Square."** Understandably.

[13.] Brooklyn Boys Boarding School/later **Public School 15 Brooklyn/**now **Board of Education Certificating Unit,** 475 State St. NE cor. Third Ave. ca. 1840.

A complex of red-painted buildings that are a far-flung outpost of the bureaucracy centered at 110 Livingston Street. Their rich color and studied forms add **a diverting note** to an otherwise colorless scene.

[14.] Brooklyn Academy of Music (BAM), 30 Lafayette Ave., bet. Ashland Place and Saint Felix St. 1908. Herts & Tallant.

Without its intricately modeled cornice, this low box of a building looks like a much later (and lesser) work, the Bronx General Post Office [W Bronx 17c.]. Perhaps one day a substitute architectural **"brow"** will grace the building's roof line. Meanwhile, within are **four great performance spaces** as well as the **imaginative ideas** and events to animate them. **BAM is a bash!**

GOWANUS

A shabby, dull, and monotonous part of Brooklyn. Among its **most interesting** physical features are the **bridges** and **viaducts** that **cross the waterway bearing its name.** Before 1911 the fetid Gowanus Canal was known derisively as **Lavender Lake.** At that time the Butler Street pumping station at its northern terminus began piping **the stale waters** into New York Harbor's **Buttermilk Channel,** inviting fresh water to enter by **tidal action.** It hasn't helped much.

Gowanus does have a few points of interest, however.

[1.] St. Marks Avenue, bet. Third and Fourth Aves. Both sides.

If this street weren't so poor it would be famous. Working-class, three-story "English basement" tenement buildings march up the incline toward Park Slope like **a provincial brigade:** in step, regimental insignia visible, well-groomed if a bit dusty.

[4.] IND Subway High Level Crossing over the Gowanus Canal in a 1967 photo

[2.] Wyckoff Gardens, N.Y.C. Housing Authority, Nevins St. to Third Ave., Wyckoff to Baltic Sts. 1966. Greenberg & Ames.

Ordinary low-rent, high-rise housing—but with two exceptions: white unglazed brick rather than the traditional Hudson River red, and stepped-back forms for the three towers. The brick color gives the project **a bleached Sahara look** even in the dead of winter. But the setbacks are **bold and effective,** a kind of Skidmore, Owings & Merrill Sears Roebuck Tower (Chicago, 1974) before its time.

[3.] Carroll Street Bridge, over the Gowanus Canal, bet. Bond and Nevins Sts. 1889.

A unique (for New York City) **retractile bridge;** the roadway slides back diagonally on special tracks in order to clear the canal for a passing boat.

[4.] IND Subway High Level Crossing, Smith and Ninth St. Station, over Gowanus Canal. 1933.

The ground in these parts proved so unsuitable for tunnel construction that the IND Subway comes out of the ground to rise over a hundred feet to meet the Canal's navigational clearances. This leaves the Smith and Ninth Street subway station **high and dry** and embraced in the lattice-work of a steel truss. **A spectacular piece of construction,** but regrettably of little visual merit save that of size.

[5.] Engine Company 204, N.Y.C. Fire Department, 299 DeGraw St., bet. Court and Smith Sts. N side. ca. 1880.

A holdover from the time when fires were fought by fire laddies stoking horse-drawn steam pumpers. This one began as **Engine 4, Brooklyn Fire Department,** as the old terra-cotta shields indicate.

[6.] St. Agnes Church (Roman Catholic), 417 Sackett St., NE cor. Hoyt St. 1905. Thomas F. Houghton.

The tallest structure in the community north of the IND crossing, St. Agnes dominates the two- and three-story row houses that hug the slopes west of the Gowanus. Note the proliferation of stone crosses along the nave roof.

[7a.] St. Mary's Star of the Sea Church (Roman Catholic), 471 Court St., bet. Nelson and Luquer Sts. Mid-19th century. P. C. Keely. **[7b.] Girl's School,** 477 Court St., NE cor. Nelson St. **[7c.] Rectory,** 467 Court St., SE cor. Luquer St.

Red painted brick humility—a parish church trio for a 19th-century immigrant working-class parish. Compare with other nearby Catholic churches by architect P. C. Keely: St. Peter's [Cobble Hill 3a.], St. Stephen's [Carroll Gardens 10.].

Don't miss taking a peek at Dennett Place, just behind St. Mary's.

Dennett Place: An atmospheric street that seems more like a stage set for Maxwell Anderson's *Winterset* than a brick and mortar reality. It lies between Court and Smith Streets and connects Luquer with Nelson Streets.

FORT GREENE/CLINTON HILL/THE NAVY YARD

"To the rear of **the boisterous city hall quarter** was Brooklyn's other **fine residential district,** the Hill. Located in the center of the city and surrounded by **diverse elements,** its position was not unlike that of the Heights; but its **elegant residences** were fewer in number and their owners slightly further removed from the traditions of **genteel respectability.** It abounded in churches and middle class houses, the majority of whose owners worked in New York, but **took pride** in living in Brooklyn." **Harold C. Syrett,** *The City of Brooklyn, 1865–1898.*

Fort Greene and Clinton Hill rank with Cobble Hill and Boerum Hill as **unsung areas of urban delight.** Clustering around Fort Greene Park and the Pratt Institute Campus are blocks of **distinguished** brownstones, occasional **mansions,** and a surprisingly **rich inventory** of churches and other institutions. Their edges at Flatbush Avenue and along the old Navy Yard are **roughened** by cheap commercial areas and areas of proposed renewal, but the body is **solid and handsome** in large part.

FORT GREENE

Fort Greene Walking Tour: Start at Hanson Place and South Portland Street, about four blocks east from either the Atlantic Avenue Station of the IRT, BMT, and Long Island Rail Road, or the Pacific Street Station of the BMT (all at Times Plaza), or the Lafayette Avenue Station of the IND Eighth Avenue Line, the faithful A train. The walk ends at Clinton Avenue below Fulton Street, one stop farther away from Manhattan on the A train. (The structures at Times Plaza are covered in the Boerum Hill/Times Plaza section, above.)

[1.] Hanson Place Seventh Day Adventist Church/originally **Hanson Place Baptist Church,** 88 Hanson Place, SE cor. S. Portland Ave. 1860. ★

Cream and white Greek Revival reminiscent of the many **churches of the Kremlin.** Victorian milk glass.

Follow Hanson Place east and turn right into South Oxford Street.

[1.] The Hanson Place S.D.A. Church   **[2b.]** St. Simon the Cyrenian Church

[2a.] Oxford Nursing Home/originally **Lodge No. 22, Benevolent Protective Order of Elks,** 144 S. Oxford St., bet. Hanson Place and Atlantic Ave. 1912. H. Van Buren Magonigle and A. W. Ross. Altered, 1955. Wechsler & Schimenti.

The bracketed cornice and still-visible polychromed terra cotta reveal the original use; changed brick color and texture give away the losses in this crude conversion.

[2b.] Church of St. Simon the Cyrenian, 175 S. Oxford St., bet. Hanson Place and Atlantic Ave. E side. ca. 1895.

A splendid mansion is now, happily, used as a church. **Black Forest Queen Anne:** ornamented stucco, ornamented terra cotta, ornamented brick.

[2c.] N.Y.C. Taxi & Limousine Commission/originally **New York & Brooklyn Casket Co.,** 187 S. Oxford St., bet. Hanson Place and Atlantic Ave. E side. 1927. Vincent B. Fox.

Charming neo-Georgian which respects the scale of the row houses on the block.

From the end of this block it's easy to see the extent (and some early outgrowths) of the Atlantic Terminal plan. Trace your steps back on South Oxford Street.

Atlantic Terminal Urban Renewal

Plotted on a map the urban renewal area looks faintly like a comet, pointing northwest to Downtown Brooklyn and the Civic Center. Its squared-off head is the decaying **Atlantic Avenue Terminal** of the Long Island Rail Road's Brooklyn spur. Its tail is contained within Hanson Place and Fulton Street on the north, and Atlantic Avenue on the south. (Like the real comet Kohoutek, this cartographic comet may never really make its presence felt—the city's 1975 fiscal crisis crippled its chances for completion.) Though intended to renew the **old passenger terminal,** eliminate the neighboring **Fort Greene meat market,** and provide a real campus for **Baruch College,** CUNY's business school on 23rd Street in Manhattan, so far only some low- and moderate-income housing and a school, all in the comet's tail to the east, have been built. The rest is **in limbo.**

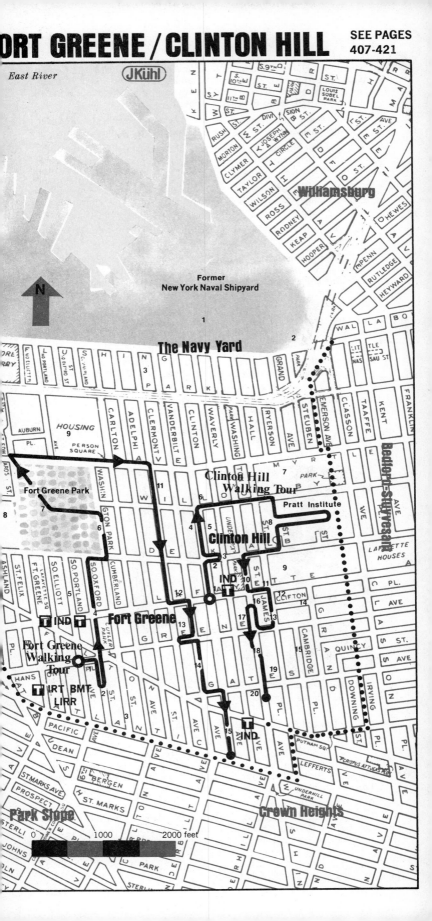

[3a.] 170 South Portland Avenue and **161 South Elliott Place (apartments),** bet. Hanson Place and Atlantic Ave. **[3b.] 455 and 475 Carlton Avenue (apartments),** bet. Fulton St. and Atlantic Ave. E side. **770 Fulton St. (apartments),** bet. Carlton Ave. and Adelphi St. S side. All buildings, 1976. Bond Ryder & Assocs.

Handsome residential towers well integrated with the play areas and **exquisitely handled** small public plazas which their volumes define.

[3c.] Atlantic Terminal Houses, N.Y.C. Housing Authority, 487, 495 Carlton Ave., NE cor. Atlantic Ave. 1976. James Stewart Polshek & Assocs.

The apartment towers to the south use contrasting bands of buff brick, seemingly to camouflage their structures' ungainly appearance, as well they might.

[4a.] Lafayette Avenue Presbyterian Church, 85 S. Oxford St. SE cor. Lafayette Ave. 1862. Grimshaw & Morrill.

Noted architecturally largely for its numerous windows by the Tiffany studios (six of eight upper windows; all but one below). The large one in the Underwood Chapel, installed in 1920, was **the last work** of the Tiffany firm. Dr. Theodore L. Cuyler, **a renowned Brooklyn preacher,** was its minister—hence Cuyler Park, the triangle across Fulton Street.

[4b.] 99 Lafayette Avenue (apartments), bet. South Portland Ave. and South Oxford Place. 1937. Jacob Mark, engineer. A. Markewich, designer.

Unusual Art Deco—in red-brown brick (rather than orange or buff)—and **making the most** of the brickmason's skills for its ornamental devices.

[4c.] The Roanoke/originally **The San Carlos Hotel,** 69 S. Oxford St., bet. Lafayette and DeKalb Aves. E side. ca. 1893.

An early Brooklyn **apartment house** (as opposed to **tenement**). Too bad about the addition above the cornice.

[4c.] The Roanoke Apts./orig. hotel   **[7a.]** Prison Ship Martyrs' Monument

[5a.] South Oxford Street and **[5b.] South Portland Avenue,,** Lafayette to DeKalb Aves.

Two handsome, tree-shaded blocks of brownstones. South Oxford's offer a range from the early 1850s to the end of the century; South Portland's are mostly from the 1860s. Note the reliance upon **fashionable London street names,** these and Adelphi, Carlton, Cumberland, and Waverly.

The end of these blocks is terminated by the rise of Fort Greene Park, a later stop on the tour. Meanwhile, turn right on DeKalb Avenue and left at the end of the park onto:

[6.] Washington Park, the portion of Cumberland St. facing Fort Greene Park, DeKalb to Myrtle Aves. **[6a.] 192 Washington Park,** bet. DeKalb and Willoughby Aves. ca. 1880. Marshall J. Morrill. **[6b.] 179– 185 Washington Park,** bet. DeKalb and Willoughby Aves. 1866. Joseph H. Townsend, builder. **[6c.] 173–176 Washington Park,** bet. Willoughby and DeKalb Aves. ca. 1867. Thomas B. Jackson, builder.

These two blocks were the most desirable addresses in Fort Greene when these mostly **Italianate brownstones** were built to overlook the park across the way. No. 192 is a **terrific Queen Anne** exception. The mansions had their notable residents: Publisher **Alfred C. Barnes** lived at No. 182 [also see Brooklyn Heights 26b.], William C. Kingsley at No. 176, and his partner Abner Keeney next door at No. 175. **Kingsley and Keeney** were among Brooklyn's **most affluent contractors,** builders of streets and sewers, a reservoir on Long Island, and much of Prospect Park. In 1867, when Kingsley bought his house, he was known to be **the driving political force** behind the Brooklyn Bridge; he was later to become its **largest individual stockholder.**

Enter Fort Greene Park and climb the hill to the base of the tall monument.

[7.] Fort Greene Park/formerly **City Park (City of Brooklyn),** DeKalb Ave. to Myrtle Ave., Washington Park to St. Edwards St. 1860. Frederick Law Olmsted and Calvert Vaux. Additions, 1908. McKim, Mead & White. Altered, 1972. Berman, Roberts & Scofidio.

From its summit there is **a prospect of Brooklyn** and the harbor that suggests this might better have been the park to be named "Prospect."

[7a.] Prison Ship Martyrs' Monument, center of Fort Greene Park. 1908. McKim, Mead & White, architects. A. A. Weinman, sculptor.

A memorial to those many thousands of **unlucky patriots** to the American cause who died in prison ships anchored in Wallabout Bay (near the Navy Yard) during the Revolution. The large, hollow **Doric column,** 148′8″, bears a brazier of bronze (which once contained an "eternal" flame) by sculptor Weinman. The tower is not open to the public. Nearby is the **world's most elegant comfort station,** a square "distyle in antis" Doric temple by the same architects.

Visible to the west and south from the commanding site of the park:

[8.] The Brooklyn Hospital, DeKalb Ave. to Willoughby St., Ft. Greene Park to Ashland Place. 1920. J. M. Hewlett. Alterations/expansion, 1967. Rogers, Butler & Burgun. **[8a.] Staff Residence (apartments),** NE corner of site, Willoughby St., SW cor. Saint Edwards St. 1976. Walker O. Cain & Assocs.

Clearly **the best** of the hospital's buildings is this tall brick tower, its newest structure, a state **UDC** product. It will house staff from the hospital as well as from the many other nonprofit institutions nearby.

[8b.] Kingsview (apartments), Willoughby St. to Myrtle Ave., Saint Edwards St. to Ashland Place. 1957. Brown & Guenther.

Neat cooperative housing surveying Fort Greene Park.

[9a.] Walt Whitman Houses and **[9b.] Raymond V. Ingersoll Houses/** originally **Fort Greene Houses, N.Y.C. Housing Authority,** Myrtle to Park Aves., Carlton Ave. to Prince St. 1944. Rosario Candela, André Fouilhoux, Wallace K. Harrison, Albert Mayer, Ethan Allen Dennison, William I. Hohauser, Ely Jacques Kahn, Charles Butler, Henry Churchill, and Clarence Stein.

Thirty-five hundred apartments (14,000 persons) on 38 acres. Within its bounds are the Church of St. Michael and St. Edward, Cumberland Hospital, and P. S. 67 Brooklyn. It was completed during World War II, despite the embargoes on construction, as **high-priority housing** for Brooklyn's wartime industrial labor force.

[10.] Church of St. Michael and St. Edward (Roman Catholic)/originally **Church of St. Edward,** within Ingersoll Houses, 108 Saint Edward's St., bet. Myrtle and Park Aves. W side. 1902. Altar, 1972. Carol Dykman O'Connor. Cross, 1972. Robert Zacharian.

Twin conical-capped towers in the manner of a **Loire Valley** 17th-century **château.** The interior is **Pop-Art plaster,** painted and gilt, with huge sheets of pictorial stained glass (done by a Norman Rockwell of the medium). The altar and the cross are new, incorporating parts of the **old Myrtle Avenue "el,"** which once rumbled by down the street. Before construction of the adjacent project the church occupied a narrow triangular site defined by now-gone Leo Place on the west.

For those who remember the dappled gloom of Myrtle Avenue as it suffocated under the "el," a walk east on the wide, sky/sunlit thoroughfare will be refreshing. Turn right at Clermont Avenue.

[11a.] Former **Third Battery Armory, N.Y. National Guard**/now **Encumbrance Warehouse, N.Y.C. Sanitation Department,** 181 Clermont Ave., bet. Myrtle and Willoughby Aves. E side. ca. 1890.

A one-time national guard armory whose unencumbered open space within is used to store (and auction) the encumbrances (household belongings) of unfortunate New Yorkers dispossessed from their homes. Next door, to the south, once stood the well-known **Clermont Skating Rink.**

[11b.] Jewish Center of Fort Greene/formerly **Simpson Methodist Episcopal Church,** 209 Clermont Ave., SE cor. Willoughby Ave. 1870.

As neighborhoods change their demographic characteristics, their buildings are adapted to new (or similar) uses. So are styles. In this case the **northern Italian raiment** of **Lombardian Romanesque** was adapted to the needs of a 19th-century Brooklyn church.

[12a.] Medgar Evers Community College, C.U.N.Y./originally **The Brooklyn Masonic Temple,** 317 Clermont Ave., NE cor. Lafayette Ave. 1909. Lord & Hewlett and Pell & Corbett.

They took the word "temple" **literally** in 1909. Some of the polychromy that archeologists believe was used on 4th century B.C. Greek temples **is recalled here** in fired terra-cotta ornament.

[11b.] Jewish Center of Ft. Greene   [12a.] Orig. Brooklyn Masonic Temple

Turn left at this corner into Lafayette Avenue.

[12b.] Our Lady Queen of All Saints School, Church, and Rectory (Roman Catholic), 300 Vanderbilt Ave., NW cor. Lafayette Ave. 1913. Gustave Steinback.

George Mundelein, later Cardinal of Chicago, commissioned this building while pastor of the local parish. A glassy church **(stained)** and a glassy school **(clear)** suggest on the one hand that stained-glass box, **the Sainte Chapelle of Paris,** and on the other, slim-mullioned, **modern school architecture.** The sculpture is impressive in both quality and quantity; 24 saints are "in residence."

[12c.] Originally **Joseph Steele Residence**/now **Skinner Residence,** 200 Lafayette Ave., SE cor. Vanderbilt Ave. 1812. Altered. ★

Extraordinary relic from the days these precincts were **farm country.** Greek Revival clapboard, weathered and shuttered, it has been inhabited by the Skinner family since 1900.

Turn right down Vanderbilt Avenue and then right again at Greene Avenue.

[13.] Former **Episcopal Residence, Roman Catholic Diocese of Brooklyn**/now **the Chancery,** 367 Clermont Ave., NE cor. Greene Ave. 1887. P. C. Keely.

Dour; Hollywood would cast it as **an orphan asylum** for a Charlotte Brontë novel. In fact, the neatly dressed granite blocks and mansard roof may be austere, but remember, they were meant to minimize the effect of this neighbor upon the **never-built great cathedral** with which it was to share this block-long site. See below.

[12b.] Our Lady Queen of All Saints   **[12c.]** Orig. Joseph Steele Residence

Memories of an unbuilt monument: The entire block bounded by Vanderbilt and Clermont Avenues, east and west, and by Lafayette and Greene Avenues, north and south, was acquired in 1860 as the site of a church that was to be one of the world's largest, Brooklyn's Cathedral of the Immaculate Conception. Architect Patrick Charles Keely, one of the 19th century's most prolific, was chosen to execute the commission. Foundations were laid, cathedral walls rose to heights of ten to twelve feet, the Chapel of St. John's, the largest of the cathedral's proposed six, was completed in 1878, and the Bishop of Brooklyn's residence was finished nine years later. And then, funds not being available, all work stopped. The incomplete walls remained for decades, a challenging play area for imaginative neighborhood children. After Keely's death in 1896, John Francis Bentley, architect of Westminster Cathedral, London, was asked to draw new plans, but he too died and his plans remained incomplete. The walls remained until 1931 when they and the chapel were demolished to build Bishop Loughlin Memorial High School, a tribute to the prelate who had dreamt the dream back in 1860. The only relic is the bishop's residence, now used by the brothers who teach in the high school.

Now, back to Vanderbilt Avenue and turn right.

[14.] **378–434 Vanderbilt Avenue (row houses),** bet. Greene and Gates Aves. W side. ca. 1880.

An **almost perfectly preserved row;** 29 Italianate brownstones stepping down the gentle hill. At either end their march is stopped in a dignified way; houses No. 378 and 434 return to the building line, creating a long narrow space between for the stoops. Note the balustrades are **cast iron painted** (in some cases) **to look like brownstone:** industrialization rears its head.

Turn left at Gates Avenue and right at Clinton Avenue for a wonderful church facade and the end of this tour.

[15a.] 487 Clinton Avenue (residence), bet. Gates Ave. and Fulton St. E side. ca. 1890.

A Loire Valley château, towered, machicolated, and mated with a Richardsonian Romanesque entry.

[15b.] Church of St. Luke and St. Matthew (Protestant Episcopal)/ originally **St. Luke's Episcopal Church,** 520 Clinton Ave. bet. Fulton St. and Atlantic Ave. W side. 1891.

The Episcopalians begat Baptist temples in the 1880s and '90s. Eclecticism gone berserk: battered Egyptian-like walls, Romanesque arches, Ruskinian Gothic granite-brownstone polychromy. **It all adds up to a great facade.**

End of Fort Greene Walking Tour: The nearest subway is the IND Eighth Avenue Line, the A train, less than a block north, at Fulton Street and Clinton Avenue. If you are hungry, or if you want a glimpse of adjacent Clinton Hill, walk farther north on Clinton Avenue till you get to Lafayette Avenue, where the Hill tour begins.

Relax, refresh, revive: Conveniently located in the "center of gravity" between the imprecisely defined communities of Fort Greene and Clinton Hill are a few places to eat and browse. Antique shops and boutiques are always opening and closing, too. On the DeKalb Avenue block between Clermont and Vanderbilt Avenues are **Sisyphus Books** and its Used Book Annex at No. 235 (telephone 638-0606); **Two Steps Down,** a restaurant at No. 240 (telephone 783-9239); and **Cino's Italian Restaurant** at No. 243 (telephone ST 9-9772). Nearby are two other Italian *trattorie,* **Venice** at 454 Myrtle Avenue off Waverly Avenue (telephone MA 5-3010), and **Joe's Place,** occupying an old carriage house at 264 Waverly, above DeKalb (telephone ST 9-9767). All are nice to visit and reasonably priced.

CLINTON HILL

Clinton Hill Walking Tour: Starts at Clinton and Lafayette Avenues, the west exit of the IND Clinton-Washington station of the GG train, the Brooklyn-Queens Crosstown Line. (If voyaging on the IND from Manhattan, change at Hoyt-Schermerhorn station for the GG—toward Long Island City—for two stops.) The tour ends at the other IND Clinton-Washington station, this time of the Eighth Avenue Line A train, at Fulton Street. In between the tour will pass what remains of the homes on "The Hill" that belonged to the merchant and industrialist kings of Brooklyn—the Bedfords, Pfizers, Underwoods, and most prominent of all, the Pratts.

Walk north along Clinton Avenue. It and Washington Avenue are the two wide avenues on which the most fashionable families settled.

[1.] 315 Clinton Avenue (residence), bet. Lafayette and DeKalb Aves. E side. ca. 1890.

Robust red brick, brownstone, and orange terra cotta. Don't miss the **intricately molded** terra-cotta soffit below the bay window.

Take a short detour to the right along DeKalb Avenue and then resume your northerly walk on Clinton.

[2.] 282, 284, 286, 288, and 290 DeKalb Avenue (residences), SW cor. Waverly Ave. ca. 1890.

Quintuplets unified by a pediment over the central trio and symmetrical cylindrical **turrets** at each end. A terrific *tour-de-force,* rare both for its design and for its state of preservation.

[3.] Waverly Avenue, bet. Gates and Myrtle Aves.

This **narrow service street** is sandwiched between the more expansive Clinton and Washington Avenues, **the proud thoroughfares** on which the

[15a.] 487 Clinton Avenue: an eclectic mating of Gothic and Romanesque styles

[15b.] The Church of St. Luke and St. Matthew: an impressive agglomeration

wealthy built their mansions. Many of the stables and carriage houses, charming mementos to the age of horse and carriage, remain.

[4.] St. Joseph's College/formerly **Charles Pratt (Sr.) Residence,** 232 Clinton Ave., bet. DeKalb and Willoughby Aves. W side. ca. 1875.

The original **manor house and gardens** of the Pratt family; Italianate, a freestanding equivalent of the brownstone row mansion.

Charles Pratt the elder, refiner of Kerosene at Greenpoint, joined his oil empire with that of John D. Rockefeller's Standard Oil Company in 1874. At the marriage of each of his five sons, the new couple was presented with a house for a wedding present. Three of the four built in Clinton Hill still remain, at Nos. 229, 241, and 245 Clinton Avenue, opposite their father's at No. 232. The last son, Harold I., responsive to the changing fashion and the consolidation of Brooklyn with New York, built *his* nuptial palace on Park Avenue at 68th Street. [See UES Manhattan 12i.].

[5a.] Caroline Ladd Pratt House (foreign student residence of Pratt Institute)/originally **Frederick B. Pratt Residence,** 229 Clinton Ave., bet. DeKalb and Willoughby Aves. E side. ca. 1898. Babb, Cook & Willard.

Attached on one side and freestanding on the other, it forms a neat and handsome **urban transition.** The pergola-ed entry supported by truncated **caryatids** and **atlantides** does the trick. The house proper is gray and white Georgian Revival.

[5b.] Residence, Bishop of Brooklyn (Roman Catholic)/originally **Charles Millard Pratt Residence,** 241 Clinton Ave., bet. DeKalb and Willoughby Aves. E side. 1893. William B. Tubby.

"Richardsonian" Romanesque of bold, strong forms, without the fussy picturesqueness of lesser acolytes than Tubby. Note the **spherical bronze lamp** at the **great arched porte cochère** and the **semicircular conservatory** to the south.

[5c.] St. Joseph's College/originally **George DuPont Pratt Residence,** 245 Clinton Ave. (north wing only), bet. DeKalb and Willoughby Aves. E side. 1901. Babb, Cook & Willard. Extensions to S by others, 1929.

A masonry cube of maroon Flemish-bond brick embellished with a variety of limestone ornament; more like an embassy than a residence. The additions by the college to the south are properly unprepossesing.

Turn right on Willoughby Avenue.

[6.] Clinton Hill Apartments, Section 1, Clinton to Waverly Aves., Willoughby to Myrtle Aves. 1943. Harrison & Abramovitz, Irwin Clavan.

World War II housing for the families of naval personnel (the old Navy Yard is only a short walk away), which remembered to include **blue and white nautical motifs** as ornament at the entrances despite wartime restrictions on everything else. (Section 2 was completed by the same architects farther south between Lafayette and Greene Avenues.)

[7.] Willoughby Walk Apartments, Hall St. to Classon Ave., Willoughby to Myrtle Aves. 1957. S.J. Kessler.

Undistinguished but very visible slabs, these marked the coming of urban renewal to the area. Federal subsidies absorbed 90 percent of the cost of land and demolition, making it feasible to build apartments for moderate-income families.

Enter the Pratt Campus at Ryerson Walk.

[8.] Pratt Institute Campus, Willoughby Ave. to DeKalb Ave., Classon Ave. to Hall St. 1887 to the present. Various architects.

Originally five blocks; renewal gave the opportunity to make a single, **campus-style superblock.** The separate buildings were built to conform to a **geometry of streets** that **no longer exists.** The in-between buildings were removed in favor of grass and parking lots, giving **a surrealistic result:** street architecture with both streets and most of the adjacent facades removed.

Pratt is **a professional school** of art, graphics, architecture, engineering, home economics, and library science. Old Charles Pratt ran it as his **personal paternalistic fiefdom** until his death in 1891.

[8a.] Memorial Hall, Pratt Institute, S of Willoughby Ave. on Ryerson Walk, E side. 1927. John Mead Howells.

Howells reversed history. Instead of grafting Byzantine capitals onto Classical columns to produce a Romanesque vocabulary, he grafted a neo-Byzantine, eclectically detailed hall onto a Romanesque revival.

[5a.] Orig. Frederick B. Pratt Res.   **[8b.]** The Main Bldg., Pratt Institute

[5b.] Orig. Charles Millard Pratt Res./now Residence, R.C. Bishop of Brooklyn

[8b.] Main Building, Pratt Institute, S of Memorial Hall on Ryerson Walk, E side. 1887. Lamb & Rich.

A gung-ho Romanesque Revival, the Main Building's innards have been tortured by **necessary surgery** as educational space-needs changed.

Looking backward: To enter the Pratt Institute engine room, located on the ground floor of the East Building (originally Machine Shop Building, 1887, William Windrim), is to pass through a time warp. Inside spin a gleaming trio of late 19th century Ames Iron Works steam engines (actually installed in 1900), whose electrical generators still supply one third of the campus buildings with 120-volt D.C. service. These and other antique artifacts form a veritable museum of industrial archeology. On display is the steam whistle of the DeLavergne Refrigerating Machine Company [see S Bronx 8.], chandeliers from the Singer Tower's boardroom, and a "No Loafing" sign from the Ruppert Brewery complex [see UES Manhattan/Yorkville 12.], among other industrial memorabilia. The chief engineer (and "curator" of the informal museum) is Conrad Milster: 636-3694.

To your right across the campus green is the library.

[8c.] Library/formerly **Pratt Institute Free Library, Pratt Institute,** Hall St. bet. Willoughby and DeKalb Aves., E. side. 1896. William B. Tubby. Alterations, 1936. John Mead Howells.

Tubby's stubby: strongly articulated brick piers give a bold face to Hall Street. A free Romanesque Revival, but with a classical plan. Originally Brooklyn's first **free** public library, it was restricted to Pratt students in 1940.

Walk east along the campus's long axis. At the far end is Pratt's newest building.

[10a.] Graham Home (photo 1967)   **[12.]** Higgins Hall, Pratt Institute

[8d.] Activity/Resource Center, Pratt Institute, E of Steuben St. Activity center (upper part), Daniel F. Tully Assocs. Resource center (lower part), Ezra D. Ehrenkranz & Assocs. 1975.

Architectural fashions traditionally **come late to Brooklyn,** across the river. This enormous hyperbolic paraboloid roofed building continues that tradition of tardiness. A decade or two after this style of construction **had its heyday elsewhere,** it appeared here with outdated precast exposed aggregate wall panels and a paltry outdoor amphitheater, a belated response to the student unrest of the early '70s.

[8e.] Pratt Row, 220–234 Willoughby Ave. S side, 171–185 Steuben St. E side, 172–186 Emerson Place. W side. ca. 1910. Hobart C. Walker.

Preserved despite the mandates of the same federal urban renewal legislation that produced Willoughby Walk [7.]: declare a certain percentage of existing units substandard. Today the 27 that remain—some were demolished—are faculty housing.

Retrace your steps and turn left at Ryerson Walk.

[8f.] Thrift Hall, Pratt Institute, Ryerson Walk, NE cor. DeKalb Ave. 1916. Shampan & Shampan.

"The Thrift," as its classical lettering and its Beaux Arts brick and limestone design proclaim, was built to be a bank though it is today used for offices. Charles Pratt, Sr., initiated the idea in 1889, a few years prior to his death—the original building was demolished to build Memorial Hall. The Thrift closed as a bank in the early 1940s.

Leave the campus and turn right on DeKalb Avenue and then left on Washington Avenue. Along the way is another example of high-rise housing.

[9.] University Terrace (apartments), DeKalb to Lafayette Aves., St. James Place to Classon Ave. 1963. Kelly & Gruzen.

The balconies are **recessed within the body** of the high rise, rather than **appliquéd.** This containment on three sides not only solves a design problem but also reduces the **possibility of vertigo.**

[10a.] Originally **Graham Home for Old Ladies,** 320 Washington Ave., bet. De Kalb and Lafayette Aves. W side. 1851.

Free Georgian with a touch of the Romanesque, it bears an incised stone plaque which speaks of **earlier days** and **earlier uses.** Applied to its facade is a newer sign: Bull Shippers Plaza Motor Inn.

[10b.] Underwood Park, Lafayette Ave., bet. Washington and Waverly Aves. N side.

Site of the former John T. Underwood mansion, the site of this mundane playground was donated to the city upon its demolition. Underwood was the typewriter tycoon.

Take a left onto Lafayette Avenue.

[11a.] Apostolic Faith Mission/originally **Orthodox Friends Meeting House,** 265 Lafayette Ave. NE cor. Washington Ave. 1868.

A simple Lombardian Romanesque box **polychromed with vigor** by its current tenants.

[11b.] Emmanuel Baptist Church, 279 Lafayette Ave., NW cor. St. James Place. 1887. Francis H. Kimball. ★

Porous Ohio sandstone was sculpted into an approximation of **French 13th-century Gothic.** The interior is a Scotch Presbyterian preaching room that is **startling in contrast,** with **radial seating** fanning from the pulpit and baptismal font.

[11a.] Apostolic Faith Mission (left) **[11b.]** Emmanuel Baptist Church (right)

St. James Place is your next routing. Turn right.

[12.] Higgins Hall, Pratt Institute/originally **Adelphi Academy,** St. James Place, bet. Lafayette Ave. and Clifton Place. North wing, 1887. Charles C. Haight. South wing, 1888. Mundell & Teckritz.

The brickmasons have been loose again with piers, buttresses, round arches, segmental arches, reveals, corbel-tables. The nature of the material is **exploited and exaggerated.** Henry Ward Beecher laid the cornerstone of the north (older) building, and Charles Pratt gave the latter.

[13.] St. James Place, the southerly extension of Hall St. **[14.] Clifton Place,** running E from St. James Place. **[15.] Cambridge Place,** starting S at Greene Ave., bet. St. James Place and Grand Ave.

Three **Places** that are really **places.** Each is a showpiece of urban row house architecture built for the Brooklyn middle class between the 1870s and 1890s. When bored by the excesses of the uniform row, architects turned to **picturesque variety,** giving identity of detail and silhouette to each owner, as in Nos. 202–210 St. James Place.

If you wish a peek at Cambridge Place, turn left at Greene Avenue for a short block and then return. If not, turn right on Greene and right again at Washington Avenue for a half-block excursion.

[16.] Mohawk Hotel/formerly The Mohawk (apartments), 379 Washington Ave., bet. Greene and Lafayette Aves. E side. 1904.

A Beaux Arts latecomer to the Hill. By the turn of the 20th century the idea of apartment living **had begun to catch on.** Nowadays an accommodation for transients.

[17.] Clinton Hill Branch, Brooklyn Public Library, 380 Washington Ave., bet. Greene and Lafayette Sts. W side. 1974. Bonsignore, Brignati, Goldstein & Mazzotta.

This lesser work, not offensive in itself, does not recognize—much less respond to—the architectural dignity of the rest of this avenue.

Retrace your steps southbound for more of Washington Avenue.

[18a.] 396 and 398 Washington Avenue (row houses), bet. Greene and Lafayette Aves. W side. Ca. 1890.

Bearded giants in the gables. Orange terra-cotta Queen Anne.

[18b.] 400, 402, and 404 Washington Avenue (row houses), NW cor. Greene Ave. ca. 1885.

A **trio** of Romanesque Revival **beauties.**

[19.] 417 Washington Avenue (single house), bet. Greene and Gates Aves. E side. ca. 1870.

Once there were expert carpenters (and shinglers, and so on), and this gem was just one result of their talents. Luckily for us its owner treasures it and its upkeep. Note this frame dwelling's monumental scale but miniature size.

[20a.] 460 Washington Avenue (single house), bet. Greene and Gates Aves. W side. ca. 1890.

A Queen Anne porch surrounds a brick and cast terra-cotta body. Boarded up in 1976, perhaps some use can be found for this one-time mansion.

[20b.] Brown Memorial Baptist Church/originally **Washington Avenue Baptist Church,** 484 Washington Ave., SW cor. Gates Ave. ca. 1895.

A pinch of Lombardian Romanesque decorates a square-turreted English Gothic body. The white **water tables** against red brick are perhaps too harsh.

End of Clinton Hill Walking Tour: The IND Eighth Avenue Subway, the A train, is a block south on Fulton Street—at the Clinton-Washington station. It connects with the IRT Lexington Avenue Line and the BMT at Broadway/Nassau-Fulton Street; with the IRT Seventh Avenue Line at Chambers Street/World Trade Center-Park Place.

THE NAVY YARD

[1.] Former **Brooklyn Navy Yard (officially The New York Naval Shipyard)/**now **C.L.I.C.K. Industrial Park,** Flushing Ave. to the East River, Hudson and Navy Sts. to Kent Ave.

Brooklyn's oldest industry, the then-shipyard was purchased by the Navy in 1801, abandoned in 1966. Seventy-one thousand naval and civilian personnel labored here, a city within the city, during World War II. Beginning in the late 1960s the area began undergoing conversion into an industrial park operated by a quasi-governmental, acronymed organization named Commerce, Labor, Industry of the County of Kings (C.L.I.C.K.).

Behind the gates of the old Navy Yard, as inaccessible to the public today as during wartime, lie these buildings:

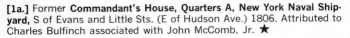

[1a.] Former **Commandant's House, Quarters A, New York Naval Shipyard,** S of Evans and Little Sts. (E of Hudson Ave.) 1806. Attributed to Charles Bulfinch associated with John McComb, Jr. ★

Only a glimpse of the rear is possible, for the **old Navy gates intervene.** In the past, a photograph had to satisfy most people except those with Admiral's rank or official business in the Yard. Abandoned in 1976, its future is cloudy.

[1a.] Formerly Commandant's House, Quarters A, New York Naval Shipyard

[1b.] Dry Dock #1 of the former New York Naval Shipyard, Dock St. at foot of 3rd St. 1851. William J. McAlpine, engineer primarily responsible. Thornton MacNess Niven, architect and master of masonry. ★

Considered one of the **great feats** of 19th-century American engineering, this granite-walled dry dock has serviced such ships as the *Niagara,* the vessel that laid **the first transatlantic cable,** and the *Monitor,* the Civil War's "cheesebox on a raft."

[2a.] Originally **U.S. Marine Hospital**/then **U.S. Naval Hospital,** Flushing Ave., bet. Ryerson St. and Williamsburg Place. N side. 1838. Martin E. Thompson. ★

Built of Sing Sing marble, this austerely modeled work is almost entirely devoid of ornament. Can it be that Mussolini's architects sought inspiration here for his University of Rome?

[2b.] Surgeon's House, Quarters R-1, Third Naval District, on grounds of U.S. Naval Hospital opp. Ryerson St. 1863. True W. Rollins and Charles Hastings, builders. ★

A spacious two-story brick house topped by a concave mansard roof in the French Second Empire style. This was the home of the naval hospital's chief surgeon.

[3.] Public School 46 Brooklyn, The Edward Blum School, 100 Clermont Ave., bet. Park and Myrtle Aves. 1958. Katz, Waisman, Blumenkranz, Stein, Weber, architects. Constantino Nivola, sculptor.

An austere white-glazed brick body, embellished with sculptured entrance canopies and chimney, and Nivola play horses in the playground. Edward Blum was the son-in-law of Abraham Abraham; each headed the Abraham & Straus department store. [See Civic Center/ Downtown Brooklyn 9a.]

[4.] U.S. Naval Receiving Station, 136 Flushing Ave. bet. Clermont and Vanderbilt Aves. to Park Ave. 1941.

Rare naval structures in that they are urban housing in its *strictest* sense, modern and permanent. They're also a bit rigid.

RED HOOK

Partly residential, partly industrial, generally squalid. The most impressive things in this area are the docks and the ships. Its immense low-rent housing project of the thirties is simply that: immense. Though these units are four stories high, like Williamsburg and Harlem River Houses, they prove that scale alone is not sufficient **to create an environment;** design must include a broader palette. For such a broad palette see Ciardullo Associates' N.Y. Urban Coalition housing [2. below].

[1.] Pioneer Street, bet. Van Brunt and Richards Sts. ca. 1840.

From out of nowhere appears this charming row of early houses; until 1972 by far the **best** bit of environment in the area.

[2a.] 71–79, 81–89 Visitation Place, bet. Van Brunt and Richards Sts. S side. **[2b.] 2–12 Verona St.** N side. **[2c.] 9–19 Dwight St.** E side. All 1972. Ciardullo Assocs.

Federally subsidized low-rent (and *low-cost*) rental housing sponsored by the **N.Y. Urban Coalition**—a terrific example of what can be done without a municipal authority as **Big Brother.** Sixty-four units in three-story-high brick-block houses. This success led to more such work in the Bronx [see S Bronx 3.].

[3.] Orig. Bklyn. Clay Retort & Firebrick Works: Van Dyke St. cor. Richards St.

[3.] Originally **Brooklyn Clay Retort and Firebrick Works,** Beard to Van Dyke Sts., bet. Van Brunt and Richards Sts. ca. 1860.

Two **sturdy** granite warehouses, on the north sides of both Beard and Van Dyke Streets just west of Richards, and a **manufactory** with original masonry chimney, on the south side of Van Dyke, are all that remain of this **major enterprise.** Clay from South Amboy, New Jersey, was barged in to nearby Erie Basin and **converted to firebrick** here.

[4a.] Originally **Beard & Robinson Stores,** along Erie Basin, 260 Beard St. SE cor. Van Brunt St. 1869. **[4b.] Van Brunt's Stores,** along Erie Basin, 480 Van Brunt St. S of Beard St. ca. 1869.

Half-round arched openings and down-to-earth brickwork commend these and other nearby post–Civil War **wharfside warehouses,** which are the epitome of **"the functional tradition."** Compare with the much better known Empire Stores [Fulton Ferry 6b.]. A cut-stone marker modestly appears at the street-side southernmost point of Beard & Robinson. **Look up.**

[5.] Todd Shipyards Corporation, Beard St., bet. Dwight and Otsego Sts. S side. Engine house, ca. 1865.

Though its arched Romanesque Revival entrance is bricked up, the remainder of this tribute to 19th-century brickwork has **much to offer the eye.** The later Todd buildings are respectful neighbors.

Erie Basin: The scythe-shaped breakwater defining Erie Basin and protecting ships docked there from ocean waves was the idea of enterprising William Beard, a railroad contractor who completed it in 1864. He charged ships seeking to haul American cargoes 50 cents per cubic yard to deposit the rock they had carried as ballast from overseas ports. The rock then went into building the breakwater. Incidentally, the longest dead-end street in New York is Columbia Street at Erie Basin. Drive out and see oceangoing vessels parallel parked in the adjacent slips and the dry docks of Todd Shipyards Corporation across the way.

[6.] Originally **Port of New York Grain Elevator Terminal, N.Y. State Barge Canal System,** Henry St. Basin. (Best seen from Columbia Street.) 1922.

Concrete silos dramatically lined up to receive grain shipments from incoming ships. The decline of grain traffic in New York harbor caused their deactivation in 1955. Endangered.

[7.] Red Hook Play Center (swimming pool and bathhouse), Bay St., bet. Clinton and Henry Sts., through to Lorraine St. 1936. N.Y.C. Parks Department, Aymar Embury II, consulting architect.

A WPA, Great Depression pool-bathhouse complex occupying a whole block. Look at those arches and cylindrical piers!

SUNSET PARK AND ENVIRONS

Sunset Park is a neighborhood named, understandably, after its park, a sloping **green baize oasis** with sweeping views of New York Harbor. Though **once heavily Scandinavian,** the community has changed and is now **equally heavily Hispanic.** On the flats between the elevated Gowanus Expressway (over Third Avenue) and the waterfront lie **Bush Terminal** at the north and the old **Brooklyn Army Terminal** at the south. Beginning a few blocks north of Sunset Park (the park) is the enormous and very beautiful Victorian burying ground, Green-Wood Cemetery.

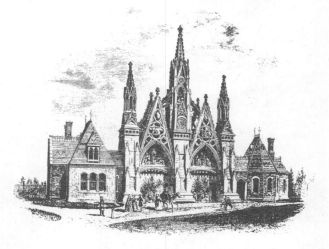

[1.] Green-Wood Cemetery, Fifth Ave. to MacDonald Ave. and Fort Hamilton Pkwy., 20th to 37th Sts. 1840. **[1a.] Main Entrance Gate and Gatehouse,** Fifth Ave. opp. 25th St. E side. 1861. Richard Upjohn & Son. **[1b.] Gate and Gatehouse,** 20th St. opp. Prospect Park West, S side. 1920. Warren & Wetmore. **[1c.] Fort Hamilton Parkway Gate and Gatehouse,** 37th St. W of Ft. Hamilton Pkwy. 1875. Richard M. Upjohn. Only the main gate is always open during visiting hours. Telephone: 768-7300.

Opened in 1840, this cemetery covers 478 acres and includes the **highest point in Brooklyn** (216 feet above sea level). It would be worth visiting merely for its hills, ponds, plantings, and its superb view of the harbor, but there is much more. Most of the more than one-half million buried here (including **Henry Ward Beecher, Currier and Ives, Peter**

Cooper, Samuel F. B. Morse, "Boss" Tweed, and Lola Montez) are memorialized by extraordinary mausoleums and monuments. A veritable **history of Victorian New York** is indexed by the gravestones and the more elaborate markers. At the **main entrance,** appropriately, is an especially fine gate and gatehouse, a Gothic Revival counterpart to a pair of Roman triumphal arches. **Alan Burnham** has called it the **"culmination" of the Gothic Revival movement** in New York. The entry structure includes offices and even a clock tower, all built of brownstone with polychromed slate roofs on the office wings. The composition has **exaggerated verticals** and is **deliberately squeezed horizontally,** the clock face barely fitting within a face of the central steeple.

[2.] Former **Weir & Co. Greenhouse,** Fifth Ave., SW cor. 25th St.

A charming miniature Crystal Palace, across from Green-Wood's main entrance.

[4.] St. Michael's Church: a prominent landmark in this low-rise community

[3.] Alku, "Alku" Toinen, Finnish Cooperative Apartments, 816–826 43rd St., bet. Eighth and Ninth Aves. S side. 1916.

No. 816, a not-too-unusual apartment building, is reputedly the **first cooperative dwelling** in New York.

[4.] St. Michael's Roman Catholic Church, 4200 Fourth Ave., SW cor. 42nd St. 1905. Raymond F. Almirall.

Brooklyn's own **Sacré Coeur,** except that the egg-shaped domes are grouped on its prominent 200-foot tower.

Bush Terminal District: Created by Irving T. Bush in 1890, this is an industrial and warehouse **city within the city** containing loft, freight depot, and pier facilities.

[5.] Bush Terminal, 28th St. to 50th St., Upper Bay to Second Ave. (irregular) ca. 1911. William Higginson.

Block after block of eight-story, white-painted concrete loft buildings are the visual evidence of this mammoth **industrial and warehousing** enterprise. Some older red brick buildings still exist in the vicinity of First Avenue and 43rd Street.

[6.] National Metal Co./now **loft space,** 4201–4207 First Ave., SE cor. 42nd St. ca. 1885.

Its ornamental red brick tower is a local landmark—and enigma.

[7.] 2nd Battalion Armory, N.Y. Naval Militia: a bold waterfront silhouette

[7.] 2nd Battalion Armory, N.Y. Naval Militia, 5100 First Ave., bet. 51st and 52nd Sts. W side. 1904. Lord & Hewlett.

Magnificent **parabolic arched** naval armory more reminiscent of **dirigible hangars** of the pre-*Hindenburg* era; no attempt here (as in other armories) to disguise the structural form, only to embellish it, with a romantic facade of crenellated towers and battlements. Abandoned, and therefore endangered.

[8.] 68th Precinct Station House, N.Y.C. Police Department, 333 65th St., bet. Third and Fourth Aves. N side. 1970. Milton F. Kirchman.

An overly expressionistic composition of volumes and voids. From this early design effort came a later, more mature development of a similar facility. [See H Manhattan/E Harlem 7.]

[9.] Originally **New York Port of Embarkation and Army Supply Base (Brooklyn Army Terminal)/**officially **Military Ocean Terminal,** Second Ave. bet. 58th and 65th Sts., W side. 1918. Cass Gilbert.

As the **Woolworth Building** by the same architect was tall and embellished, these utilitarian warehouses are long and devoid of extraneous ornament. The innards parallel a **skylighted** central gallery.

[10.] State Arsenal, N.Y. National Guard, Second Ave. bet. 64th and 65th Sts. E side.

If the nearby Brooklyn Army Terminal buildings lack extraneous ornament, this quartermaster and ordnance facility is downright grim. The ivy-covered walls, however, happily temper the severity.

PARK SLOPE

A somber-hued wonderland of **finials, pinnacles, pediments, towers, turrets,** and **bay windows:** a *smörgasbord* of late Victoriana, and the successor to the **Heights** and the **Hill** as bedroom to the middle class and wealthy. These three districts are, together, the prominent topographic precincts of old brownstone Brooklyn (the **Heights** is a *bluff* over the harbor; the **Hill** a major *crest* to the northeast; and the **Slope** *slopes* from the **Gowanus Canal** up to **Prospect Park**).

Despite its proximity to the park, the area was slow to develop. As late as 1884 it was still characterized as "fields and pasture." **Edwin C. Litchfield's Italianate villa,** completed in **1857,** alone commanded the view to the harbor from the hill it occupies today off Prospect Park West. The primary stage of the park had been already complete in **1871,** yet the **Slope** lay quiet and tranquil, bypassed by thousands of persons on the Flatbush Avenue horsecars making their way to the newly created recreation area. By the mid-**80s,** however, the potential of the **Slope** became apparent, and mansions began to appear on the newly built grid of streets.

The lavish homes clustered along **Plaza Street** and **Prospect Park West** eventually were christened *The Gold Coast.* Massive apartment buildings invaded the area after **World War I,** feeding upon the large, underutilized plots of land occupied by the first growth. These austere **Park-Avenue-like** structures, concentrated at **Grand Army Plaza,** are in contrast to the richly imaginative brick dwellings of **Carroll Street** and **Montgomery Place,** the mansions and churches and clubs that still remain, and the remarkably varied row houses occupying the side streets as they descend toward the skyscrapers of **Manhattan** to the west.

[1.] Park Slope Historic District, generally along the S flank of Flatbush Ave. and Plaza St. and the W flank of Prospect Park West; W to Sixth Ave. N of Union St., W to Seventh Ave. N of 5th St., and W to Eighth Ave. N of 15th St. District designated, 1973. ★

When discussions began, in the late 1960s, to determine the boundaries of a Park Slope historic district, they were to include only the "park blocks," perhaps influenced by the park blocks that flank Prospect Park's older sibling in Manhattan, Central Park. The Slope, emerging as a newly rediscovered brownstone area in that period, was recognized as having a rich fabric of row housing both inside and outside that arbitrary boundary. The district eventually designated reaches northwesterly from the park blocks to encompass part of the richness of Sixth Avenue between Berkeley and Sterling Places.

Note: All the Park Slope entries lie within the historic district unless otherwise noted.

Park Slope Walking Tour A: From the newsstand where Flatbush Avenue joins Grand Army Plaza (at the surface of the IRT Seventh Avenue Subway's Grand Army Plaza Station) south into Park Slope and return. Cross Plaza Street and admire:

[1a.] The Montauk Club, 25 Eighth Ave., NE cor. Lincoln Place. 1891. Francis H. Kimball.

A **Venetian Gothic** palazzo, whose canal is the narrow lawn separating it from its Indian-head-encrusted, cast-iron fence. Remember the *Ça d'Oro*? But here in brownstone, brick, terra cotta, and verdigris copper. It bears the name of a local tribe, which explains the varied Indian motifs. Continue south on Plaza Street and turn right into Berkeley Place.

[2.] Originally **George P. Tangeman Residence,** 276 Berkeley Place, bet. Plaza St. and Eighth Ave. S side. 1891. Lamb & Rich.

Brick, granite, and terra-cotta **Romanesque Revival,** paid for by Cleveland Baking Powder. Cupid caryatids hold up the shingled pediment.

[3.] 64–66 Eighth Avenue (row houses), bet. Berkeley Place and Union St. W side. 1889. Parfitt Bros.

Two bold whitestone and granite residences by popular architects of the period: they bear carved foliate bas-reliefs worthy of **Louis Sullivan.**

Take a peek to the right down Union Street.

PARK SLOPE / PROSPECT PARK

N

Park Slope

Crown Heights

ST MARKS AVE
28
PROSPECT
27
PARK
STERLING
26
ST JOHNS
25
21 20
LINCOLN
BERKELEY
UNION
24
23 19
17 18
PRESIDENT
CARROLL
22
Walking Tour B
GARFIELD

T IRT

BERGEN
ST. MARKS
PL.
PROSPECT
STERLING
PL.

T BMT/IND

T IRT
1b
Grand Army Plaza
1c

ST. 4
8
2
5a
11
5b
12
6 5c
10 8
Walking Tour A
13
1

1a
1

Central
Library

ST. JOHNS
LINCOLN

EASTERN

T IRT
BROOKLYN
MUSEUM
23

BOTANIC

1d

4a
4b

14
15
16a
16b

5

6

Institute Park Walking Tour
22
21
20

GARDENS

The Zoo
8 7

16b
16a 19
17

9

Prospect Park Walking Tour

32
11th St.
12th St.
13th St.
30

10

PROSPECT PARK

BMT IND T

11

BEEKMAN

12

J K L M

13

WESTBURY

SHERMAN
AVE

The Lake

BMT IND T

KENMORE

IND T

PARKSIDE
15

PARADE GROUNDS

CATON

0   1000   2000 feet

[4a.] 889–903 Union Street, bet. Eighth and Ninth Aves. N side. 1889. Albert E. White.

A picturesque **octet** of eclectic medieval and Classical parts.

[4b.] 905–913 Union Street, bet. Eighth and Ninth Aves. N side. 1895. Thomas McMahon.

Brick, brownstone, and shingle Queen Anne **quintet.**

[5a.] Missionary Servants of the Most Holy Trinity Residence/originally **Stuart Woodford Residence,** 869 President St., bet. Seventh and Eighth Aves. 1885. Henry Ogden Avery.

Painted red brick is here punctuated by two oriel windows bracketed from the wall on **Viollet-le-Duc**-inspired struts. Woodford was onetime ambassador to Spain.

[5b.] 876–878 President Street (row houses), bet. Seventh and Eighth Aves. S side. 1889. Albert E. White.

Roman brick and brownstone, bay-windowed Queen Anne.

[5c.] 944–946 President Street (row houses), bet. Prospect Park W. and Eighth Ave. S side. 1886–1890. Attributed to Charles T. Mott.

Brick and brownstone picturesque pair. Note the rich wrought iron, stained glass, and terra-cotta tile.

[6.] 105 Eighth Avenue (residence), bet. President and Carroll Sts. E side. 1916. Helmle & Huberty.

A neo-Classical mansion.

[7.] 18 and 19 Prospect Park West (residences), SW cor. Carroll St. 1898. Montrose W. Morris.

An eclectic Renaissance Revival in limestone. Note the second and third floor Ionic pilasters and the hemispherical glass and bronze entrance canopy at No. 18.

[8.] Carroll Street, bet. Prospect Park W. and Eighth Ave. 1887–1911. Various architects.

The *north* side of this street is as **calm, orderly, and disciplined** in its row housing as the *south* side is **picturesque.** This block of Carroll Street is visual evidence of a significant change in style. Some samples:

North Side

863	1890	Napoleon LeBrun & Sons.
861–855	1892	Stanley M. Holden. A quartet of yellow Roman brick and brownstone Romanesque Revival: stained glass, carved faces, and decoration.

South Side

878–876	1911	Chappell & Bosworth. Victorian "Georgian."
872–864	1887	William B. Tubby. Queen Anne shingles and brick.
862	1889	F.B. Langston. Dour polychromed brick and sandstone.
860	1889	Romantic in the spirit of Philadelphia's Wilson Eyre.
858–856	1889	Brownstone supports orange Roman brick.
848	1905	William B. Greenman. A narrow bay window.
846–838	1887	C.P.H. Gilbert. Three forty-foot brownstone and Roman brick beauties and the beast.

[9.] Thomas Adams, Jr., Residence, 119 Eighth Ave., NE cor. Carroll St. 1888. C.P.H. Gilbert.

A brownstone arch worthy of **Louis Sullivan,** and incised with naturalistic bas-reliefs in his fashion, supported by two **Romanesque**-capped columns. The important did or do enter here to visit this mansion built for the inventor of **Chiclets.**

[10.] 123 Eighth Avenue (residence), SE cor. Carroll St. 1894. Montrose W. Morris.

Dirty gray brick and terra cotta in a free version of **Italian Renaissance Revival.**

[11.] Old First Reformed Church, 126 Seventh Ave., NW cor. Carroll St. 1893. George L. Morse.

A bulky granite and limestone **neo-Gothic.**

[12.] 12, 14, and 16 Fiske Place (row houses), bet. Carroll St. and Garfield Place, W side. 1896.

A trio where "bay" windows are handled like an academic exercise in design: a *square*, a *semicircle*, a *triangle.* Very neat. The developer thought so too—the same grouping occurs in the same sequence one block west at **11, 15, and 17 Polhemus Place.**

[5a.] Orig. Stuart Woodford Residence

[7.] Eighteen Prospect Park West

[9.] Thomas Adams, Jr., Residence

[12.] 12, 14, and 16 Fiske Place

Turn left onto Garfield Place and left again onto Eighth Avenue. As you do, take note that James A. Farrell, elected president of the United States Steel Corporation in 1911, lived at 249 Garfield Place during his tenure.

What shall we call it? Naming apartment buildings to give them personality may have begun with Manhattan's **Dakota.** At the northwest corner of Garfield Place and Eighth Avenue are four more modest works: the **Serine,** the **Lillian,** and the **Belvedere,** but the Gallic influence won out on number four: the **Ontrinue.**

Park Slope: see map p. 427

[13.] Montgomery Place, bet. Eighth Ave. and Prospect Park W. 1888–1904.

A grand street, only a block long, displaying a rich texture of houses built as a real estate scheme by **Harvey Murdock.** He sought the picturesque, and commissioned the noted architect **C.P.H. Gilbert** to create the product. An *Art Moderne* amber brick apartment house closes the vista at Eighth Avenue—an accidental and successful closing of the street's space.

North Side: 11, 17, 19, 1898. C.P.H. Gilbert. **21, 25,** 1892. C.P.H. Gilbert. **27, 29,** 1904. Unattributed. **31,** 1889. Hornium Bros. **37–43,** 1891. George B. Chappell. **45,** 1899. Babb, Cook & Willard. **47,** 1890. R.L. Daus.

South Side: 14–18, 1888. C.P.H. Gilbert. **20–28,** 1898. Unattributed. **30–34,** 1896. Robert Dixon. **36–46,** 1889. C.P.H. Gilbert, **48–50,** 1890. C.P.H. Gilbert. **52,** 1890. T. Williams. **54–60,** 1890. C.P.H. Gilbert.

Turn right at Prospect Park West and proceed south.

[13.] Montgomery Place (houses)

[19.] Orig. Lillian Ward Residence

[14.] Brooklyn Ethical Culture School/formerly **Henry J. Hulbert Residence,** 49 Prospect Park W., bet. 1st and 2nd Sts. W side. 1892. Montrose W. Morris.

A bland and pasty mansion more noted for its size and historical role than any great architectural distinction.

[15.] Brooklyn Ethical Culture Society Meeting House/originally **William H. Childs Residence,** 53 Prospect Park W., NW cor. 2nd St. 1901. William B. Tubby.

A Jacobean loner in these turgid stone precincts. Built for the inventor of **Bon Ami** (cleansing powder, as opposed to the baking powder of [2.]).

Continue south along Prospect Park West to 4th Street. On your left in the park you will see:

[16a.] Third Street Playground, in Prospect Park SE of 3rd St. 1975. Richard Dattner & Assocs.

A Central Park **adventure playground** transposed to Prospect.

[16b.] Litchfield Villa/or **Ridgewood**/or **Grace Hill Mansion**/now **Brooklyn Headquarters, N.Y.C. Parks and Recreation Department,** Prospect Park W., bet. 4th and 5th Sts. E side. 1857. Alexander Jackson Davis. ★ Annex, 1913. Helmle & Huberty.

The villa of **Edwin C. Litchfield,** a lawyer whose fortune was made in midwestern railroad development. In the 1850s he acquired a square mile of virtually vacant land extending from **1st** to **9th Streets** and from the

Gowanus Canal to the projected line of **Tenth Avenue,** just east of his completed mansion: a territory that includes a **major portion** of today's **Park Slope.**

The mansion is the **best surviving example** of Davis's Italianate style, but more than 80 years as a public office **have eroded much** of its original richness: the original exterior stucco, simulating cut stone, has been **stripped off,** exposing **common brick** behind. Note the **corncob capitals** on its porches: an Americanization of things Roman? Corinthian, or *Corninthian?*

End of Park Slope Walking Tour A: Walk north on Prospect Park West to the Grand Army Plaza Subway Station.

Park Slope Walking Tour B: From the newsstand where Flatbush Avenue joins Grand Army Plaza (at the surface of the IRT Seventh Avenue Subway's Grand Army Plaza Station) to the Bergen Street Station of the same subway. Proceed south on St. John's Place. The silhouetted church spires you see on this lovely street are those of:

[16b.] The romantic Italianate Litchfield Villa by Alexander Jackson Davis

[17.] Memorial Presbyterian Church, 42–48 Seventh Ave., SW cor. St. John's Place. 1883. Pugin & Walter. **Chapel,** 1888. Marshall & Walter.

An ashlar brownstone sculpted monolith. Tiffany glass windows embellish both church and chapel.

[18.] Grace United Methodist Church and Parsonage, 29–35 Seventh Ave., NE cor. St. John's Place. 1882. Parfitt Bros.

View particularly the *Moorish-Romanesque* detailing along the St. John's Place facade.

[19.] Originally **Lillian Ward Residence,** 21 Seventh Ave., SE cor. Sterling Place. 1887. Lawrence B. Valk.

A **fanciful cylindrical tower** worthy of the French Renaissance guards this corner: all crowned with a polychromed and finialed roof. This special place (called *mansion* locally) and its neighbors at **23–27** were built by **Valk** for investor **Charles Pied;** a rare and rich group to be still so well preserved. **Miss Ward** was a **noted opera star** of the early 20th century.

Plane Crash: In the morning mist of **December 16, 1960,** two airliners collided in the air over Staten Island. The pilot of one attempted an emergency landing in Prospect Park, but made it only to the intersection of Seventh Avenue and Sterling Place. The plane sliced the cornice off a small apartment building west of Seventh Avenue (the light-colored brick marks the spot) and came to rest with its nose at the doorstep of the old Ward Mansion. A church on Sterling Place was destroyed by the resulting fire, but, miraculously, the mansion was untouched.

Retrace your steps on Seventh Avenue south to St. John's Place. On your right between Sixth and Seventh Avenues are St. John's Episcopal Church at No. 139, and two robust Victorian town houses across the way at Nos. 176 and 178.

[20.] St. John's Episcopal Church, 139 St. John's Place, bet. Seventh and Sixth Aves. 1870.

Victorian Gothic in varied-color brownstone: another **English country church** for Brooklyn.

[21.] William M. Thallon and Edward Bunker Residences, 176 and 178 St. John's Place, bet. Seventh and Sixth Aves. S side. 1888. R.L. Daus.

Brownstone and brick eclectic mélange: some flavor from the **Loire Valley,** some from the **Black Forest.** Note **the caduceus** in No. 178's gable; both Thallon and Bunker were physicians.

[22.] Helen Owen Carey Child Development Center, 71 Lincoln Place, bet. Seventh and Eighth Aves. N side. 1974. Beyer Blinder Belle.

A friendly brown brick form in **happy scale** with its neighbors.

[22.] Helen Owen Carey Child Center   **[26.]** Saint Augustine's R.C. Church

[23a.] Brooklyn Conservatory of Music/formerly **Park Slope Masonic Club**/originally **M. Brasher House,** 58 Seventh Ave., NW cor. Lincoln Place. 1881. S.F. Evelette.

Austere brick and brownstone.

[23b.] Originally **John Condon Residence,** 139 Lincoln Place, bet. Sixth and Seventh Aves. N side. 1881.

Romanesque Revival. Note the **lion's-head corbel.** Condon was a florist whose place of business was on Fifth Avenue opposite Green-Wood Cemetery.

[23c.] Lincoln Hotel/formerly **F.L. Babbott Residence,** 153 Lincoln Place, bet. Sixth and Seventh Aves. N side. 1887. Lamb & Rich. Enlarged, 1896.

Romanesque Revival *reincarnated* in **black and gold jazz.**

[24.] 214 Lincoln Place (residence), bet. Fifth and Sixth Aves. S side. 1883. Charles Werner.

Queen Anne for Charles Fletcher, a gas company president.

[25.] Sixth Avenue Baptist Church, Sixth Ave., NE cor. Lincoln Place. 1880. Lawrence B. Valk.

A small-scaled brick church, **de-steepled** in the 1938 hurricane.

[26.] St. Augustine's Roman Catholic Church, 116 Sixth Ave., bet. Sterling and Park Places. W side. 1888–1892. Parfitt Bros.

Sixth Avenue is one of **Park Slope's** finest streets, block after block containing rows of amazingly well preserved row houses. **St. Augustine's** provides a bulky monument along the stately avenue. The crusty tower with its mottled, rockface brownstone contrasts with the smooth row housing. The tower's finials include an elegant angel **Gabriel.**

[27.] Cathedral Club of Brooklyn/originally **The Carlton Club,** 85 Sixth Ave., SE cor. St. Mark's Place. 1890. Not included within the historic district.

Built as an exclusive clubhouse, it changed hands to become successively the **Monroe Club,** the **Royal Arcanum Club,** and, in 1907, through the efforts of a young priest, the **Cathedral Club,** a Roman Catholic fraternal organization. The priest went on to become Cardinal Mundelein of Chicago.

[28.] "Pintchikville," Flatbush Ave. and Bergen St. in every direction. Not included within historic district.

If **"Pop Art"** had its origins in New York, certainly this area must have been influential in giving it impetus. Building after building has been raucously decorated in bright colors all calling attention to **Pintchik's,** a series of emporiums for every sort of home decoration material: *linoleum, tile, paint, carpeting, lamps, and what-have-you.* There is an **immense scale** to the advertising which covers every inch of the old facades on both sides of the street.

End of Park Slope Walking Tour B: The Bergen Street stop of the IRT Seventh Avenue Subway is close by.

Miscellany:

Note: The entries which follow are all *outside* the historic district unless otherwise noted.

[29.] Public School 39 Brooklyn, The Henry Bristow School, 417 Sixth Ave., NE cor. 8th St. 1877. Samuel B. Leonard, superintendent of buildings, City of Brooklyn Board of Education. ★

A **petite** Victorian schoolhouse of red brick. Park Slope was largely undeveloped at the time.

[30.] Public School 107 Brooklyn, The John W. Kimball School, 1301 Eighth Ave., SE cor. 13th St. 1894. J. M. Naughton. Included within the historic district.

An **overblown** Victorian schoolhouse of buff brick. The population of the community had begun to mushroom.

[31.] 14th Regiment Armory, N.Y. National Guard, 1402 Eighth Ave., bet. 14th and 15th Sts. W side. 1895. William A. Mundell. Altered.

Picturesque massing and **heroic** brick detailing make this a **special event** among the rows of brownstones in the community. The statue of the doughboy out front dates from after World War I.

World's Largest Clock Factory: In 1877 the Ansonia Clock Company established a factory on the east side of Seventh Avenue between 12th and 13th Streets, employing 1,500 workers. It was the world's largest clock factory in its time. The brick "functionalist" tradition buildings still exist at the site.

[32a.] Ladder Company 122, N.Y.C. Fire Department, 532 11th St., bet. Seventh and Eighth Aves. S side. 1883. **[32b.] Engine Company 220, N.Y.C. Fire Department,** 530 11th St. 1907.

The older Italianate firehouse (which occupies its entire lot) once was **adequate** for the neighborhood's needs. As the row houses **filled every vacant parcel** up to Prospect Park's edge, the **Classical adjunct** to the west was added. They make **a fine pair** of architectural contrasts.

[33.] Vechte-Cortelyou House, in James J. Byrne Memorial Playground, 3rd St., SW cor. Fifth Ave. Originally built, 1699. Replica, 1935.

Known as the *Old Stone House at Gowanus,* the building now occupying the site was **recreated** by the city's Parks Department in 1935 using old sketches and what were believed to be **the old stones**—the original house has long ago **fallen into total ruin.** In its recreated state it served as a playground office and comfort station until **it too was vandalized.** There are plans for reconstruction—again.

The most severe fighting in the Revolutionary War's Battle of Long Island took place here, **General Stirling's** Continental troops fighting a delaying action with Cornwallis' superior number of redcoats, thus permitting Washington's successful retreat.

[33.] Old Stone House at Gowanus/now called the Vechte-Cortelyou House

Where the Dodgers played: The James J. Byrne Memorial Playground (the west side of Fifth Avenue below Third Street) is named for the owner of the forebears of the Brooklyn Dodgers baseball club at the time they played there, the first Washington Park ballfield. Byrne then moved them to Eastern Park, near today's Broadway Junction. Failing to attract crowds to what was then a remote location, Charley Ebbet persuaded the team to return to these precincts, to a new Washington Park, this time on the west side of Fourth Avenue between First and Third Streets. It is from there that the Dodgers moved to the more commodious stadium on Bedford Avenue named for their new owner, Ebbets Field, which Brooklynites will never forget.

PROSPECT PARK/GRAND ARMY PLAZA/"INSTITUTE PARK"

[1.] Grand Army Plaza, within Plaza St. at the intersection of Flatbush Ave., Prospect Park W., Eastern Pkwy., and Vanderbilt Ave. 1870. Frederick Law Olmsted and Calvert Vaux. Scenic landmark. ★

Olmsted & Vaux designed this monumental oval plaza in the spirit of Paris' **Étoile** (that circular traffic island bearing the Arc de Triomphe). The triumphal arch here, however, did not arrive for 26 years: the **Soldiers' and Sailors' Memorial Arch [1a.],** by John H. Duncan, architect of Grant's Tomb, completed in **1892,** commemorating Union forces in the Civil War. The arch provides an elegant armature for sculpture, most spectacular of which is **Frederick MacMonnies'** huge *quadriga* on top **(1898).** Inside the arch itself is more subtle work, bas-reliefs of *Lincoln* (by Thomas Eakins), and *Grant* (by William O'Donovan), both placed there in **1895.** On the south pedestals are two bristling groups representing *the Army and the Navy* by MacMonnies, dating from **1901.**

The oval island to the north of the arch (difficult to reach on foot in the streaming traffic) is of a more homely scale, with a double ring of formally trimmed London plane trees surrounding a generous complex of stairs and terraces, and a fountain. Around the **John F. Kennedy Memorial [1b.]** at the north end (1965. Morris Ketchum, Jr. & Assocs., architects; Neil Estern, sculptor), the scale shrinks noticeably. This little memorial,

New York's only official memorial to **President Kennedy,** was originally designed as a marble cube with a flame on top, later abandoned as an unsuitable duplication of the perpetual flame in Arlington Cemetery; its present form is a compromise, Kennedy's bust bracketed from the side. Budget-makers here demeaned it all by causing the cube to be merely a box of thin butted marble slabs rather than the monolithic cube it should have been. The **Bailey Fountain** (1932. Edgerton Swarthwout, architect; Eugene Savage, sculptor) **[1c.]**, a lush mass of verdigris bronze **Tritons** and **Neptune,** is a *delight* when turned on, a *pleasure* all the time.

While the arch was being embellished, **a necklace of Classical ornaments** were being strung across the park entrances facing it **[1d.]**. Four 50-foot Doric columns rising out of entangling fasces, and topped with harpy-like eagles (by MacMonnies), railings, bronze urns, and lamp standards, and two **twelve-sided "temples,"** were all designed by Stanford White, and completed in **1894.** Of the whole ensemble, the temples—with their polished granite **Tuscan** columns, **Guastavino** vaulting, and bronze finials—probably show **White's** abilities best: note particularly the lamp standards.

[1a.] The Neo-Roman Soldiers' and Sailors' Arch, memorial to the Union Army

[2.] Main Branch (Ingersoll Memorial), Brooklyn Public Library, Grand Army Plaza at the intersection of Flatbush Ave. and Eastern Pkwy. 1941. Githens & Keally, architects; Paul Jennewein, sculptor of bas-reliefs; Thomas H. James, sculptor of screen over entry.

Streamlined Beaux Arts, or an example of how the **École des Beaux Arts** confronted the **Art Moderne** of the **Paris Exposition** of **1937.** In effect, it is a formal participant in the geometry of avenues radiating from the **Soldiers' and Sailors' Arch,** but styled after the 1937 Exposition idiom. Inside is lots of grand space.

Prospect Park

Once past **Stanford White's** ring, one sees **Olmsted and Vaux's** park much as they conceived it. They considered it a better work than their first collaboration, **Central Park.** There are several reasons, none of which reflect on **Central Park.** The main one is that since the commission did not result from a competition (with its inevitably fixed site and program), **Olmsted and Vaux** had a chance to change the problem given, and they did. Delay of construction due to the Civil War aided their efforts. Almost half of the land the City set aside for a park in the **1850s** lay to the northeast of **Flatbush Avenue,** the main artery to **Flatbush** (then a town in its own right); it centered about the reservoir on **Prospect Hill** (since filled in and used as a playground). **Olmsted and Vaux** rejected a scheme **[Figure a.]** that completely bisected the projected park, recommending instead that the allotted land be expanded to the south and west **[Figure b.]**. In lopping off the land to the northeast, they lost the hill that gave the park its name, but they also got rid of the reservoir (a major part of Central Park to this day), and provided a tract on which related institutions (the **Library,** the **Brooklyn Museum,** and the **Brooklyn Botanic Garden**) could be located without consuming park space (as the Metropolitan Museum does in Manhattan). Another encumbrance reduced considerably here is road area; with a more compact shape, and without transverse roads, **Prospect Park** gives up a much smaller portion of its area to cars (of course originally to carriages).

[3.] Prospect Park, Grand Army Plaza, Prospect Park W., Prospect Park SW., Parkside Ave., Ocean Ave., and Flatbush Ave. 1866–1874. Frederick Law Olmsted and Calvert Vaux. Altered since. Scenic landmark. ★

[a.] Original land allocation for Prospect Park, prior to Olmsted & Vaux

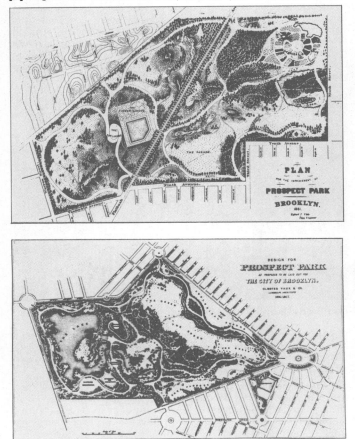

[b.] Olmsted & Vaux' revised "taking" of land for the proposed Prospect Park

Prospect Park Walking Tour: Grand Army Plaza (IRT Seventh Avenue Subway to the station of the same name), to southeast entrance at Parkside and Ocean Avenues (BMT/IND Brighton Line's Parkside Avenue stop. Connections to IRT at Atlantic Avenue).

Enter between the east (left) pair of Doric columns. Note the statue of **James Stranahan** (1891. Frederick MacMonnies, sculptor), whose personal 24-year crusade is largely responsible for both **Prospect Park** and Brooklyn's "*Park*ways" **(Eastern and Ocean).** Note also the pine grove along the walk, which is repeated on the opposite corner as the symmetry of the entrance composition blends into the picturesque layout of the park. Like all walks entering this park, it quickly loses visual connection with the point of entrance through its twisting route and the modeling of the terrain.

Turn right at the first fork to **Endale Arch [4a.],** the first structure completed in the park **(1867),** a dramatic tunnel transition into bright sunlight and a half-mile vista down the Long Meadow. The arch is a bucolic vault of **Ruskinian Gothic** in sandstone, festooned with **crockets,** bosses, and **finials.** Only vestiges of the wood interior remain (there were once benches in the niches).

Once through the arch, note the corresponding (but architecturally distinct) **Meadow Port Arch [4b.]** to the right at the west entrance to the meadow: a barrel rather than a Gothic vault here. Follow the path to the left along the edge of the meadow. Note that active (but not regimented) recreation on the meadow itself is deftly separated, but still visible, from the tree-dotted hillsides along the encircling walks.

About 500 feet ahead a set of steps rises to the left; go a bit beyond them for a better view of the meadow, then back, up the steps, and across the road. On the other side go left, then right at the next fork down a curving walk to the **Rose Garden [5.]** (**1895.** designer unknown), now somewhat forlorn, with a few rosebushes and the empty round and oval concrete basins that once held exotic water lilies. Turning right across the center of the rosebed circle, take the steps leading down to the **Vale of Cashmere [6.]**, an unusual melding of Classical architectural elements (1894. *Possibly* by McKim, Mead & White) and picturesque landscaping (*older* Calvert Vaux). Here are romantic, meandering free-form pools with Classical piers. Deep in a hollow facing due south the **Vale** supports lush groves of bamboo (green year round), and multitudes of birds—some uncommon in New York (there are almost always bird-watchers).

Follow the brick path along the east side of the **Vale** (left as you enter) straight out into a little meadow from which there are glimpses of the **Long Meadow** across the road. Continue over the crest of a rise (part of the terminal moraine ridge that cuts across the park from northeast to southwest) and down the wooded slope to **Battle Pass.** The park road at this point follows roughly the alignment of the original road from Flatbush to Brooklyn, and it was at this pass that Revolutionary volunteers put up brief resistance against British troops advancing toward New York in 1776.

[7.] The Zoo's central octagonal domed pavilion: pachyderms under a pantheon

The Zoo [7.]: An optional (and recommended) detour at this point is to the **Prospect Park Zoo,** just to the south, which offers small-scaled formal, but intimate, confrontations with animals. (It also offers, for those in need of other services, rest rooms and fast food.) Its neat semicircle of brick, Beaux Arts vernacular buildings (1935. Aymar Embury II) was decorated with bas-reliefs and murals by **WPA** artists, representing scenes from **Rudyard Kipling's** *Jungle Books.*

Of particular architectural interest is the central pavilion: an octagonal blue tiled dome of **Guastavino** vaulting with 24 oculi windows. **Pachyderms** under a pantheon; *rhinoceroses, hippos* and *heffalumps.*

To the west along the park drive is a charming sculpture of a lioness and her cubs by Frederick MacMonnies.

At **Battle Pass,** cross the road and climb the stairs ahead to a plateau that is the site of the **Dairy [8.]** (1869. Calvert Vaux), an original feature of the park. Turn left at the top of the stairs and follow the brow of the plateau across the bridle path (careful!) and past the old red brick service building, then turn right and cross the high **boulder bridge** (*romantic rock-rock*) over a return loop of the bridle path. From the bridge, bear right and then left up steps, then left at a **T**-intersection along a walk that skirts the knoll on which the **John Howard Payne Monument [9a.]** stands (1873. Henry Baerer, sculptor). Climb to the crest for a sweeping view of the Long Meadow; the red brick picnic house is directly across the meadow, the more elegant Palladian **Tennis House [9b.]** (1910. Helmle & Huberty) to its left. Return to the walk below and take your first left on the walk along the slope's edge. At the next **T,** go right, down steps, and stop where the walk takes a sharp right for a view of the **boulder bridge** crossed earlier.

Continue your descent into a deep rocky glen, through which a brook usually trickles. Turn left at the bottom, crossing a smaller boulder bridge, and follow the path along the brook. Turn right at the end of this walk and pass through the triple **Nethermead Arches [10.]** (1870. Calvert Vaux) where walk, brook, and bridle path all pass under the Central Drive. The **Arches** are crowned with a trefoil sandstone balustrade, and supported by barrel vaults of granite, brick, and stone. Continue along the brook, past some specimen trees into the **Music Grove.** The unhappily remodeled **bandstand** here has been the site of summer **Goldman Band** concerts for decades, the gracious Victorian bandstand now sullied by crass "modernization." Cross **Music Grove** and bear right on the walk that crosses **Lullwater Bridge.** From the bridge there is a fine view of the white terra-cotta-faced **Boathouse [11.]** (1905. Helmle & Huberty). ★ From the other side of the bridge there is a long view down the **Lullwater,** meandering toward the lake (note that the sides of the Lullwater are hard-edged stone). At the end of the bridge turn left for a closer look at the Boathouse (note, in particular, the bronze lamp standards). The **Boathouse** is a pleasant terra-cotta remembrance of **Palladian** architecture, as recorded by **Sebastiano Serlio.** From the Boathouse take the path south past the **camperdown elm** (a weeping, drooping Japanese super-bonsai of a tree: gnarled, arthritic, wonderful), then turn left through the **Cleft Ridge Span [12a.]** (1872. Calvert Vaux) with its polychrome tile inner surface easily visible in this lofty barrel vault.

[11.] Boathouse on the Lullwater: pleasant terra cotta remembrance of Palladio

Through this span is the formal **Garden Terrace [12b.],** with oriental eclectic floral-vegetable decorated walls by Calvert Vaux. Bear right and then left to the **Oriental Pavilion** (1874. Calvert Vaux), now mutilated by fire. As much as this structure has suffered from degrading uses in recent years, and fire damage, the view down the axis to the lake has suffered even more, for the semicircular cove at the foot of the terraces is now filled by the **Kate Wollman Memorial Skating Rink,** a banal place, an intruding scar on the park. Walk down the axis of the garden, past the statue of **Lincoln** (1869. H.K. Brown, sculptor), and look, with Lincoln, at the high wire fence and exposed refrigeration equipment that stand at what was, until 1961, the edge of the lake. Lincoln is gesturing with his right hand: *"Take it away?"* To the left is the **Skating Shelter [13.]** (1960. Hopf & Adler).

[15.] *The Horse Tamers:* sculpture by MacMonnies, base by McKim, Mead & White

After a short detour to the right, to an area where the lake edge is in its original condition, return across the axis of the garden and the skating shelter, turning right at the parking lot (which was a "carriage concourse" from the very beginning, and undoubtedly influenced the siting of the rink) and continue to the edge of the lake. Pass a **World War I Memorial** (1920. A.D. Pickering, designer) and continue around the edge to the landing shelter—a 1971 reconstruction of **the original** (1870. Calvert Vaux), sole survivor of the many log-braced rustic shelters that once bordered the lake. From here, follow the path parallel to the lake edge, then bear left across the drive, and continue straight out of the park through the **Classical porticos** with redwood trellises (1904. McKim, Mead & White) to the intersection of Ocean and Parkside Avenues.

End of tour: To the left across Ocean Avenue is the BMT/IND Brighton Line Parkside Avenue Station. Change at Atlantic Avenue for the IRT.

For further views of the lake and a look at some of the park's finest Classical structures, instead of leaving the park at this point follow the walk along the south side of the park, between Parkside Avenue and the park drive, to the **Croquet Shelter [14.]** (1906. McKim, Mead & White. Stanford White, designer. Restored, 1967) ★, a Corinthian-columned pavilion of limestone and terra cotta; then on to **Park Circle Entrance [15.]** (1897. McKim, Mead & White, architects; Frederick MacMonnies, sculptor of *The Horse Tamers*), a remarkably successful Classical composition.

"Institute Park"

The green triangle contained by Eastern Parkway and Flatbush and Washington Avenues, formerly known as **Institute Park** (after the Brooklyn Institute of Arts and Sciences), which Olmsted & Vaux rejected in their plan for Prospect Park, was **reserved for related institutional uses.** It now accommodates the **Brooklyn Botanic Garden,** the **Brooklyn Museum,** and the main branch of the **Brooklyn Public Library.** The garden and museum are contiguous, and offer more than the expected horticultural specimens and works of art. The garden has some interesting examples of landscape architecture, and the museum (which is not just an art museum, but an art school and an anthropological museum as well) houses extensive decorative craft collections, **25** period rooms, a *whole* **Dutch Colonial** house, one of the *great* **Egyptian collections** of the world, and, in a garden behind, a collection of **exterior architectural building parts** (columns, friezes, sculptures, plaques) from demolished New York buildings.

Botanic Garden to Brooklyn Museum Walking Tour: From the BMT/IND Brighton Line Prospect Park Station (the D train) on Flatbush Avenue near Empire Boulevard (can also be reached from Grand Army Plaza Station of IRT Seventh Avenue Subway by B41 bus) to the IRT Seventh Avenue Subway Eastern Parkway Station. Cross the street to the Lefferts Homestead, go back along Empire Boulevard to the Fire Department Bureau of Communications, and *then* enter the Botanic Gardens.

[16a.] Flatbush Turnpike Tollgate, Empire Blvd. entrance road to Prospect Park. N side. ca. 1855.

A wooden guardhouse moved from its old position at **Flatbush Turnpike** (*now Flatbush Avenue*) is all that remains of the days when roads were privately built and tolls were charged for their use.

[16b.] Lefferts Homestead, "Dutch" house built 119 years after New Amsterdam

 [16b.] Lefferts Homestead, Flatbush Ave. N of Empire Blvd. W side. In Prospect Park. 1783. ★ Telephone: SO 8-2300.

Six slender **Tuscan** colonnettes support a **"Dutch"** eave, the edge of a gambrel roof. Painted shingle body, stained shingle roof. The English built many such copies of the basic Dutch house.

 [17.] Brooklyn Central Office, Bureau of Fire Communications, N.Y.C. Fire Department, 35 Empire Blvd., bet. Flatbush and Washington Aves. N side. 1913. Frank J. Helmle. ★

Brunelleschi in Brooklyn: its arcades are those of his foundling hospital in Florence.

[18.] 71st Precinct Station House, N.Y.C. Police Department, 421 Empire Blvd. NE cor. New York Ave.

A **Florentine** palace in *un*-Florentine brick: there are many of these vigorous stations around the city.

[19.] Brooklyn Botanic Garden, 1000 Washington Ave., bet. Empire Blvd. and S side of Brooklyn Museum, W to Flatbush Ave.

Enter the garden through the Palladian south gate at Flatbush Avenue and Empire Boulevard. Its 50 acres are intensively planted with *almost every* variety of tree and bush that will survive in this climate. The most popular attraction, and one that generates traffic jams at the end of

April, is the grove of **Japanese cherry trees,** the finest in America. For a simple tour of the garden follow the east side, consistently staying to your right. For seasonal attractions (the *cherry blossoms, roses, lilacs, azaleas*) not on this route, ask the guard (on a motor scooter) for directions. On the east edge of the garden a few hundred feet from the south entrance is a reproduction of the garden from the **Ryoanji Temple, Kyoto [20.].** Constructed with painstaking authenticity in **1963,** this replica lacks all of the atmosphere that history and a natural setting give to the original, but it offers an opportunity unique in this area to contemplate a **Zen-inspired,** virtually plantless landscape composition: rock islands in a sea of raked pebbles.

[20.] The Brooklyn Botanic Garden reproduction of the Ryoanji Temple garden

[22.] Japanese Garden: eclectic design resembling a Momoyama stroll garden

Just north of the **Ryoanji** are the greenhouses, facing a plaza with pools of specimen water lilies. This conservatory has a tropical jungle section, and a desert section, but its prize exhibit is the collection of *bonsai* (Japanese miniature trees) **unequalled** in the Americas. North of the conservatory is another formal terrace planted with magnolias (a *dazzling* display in **early to mid-April**) in front of the garden's **School-Laboratory-Administration Building [21.]** (1918. McKim, Mead & White) originally painted white, but now aquatic green. Farther north is the **Japanese Garden [22.]** (1915. Takeo Shiota, designer), gift of philanthropist **Alfred Tredway White.** It resembles a stroll garden of the **Momoyama** period but it is not copied from any one particular example. Around its small pond are examples of almost every traditional plant and device; this overcrowding fails to achieve the serenity of really good Japanese prototypes. North of the **Japanese Garden** is the gate to the parking field which leads to the Brooklyn Museum. Walk out to Washington Avenue and enter the museum via its front entrance on Eastern Parkway, now sans its monumental staircase removed in the 1930s.

 [23.] Brooklyn Museum, 200 Eastern Pkwy., SW cor. Washington Ave. 1897–1924. McKim, Mead & White. ★ Addition, 1978. Prentice & Chan, Ohlhausen.

One quarter of the grand plan envisioned for **Brooklyn** in the year before consolidation with New York. As a borough in the larger metropolis, support for the museum waned. But what it *lacks* in sheer size, it *makes up for* in quality. Inside is one of the world's greatest **Egyptian** collections.

[23.] McKim, Mead & White's presentation rendering of the Brooklyn Museum

Enter the museum by the main entrance on Eastern Parkway. Note the two sculptured female figures representing **Manhattan** and **Brooklyn** (1916. Daniel Chester French, sculptor). Although they look as if created for this location, they were placed here in 1963 when their seats at the **Brooklyn** end of the Manhattan Bridge were destroyed in a roadway improvement program.

The austere architecture of the lobby dates from its remodeling in the **1930s** under **WPA** sponsorship. The lobby was moved downstairs from the "parlor floor" to the basement, and the monumental exterior stairway was removed. **Stark functionalism** replaced **Classical monumentality:** a *sorry loss.* The information desk will offer directions to the collections as well as information on concerts, lectures, and movies in the museum. Among the outstanding exhibits in architecture and interior design are the **Jan Martense Schenck House** (originally built in 1675 in the Flatlands section of Brooklyn), dismantled in 1952 and reconstructed inside the museum, and a suite of rooms from the **John D. Rockefeller, Sr., Mansion,** built in 1866 at 4 West 54th Street, Manhattan, and redecorated in 1885 in the "Moorish" style by **Arabella Worsham.**

In the rear, adjacent to the new addition and parking lot is the **Frieda Schiff Warburg Sculpture Garden** (*1966. Ian White, designer*). Here are pieces of McKim, Mead & White's **Pennsylvania Station** (a column base and a capital; a figure that supported one side of a huge clock), Coney Island's **Steeplechase** Amusement Park (a roaring lion's head and a lamp standard) and capitals from the first-floor columns of Louis Sullivan's **Bayard** (Condict) building, still standing on Manhattan's Bleecker Street [see V Manhattan/Astor Place].

Curios and antiquities: Just inside the south (parking area) entrance of the museum is the **Gallery Shop,** once the largest museum shop in the U.S., with an extensive stock of handcrafted toys, jewelry, textiles, ceramics from all over the world. Note the cut-out paper architectural models.

End of Botanic Garden-Brooklyn Museum Walking Tour: The Eastern Parkway stop of the IRT Seventh Avenue Subway is directly in front of the museum. Transfer to the BMT/IND D train at Atlantic Avenue Station.

BEDFORD-STUYVESANT

An amalgam of two communities of the old **City of Brooklyn:** Bedford, its western portion, and Stuyvesant Heights, its eastern. Today Bedford-Stuyvesant is **New York's** second largest black enclave, eclipsed by **Harlem** because of the latter's prominent location on **Manhattan Island.** It differs markedly from its **Manhattan** counterpart in its large percentage of home-owners, and is, therefore, more *conservative* in its politics. The southern and western portions consist of masonry row housing of **great quality,** and of fine churches whose spires create this community's often **lacy skyline.** The northeastern reaches have considerable numbers of wooden tenements containing some of the *worst* slums in the country—fire traps and *vermin-infested* **hovels** that are a **disgrace** to the city and an insult to those whose bare subsistence incomes force residence there.

Where **Bedford-Stuyvesant** has good housing, however, it is *very good.* Particularly from the **outside,** where the facades of its brownstones and brickfronts create a magnificent townscape, it is as good, or better, than many *fashionable* parts of **Brooklyn** and **Manhattan.** Parts of **Chauncey, Bainbridge, Decatur, McDonough** and **Macon Streets** and the southern end of **Stuyvesant Avenue** are superb. **Hancock Street,** between **Nostrand and Tompkins** Avenues, was considered a showplace in its time; it exhibits much of this same quality even today. **Alice** and **Agate Courts,** short streets isolated from the macrocosm of the street pattern, are particularly special places in the *seemingly* never-ending anonymous grid.

Bed-Stuy comprises **500** acres and houses about **400,000** people, placing it among the **30** largest **American** cities. It should be toured by car, the sights being dispersed.

[1.] Brevoort Place, S of Fulton St., bet. Franklin and Bedford Aves. 1860s.

A handsome block of brownstones in **mint** condition, with original detail undamaged by the crass modernizations of richer areas of the city.

[1a.] Bethel 7th-Day Advtst. Church   **[1b.]** The Mechanics Building

[1a.] Bethel Seventh Day Adventist Church/originally **Church of Our Father,** 457 Grand Ave. NE cor. Lefferts Pl. ca. 1885.

The **obtuse** intersection of Lefferts and Grand suggested a stepped form to this architect. The **piered, arched, corbeled,** and **articulated** brickwork has a fresh modern flavor.

[1b.] Mechanics Building/formerly **Lincoln (Republican) Club,** 67 Putnam Ave., bet. Irving Pl. and Classon Ave. N side. 1890. R. L. Daus.

Elegant **Republicans** left this florid structure, marking the memory of these streets with remembrances of better times. The bracketed tower is in the **Wagnerian Victorian** idiom popularized by the fantastic Bavarian royal castle, **Neuschwanstein.**

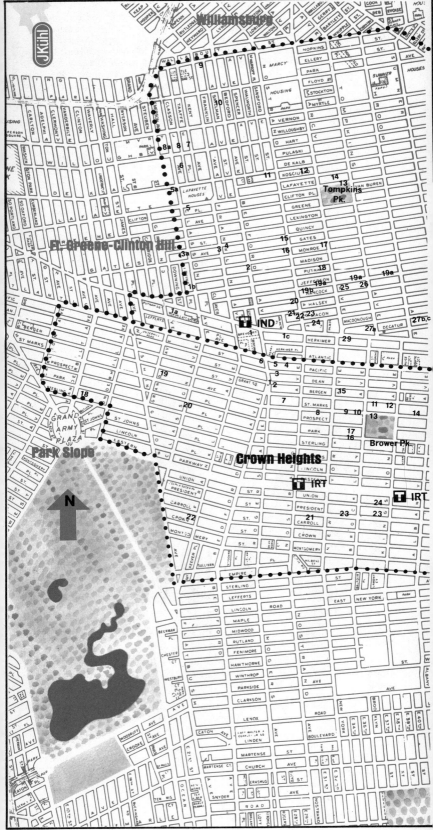

BEDFORD-STUYVESANT

[1c.] Friendship Baptist Church, 92 Herkimer St., bet. Bedford and Nostrand Aves. ca. 1900.

A *Moorish* facade for, it turns out, more than one religious congregation.

[2.] Aurora-Grata Scottish Rite Cathedral/originally **East Reformed Church,** 1160 Bedford Ave., NW cor. Madison St. Rebuilt, 1888.

Bedford Avenue nearby is nondescript commercial. This gray and buff fantasy is welcome relief. Its history dates back to **1877** when the **Aurora-Grata Lodge of Perfection,** a Masonic local, bought the old **East Reformed Church** and Parsonage on this site. It was rebuilt for **Masonic** purposes. The belfry is capped by the flat silhouette of a *mystic, mythic* bird: the Scottish Rite emblem in bronze.

[3.] Evening Star Baptist Church/originally **Latter Day Saints Chapel,** 265 Gates Ave., NW cor. Franklin Ave. 1917. Eric Holmgren.

Superficially reminiscent of **Frank Lloyd Wright's Unity Temple** (*Oak Park, Illinois. 1904*), this church is unique for **New York:** early cubism in stucco.

[3a.] 418 Classon Avenue, bet. Gates Ave. and Quincy St. W side. ca. 1885.

A **Romanesque** trio arranged as a single composition.

[4.] 118 Quincy Street, SE cor. Franklin Ave. ca. 1890.

A *modest* example of the lavish apartments built in this community in the last decade of the **19th** century. Battered walls of stone support arched and rock-linteled brick.

[2.] Aurora-Grata Scot'sh Rite Cath.   **[6.]** Romanesque Revival warehouse

[5.] 361 Classon Avenue and **386–396 Lafayette Avenue,** SE cor. of the two avenues. ca. 1888.

A **picturesque and romantic** Victorian terrace. Compare this rich massing with the high-rise public housing across the street: charm and personality confronted by **super-tombstones.**

[5a.] 88th Precinct Station House, N.Y.C. Police Department, 300 Classon Ave. SW cor. DeKalb Ave. ca. 1890; south half, 1924.

Mini-Romanesque Revival, it packs an arcuated castle into a tight site, with small scale.

[6.] Warehouses, 220–232 Taaffe Place, W side, bet. Willoughby and DeKalb Aves. ca. 1885.

No-nonsense **Romanesque Revival: virile,** vigorous brickwork. Arches *bound and abound.* **H. H. Richardson** would have been pleased.

[7.] St. Patrick's Roman Catholic Church, Kent Ave., NW cor. Willoughby Ave. **Rectory,** 285 Willoughby Ave. **Academy,** 918 Kent Ave. 1856. P. C. Keely

The rectory is a perfect, arch-windowed, mansarded brick-and-brownstone **Charles Addams.**

[8.] Convent of the Sisters of Mercy, 273 Willoughby Ave., bet. Classon Ave. and Taaffe Pl. N Side. ca. 1880.

A *gloomy* mansarded red brick pile.

[8a.] St. Mary's Episcopal Church, 230 Classon Ave., NW cor. Willoughby Ave. ca. 1920.

Very comfortable English country chapel. It looks peaceful.

Rope walks: Not for crossing jungle swamps, but long narrow buildings used for the spinning of rope. In **1803** one was erected **1200 feet long** in the two blocks north of the **Convent of the Sisters of Mercy.** It was so long that a tunnel was built for it to pass beneath intersecting **Park Avenue.**

[9.] Wallabout Warehouse/formerly **Franklin Brewery/**originally **Malcolm Brewery,** 394–412 Flushing Ave., bet. Franklin and Skillman Aves. S side. ca. 1885.

A truncated pyramid crowns this **robust pile,** giving it a distinct silhouette; a **landmark** to the thousands of motorists who pass it daily on the **Brooklyn-Queens Expressway** nearby.

[10.] Engine Company 209, Ladder Company 102, 34th Battalion, N.Y.C. Fire Department, 850 Bedford Ave., bet. Myrtle and Park Aves. W side. 1965. Pedersen & Tilney.

One of the first modern public buildings of New York to share in the new concern for architectural design quality that burgeoned in city government in the sixties. It replaced an **1869** station that can still be seen on the west side of **Bedford** between **Myrtle** and **Willoughby.**

[11.] CABS (Community Action Program for Bedford Stuyvesant) Nursing Home and Related Health Facility, 270 Nostrand Ave., bet. Kosciusko and Dekalb Aves. 1976 William Breger. Interiors by Harold Leeds.

A **stylish, elegant** stacking of cubist brickwork crowned with a space-frame skylight. **Superb.** The atrium within is a *delightful* greenhouse filled with a **bamboo jungle.**

[12.] Bedford-Stuyvesant Community Pool, also known as the **People's Pool, N.Y.C. Department of Parks & Recreation,** Marcy Ave. bet. Kosciusko and DeKalb Aves. W side. 1969. Morris Lapidus & Assocs.

A reinforced concrete swimming stadium—an unfortunate and brutal material to use in the land of graffiti. It is a relief valve for these crowded streets.

[13.] Tompkins Park Recreation and Culture Center, N.Y.C. Department of Parks and Recreation, in the center of Tompkins Park, surrounded by Lafayette, Tompkins, Greene, and Marcy Avenues. 1971. Hoberman & Wasserman.

Stylish concrete forms with pitched roofs in another park borrowed from London's Bloomsbury (remember Russell Square?). (Originally the park was a design of Olmsted and Vaux—you couldn't tell today.)

[14.] Magnolia Grandiflora, 679 Lafayette Ave., bet. Marcy and Tompkins Aves. N side opp. Tompkins Park. ca. 1880. ★

Not a building, but a tree—an expatriate southern veteran of the **1880s** that survived its brownstone neighbors of the same vintage. Other noted New York trees include the **Weeping Beech** in Flushing [see Northeastern Queens] and the **Camperdown Elm** in **Brooklyn's Prospect Park.**

[15.] John Wesley United Methodist Church/originally **Nostrand Avenue Methodist Episcopal Church,** Quincy St., SW cor. Nostrand Ave. 1880.

A church of many gables, brick with **Gothic** timbering, and milky **Tiffany-style** stained glass.

Governors: Between Marcy and Stuyvesant Avenues, streets were named after New York governors: **William L. Marcy, Daniel D. Tompkins, Enos T. Throop, Joseph C. Yates, Morgan Lewis,** and, of course, **Peter Stuyvesant.** Yates Avenue became Sumner when confusion arose between it and Gates.

[16.] IBM Systems Products Division/formerly **Empire State Warehouse**/originally the **Long Island Storage Warehouse and Jenkins Trust Co.,** 390 Gates Ave., SW cor. Nostrand Ave. 1906. Helmle, Huberty & Hudswell.

A rusticated, iron-grilled base supports the patterned brickwork of this sturdy monolith crowned with a **neo-Baroque** tower.

[9.] The Wallabout Warehouse, a robust pile that started life as a brewery

[11.] Lyndon Johnson Nursing Home

[18.] Old Boys' High School, Brooklyn

[17.] St. George's Episcopal Church, 800 Marcy Ave., SW cor. Gates Ave. 1887. Richard Upjohn.

A *fat and friendly* country church in the city: the small octagonal tower is **delightful lilliput.**

[18.] Formerly **Boys' High School,** 823 Marcy Ave., bet. Putnam Ave. and Madison St. W side. 1891. James W. Naughton. ★

Splendid **Romanesque Revival;** arched, quoined, towered, lushly decorated in terra cotta in the manner of **Sullivan.** Glassy for its ilk. [See architect Naughton's own house: WC Brooklyn/Cobble Hill 8b.]

[19a.] Brownstone Blocks, along Jefferson Ave., bet. Nostrand and Throop Aves. ca. 1885–1890.

Merely three blocks out of dozens in the area with staid Renaissance brownstones. **F. W. Woolworth** moved here in **1890 (No. 209).** Changing fashion and vastly increasing wealth caused him to move to **Manhattan.** Compare the similar migration of **Harold I. Pratt** to **68th** Street and **Park Avenue.** [See Manhattan UES 12i.]

[19b.] Most Worshipful Enoch Grand Lodge/originally **Reformed Episcopal Church of the Reconciliation,** Jefferson Ave., SE cor. Nostrand Ave. 1890.

A *churchly* place of brick and milky stained glass now used by the local **Masons.**

[20.] Renaissance Apartments, 488 Nostrand Ave., SW cor. Hancock St. ca. 1890. Montrose W. Morris.

Cylindrical, conically capped towers are borrowed from **Loire Valley** chateau country (*Chaumont, Langeais*). The "modernized" entrance is misguided "colonialization."

[21.] 74 Halsey Street, bet. Nostrand Ave. and Arlington Pl. S side. ca. 1890.

Fine brick residence with exuberant iron railings: imagine *bounding* up those front steps!

[21.] 74 Halsey Street iron railings   **[26.]** Neo-Renaissance Kelley Res'dce

[22.] Alhambra Apartments, 29 Macon St., 86 Halsey St. W side of Nostrand Ave. ca. 1890. Montrose W. Morris.

Morris did better here than at the Renaissance nearby: a richer collection of terra cotta and brick, arcaded, pedimented, mansarded, chimneyed, dormered. **Morris** is more renowned for the **Hulbert Mansion** (now Brooklyn Ethical Culture School) in **Park Slope.** [See Park Slope 14.]

[23.] New York City Board of Education Adult Training Center/formerly **Girls' High School/**originally **Central High School,** 475 Nostrand Ave., bet. Halsey and Macon St. E Side. 1885, 1891, 1911.

Gothic Revival **hulk.**

[24.] 64 and 68 Macon Street, bet. Nostrand and Marcy Aves. 1880s.

The "garden" space between sets off these two classy houses, allowing No. **64's** oriel window a place to view this urbane street from its brick and brownstone, Virginia-creepered body. No. 68 is Romanesque Revival brick and terra cotta: look for the face in the entrance pediment.

[25.] Hancock Street, bet. Marcy and Tompkins Aves. 1890s. Various architects.

No. **232** is a corner mansarded palace: oriels, gables, pediments, and corbels. Nos. **236–242:** Pompeiian-red terra cotta and brick worthy of **George B. Post.** No. **239** (N.Y.C. Dept. of Health, Child Health Station): brownstone, whitestone, gray brick **Romanesque Revival.** No. **247:** the Kelley house, see below. Nos. **246–252:** terra cotta, stained glass, elliptical arches, **Byzantine** columns. No. **273:** Lion-faced voussoir guards this entry.

[29.] Bedford-Stuyvesant Restoration Center: Brooklyn's "Ghirardelli Square"

[26.] John C. Kelley Residence, 247 Hancock St., bet. Marcy and Tompkins Aves. N side. ca. 1895. Montrose W. Morris.

A formal neo-Renaissance town house (the **Renaissance Romans** would have termed it a palazzo) on a wide site (**81** feet) for an **Irish** immigrant who made good. Legend claims that the brownstone was selected, piece by piece, to guarantee its quality. The *irony* is that it is now crumbling and painted white!

[27a.] First African Methodist Episcopal Church/originally **Tompkins Avenue Congregational Church,** 480 Tompkins Ave. SW cor. McDonough St. 1889. George B. Chappell.

The *immense* campanile dominates the neighborhood in a form reminiscent of that of **St. Mark's** in **Venice's Piazza San Marco.** *Brick, brick, brick.*

Once the nation's largest Congregational congregation, it was often referred to as Dr. Meredith's church after its well-known preacher.

[27b.] Fulton Storage Building/originally **New York and New Jersey Telephone Company** (branch office), 613 Throop Ave., NE cor. Decatur St. ca. 1895.

Roman brick and **Renaissance** arches; the spandrels between are richly decorated with terra cotta.

[27c.] 81 Decatur Street/formerly the **Clermont Apartments,** bet. Throop and Sumner Aves. N side. 1900.

A *shrunken* palace: **Azay-le-Rideau** for multi-families.

[28.] Stuyvesant Heights Historic District, an L-shaped area between Chauncey and Macon Sts. from Stuyvesant to Tompkins Aves. 1870–1920. District designated, 1971. ★

Blocks illustrating a cross section of Bedford-Stuyvesant architectural history. Locally designed and built, they encompass styles from free-standing suburbia to Victorian row houses and modest apartment buildings.

[29.] Bedford-Stuyvesant Restoration Center, 1360 Fulton Street, SE cor. New York Ave. 1976. Arthur Cotton Moore.

Brown brick, brown glass, banners, and a floating **Victorian** facade recalling this block's history give a simple face to the street but embrace an *urban* compound-plaza: **Brooklyn's** answer to **San Francisco's Ghirardelli Square.** Stylish new and carefully renewed old buildings mix on this block.

Ice skating rink, shops, boutiques. **Excellent.**

[30.] 13th Regiment Armory, New York National Guard, 357 Sumner Ave., bet. Jefferson and Putnam Aves. E side. 1894. R. L. Daus.

A **great granite arch** gives support to twin battlemented towers.

[31.] Mount Lebanon Baptist Church, 228–230 Decatur St. SE cor. Lewis Ave. 1894. Attributed to William Tubby.

Richardsonian Romanesque, Roman brick and brownstone. Round-towered, terra-cotta-shingled.

[32.] Bainbridge Street, bet. Lewis and Stuyvesant Aves. N side. 1890–1900.

A *studied* variegation of houses picturesquely composed: in sharp contrast to the normally sober, sometimes dull regularity of Renaissance Revival brownstone rows. [See 37. below as well.]

[32.] Bainbridge Street town houses: a picturesque Victorian silhouette

[33.] Fulton Park, Chauncey and Fulton Sts. at Stuyvesant Ave.

The rumble of the A train below doesn't affect the serenity of this sliver of green space along Fulton Street. The neighborhood to the north of the park is named after it, and, because of its well-maintained and stable population, is considered an important asset in the work of renewing **Bedford-Stuyvesant.** North of the **park** along **Chauncey Street** is a fine set of small-scale row houses with stoops intact.

City Center: The geographical center of New York City lies within Bedford-Stuyvesant. To be exact, it occurs within the block bounded by **Lafayette, Reid, Greene,** and **Stuyvesant Avenues,** the present site of a less-than-distinguished public school.

[34.] 1660–1670 Fulton Street, opp. Fulton Park, bet. Troy and Schenectady Aves. 1976. Henri Legendre.

Medium-rise housing with a broken and incised form that works **happily** with this predominantly low housed neighborhood. Tan brick, elegant.

[35.] Lawrence H. Woodward Funeral Home, 1 Troy Ave. SE cor. Fulton St. 1976. Henri Legendre.

A tan brick satellite of **No. 1660** above.

[36.] Remsen Court, 120 Chauncey St., bet. Reid and Stuyvesant Aves., Chauncey and Fulton Sts. 1976. L. E. Tuckett & Thompson.

Broken brick forms enclose private courtyards. A New York State Urban Development Corporation (UDC) project, as is **1660 Fulton Street** above.

McDonald's Dining Room, 327 Stuyvesant Ave., NE cor. Macon Street. Telephone: 773-2774.

A good eating and drinking place in a community that can't afford elegant bars or restaurants.

[37.] Decatur Street, bet. Howard and Saratoga Aves. N side. 1890–1900.

Pyramids and arches **punctuate** this picturesque group.

[38.] Saratoga Park, bet. Halsey and Macon Sts., Saratoga and Howard Aves.

A **Bloomsbury**-scaled park with *appropriate* low-scaled houses surrounding. None distinguished. All pleasant.

[34.] 1660 Fulton Street (apartments)

[1.] U.S. Grant equestrian statue

CROWN HEIGHTS

The term **Crown Heights** is today applied to the area east of Washington Avenue between **Atlantic Avenue** on the north and **Empire Boulevard** and **East New York Avenue** on the south. Included is the handsome portion surrounding **Grant Square** at **Bedford Avenue** and **Bergen Street** that was originally considered part of the **Bedford** community whose southern boundary we now define as **Atlantic Avenue.**

Crown Heights, the 19th-century **Crow Hill,** actually includes a succession of hills south of **Eastern Parkway.** The old designation derisively recalls the black colony along **Hunterfly Road,** now termed **Weeksville,** with extant buildings in the process of preservation and restoration. In addition to Hunterfly another old thoroughfare is **Clove Road,** a two-mile, north-south link from the Village of **Bedford** to **Flatbush,** dating from **1662.** (A bit still remains above **Empire Boulevard** east of **Nostrand Avenue.**)

The community is in transition, with *burgeoning* black and *diminishing* Jewish populations. Many **West Indian** immigrants reside in the area; **Haitian** French and **"British"** English are often heard in the streets.

[1.] Ulysses S. Grant Statue, Grant Square at Dean St. and Bedford Ave. 1896. William Ordway Partridge, sculptor.

A youthful **Grant** astride his charger.

[2.] Former Union League Club of Brooklyn, Bedford Ave., SE cor. Dean St. 1892. Lauritzen & Voss.

Brooklyn's most resplendent club built to serve the social needs of Republican Party stalwarts of **Bedford** (of which this area was then considered part). Brownstone **Richardsonian Romanesque** arches support an eclectic body above; note **Lincoln** and **Grant** in the arches' spandrels and the monumental American eagle supporting the great bay window.

[3.] Imperial Apartments, 1198 Pacific St., SE cor. Bedford Ave. ca. 1892. Montrose W. Morris.

Of an *imperial* scale, with great paired Corinthian terra-cotta columns and arches along both **Pacific Street** and **Bedford Avenue.** Advertised in its time as an "elegant and well conducted apartment hotel in the fashionable part of Bedford," its immense apartments have been subdivided. For more **Morris** see **Bedford Stuyvesant** 20. and 22.

[2.] Formerly the Union League Club of Brooklyn, a Republican stronghold

[3.] The Imperial Apartments

[6.] 23rd Reg'mt. Armory, Nat'l Gd.

[4.] St. Bartholomew's Episcopal Church, 1227 Pacific St., bet. Bedford and Nostrand Aves. N side. ca. 1893. George B. Chappell.

A charming and romantic place: **squat and friendly,** brick with terra-cotta trim and roof tiles. The tower (in summer) seems constructed of **Virginia creeper.** All in a **bosky bower.**

[5.] Medical Society of the County of Kings, 1313 Bedford Ave., bet. Atlantic Ave. and Pacific St. E side. 1903. D. Everett Waid and R. M. Cranford.

A safe institutional **neo-Georgian.**

[6.] Twenty-Third Regiment Armory, New York National Guard, 1322 Bedford Ave., bet. Atlantic Ave. and Pacific St. W side. 1892. Fowler & Hough. ★

This crenellated fortress for the **National Guard,** with its great round tower and arched entry complete with portcullis, lacks only a moat to be right out of **King Arthur's** realm.

[7.] 669, 673, 675, 677 St. Marks Place, bet. Rogers and Nostrand Aves. N side. ca. 1890.

Somber brick and brownstone. **No. 669** is of the "shingle-style" period. **Nos. 675** and **677** are Romanesque Revival.

[8.] 758 St. Marks Avenue, bet. Nostrand and New York Aves. S side. ca. 1890.

Now called **Buford's Haven.** Note the oriel window overseeing street life.

 [9.] Marcus Garvey Nursing Home, 800 St. Marks Ave., bet. New York and Brooklyn Aves. S side. 1977. William N. Breger Assocs.

Simple terra-cotta-colored brick box that replaced three major mansions, including that of Abraham Abraham, co-founder of A & S.

Abraham Abraham was first a partner in **Wechsler and Abraham,** the forerunner of today's **Abraham & Straus,** Brooklyn's largest and classiest department store. Among his many philanthropic accomplishments was the founding of the Brooklyn Jewish Hospital, built in **1894** as Memorial Hospital for Women and Children. His son-in-law **Edward Blum** and grandson-in-law **Robert A. M. Blum** carried on both the business and philanthropic tradition, the latter by being at once board chairman of both **Abraham & Straus** and the **Brooklyn Institute of Arts and Sciences.**

[10.] 828–836 St. Marks Avenue, bet. New York and Brooklyn Aves. S side. ca. 1914.

Six small neo-**Georgian** houses. Note how **No. 828's** eaves have been received by an incision into the nursing home next door!

[11.] St. Louis Senior Citizens' Center/formerly **St. Louis Convent**/originally **Dean Sage Residence,** 839 St. Marks Ave., NE cor. Brooklyn Ave. ca. 1898. Russell Sturgis.

Rockface brownstone Gothic Revival. **Sturgis** was most noted as a critic and writer, particularly for his **1902** *Dictionary of Architecture.*

[13.] The Brooklyn Children's Museum: a delightful and exciting "iceberg"

[12.] 855 St. Marks Avenue, bet. Brooklyn and Kingston Aves, N side. 1890.

An eclectic brick and limestone mansion with an elegant corner tower capped by a belled cupola.

[13.] Brooklyn Children's Museum, in Brower Park, bet. Brooklyn and Kingston Aves., St. Marks Ave. and Park Pl. 1976. Hardy, Holzman, Pfeiffer. Telephone: 735-4400.

Earth- and metalworks reminiscent of a missile launching station, but less rugged against the onslaught of the neighborhood than a **NASA** installation would be! **Pop architecture,** and the museum as an amusement park.

A delightful and exciting iceberg, whose visible parts give little anticipation of its underground wonders. Smashing. Bring a child.

Old mansions: The new Brooklyn Children's Museum replaces the original one organized in **1899** that occupied two Victorian mansions on this site: the **L. C. Smith** (typewriter) **Residence,** an Italianate villa of ca. **1890;** and the **Adams Residence** of **1867,** a low mansarded place, once home of historian **James Truslow Adams.**

[14.] St. Marks Avenue, bet. Kingston and Albany Aves. 1966. I. M. Pei & Assocs., architects. M. Paul Friedberg & Assocs., landscape architects.

Plaza-playground interrupting **St. Marks Avenue.** It seems more an *incidental place* in a parking lot than a contribution of any substantial pedestrian urbanity.

[15.] Union Methodist Church/originally **New York Avenue Methodist Church,** 121 New York Ave., bet. Bergen and Dean Sts. E side. 1896. J. C. Cady & Co.

Smooth and rounded monumental **Romanesque Revival.**

[16.] Brooklyn Methodist Church Home, 920 Park Pl., bet. Brooklyn and New York Aves. S side. ca. 1875.

It has the *look* of an asylum in its literal sense: a place of refuge for the indigent **Victorian.** Victorian brick, with appropriate Victorian planting: **hydrangeas abound.**

[17.] 975 and 979 Park Place, bet. Brooklyn and New York Aves. N side. ca. 1885.

No. 979 could well serve as an illustration in Vincent Scully's *The Shingle Style.*

Loehmann's, 1476 Bedford Ave., NW cor. Sterling Pl.

This was humanity's gift to the middle-class matron, the outside an *extravagantly decorated* bit of orientalia, the work of its founder, **Mrs. Frieda Loehmann.** On her death in **1963** it was closed, then reopened under new management, but the loss of the migrating middle class, and competing shopping center, caused its second demise. It had been noted for **fantastic buys:** one-of-a-kind samples, and manufacturers' overstocks of chic women's fashions.

Further Afield: in Crown Heights, but scattered away from the cluster of **[1.]** through **[17.],** are several buildings and blocks of interest.

[18.] Public School 9 Brooklyn, NE cor. Vanderbilt Ave. and Sterling Pl. 1895.

A brownstone and brick **Renaissance Revival** building with, however, some **Romanesque** detail. *Grand* Corinthian pilasters stride around the third and fourth floors.

[19.] Former **Knox Hat Factory,** 369–413 St. Marks Ave., NE cor. Grand Ave. ca. 1885.

Where one of Brooklyn's once major industries flourished—hat-making. [The main office of Knox was at Fifth Avenue and 40th Street—see M Manhattan/Bryant Park 6.].

[20.] Nursing Home, Jewish Hospital Medical Center of Brooklyn, Classon Ave., bet. Prospect and Park Pl. 1977. Puchall & Assocs. and Herbert Cohen.

The former site of the Romanesque Revival Brooklyn Home for Aged Men, it continues to serve the elderly community as one of a number of nursing homes in the Crown Heights/Bedford Stuyvesant communities. Handsome.

[21.] Crown Gardens, Nostrand Ave., bet. President and Carroll Sts. E side. 1971. Richard Kaplan. Stevens, Bertin, O'Connell & Harvey, assoc. architects.

Sponsored by the Association for Middle-Income Housing. Stacked town houses surround three sides of a handsome center courtyard, a slender slab forms the fourth side. One of New York's most urbane sets of modern housing.

[22a.] 49–57 Crown Street, bet. Carroll and Crown Sts. on Franklin Ave.

Concrete frame and tan brick: this apartment house forms a slender but **dominant silhouette** on the local skyline.

[22b.] 42nd Supply and Transport Battalion, N.Y. National Guard/originally **Troop C Armory,** 1579 Bedford Ave., bet. President and Union Sts., E side. 1908. Pilcher, Thomas & Tachau.

The last stand of the cavalry—and a **mighty fortress** to this day! The interior of the great arched roof, silhouetted on the outside, is an early 20th-century tribute to the principles of the late Victorian steel-framed train shed.

[21.] Crown Gardens (apt. complex)   **[28.]** Ocean Hill Intermediate School

[23.] President Street, bet. Kingston and New York Aves. Both sides. 1905–1920.

Both sides of this two-block stretch are lined with lavish brick and limestone early 20th-century mansions, largely **neo-Georgian.** It is a section of grand freestanding suburbia in the midst of the surrounding cheek-by-jowl city.

[24.] Union Street, bet. Brooklyn and Kingston Aves. Both sides. ca. 1910.

Double brick houses in a variety of styles: neo-Tudor, neo-Romanesque, and just plain eclectic.

[25.] Public School 390 Brooklyn, Sterling Place, NW cor. Troy Ave. 1977. Giorgio Cavaglieri.

A highly articulated design. Stair towers have tall and elegant corner windows. Exposed concrete frame infilled with giant beige brick.

[26.] St. Mary's Hospital, Division of Catholic Medical Center of Brooklyn & Queens, 1298 St. Marks Ave. bet. Rochester and Buffalo Aves. S side. ca. 1890.

Brick with mansard rooflets. DEMOLISHED

[27.] Weeksville, along old Hunterfly Road, off Bergen St. 1830. ★

Remnants of an early **black** community in this part of town that will be restored to their simple architectural origins by private contributions.

[28.] Intermediate School 55 Brooklyn/The Ocean Hill Intermediate School, Bergen and Dean Sts., Hopkinson and Rockaway Aves. 1968. Curtis & Davis.

Grim, fortified place of brown brick with narrow slit windows. Its edge against the sky simulates crenellations.

NORTHERN BROOKLYN

Town of Bushwick/Boswijck-Town of the Woods

Established as a town in 1660; the Town of Williamsburg separated from it in 1840; annexed to the City of Brooklyn in 1855.

This area, including the three communities of **Bushwick-Ridgewood, Williamsburg,** and **Greenpoint,** was often referred to as the **Eastern District** after the merger of **1855,** to distinguish it from the original area of the **City of Brooklyn,** the **"western."** In general the term has fallen into disuse except in connection with the names of a local high school and a freight terminal (with some logic, as the **Eastern** District is now the **northern** tip of Brooklyn and **South** Brooklyn is, in fact, at Greater Brooklyn's **northwest** corner).

Much of this part of Brooklyn is devoted to working-class residential areas clustered between industrial concentrations strung along the **East River** and **Newtown Creek.** It is in this precinct that many fortunes were made in sugar, oil, rope, lumber, shipbuilding, brewing, and glue.

BUSHWICK-RIDGEWOOD

Malt and hops, barley and barrels, beer and ale. **Obermeyer and Liebmann, Ernest Ochs, Claus Lipsius, Danenberg and Coles.** The history of the Bushwick we see today has been the history of brewing. **Beer** came to **Bushwick** in the middle of the **19th** century when a large **German** population emigrated here after unsuccessful uprisings in **the Fatherland** in **1848** and **1849.**

In its early years the community was noted largely for farming, the produce being sold locally as well as ferried to Manhattan's markets. By the 1840s **Peter Cooper** had moved his glue factory here, land values in **Manhattan's Murray Hill** having risen so sharply that an odoriferous glue factory was no longer of economic sense there. **Cooper,** always a shrewd businessman, chose this undeveloped area of Brooklyn near main roads connecting the ferries to **New York** with the farms on **Long Island.** His site today is that of **Cooper Park Houses,** a low-rent housing project. It is named after the adjacent park given to the City of Brooklyn in **1895** by the Cooper family.

Bushwick-Ridgewood: see map pp. 458–459   **457**

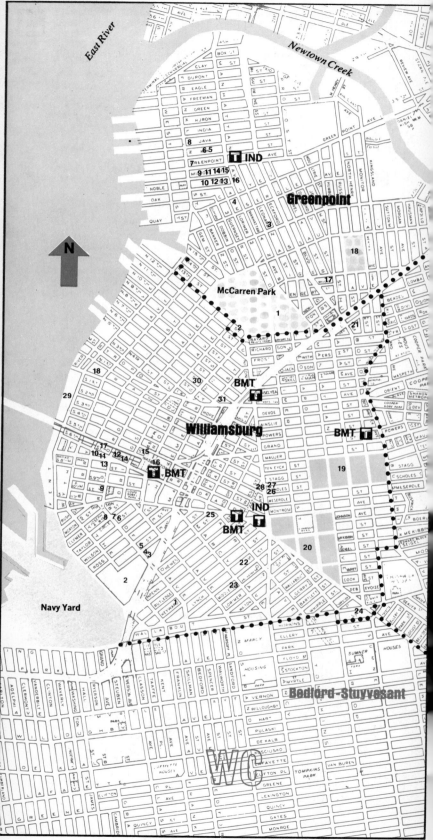

NORTHERN BROOKLYN

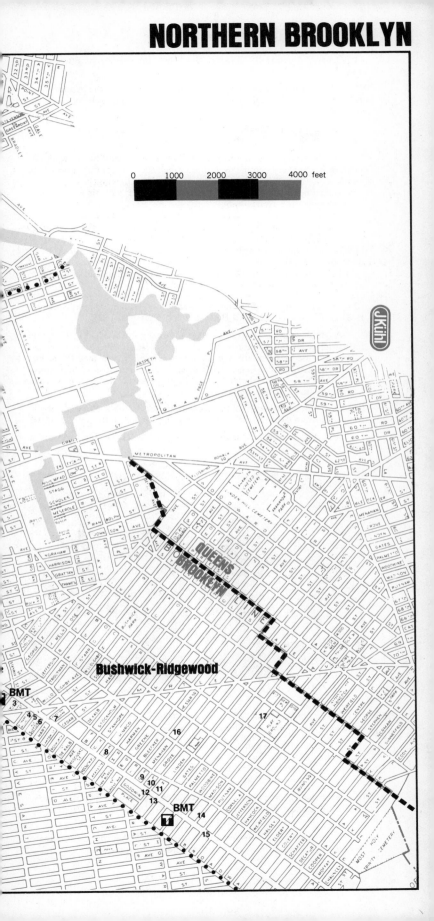

0   1000   2000   3000   4000 feet

JKuhl

QUEENS
BROOKLYN LINE

Bushwick-Ridgewood

BMT

Metropolitan

Aspeth

[1.] Original **Arion Hall,** 13 Arion Place, bet. Bushwick Ave. and Broadway. E side. 1887.

Rich embellishment redolent of those days when the Arion Männerchor, the Eastern District's leading German singing society, met and sang here.

[2a.] Breweries for Rheingold and Schlitz, off Bushwick Ave., bet. Forrest and Jefferson Sts. off Evergreen Ave.

On **Forrest, George, Noll,** and **Stanwix Streets** stand two now almost abandoned brewery complexes that interlock the original buildings of the **1880s** with their **20th-century** counterparts. The brewing has moved to suburban places, leaving these **gargantuas** behind, still places for shipping, storage, and distribution.

Bushwick Avenue displays twenty blocks of stolid mansions, freestanding town palaces advertising the wealth and taste of the local industrial magnates. A *gloomy* set of buildings, they nevertheless reveal the spirit of their time: wealth was a *burden,* and its owner had the duty to *uplift* the masses—here to a somber level of **Victorian morality** through dour stonework. No joy here, just heavy-handed sermonizing.

[2b.] Former **Vicelius & Ulmer Brewery**/later **William Ulmer Brewery,** Beaver St., bet. Locust and Belvidere Sts. SW side. 1872.

A ghostly brick brewery complex. Note particularly the romantic industrial brick cum mansard cum cast iron crested "office" of the brewery on Belvidere Street, and the carved stone plaque overhead ("Vicelius & Ulmer's Continental Lagerbier Brewery") on the multistory brewhouse on Beaver Street near the Belvidere corner. [See 4. below for William Ulmer's mansion a few blocks east.]

[3.] St. Mark's Lutheran Church/originally **St. Mark's Evangelical Lutheran German Church,** 626 Bushwick Ave., SE cor. Jefferson St. 1892.

The verdigris-covered spire dominates **Bushwick Avenue** for most of its length.

[4.] Orig. William Ulmer Residence

[7.] Old Bushwick Democratic Club

[4.] Davis Medical Building/originally **William Ulmer Residence,** 670 Bushwick Ave., SW cor. Willoughby Ave.

A stolid, solid Romanesque Revival brick fortress, as befits its brewer builder [see 2b.]. **Dr. Frederick A. Cook,** a later owner, was a well-known but not too well-heralded **Arctic** explorer in the **1900s.** He claimed to have discovered the North Pole, but lost in court to Admiral Robert E. Peary.

[5.] Franciscan Residence-Pranciskonv Vienuolynas/originally **Mrs. Catherine Lipsius Residence,** 680 Bushwick Ave., SE cor. Willoughby Ave. ca. 1886. Theobald Engelhardt.

A brewer's widow commissioned this poorly proportioned **Italianate Renaissance Revival** house. Note the windows in the frieze.

[6.] 696 Bushwick Avenue, SW cor. Suydam St.

Italianate Renaissance Revival frame house with a many-columned porch.

[7.] Bushwick Democratic Club/most recently used as the **Bethesda Pentecostal Church,** 719 Bushwick Ave., NW cor. Hart St. 1892. Frank Freeman. ★

Ravaged by a second great fire, this brick shell is one of the two *greatest works* of Brooklyn's greatest architect [the other is the **Jay Street Fire House;** see WC Brooklyn/Civic Center a.]. The ornament is worthy of **Louis Sullivan,** but the forms, such as the negative bay windows behind arches along Hart Street, are breathtaking, anticipating those that Robert Venturi speaks of in his book *Complexity and Contradiction in Modern Architecture,* and those **Louis Kahn,** in fact, built.

[10.] Gustav Doerschuck Residence   **[13.]** 1020 Bushwick Ave. (town house)

[8.] South Bushwick Reformed Church, Bushwick Ave., NW cor. Himrod St. 1853. ★

A grand late **Greek Revival** wood church with imposing **Ionic** columns. Note the Parish house to the rear along **Himrod Street:** large-scaled pilasters, *delicate* clapboard, purple and white milk glass. Its first minister was **John Himrod,** after whom this side street was named.

[9.] John F. Hylan Residence, 959 Bushwick Ave., bet. Bleecker and Menahan Sts. N side.

One in a row of *unpretentious* brownstones, noted only because it was the home of a mayor of **New York** (1918–1925).

[10.] Gustav Doerschuck Residence, 999 Bushwick Ave., NW cor. Grove St. ca. 1890.

Another brewer's substantial mansion. Brick **Romanesque Revival.**

[11.] Charles Lindemann Residence, 1001 Bushwick Ave., NE cor. Grove St. ca. 1890.

Shingle style, turreted, porched, dormered, and decrepit.

[12.] Frederick Williams Child Care Center/formerly **Arion Singing Society**/originally **Louis Bossert Residence,** 1002 Bushwick Ave., SE cor. Grove St. ca. 1890.

A dour red-brick box enlivened by extraordinary triangular dormer windows. **Bossert** was a successful local millwork manufacturer, who later built **Brooklyn Heights'** Bossert Hotel.

Grove Street: It owes its name to a park called **Boulevard Grove** at the intersection of that street with **Bushwick Avenue.** Picnics were held there as early as **1863.**

[13.] 1020 Bushwick Avenue and **37–53 Linden St.,** SW cor. Linden St. ca. 1885.

Richly decorated and carefully crafted row houses, the corner house treated as a special place. The friezes (brow and waist) are superb.

[14.] Bushwick Avenue Central Methodist Episcopal Church, 1130 Bushwick Ave., NE cor. Madison St. 1886–1912.

The octagonal Italianate Renaissance Revival corner tower is a local landmark.

[15.] Bethesda Baptist Church/formerly the **Bushwick Avenue Congregational Church,** 1160 Bushwick Ave., SW cor. Cornelia St. 1896. Parfitt Bros.

A powerful octagonal campanile corners this handsome church.

[15.] The Bethesda Baptist Church: note the powerful octagonal "campanile"

[17.] The Spanish-Baroque-Revival Saint Barbara's Roman Catholic Church

[16.] 20 Bleecker Street, bet. Bushwick and Evergreen Aves. E side. ca. 1890.

A magnificent **Victorian** cream and brown painted wood and bay-windowed tenement. Perhaps the best of its ilk in the city. *Tenement* is a pejorative word today: in fact it describes a walk-up apartment house that covers most of its building site. Here the light in the back rooms is minimal, but the visible architecture **magnificent.**

[17.] St. Barbara's Roman Catholic Church, Central Ave., NE cor. Bleecker St. 1910. Helmle and Huberty.

Gleaming white and cream **Spanish Baroque.** The towers are wedding-cake icing: edible. Built to serve a **German Catholic** parish that later became **Italian** and is now largely **Hispanic.** Named not only for the saint, but for brewer Leonard Eppig's little daughter Barbara—Eppig contributed to the parish. Nearby St. Leonard's has a similar history of naming.

[18.] New Life Child Development Center, 295 Woodbine St., bet. Knickerbocker and Irving Aves. W side. 1973. Paul Heyer.

Carefully arranged brown brick clads a carefully *understated* building of high architectural quality.

[19.] 83rd Precinct Station House, N.Y.C. Police Department/originally **20th Precinct, Brooklyn P.D.,** 179 Wilson Ave. NE cor. DeKalb Ave. 1895. William B. Tubby. ★

At its dedication, the commissioner of the **Brooklyn Department of Police and Excise** declared it to be "commodious, architecturally ornate, and thoroughly equipped, . . . the handsomest and most convenient police office in the world." The remark is a forgivable exaggeration—a fine provincial station house.

WILLIAMSBURG

Right! Without the final "h," even though the Williamsburgh Savings Bank spells its name the old way (the "h" fell when it consolidated with the **City of Brooklyn** in **1855.**)

Though it shares its current spelling with the well-known restoration in **Virginia,** the resemblance ends there. This **Williamsburg,** formerly part of the **Town of Bushwick,** later a village and city in its own right, was named after **Col. Jonathan Williams,** its surveyor and grandnephew of **Benjamin Franklin. Richard M. Woodhull** started the community when he purchased thirteen acres of land at the foot of today's **South 2nd Street,** in **1802.** He commissioned **Williams** to survey it, established a ferry to **New York** (Manhattan), and quickly went into bankruptcy **(1811).**

Thomas Morrell and **James Hazard** picked up where **Woodhull** had failed. They also established a ferry, this time to the **Grand Street Market** at **Corlear's Hook,** providing an outlet for the farmers of **Bushwick** to sell their produce in New York. The impetus to growth of the area, however, was the establishment of a distillery in **1819.** The distillery is gone (and the **Schaefer** brewery that followed it on the same site too). Booze and beer helped build **Williamsburg,** but now are only drunk here, not distilled or brewed.

The most telling impact on the community came from the opening of the **Williamsburg Bridge** in **1903.** Overnight the community changed from a fashionable resort with hotels catering to such sportsmen as **Commodore Vanderbilt, Jim Fisk,** and **William C. Whitney** to an immigrant district absorbing the overflow from **New York's Lower East Side.** (*The New York Tribune* of the period characterized the bridge as **"The Jews' Highway."**) Its elegant families moved away, and its mansions and handsome brownstones from the post–**Civil** War era first fell into disuse, then were converted to multiple dwellings.

Hasidic Community: Along **Bedford Avenue** are arrayed a group of brownstones, mansions, and apartment houses such as described above. Occupying these precincts is one of New York's most concentrated **Hasidic** (Jewish) communities. This unique settlement of the Satmarer Hasidim, recalling late medieval **Jewish** life in dress and customs, is a result of the persecution of the Eastern European Jewish community during **World War II.** In **1946, Rebbe Joel Teitelbaum** and several of his flock reached these shores and chose **Williamsburg**—even then a heavily **Orthodox** area—as their home. At the end of the war, the remaining survivors from **Poland** and **Hungary** migrated to the new settlement and reestablished their lives there. As the community grew, parts of it split off and moved to other parts of Brooklyn and to the suburbs. *Beards and uncut forelocks* of hair identify the men; *shaven but wigged heads* identify the women. Long frock coats and skull caps are in evidence everywhere among its male population, young and old, and in the winter, the fur-trimmed hat, the *shtreiml,* is certain to make its appearance. Evidence of its residents' heritage is everywhere apparent, from the proliferation of **Hebrew** signs on the mansions to the identification of small business establishments catering to the group.

Williamsburg: see map pp. 458–459 **463**

The Tree that Grows in Brooklyn: Williamsburg, a swampy, low-lying area, became the ideal spot for the culture of the *ailanthus* tree (a tree of fernlike leaves similar to those of the *mimosa* and *locust*). First imported from China about 1840, its intended use was as the grazing ground of the *cynthia moth's* caterpillar, a great, green, purple-headed, horned **monster** (³⁄₄ inch in diameter, 3 inches long) that spins a cocoon prized for its silk threads. The **mills of Paterson, New Jersey,** were to be its beneficiaries. Its grazing role proved uneconomical (the grazing still goes on, however, without cocoon collection), but the tree was believed to have another virtue for the locals: supposedly providing power to dispel the "disease-producing vapors" presumed to come from swampy lands. See **Betty Smith's** novel of **Williamsburg** life, *A Tree Grows in Brooklyn.*

Bedford Avenue: The sequence is north, with the direction of traffic; the house numbers decrease as we proceed.

[1.] 665–677 Bedford Avenue, bet. Heyward and Rutledge Sts. E side.

An entire blockfront of tenements magnificently encrusted with stone following in the footsteps of the more elegant mansions further north on the avenue. Granite columns with Byzantine capitals.

[2.] Bedford Gardens, generally bet. the Brooklyn-Queens Expressway, Wythe Ave. and Ross St. Most addresses are along Ross St. 1975.

A project of the **federal Housing and Urban Development Department's** *Operation Breakthrough* attempting precast, prebuilt, prefabricated housing. These are built of concrete parts and bear the stamp of crudeness. They look cheap but aren't.

[3.] Yeshiva Jesode Hatorah of Adas Yereim, 571 Bedford Ave., bet. Keap and Rodney Sts. E side.

Rockface brownstone, and an obviously affluent client, made this a showplace. The elliptical bay window is elegant. Note the cherubs, copper frieze, roof finials and balls.

[4.] Young Israel of Brooklyn/formerly **Hanover Club/**originally **Hawley Mansion,** 561 Bedford Ave., SE cor. Rodney St. ca. 1875. Conversion, 1891. Lauritzen & Voss.

Yellow brick with brownstone quoins; cast iron against the sky. **William Cullen Bryant** was the first president of the **Hanover Club.**

[5.] Congregation Arugath Habosem, 559 Bedford Ave., NE cor. Rodney St. ca. 1890.

An imposing terra-cotta "castle," now minus the conical **Spanish** tile roof over its round corner tower's crown. The sunbay on **Rodney Street** and the smaller bay on **Bedford Avenue** give glassy contrast to the basic body. An *owl* is perched on **Rodney's** pediment.

[6.] Yeshiva Yesoda Hatora of K'Hal Adas Yereim/formerly the **Congress Club**/originally the **Frederick Mollenhauer Residence,** 505 Bedford Ave., NE cor. Taylor St. 1896. Lauritzen & Voss.

Neo-Renaissance limestone mansion built by a son of **John Mollenhauer,** founder of the Mollenhauer Sugar Refinery **(1867),** which became the **National Sugar Refining Company** (Jack Frost). The original refineries were first at **Kent Avenue** and **Rush Street,** then at **South 11th Street.**

[7.] Congregation Tifereth Israel, 491 Bedford Ave., SE cor. Clymer St. 1976. Castro-Blanco, Piscioneri & Feder.

A ribbed-block, streamlined *"taxpayer"* of a synagogue.

[8.] National Committee to Aid New Immigrants/formerly the **Rebbe's House (Grand Rabbi Joel Teitelbaum Residence),** 500 Bedford Ave., NW cor. Clymer St.

The American home of the rebbe who led the bulk of the Hasidim to Williamsburg.

[9a.] George Washington Building, SW cor. Bedford Ave. and S. 8th St.

A cast iron elliptical panel bas-relief of George Washington set in an ornate cast-iron balustrade.

[9b.] 390 Berry Street, NW cor. Berry St. and S. 8th St. ca. 1885.

A *smooth* terra-cotta and brick warehouse: a **monolith** of narrow joints and virtuoso brickwork.

[10.] 97 Broadway, bet. Bedford Ave. and Berry St. N side. 1870.

A cast-iron Second Empire facade with mansard roof, formerly the **Kings County Fire Insurance Company.** The three-story **Victorian-Baroque** porch is in the manner of A. B. Mullett (cf. *Executive Office Building, Washington*), but in **iron,** rather than the latter's **stone.**

[11.] 103 Broadway, bet. Bedford Ave. and Berry St., N side. ca. 1875.

Elegant *glassy* elliptical bays: studio-lofts. Note the console brackets (scrolls) that form visual keystones. Great **Corinthian** columns.

[6.] Orig. Frederick Mollenhauer Res.   **[12.]** The United Mutual Savings Bank

[12.] United Mutual Savings Bank/formerly **Kings County Savings Bank,** 135 Broadway, NE cor. Bedford Ave. 1868. King & Wilcox, William H. Wilcox. ★

Bands of smooth and vermiculated **Dorchester** stone alternate to enliven the exterior of the banking floor of this splendid **Second Empire** masterpiece. **Victorian** at its best, even the interior is carefully preserved, the gas-lit chandeliers all present (but wired for electricity). Look at the plaited Indian hut in the entry pediment.

[13.] 134–136 Broadway/formerly the **Nassau Trust Company,** SW cor. Bedford Ave. 1888. Frank J. Helmle.

Neo-Renaissance limestone and granite.

Peter Luger Steak House, 178 Broadway, west of Driggs Avenue. Telephone: EV 7-7400.

Spartan place of polished oak and white aprons in a precinct far from the habitat of its elegant clientele: next to the **Williamsburg Bridge.** Steak reigns, all else being decoration surrounding it, or fodder for those who can't contend with greatness. It all began as **Charles Luger's Cafe, Billiards and Bowling Alley** in **1876.** The side entrance on **Driggs Avenue** wears some of the original architecture. Expensive. No credit cards.

Crisci's Restaurant (Italian), 593 Lorimer St. Telephone: 384-9204.

Hearty **Italian** food in the center of a neatly kept Italian community within the **polyglot** eastern part of **Williamsburg.** It's good to see businessmen (at lunch) and families (at dinner) enjoying the flavorful food and atmosphere. A busy bustling place.

Bamonte's Restaurant (Italian), 32 Withers St., E of Union Ave. Telephone: 384-8831.

The front is a dark bar cum color TV. But the back is like a theater, and the brightly lighted, glass-fronted, sparkling white kitchen is *on-stage* in every way. Lower keyed than **Crisci's**—more relaxed. Good sauce-y food.

 [14.] Williamsburgh Savings Bank, 175 Broadway, NW cor. Driggs Ave. 1875. George B. Post. ★ Additions, 1906, 1925. Helme, Huberty & Hudswell.

An eclectic **Victorian** crossbreeding of **Renaissance** and **Roman** parts that is one of the major landmarks of Brooklyn, particularly to the tens of thousands who pass it daily on the **BMT** Jamaica Elevated Line. It is a sharp, hard, gray place reminiscent of the work of **Philadelphia's** great architect **Frank Furness** (below the dome).

[15.] Holy Trinity Cathedral of the Ukrainian Autocephalic Orthodox Church in Exile/formerly **Williamsburg Trust Co.,** 117–85 S. 5th St., NW cor. New St. 1906. Helmle & Huberty.

The more common progression from religious to sectarian use in a building's life is here reversed. Built as a bank, this *opulent* terra-cotta monument is now a **cathedral:** the building is a natural result of the **World's Columbian Exposition** (*Chicago World's Fair,* 1893), vendor, or catalyst, of the **American** Renaissance.

[16.] Washington Plaza, S. 4th St. to Broadway, New St. to Havemeyer St.

Formerly a ganglion for half the trolley empire in **Brooklyn,** the **Plaza** is now a depot for nondescript buses belching forth diesel fumes even though resting between runs. Some of the old sheds and a signal tower remain, but the mass of overhead copper wires is now only a memory. Furthermore, the space is cut into pieces by the elevated **BMT** and **Brooklyn-Queens Expressway,** slicing through it with melancholy abandon. In the northwest corner, a forecourt for the **Ukrainian Cathedral** is a formally executed plaza which is the only part of the whole deserving the plaza title. It contains, among disintegrating **Renaissance Revival** ornaments, a fine verdigris equestrian statue, *George Washington at Valley Forge* (Henry M. Shrady. 1906.).

[17.] Fruitcrest Corporation/formerly **Bedford Avenue Theater,** 109 S. 6th St., bet. Bedford Ave. and Berry St. 1891. W. W. Cole, builder.

Opened by actress **Fannie Rice** in a farce, *The Jolly Surprise.* Its history as a theater was short-lived.

Grand Street

[18.] J. Nikolas Guaranteed Lacquers/formerly **Manufacturers Trust Co.**/originally **North Side Bank,** 33–35 Grand St., bet. Kent and Wythe Aves. N. side. 1889. Theobald Engelhardt.

Lusty, gutsy, rockface, **Romanesque**-arched, cast-iron corniced wrought iron.

The Fourteen Buildings: The turn Grand Street takes at Union Avenue marks the beginning of the site of the **Fourteen Buildings.** The street was laid out between **Union** and **Bushwick Avenues** so that it would pass through the property of a group of men who then built for themselves a series of **Greek Revival** frame dwellings. Each had a dome and a colonnaded porch of fluted wood columns. The houses were arranged one per block on both sides of **Grand Street** with two extras slipped in. This was in **1836.** By **1837** each of the men had suffered the consequences of that year's financial panic and the houses changed hands. In **1850** all still remained, but by **1896** only one was left. Today there is no sign on this busy shopping street of that *bygone elegance,* save the bent street.

[15.] Formerly Williamsburg Trust Co.   [19.] Williamsburg Houses (apts.)

[19.] Williamsburg Houses, Maujer to Scholes Sts., Leonard St. to Bushwick Ave. 1937. Board of Design: Richmond H. Shreve, chief architect; with James F. Bly, Matthew W. Del Gaudio, Arthur C. Holden, William Lescaze, Samuel Gardstein, Paul Trapani, G. Harmon Gurney, Harry Leslie Walker, and John W. Ingle, Jr., assoc. architects.

The *best* public housing project *ever built* in **New York,** but also the first and most expensive (in adjusted dollars). Its four-story buildings embrace semi-private spaces for both passive and active recreation. Reinforced concrete and brick infill is **punctuated** by pedestrian ways that connect courtyards through stepped and columned portals. The apartments themselves are reached without benefit of corridors by an entry system that opens directly off stair landings (as in **Princeton Collegiate Gothic,** here in serene modern dress).

[20a.] Lindsay Park Houses, Montrose Ave. to Moore St., Union to Manhattan Aves. 1967. Kelly & Gruzen.

A middle-income urban renewal project **30 years** younger than **Williamsburg Houses,** but without the latter's style. Freestanding slabville.

[20b.] New York Telephone Company Communications Center, 55 Meserole St., NE cor. 1975. John Carl Warnecke & Assocs.

Fancy and **inhuman** place for telephone equipment—stylish form gives **Ma Bell** points in its never-ending rate battle.

[21.] 492–494 Humboldt St., bet. Richardson and Herbert Sts. E side. and **201 Richardson St.,** bet. Humboldt and N. Henry Sts. N side. ca. 1850.

Three houses participating in what was once one of four of **Brooklyn's** colonnade rows. (Two were in **Brooklyn Heights,** one is still in existence; the other was also in **Williamsburg**). Note the **Doric** order at **No. 492.**

Colonnade Row: Only records remain of the least-known of Brooklyn's four colonnade rows. It was on the east side of Kent Avenue, between **South 8th** and **South 9th Streets,** in **Williamsburg.** (The last of the group was removed in the **1920s.**) Among the families who shared the extraordinary views across the river were the **Walls** and the **Berrys. Dr. Abraham Berry** became the first mayor of the City of Williamsburgh in **1852; William Wall** became the second and last in **1854.**

[22.] 17th Corps Artillery Armory/formerly **47th Regiment Armory**/ originally the **Union Grounds,** Marcy to Harrison Aves., Heyward to Lynch Sts. 1883. William A. Mundell.

The **Harrison Avenue** end is a short fort: double-clerestoried, triple-hipped brick with crenellated and machicollated corner towers.

The **Union Grounds** were the site of early baseball games in the **1860s** between the **Cincinnati Red Stockings,** the **Philadelphia Athletics,** the **New York Mutuals,** and the **Brooklyn Eckfords.**

[23.] Primary School 380 Brooklyn, Marcy Ave., bet. Lynch and Middleton Sts. 1977. Richard Dattner.

A somber **Pompeiian-red** brick construction: broken multipolygons. Strangely appropriate modern intrusion for this neighborhood.

[24.] Woodhull Medical and Mental Health Center, a New York City hospital

[24.] Woodhull Medical and Mental Health Center, SW cor. Broadway and Flushing Aves. 1977. Kallmann & McKinnell/Russo & Sonder, Assoc. Architects.

The biggest thing around these parts, it anchors the intersecting corner of **Williamsburg, Bushwick,** and **Bedford-Stuyvesant.** Self-weathering steel, which will eventually achieve a purple-brown color, and glass clad this bold, cubistic place, where great human-high trusses span **69** feet, within which workers can adjust the complex piping and tubing that serve the rooms and laboratories above and below. **Kallmann & McKinnell's** first and major monument is the competition-winning **Boston City Hall.** *Here* they have created a *superbuilding,* a machine for medicine, inhuman, centralized; a scary monument of health, more dedicated to the efficiency of health economics than the happiness of its clients.

In competition it has won, and will win, many prizes.

[25.] Talmud Torah Pride of Israel School/originally **Temple Beth Elohim,** 274 Keap St., bet. Marcy and Division Aves. 1876.

Its Hebrew congregation was the first in Brooklyn, dating from 1851. **Ruskinian Gothic** Revival polychromy in brick, brownstone, sandstone, terra cotta, stained glass, and tile. Now sadly neglected.

[26.] Iglesia Pentecostal Misionera/originally **Deutsche Evangelische St. Petri Kirche,** 262 Union Ave., NE cor. Scholes St. 1881.

That *dour* **German** brickwork again.

[27.] District Office N.Y.C. Department of Sanitation/formerly **P.S. 69 Brooklyn,** 270 Union Ave., bet. Scholes and Stagg Sts. E side.

Italian Romanesque miniature for a school flock of Williamsburg's more rural days.

[26.] Iglesia Pentecostal Misionera   **[31.]** R.C. Church of the Annunciation

[28.] United Methodist Church/originally **South Third Street Methodist Church,** 411 S. 3rd St., bet. Union Ave. and Hewes St. N side. 1855.

Simplified **Italian Romanesque:** painted buff.

[29.] American Sugar Refining Company/formerly **Havemeyer and Elder's Sugar Refining Company,** 292–350 Kent Ave., bet. S. 5th and S. 2nd Sts. W side.

Bulky, bold, and brutal masonry behemoths.

[30.] Iglesia Bautista Calvario/formerly **St. Matthew's First Evangelical Lutheran Church,** 197–199 N. 5th St., bet. Roebling St. and Driggs Ave. 1864.

Battered buttresses flank this painted brick church.

[31.] Church of the Annunciation (Roman Catholic), 255 N. 5th St., NE cor. Havemeyer St.

A crisply detailed and lovingly maintained **Lombardian Romanesque** basilica. Note the two **Romanesque Revival** parochial school buildings across Havemeyer Street to the west.

Subway kiosks: The famous and late-lamented cast-iron **IRT** subway kiosks were cast in a foundry that once existed in **Williamsburg.** The **Hecla Iron Works** flourished on **Berry Street** in the northern part of the community.

GREENPOINT

Greenpoint (movie pronunciation: "Greenpernt") is a quiet, ordered, and orderly community of discrete ethnic populations, with a central charming area all but unknown to outsiders (the uncognoscenti).

Its modern history began with the surveying of its lands in **1832** by **Dr. Eliphalet Nott,** President of **Union College, Schenectady** (America's first architecturally planned campus), and **Neziah Bliss.** Within two years the whole area was laid out for streets and lots. Much of it was then purchased for development by **A. C. Kingsland,** a mayor of New York, and **Samuel J. Tilden,** who went on to fame in politics (gubernatorial and presidential candidate) but who is also happily remembered for the establishment of a free public library system in **New York City.**

The area became a great ship-building center soon afterward, and it is here at the **Continental Iron Works,** in a building which stood at **West** and **Calyer Streets,** that **Thomas F. Rowland** built the ironclad *Monitor* from designs by **John Ericsson.** The "Yankee cheese box on a raft" was launched **January 30, 1862,** and battled the Confederate *Merrimac* at **Hampton Roads, Virginia,** two months later. That same year the *Monitor* foundered off **Cape Hatteras** and was lost. [See the *Monitor* Monument in Monsignor McGoldrick Park, Greenpoint 18.]

By **1860** the so-called five black arts (printing, pottery, gas, glass, and iron) were firmly established in **Green Point,** as it was first known. In **1867, Charles Pratt** established his kerosene refinery. (The first successful tapping of oil had been in **1859** in Titusville, Pa.) **Pratt's** product later gave rise to the slogan, "The holy lamps of **Tibet** are primed with **Astral Oil.**" The sale of **Astral Oil** provided the wealth which later made possible **Pratt Institute,** as well as Greenpoint's **Astral Apartments.**

[1.] Entrance Pavilion, McCarren Park Play Center (swimming pool complex)

[1.] McCarren Park Play Center, McCarren Park, Lorimer St., bet. Bayard St. and Driggs Ave. E side. ca. 1936. N.Y.C. Department of Parks. Aymar Embury II, consultant.

One of four **WPA**-built swimming pools erected in Brooklyn during the Depression (**Red Hook, Sunset Park,** and **Betsy Head** are the others). The ceremonial arch and clerestory announce the grand dip beyond.

[2.] Russian Orthodox Cathedral of the Transfiguration, 228 N. 12th. St., SE cor. Driggs Ave. 1921. Louis Allmendinger.★

The five verdigris-copper onion-domed cupolas on this church are visible from far and wide. The real treat, however, is within: the area is small (it seats but **250**), and the central cupola is supported on four great columns painted to simulate richly veined marble. The triple-altared eastern end is screened from the body of the church by the *iconostasis,* a hand-carved wooden screen on which icons were painted by the monks in the **Orthodox Monastery of the Caves** in **Kiev.** Around the screen are miniature light bulbs—those around the door flicker off and on as it is opened into the sanctuary.

A visit should include the celebration of the **Mass.** The architecture, the incense, the service sung and chanted in many tongues, together are overwhelming: a deeply moving *saturation of the senses.*

[3.] Greenpoint Branch, Brooklyn Public Library, Leonard St., NE cor. Norman Ave. 1972. Hausman and Rosenberg.

A white "mansard" concrete hat floats over a brick base on light and glass.

Brackets, asphalt, and pictorial masonry: The wood entrance canopy brackets at **117 Norman Avenue** next door are a pair of the most monumental in Brooklyn. Such parts are unsung heroes of **Victoriana-Brooklyniana** that made endless rows of simple houses rich. Unfortunately the relentless process of "modernization" rips these handsome ornaments off houses at the same time that it veneers the formerly wood-clapboarded sides with *picture-book asphalt* intended to look like stone, or brick, or anything other than what it really is. It's all neat, but depressing. One must go to the poorest neighborhoods to find **real,** but decrepit, materials.

[5.] Former Greenpoint Reformed Church (from a 19th-century engraving)

[4.] Green Point Savings Bank, 807 Manhattan Ave. SW cor. Calyer St. 1908. Helmle & Huberty.

Roman pomp under a pantheon dome: limestone **Doric** on a granite base.

[5.] St. Elias Greek Rite Catholic Church/formerly **Greenpoint Reformed Church,** 149 Kent St., bet. Manhattan Ave. and Franklin St. N side. Church, 1870. Chapel, 1880.

Bulky brick, whitestone and brownstone (now in paint) in a neo-**Gothic** polychromy promoted by the writer-historian **John Ruskin** (hence "Ruskinian Gothic").

[6.] Church of the Ascension, 129 Kent St., bet. Manhattan Ave. and Franklin St. N side. 1866.

A granite ashlar building with brownstone trim, a double-pitched silhouette and red Episcopal doors!

[7.] Metmaint Electric Company/formerly **Greenpoint Branch, Corn Exchange Bank,** 144 Franklin St., NE cor. Greenpoint Ave.

Gloomy burnt red Renaissance Revival: terra cotta, brick, and brownstone with great composite (Ionic and Corinthian) pilasters.

[8.] The Astral Apartments, 184 Franklin St., bet. Java and India Sts. E side. 1886. Lamb & Rich.

Commissioned by **Charles Pratt** as housing for his refinery workers, this six-entried building was patterned after the earlier **Peabody Apartments** in **London. Alfred Tredway White** had already pioneered in similar projects south of Brooklyn Heights [see WC Brooklyn/Brooklyn Heights 6b. and Cobble Hill 4.]. Here are patterned brickwork, rockface brownstone arches and lintels, structural steel storefronts with the very rivets as decoration. All now *seedy.*

Milton Street: This rich block between **Franklin Street** and **Manhattan Avenue** is crowned on its axis by **St. Anthony's Church.** It sums up the finest urban values in **Greenpoint.**

[9.] 93–103 Milton Street, N side. ca. 1875.

Six brickfront houses with delicate archivolts over the doors, curved **Renaissance Revival** window lintels.

[10.] 118–120 Milton Street, S side. ca. 1880.

Mansarded pair on a tiny scale. Note that entries are along building *sides,* rather than at front.

[11.] 119–121, 123–125 Milton Street, N side.

Each pair is handled as one composition, with nos. **123–125** insensitively altered.

[12.] 122–124 Milton Street, S side. ca. 1880.

Brick and brownstone eclectic: the bracketed canopies over the entries are vigorous.

[13.] Greenpoint Reformed Church, 138 Milton St., S side. ca. 1880.

Italianate Greek Revival (those warring peoples could combine in style on occasion). Before **1891** this congregation occupied what is now **St. Elias Church** two blocks north on Kent Street.

[14.] 141–149 Milton Street, N side.

Arched and recessed terraces at the third floor.

[15.] St. John's Lutheran Church, 155 Milton St., N side. 1892.

Painted brick **German Gothic** Revival: stolid. Incised is its original name: **Evangelisch-Lutherische St. Johannes Kirche.**

[16.] St. Anthony of Padua Church (Roman Catholic), 862 Manhattan Ave. at the end of Milton St. E side. 1874. P.C. Keely.

Red brick and white limestone: a little *fancy dress* in this dour neighborhood. Its **190-foot spire,** at a bend in **Manhattan Avenue,** is a visual pivot not only for **Milton Street** and **Manhattan Avenue** but for much of **Greenpoint** as well.

Little Europe Restaurant, 888 Manhattan Ave., S of Greenpoint Ave. Telephone: 383-5063.

With a theater called the **Chopin** up the street, and a wedding caterer named the **Polonaise Terrace,** it should come as no surprise that there is a modest restaurant here serving Middle- and Eastern-European food. Try the fruit-filled dumplings.

[17.] St. Stanislaus Kostka Roman Catholic Church, 607 Humboldt St. SW cor. Driggs Ave. ca. 1878.

The tan brick, octagonal spires of this, the largest **Polish Catholic** congregation in **Brooklyn,** dominate the local skyline. It bears a heavy encrustation of stone ornament, in rich contrast to the row houses that line local streets (wood-framed, with painted aluminum "clapboard" and asbestos shingles, like neat exterior wallpaper, *Archie Bunker style*).

[18.] Monsignor McGoldrick Park, Driggs to Nassau Aves.. Russell to Monitor Sts. **[18a.] Shelter Pavilion,** Helmle & Huberty. ★

A park on the scale of **London's Bloomsbury,** but the surrounding buildings are too low to supply the same impact. Within is a monument to the *Monitor* and its designer, **John Ericsson (Antonio de Filippo, sculptor).**

C

CENTRAL BROOKLYN

Town of Flatbush/Vlackebos

Established as a Town in 1652; Town of New Lots separated from Flatbush in 1852; annexed to the City of Brooklyn in 1894.

Until the **1880s Flatbush** was a quiet place with a rural character. The introduction of the **Brooklyn, Flatbush, and Coney Island Railroad,** now the Brighton Line of the **BMT/IND,** encouraged real estate speculation and development that, by the turn of the century, had transformed the farmland into a *fashionable suburb.* The names of these subdivisions are still used in some cases, only dimly remembered in others: **Prospect Park South,** the most affluent of those extant, **Vandeveer Park, Ditmas Park, Fiske and Manhattan Terraces,** and a host of others like **Matthews Park, Slocum Park,** and **Yale Park.**

Earlier there were a series of abortive attempts to establish grids of houses on the countryside, such as **Parkville,** the off-axis grid surrounding **Parkville Avenue (1852),** and **Windsor Terrace,** between **Vanderbilt Street** and **Greenwood Avenue** in the corridor separating **Green-Wood Cemetery** from **Prospect Park (1862).** These projects were never as successful as those that hugged the natural interruption of through streets caused by the cut of the railroad to Brighton Beach.

[1.] 111 Clarkson Avenue: "berserk eclecticism," complete with onion domes

[1.] 111 Clarkson Avenue, bet. Bedford and Rogers Aves. N side.

A fairyland place that might be termed *berserk-eclecticism.* The onion domes remind one of **John Nash's Royal Pavilion** at **Brighton** (England, not Beach).

[2a.] Flatbush Reformed Dutch Church and Parsonage, 890 Flatbush Ave., SW cor. Church Ave. **Church,** 1793–1798, Thomas Fardon. ★**[2b.] Parsonage,** Kenmore Terrace, NE cor. E. 21st St. 1853.

Stone ashlar (the stone is **Manhattan schist**) with **Romanesque** arched windows and doors: all crowned with a **Georgian** white wood tower. Third building to occupy this site, of which the first was one of three built according to the mandate of **Gov. Peter Stuyvesant.** (The other two were the **Flatlands Dutch Reformed Church** and the **First Reformed Church.**)

Central Brooklyn: see map pp. 362–363   **473**

The parsonage is a delicately detailed late Greek Revival house surrounded by a gracious **Corinthian**-columned verandah, but with Italianate house- and porch-cornice detailing.

[2a.] The eclectic Greek Revival parsonage of the Flatbush Reformed Church

[3a.] Erasmus Hall Academy, in the courtyard of **Erasmus Hall High School,** Flatbush Ave., SE cor. Church Ave. 1786. ★ **[3b.] Erasmus Hall High School.** 1903. C. B. J. Snyder.

Established as a private academy by the **Flatbush Reformed Dutch Church** across the street. **Georgian-Federal,** it has a hipped-gambrel roof; **Palladian** window over a delicate **Tuscan-**columned porch.

Those later adversaries, **Hamilton and Burr,** both contributed to its building fund. It became the first secondary school to be chartered by the **State Board of Regents.**

Warning: Rule 9, Erasmus Hall Academy, 1797, stated *"No student shall be permitted to practice any species of gaming nor to drink any spiritous liquors nor to go into any tavern in Flat Bush without obtaining consent of a teacher."*

[4.] Flatbush Town Hall, 35 Snyder Ave. 1876. John Y. Culyer. ★

Flatbush became part of Brooklyn in **1894,** and Brooklyn part of New York City in **1898.** This lusty **Ruskinian Gothic** building is, happily, being preserved.

[5.] Kenmore Terrace, E of 21st St., bet. Church Ave. and Albemarle Rd.

The **Flatbush Reformed Dutch Church** parsonage forms one flank, and pleasant eclectic brick row houses the other.

[6.] Albemarle Terrace, E of 21st St., bet. Church Ave. and Albemarle Rd. S of Kenmore Terrace.

Charming, **Georgian** Revival dormered row houses in a cul-de-sac that says "dead end" but is far from dead.

[7.] Loew's Kings, Flatbush Ave., bet. Tilden Ave. and Beverly Rd., E side.

Ornate eclectic terra-cotta facade. One of the last of the **movie palaces** of the twenties still in operation.

PROSPECT PARK SOUTH

The streets between **Church Avenue** and **Beverly Road** and between **Coney Island Avenue** and the open cut for the **BMT/IND Brighton Line** contain as unique a community as any in the city. The entrances to most of the streets are guarded by pairs of sturdy brick piers containing cast-concrete plaques with the letters **PPS** formed into a monogram. The area is **Prospect Park South,** characterized at the time of its initial development as *"rus in urbe"* ("country in the city"), an expression not inappropriate even today. Lining its streets are a series of lavish, turn-of-the-century single-family residences that have somehow withstood the pressures of change.

PPS is a monument to the vision of **Dean Alvord.** What he conceived was a rural park within the confines of the grid. He wanted to abandon the row house concept and build detached houses under careful restrictions. To this end he installed all the utilities and paved all the streets before selling one plot of land. Trees were planted, not along the curb but on the building line, in order to give the streets a sense of breadth. The species were carefully chosen. Alternating every **20** feet were **Norway maples,** for permanence, and **Carolina poplars,** for immediate shade. The poplars, **Alvord** and his architect, **John Petit,** reasoned, being short-lived, would die out as the maples reached maturity.

[8a.] 84 Buckingham Road, SW cor. Church Ave.

Tudoresque.

[8b.] 85 Buckingham Road, bet. Church Ave. and Albemarle Rd. E side.

Note the **Palladian** window over the entrance and the harmonizing swell in the eave.

[8c.] 104 Buckingham Road, bet. Church Ave. and Albemarle Rd. W side.

Originally the **Russell Benedict** residence. As stately a portico as one could wish; shingled and bay windowed, imagine the *glassy elegance* without the intervening ironwork.

[8d.] 115 Buckingham Road, bet. Church Ave. and Albemarle Rd. E side. ca. 1885.

A *volumetric exercise* in shingle-style design: a gambrel-roofed volume incised for a porch and extended by a corner, bell-capped tower. Originally the **M. G. Gillette** residence.

[8d.] 115 Buckingham Road (house)   **[8f.]** 131 Buckingham Road (house)

[8e.] 125 Buckingham Road, bet. Church Ave. and Albemarle Rd. E side.

Corinthian columns and finely scaled clapboard. An **Americanized Roman** temple (as seen through **Renaissance** eyes).

[8f.] 131 Buckingham Road, bet. Church Ave. and Albemarle Rd. E side. 1903. Petit & Green.

Built by **Dr. F. S. Kolle,** a German émigré radiologist. It wears **Japanese** fancy dress of a sophisticated sort, unlike the Chinese and Japanese Moderne elsewhere in **Brooklyn.** Sticks and struts, corbels and brackets give a timber-structuralist look to what is, underneath, a *rather plain* box.

Prospect Park South: see map pp. 362–363   **475**

[8g.] 1519 Albemarle Road, NW cor. Buckingham Rd.

A later, masonry dwelling, somewhat influenced in both form and detail by the work of the *Chicago School* of architects. Note the ornate bay windows on **Buckingham,** and the terra-cotta corbeled caryatids.

[8i.] 1305 Albemarle Road (house)   **[10a.]** George W. Van Ness Residence

[9c.] Flatbush-Tompkins Congregational Church Parish House (photo, 1967)

[8h.] 1510 Albemarle Road, SE cor. Marlborough Rd.

A **stately mansion,** with grand conservatory and stable: in the latter composite columns on a huge scale support the roof in the manner of many Roman buildings (like the **Temple of Vesta**) where old columns got a new hat too small for them.

[8i.] 1305 Albemarle Road, NE cor. Argyle Rd.

Perfectly preserved **Queen Anne** house; the only change is the second-story balcony behind the colonnade, like **Harry Truman's** at that other **White House.**

[8j.] 1440 Albemarle Road, SW cor. Marlborough Rd.

Another **Queen Anne,** beautifully cared for, but veneered with ghastly asbestos sheeting—intended to look like stone?

[9a.] Stratford Road, between Beverly and Church Aves. Both sides.

Another street of grand and variegated mansions.

[9b.] 156 Stratford Road, bet. Hinckley and Turner Places. W side.

Four-columned **Roman temple** with a bedroom in its pediment! *Elegant* narrow clapboard, great **Corinthian** columns and pilasters.

Street furniture: An original **Prospect Park South** cast-iron street sign still stands at the southeast corner of **Beverly** and **Marlborough roads:** hard to see, hidden by leafery in the summer.

[9c.] Flatbush-Tompkins Congregational Church Parish House/formerly that of the **Flatbush Congregational Church,** 451 E. 18th St., SE cor. Dorchester Rd. ca. 1890s.

A bold, polygonal, dark, shingle-style parish house, that, if it were a complete form, would have **16** sides.

[10a.] George W. Van Ness Residence, 1000 Ocean Ave., bet. Ditmas and Newkirk Aves. W side. 1899.

What was a grand **Corinthian-columned and pilastered** house is now an incipient ruin.

[10b.] Community Temple Beth Ohr/formerly **Thomas H. Brush Residence,** 1010 Ocean Avenue, NW cor. Newkirk Ave. 1899.

What the house next door once was: a grand **Georgian** mansion with red brick, white limestone, and composite Ionic columns and pilasters. Note the **Palladian** window in the pediment.

[11.] 900 Ocean Avenue, bet. Dorchester Ave. and Ditmas Ave. W side.

Classy **Queen Anne** house. *Delicate* clapboard, and an **Ionic** porte cochère.

[12.] 2693 Bedford Avenue (house) **[13a.]** The Downstate Medical Center

[12.] 2693 Bedford Avenue, bet. Foster Ave. and Farragut Rd. E side.

The juxtaposition of circular recesses in an otherwise rectalinear house produces a feeling of cut-out paper dolls. Delightful **shingle-style** showpiece.

EAST FLATBUSH/RUGBY

[13.] Downstate Medical Center of the State University of New York. Complex occupies area roughly bounded by Clarkson, New York, and Albany Aves. and Winthrop St.; stepping down to Lenox Rd., bet. New York and Brooklyn Aves.

[13a.] Hospital and Intensive Care Unit, 445 Lenox Rd. N side. 1966. The Office of Max O. Urbahn.

Concrete graph paper.

East Flatbush/Rugby: see map pp. 362–363   **477**

[13b.] Dormitories, New York Ave., bet. Lenox Rd. and Clarkson Ave. E side. 1966. The Office of Max O. Urbahn.

Stacked picture frames, some without pictures, but stylish in its day.

[13c.] Kings County Hospital, Clarkson Ave. bet. Brooklyn and Albany Aves. N side. 1931. Leroy P. Ward, architect. S.S. Goldwater, M.D., consultant.

The "Bellevue" of Brooklyn. High-rise, bay windows, brick with Spanish tile roofs, and marvelous towers and finials.

[13d.] Student Center, 394 Lenox Rd., bet. New York Ave. and E. 34th St. 1969. Victor Christ-Janer & Assocs.

"Brutalist" concrete embracing a pleasant garden courtyard.

WINDSOR TERRACE

[14.] Engine Company 240, N.Y.C. Fire Department, 1309 Prospect Ave., bet. Greenwood Ave. and Ocean Parkway. E side. 1896.

Brick, rockface limestone and slate: Romanesque Revival with a corner oriel (its hat gone) and an arched corbel table.

PARKVILLE

[15.] Parkville Congregational Church, 18th Ave., NW cor. E. 5th St. 1895.

The stepped and shingled brackets of the gable end, with its hipped-roofed belfry, give this friendly church exotic detail.

[15.] Parkville Congregational Church   **[2.]** Flagg Court (apartment bldgs.)

[16.] Philip Hirth Academy, Beth Jacob School, 4419 18th Ave. bet. McDonald Ave. and Dahill Rd. S side. 1971. William N. Breger Assocs.

More stylish and smartly scaled brickwork by Breger. Look up his similar works in the index.

Boccie: Using the sandy roadbed of the dormant railroad tracks as their court (4 feet 8½ inches is a perfect width) and portable wooden planks as their backstops, a group of die-hard Italians still play their game of Latin bowls under the structural steel of the now-abandoned BMT Culver shuttle at 37th Street and Church Ave. You can find them there any weekend, and many weekdays, weather permitting.

SW

SOUTHWESTERN BROOKLYN

Town of New Utrecht/Nieuw Utrecht

Established as a town in 1662; annexed to the City of Brooklyn in 1894.

The old **Town of New Utrecht** includes the present-day communities of **Bay Ridge, Fort Hamilton, Dyker Heights, Borough Park, Bath Beach,** and much of **Bensonhurst.** At various times in its past, other, barely remembered communities were identified within its boundaries: **Blythebourne, Mapleton, Lefferts Park,** and **Van Pelt Manor;** and the area was largely rural until the beginning of the **20th** century.

BAY RIDGE/FORT HAMILTON/DYKER HEIGHTS

Some of Brooklyn's most desirable residential sites lay along the high ground overlooking the **Narrows** and **Gravesend Bay.** Inevitably this best of topography became the site of magnificent mansions along **Shore Road** and the sometimes higher ground behind and along **Eleventh Avenue** in **Dyker Heights.** The ornate villa of **E. W. Bliss,** of **Greenpoint** fame; Neils **Poulson's** cast-iron fantasy, by the founder of Williamsburg's **Hecla Iron Works; Fontbonne Hall,** the home of **Tom L. Johnson,** the "three-cent mayor of Cleveland"; and many others lined the bluff overlooking the harbor. In the **Chandler White** residence the group headed by **Cyrus Field** and **Peter Cooper** first gathered to discuss the laying of the **Atlantic Cable.** The **Bliss** mansion was once the home of **Henry Cruse Murphy,** where, in 1865, **Murphy** met with **William C. Kingsley** and **Alexander McCue** to formulate the original agreement for the construction of the **Brooklyn Bridge.** Except for **Fontbonne Hall,** now a private school, all the mansions have been supplanted by endless ranks of elevator apartment buildings, forming a palisade of red brick along the edge of **Shore Road.**

[1.] Bay Ridge Masonic Temple/originally **New Utrecht N. Y. Exempt Firemen's Association,** 257–259 Bay Ridge Ave., bet. Second and Third Aves. N side. ca. 1897. Addition to west and conversion to Masonic Temple later.

A *fine exercise* in above-ground archeology. Look carefully at the entrance cornice and the keystones over the windows. They bear the old volunteer fire company's seals and names (including the now-disappeared community of **Blythebourne**) on the east portion of the building, and the **Masonic** symbols (in the stained glass, too) only in the west. The structure was once symmetrical about its ornate entrance. Note subtle changes in the brick coloring to find the line of the addition.

Pollio's Restaurant (Italian), 6925 Third Ave., near Bay Ridge Ave. (69th St.) Telephone: SH 5-4877.

If you have longed for *real* **Italian** home cooking, drop in. Very modest. Authentic, down to the chilled burgundy [sic.]. Check hours . . . they close early in Bay Ridge.

[2.] Flagg Court, 7200 Ridge Blvd., bet. 72nd and 73rd Sts. W side. 1933–1936. Ernest Flagg.

Flagg Court, named for its well-known architect, is a 422-unit housing development contained in six contiguous buildings. Within the complex is an arcaded courtyard and swimming pool served by a diving tower in the form of a **Hindu** chatri (*good grief*). Among the project's avant-garde features: reversible fans below windows (now gone), windowshades on the outside of windows, concrete slabs serving as finished ceilings, and an auditorium of vaulted concrete. Note the pendant **carpenter-Gothic cornice** on the eighth floor. [See the index for earlier Flagg elsewhere in the city.]

[3.] The Ridge, 129 Bay Ridge Parkway, bet. Ridge Blvd. and Colonial Rd. N side. 1900.

A **shingle-style** mansion in the sky: red cedar shingles, crisp white trim, perched on a lawn retained by a giant rubble wall.

[4.] 112 Bay Ridge Parkway, bet. Ridge Blvd. and Colonial Rd. ca. 1900.

A formal stucco near-mansion with a handsome **Palladian** window and a cleverly suppressed garage.

[5a.] 131 76th Street, bet. Ridge Blvd. and Colonial Rd. N side. ca. 1900.

Neo-Georgian stucco, **Bermuda style.**

[5b.] 122 76th Street, bet. Ridge Blvd. and Colonial Rd. S side. ca. 1900.

Stucco, copper, and tile. This house and **No. 131** above are perched on a bluff rising **61** steps from **Colonial Road:** the pedestrian, for once, is king.

[6.] 8220 Narrows Avenue, NW cor. 83rd St.

A mansion disguised as a witch's hideaway; **Black Forest Art Nouveau.** Bumpety stone and simulated thatch make this one of **Brooklyn's** greatest private fantasies.

[7.] 175 83rd Street, bet. Ridge Blvd. and Colonial Rd. N side. ca. 1880.

Shingle style, conical capped, stepped gables. Note the round-cut shingles on the brick body.

[8.] 215 86th Street, bet. Ridge Blvd. and 3rd Ave. N side. ca. 1910.

A **Georgian Revival** house perched on a cut-stone retaining wall adjacent to **Adelphi Academy.**

[9.] Shore Hill Apartments, Shore Rd., bet. 90th and 91st Sts. E side. 1976. Gruzen & Partners.

Schematic facades on a building that is overbearing in this low-scaled neighborhood. The views from within, however, are fantastic.

[10.] Visitation Academy, 91st to 93rd Sts., Colonial Rd. to Ridge Blvd.

A twenty-foot stone and concrete wall protects the first through eighth grades from sight. The attached church is brick **Italian neo-Renaissance.**

[11.] James F. Farrell Residence, 119 95th St., bet. Marine Ave. and Shore Rd. N side. ca. 1845.

A splendid **Greek Revival** wood house inundated, but not drowned, by an adjacent sea of red brick apartment blocks. White painted, no detail changed, this miraculously preserved building sits next to an unpretentious outbuilding **(No. 125)** askew from the line of 95th Street. Presumably the main building was moved to this point and set parallel to the street next to its humble neighbor.

[12.] St. John's Episcopal Church, 9818 Fort Hamilton Parkway. NW cor. 99th St. 1834.

A *homely* cottage-scaled country church: stone and shingles clad a timbered body enriched with red, white, and gold polychromy. Called the "**Church of the Generals,**" it had attracted numerous military leaders from adjacent Fort Hamilton, including **Robert E. Lee** and **Stonewall Jackson.**

[13a.] Fort Hamilton Veterans' Hospital, 800 Poly Place, bet. Seventh and Fourteenth Aves. S side. 1950. Skidmore, Owings & Merrill.

Sleek slab with soothing views for ill veterans.

[13b.] Fort Hamilton Officers' Club/originally **Casemate Fort,** in Fort Hamilton Reservation, Shore Pkwy. E of Verrazano Bridge approaches. 1825–1831. Altered. ★

A granite military fortification now used as an officers' club. Not open to the public.

[14.] Poly Prep School, 92nd St., bet. 7th Ave. and Dahlgreen Ave. 1924.

A **collegiate-Georgian** boys' school on a generous campus, now coeducational.

[15.] 8205 11th Avenue, SE cor. 82nd St., Dyker Heights. ca. 1870.

A towered **Italianate** country villa, clapboarded with a generous **Tuscan**-columned porch. The view from on high is spectacular.

[6.] 8220 Narrows Avenue (house): in bumpety stone and simulated thatch

[11.] James F. Farrell Residence, an extraordinary Greek Revival remnant

[16a.] 8302 11th Avenue, SW cor. 83rd St. **[16b.] 8310 11th Avenue,** bet. 83rd and 84th Sts., W side. **[16c.] 1101 84th Street,** NE cor. 11th Ave., All in Dyker Heights.

The **mad dwarves** who built the manse [6.] above, moved a mile to build these country cousins. Note, particularly, the amber conservatory on **No. 8310.**

[17.] 1259 and 1265 86th Street, bet. 12th and 13th Aves. N side. ca. 1885.

Two unloved but handsome shingle-style houses facing **Dyker Beach Golf Course.**

[18.] National Shrine Church of St. Bernadette (Roman Catholic), 8201 13th Ave., bet. 82nd and 83rd Sts. E side. 1937. Henry V. Murphy.

A *streamlined surprise:* a parabolic, verdigris-copper-covered roof over chunky brick. **Go in** to a space washed in rich colored light.

BOROUGH PARK

Largely built up during the **1920s** with numerous one- and two-family houses as well as apartment buildings, this section was rural, save for scattered villages, at the turn of the century. Perhaps the most interesting of these settlements was **Blythebourne,** which lay southwest of the intersection of **New Utrecht Avenue** and **55th Street** along the old **Brooklyn, Bath Beach & West End Railroad,** today's **BMT/IND** West End Line. It was founded in the late **1880s** by **Electus B. Litchfield,** the son of **Edwin C. Litchfield** of **Prospect Park** fame. A number of houses were quickly built, as well as a series of **Queen Anne** cottages and two churches, but before the community could take hold, a politician purchased the area north of **Blythebourne** and east of **New Utrecht Avenue** and named it **Borough Park.** A real estate agent at the time warned the **Litchfield** family to sell its holdings, explaining that the *pogroms* of **Eastern Europe** would soon cause a mass migration to the outskirts of **Brooklyn,** forcing land values down. **Mrs. William B. Litchfield,** who controlled the property at the time, decided not to sell. The prediction was partially fulfilled; the **Borough Park** section did become a heavily **Jewish** community, but the land values, instead of falling, *rose* tremendously. As a result, **Blythebourne** was swallowed by **Borough Park** and is remembered today only in the name of the local post office, **Blythebourne Station.** The area also embraces a second-generation **Hasidic** community, transposed from **Williamsburg.**

[18.] National Shrine, St. Bernadette   [19.] Franklin D. Roosevelt School

[19.] Franklin Delano Roosevelt High School, 5801 19th Ave., bet. 59th and 55th Sts. 1965. Raymond & Rado.

Its **bold** precast concrete facade adds a note of architectural vigor to this otherwise visually monotonous area.

BENSONHURST/BATH BEACH

This lower-middle-class residential area preserves the family name of **Charles Benson,** whose farm was subdivided into the gridiron we see today. At **New Utrecht** and **18th Avenues** the original village of **New Utrecht** was settled in **1661,** on a site now marked by the **New Utrecht Reformed Church.**

[20a.] New Utrecht Reformed Church, 18th Ave., bet. 83rd and 84th Sts. E side. 1828. ★

A **Georgian Gothic** granite ashlar church, its brick-framed Gothic windows filled with **Tiffany-like Victorian** milk glass. An eneagled (gilt)

liberty pole stands in front of the church; its predecessors date back to **1783** and have been replaced six times since.

[20b.] New Utrecht Reformed Church Parsonage, 83rd St., bet. 18th and 19th Aves. ca. 1885.

A **shingle-style** home for the pastor, with a generous **Tuscan**-columned porch.

[20c.] New Utrecht Reformed Church Parish House, 84th St., bet. 18th and 19th Aves. 1892.

Robust **Romanesque Revival** in a class with **Frank Freeman's** Jay Street Fire House [WC Brooklyn/Civic Center 7a.].

Liberty Poles: To harass **British** garrisons, or to signify their defeat, Revolutionary patriots erected flagpoles, called **liberty poles,** on which to raise the flag of independence. Lightning and dry rot have taken their toll of the originals, but in some communities a tradition has developed to replace them.

[20d.] 8756 21st Avenue, just north of Bath Ave. W side. ca. 1888.

A *shingle-style* volume cut away for porches and crowned with a bell-like tower. White shingles, blue trim. **Threatened** by the gas station adjacent.

S

SOUTHERN BROOKLYN

Town of Gravesend/'s Gravensande

Established as a town in 1645; annexed to the City of Brooklyn in 1894.

Of the six original towns of **Brooklyn, Gravesend** is unique in a number of ways. First of all, it was settled by a group of *English* rather than *Dutch* colonists. Second, its list of patentees was headed by the name of a **woman,** a precocious admission of the equality of the sexes. Third, **Gravesend Village** was laid out using a set of sophisticated town-planning principles resembling those of **New Haven** and **Philadelphia.** Remnants of the plan are still visible today, but only in the street layout.

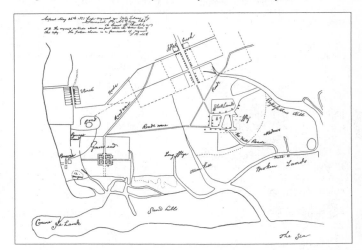

[5a.] Gravesend (Dutch) Reform Church: neo-Gothic with Art Nouveau detail

In **1643, Lady Deborah Moody** and her flock chose to found **Gravesend** after a bitter sojourn in **New England**, where they encountered the same religious intolerance from which they had fled in their native land. The free enjoyment of most opinion in religious matters, which characterized the **New Amsterdam** colony, made **Gravesend** an obvious haven for them.

In the **19th** century the territory of **Gravesend** became a great resort. No less than three racetracks were built within its bounds at various times, one northeast of **Ocean** and **Jerome Avenues** in **Sheepshead Bay,** another southeast of **Ocean Parkway** and **Neptune Avenue** in **Brighton,** and a third southwest of **Ocean Parkway** and **Kings Highway,** just north of the original village square. Before the development of **Coney Island** as a public beach and amusement area, it was the location of a number of fashionable hotels and piers, immense pinnacled wooden structures benefiting from the imagination and wit of **Victorian** decoration. Regrettably, there is little left of its raucous spirit and lively architecture. **Coney** was revived in the **1920s** with the completion of subway connections to **Manhattan,** but as a recreation area it has lost popularity and been surpassed by more attractive resorts accessible by automobile on **Robert Moses**-built highways. Only the dismembered corpse remains—the soul is gone.

[1.] The Old Village of Gravesend, Village Rd. N. to Village Rd. S., Van Siclen St. to Village Rd. E., its center at the intersection of Gravesend Neck Rd. and McDonald (formerly Gravesend) Ave. 1686.

The bounds of **Lady Moody's** town plan, now remembered only in the streets and the turf on the cemetery.

 [2.] Hicks-Platt House/also called Lady Moody House, 27 Gravesend Neck Rd., bet. McDonald Ave. and Van Siclen St. N side. Mid-17th century.

First publicized as **Lady Moody's** own home in the **1890s** by **William E. Platt,** a real estate developer, for publicity purposes. The fake stone veneer is ludicrous: *bring back the clapboard!* The fluted white **Tuscan** columns contribute a visual strength that even permastone can't kill.

[3.] Ryder-Van Cleef House, 38 Village Rd. N., bet. McDonald Ave. and Van Siclen St. S side.

A narrow **"Dutch"** gambrel-roofed house.

[4.] Hubbard House, 2138 McDonald Ave., bet. Avenue S and Avenue T. W side.

In a *vegetable jungle* next to the "el." The two-story wing is a **1925** addition.

[5a.] Gravesend Reform Church, 145 Gravesend Neck Rd. NW cor. E. 1st St. 1894.

The congregation's original building at **Neck Road** and **McDonald Avenue** was built in **1655.** This **Victorian Gothic** place is quite a departure from the original plain white churches of **Dutch Reform Congregations.** Note the **Art Nouveau** lettering and the porte cochère.

[5b.] Gravesend Cemetery, Gravesend Neck Rd., bet. McDonald. Ave. and Van Siclen St. S side. 1650. ★

One of the oldest and dingiest cemeteries in the city; **Lady Moody's** grave is somewhere within its boundaries, but its exact location is lost. Many old markers still remain; the cemetery can be viewed only by special arrangement.

[6.] Brooklyn School for Special Children, 376 Bay 44th St., SW cor. Shore Pkwy. service road. 1975. Edgar Tafel & Assocs.

A low institutional structure seemingly at the edge of the world. Surrounding it is an exquisitely detailed metal fence.

SHEEPSHEAD BAY

[7.] Wyckoff-Bennett House, 1669 E. 22nd St. SE cor. Kings Highway. ca. 1766. ★

A *rural idyll:* the **most impressive** of all early **Brooklyn** houses still in private ownership, this one is dated by a number cut into one of the wooden beams. Used as quarters by the Hessians during the Revolutionary War, it contains this inscription scratched into a **4-** by **7-inch** window-pane:

> Toepfer Capt of Regt de Ditfurth
> MBach Lieutenant v Hessen Hanau Artilerie

Savor the six-columned porch, the picket fence, ample grounds, and trees.

[7.] The Wyckoff-Bennett House: the most impressive early house still in use

[8.] Elias Hubbard Ryder House, 1926 E. 28th St., bet. Avenue S and Avenue T. W side. ca. 1834. ★

Funky shutters and gaslights do not a "Dutch Colonial" make! Look at those eaves! Squeezed between a group of two-and-a-half-story row houses.

Gerritsen: A community of **1600** year-round **lilliputian** bungalows on **lilliputian** plots, narrow streets barely wide enough for two cars to pass, a volunteer fire company, and lots of community spirit. Off **Gerritsen Avenue** along undeveloped **Marine Park.**

[9.] Junior High School 43 Brooklyn/The James J. Reynolds School,
1401 Emmons Ave., bet. E. 14th and E. 15th Sts. N side. 1965. Pedersen & Tilney.

Cast-in-place concrete. The long, low facades along the side streets, often the downfall of recent public school design, are here the most successful parts of a serious modern building.

[9.] Junior High School 43 Brooklyn, the James J. Reynolds School

Lundy Brothers Restaurant, Ocean and Emmons Avenues. Telephone: 646-9879.

Pointing like an arrow toward **Sheepshead Bay,** Ocean Avenue terminates at the water's edge and at **Lundy's.** Big, brash, noisy, crowded, but oh, what seafood! Quartered in two stories of a huge, **Spanish mission-style** stucco building, and serving as many as **5000** meals a day; a visit to **Lundy's** is a special treat for anyone in New York. Don't mind the brusque waiters—just dig in and enjoy!

Sheepshead Bay Fishing Fleet: Emmons Avenue east of Ocean Avenue to East 27th Street. A flotilla of fishing boats offers you the chance to catch *blues, stripers,* and *miscellany* if you rise early or go to bed late. You may return with more fish than you can possibly cook or eat.

MANHATTAN BEACH

The eastern peninsula of what was once **Coney Island.** *Very* isolated, very affluent (in late 20th century terms), very green, very **dull.** At the eastern tip was the old **Naval Training Station** from **World War II,** now replaced by the campus of **Kingsborough Community College.**

[10.] Kingsborough Community College, main gate at end of Oriental Blvd., bet. Sheepshead Bay and the Atlantic Ocean. Master Plan, 1968. Katz, Waisman, Weber, Strauss. Various buildings by KWWS; James Stewart Polshek; Lundquist & Stonehill; Warner, Burns, Toan & Lunde.

A large and *complex* complex, with some stylish modern forms.

CONEY ISLAND

[11.] Coney Island Hospital, Ocean Parkway, NE cor. Shore Parkway. 1953–1957. Katz, Waisman, Blumenkranz, Stein & Weber, Architects Associated.

Renowned as a landmark to vast numbers of motorists, it announces arrival at **Coney Island** even though it is over the district's boundary. Off-white brick masses are fussily articulated, its southern facade, seasoned with sunshades, a symbol of its period. From the period of modern architecture when *removal of ornament* was a holy mission.

[12.] William E. Grady Vocational High School, 25 Brighton 4th Rd., bet. Brighton 4th and Brighton 6th Sts. N side. 1956. Katz, Waisman, Blumenkranz, Stein, Weber, Architects Associated.

Great barrel-vaulted gymnasium and auditorium: limestone, brick, and concrete that already seem of a dated style. On the south facade is a bas-relief by **Constantino Nivola;** on the west, a mosaic by **Ben Shahn.**

[12.] The William E. Grady Vocational High School: note the barrel-vaulted gym

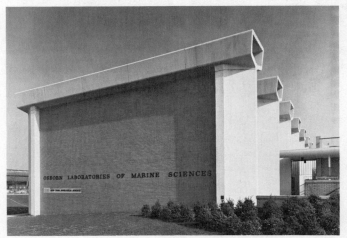

[13.] The Osborn Laboratories of Marine Sciences at the New York Aquarium

[13.] New York Aquarium, Boardwalk, NE cor. W. 8th St. **Exhibit Building,** 1955. Harrison & Abramovitz. **Osborn Laboratories of Marine Sciences,** 1965. Goldstone & Dearborn.

A must visit for the sealife displayed within and without. It is equivocal, and therefore less than successful, in its attempts to reconcile the opposing needs of a museum and an amusement park. White whales, seahorses, penguins, octopi, sea anemones, electric eels make the trip abundantly worthwhile, particularly with and for children (handle your own horseshoe crab!). Parking available, or take the BMT/IND "D" train to the West 8th Street stop. Telephone: 266-8500.

[14.] Amusement Area, bet. W. 8th St. and W. 16th St., and bet. Surf Ave. and the Boardwalk.

As each Memorial Day rolls around, signifying the opening of a new season at **Coney Island,** the number of amusements decreases. The immense spiderweb of the *Wonder Wheel* still remains, but *Steeplechase* is gone. *Luna Park* is gone. *Dreamland* is gone. The inoperative parachute jump is still a spidery silhouette if a bit rusty. A number of roller coasters and carousels remain. The **Bowery,** a circus midway of a street located between the **Boardwalk** and **Surf Avenue,** still provides some life. (Note the great **Greek Revival** autoscooter rink between 12th Street and Stillwell, along the Bowery, south side.) The automobile has taken the middle class to other pleasures.

Nevertheless many rides remain, as do **games of "skill," corn-on-the-cob, slices of watermelon,** and **cotton candy.** The rides and buildings reveal all sorts of architectural styles and fantasies, many vernacular in origin, the work of local carpenters. It would be pointless to single out any special events since "change" is the battle cry. Look around—there is plenty to see and enjoy.

[15.] Nathan's Famous (the original)   **[22.]** The Tower & Town houses

[19.] Sea Rise I (apartments): the best of the Coney Island UDC projects

[15.] Nathan's Famous (the original), Surf Ave., SW cor. Stillwell Ave.

With **Steeplechase Park** gone, **Nathan's Famous** remains Coney's greatest institution. Once upon a time it cost a nickel on the subway to get to **Coney,** and a nickel bought a hot dog at Nathan's (**1976: 50¢** and **60¢,** respectively). Open all year for stand-up, delectable treats, such as delicatessen sandwiches, clams on the half-shell, "shrimp boats" (shrimp cocktails in miniature plastic dinghies), and sundry other appetizing morsels. Our mouths are watering!

[16.] Steeplechase Pier, Boardwalk at W. 17th St.

Ravaged by fire numerous times (like most of Coney Island), this pier is no longer as elegant as it was years ago. It is now a **favored fishing dock** operated by the city. A walk along its thousand feet provides cool breezes and wonderful vantage points for the summer fireworks or the setting sun. Try your hand at catching *fluke, blues, flounder, stripers,* or other fish in season.

[17.] Abe Stark Center, N.Y.C. Department of Parks and Recreation, W. 19th St. at the Boardwalk. 1969. Daniel Chait.

A **would-be Nervi** created these **Y**-shaped column-buttresses to support a great dished-trussed roof. An ice-skating rink.

[18.] Our Lady of Solace Church, NW cor. Mermaid Ave. and W. 17th St. 1925. Robert J. Reiley.

A plain brick **neo-Romanesque** church. The interior is *refreshingly* austere: exposed brick, arches, limestone columns, timbered roof.

Gargiulo's Restaurant, 2911 15th St., bet. Mermaid and Neptune Aves. Restaurant founded 1907; located here since 1928.

A **princely place** in its **plebeian** surroundings. It would be just another Italian restaurant on Second Avenue. Here it is **Mecca.** The works—**wine, pasta, appetizer, entree, dessert, and coffee**—are expensive.

UDC Land: The New York State **Urban Development Corporation,** under Edward J. Logue, chose Coney Island's urban renewal area as one of three principal precincts for its New York City experiments (Twin Parks in the Bronx and Roosevelt Island are the other two). The many projects listed below are all *risk-taking* experiments in **quality** *urban design:* experiments that had not been attempted or matched by the **New York City Housing Authority** since early glories at **Williamsburg Houses** and **Harlem River Houses,** but were anticipated by such excellent **Housing and Development Administration** projects as *Riverbend, Waterside,* and *East Midtown Plaza* (all **Davis, Brody & Assocs.)**

Among Coney Island's UDC projects are:

[19.] Sea Rise I, Neptune and Canal Aves., bet. W. 33rd and W. 37th Sts. 1976. Hoberman & Wasserman.

Warm gray brick, open access corridors, stepped and terraced forms. The best of the Coney Island **UDC** high-rises: it appears more a successful architectural school design project than a piece of urban reality: a theoretical possibility built full size.

[20.] 2730 W. 33rd Street, bet. Bayview and Neptune Aves. 1975. Skidmore, Owings & Merrill.

Stacked **cubist** balconies on a white concrete tower: clever and dull.

[21.] Town houses, Bayview Ave., SW cor. W. 33rd St. 1975. Davis, Brody & Assocs.

Brown brick, concrete-corniced, unassuming, understated row houses; their broken forms surround a garden court. Lovely.

[22.] Tower and Town houses, W. 24th to W. 25th Sts., S side of Neptune Ave. 1975. Tower, Skidmore, Owings & Merrill. Town houses, Davis, Brody & Assocs.

See comments on mates at [20.] and [21.] above.

[23.] Housing for the Elderly, Surf Ave., bet. W. 36th and W. 37th Sts. N side 1975. Hoberman & Wasserman.

Stepped terraces are empty: the residents wilfully cluster about the trafficked streets below where the action is, rather than where the architects assigned them space.

[24.] Sea Park East, bet. W. 28th and W. 29th Sts. Midblock bet. Mermaid and Surf Aves. 1975. Tower, Skidmore, Owings & Merrill. Town houses, Davis, Brody & Assocs.

See comments on mates at [20.], [21.], and [22.] above.

[25.] Sea Park East, bet. W. 27th and W. 29th Sts. N side Surf Ave. 1975. Hoberman & Wasserman.

Lesser versions of Sea Rise I above [19.].

[26.] Ocean Towers, N side Surf Ave., bet. W. 24th and W. 25th Sts. 1975. Prentice & Chan, Ohlhausen.

Beige, semiglazed brick; black sliding sash. An unbroken monolith.

[27.] 2920 and 2940 W. 21st Street, NW cor. Surf Ave. 1974. James Doman & Emil Steo.

Simple **7-story** warm gray brick.

[28.] Fire Service Pumping Station/Coney Island High Pressure Pumping Station, N.Y.C. Department of Water Resources, 2301 Neptune Ave., bet. W. 23rd and W. 24th Sts. N side. 1937. Irwin S. Chanin.

Wraparound lights of fixed glass and a lozenge plan tie this work to the same European influences vividly realized in the **Paris Exposition** of **1937.** Guarding the entrance of this pure white bilaterally symmetrical structure are two pairs of moderne prancing steeds.

[29.] 2835–37 W. 37th Street, bet. Neptune and Canal Aves. E side.

Mykonos in Brooklyn, complete to the textured stucco and white-washed surfaces. Mediterranean memories must have been vivid among the masons responsible for this **vernacular conversion** of two adjacent two-family houses of standard design.

SOUTHEASTERN BROOKLYN

Town of Flatlands/Nieuw Amersfoort

Established as a town in 1666; annexed to the City of Brooklyn in 1896.

The name **Flatlands** aptly describes this area. It is billiard-table flat, much of it still marshy. A considerable part bordering Jamaica Bay is landfill. The area includes much of **Midwood;** the inland portion still known as **Flatlands,** part of which has been developed as an industrial park; and the shorefront areas of **Floyd Bennett Field, Bergen Beach, Mill Basin,** and **Canarsie.**

MIDWOOD

[1.] Van Nuyse-Magaw House, 1041 E. 22nd St., bet. Avenues I and J. E side. ca. 1800. ★

Built at **East 22nd Street** and **Avenue M,** this farmhouse was moved about 1916 and turned perpendicular to the street in order to fit its narrow lot. The distinctive "Dutch Colonial" gambrel roof is, therefore, the street facade. Woodwork and the oval window into the front hall are Federal. The silly columns at the entrance date from a 1952 "restoration."

[2.] Johannes Van Nuyse House, also called the **Coe House,** 1128 E. 34th St., bet. Flatbush Ave. and Ave. J. W side. 1744, 1793, 1806. ★

It manages to look like a well-dressed man on an assembly line: *too neat* for its neighbors.

FLATLANDS

[3.] Pieter Claessen Wyckoff House, 5902 Clarendon Rd. at intersection of Ralph and Ditmas Aves. SW cor. ca. 1641. ★ Restoration architects, Oppenheimer, Brady and Vogelstein.

Hard to find in this confused stretch of street intersections, it is a *tired hulk* badly in need of the restoration promised. Not worth a visit now, its remnants are largely screened from view by a contractor's protective fence.

[4.] Vitagraph Company, Inc./Warner Brothers Pictures Inc., 791 E. 43rd St., bet. Farragut and Glenwood Rds. E side. ca. 1925.

Atop these storage vaults built for highly inflammable motion picture film is a ventilation system that creates a roofscape of **startlingly dramatic form.**

[29.] "Mykonos" in Brooklyn stucco   **[6.]** The Dutch Colonial Lott House

[4.] Vitagraph Company's ventilators provide a strong architectural statement

[5.] Flatlands Dutch Reformed Church, 3931 Kings Highway, bet. Flatbush Ave. and E. 40th St. 1848. Henry Eldert, builder. ★

One of three Brooklyn churches established by order of **Gov.** Peter Stuyvesant (the other two are the **Flatbush Reformed Dutch** and the **First Reformed**). Handsomely sited in a tree-filled park, this simple **Georgian-Federal** church stands where two earlier buildings stood: the first, built in **1663,** octagonal in plan. Note names in the adjacent cemetery: **Lott, Sprong, Voorhees, Kouwenhoven, Wyckoff.**

[6.] Hendrick I. Lott House, 1940 E. 36th St., bet. Fillmore Ave. and Avenue S. W side. 1676, 1800.

This happy **"Dutch Colonial"** house presents its end to the road in a garden bounded by a picket fence. The small wing is the original structure of **1676,** the main body built by Lott himself in **1800.** The projecting "Dutch" eaves are supported by columns that are square on one side and round on the other.

[7.] Stoothof-Baxter House, 1640 E. 48th St., bet. Avenue M and Avenue N. W side. Before 1796. ★

Trim, neat and **Williamsburgy.** Face to street.

[8a.] Douwe Stoothoff/John Williamson House, 1587 E. 53rd St., bet. Avenue M and Avenue N. E side.

Poorly altered "Dutch Colonial" farmhouse; asphalt printed "brick." End to street.

[8b.] Mill Baśin Branch, Brooklyn Public Library, 2385 Ralph Ave., NE cor. Ave. N. 1974. Arthur A. Unger & Assocs.

A serene box (compare the **Jamaica Bay Branch**) of brick, curved and carved without overkill.

[8b.] The new Mill Basin Branch of the Brooklyn Public Library System

CANARSIE

[9a.] Bay View Houses, Shore Parkway, NE cor. Rockaway Parkway. 1955. Katz, Waisman, Blumenkranz, Stein, Weber, Architects Associated.

In its time a **better-than-average** housing project.

[9b.] Jamaica Bay Branch, Brooklyn Public Library, Seaview Ave., NW cor. E. 98th St. 1972. Leibowitz, Dobuva & Assocs.

A **histrionic** little building for such a noble, simple purpose—ribbed block, slots, notches, cantilevers, splayed sills. An **advertisement for books?**

[9c.] Seaview Jewish Center, 1440 E. 99th St., bet. Seaview Ave. and Avenue N. W side. 1972. William N. Breger Assocs.

White stucco carved ice cream. Stylish and in another world than the surrounding *ticky-tacky* 2-family row houses. Make certain to see it from the south.

[9d.] Harry and Sidney W. Waxman Building, Hebrew Educational Society of Brooklyn, 9502 Seaview Ave., SE cor. E. 95th St. 1968. Horace Ginsbern & Assocs.

Concrete and brown brick, understated, yet still bold in scale. This institution, in a considerably less sophisticated building, was an important educational and social force in **Brownsville.** It moved to **Canarsie** with its community.

[10.] Canarsie Pier, Gateway National Recreation Area, S. of Shore Parkway at the foot of Rockaway Pkwy.

A pier to fish, rent boats, or just bask—at the edge of Jamaica Bay, where one day, perhaps, clams and oysters may again be taken.

[11.] Bankers Federal Savings Bank, 1764 Rockaway Parkway, SW cor. Avenue L. 1961. LaPierre, Litchfield & Partners.

A sophisticated modern building all but destroyed by a later brutal air-conditioning penthouse.

[9c.] Seaview Jewish Center: stylish in white stucco, like carved ice cream

[12.] Pepsi-Cola Bottling Plant, 9701 Avenue D, NW cor. Rockaway Ave., 1956. Skidmore, Owings & Merrill.

A now **grimy** classic curtain wall overlooks what is still a primordial *zumpf:* a low-lying marsh on one side and a railroad siding on the other. The rock-throwing *zumpf* inhabitants have caused **Pepsi** to add screens to fend off the rocks, producing a degraded elegance.

[13.] Playground, Public School 114 Brooklyn, Remsen Ave. NE cor. Glenwood Rd. 1972. Norman Jaffe, architect. Robert Malkin, landscape architect.

A ski-slope-roofed comfort station in cast concrete dominates this cold play area developed for joint operation by the city's Board of Education and the Parks and Recreation Department.

EASTERN BROOKLYN

Town of New Lots

Separated from the Town of Flatbush in 1852; annexed to the City of Brooklyn in 1886.

Three major neighborhoods exist within this sector. **Highland Park,** also called **Cypress Hills,** lies north of Atlantic Avenue; **Brownsville** occupies the roughly triangular area between **Remsen Avenue, East New York Avenue,** and the tracks of the **Long Island Railroad; East New York** makes up the remainder south to **Jamaica Bay** and east to the **Queens** boundary, or "City Line," as its residents often call it, a relic of the days when **Brooklyn** was a separate city.

HIGHLAND PARK/CYPRESS HILLS

[1.] 279 and 361 Highland Avenue, bet. Miller Ave. and Barbey St.

Two mini-mansions out of a larger number, many now displaced by apartment houses seeking these spectacular views. **No. 279,** in gray Roman brick and white limestone, bears a great composite Ionic porte cochère. **No. 361** is now a **Lithuanian Cultural Center.**

[2.] 101 Sunnyside Avenue, bet. Hendrix St. and Miller Ave. N side. ca. 1930.

Nestled against a sharp precipice, this brick apartment house is entered through a **neo-neo-Romanesque** courtyard.

[3.] 130 Arlington Avenue, 65 Schenck Avenue, SE cor. ca. 1900.

Two similar eclectic houses of **Roman** brick, with great Ionic-columned porches. Wealth was once here.

[3.] Houses, SE corner Arlington Ave.   **[1.]** Rutland Plaza (apartments)

[4.] House, NW cor. Barbey St. and Sunnyside Ave. ca. 1882.

Shingle-stick style house with an octagonal tower viewing the sea. Note the great yard with **Victorian** planting, a copper beech, and a flagpole.

[5.] Trinity Episcopal Church, Arlington Ave., NE cor. Schenck Ave. 1850.

Gothic Revival brick church, with a friendly squat, low scale.

BROWNSVILLE

Brownsville is at the bottom of the economic ladder. It is a poor area, largely non-white, with old and dilapidated housing predominating, much nondescript public housing, and some quite elegant new intrusions by the **State Urban Development Corporation** (U.D.C.). The neighborhood was first subdivided from farmland by **Charles S. Brown** in **1865,** and the community owes its name to him. In **1887** a group of real estate men purchased land and began to encourage **Jewish** immigrants in the congested **Lower East Side** to move here. The arrival of the **Fulton Street "el"** in **1889** stimulated the influx, and the settlement became a great concentration of poor **Eastern European Jews.** The community was not free of problems normally associated with deprived areas. Some of *Murder Incorporated's* most notorious leaders grew up in its streets. The completion of the **New Lots** branch of the **IRT** in **1922** further improved rapid transit connections to **Manhattan,** and the area grew mildly prosperous. **Pitkin Avenue** is still a major shopping street which, in the **1920s** through **1940s,** attracted shoppers from a much larger region. The movie house (now **Hudson Temple Cathedral**) at **Pitkin and East New York Avenues** was one of the great ornate picture palaces of **New York.** Following **World War II** the **Jewish** population began to leave, and the area, never very well maintained, settled into a neglected *miasma* of apartments, tenements, and two- and four-family housing. "Slum clearance" has been only partially effective, peaking at the new U.D.C. **Marcus Garvey Village** and **Rutland Plaza,** but leaving scars between that may never be eradicated.

[1.] Rutland Plaza, E. New York Ave. and Rutland Road, E. 92nd to E. 94th Sts. 1976. Donald Stull and Assocs.

Precast concrete rough aggregate panels: a building of considerable visual style, without some of the subtleties of other **U.D.C.** works: cf. **Sea Rise I** (Hoberman & Wasserman) at **Coney Island** [see S Brooklyn 19.].

[2.] Public School 398 Brooklyn, The Rutland Road School, S side E. New York Ave., bet. E. 93rd and E. 94th Sts. 1976. Perkins & Will.

Barrel-vaulted "barn" allowing total flexibility of partitioning on the upper level. Terra-cotta-colored brick, with bronze-anodized aluminum sash.

[3.] Hudson Temple Cathedral/formerly **Loew's Pitkin Theater,** 1501 Pitkin Ave., NW cor. Saratoga Ave. ca. 1925. Thomas Lamb.

A landmark on this brassy shopping street. Its carefully ornate masonry exterior screens one of those outlandish, fairy tale auditoriums of the great era of the picture palace, complete with twinkling stars and moving clouds across its ceiling-sky.

[4.] Mobile Home Park, Sutter to Pitkin Aves., Herzl St. to the W side of Strauss St. 1970. M. Paul Friedberg & Assocs., site planners.

Surprisingly, these bleak dwellings, built by the U.D.C. in early-Fort **Bragg style,** are popular among their residents; each is a private, free-standing house-object, an *idea* more potent to the poor than any attitude about architectural aesthetics.

[5.] East New York Savings Bank, Kingsboro Branch, Kings Highway and E. 98th St. 1962. Lester Tichy & Assocs.

A little bit of **Hollywood** in **Brownsville:** a parasoled brick cylinder.

[6.] Engine Co. 238, Squad Co. 4, N.Y.C. Fire Department, 885 Howard Ave., SE cor. Livonia Ave. 1974. Giovanni Pasanella.

Modest, modern brown brick fire station with skylights at its rear.

[5.] East New York Savings Bank: a little bit of Hollywood in **Brownsville**

[7.] Belmont Avenue Pushcart Market, Belmont Ave., bet. Rockaway and Christopher Aves.

One of the few remaining street markets in the city. This one originated because the **Long Island Rail Road** siding at nearby **Junius Street** was the center of a wholesale fruit and vegetable market. The tradition evolved of selling the less-appetizing remainders of the early morning bargainings in the vicinity. To provide a vehicle for such sales to the local community, the pushcart market was created. Though efforts are constantly being made to displace these activities from the streets, this brash, noisy, and pungent marketplace has weathered all storms, its population slowly transmogrified from **Jewish** to **Hispanic.**

[8.] Betsy Head Memorial Playground Bathhouse, Strauss St. to Hopkinson Ave., Dumont to Livonia Aves. 1940. John Matthews Hatton.

Liberal use of glass block and a parasol roof delicately balanced on parabolic ribs distinguish this **WPA** bathhouse serving a large swimming pool.

The Shtetl: What Brownsville lacked in physical amenities it more than made up in the richness of its social life. It recalled the life of the *shtetl,* the small **Jewish** community in **Eastern Europe. Pitkin Avenue** was the street for the grand promenade, its Yiddish-speaking community addicted to thrashing out the social and political problems of the hour while *spatziering* down the avenue. At one time, a cafeteria called **Hoffman's** was the area's glittery but modest version of a **Delmonico's** of another era and an entirely different social class. **Amboy Street,** the home of a youth gang immortalized by Irving Shulman's *The Amboy Dukes,* became, in **1916,** the home of the first birth control clinic in **America,** established by the pioneer in this field, **Margaret Sanger.** Almost no Jewish population remains.

[8.] The Betsy Head Memorial Playground Bathhouse: early Art Moderne

[9.] Marcus Garvey Village: a pretentious experiment in low-rise housing

[9.] Marcus Garvey Village, Dumont Ave. to a point S of Riverdale Ave., from W of Bristol St. to Chester St., and, at a portion, Rockaway Ave. 1976. Institute for Architecture and Urban Studies and David Todd & Assocs.

The **U.D.C.'s** pretentious experiment in low-rise high-density housing: row houses with stoops, embracing paved and planted play and sitting areas. Austere and reminiscent of the fanatically regimented Amsterdam housing of the late 1920s, it is more an architectural idea than housing for humans.

[10.] Holy Trinity Russian Orthodox Church, SE cor. Pennsylvania and Glenmore Aves. 1935.

One great and one minor onion dome sheathed in verdigris copper on a salmon-brick base. The porch on **Glenmore Street** is an eclectic fantasy.

[11.] "Clinic" Building, SE cor. Pennsylvania and Pitkin Aves. 1976.

Orange-brown brick, deeply incised windows in the current "carved brick" style.

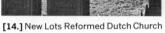

[14.] New Lots Reformed Dutch Church   **[15.]** Essex Terrace (apt. complex)

[12.] Bradford Street, bet. Sutter and Blake Aves.

This street preserves a sense of the early settlement of **East New York.** Gaily painted, the block conveys a charm that must have been attractive to the families that moved here from more crowded adjacent areas during the period of peak development.

[13.] Christian Duryea House, 562 Jerome St., bet. Dumont and Livonia Aves. ca. 1787.

Another "Dutch" farmhouse, now denuded of its hallmark, the eaves.

[14.] New Lots Reformed Dutch Church, 630 New Lots Ave., SE cor. Schenck Ave. 1823. ★

Built by the **Dutch** farmers of this area when weekly trips to the **Flatbush Church** became too arduous. A wood-shingled body, with Gothic Revival openings. The old **Parish House,** in design concert with the church, has been demolished in favor of an **unfortunately heavy-handed** replacement.

[15.] Essex Terrace, bounded by Linden Blvd., Hegeman Ave., Linwood and Essex Sts. 1970. Norval C. White.

A **low-rise high-density** project surrounding its private outdoor space. The corner gates allow residents to admit or restrict the neighborhood at their own discretion. Critic **Carolynn Meinhardt** cites it as "the best of its kind in the city."

[16.] City Line 1 Turnkey Public Housing, 460–470 Fountain Ave. and 1085–1087 Hegeman Ave. NW cor. Fountain Ave. and 1052–1064 Hegeman Ave. and 768–774 Logan St. SW cor. Hegeman Ave. 1975. Ciardullo-Ehmann.

Duplexes over flats that attempt to emulate, in modern terms, the *fussy scale* of their row house neighbors.

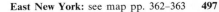

[17.] Brooklyn Developmental Center, Fountain Ave. W side., S of Flatlands Ave. 1974. Katz, Waisman, Weber, Strauss.

A center for the **care, residence,** and **education** of retarded children. A handsome, sprawling group of ribbed concrete block buildings with a hipped skylight over its central social space.

[18.] Public School 306 Brooklyn, 970 Vermont St., NW cor. Cozine Ave. 1966. Pedersen & Tilney.

A superb cast-in-place concrete school. In an area of flat monotony and long eerie vistas down empty streets, the boldly raked stair towers and handsome massing of the long, low volumes of this building add richness and an air of mystery.

[17.] Brooklyn Developmental Center   **[18.]** Public School 306 Brooklyn

[19.] Starrett City, bet. Flatlands Ave. and Shore Pkwy., Seaview and Louisiana Aves. 1976. Herman Jessor.

A *surreal* experience. Great building blocks placed like a **supermodel** in the boondock landscape. Jessor's other giant fantasies include Co-op City [See N Bronx 39.].

[20.] Arnold and Marie Schwartz Comprehensive Health Care Center, Brookdale Hospital Medical Center, Rockaway Pkwy., NE cor. Linden Blvd. 1974. William Breger & Assocs. and Unger/Napier Assocs.

Its large pale brown bulk is festooned with vanes that swoop out from its facade.

[21.] Josephine B. Baird Special Care Pavilion, Brookdale Hospital Medical Center, 1235 Linden Blvd., NW cor. Rockaway Pkwy. 1968. Horowitz & Chun.

Brown brick here makes a strong, well-scaled and appropriately **serene** statement in this innocuous area. Both private physicians' offices and clinics are herein contained.

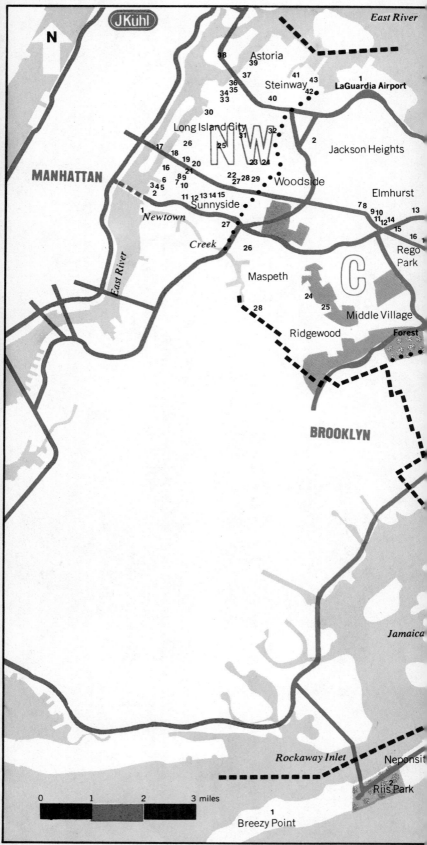

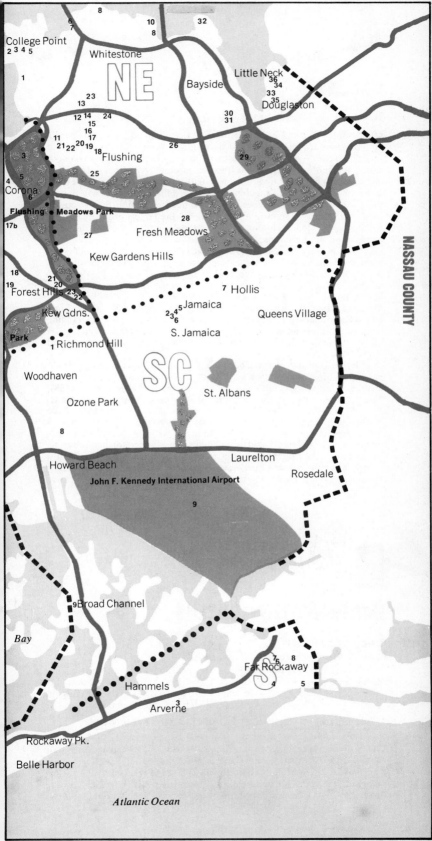

College Point
2 3 4 5

8
6
7

10
8

32

1

Whitestone

NE

Bayside

Little Neck
36
34
33
35
Douglaston

23
13

12 14 24
15
16
17
11
21 22 20 19 18 Flushing
3

30
31

26

29

25

4
5
Corona
6
Flushing ● Meadows Park
17b

28

Fresh Meadows

27

Kew Gardens Hills

18
19
21
20
Forest Hills 23 22
22

Kew Gdns.

Park

7 Hollis

5
2 3 4 Jamaica
6

Queens Village

S. Jamaica

1 Richmond Hill

Woodhaven

SC

St. Albans

Ozone Park

8

Laurelton

Howard Beach

Rosedale

John F. Kennedy International Airport

9

9 Broad Channel

Bay

7 6 8
Far Rockaway
4

Hammels

5

3
Arverne

Rockaway Pk.

Belle Harbor

Atlantic Ocean

NASSAU COUNTY

4

QUEENS

Borough of Queens/Queens County

Queens is the home of *two* of the three metropolitan airports—**LaGuardia**
and **Kennedy International**—and its residents are unable to forget that
fact, the drone of jets and props ever-reminding them as planes swoop out
of the sky and into these all-weather aerodromes. Awareness of modern
technology is balanced by contact with nature—postage-stamp-sized front
lawns or the vastness of the **Jamaica Bay Wildlife Refuge** (now a part of
the **Gateway National Recreation Area**), not to mention the borough's
other parks: **16,397** acres in all. **Queens** has the largest gross area, **114.7**
square miles (**126.6** including inland waters), almost a *third* of the city's
entire area. In population, it ranks second only to **Brooklyn.**

As a borough it is predominantly a bedroom community. The last
great open spaces of **New York** were here until the forties, allowing the
great pressure of returning World War II veterans' desires for detached
dwellings to be fulfilled here: suburbia within the city limits. However, a
good deal of industry also thrives within its boundaries. In **Long Island
City** and **Maspeth** and along the extensive rights of way of the **Long
Island Rail Road** are manufacturers of a wide variety of products ranging
from surgical instruments to pianos, from biscuits to perfume. The **LIRR**
makes it a transportation center as well, aided by **Conrail, Amtrak** and
many truck operations.

Before **Queens** became a borough, it was a far larger county, encompassing its present-day area as well as that of **Nassau** (a new county
created as a by-product of consolidation into greater **New York** in **1898**).
The borough is named for **Catherine of Braganza, Queen of Charles II.**

The vastness of **Queens** and its relatively late development have
encouraged the retention of the old town, village, and subdivision names
for its various communities. From a strong sense of pride and identification with the outlying suburbs, residents never refer to themselves as
"Queensites" but rather as living in **Jamaica,** or **Flushing,** or **Forest Hills,**
or **St. Albans.** If pressed further, the response to "Where do you live?"
becomes **"Long Island."**

NORTHWESTERN QUEENS

Long Island City
Separated from the Town of Newtown in 1870.

Between **1870** and **1898,** the year of consolidation into greater **New
York, Long Island City** was, in fact, a city. It encompassed not only the
area we still identify with its name but the adjacent communities of
Hunter's Point, Ravenswood, Astoria, Steinway, and **Sunnyside.**

LONG ISLAND CITY, HUNTER'S POINT, AND RAVENSWOOD

These three areas form the industrial concentration of **New York
City,** in appearance, if not in fact. Laced by **IRT** and **BMT** elevateds, the
passenger yards of the *old* **Penn Central** (now **Conrail**) and the Long Island
Rail Road (now part of the **Metropolitan Transit Authority**) are in an
open cut, and the **IND** underground. It is a great transportation nexus.
From the "els," from a car, or on foot, the factory agglomeration makes

itself felt: above, alongside, and even below you as you cross endless trestles over deep scars in the flat landscape.

Hunter's Point, in the southwest corner, is a mixed factory and residence district. **Ravenswood,** along the **East River** above the **Queensboro Bridge,** has a number of high-rise housing projects in its midst, as well as a major **Con Edison** power generator, whose candy-striped stacks (and their produce) are landmarks on both sides of the river.

[1.] New York News Gravure Inserting Plant, 2nd St. at Newtown Creek. 1972. Harrison & Abramovitz.

A great concrete box housing operations for the world's largest newspaper.

[2.] Prudenti's Vicino Mare Restaurant/formerly the **Queens County Bank,** 2nd St. NW cor. Borden Ave.

This fine **Romanesque Revival** building is happily preserved as a restaurant.

[6.] Engine Company 258, Ladder 115: firehouse with stepped super-Dutch gable

[3.] Tennisport, behind Prudenti's, 2nd St., NW cor. Borden Ave.

The major tennis space here is a space-frame barrel vault. Fabric in tension against an aluminum frame: **Bucky Fuller** made real by the affluent—a sad note.

[4.] Formerly **New York and Queens Electric Light and Power Plant,** 2nd St., bet 50th and 51st Aves. ca. 1890.

This brick **Renaissance Revival** plant bears four great stacks, rampant on the **Queens** skyline. Note the Renaissance window guards in its granite base. Occupants include assorted manufacturing establishments and indoor tennis courts.

[5.] St. Mary's Roman Catholic Church, 10-08 49th Ave., SE cor. Vernon Blvd. ca. 1870. P. C. Keely.

A painted brick church, its steeple the local landmark.

[6.] Engine Company 258, Ladder Company 115, N.Y.C. Fire Department. 10-40 47th Ave., bet. Vernon Blvd. and 11th St. S side. 1903. Bradford L. Gilbert.

Robust multistory firehouse with stepped super-Dutch gable.

[7.] P. S. 1 (artists' studios)/formerly **P. S. 1 Queens**/originally **Ward 1 School,** 21st St., bet. 46th Rd. and 46th Ave. 1892. Altered, 1976, Shael Shapiro.

Now converted to lofts in a continuing process of adaptive reuse for the city's artists' community, this stolid **Romanesque Revival** building was built when *"Battle Ax"* **Gleason** was mayor of **Long Island City.** It once supported a clock tower.

The Steinway Tunnels: The twin tubes of the **IRT Flushing Line** under the **East River** were originally begun in **1892** by piano king **William Steinway** as a trolley car connection to **Manhattan.** The **Panic** of **1893** and **Steinway's** death in **1896** interrupted the project until **August Belmont,** the **IRT** financier, revived it in **1902.** The tunnel, with reversing loops at each end (the loop under the Grand Central IRT Station still exists) became the first connection between **Manhattan** and **Queens** in **1907,** though it was not put into regular use until converted to subway operation in **1915.**

[8.] Hunter's Point Historic District, much of 45th Ave., between 21st and 23rd Sts. District designated, 1968. ★

A street of virgin row houses complete with original stoops and cornices. Off-white *brown*stones!

[9.] 21-49 45th Road, bet. 21st and 23rd Sts. N side. ca. 1890.

Romanesque Revival; bowed, arched, bold terra cotta—grand old house.

[10.] Supreme Court of the State of New York/formerly **Queens County Court House,** Court Square at Jackson Ave. 1874. 1908. ★

Beaux Arts Baroque: limestone, brick, and three kinds of granite (smooth gray, rockface pink, and rockface slate gray). The present building was built on the foundations of its burnt ancestor.

[10.] Supreme Court, State of N.Y.   **[16.]** Old Amer. Arch. Terracotta Co.

[11.] Russ Toggs Manufacturing and Distribution Center, 27-09 49th Ave. NE cor. 27th St. 1965. Robert E. Levien.

A bulky, "brutal" brick box that reaches for the top of the nearby elevated viaduct of the **Long Island Expressway.** Its roof becomes the *obvious* place for a giant neon sign on a delicate latticework of steel. From the street the factory reads strongly against its confused industrial background. From the highway, the sign is all that can be captured at **50** mph.

[12.] Thypin Steel Co., 49-49 30th St. at the Long Island Expressway. 1950. Saul Goldsmith.

Glassy, daylit steel warehouse. An industrial giant worthy of the great **Detroit** work of **Albert Kahn.**

[13.] Executone Building/originally **Loose-Wiles, Sunshine Biscuit Co.,** 29-10 Thomson Ave. bet. 29th and 30th Sts. 1913. William Higginson.

504   Northwestern Queens [NW]

A gargantua of warehouses in white-glazed terra cotta. This building, drawn and stylized, formed the logo on the **Sunshine Biscuit** box for years: "The plant of a thousand windows." Higginson was an important industrial architect of the time. [See his **Bush Terminal,** WC Brooklyn/ Sunset Park 5.]

[14.] American Chicle Division of Warner-Lambert Co./The Adams Gum Building, 30-30 Thomson Ave., bet. 30th Pl. and 31st St. 1919. Ballinger and Perot.

Neon giants to the glory of **Dentyne** and **Chiclets** vie with Ballinger and Perot's **Jugenstijl:** Germanic Art Nouveau in the manner of **Otto Wagner.**

[15.] LaGuardia Community College, Thomson Ave. bet. 31st Pl., 31st St., and 47th Ave. 1977. Stephen Lepp & Assocs.

A renovation and addition in brown brick and glassy, classy red sash. Low key, high style.

[16.] Kilmoyler Realty Corp./originally **The American Architectural Terracotta Co.,** 42-16 Vernon Blvd., bet. Bridge Plaza South and 43rd Ave. W side. 1892.

Tudor Revival amber brick jewel with Sullivan-like terra-cotta trim. It stands proudly among the artifacts of industrial blight. Look at the chimney pots.

[17.] Queensboro Bridge, from Queens Plaza to 59th–60th St. in Manhattan. 1909. Gustav Lindenthal, engineer. Palmer & Hornbostel, architects. ★

This ornate (note the **Hornbostel** finials) cantilevered bridge formed the backdrop for views in countless **Hollywood** films from swank **New York** apartments of the forties. Surprisingly, its completion in **1909** did not cause the migration across the river that the **Williamsburg** and **Manhattan Bridges** before it had caused. The last trolley car to see service in New York shuttled across the **Queensboro,** stopping at the (now-demolished) elevator tower on **Welfare** (now **Roosevelt**) Island. The trolley and vehicular elevators were discontinued in **1955** when a bridge was completed between the island and **Queens.** Passenger elevator operation continued until **1975.**

[18.] Queensbridge Houses, Vernon Blvd. to 21st St., 40th Ave. to Bridge Plaza N. 1939. William F. R. Ballard, chief architect. Henry Churchill, Frederick G. Frost, Burnett C. Turner, assocs.

One of the *best* of city housing projects, in a handsome light brown brick with red window frames. Once it was the largest public housing project in the country: **3149** units in **26** six-story buildings, occupying six superblocks.

[19.] Brewster Building, 27-01 Bridge Plaza North, bet. 27th and 28th Sts. 1910. Stephenson & Wheeler.

Bulky brick, surmounted by a "constructivist" clock tower, the clock long since departed. This is where **Brewster** produced his carriages and later assembled **Rolls-Royces,** shipped knocked down from **England.**

[20.] Chase Manhattan Bank Building/originally **Bank of the Manhattan Co.,** 29-27 41st Ave. at Queens Plaza. 1927. Morrell Smith.

The crenellated clock tower commands this giant tangle of elevated train viaducts.

[21.] Municipal Parking Garage, Bridge Plaza South, 28th St., 42nd Rd., and Jackson Ave. 1976. Rouse, Dubin & Ventura.

They worked hard to raise a common garage to an uncommon status. Stylish smooth and ribbed concrete: *too stylish.*

[22.] Naarden-UOP Fragrances/formerly **Knickerbocker Laundry,** 43-23 37th Ave. 1936. Irving M. Fenichel.

Art Moderne concrete, seemingly moulded of streamlined ice cream: a monument for the traveller on the adjacent **LIRR** into **Pennsylvania Station.**

[23.] New York and Queens Railroad Company Station, Northern Blvd. SE cor. Woodside Ave. 1885.

The main station for a street railway and railroad company later absorbed by the **LIRR** system. Twin masonry towers and a robust archway (now filled in) *joyfully* announced the then-impending trip to Queens.

[24.] Queensboro Motors Corporation, 51-30 Northern Blvd., bet. Woodside Ave. and 54th St. S side. 1959. Hugh Stubbins.

A **Miesian** (i.e., in the manner of the great German-American architect **Ludwig Mies van der Rohe**) place of commerce for Volkswagen. Neat but not notable.

[23.] The old Romanesque Revival N.Y. and Queens Railroad Company Station

[25.] United States Army Pictorial Center/formerly Paramount Pictures Corp.

[25.] U.S. Army Pictorial Center/formerly **Eastern Service Studios**/originally **Famous Players Lasky Corp. (Paramount Pictures),** 35th Ave., bet. 34th and 38th Sts. N side. 1919.

Ernst Lubitsch, Ben Hecht, and Charles MacArthur produced films here, one of a number of old film studios that can still be found in the city. The porte cochère (at 35-11 35th Avenue) is the only architectural statement here.

 [26.] Structural Display Co./originally **Barkin-Levin Factory (Lassie Coats),** 12-12 33rd Ave., bet. 12th and 13th Sts. 1958. Ulrich Franzen.

Built for an expatriate clothing manufacturer from the overcrowded garment district of Manhattan. Crisp architecture that has been ill maintained.

To Roosevelt Island: At the end of **36th** Avenue as it crosses **Vernon Boulevard** is the bridge to **Roosevelt Island** (formerly **Welfare Island**): painted blue and purple, a welcoming spectrum in contrast to its earlier grim **Department-of-Public-Works-*eye-ease*** green.

SUNNYSIDE

A residential area triggered by the arrival of the **IRT Flushing Line** along **Queens Boulevard** and **Roosevelt Avenue** in **1917.** Though surrounded by industry and cemeteries, proximity and excellent access to **Manhattan** have assured its stability. Its most noted feature is **Sunnyside Gardens.**

[27.] Sunnyside Gardens, 43rd to 50th Sts., Skillman to 39th Ave. First units, 1924. Henry Wright, Clarence Stein, and Frederick Ackerman.

Seventy acres of **barren, mosquito-infested land** were transformed into a great and successful experiment in urban housing design. Using the street grid, row housing is arranged facing both the street and interior garden spaces. Walk through the paths that penetrate each block under umbrellas of **London plane trees:** an urbane delight, where the architecture is unimportant, even insipid, but the urban arrangements a source of great community delight.

[26.] Originally Barkin-Levin (Lassie Coat) Co. (note concrete umbrellas)

[28.] Phipps Garden Apartments, 5101 39th Ave., bet. 39th Ave., 50th and 52nd Sts., and Barnett Ave. 1931. Clarence Stein.

Four-, five-, and six-story *incunabulum,* surrounding a lush green, private, center-courted world. The architecture, again, is *secondary* to the sense of place.

[29.] J. Sklar Manufacturing Company/formerly **Lathan Lithography Co.,** 38-04 Woodside Ave., bet. Barnett and 39th Aves. W side. 1923. McDonnell and Pearl.

A **Tudor** campus set on manicured lawns disguises this manufactory of surgical instruments. *For once* a factory becomes a visual amenity in the community.

ASTORIA AND STEINWAY

The original settlement in these parts was **Hallet's Cove** along the **East River** at the foot of **30th Avenue,** named after **William Hallet** to whom **Governor Peter Stuyvesant** gave a patent for **1500** acres in **1654.** As a suburb its growth coincided with the introduction of the steam-powered ferry in **1815.** By **1839** the area was incorporated, friends of **John Jacob Astor** winning a bitter factional fight in naming Astoria for him.

The year **1842** saw the completion of the turnpike to **Greenpoint.** Soon shipping trade was established in lumber, particularly in exotic foreign woods. Shipping and lumber magnates built mansions just north of the **Cove** on the mount called **Hallet's Point,** two of which still existed as late as 1966. The availability of both lumber and cheap land persuaded **William Steinway** to establish a **400**-acre company town in the seventies near the foot of **Steinway Street.** The piano factory, some row housing, and his mansion all remain.

[30.] Sohmer Piano Company, 11-02 31st Ave., SE cor. Vernon Blvd. ca. 1875.

Steinway's competitor also established himself in this area in a many leveled factory crowned with a mansarded clock tower that could have been borrowed from the later pavilions of the **Louvre.**

[31.] American Savings Bank, 31-02 Steinway St., SW cor. 31st Ave. 1974. Edward Larrabee Barnes.

Dark brown brick and sheer glass; *elegance,* urbanity, and chic amidst an older, stolid, somber, middle-class community.

[32.] Boulevard Gardens, 31st Ave., Hobart St., 60th St., and 27th Ave. 1934. Theobald Engelhardt.

Early publicly assisted housing, meticulously maintained in this stable precinct. The **neo-Georgian** detailing gives it more character than the stripped nonarchitecture of later public boxes.

[33.] Good Church of Deliverance, Pentecostal, and the First Reformed Church of Astoria/formerly **Reformed Dutch Church of Hallet's Cove,** 27-26 12th St., bet. 27th and 28th Aves. 1888.

A terra cotta, brick, and verdigris copper squat **Goth.** Bold, monolithic, and homely.

[34.] Doctor Wayt House, 9-29 27th Ave., NW cor. 12th St. ca. 1845.

Crumbling **Italianate** mansion.

[31.] American Savings Bank Branch, Astoria (brown brick and sleek glass)

[35.] Remsen House, 9-26 27th Avenue, SW cor. 12th St. ca. 1835. ★

Greek Revival house, handsomely maintained with rural grounds, rubble garden walls, iron fence, slate sidewalk.

Walk north down 12th Street past faded grandeur to a smashing view of the Triborough Bridge, Wards Island, and Manhattan.

[36.] 25-37 14th Street, bet. Astoria Park S. and 26th Ave. E side.

Two-story **Doric,** a grand southern mansion in the midst of **Archie Bunker** land. Hard to find since it is screened by a copper beech that is, itself, a grand piece of tree architecture.

[37.] Astoria Park, Shore Blvd. to 19th St., Ditmars Blvd. to Astoria Park S. **[37a.] Astoria Play Center and Swimming Pool,** in Astoria Park. 1936. J.M. Hatton.

A tilted piece of green giving picnic views of the Triborough Bridge and the Manhattan skyline. Within is an expansive WPA-era pool complex and bathhouse.

[38.] Triborough Bridge, O. H. Ammann, engineer. Aymar Embury II, architect. 1936.

A whole highway system, trestled and bridged, of which this, the **Hell Gate** span, is the greatest part.

[36.] 25-37 14th Street, Astoria (a trick to find this two-story mansion)

[39.] **Hell Gate Bridge/**officially the **East River Arch Bridge of the New York Connecting Railroad.** 1917. Gustav Lindenthal, engineer. Henry Hornbostel, architect.

The through connection for the **Penn Central** (now **Conrail**) on its way from **Washington** through **New York** to **Boston** (it tunnels under both the **Hudson** and **East Rivers,** rising in **Queens** to pass over and through these great over- and under-slung bowstring trusses).

[40.] **Lawrence Family Graveyard,** 20th Rd. SE cor. 35th St. 1703. ★

A memorable location in history. Don't bother to look.

[41.] **William Steinway Mansion,** 18-33 41st St., bet. Berrian Blvd. and 19th Ave. 1865. ★

On a minimountain in a deciduous jungle inhabited by barking dogs, old cars, and trucks. **William Steinway's** (originally optician Benjamin Pike, Jr.'s) dark gray granite house was a showplace in its time. (The piano company factory [1872] is still at the northwest corner of **19th Avenue** and **39th Street.**)

[41.] William Steinway Mansion: brick Italianate mansion for the piano maker

[42.] Steinway (company town) Row Housing, 20th Ave., bet. Steinway St. and 41st St. S side. ca. 1880.

Trim, painted **Victorian** brick houses. Loved.

[43.] Lent Homestead, 78-03 19th Rd. at 78th St. N side. ca. 1729. ★

Weathered shingles, dormers, nestling in lush foliage: a well-preserved **"Dutch"** farmhouse.

NORTHEASTERN QUEENS

Town of Flushing/Vlissingen

Settled in 1642; chartered in 1645.

The town **Flushing** is commonly associated with the growth of religious freedom in the **New World.** Founded by **English** settlers, it received its patent from **Dutch Governor Kieft,** who stipulated in its text that the freedom of conscience of its townspeople was to be guaranteed. **Kieft's** successor, **Peter Stuyvesant,** attempted to suppress the **Quaker** sect, a number of whose adherents had settled in **Flushing. Quaker** and **non-Quaker** residents banded together against **Stuyvesant** and were successful in having the patent's stipulation recognized and observed. Among these settlers was the **Bowne** family whose house, dating from the **17th** century, can still be seen. The old **Quaker Meeting House** of the same period also remains as a testament to this struggle for religious liberty.

COLLEGE POINT

This community is named for an ill-fated Episcopal divinity school founded in **1836** by the **Rev. William A. Muhlenberg,** but never opened. Before religion found it, it was called Strattonsport, after **Eliphalet Stratton,** who had purchased the land in 1790 from the **Lawrence** family, noted early settlers. See their graveyard in **Astoria/Steinway** [NW Queens 40.]. At first, **College Point** was virtually an island separated from the **Village of Flushing** by creeks and flooded marshland and connected by a route known to this day as **College Point Causeway** (Boulevard). Landfill and recent developments have begun to change this, but the isolation of the area is still visible in the flats near Flushing Airport, a private aircraft facility.

In the Civil War era the district became a lusty industrial community, only a few vestiges of which remain. It attracted large **German** and **Swiss** populations whose beer gardens and picnic groves were the focus of Sunday outings by German-born **Manhattanites.** Following the war the **Poppenhusen** family (**Adolph** was majority stockholder in the **Long Island Rail Road**) purchased large amounts of property and established an institute still bearing its name.

[1.] 23-27 College Point Boulevard, bet. 23rd and 25th Aves. E side, ca. 1870.

A well-kept mansarded **Victorian** country house, blue-roofed and corniced, typical of late 19th-century **College Point. No. 23-41** down the block is a smaller and poorer brother.

[2.] Poppenhusen Institute, 114-04 14th Rd., SE cor. 114th St. 1868. Mundell & Teckritz. ★

A somber **Second Empire** place painted black and maroon. It was one of the earliest free kindergartens in this country, established by **Conrad Poppenhusen.**

[3.] First Reformed Church of College Point and Parish House, 14th Ave., NW cor. 119th St. 1872.

A lovely, white, eclectic wood country church with an extraordinary **Carpenter-Gothic** 3-D parish house (no flat cutting of boards here!).

[4.] Beech Court, off 14th Ave., N side opposite 121st St.

A kempt and venerable oasis: large and comfortable houses surround a common, grassy, treed park. Art Moderne, glass block, stucco and steel sash at **No. 9.**

[5.] 11-41 123rd Street at 13th Ave.

A mansarded brick **Victorian** mansion (now an apartment house) on an island; the streets came and swept around it.

[3.] The lovely, white, eclectic wood First Reformed Church of College Point

WHITESTONE

The original community saw its major growth in the streets radiating from **14th** Avenue and **150th** Street. Though it was settled in **1645,** it took the establishment of a tinware factory to convert it from a rural settlement into a thriving manufacturing center. A bit of industry survives, but the area is best known for its housing resources, such as the private community of **Malba,** west of the **Bronx-Whitestone Bridge; Beechhurst;** and the **Levitt House** development, now known as **Le Havre,** in the shadow of the **Throgs Neck Bridge:** upper-middle-income enclaves of special qualities and character.

[6.] Malba Pier, at the end of Malba Dr. next to the Whitestone Bridge.

A private fringe benefit for this upper-middle-class community. The view of the bridge is melodramatic.

 [7.] House, 143-08 Malba Dr., at the East River. ca. 1937.

Rounded, stuccoed concrete block in the **Art Moderne** style of the **Paris Exposition** of **1937.**

[8.] Dr. George W. Fish Residence and Carriage Houses, 150-10 Powell's Cove Blvd. at 150th St. S side. ca. 1860. ★

A mansarded, emporched **General Grant** house, magnificently sited to overlook this inland sea. To gain a peek it is necessary to take a circuitous route: take 149th Street north from 3rd Avenue; continue to bear right in a broad arc to the cul-de-sac at its end. Note the lovely views of the Throgs Neck Bridge from this area.

[7.] House on Malba in the Art Moderne style of the Paris Exposition, 1937

[9.] Le Havre Houses/formerly **The Levitt House Development,** 162nd St. to Utopia Pkwy., Powell's Cove Blvd. to 12th Ave. 1958. George G. Miller.

Thirty 8-story apartment buildings built by (Levittown) William Levitt's brother Alfred, an amateur architect working with professional architect Miller. Their beige and brown paint gives a fresh and sober look.

 [10.] Cryder House, 166-25 Powell's Cove Blvd., at 116th St. N side. 1963. Hausman & Rosenberg.

A *lone* slab apartment standing out dramatically from lesser construction in its vicinity. Great views of **Long Island Sound** and the **Throgs Neck Bridge.**

FLUSHING

Until the end of World War II, **Flushing** was a charming **Victorian** community laced with some six-story **Tudor** apartments constructed in the late twenties and early thirties. Many of its streets were lined with rambling white clapboard and shingle (**Classical Revival** and **shingle style**) houses dating from the last quarter of the **19th** century. On its outskirts were vast reaches of undeveloped rolling land.

The construction of the **Bronx-Whitestone Bridge** together with its connecting highways for the **1939 New York World's Fair** set the stage for a change that was nipped in the bud by the war emergency. After the end of the conflict the rush to build was on.

[11.] St. George's Episcopal Church, Main St., bet. 38th and 39th Aves. W side. 1854. Wills & Dudley. ★

Miraculously, this stately **Gothic Revival** church has withstood the commercial, cacophonous onslaught on **Main Street. Francis Lewis,** a signer of the **Declaration of Independence,** was a church warden in the original building, completed in **1761.**

Manhattan schist ashlar and brownstone; it would be more convincing without the later wood-shingled steeple: timid.

[12.] Friends' Meeting House, 137-16 Northern Blvd., bet. Main and Union Sts. S side. 1694–1717. ★

Austere and brooding, this medieval relic timidly looks out upon the never-ending stream of cars on **Northern Boulevard.** On its rear facade, facing the quiet graveyard, are two doors, originally separate entrances to the meeting house for men and women. The wood-shingled, hip-roofed structure has been used continuously since the **17th** century for religious activities by the **Society of Friends,** except for a hiatus as a **British hospital,** prison, and stable during the **Revolution.**

[13.] Flushing's Town Hall, 1862–1900, now a public restaurant and theater

[13.] Flushing Town Hall, 137-35 Northern Blvd. NE cor. Linden Pl. 1862. Cornelius Howard, builder. ★

A well-preserved **Romanesque Revival** brick pile of the **Civil War** era. It served as **Flushing's Town Hall** until **1900,** when **Flushing** became part of **New York City.** A theater and restaurant now make this splendid building part of community life once more.

[14.] Flushing Armory, 137-58 Northern Blvd., bet. Main and Union Sts. 1905.

A minifort, brick over brownstone, battered and crenellated and machicolated tower.

[15a.] The Weeping Beech Tree, 37th Ave. W of Parsons Blvd. 1847. ★

An immense canopy of weeping branches hangs about its broad trunk, almost making a natural shelter. On a cul-de-sac that makes a peaceful place for it and the adjacent **Kingsland Mansion.**

[15b.] Kingsland Mansion/once **William K. Murray House,** 143-35 37th Ave., on 37th St. W of Parsons Blvd. 1775. ★ Moved to this site 1968.

A gambrel-roofed **English** shingle (painted) house, once the home of the family for which **Manhattan's Murray Hill** was named. Open to the public. Exhibits installed by the **Queens County Historical Society,** quartered here, are of **Queens** life. Hours, information: #939-0647.

[16.] Bowne House, 37-01 Bowne St., bet. 37th and 38th Aves. E side 1661, with later additions. ★

Built by **John Bowne,** a **Quaker,** this house was the first indoor meeting place of the forbidden **Society of Friends;** earlier they had met clandestinely in the nearby woods. **Bowne** was a central figure in the dispute with **Gov. Peter Stuyvesant** over religious freedom. The interiors are carefully maintained and contain a wide variety of colonial furnishings. Hours and information: FL9-0528.

[17.] Bowne Street Community Church/formerly the **Reformed Church of Flushing,** Roosevelt Ave. NE cor. Bowne St. 1891.

Northern **European** brick **Romanesque** with a tower from **Prague.**

[15b.] Orig. William K. Murray House   **[17.]** Old Reformed Church, Flushing

[18.] The East Flushing Residential Blocks, bounded by Franklin Ave., Parsons Blvd., a line between Cherry and 45th Aves., and Bowne St. 1875–1900.

Porches, chimneys, mansards, and gambrels; shingle-style, **Queen Anne,** and eclectic miscellany: a wonderful small district that our apocrypha says was preserved by the first "preservation" bill in the late twenties after an apartment house was built on **Phlox** Place: an anticipation of the **Landmarks Preservation Commission** forty years later.

Wander off **Bowne** down **Ash.** No. **143-10 Ash Ave.,** in "Moorish" stucco; No. **143-13 Ash Ave.,** shingle-style, well-hedged; No. **143-32 Ash Ave.,** a bungalow with bumpety stone and a **Palladian** window; No. **143-40 Ash Ave.,** (1908.) early concrete block; No. **143-50 Ash Ave.,** shingles and more bumpety stone; No. **143-63 Ash Ave.,** awkward **Classic Revival;** No. **143-74 Ash Ave.,** SW cor. Parsons Blvd: there were 10 gutsy **Ionic composite** columns supporting this shingled gambrel; now there are nine: a **junior Newport House.**

[19.] 143-43 and 143-46 Sanford Avenue, bet. Bowne St. and Parsons Blvd. S side. ca. 1860.

Two lovely veterans of the mid-19th century lurking behind wisteria, blue spruce, and hydrangea. Mansarded **General Grant** with details intact.

[20.] Korvette's, Kissena Blvd., bet. Sanford and Barclay Aves. 1974.

Smooth, light brown monolith. Its very understatement stands out as a classy commercial operation in the midst of commercial anarchy.

[21.] The Windsor School, 136-23 Sanford Ave. bet. Main St. and Kissena Blvd. N side. ca. 1845.

Greek Revival mansion (the capitals have gone back to **Corinth**) with a mansarded, balustraded roof.

[22.] United States Post Office, Flushing, NE cor. Main St. and Sanford Ave. 1932. Dwight James Baum and William W. Knowles, architects. James A. Wetmore, supervising architect.

A tasteful **Georgian** building from an era when taste was all one had to hold onto: a *safe and comforting* neighborhood monument.

Shushikaza Japanese Restaurant, 41-32 Main St., bet. 41st Rd. and Sanford Ave. W. side.

Pleasant, low-key, modern light-wood interior with place for three styles of dining: tatami-matted niches, western tables, and a counter. Moderate prices.

[22.] United States Post Office, Flushing (a safe and comforting monument)

Prince's Nursery: North of **Northern Boulevard,** from the site of today's **RKO Keith** theater, was a tree nursery, the first in the country, established by **William Prince** in **1737.** The eight acres had, by **1750,** become the **Linnaean Botanic Garden.** All traces of the site are erased, but not its produce. To this day **Flushing** displays **140** genera, consisting of **2000** species of trees that are, in large part, the progeny of **Mr. Prince.**

[23.] St. John Vianney Church, Union St. SE cor. 34th Ave. 1974. Bentel & Bentel.

A simple, powerful, dark brick box form modified by a curved garden wall.

More Mansions: Along the north side of **Bayside Avenue** between **Parsons Boulevard** and **146th Street,** and along **146th Street** between **Bayside Avenue** and **29th Road.** Modest but affluent mansions, luxurious, manicured; those along 146th Street are a piece of twenties Tudor.

[24.] North Shore Oldsmobile, 149-04 Northern Blvd. SE cor. 149th St. 1963. Rigoni & Reich.

An elegant modern pavilion for the sale of cars: four cruciform piers bear a hovering, bulky roof.

[25.] Kissena II Apartments, 137-47 45th Ave. off Kissena Blvd., bet. 45th Ave. and Geranium Ave. 1970. Gruzen & Partners.

Articulated, well-proportioned, and, *happily,* not an architectural statement in excess of its duties. The exposed brick, glass, and sash are beautifully detailed.

[26.] St. Nicholas Greek Orthodox Church, 196-10 Northern Blvd. SE cor. 196th St. 1974. Raymond and Rado.

A spartan octagonal auditorium is crowned with a spherical dome: bold concrete and brick. The chapel is a lilliputian version of the main church. A sort of romantic *"brutalism."*

[27.] Public School 219 Queens, 144-39 Gravett Rd. E of Main St. 1966. Caudill, Rowlett & Scott.

A domed set of open classrooms.

[28.] Fresh Meadows Housing Development, 186th to 197th Sts., Long Island Expwy. to 73rd Ave. (irregularly). 1949. Voorhees, Walker, Foley & Smith; 20-story addition, 1962. Voorhees, Walker, Smith, Smith & Haines.

This **166-acre** development on the site of the old **Fresh Meadows Country Club** was a post–World War II project of the **New York Life Insurance Co.** Its (then) avant-garde site plan, including a mix of row housing, low- and high-rise apartments, regional shopping center, theater, schools, and other amenities, scores as excellent planning but *dull* architecture.

BAYSIDE, DOUGLASTON, AND LITTLE NECK

Bayside is an outlying portion of **Flushing** with an attractive suburban character maintained by an abundance of detached houses and low-rise apartments. It was originally settled by **William Lawrence** in **1664,** and remained largely rural until linked to **Manhattan** by the **LIRR's East River Tunnels** in **1910.**

Both **Douglaston** and **Little Neck** lie east of the **Cross Island** (Belt) **Parkway,** New York's circumferential highway, and, as a result, many assume they are part of adjacent **Nassau County.** The part above **Northern Boulevard** certainly lends credence to this assumption, since the area physically resembles the prosperous commuter towns on the adjacent **North Shore.** Originally the peninsula was **all Little Neck,** but in **1876** the western part was renamed **Douglaston** after **William B. Douglas,** who had donated the LIRR station there. It is a rocky, treed knoll with sometimes narrow, winding streets chockablock with Victorian, stucco, shingled, myriad individual houses of romance, many with splendid views of water, sunsets, and sailboats.

[29.] Queensboro Community College/formerly the **Oakland Golf Course and Club,** 56th Ave., Kenilworth Rd. to Cloverdale Blvd. 1967 Master Plan, Frederick Wiedersum & Assocs. and Holden, Egan, Wilson & Corser. 1970–1975 Master Plan, Percival Goodman.

Built from scratch in **10** years on a large portion of the grand old **Oakland Golf Course.** The first round of buildings by the **Wiedersum/ Holden** group is precast concrete and brick, straightforward and simple (Library, Science, Humanities, Gymnasium, Campus Center, **1967–1970**). New buildings under the new master plan include the **Administration Building** (*1977. Percival Goodman.*) and the **Medical Arts Building** (*1977. Armand Bartos and Assocs.*). The former bears slit windows in a broken form of tan/salmon brick: stylish artifice. The grand outdoor stair leads to the old **Oakland Golf Club** at the crest. The latter is a chunky form in the same brick, but involved in stylish form-making.

[29a.] Creedmoor Farmhouse/originally **Cornell Farmhouse,** 73-50 Little Neck Pkwy. W side (on property of Creedmoor State Hospital). ca. 1750. Additions, ca. 1840, 1875, 1885, 1900. ★

A colonial farmhouse preferred by the happy accident of its location: protected by the enveloping state institution.

[30.] Lawrence Family Graveyard, 216th St., bet. 43rd and 42nd Aves. W side. 1830. ★

A tiny private cemetery of this ubiquitous Queens family [see NW Queens 39.]. Not open to the public.

[31.] 215-37 43rd Avenue, NW cor. 216th St. 1931. Benjamin Braunstein.

Half half-timbered, stucco and brick: a charming meandering medieval close gives access, light, and great charm to this group. Go in.

[32a.] Fort Totten Battery, U.S. Government Reservation, Willets Point. Accessible via Bell Blvd. 1864. William Petit Trowbridge, engineer. ★

A monumental tooled-granite-block fortification: arched ways along its embrasured walls and a bastion at its prow worthy of **ancient Rome.** Magnificent site and view. Ask permission to view it at the entry gate.

[32b.] New York City Job Corps Center/formerly **Fort Totten Officers' Club, U.S. Government Reservation,** Fort Totten Rd. Accessible via Bell Blvd. 1870. Enlarged 1887. ★

Castellated Gothic Revival in the spirit of **Alexander Jackson Davis** and **Andrew Jackson Downing.** Wood here *simulating* masonry grandeur.

[33.] Cornelius Van Wyck House, 37-04 Douglaston Pkwy. (126 West Drive) SW cor. Alston Pl. 1735. ★

The roof is a magnificent plastic shingled exercise: Hansel and Gretel style.

[34.] 29 Center Drive, SW cor. Forest Rd. ca. 1845.

Greek Revival house in bed with the new Italianate of the time. White shingles, Tuscan porch, octagonal widow's walk overseeing Little Neck Bay.

[25.] Kissena II (apts. for elderly)   **[29.]** Queensboro Community College

[35.] Three Houses, S side Bay St., bet. 234th St. and Douglaston Pkwy.

Find the three shingle-style Victorian gems tucked away along this bosky lane.

[36.] Douglaston Club/formerly **George Douglas Residence**/originally **Wynant Van Zandt Residence,** West Drive SE cor. Beverly Rd. Before 1835, with numerous additions.

A large, homely country house with a Tuscan-columned porch: now a tennis club.

C

CENTRAL QUEENS

Town of Newtown/Middleburg

Settled in 1642; chartered by the Doughty Patent of 1640.

The old **Town of Newtown** encompasses the present-day communities of **Jackson Heights, Corona, Elmhurst, Rego Park, Forest Hills, Maspeth, Middle Village, Ridgewood,** and **Glendale.** Its western reaches comprise endless blocks of old frame buildings, whereas the eastern and northern parts have become dense apartment districts. **Jackson Heights** developed between the two world wars, and the spine along **Queens Boulevard** in both **Rego Park** and **Forest Hills** after World War II. **Forest Hills** was named (1901) by developer **Cord Meyer,** and immortalized by **Forest Hills** *Gardens,* the magnificent town-planning/real estate scheme of the Russell Sage Foundation to whom Meyer had sold vast land. **Rego Park** is named for the developing/building **Rego** (*Real Good*) **Construction Company** that pioneered building in that area.

The center of **"New Towne,"** the outgrowth of **Middleburg** by **1665** and an **English Puritan** settlement under **Dutch** auspices, occupied the winding stretch of **Broadway** north of **Queens Boulevard.** Vestiges of the community remained well into the **20th** century, but only a single church building remains today.

After consolidation with **New York** in **1898** the name, **Newtown,** quickly fell into disuse, the immediate community becoming known as **Elmhurst.** "Newtown Pippins," grown in the apple orchards of this area, were prized by the English, to whom they were exported for the manufacture of cider!

[1c.] The new Central Garage, LaGuardia Airport, with helical access ramps

[1.] LaGuardia Airport, Grand Central Pkwy. at 94th St., Jackson Hts. **[1a.] Original Buildings and Marine Terminal,** 1939. Delano and Aldrich. **[1b.] New Central Terminal and Control Tower,** 1965. Harrison & Abramovitz. **[1c.] Central Garage,** 1976. Staff of the Port of New York Authority.

Built for the **New York World's Fair** of **1939–1940** as New York's second (chronologically) municipal airport (after **Floyd Bennett Field** in **Brooklyn**). The **1965** main terminal, in a great glass arc, bears a parasol roof as a symbol of flight—no function intended for it—while the control towers wears a stylish hyperbolic shape. Within the terminal's curved embrace now rests the new garage, a weathered steel grillage accessible by helical concrete ramps (the steel weathers by rusting to a final hard purple-brown patina).

Flanking the main terminal are the old hangars of **1939** vintage (the original main building, too small for post–**World War II** traffic, was demolished) and the **Marine Terminal,** lurking on the northwestern edge of the field. Originally built to serve flying boats of the thirties (remember the **China Clipper?**), today the **Marine Terminal,** a *fantastic* **Art Deco** extravaganza, is a facility for private aircraft (without benefit of water).

[2.] Lexington School for the Deaf, 30th Ave., bet. 73rd and 75th Sts. N side. Jackson Heights. 1967. Pomerance & Breines.

A modern campus for the schooling of deaf children.

Flushing Meadows Park, Park from a Dump: Straddling the Flushing River, one-time navigational facility into the village of **Flushing** and boundary between the towns of **Flushing** and **Newtown,** is present-day **Flushing Meadows Park.** Originally a swamp, it became known as the "Corona Dump" after "sanitary landfill" operations were started. It gained park status by means of its selection as site for the **1939–1940 New York World's Fair,** with a repeat performance at the same location in **1964–1965.** Some remnants remain of both fairs.

[3.] Shea Stadium, Grand Central Pkwy. to 126th St., Northern Blvd. to Roosevelt Ave. 1964. Praeger-Kavanagh-Waterbury.

The simple form and sheer bulk of this home for the **N.Y. Mets** dominate the flat landscape for miles. The exterior gives the impression of scraps of colored paper caught on a giant wire basket after a windstorm—the product of an arbitrary appliqué of pastel panels. A unique functional feature is the rotating infield seating that permits conversion to a football stadium.

[4.] Hall of Science, City of New York, Flushing Meadows Park at 111th St. and 48th Ave. 1964. Harrison & Abramovitz.

An **undulating tapestry** of stained glass set in precast panels exhibiting within a variety of *funky* crowded displays on space travel and atomic energy. Now ill-maintained and seedy, it was to have enjoyed a substantial addition to the west, the foundations of which remain like an archeologists excavation, the city having lost interest. **Telephone: 699-9400.**

[5.] United States Pavilion, 1964–1965 World's Fair, Flushing Meadows Park, 1964. Charles Luckman Assocs.

An **immense square doughnut** with colored plastic walls built on four great piers surrounding a pyramidal entrance form: a sorry symbol for **America.** Various groups yearn to use its space for good works, but it would be *happier* for the park and the city to quietly take it down.

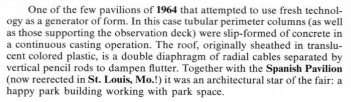

A panorama of New York City: An impressive model of the whole of the city—835,000 buildings—plus streets, rivers, bridges, piers, and airports—is on view at the **Queens Museum** in the old New York City Building in Flushing Meadows Park. Well worth a special visit. An elevated platform offers an airliner's view of the enormous diorama, updated regularly since built for the 1964–1965 World's Fair. The rest of the museum is also a treat. Telephone: 592-2405.

[6.] New York State Pavilion, 1964–1965 World's Fair, Flushing Meadows Park. 1964. Philip Johnson and Richard Foster, architects. Lev Zetlin, structural engineer.

One of the few pavilions of **1964** that attempted to use fresh technology as a generator of form. In this case tubular perimeter columns (as well as those supporting the observation deck) were slip-formed of concrete in a continuous casting operation. The roof, originally sheathed in translucent colored plastic, is a double diaphragm of radial cables separated by vertical pencil rods to dampen flutter. Together with the **Spanish Pavilion** (now reerected in **St. Louis, Mo.!**) it was an architectural star of the fair: a happy park building working with park space.

Dough sculpture: The fine Italian art of bread sculpture is practiced at **S. Purpura's Bakery, 40-09 111th St.** (just south of **Roosevelt Avenue**) in **Corona. Bosomy** maidens and other ebullient works are usually on display in the window. It isn't a museum, but it might as well be. Bread baked to order. **Telephone: 672-6800.**

[7.] Reformed Dutch Church of Newtown, and Fellowship Hall, 85-15 Broadway, SE cor. Corona Ave., Elmhurst. **Church,** 1831. **Hall,** 1858. ★

Georgian-Greek Revival in white clapboard, wearing **Tuscan** columns. The stained glass is **Victorian.**

[8.] St. James Fellowship Hall/formerly **St. James Episcopal Church,** Broadway, SW cor. 51st Ave., Elmhurst. 1734.

Carpenter Gothic additions updated this, the original **St. James,** built on land granted by the town. The steeple on the west end of this somber gray-painted Colonial relic was removed at the turn of the century. A new **St. James** at the northeast corner of **Broadway** and **Corona Avenue** was built in **1849:** now burned.

[9.] Queens Boulevard Medical Building, 86-15 Queens Blvd., bet. Broadway and 55th Ave. N side. Elmhurst. 1957. Abraham Geller & Assocs.

This medical building sits atop the **IND** subway tunnel, thus requiring heating and air-conditioning equipment normally placed in a basement to be on the roof. The splendid resulting form, a sophisticated cubist construction, bears good materials and detailing. It *suffers* from poor maintenance and ugly signs. A cemetery, to its east, was a welcome forelawn until some enterprising exploiter bought the space, moved the bodies, and built a **gross** 6-story apartment house.

[10.] Macy's Queens, 87-11 Queens Blvd. bet. 55th and 56th Aves. N side. Rego Park. 1965. Skidmore, Owings & Merrill.

Take a difficult site, consider that a department store requires exterior walls only as enclosure, calculate the parking problem, add the **SOM** touch, and you get **Macy's Queens,** a circular department store girded by a concentric parking garage. What could be more logical? Luckily, a recalcitrant property owner refused to part with the southwest parcel, forcing a notch to be cut into the squat cylinder of precast concrete panels; a welcome punctuation.

[11.] First National City Bank, 87-11 Queens Blvd. (next to Macy's Queens). 1966. Skidmore, Owings & Merrill.

A small, bronze-colored aluminum and glass cylinder **aping** the larger concrete cylinder of Macy's.

[12.] Jamaica Savings Bank, 89-01 Queens Blvd. NE cor. 56th Ave., Rego Park. 1968. William Cann.

A **showy form** (hyperbolic paraboloid) more concerned with advertising than useful space.

[13.] Lefrak City, Junction Blvd. to 99th St., 57th Ave. to Long Island Expwy. Elmhurst. 1962–1967. Jack Brown.

Hardly a city, it is *redbrick forever.* Entrepreneur **Sam Lefrak** is New York's largest private taxpayer.

[14.] Queens Center, Queens Blvd. NE cor. 59th Ave. 1973. Gruen Assocs.

A sparkling three-story space within is clad in glazed brick and metal panels without: a *modernistic* reprise to the thirties. The concrete garage behind is no-nonsense. Branches of **Ohrbach's** (ladies' inexpensive fashions), **A & S** (Brooklyn's Bloomingdale's), and **Herman's** ("discount" sporting goods) dominate.

[15.] New York Telephone Company, Rego Park Communications Center, Queens Blvd., bet. 62nd Ave. and 62nd Dr. N side. 1976. Kahn & Jacobs.

A bold, monumental brick mass set on a battered granite base. Telephone equipment in fancy dress.

[16.] Alexander's Rego Park, Queens Blvd. NW cor. 63rd Rd., Rego Park. 1960.

The first of the branch department stores to invade this part of **Queens.** Vermilion glazed brick.

[7.] Ref. Dutch Church of Newtown   **[15.]** N.Y. Telephone Co., Rego Park

[9.] Queens Boulevard Medical Building (a sophisticated exercise in cubism)

[17a.] Walden Terrace, 98th to 99th Sts., 63rd Dr. to 64th Rd. Rego Park. 1948. Leo Stillman.

Exposed concrete structure gave these precocious modern apartments a *continental* look when erected in **1948.**

[17b.] Max and Dorothy Cohn High School, 66-35 108th St. E side. bet. 66th Rd. and 67th Ave. 1971. William N. Breger Assocs.

Stylish brown brick forms with artfully composed openings. A private religious school.

[18.] Arbor Close and Forest Close, from the back of Queens Blvd. storefronts to Austin St., 75th Ave. to 76th Ave. 1925–26. Robert Tappan.

Brick, slate, and half-timbering clad picturesquely profiled row houses surrounding a garden. Privacy hedged at its edges; a charming, urbane place.

[19.] Forest Hills Gardens, 71st (Continental) Ave. to Union Tpke., Long Island Railroad right-of-way to an uneven line south of Greenway South. 1913–present. Grosvenor Atterbury, architect. Frederick Law Olmsted, Jr., landscape architect.

"Apart from its convenient location, within a quarter of an hour of the center of Manhattan Island, the Forest Hills Gardens enterprise differentiates itself . . . from other suburban development schemes most notably in that its size permits a *unique layout* of winding streets, open spaces and building lots and thus permits the development of an ideally attractive neighborhood, while its financial backing is such that the realization of the well studied plans is assured in advance beyond peradventure." **Alfred Tredway White** in a promotional booklet of 1911.

White, who had pioneered in housing for the working class [see WC Brooklyn/Cobble Hill 4.] would not have been disappointed. This project, sponsored by the Russell Sage Foundation, has become one of Queens's most exclusive residential enclaves. It is also a splendid combination of good planning and of romantic, picturesque architecture.

[20.] The "Pretzel" Highway Intersection, Grand Central Pkwy., Union Tpke., Van Wyck Expwy., Interboro Pkwy. 1939–1964.

A highway engineer's fantasy come true. The best view is from the upper-floor windows of the Queens Borough Hall, or from a helicopter passing from Manhattan to Kennedy Airport.

[21.] Forest Hills South, bet. Queens Blvd. and Grand Central Pkwy. Service Rd., 76th Dr. and 78th Ave. 1941. Philip Birnbaum.

Neo-Georgian architecture surrounding and serving the real purpose and joy of this complex: a grand mall that presents a lush park to the pedestrian in the spring, in the space **113th Street** would have passed, here claimed for people.

[18.] Arbor Close and Forest Close   **[23.]** MacMonnies' exiled *Civic Virtue*

[22.] Queens Borough Hall, Queens Blvd. bet. Union Tpke. and 82nd Ave. N side. 1941. William Gehron & Andrew Thomas.

A pompous neo-**Classical** building in red brick and limestone.

[23.] Civic Virtue (statue), NE cor. Queens Blvd. and Union Tpke. 1922. Frederick MacMonnies, sculptor.

Once directly in front of **City Hall** in **Manhattan,** this **Nordic** male chauvinist was banished to these boondocks by popular pressure (note that the writhing women are not being stepped upon, however). **MacMonnies,** Brooklyn's great sculptor (see *The Horse Tamers* at **Prospect Park**), was in his dotage when this was carved: a sorry reprise to a brilliant career.

[24.] Fresh Pond Crematory/formerly **United States Columbaria Co.,**
61-40 Mt. Olivet Crescent, NW cor. 62nd Ave. Middle Village. ca. 1905.

A pompous tan brick and limestone crematory in an undistinguished area of Queens. Note the adjacent (abandoned) church whose cornerstone reads 1837.

[19.] Forest Hills Gardens, New York's superb planned in-town garden suburb

[25.] Rentar Plaza, Metropolitan Ave. at 65th Lane, Middle Village. 1974. Robert E. Levien Partners.

An aircraft carrier astray that parks 1200 cars on its flight deck. Glazed brown brick, rounded stair forms. One floor of this is equal in area to half the Empire State Building; three floors—one tower of the World Trade Center.

[26.] United Parcel Service Distribution Center, 56th Rd., bet. 44th and 48th Sts. N side. Maspeth. 1967. Francisco & Jacobus.

Super-scaled distribution by conveyor belts dictated the fingered form of this pink-mansarded complex.

[27.] Old Calvary Cemetery Chapel, entered off Laurel Hill Blvd. in an area generally between the Brooklyn Queens Expwy., Long Island Expwy., Newtown Creek, and Greenpoint Ave. ca. 1875.

A squat set of limestone beehives with Spanish tile roofs, surrounded by huddled small Roman temple-mausoleums.

On axis (cemetery section 3b) the **Halloran Mausoleum** is **Victorian neo-Grecian:** Philadelphia's **Frank Furness** and Berlin's Karl Schinkel could have been in partnership for this.

The **Johnston Mausoleum,** a small domed neo-Baroque "chapel," crowns a hill a thousand feet away.

Niederstein's Restaurant, 69-16 Metropolitan Ave., at 69th St. 1854. Badly remodeled, 1974. Telephone: 326-0717.

A roadside tavern on the road from **Greenpoint** to **Jamaica,** now architecturally destroyed by a plastic mansard roof, fake leaded windows: the *philistines* were here without knowing they were philistines. We mention it only because it had a generous history and is the only place in these parts with pretentions to the service of food.

The **Niederstein family** took over in **1888** to serve the **German** population making pilgrimages to the **Lutheran Cemetery** nearby.

[28.] Adrian Onderdonck House, 1820 Flushing Ave., bet. Cypress and Onderdonck Aves. S side. 1731.

A burnt and mutilated hulk that is the only remaining example of the group of **"Dutch" Colonial** farmhouses in this area that had withstood the onslaught of heavy industry onto their farmlands in the early part of this century. Restoration is hoped for by the **Greater Ridgewood Historical Society.**

SOUTH CENTRAL QUEENS

Town of Jamaica/Rustdorp

Settled in 1656; chartered in 1660.

The communities lying within the boundaries of the old **Town of Jamaica** contain as a group the widest contrasts of any in **Queens.** Some, like **Ozone Park, Richmond Hill,** and **Woodhaven,** are quiet residential communities; **Jamaica** itself, on the other hand, is a bustling marketplace with department stores, specialty shops, and theaters. Affluence is markedly visible in **Jamaica Estates** along **Grand Central Parkway;** poverty and squalor mark the black slums of **South Jamaica;** in the **St. Albans** area, though, is a lovely, tree-lined, middle-income black community. Parts of **Jamaica** date from the **17th** and **18th** centuries; **Richmond Hill, Queens Village,** from the **19th;** the eastern and southern areas like **Howard Beach** and **Cambria Heights** saw their most intensive growth in the last two decades.

RICHMOND HILL

[1.] Houses along 85th Avenue, bet. 112th St. and Myrtle Ave. ca. 1890.

Great nest of shingle-style houses; ballooning, sweeping porches; bold form.

Frappes and sundaes: Frank Jahn's is a neo-real **1890s** ice cream parlor at 117-03 Hillside Avenue (near 117th Street and Jamaica Avenue). Complete with marble countertops, leaded-glass **Coca Cola** chandeliers, and wild, just wild, ice cream concoctions.

JAMAICA

[2a.] King Mansion, King Park, Jamaica Ave. bet. 150th and 153rd Sts. N side. North section, 1730; west section, 1755; east section, 1806. ★

A large bland white house, more interesting for its *social* history than its architecture, set on a greensward next to the "el." Peaceful eyes, noisy ears.

[2b.] First Reformed Church of Jamaica, 153-10 Jamaica Ave., bet. 153rd and Standard Place. S side. 1859.

Almost entirely of red brick used in a variety of Romanesque Revival arched forms as doorways, windows, corbel tables, relieving arches, all three-dimensional. Unfortunately it sits on a bleak site, the LIRR embankment its neighbor to the rear.

[3.] Grace Episcopal Church and Graveyard, 155-03 Jamaica Ave., bet. 153rd St. and Parsons Blvd. 1862. Dudley Field. Additions, 1901–1902. Cady, Berg & See. **Graveyard,** ca. 1734. ★

A brownstone monolith from grass to finial. English country **Gothic.**

[4a.] Jamaica Arts Center/formerly **Jamaica Register Building,** 161-06 Jamaica Ave., bet. 161st and 162nd Sts. S side. ca. 1890. ★

A Renaissance Revival **English** club, now happily preserved as an arts center.

[4b.] N.Y.C. Department of Social Services Center/formerly **Jamaica Savings Bank,** 161-02 Jamaica Ave., bet. 161st and 162nd St. S side. ca. 1890.

Second Empire **Beaux Arts** cheek by jowl with the Renaissance Revival club above.

[4c.] Title Guarantee Company/formerly **Suffolk Title & Guarantee Building,** 90-04 161st Street. 1929. Dennison & Hirons.

The decoration here is more important than the building: Art Moderne at the third-floor spandrels and the sky: blue, beige, orange and black.

[5a.] Roxanne Swimsuits, 90-33 160th St., bet. Jamaica and 90th Aves. E side. ca. 1936.

A sophisticated mastaba of Art Deco origins which has seen better days.

[5b.] First Independent Hebrew Congregation, 90-21 160th St., bet. Jamaica and 90th Aves. E side. ca. 1910.

A twin, ogee-domed frame synagogue, like the many so styled in masonry in **Manhattan** after the turn of the century. Reshingled in drab green.

Annam Brahma Restaurant (Vegetarian Indian), 83-43 164th St., S of Grand Central Parkway. Telephone: 523-2600.

A clear bright springlike interior announces a restaurant operated by the American adherents of guru **Sri Chimnoy's** Indian teachings. Very *flavorful* and very reasonably priced. A must if exploring Jamaica.

[2a.] King Mansion, more interesting for social history than architecture

[6.] Prospect Cemetery, 159th St. SW cor. Beaver Rd. 1662.

The first public burial ground of **Jamaica.** In the early years of this community the wealthy were mostly buried in church—laymen under their pews, clergymen in the chapel or beneath the pulpit. Less affluent parishioners were interred in the churchyard. The rest were buried in **Prospect Cemetery.**

HOLLIS

[7.] Hollis Unitarian Church, 195-39 Hillside Ave., Hollis. 1961. Blake & Neski.

A *spartan* white brick box.

OZONE PARK/SOUTH OZONE PARK

[8.] Aqueduct Race Track, Rockaway Blvd. to Southern Pkwy., IND Rockaway Line right-of-way to 114th. 1894. Reconstruction, 1959. Arthur Froehlich & Assocs.

The **Big A,** as it is currently known, is the last race track entirely within the city limits. As land values increase, these enormous operations sell to developers (cf. **Jamaica Race Track,** now **Rochdale Village**). The name relates to the **Ridgewood Aqueduct, Brooklyn** and **Queens's** first large-scale water system, which still follows **Conduit Avenue,** the service road of Southern Parkway, in from its reservoirs on **Long Island.**

[9.] John F. Kennedy International Airport/formerly **Idlewild Airport,** Van Wyck Expwy., Southern Pkwy., Rockaway Blvd., and Jamaica Bay. 1942 to present.

With land claimed by fill in the swampy waters of **Jamaica Bay,** Kennedy's **4900** acres are roughly equivalent in area to Manhattan Island south of **34th Street.** It is so large that it's possible to run up several dollars' tariff on your taxi meter between the terminal and the airport's edge: **Manhattan** lies **15** miles further west. The fare will be well spent, however, for the trip will take you past every architectural cliché of the past two decades, some very handsome works, and some less-distinguished hangovers from earlier periods as well.

Kennedy is best known for its **Terminal City,** housing the various passenger terminals, a control center, a central heating and cooling plant, three chapels, a multitude of parking places. In addition the airport has many cargo complexes and service and storage facilities for the airline companies, as well as a hotel, a federal office building, and other service structures.

[9a.] International Hotel, Van Wyck Expwy. at Southern Pkwy. 1958. Additions, 1961. William B. Tabler.

The *gateway* building, by default, to this aircraft empire.

[9f.] Pan American World Airways' original building (great concrete parasol)

[9b.] Federal Office Building. 1949. Reinhard, Hofmeister & Walquist.

Neo-frumpy, by some of the guys who helped build New York's greatest commercial wonder: **Rockefeller Center.**

[9c.] First National City Bank, along main access road. 1959. Skidmore, Owings & Merrill.

The stilts holding this exquisite glass box above its roadside site express just the right amount of diffidence about becoming associated with the rest of **Terminal City.**

[9d.] Eastern Airlines/Mohawk Airlines. 1959. Chester L. Churchill.

Skip it.

[9e.] Northwest Airlines et al. 1962. White & Mariani.

A forest of mushroom columns at its portals masks this simple box behind.

[9f.] Pan American Airways et al. 1961. Tippetts-Abbett-McCarthy-Stratton; and Ives, Turano & Gardner, assoc. architects. Zodiac Figures: Milton Hebald, sculptor.

A **tour-de-force** produced a parasoled pavilion unfortunately marred from the beginning by gross details (i.e., the meandering drainpipes around the great piers). Now, expanded manyfold into a complex as large and confusing as the **Palace of Knossos** (the Minotaur's labyrinth), the parasol is but an entrance canopy to this depressing maze.

[9g.] International Arrivals Building, 1957. Skidmore, Owings & Merrill.

The principal place of **Customs,** and hence a string of international airlines flank a grand, vaulted central pavilion. Once a place of sumptuous lounges and bars where one could stroll past the glass arrivals hall to see and greet incoming passengers passing through Customs, it is now *drab and dull*. A screen bars the arrivees' view, and the international airline bars are degraded or gone. The affluent travelers of the fifties have been overwhelmed by the populist travelers of the seventies, who seek a **MacDonald's** world: noisy, dirty, inelegant, crowded—fast food amidst cacophony.

[9g.] Internat'l. Arrivals Building

[9i.] The National Airlines Sundrome

[9h.] Trans World Airlines Building: romantic voluptuary, soaring & sinuous

[9h.] Trans World Airlines. 1962. Eero Saarinen & Assocs.

Romantic voluptuary: soaring, sinuous, sensual, surreal, and always controversial. Well worth a visit to judge for yourself. Unfortunately, trips through the "umbilical cord" to the plane-loading lounge are forbidden to all but ticketed passengers, because of security against hijackings in the seventies.

[9i.] National Airlines Sundrome. 1972. I. M. Pei & Partners.

A classy, classic building, the best architecture at Kennedy. This serene temple to transport is the *portal to Florida* for many: rich travertine floors and walls under a great columned and corniced roof.

[9j.] British Airways Terminal. 1970. Gollins Melvin Ward & Partners.

Heavy-handed battered concrete over heavy-handed battered glass. An awkward tour-de-force.

[9k.] Chapels. 1966. **Our Lady of the Skies (Roman Catholic),** George J. Sole. **Protestant,** Edgar Tafel & Assocs. **Jewish,** Bloch & Hesse.

All three are labored and self-conscious "modern": the **Protestant** is the best of the three.

 [9l.] Central Heating and Refrigeration Plant. 1957. Skidmore, Owings & Merrill.

On axis with the **International Arrivals Building,** across the fountain-studded megamall, this glass display case for condensers, compressors, pumps, and pipes is a multicolored fantasy: splendid and wonderful.

[9l.] The Kennedy Airport Central Heating & Refrigeration Plant (1966 Photo)

[9m.] The American Airlines Building   **[9n.]** United/Delta Airlines Building

[9m.] American Airlines. 1960. Kahn & Jacobs. Stained glass, Robert Sowers.

The world's largest stained-glass wall is screened from the public passenger by private offices, small rooms that enjoy its colored light privately: a strange and frustrating experience for the uninitiated observer.

 [9n.] United/Delta Airlines Building. 1961. Skidmore, Owings & Merrill.

A fastidiously detailed, subtly curving building that is, at Kennedy, second only to the **National Airlines "Sundrome"** for classic serenity.

[9o.] Gulf Station. 1959. Edward D. Stone & Assocs.

A pretentious and unintended joke in the form of a miniature of Stone's **American Embassy, New Delhi.**

SOUTHERN QUEENS

Portion of Town of Hempstead/Hemstede

Settled and chartered in 1664.

This narrow spit of land, a breakwater for **Jamaica Bay** (Floridians would term it a *key*), was so inaccessible prior to the coming of the railroads in **1868–1878** that it was an exclusive resort second only to **Saratoga Springs.** The accessibility afforded by rail connections by **1900** drove society leaders to more remote parts of Long Island's south shore in and around the **Hamptons.** Neponsit and **Belle Harbor** retain traces of this former splendor. (The IND subway, here not sub-, but on grade or in the air, replaced the LIRR as the operator of the trestled connection to Long Island and the continent!)

After the departure of high society the area became a resort for the middle class. But in much of the peninsula, this too has changed: the **Hammels** and **Arverne,** both east of the terminus of the **Cross Bay Bridge,** became squalid slums. **Arverne** never achieved the aims intended by urban renewal, its renewing momentum crushed by the cost spiral and the disinterest of **Presidents Nixon** and **Ford** in public and publicly assisted housing. Some public and publicly assisted housing for low- and middle-income families dot the area. Unfortunately all but **Roy Reuther Houses** are grim in appearance and amazingly unresponsive to the beachfront sites they occupy. The potential development of a great recreational area at **Breezy Point,** thanks to the successful fight waged by a number of civic-minded citizens, holds out the greatest promise for the area. **Breezy Point** is a unit of the **Gateway National Recreation Area.**

[1.] Breezy Point, Tip of Rockaway Peninsula W of Beach 193rd St.

Appropriately named, these windswept dunes are the site of a private shorefront community with ferry access to **Sheepshead Bay, Brooklyn.** Its most conspicuous landmarks are the abandoned steel and concrete frames for a high-rise apartment development. In **1963,** owing to pressure from a group of public-spirited citizens, municipal authorities courageously acquired title to the site for future beachfront development and saved **Breezy Point** from becoming another high-rise jungle. With **Fort Tilden** to the east, it creates an uninterrupted public beach and park stretching $3\frac{1}{2}$ miles from **Riis Park** to the western tip of the peninsula. With legislation forming the **Gateway National Recreation Area, Breezy Point** became a unit in that complex. *Smokey the Bear* is now the manager in residence.

[2.] Jacob Riis Park, Beach 149th to Beach 169th Sts. 1937. N.Y.C. Department of Parks, Aymar Embury II, consultant.

A *mile* of sandy beach graced by simple, handsome, WPA-era buildings. In addition to swimming, there are other recreational possibilities, such as handball, paddle tennis, and shuffleboard, as well as a boardwalk for strolling. In the winter this is haven for **Polar Bear Club** enthusiasts, and the **13,000**-car parking lot an aerodrome for radio-controlled model aircraft flights. Now a gateway unit, refreshments are available year round, as are lockers during the swimming season (nominal charge).

[3.] Ocean Village, Rockaway Beach Blvd. to the Boardwalk, bet. Beach 59th St. and Beach 56th Pl. 1976. Carl Koch & Assocs.

Prefabricated, precast concrete and brick slabs and towers surrounding a central courtyard at the edge of the sea: a multifamily island in a sea of unrenewed weeds.

[4.] Hebrew Institute of Long Island, N side Seagirt Blvd. bet. Beach 17th and Beach 19th Sts. ca. 1900.

Four Classical Revival white stucco and Spanish tile mansions from the era when the **Rockaways** had real class. A *banal,* institutional, modern replacement is ominously heralded by the Institute's fund-raising sign.

 [5.] Roy Reuther Houses, 711 Seagirt Ave., bet. Beach 8th and Beach 6th Sts. 1971. Gruzen & Partners.

Middle-income housing sponsored by the **United Auto Workers:** a great, stepped series of monolithic slabs face the ocean across Atlantic Beach, **Nassau County's** first key.

[4.] Hebrew Institute of Long Island   **[5.]** Roy Reuther Houses (apartments)

 [6.] Intermediate School 53, Queens, The Brian Piccolo School, Nameoke St., bet. Cornaga Ave., Mott Ave. and Beach 18th St. 1972. Victor Lundy.

A many bay-windowed volume surrounding a central courtyard to which there is a grand, monumentally staired entry—the intended main entrance—now barred because of security problems.

[7.] National Bank of Far Rockaway, 1624 Central Ave., bet. Mott St. and Foam Place N side. ca. 1900.

Renaissance Revival in white-glazed terra cotta with great Corinthian pilasters.

 [8.] Congregation Knesseth Israel, 728 Empire Ave. NW cor. Sage St. 1964. Kelly & Gruzen.

An octagonal sanctuary: the **local monument** is now somewhat dated stylistically.

[9.] Jamaica Bay Wildlife Refuge Visitors' Center, Gateway National Recreation Area, Cross Bay Blvd. Broad Channel. 1971. Fred L. Sommer & Assocs., with Elliot Willensky.

Serene, concrete and fluted concrete block, appropriately noncompetitive with its surrounding vegetation.

Hawtree Basin: A tiny, forked inland waterway serving modest houses, spanned at 163rd Avenue by a new steel pedestrian bridge, replacing a charming old wooden lift bridge. The local Tom Sawyers leap into the murky depths off its center on hot August afternoons.

[10.] Richard Cornell Graveyard, 1457 Greenport Rd., Far Rockaway. 17th century. ★

Graveyards outlast architecture.

SEE PAGES 534-560

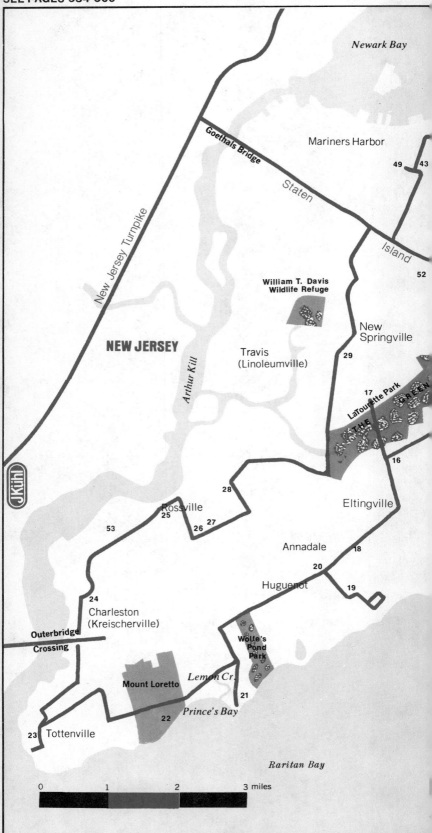

STATEN ISLAND

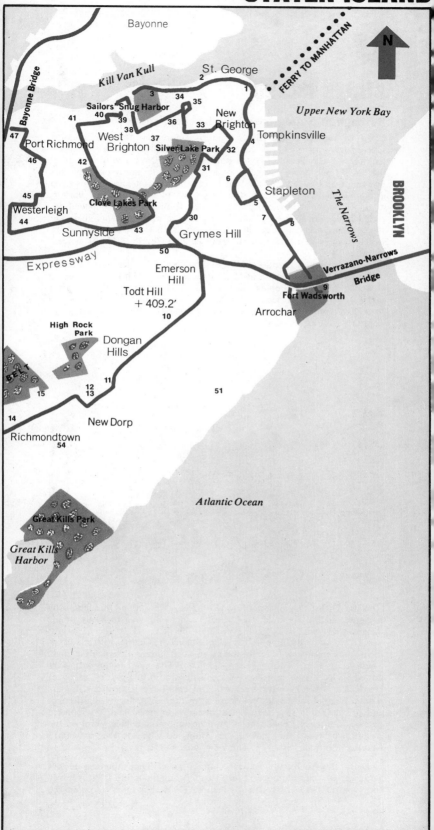

Bayonne

Kill Van Kull

St. George

2

1

FERRY TO MANHATTAN

N

Upper New York Bay

Bayonne Bridge

Sailors' Snug Harbor
3
34
35

41
40
39
38

West
Brighton
37
36
33

New
Brighton

Tompkinsville

4

47

Port Richmond
46

Silver Lake Park
32

42
31

45

Clove Lakes Park

30

6

5

Stapleton

The Narrows

BROOKLYN

Westerleigh
44

Sunnyside
43

Grymes Hill

50

7

8

Expressway

Emerson
Hill

Todt Hill
+ 409.2'

10

Fort Wadsworth
9

Verrazano-Narrows
Bridge

Arrochar

High Rock
Park

Dongan
Hills

BELT

11

51

15

12
13

14

New Dorp

Richmondtown
54

Atlantic Ocean

Great Kills Park

Great Kills
Harbor

5

STATEN ISLAND

Borough of Staten Island/Richmond County

For most tourists, Staten Island is nothing more than the terminus of a **spectacular ferry ride.** Few venture ashore to explore. From such thoroughfares as Bay Street or Hylan Boulevard the views are very discouraging: drab brick houses, huge gasoline stations, and gaudy pizza parlors predominate. Persevere. Behind the listless dingy facades are **hills as steep as San Francisco's,** with breathtaking **views of the New York harbor;** mammoth, crumbling mansions surrounded by **mimosa and rhododendron,** rutted dirt roads, four-foot blacksnakes and fat, **wild pheasant.** There are ridges where archeologists still find Indian artifacts, Dutch farmhouses, **Greek temples,** and Victorian mansions beyond Charles Addams' wildest **fantasies.**

The triangular island is 13.9 miles long and 7.3 miles wide. It is two and one-half times the size of Manhattan and ranks **third in area** among the city's boroughs. **Population** is equal to Manhattan's in 1840—over 300,000, a mere eight persons per acre. This **low density** can be expected to change rapidly as a result of the completion of the Verrazano Bridge, to approach 500,000 by 1985.

11961—*Board Walk at Midland Beach,* STATEN ISLAND, N. Y.

Hills and Dales: One always is aware of being on an island. A slight, salty **dampness** in the air, a **brackish** smell, a buoy **braying forlornly** in the distance, a feeling of isolation, proclaim the fact.

Down the backbone of the island, from St. George to Richmond-town, runs a range of hills formed by an outcropping of **serpentine rock.** These hills—Fort, Ward, Grymes, Emerson, Todt, and Lighthouse—are dotted with elegant mansions of the 19th and 20th centuries, many of them taken over by **private schools** and **charitable institutions.** Others remain palatial residences protected from the hoi polloi by high fences and private roads. (Private associations pay for street lamps, telephone poles, and upkeep.) **Todt Hill,** often proclaimed the **highest point** on the Atlantic coast, is a dinky 409.2 feet compared with Mt. Desert Island's Cadillac Mountain at 1,532. The view, however, is justly famous.

Links to the Mainland: Staten Island is an **Othmar Ammann lover's paradise.** All four automobile bridges connecting the island to New Jersey and to Brooklyn were constructed under his design supervision. In the north, the steel arch of the **Bayonne Bridge,** opened in 1931, connects Port Richmond and Bayonne. In the northwest, the **Goethals Bridge,** a cantilever structure built in 1928, joins Howland Hook and Elizabeth. In the southwest is the **Outerbridge Crossing**—named not for its remoteness from Manhattan but for Eugenius Outerbridge, first chairman of the Port of N.Y. Authority. It also opened in 1928 and spans the Arthur Kill between Charleston and Perth Amboy. The **Verrazano Bridge,** completed in 1964, provides a crossing to Brooklyn and is responsible for the land (and people) boom which has swelled Staten Island's population ever since.

Once Upon a Time: The island is rich in historical associations. Indians and Dutch colonialists seem absurdly distant and irrelevant in Manhattan. The crush of **towering skyscrapers** inhibits the play of the imagination on which a sense of history thrives. On Staten Island, however, a **Dutch Colonial farm** is still set out in fields surrounded by old apple trees. Here it is still possible to envision the life of our forebears.

History books notwithstanding, Staten Island was first "discovered" by the Algonquin Indians. It was first *seen* by a European, **Giovanni da Verrazano,** in 1524, and named **Staaten Eylandt** 85 years later by Henry Hudson while on a voyage for the **Dutch East India Company.** Following a number of unsuccessful attempts, the first permanent settlement by 19 French and Dutch colonists was established in 1661 near the present **South Beach.** The island was renamed **Richmond** (after King Charles II's illegitimate son, the Duke of Richmond) following the English capture of New Amsterdam in 1664.

Until the Revolution, inhabitants went quietly about their business, farming, fishing, oystering, shipbuilding. The revolution brought 30,000 hungry, lusty **redcoats** and **Hessian mercenaries** who occupied the island from 1776 to 1783. Initially Loyalist in sentiment, islanders greeted **Admiral Howe** with boisterous celebrations. But the 3,000 islanders were hard put to provide food, fuel, hay for the occupying army and rapidly lost some of their fondness for the British. The island was the scene of several **skirmishes** between patriots, encamped on the Jersey shore, and the King's troops.

At the beginning of the 19th century a sixteen-year-old's $100 investment in a passenger-and-produce ferry across New York harbor marked the first successful business venture of a native-born islander, Cornelius Vanderbilt. [See 8d, 11c.] As a result of such improved access across New York Bay the island began, in the 1830s, to develop into a **summer retreat** for wealthy, if not particularly prominent, families from New York and the South, who moved into the New Brighton area. A small literary colony sprang up around the eminent eye specialist, **Dr. Samuel MacKenzie Elliott.** [See 39a.] James Russell Lowell, Henry Wadsworth Longfellow, Francis Parkman came to Elliott for treatment and stayed on the island to recuperate. Here Italy's patriot, **Giuseppe Garibaldi,** lived in exile for three years, and **Frederick Law Olmsted** opened a wheat farm. But Staten Island's connection with famous people has always been rather tenuous; more typical were **gentleman farmers, shipbuilders,** and **oyster captains.**

The **Civil War** may have benefited oyster captains, but other islanders suffered the dislocation of a new army. The island became the **assembly point for Union regiments** in the process of organization. Fields and orchards were turned into **camps** and **training fields.** This exacerbated an already touchy situation. Confederate sympathies were strong on the island—many Southerners had sent their wives and children up from Virginia and Maryland to the comparative safety of Staten Island's hotels. Lootings, burnings, and riots of the **anti-draft citizenry** plagued the island, and **abolitionists** had a hard time protecting their homes from the **angry mobs.**

After the war the island continued to develop, albeit slowly. The industrial revolution brought to the island's shores **brick and linoleum factories,** breweries, dye and chemical plants, **wagon and carriage makers.** Farming continued to be a leading occupation. Growth was so sluggish, however, that in 1871 the Legislature appointed a committee to study the problem. This report, penned by Olmsted and amazingly fresh even today, was the first of endless analyses of Staten Island's **lack of growth** or (as is more popular today) **excessive growth.** It pointed to the **prevalence of malaria** (mosquitos prospered in the island's marshes) and **poor ferry** service. Indeed, the preceding decades had seen one ferry's hull crushed by ice, another blown up as the result of a boiler explosion. Prospective passengers were understandably alarmed.

The rural nature of the island, however, did attract the sporting set from across the bay. Here the **first lawn tennis court in America** was built in 1880, and the **first American canoe club** founded. Lacrosse, cricket, rowing, fox hunting, fishing, bathing, and cycling engaged **weekend enthusiasts.** But by the beginning of the 20th century, the island's popularity had begun to wane. Fantastic schemes worthy of **Barnum and Bailey** were developed in a last-ditch attempt to lure the tourist trade. One promoter imported **Buffalo Bill's Wild West Show,** complete with **sharpshooting Annie Oakley,** "Fall of Rome" spectacles, and herds of girls and elephants.

Advice for Touring: A map is absolutely necessary. Buy one in advance to be safe. A newspaper stand inside the terminal may have one. A better bet, however, is an inexpensive Chamber of Commerce map sold at Toder's Newspaper Store, 32 Bay Street, or the Chamber itself, 130 Bay Street (weekdays only at both places, unfortunately). A car is not a necessity but offers distinct advantages.

Carless tour: See St. George, then take Bus 114 to Richmondtown, look around restoration project, proceed to Tottenville on Bus 113 to see Conference House. Return by Staten Island Rapid Transit to St. George, a 45-minute trip.

Driving Tours: The island can't be done in one day . . . it is after all the third largest borough of the city. Distances are deceptively long, roads poorly marked, and buildings hard to find. Specific driving instructions are given to save time. If you must be independent, go ahead but with fair warning. The driving tours are divided this way:

St. George-Fort Wadsworth: Entries 1–9. Starts with the ferryboat ride, takes in Sailors' Snug Harbor, the historic markers in Stapleton, Garibaldi's exile, and a military museum.

Dongan Hills–Richmondtown: Entries 10–17. Encompasses two inland lighthouses, a natural forest preserve, a house by Frank Lloyd Wright, and historic Richmondtown Restoration.

Eltingville-Tottenville: Entries 18–23. Includes some modern schools, Olmsted's homestead, an old fishing settlement, and the Conference House museum.

Charleston–New Springville: Entries 24–29. From a brick manufacturing area to planned unit developments . . . a trip through the least well-known parts of Staten Island.

Grymes Hill/New Brighton/West Brighton: Entries 30–42. Three 19th-century residential communities with a few 20th-century additions.

Sunnyside/Westerleigh/Port Richmond: Entries 43–50. A *potpourri:* modern churches, an old synagogue, a radically designed seminary—and an early gas station for contrast.

Today and Tomorrow: During the last half-century the dangers threatening the island's natural advantages of space, air, grass, and trees have increased. Park areas are being **menaced by expressways.** On humid, stagnant days, lawns shrivel up and die from chemical fallout, and citizens hastily retreat to the safety of air conditioned homes. Meadows have been **scraped clean of trees,** natural streams buried, **hills leveled** in preparation for jerry-built housing developments. Wild salt marshes are now city garbage dumps. The outlook is grim—particularly to a person who remembers what rural Staten Island was once like. But to a person who knows how rare **a blade of grass** is in Manhattan or Queens, the island, by contrast, is positively pastoral. The recession of the 1970s has slowed highway development. The National Park Service, through its Gateway National Recreation Area, now controls a large amount of the island's ocean and bay shoreline. The state wetlands act offers protection against indiscriminate destruction of marshlands. South Richmond, the least-developed part of the island, has been the subject of many studies to control its growth. And first steps to protect the greenbelt have been taken by enacting zoning legislation for a special natural area district. Whether the island's remaining opportunities will be used with care or recklessly squandered is the big question for Staten Islanders (and New Yorkers) in the next decade.

Restaurants: The island is not known for its restaurants, but increased population has expanded the choices in recent years. Call about reservations for weekend and holiday dinner.

Carmen's, 750 Barclay Ave., southern section of the island off Hylan Blvd. near Arden Ave. Spanish and Mexican food in a charming hacienda setting overlooking Raritan Bay. A bit on the expensive side. Lunch and dinner seven days a week. Parking. **984-9786.**

Grandma's Table, 33 Water St., Stapleton. Informal dining, lunch and dinner. Closed Thursdays. Inexpensive American standbys. Unpredictable service is compensated for by warmth of the surroundings. Park on street or in nearby municipal parking area. **447-9405.**

Demyan's Hofbrau, 742 Van Duzer St. on the hill overlooking Stapleton. Occupies a building which was once a brewery. The restaurant walls are covered with memorabilia. (Demyan's was used as the commissary during the filming on location of *The Godfather.*) Lunch and dinner every day. On the expensive side. Lots of parking. **GI 8-7337.**

Montezuma's Revenge, 103 Stuyvesant Pl., St. George. Don't be put off by the name . . . terrific Mexican food, subtle to spicy. Lots of fun in a cozy setting. Lunch and dinner except Mondays. Street parking only, or try nearby municipal parking area. **442-9612.**

Forest Inn Restaurant, 834 Forest Ave. off Broadway and near the zoo. An unpretentious place for snacks and simple American meals. Lunch and dinner every day. Parking in rear. **727-6060.**

Staten Island Mall, Richmond Ave. at Richmond Hill Rd., not too far from Richmondtown. Plenty of parking around this indoor shopping center and a range of eateries to choose from: Zum Zum, Chinese, Italian, pizza, McDonalds, Baskin-Robbins, and don't forget the department store cafeterias.

Staten Island Ferry Ride

> *We were very tired, we were very merry—*
> *We had gone back and forth all night on the ferry.*
> —Edna St. Vincent Millay

Drawbridges and rusty chains clank, engines shudder and grunt, the throaty whistle blasts, and the ferry churns out into the oily waters of New York harbor. Petulant gulls hover aloft, commuters, inured to the spectacular, settle behind newspapers while tourists crowd to the rail. Children and even some adults become very merry.

Ferries leave frequently during daylight hours (calling **566-8633** will get the exact schedule). Upon boarding, move to the far end of the second deck. From this position, Brooklyn lies to the left, and Governors Island is immediately ahead; Ellis Island, the old immigration station, and the **Statue of Liberty,** bound to produce **a lump in the throat** for even the most callous, appear in succession on the right.

The **first glimpse** of Staten Island is attractive. Steep, wooded hills rise behind the civic center of St. George; **Greek Revival porticos** appear along the waterfront, and **Gothic spires** and **Italianate towers** of schools and churches top hills on the right. On a misty or, more likely, smoggy day, the aspect is momentarily reminiscent of **a small Italian town.** Romance is quickly dispelled by the brutally efficient red brick ferry terminal at St. George, with its pea green tile interior—more suggestive of an athletic shower room than of a **gateway.**

ST. GEORGE-FORT WADSWORTH

[1a.] Originally **Chief Physician's House, U.S. Coast Guard Base,** 1 Bay St., adjacent to ferry. 1815. (Visiting by appointment.)

Gambrel roof of handsome, Federal-style building can be seen from Richmond Terrace, picturesquely peeking over base's high brick wall. Fussy bay windows capped by scalloped roof added to facade later.

[1b.] Borough Hall, Richmond Terrace, S side, opposite ferry terminal. 1906. Carrère & Hastings.

This elegant brick structure in the style of a French town hall welcomes the passenger emerging from the ferry building.

[1c.] County Court House, 30 Richmond Terrace, next to Borough Hall. 1919. Carrère & Hastings.

Slightly pretentious Italian Renaissance structure with Classical Revival portico. Designed in totally different style from its neighbor. Purists may object, but effect is pleasing.

[1d.] Family Court House, 100 Richmond Terrace bet. Wall St. and Hamilton Ave. S side. 1930. Sibley & Fetherston.

Has finely detailed Ionic columns and delicately ornamented facade. Looks pleasantly remote from the heavy problems that are pondered within.

REAR VIEW OF BOROUGH HALL, ST. GEORGE, STATEN ISLAND, N. Y.

[1b.] Staten Island Borough Hall: as depicted on a pre-World War I postcard

If driving, continue west along Richmond Terrace, once fashionable for Sunday outings in horse and carriage, now blighted by oil refineries in New Jersey, factories and railroad further down. If walking, go back toward Borough Hall to see Brighton Heights Reformed Church, then take bus to Richmondtown. [See 16.]

[1e.] Staten Island Museum, 75 Stuyvesant Pl. NE cor. Wall St. 1918, 1927. Robert W. Gardner. Telephone: 727-1135.

A sleepy museum bulging from its small Georgian Revival building. Sometimes has interesting temporary exhibitions. Call for schedule.

[1f.] N.Y.C. Health Department Building, 51 Stuyvesant Pl. bet. Wall St. and Hamilton Ave. E side. ca. 1935. Henry C. Pelton.

A modest but effective example of the Art Deco style as applied to a mid-Depression municipal edifice.

[1g.] Brighton Heights Reformed Church, 320 St. Marks Pl. SW cor. Fort Pl. on hill one block above Borough Hall. 1866. ★

This delicate white wood-framed church is almost overwhelmed by the competition from less thoughtful 20th-century intrusions.

[2a.] Columbia Hall/formerly **William J. Taylor Residence**/now **Pavilion on the Terrace,** 404 Richmond Terrace bet. St. Peter's Pl. and Westervelt Ave. S side. 1835.

This is the last vestige of **Temple Row,** the name given to ten Greek Revival mansions built by wealthy New Yorkers and Southern planters along Richmond Terrace when the view across the Kill Van Kull was more pastoral. Its handsome Doric columns and stately pediment are compromised by its pink and white paint job, no doubt intended to attract business to its current use as a catering establishment.

[2a.] Pavilion on the Terrace, the last of Temple Row, in a 1967 photograph

[2b.] **Neville House,** 806 Richmond Terrace bet. Clinton Ave. and Tysen St. S side. ca. 1770. ★

Identified by its slender-columned two-story-high veranda, it is said that the house reflects the Caribbean journeys of its retired sea captain owner, John Neville. Its proximity to Sailors' Snug Harbor, just down the Terrace, caused it to have a period of success as a local tavern, the Old Stone Jug.

[3.] Sailors' Snug Harbor, Bldg. C and neighbors: *Valentine's Manual,* 1869

[3.] **Sailors' Snug Harbor,** Richmond Terrace bet. Tysen St., Snug Harbor Rd., and Kissel Ave. S to Henderson Ave. **Bldg. C** (central building facing Richmond Terrace), Minard Lafever, Samuel Thompson & Son. 1831–1833. **Bldg. A,** 1879. **Bldg. B,** 1839–1840. **Bldg. D,** 1840–1844. **Bldg. E,** 1880. **Gatehouse,** ca. 1860, 1880. **Fence,** 1842, Frederick Diaper. **Chapel,** 1856. ★

Five Greek temples serenely surveying an immaculately groomed lawn made the **vision** of Sailors' Snug Harbor an obvious **landmark choice** back in the 1960s. A court action by the Harbor's trustees against designation, their initial victory, and their ultimate defeat on appeal by City attorneys presaged New York City's purchase of the buildings—and then the remainder of the picturesque site. Whether the vision can, through **adaptive reuse,** be made into a tangible cultural center for Staten Island is a great local question.

The Harbor was founded by Robert Richard Randall, who converted his Revolutionary War privateer-father's bequest into a fund for the support of **"aged, decrepit and worn-out sailors."** For many years, the proceeds from Randall's property in Manhattan's Greenwich Village supported the Harbor. Following the court of appeals support of landmark designation, the Harbor's trustees moved the institution to a new site on the North Carolina coast. This paved the way, in 1976, for the reuse of the **rich complex** of Greek Revival, Victorian, and early 20th-century edifices, and 60 acres of romantic grounds to the south, for **a new public benefit.**

Retrace your route back along Richmond Terrace and gently bear right beyond Borough Hall onto Bay Street. Take a left turn at Hannah Street (fake lighthouse will be on your right) and cross viaduct over Staten Island's commuter line, the SIRT, to a curious melange of dockside municipal architecture. From north to south:

[4a.] Joseph H. Lyons Pool, Murray Hulbert Ave. SW cor. Victory Blvd. 1936. N.Y.C. Parks Department. Aymar Embury II, consultant.

Squat cylinders of economical red-brick masonry, helical concrete stairways, and Art Deco detailing identify this as one of eight city swimming pools built in the heyday of municipal construction, the Great Depression of the 1930s. Named for the commander of local V.F.W. and American Legion units.

Great Depression Bathhouses: Public works—and works for the public— were a great civic concern during the Great Depression. This concern, plus the availability of subsidized skilled labor, resulted in the building of a group of great public swimming pools and even greater public bathhouses. The superior architectural design of the bathhouses (actually locker and shower facilities for pool users) makes them monuments to their period even decades later. Bronx: Crotona Park; Brooklyn: Betsy Head Park, McCarren Park, Red Hook Park, and Sunset Park; Manhattan: Colonial Park and Highbridge Park; Staten Island: Joseph H. Lyons Pool.

[4b.] George Cromwell Center, Pier 6, Murray Hulbert Ave. at Victory Blvd. E side. Facade 1936. N.Y.C. Parks Department.

A port pier converted to recreational use in the 1930s, it sports a fine Art Deco front. Named for the island's first borough president.

[4c.] Richmond Tunnel Chlorination Station, Murray Hulbert Ave. SW cor. Hannah St. viaduct. 1974. N.Y.C. Board of Water Supply.

Free Port: Between Tompkinsville and Stapleton there remain the remnants of deep-water piers with signs that can still be made out to read "Free Trade Zone No. 1." Built between 1921 and 1923 by Mayor John Hylan (for whom Hylan Boulevard was named), the piers were the first of several attempts to boost Staten Island's maritime economy. As in the case of the Bronx Terminal Market [see W Bronx 16.], the scheme failed and the docks (and market) were dubbed "Hylan's Folly." In 1937 the area was designated a free port—a place where international cargo could be stored for transshipment without the payment of duty. Freshly picked coffee, for example, taxed by weight, was stored till it dried out and then was charged a lower import duty when received at its ultimate destination. Strangely enough, this special privilege also failed to activate the dormant piers. In the mid-seventies the 135 acres were converted to container port use.

[4d.] Tompkinsville Water Pollution Control Facility, Murray Hulbert Ave. at Pier 7. W side. 1976. Warren W. Gran & Assocs.

What a contrast in these two municipal works built only a few years apart. The sophisticated if too self-conscious shed-roofed control facility cast in brutalist gray concrete is for society's waste products. The prim, handsomely crafted neo-Georgian chlorination station of carefully laid brick, pink granite, and monumental aluminum trim is for another vital need: pure water. The architectural message seems clear, or does it?

Return to Bay St. via the viaduct and turn left.

[5.] Edgewater Village Hall, in Tappen Park, Bay St. to Wright St., Water St. to Canal St. 1889. ★

Though it bears the name of Edgewater, a 19th-century village all but forgotten today, this fine Victorian edifice is an anchor for another community not at all forgotten, **Stapleton.** The intricately detailed masonry structure sits within Tappen Park, shaded by stately old trees which temper the loudness of the many small businesses which on every side attempt to destroy the peacefulness of its setting. A picturesque **Victorian** landmark.

Discover Stapleton: To provide both residents and visitors with insight into the history and environment of Stapleton, a team from High Rock Park's environmental center [see 15f.] developed and installed more than a hundred permanent illustrated markers along the community's streets during the 1976 national bicentennial. They tell of the area's growth and change, recollect people and events, and call attention to the buildings, spaces, and views.

If an Official Landmark buff, detour west to Van Duzer Street to see two unusual two-story houses in a 19th-century version of the Dutch Colonial style and a fine church.

[6a.] 364 Van Duzer Street, bet. Wright and Beach Sts. W side. ca. 1835. ★

[6b.] 390 Van Duzer Street, bet. Beach and Prospect Sts. W side. ca. 1835. ★

[6c.] St. Paul's Memorial Church (Protestant Episcopal), 225 St. Paul's Ave. bet. Taxter Pl. and Clinton St. E side. 1870. Edward Tuckerman Potter. ★

A lovingly crafted English country church whose traprock walls have weathered beautifully over the years.

Continuing south on Bay Street brings you to:

[7a.] U.S. Public Health Service Hospital/formerly **U.S. Marine Hospital**/ formerly **Seamen's Fund and Retreat,** Bay St. NW cor. Vanderbilt Ave. Earliest building, 1834–1837. Later buildings, 1933–1936. Kenneth M. Murchison, William M. Bompert, Tachau & Vaught, associate architects; J. H. de Sibou, consultant; James A. Wetmore, Louis A. Simon, supervising architects.

Hard to spot through the trees from the exit driveway on Bay Street (but worth the effort) is the old hospital's **imposing stone facade** with two-story **pierced galleries** and **pedimented pavilions.** Operated by the state and federal governments since its inception—unlike the privately run Sailors' Snug Harbor on the island's north shore [see 3.]—it was this early marine hospital building that spawned the large complex of 1930s buildings which now dominates the site. The well-known **National Institutes of Health,** located in Bethesda, Maryland, had their modest beginnings here in a small laboratory of this old structure.

[7b.] Mariners' Family Asylum of the Port of New York, 119 Tompkins Ave. bet. Vanderbilt Ave. and Tompkins St. E side. 1855.

Contiguous with the rear of the Public Health Service Hospital is this building constructed to care for the widows, wives, sisters, and daughters of the seamen of the port.

If interested in Italian history, make a right on Chestnut Avenue to visit Garibaldi Memorial; otherwise continue south on Bay.

[8a.] Garibaldi Memorial, 420 Tompkins Ave. SW cor. Chestnut Ave. 1840. ★ Telephone: GI 2-1608.

An unlikely refuge for fiery Italian patriot Giuseppe Garibaldi, who lived here with his friend **Antonio Meucci** between 1851 and 1853. Restlessly awaiting an opportunity to return to Italy, Garibaldi made candles in a nearby factory, killed time fishing and "shooting thrushes." **Museum,** housed in altered Federal farmhouse, has letters, photographs describing Garibaldi's life and documenting Meucci's claim to **invention of the telephone** prior to Alexander Graham Bell.

Fig Trees: Italians on the island love ripe figs. Consequently, many backyards are decorated with weird trees bundled up like mummies in winter, laden with clusters of ripe figs in summer. Presence of this tree is foolproof clue to nationality of its owner. Garibaldi memorial is no exception—an Italian caretaker lives on the second floor.

Turn left on Hylan Boulevard for Austen Cottage and old New York Yacht Club.

[8b.] Austen Cottage, "Clear Comfort," 2 Hylan Blvd. E of Bay St. overlooking Upper New York Bay. S side. ca. 1691–1710. North extension, porch, dormers added 1844. ★

The original portion having been built by a Dutch merchant (to take advantage of the still breathtaking view?) this house was purchased and altered by John Austen, a wealthy and cultivated New Yorker, in 1844. His granddaughter, **Alice Austen,** came here in 1868 at the age of two. She is remembered today for her **pioneering work** in what was in her early years a new art and a new science, **photography.** More than seven thousand of her glass plate negatives are preserved at the Staten Island Historical Society. They depict, with consummate artistry, the world she knew between 1880 and 1930.

[8b.] "Clear Comfort," as photographed in the 19th century by Alice Austen

[8c.] F. Bredt House/formerly **N.Y. Yacht Club,** 30 Hylan Blvd. E of Bay St. ca. 1859.

Behind the Austen house, set back from road. Another incredible view, enhanced here by meadows and horse paddock. Its tenure as a club ended in 1880; now an apartment house. Rambling plan with spacious bay windows framed by Egyptoid forms.

[8d.] St. John's Protestant Episcopal Church, 1331 Bay St. SE cor. New Lane. 1871. Arthur D. Gilman. ★ **Rectory,** 1862. **Parish House,** 1865.

More likely to be found at Yale University than on Staten Island. A fine example of Victorian Gothic style built of rose-colored granite with handsome stained-glass windows. Unfortunately, original steeple has been altered. The first child baptized in the original frame building of this parish was Cornelius Vanderbilt, born in nearby Stapleton in 1794.

Backdoor to America: An important strategy conference brought Winston Churchill to the island's shores during World War II. The Prime Minister secretly debarked from British cruiser anchored off Stapleton and took the B&O Railroad directly to Washington to confer with President Roosevelt. Thus you might say the island is the backdoor to America.

[9a.] Von Briesen Park, Bay St. at School Rd. E side.

Once the estate of Arthur Von Briesen, the first president of Citizens' Union, this park enjoys **unparalleled views** of New York harbor, the Verrazano Bridge, and the courtyard of Battery Weed next door. The small parking area at Bay Street is rarely full. Stop and **take a walk** to the edge of the cliff for the great view. Across the northern boundary of the park you will glimpse one of Staten Island's many ponds, this one in the adjacent shorefront residential community of **Shore Acres.**

[9b.] Battery Weed at Fort Wadsworth in a view from the Verrazano Bridge

[9b.] Battery Weed/formerly **Fort Richmond,** Fort Wadsworth Military Reservation, S end of Bay St. 1847–1861. ★ Military Museum at **[9c.] Fort Tompkins,** 1861. ★ Telephone: 447-5100.

Gate and guards look ominous, but actually visitors are welcome. Drive straight ahead; turn left beyond the bridge; follow signs to **Military Museum** and closeup view down into the landmarked Battery Weed built at the water's edge before the Civil War. The three tiers of arched galleries make the interior of the polygonal fortress far less formidable in appearance than its severe exterior walls.

Romantic legend depicts Algonquin Indians standing here spellbound by the sight of Hudson's ship, the *Half Moon,* entering the Narrows in 1609. Since those sylvan times, Dutch, British, and Americans in times of war have stood watch here, scanning the horizon for enemy ships.

Known well into the 1970s as the oldest continuously staffed military post in the United States, there are plans to add the site to the holdings of the **Gateway National Recreation Area** once the Army decides to relinquish it. The Military Museum is a fascinating storehouse of armed forces trivia displayed in the galleries of another old fortress, **Fort Tompkins,** built at the top of the escarpment guarding the Narrows. Call for hours museum is open.

H. H. Richardson house. On Staten Island? It's hard to believe (and looking at it today minus its original shingles makes it harder), but the house at 45 McClean Avenue at the northeast corner of Lily Pond Avenue (south of the Verrazano Bridge toll plaza) is an early (1868–1869) design of Henry Hobson Richardson, later the architect of such masterpieces as Boston's Trinity Church and considered one of this country's architectural geniuses. Richardson lived in Staten Island between 1867 and 1874.

We suggest you now take the Verrazano Bridge home and come back another day *via the bridge* to continue touring. When you do, take the Richmond Road exit off the Expressway. To see the southern sections of the island turn left at Richmond Road and proceed to the Billiou House. To see more of the northern part of the island, continue on the service road to Clove Road and skip to [29.].

DONGAN HILLS-RICHMONDTOWN

[10a.] Billiou-Stillwell-Perine House, 1476 Richmond Rd. bet. Delaware and Cromwell Aves. E side. 1662–1830. ★

Like the **house that Jack built,** this one has additions sprawling in every direction. Looking at the building from the front and reading from left to right, you see rooms dating from 1790, 1680, 1662, and 1830. The original one-room **fieldstone farmhouse** with steep pitched roof built in 1662 is best seen from the back. Walk around the house; take a look inside and in particular at the magnificent open-hearth fireplace. Open to the public. Telephone: 987-7379.

Continue south on Richmond Road to Flagg Place, a fork to the right up a steep stretch of hill. Look for the traffic light at Four Corners Road intersection—there will be a firehouse on the far left.

Country Club Area: This area of Dongan Hills, roughly bounded by Flagg Place and Todt Hill Road, is a very prestigious residential area of the island. It once contained a group of large estates; now it is the site for many of the island's most elaborate residences, both traditional and modern; for the Staten Island Academy, a private school; and for the Richmond County Country Club and its golf course.

[10b.] Ernest Flagg Residence, Gatehouse, and Gate/now **St. Charles Seminary,** 209 Flagg Pl. W side. 1898. Ernest Flagg. ★

For many years the palatial residence of architect Ernest Flagg, designer of Manhattan's Singer and Scribner buildings [see index]. The **lavish estate** with enormous swimming pool, stone water tower, and row upon row of fruit trees owes its unusual design to Flagg's familiarity with the architecture of the Dutch colonies of the Caribbean. The main house contrasts white clapboard siding with locally quarried serpentinite walls. At one time Flagg is said to have been Staten Island's largest land-owner—in 1946 he offered a large parcel of his land to the United Nations organization for use as its permanent headquarters.

[10c.] Charles Azzue Residence, at westerly border of Country Club Area, 785 Todt Hill Rd. bet. Four Corners Rd. and Cromwell Circle. E side. 1975.

White stucco walls and sharply pitched roof lines set this house dramatically apart from its more subdued neighbors. Designed by its self-taught owner-builder.

[11a.] New Dorp Moravian Church, 1256 Todt Hill Rd. N of Richmond Rd. W side. 1844. **Parsonage,** ca. 1870. **Parish House,** 1913.

This "new" church is older than many of New York's "old" ones. The pretentious, gray stucco parish house in Classical Revival style was the gift of William H. Vanderbilt, son of Cornelius.

[11b.] Old New Dorp Moravian Church, in the Moravian Cemetery. 1763.

A good example of Dutch Colonial style. Has sweeping roof extending over eaves to form porch. Building originally served as church and parsonage; now catering to the very young as well as the very old, it is both church school and cemetery office.

[11c.] Vanderbilt Mausoleum, rear of Moravian Cemetery. 1886. Richard Morris Hunt, architect. Frederick Law Olmsted, landscape architect.

Seemingly carved out of the "living rock" with ornate granite entrance added. Buried within are **"Commodore" Cornelius Vanderbilt** (who paid for the tomb) and members of his family. A trip through the rest of the cemetery also provides beautiful landscapes, walks, and drives.

Leaving the cemetery, take a right turn onto Richmond Road. A detour at the first right turn, Altamont Avenue, will give you a view of an old wood-frame navigation light:

[11c.] The Vanderbilt Mausoleum, on a site adjacent to Moravian Cemetery

[12.] New Dorp Light Station/now **private residence,** N end of Altamont Ave. Best viewed from Beacon Ave. and Boyle St. ca. 1854. ★

A former Coast Guard navigation beacon, it acted as an aid to ships entering New York harbor. Its white clapboard tower is hardly reminiscent of the traditional lighthouse form. Now decommissioned, it will see adaptive reuse as a house.

Retrace route to Richmond Road and continue south.

[13.] Mayer House/formerly **J. M. Davis House,** 2475 Richmond Rd. bet. New Dorp Lane and Odin St. W side. ca. 1854.

Set back from the road behind landscape lush in winter as well as summer is this grand old mansion with a distinctive monitor on its roof from which much of this part of the island can be seen.

[14.] Moore-McMillen House/formerly **Rectory of the Church of St. Andrew,** 3531 Richmond Rd. opposite Kensico St. W side. 1818. ★

A very good example of Federal style. Extremely handsome doorway and neatly articulated cornice. Behind house is a good view of the Staten Island Lighthouse [See 15b.].

If pressed for time, hurry on to Richmondtown. Otherwise, turn right on Lighthouse Avenue to see a Frank Lloyd Wright house, another lighthouse, a Tibetan museum, and a public forest, all within the city's boundaries.

[15a.] Cass House, "Crimson Beech," 48 Manor Court W of Lighthouse Ave. 1959. Frank Lloyd Wright.

Best seen driving up Lighthouse Avenue toward the lighthouse. Long, low building clings precariously to cliff edge, taking full advantage of the view. A late work in Wright's career, it is certainly not of the quality of his prairie houses. However, it is the only Wright-designed residence within city limits.

[15b.] Staten Island Lighthouse, Edinboro Rd. 1912. ★

Can be seen from Lighthouse Avenue. This lighthouse, strangely distant from rocks and pounding waves, stands calmly amid lawns and homes. The octagonal structure of yellow brick with fanciful Gothic carpentry supporting walkway is a pleasant change from pure white cylindrical lighthouses familiar to yachtsmen. The beacon, on high ground and visible for miles at sea, provides range lights to guide ships into Ambrose Channel.

[15c.] Jacques Marchais Center of Tibetan Art, 338 Lighthouse Ave. near Windsor Ave. S side. Telephone: 987-3478 or 448-7877.

The largest privately owned collection of Tibetan art outside of Tibet. A rare treat—if you enjoy Tibetan sculpture, scrolls, paintings.

Continue east on Lighthouse Avenue; make a left on Ascot, a right on Meisner.

[15d.] Nathaniel J. Wyeth, Jr., Residence, 190 Meisner Ave. bet. Lowell Court and Scheffelin Ave. S side. ca. 1850.

A lovely, seemingly deserted, two-story cube of brick masonry topped by a many-sided, many-windowed monitor in the center of its roof. Heavily engulfed on the road side by lush landscaping, a siting that offers the privacy that newer homes have sacrificed to wide, showy lawns. On the far side (private) it enjoys a fantastic panorama of the approaches to New York harbor.

[15e.] Eger Home, 120 Meisner Ave. bet. London Rd. and Rockland Ave. S side. 1971. Quanbeck & Heeden.

The prismatic gray multistory masonry nursing home is too large, too noticeable, and too artificial an intrusion into the natural rhythms of the Staten Island greenbelt.

Take Meisner Avenue down the hill to the traffic light; take a right turn and then a left at Nevada Avenue.

[15b.] The Staten Island Lighthouse   [17b.] St. Andrew's Episcopal Church

[15f.] High Rock Park Conservation Center, 200 Nevada Ave. at summit of hill. Telephone: 987-6233.

A primarily natural rather than built environment, this hardwood forest preserve is a rarity among New York City's protected green spaces. With 72 acres it is only a small part of the 1,000-acre Staten Island greenbelt. There are marked, self-guiding trails (including one with Haiku verse changed every season), a loosestrife swamp, a pond, and a visitors' center where more information is available about this nationally recognized environmental education center.

Proceed to Richmondtown by taking a left at the foot of Nevada Avenue and then bearing to the right at the traffic light onto Richmond Road southbound.

Richmondtown: The site of an ambitious project involving the **restoration** and **reconstruction** of approximately 31 buildings, and hopes for a trolley museum and operating streetcars, all under the direction of the Staten Island Historical Society.

At its founding in 1685 Richmondtown was humbly known as **"Cocclestown"**—presumably after oyster and clam shells found in streams nearby. Here, in 1695, the Dutch erected the Voorlezer House, their **first**

meeting house, used for both church services and teaching school. Subsequently a **town hall** and **gaol** were built. By 1730 the town was thriving. It had a new court house, one tavern, about a dozen homes, and the Church of St. Andrew. This tiny town was now the largest and most important town on the island. As such, the name Cocclestown was considered inappropriate and changed to the more staid Richmondtown. By the time of the **American Revolution,** when British occupied it, Richmondtown had a blacksmith shop, a general store, a poorhouse, a tanner's shop, a Dutch Reformed Church, a grist mill, and several more private homes.

[16a.] Staten Island Historical Society Museum/formerly **Second County Clerk's and Surrogate's Office,** 302 Center St. NW cor. Court Pl. 1848. ★ Telephone: 351-1611 or 351-9414.

This charmingly scaled red brick building which once served a governmental purpose is today a low-key museum. On display are odd bits of Americana of varying interest—china, lithographs, furniture, toys, a marvelous collection of tools. Note photos around gallery (second floor) of Staten Island buildings, most of which have met wrecking ball fate. To get your bearings, study the model of the Richmondtown Restoration project and get a map showing the buildings open to the public the day you visit.

[16b.] Third County Court House, Center St. opp. S end of Court Pl. ca. 1837. ★

Frumpy but grand. Succeeds in making clear that it is the architectural dowager of this community.

[16c.] Stephens House and General Store, Court Pl. cor. Center St. 1837. ★

Fascinating reconstruction of 19th-century store—everything from ginger beer to quinine pills. Musty smell of soap and candles delights modern-day shopper used to antiseptic, cellophane-wrapped goods in supermarkets. Storefront is perfectly plain—no neon signs, no billboards.

[16d.] Lake-Tysen House, Richmond Rd. bet. Court and St. Patrick's Pl. N side. ca. 1740. ★

One of the best examples of the Dutch Colonial style remaining in the metropolitan area and luckily saved at the last minute from destruction when it was moved in 1962 from original site in New Dorp.

[16e.] Voorlezer's House, Arthur Kill Rd. bet. Center St. and Clarke Ave. W side. 1695. ★

Archetypical "little red schoolhouse," called Voorlezer because in Dutch communities unable to obtain a minister, a layman named a voorlezer was chosen by the congregation to teach school and conduct church services. It is the **oldest known elementary school building** in the United States.

Other Richmondtown official city landmarks:

[16f.] Basketmaker's Shop, ca. 1810; **Bennett House,** ca. 1837; **Boehm-Frost House,** ca. 1770; **Christopher House** (disassembled and awaiting re-erection), ca. 1756; **Cooper's Shop,** ca. 1790–1800; **Grocery Store,** ca. 1860; **Parsonage,** ca. 1855; **Treasure House,** ca. 1700; and the **Van Pelt-Rezeau Cemetery,** one of the city's few remaining private burial grounds. **Cubberly-Britton Cottage,** ca. 1670. Additions, ca. 1700, ca. 1750. ★

In or near Richmondtown but not part of the Restoration:

[17a.] St. Patrick's Roman Catholic Church, 53 St. Patrick's Pl. bet. Center St. and Clarke Ave. E side. 1862. ★

A white-painted brick church whose window openings carry Romanesque Revival half-round arches but whose narrow proportions are more in keeping with a Gothic Revival verticality.

[17b.] St. Andrew's Protestant Episcopal Church, 4 Arthur Kill Rd. SE cor. Old Mill Rd. 1872. William H. Mersereau. ★

A picturesque English country church set in a picturesque Staten Island setting complete with graveyard. Borders the marshlands of LaTourette Park.

Detour up Richmond Hill Road. The drive back down gives an unbelievable view of Richmondtown; it looks almost like a tiny model from the steeply winding road.

[17c.] David LaTourette Residence/now LaTourette Park Clubhouse, LaTourette Park E of Richmond Hill Rd. 1836. ★

In silhouette on the brow of the hill or studied more carefully up close, this (minus its 1936 porch addition) is a fine masonry Greek Revival mansion. As the clubhouse for a City-owned golf course, however, its interior is a great letdown, mostly barren, dim rooms used for snackbar purposes.

[17d.] Sylvanus Decker Farm, 435 Richmond Hill Rd. bet. Forest Hill Rd. and Bridgetown St. N side. ca. 1800. ★

A cozy clapboard Dutch-inspired white-painted farmhouse with barn-red outbuildings. Owned by the Staten Island Historical Society, it will be restored, in conjunction with nearby Richmondtown, as a farm of the 1830s.

If you've had enough sightseeing for the day, continue along Richmond Hill Road to Richmond Avenue, turn right and follow the signs to Interstate 278, the Staten Island Expressway. At the turn you will pass the Staten Island Mall where a variety of restaurants and fast-food opportunities are available.

If continuing the tour, retrace your route down Richmond Hill Road, past Richmondtown, directly into Arthur Kill Road. Then take the left fork at the traffic light onto Giffords Lane and a right turn at another traffic light onto Amboy Road toward Tottenville.

ELTINGVILLE-TOTTENVILLE

[18.] St. Alban's Protestant Episcopal Church and Rectory, 76 Old Amboy Rd. bet. Ridgecrest Ave. and Beach Rd. S side. ca. 1855. Richard Upjohn.

A gem. Board-and-batten Carpenter Gothic style with a steeply pitched roof. Entrance is not opposite the apse area but from one side—an interesting variation.

[18.] St. Alban's Episcopal Church: the skill of early carpenters is evident

Continue south on Amboy Road unless you wish to take a detour to see a modern school playground and a house once lived in by Frederick Law Olmsted. If so, consult your map.

[19a.] Public School 55 Richmond, and Playground, Koch Blvd. NE cor. Woods of Arden Rd. School, 1965; Playground, 1967. Richard G. Stein.

The playground, with sculpture by Nivola, was heralded at the time of its construction as a design breakthrough. Upon completion it proved to be a booby trap, its steep changes of grade and high walls challenging neighborhood children into dangerous acrobatic feats. The "zoo bars," installed afterward as a safety measure, create an unintentional but pleasing moiré effect for anyone in motion.

[19b.] Poillon House, 4515 Hylan Blvd. bet. Hales Ave. and Woods of Arden Rd. ca. 1720. ★

Hard to find—set back from road. Extensively remodeled in the 19th century. Before he became a park designer, Frederick Law Olmsted lived here, running a fruit farm, planting trees, experimenting with landscaping. Later, when Olmsted began work on Prospect Park, he moved up to Clifton, commuting daily to Brooklyn via the nearby ferry.

Return to Amboy Road. Go south.

[20a.] Holy Child Church (Roman Catholic) and Parish Center, 4747 Amboy Rd. NW cor. Arden Ave. 1970. Mignone, Coco & Smith.

An unusual shape, pristine white in color, surrounded by lots of open space, and at a major intersection. Close up, however, this modern church loses a lot of its impact.

[20b.] Huguenot Reformed Church, 5475 Amboy Rd. NW cor. Huguenot Ave. 1924. Ernest Flagg.

A refreshingly different church design for its time (and place) by one of America's most original architects. Built of native serpentinite, a stone quarried on the architect's estate in the Todt Hill section of the island [see 10b.], the church was dedicated as the national monument of the Huguenot-Walloon Tercentenary celebration in 1924.

[20c.] Tottenville High School, S of Amboy Rd. at Luten Ave. NW cor. Deisius St. 1972. Daniel Schwartzman & Assocs.

Located in the community of Huguenot but renamed for the high school it replaced, in nearby Tottenville, one of the first problems confronting the school was the removal of the letters H U G U E N O T cast into the cast-in-place concrete facade. A reserved, monochromatic design, the open spaces under its elevated wings seem unnecessary in this low-density part of the island—also they are dark and not very inviting.

Continue on Amboy Road and take a left on Seguine Avenue to reach Prince's Bay. Visit Carmen's Restaurant, if it's the right time of day.

Prince's Bay: Once a prosperous fishing and oystering village. Oysters from here were so famous that fashionable restaurants in New York and London carried "Prince's Bays" on their menus. Now an area of run-down shacks with tar paper flapping, paint peeling.

[21a.] Seguine House, 440 Seguine Ave. bet. Wilbur St. and Purdy Pl. W side. ca. 1840. ★

Grand, but ugly; two-story pillars are fat and chunky, fanlight in middle of pediment, awkward. Still, building's Southern-style grandeur in this run-down setting is appealing. Splendid site—look back at the house from marina area.

[21b.] Purdy Hotel, 509 Seguine Ave. NE cor. Purdy Pl. ca. 1690.

Looking from Purdy Place, the small-scale structure on the left dates from ca. 1690; the larger-scale one is later. Once upon a time guests had a lovely view of clipper ships and schooners sailing into the Narrows; now, an unlovely vista of smokestacks.

Take Seguine Avenue back to Hylan Boulevard; make a left.

[22a.] Prince's Bay Lighthouse and Keeper's House/now Residence for the Mission of the Immaculate Virgin, Mount Loretto Home for Children, Hylan Blvd. bet. Sharrott and Richmond Aves. S side. ca. 1868.

From Hylan Boulevard just west of Sharrott Avenue there is a good view of the **rusticated brownstone** lighthouse which sits on a rise at the water's edge. Its beacon is now replaced by a statue of the Virgin Mary. It makes an enviable residence and dining hall for priests who care for nearly a thousand children from broken homes.

[22b.] Church of St. Joachim and St. Anne, Mount Loretto Home for Children, Hylan Blvd. bet. Sharrott and Richmond Aves. N side. ca. 1882. Nave reconstructed 1976.

A disastrous fire in December 1973 destroyed the church except for its main facade. In an imaginative architectural solution, the towered Gothic Revival front was saved and a simple **new A-frame nave** was built against it. Economy, simplicity, harmony. The original church was commissioned by Father John G. Drumgoole, the founder of the 650-acre home—originally for homeless newsboys.

For two off-the-beaten-path structures, take a right turn at Page Avenue and a left at Amboy Road. If in a rush proceed along Hylan Boulevard directly to the Billopp/Conference House.

[23a.] Bethel Methodist Episcopal Church, NE cor. Amboy Rd. and Bethel Ave. 1886.

The bigger-than-life masonry facade of this church is embellished with unglazed terra-cotta trim which no doubt came from the well-known clay works in Kreischerville (now Charleston) a mile north of here.

[23b.] Formerly **Dr. Henry Litvak Residence and Office,** 7379 Amboy Rd. NW cor. Lee Ave. ca. 1940.

If this white stucco and glass block flat-roofed two-story Corbusier-inspired *maison* looks as though it was lifted from the 1939–1940 New York World's Fair, it should. Because that's exactly where the idea came from—from the Town of Tomorrow exhibit which featured no less than 15 full-size (but mostly not Corbusier-inspired) homes of the future.

Take a left at Craig Avenue and a right at Hylan Boulevard.

[23c.] Billopp/Conference House: an important Revolutionary War landmark

[23c.] Billopp House/Conference House, W end of Hylan Blvd. N side. ca. 1680. ★

This manor house was built by British naval captain Christopher Billopp, the gentleman responsible for Staten Island's inclusion in New York State. He sailed around the island in less than the stipulated 24 hours, thereby winning the island from New Jersey. The house was the site of a **Revolutionary War conference** (hence the name) during which the British representatives offered "clemency and full pardon to all repentent rebels" should they lay down their arms. Ben Franklin, John Adams, and Edward Rutledge, representing the unrepentant rebels, politely demurred and the war continued. Had the conference been a success we might have remained a British colony.

Make a U-turn, a left on Craig Avenue, and a left on Bentley Street. If you've had it for the day, take Arthur Kill Road (which begins at Bentley Street) to the Outerbridge Crossing toll plaza and then Richmond Parkway and Richmond Avenue back to Interstate 278, the Staten Island Expressway.

CHARLESTON-NEW SPRINGVILLE

This tour begins on Arthur Kill Road just north of the Outerbridge Crossing and its nearby toll plaza. Don't get confused and wind up taking the bridge!

Arthur Kill Road, a fascinating drive, runs past Charleston, a marine graveyard, Rossville, Fresh Kills reclamation project, desolate salt marshes—the real backwoods of Staten Island. Charleston, formerly known as Kreischerville, after Balthazar Kreischer, who started a brick factory in 1854, is an area rich in clay. Old clay pits can still be visited; several brick-making firms operated here during the 19th century. Rossville, now an eastern ghost town, was the site of the old Blazing Star Ferry to New Jersey, in service from 1757 to 1836. Stage coaches going between New York City and Philadelphia took the ferry, propelled by sail or oars, here and in Tottenville.

[24.] The Kreischer House: hilltop home of a Staten Island brickmaker

[24.] Kreischer House, 4500 Arthur Kill Rd. at Kreischer St. bet. Allentown Lane and Englewood Ave. E side. ca. 1885. ★

In an otherwise flat, sea-level setting juts up a mound of earth topped with this **Stick style house** whose lacy details and delicate turret with open-air balcony might be made of sugar, covered with white icing. To the east is the former terra cotta- and brick-making area once called Kreischerville.

Graveyards, industrial and otherwise: On this stretch of Arthur Kill Road between Zebra Place and Rossville Avenue lie three waterside graveyards: two burial grounds bearing the remains of the area's earliest European settlers, and another kind, for maritime castaways. First to be seen is St. Luke's Cemetery, opposite Zebra Place. Elevated above the dampness of the neighboring salt marshes, its tiny plot is overwhelmed by the enormous steel cylinders of the adjacent Distrigas Corporation. Next, at St. Lukes Avenue, is the Witte Marine Equipment Company. It is here that rusting ships and leaky barges spend their last days on the mud flats of the murky Arthur Kill. Such tenants as retired two-stack Staten Island ferryboats in their now barely remembered crimson and black paint jobs can best be seen from the rise of the other small cemetery, the Sleight Family Graveyard just east of Rossville Avenue. Better known as the Rossville or Blazing Star Burial Ground (after the nearby Blazing Star ferry that crossed over to New Jersey at this point), this tiny relic of the 18th century still contains tombstones bearing family names remembered today by Staten Island streets: Winant, Poillon, Seguine, and of course, Sleight. This burial ground is an official City landmark. ★

[25.] J. Winant House/formerly **Blazing Star Tavern,** 2390 Arthur Kill Rd. bet. St. Lukes and Engert Aves. S side. ca. 1750.

A comfortable stopping place for stagecoach travelers weary of bouncing over rutted roads.

Go south on Rossville Avenue, left on Woodrow Road.

[26.] Woodrow United Methodist Church, 1109 Woodrow Rd. bet. Rossville Ave. and Vernon Ave. N side. ca. 1842. ★

This lovely example of Greek Revival style is almost, but not quite, spoiled by ungainly arcaded bell tower added in late 19th century.

[27.] Captain Cole House, 1065 Woodrow Rd. next to Woodrow Methodist Church. ca. 1836.

This house and church next door nicely complement each other; let us hope they will continue to do so.

Return to Arthur Kill Road northbound by taking a left on Arden Avenue.

[28a.] Village Greens, Arden Ave. bet. Bunnell St. and Arthur Kill Rd. W side. 1972–1974. Norman Jaffe.

Begun in 1970 as a 2,000-family, 160-acre **"planned unit development"** (PUD) as a result of special N.Y.C. zoning legislation intended to foster cluster housing and to thereby optimize available open space for neighborhood needs. Less than a third of the units were completed. These appear to be very busy visually thus intensifying the **cheek-by-jowl** feeling. Such simple expedients for adding variety as color change were avoided—the clusters are all of white aluminum siding. Though not successful visually, the project is far more satisfying than the land-wasting detached tract housing prevalent elsewhere on the island.

[28b.] Greenbrook, Arthur Kill Rd. bet. Annadale and Crossfield Aves. S side. 1973–1975.

Another cluster development northeast of Village Greens. A more romantic appearance was achieved here through use of varied earth colors. This project too suffered Village Green's fate. It faced construction, scheduling, and marketing problems and so was reduced in scope prior to completion.

Continue on Arthur Kill Road till you pass under the superhighway. At the traffic light just beyond take a left turn north on Richmond Avenue. On your right is LaTourette Park; on your left is the Fresh Kills landfill, the largest municipal garbage dump in the world.
This is a convenient place to stop touring for the day. The Staten Island Mall, a bit further on the right, has a number of simple eateries along its indoor concourse. A left on Travis Avenue will take bird lovers to a secluded and hauntingly beautiful spot, the William T. Davis Wildlife Refuge. Straight ahead is the old Asbury Church and the Expressway home.

[29a.] Staten Island Mall, Richmond Ave. SE cor. Richmond Hill Rd. 1973. Welton Becket & Assocs.

Compared to the chaotic roadside commercial development everywhere else on the island, the mall is a welcome exercise in responsibility and discipline in design. A walk inside will be enlightening, too.

[29b.] Asbury Church of the Nazarene/originally **Asbury Methodist Episcopal Church,** 2100 Richmond Ave. bet. Rivington Ave. and Amsterdam Pl. W side. 1849, 1878. ★

The side walls of this humble church date from 1849; the arch-windowed front and tower were constructed later, in 1878. In the graveyard lies **Ichabod Crane,** whose name was used by his friend Washington Irving in the story of the **headless horseman.** The church itself is named for the circuit-riding Reverend Francis Asbury, the **first American Methodist bishop,** who made his first "circuit" on Staten Island in 1771.

A good street map is a must for this tour of the northern sections of the island. **Prepare in advance.**

Take the Richmond Road exit from the Expressway and continue on the service road. The escarpment ahead of you on the right is Grymes Hill; the modern buildings silhouetted on its summit will be your first destination: Wagner College. Take the right turn onto Clove Road after the hill subsides and then the first right turn afterward onto Howard Avenue. This thoroughfare was once known as the Serpentine Road; you'll soon see why.

Wagner College: Founded in Rochester, N.Y., in 1883, Wagner Memorial Lutheran College came to Staten Island in 1918 after purchase of the Cunard property 370 feet above sea level on the brow of Grymes Hill. The Cunards were a branch of the English steamship family. The college today is coeducational and nonsectarian.

If you plan to go exploring, it's best done on foot . . . put your car in the parking area on the west side of Howard Avenue.

[30a.] Gen. William Greene Ward Residence, "Oneata"/now Wagner College Music Building, West Campus, Howard Ave. W side next to athletic field. ca. 1865.

The gorgeous view to the east is no doubt responsible for the naming of this house "Oneata," Seminole for "kissed by the dawn." A charming mansard-roofed house which may soon be kissed by the wrecker's ball to make way for college expansion.

[30b.] Science and Communications Center. 1968. Perkins & Will. **[30c.] August Horrmann Library.** 1961. Perkins & Will. **[30d.] Towers Dormitory.** 1964. Sherwood, Mills & Smith. **[30e.] Harbor View Dormitory.** 1968. Sherwood, Mills & Smith. **[30f.] Student Union.** 1970. Perkins & Will.

These recent additions to the Wagner campus were designed over a period of years by various architects working within two different architectural firms. The diversity of approach is apparent—but a visual unity is nevertheless achieved by the acceptance of an imposed discipline of unglazed red face brick as the predominant building material.

[30g.] Sir Edward Cunard Residence, "Bellevue"/now Cunard Hall, Wagner College Administration Building. East Campus, Howard Ave. E side. ca. 1851.

This old mansion, whose name referred to the glorious view now diminished by new construction, is today used for college offices.

Serpentine Road, the original name of Howard Avenue, is a self-guiding tour of one of Staten Island's poshest areas. Both sides of the thoroughfare are lined with mansions left over from earlier days, the spaces between filled in with less distinguished, more recent works of domestic architecture. The residences on the harbor side of the road have spectacular views. The other, inland side is the site for two educational institutions, the Staten Island Campus of **St. John's University** at No. 300 and **Notre Dame Academy** at Nos. 78–134. At the end, at Louis Street, is **Hero Park,** a beautifully landscaped small city park donated by Dr. and Mrs. Louis A. Dreyfus as a monument to World War I's victims. Dr. Dreyfus had contributed to the development of cold-water paint and artificial chicle for chewing gum.

Turn left on Louis Street and then right on Victory Boulevard.

[31.] Our Lady of Good Counsel Church and Rectory (Roman Catholic), Victory Blvd. SE cor. Austin Pl. 1968. Genovese & Maddalene.

Articulated dark-red brick piers contrast with cast-in-place reinforced concrete to create a **powerful sculptural statement** that effectively controls a difficult hillside site along one of the island's busiest thoroughfares. The three-story rectory on the Austin Street side is linked to the sanctuary by use of a **handsome brick and concrete bell tower.** Unfortunately, the edifice's careful composition has been marred by the thoughtless addition of painted sheet metal signs.

Turn right on Austin Place to see original building at No. 42, erected as a convent in 1894. Take the next left on Ward Avenue and then a right on Nixon Avenue.

[32.] Ward-Nixon Residence, 141 Nixon Ave. on hill above and behind the street-side houses. Entrance via driveway bet. Nos. 135 and 143. ca. 1835.

One of the finest **Palladian villas** remaining in America, now an apartment house and in sad disrepair. Imposing Ionic portico, finely detailed cornice, applied pilasters, and chintz curtains at windows. Brick bungalows are creeping up on all sides ready to vanquish their Old World rival.

Retrace your route on Ward Avenue and take Cebra Avenue down the hill.

[33.] Orig. S.R. Smith Infirmary: as remembered on a postcard, circa 1905

[33.] Staten Island Hospital Outpatient Clinic/originally **S.R. Smith Infirmary,** Castleton Ave. at Cebra Ave. N side. 1889.

Four orotund towers each surmounted by a shingled dunce cap of a roof, machicolated dormers with stepped brick gables, thick masonry walls freely pierced by varying sizes of windows, and a commanding, hilltop site contribute to making this one of the city's most delightful Victorian fantasies.

A few zigzag turns will get you to the next stop: left on Castleton, right on Webster, left on Brighton, right at the fork onto Lafayette, and then straight ahead a few blocks to the old village hall.

[34.] New Brighton Village Hall, 66 Lafayette Ave. SW cor. Fillmore St. 1871. ★

Years of neglect and the boarded-up windows fail to conceal the prim dignity of this mansard-roofed brick delight. Designated as an official landmark but never successfully recycled for a viable contemporary use.

[35a.] Hamilton Park Cottage, 105 Franklin Ave. bet. Buchanan St. and Park Pl. E side. 1859–1872. ★

Built at a time when suburban or country dwellings of ten to fourteen rooms were dubbed **cottages.** This Italianate residence is a reminder of a 19th-century planned community, **Hamilton Park,** the dream of Charles K. Hamilton, who not only laid out the site along the precepts of landscape gardener Andrew Jackson Downing but also was reputed to have proposed a bridge from the heights above York Avenue across Kill Van Kull to improve access to Manhattan. Another relic of the community is nearby **29 Harvard Avenue.**

[35b.] W. S. Pendleton Residence, 22 Pendleton Pl. bet. Franklin and Prospect Aves. W side. 1855. ★

A remarkable wood-shingled villa, one of many which once adorned Staten Island, this is known as **the "first" Pendleton house.** As his business ventures prospered—Pendleton was president of the local ferryboat company and dabbled in real estate—he forsook this Gothic Revival gem and built another in about 1870 in the Stick style. **The "second" Pendleton house [35c.]** is still standing at No. 1, at the northwest corner of Franklin Avenue.

[35d.] Pritchard Residence, 66 Harvard Ave. NW cor. Park Pl. 1845. ★

Hidden behind privet hedge, birch trees, and wisteria is this expansive, grand, yellow stucco house with gray trim. Note that its front entrance was placed to command the downhill view to the west—today its large backyard.

Two right turns from Park Place will take you to Prospect Avenue westbound.

[36a.] Jonathan Goodhue Residence, "Woodbrook"/now **Goodhue Children's Center Recreation Building,** 304 Prospect Ave. at Clinton Ave. S side. ca. 1845. **[36b.] William H. Wheelock Residence Facility, Goodhue Center,** 290 Prospect Ave. at Clinton Ave. S side. 1970. Davis, Brody & Assocs.

The driveway at the west end of Prospect Avenue leads to an unusual pair of buildings used by the Children's Aid Society for their work. **Woodbrook,** though it shows its age, still conveys some of the elegance it must have possessed when it was a villa commanding the vast acreage of the Goodhue estate, still largely intact. The **Wheelock Building,** named for a trustee of the center, is an experiment in group living for eight teenagers. Woodbrook's tarnished elegance contrasts with the carefully contrived utilitarian statement of its modern neighbor.

[36c.] Residence for St. Peter's Boys High School/originally **Nicholas Muller Residence,** 200 Clinton Ave. at Prospect Ave. W side. 1855.

Neat and crisp in dark red with white trim, this house is the most distinguished building on the small St. Peter's campus.

[36b.] The William H. Wheelock Residence Facility at the Goodhue Center

Take a pair of lefts onto Henderson Avenue and again at Brentwood. Zigzag south and turn right onto Castleton Avenue; follow the edge of St. Vincent's Hospital's grounds around onto Bard Avenue to see the old Garner mansion and also its gatehouse.

[37.] St. Vincent's Medical Center Convent/originally **W. T. Garner Residence,** Castleton Ave. at Hoyt Ave. N side. 1887. **Gatehouse,** Bard Ave. S of Moody Pl. E side. 1887.

Huge Victorian mansion proclaims by size, if not by beauty, the prodigious wealth garnered by businessmen in the late 19th century. Ulysses S. Grant considered retiring here but his wife, visiting the house on a warm damp day, was plagued by mosquitos that thrived in Staten Island's marshes and swamps.

[38.] George W. Curtis Residence, 234 Bard Ave. NW cor. Henderson Ave. 1850.

Curtis was a dedicated abolitionist and supporter of Lincoln. In this house he hid Horace Greeley from mobs of angry Staten Islanders, who generally supported the Southern cause. **Curtis High School** is named for this historic figure.

Follow Bard Avenue almost to its source near Kill Van Kull and take a left just beyond Walker Park onto Delafield Place. (The land occupied by Walker Park was the second home of the Staten Island Cricket and Tennis Club and the site of some of the earliest—but not the first—lawn tennis matches in this country.)

[39a.] Dr. Samuel MacKenzie Elliott Residence, 69 Delafield Pl. bet. Bard and Davis Aves. N. side. 1850. ★

An early eye surgeon of wide repute, Dr. Elliott, as a result of his distinguished patients, became the focal point of a small but far-flung literary colony: James Russell Lowell, Henry Wadsworth Longfellow, and Francis Parkman, among others. The house itself, one of some thirty he built in this area, is a straightforward ashlar box whose only exterior charm is a frilly, serpentine verge board along its gabled roof.

A short walk away on narrow Richmond Terrace stands a venerable structure:

[39b.] Kreuzer-Pelton House, 1262 Richmond Terrace nr. Pelton Pl. E. side. 1722–1836. ★

Typical of the area's colonial residences. First, islanders built a one-room structure, usually of local fieldstone; in later years rooms were added when needed. Stone cottage on the right dates from 1722; central shingled section was added in 1770; two-story brick section on the left was built in 1836. The man who was to become England's **King William IV** was entertained here during the Revolution.

Resuming the tour, take Davis Avenue south to Henderson; then Henderson Avenue west (right turn) to Broadway.

[40a.] West Brighton Pool, N.Y.C. Department of Parks and Recreation, Henderson Ave. bet. Broadway and Chappell St. N side. 1970. Heery & Heery.

One of some dozen crash-program precast concrete swimming pool complexes to be found throughout the city, commissioned on the eve of a **mayoral election campaign** and rapidly built using sophisticated construction management techniques. Its **distinctive composition** and glossy graphics make it far more successful than most City-commissioned works more ponderously conceived by less-skilled minds.

West Brighton: The official name of this community is West *New* Brighton, lying as it does to the west of New Brighton. But the "New" has been dropped by all save fuddy-duddy mapmakers and the government officials who advise them. One of the few official recognitions of the vernacular is in the foot-high lettering of the entrance sign of the West Brighton Pool.

[40b.] Public School 18 Richmond, Broadway NE cor. Market St. 1890. Addition, 1898.

It is the old, intricate, multistory building which is of interest here—not its pallid 1963 low-rise addition to the north. Since before the turn of the 20th century P.S. 18 has been proclaiming to the surrounding community such eternal verities as the correct time (when the clock in its tower was working), and the date of its construction emblazoned high on its facade. Take a leisurely walk around the school and savor its collection of richly configured hip-roofed red brick pavilions, which tilt with one another along Market Street all the way back to Campbell Avenue.

A right turn on Castleton Avenue will take you past one of Staten Island's array of modern churches.

[41.] Our Lady of Mt. Carmel-St. Benedicta Church and Rectory (Roman Catholic), 1265 Castleton Ave. NE cor. Bodine St. 1969. Genovese & Maddalene.

Topped by an intricately textured brick screen, this severe geometric edifice is very prominent on this commercial strip of Castleton Avenue. Its boldness, however, has a tendency to clash with (rather than dominate) the used car emporia and two-story frame houses that are its neighbors. The sheet metal sculpture of the saint that looks down upon parishioners entering the church and the dramatic sky-lit altar and rich modern stained glass of the interior are very effective.

[40b.] Public School 18 Richmond: portrayed on an early 20th century postcard

Take a left on Clove Road and stop at Delafield Avenue, at the zoo, and at Tyler Street.

[42a.] Scott-Edwards House, 752 Delafield Ave. bet. Clove Rd. and Raymond Pl. S side. ca. 1730. Remodeled ca. 1849.

A century after its original construction as a colonial farmhouse with a so-called **Dutch kick roof,** a formal Greek Revival colonnaded porch was added. The original unwhitewashed fieldstone walls are still visible on the side. It's too bad about the addition of dormer and vents to the graceful roofline.

[42b.] Staten Island Zoo, Clarence T. Barrett Park, 614 Broadway at Colonial Court. W side. Rear entrance from Clove Rd. S of Martling Ave. 1936. N.Y.C. Parks Department. Telephone: 442-3100.

Small zoo, specializing in snakes, and an accompanying children's zoo. Only zoo in America exhibiting **all 32 species** of rattlesnakes. Snake lovers are reassured by the notice: "None of these snakes is fixed—all have full possession of fangs."

[42c.] Gardiner-Tyler Residence, 27 Tyler St. bet. Clove Rd.–Broadway intersection and Bement Ave. N side. ca. 1835. ★

Opposite St. Peter's Cemetery. The elegant portico of this fine home faces west toward a great view. Note the crisply fluted columns with their florid capitals and the chunky scroll brackets that connect the portico to the house proper. President John Tyler's widow, a woman of Southern sympathies, resided here during the Civil War. During the conflict it is said that she was relieved, by outraged Unionists, of a Confederate flag which she had displayed.

Tired? This is a convenient place to stop for the day. Hungry? Try the Forest Inn Restaurant not too far away at Forest Avenue west of Broadway for a snack or something heartier. The entrance to the Expressway is a short drive south on Clove Road.

This tour starts along Victory Boulevard at its intersection with Clove Road. The Richmond Road exit from the Expressway will take you, eventually, to Clove Road; turn right to Victory Boulevard and turn left (west).

[43a.] New Clove Road Pumping Station, N.Y.C. Department of Water Pollution Control, Victory Blvd. bet. Ontario and Laban Aves. S side. 1976. Yaroscak & Sheppard.

It is rare that a utilitarian municipal water facility rises to the level of worthy architecture. This poured-in-place reinforced concrete structure does. It uses 20th-century technology as effectively as its older neighbor to the east used red brick and cast stone. But it does so with greater panache. Tsk, tsk to the ugly transformer and cage thoughtlessly plunked right in front!

[43b.] Staten Island War Memorial Outdoor Skating Rink and Locker Pavilion, Victory Blvd. at Laban Ave. N side. 1972. Brodsky, Hopf & Adler.

A polygonal wood-shingled roof peeks up from the hollow in Clove Lakes Park in which the pavilion was sited. Though the designer exercised care in the choice of ruddy brick and dark wood shingles, the shiny aluminum railings which form a maze for crowd control are out of keeping with the setting. So is the exposed cooling tower for chilling the ice: an afterthought?

[43c.] Staten Island Obstetrics & Gynecology Associates Building, 1384 Victory Blvd. SW cor. Marx St. 1975.

A well-handled wood frame professional building that calls attention to itself through its skillful use of contrasts: vertical and diagonal siding, sweeping circular and tall slit windows, and a distinctive roofline.

[43d.] Physicians and Surgeons Building, 1460 Victory Blvd. bet. Albert St. and Little Clove Rd. S side. 1975.

Swaybacked, skylighted, and stuccoed, this structure does catch your attention but fails to hold it for very long. Designed by its builder, Charles Azzue. [Also see 10c.].

[44.] Society of St. Paul Seminary, 2187 Victory Blvd. NW cor. Ingram Ave. 1969. Silverman & Cika. Telephone: 761-0085.

Perhaps Staten Island's most unusual institutional building: a combination of architecture and monumentally scaled sculpture. Its large size and prominent location make it visible from great distances. Though it conveys an **intriguing appearance** from afar, it is **less satisfying** up close—but still well worth a visit. The society is devoted to religious publishing and operates a bookstore and media center open to the public.

At Wooley Avenue turn right, and right again at Watchogue Road. Watch for St. John Avenue on your left.

[45.] Housman House, 308 St. John Ave. NW cor. Watchogue Rd. ca. 1730–1760.

Turned catercorner to the more recent street grid, this house was the home of Loyalist Garrett Housman during the Revolution. The tiny one-room stone house on the right was built first; the clapboard addition followed thirty years later.

A jaunt up St. John Avenue, a right turn on Leonard, and a left on Jewett will give you a brief glimpse of the Westerleigh community.

Prohibition Park, a wooded tract of 25 acres, was set up in 1898 for teetotalers. Lots were sold to prohibitionists throughout the country. Some streets were named for dry states—Maine, Ohio, Virginia; others for Prohibition Party presidential candidates—Bidwell, Wooley, Fiske. A huge auditorium, now gone, was built for lectures and sermons on religion and science. The area is known today as Westerleigh, but the original street names remain to admonish unwary residents of the evils of alcoholic spirits.

Bear left from Jewett Avenue onto Post Avenue past Temple Emanu-El (on your left) and then turn right onto Richmond Avenue once you reach the Port Richmond business section.

[46.] Temple Emanu-El, 984 Post Ave. bet. Heberton and Decker Aves. S side. 1907. Harry W. Pelcher.

A small-town version of a Classical Revival facade: **heavy Roman columns and pediment,** an octagonal domed cupola, even the carefully spelled-out name in relief over the entrance—complete with hyphen. Yet there is **strength of purpose** in both the innocent pretentiousness of the white-painted street facade and the more straightforward cladding of the remainder of the edifice's wood frame, **shingles** stained a **deep forest green.** A wonderful relic of this community's earlier days.

[47.] Reformed Church of Staten Island, 54 Richmond Ave. opp. Church St. ca. 1854. **Chapel,** 1898.

Site of the first religious congregation on Staten Island, organized in 1663. The present church replaced three earlier ones on the site. Read the various plaques outside the church and walk through the **old graveyard.**

Take a left onto Richmond Terrace and follow it along this desolate stretch under the overpowering Bayonne Bridge; take the first left turn immediately following the bridge onto Morningstar Road.

[48.] Church of St. Adalbert (Roman Catholic), 30 St. Adalbert Pl. NE cor. Morningstar Rd. 1968. W. O. Biernacki-Poray.

One of a number of **radically modern** Roman Catholic churches to be found on Staten Island, this structure is **dramatically sited** to be seen by traffic on the Willowbrook Expressway, which it abuts. A more reserved facade greets those entering the church from the local street . . . and the interior, with its upswept ceiling and modern stained glass, is the best feature of all.

A detour to the right at Forest Avenue will reveal an antique from the early days of the motor car. Then follow Forest Avenue back to the east to signs which mark entrance to Route 440, the Willowbrook Expressway; the route to Interstate 278 East to the Verrazano Bridge is well marked.

[49.] Forest Discount Getty / formerly **Herb & Lloyd Service Station,** 1881 Forest Ave. at Sanders St. N side. ca. 1920.

Subtly painted in earth tones and still bearing its Spanish-tile roof, this gas station is a relic of the early days of the automobile. It appears to be right out of a Hollywood version of *The Great Gatsby.*

[50.] Staten Island Community College "Learning Town" Expansion Plan, S of Staten Island Expressway, 715 Ocean Terrace bet. Milford Dr. and Staten Island Blvd. Master plan 1975 by Max O. Urbahn Assocs., Inc., coord. archts., Johansen and Bhavnani/Alexander Kouzmanoff Assoc. Archts., Paul Rudolph. Earlier buildings, 1967, Moore & Hutchins.

Nipped in the bud by N.Y.C.'s fiscal crisis, the "learning town" contemplated in the master plan would have added some distinguished buildings to the existing, architecturally mediocre campus. Staten Island's population growth and the unification of SICC with Richmond College may one day move the project into a construction phase.

Emerson Hill: Emerson Drive, which appears to be an uphill narrow extension of Clove Road just south of the Expressway, is the easiest way to see (and to get lost on) Emerson Hill. Named for a famous resident, poet Ralph Waldo Emerson's brother, Judge William Emerson, the narrow roads and curious homes were largely developed in the 1920s by Cornelius G. Kolff, a local civic leader remembered today for the ferryboat named in his honor. Nos. 3, 93, and 205 Douglas Road are among the more interesting newer houses to be found here. (Don't be surprised if practically every lane you turn onto is called Douglas Road . . . it just is that way.) Emerson Hill's quaintness results from the constricted yet rustic development patterns and a never-ending feeling of closeness with nature . . . but don't miss the spectacular long distance views between the houses and the dense foliage. A memorable spot.

End of tour.

[51.] South Beach Psychiatric Center, N.Y. State Department of Mental Hygiene, 777 Seaview Ave. NW cor. Seaside Blvd. 1974. John Carl Warnecke.

[52.] N.Y. State Research Institute for Mental Retardation, 1050 Forest Hill Rd. S of Willowbrook Rd. W side (on grounds of the Willowbrook State School). 1967. Fordyce & Hamby.

[53.] Arthur Kill Community Rehabilitation Center, State of New York, 2911 Arthur Kill Rd. bet. Chemical Lane and Clay Pit Rd. N side. 1970. Ira Kessler & Assocs.

[54.] Monsignor Farrell High School (Roman Catholic): a dramatic building

[54.] Monsignor Farrell High School (Roman Catholic), 2900 Amboy Rd. SW cor. Tysen's Lane. 1962. Charles Luckman Assocs.

[55.] Residence, 5910 Amboy Road, bet. Seguine and Bayview Aves. S side. ca. 1840. ★

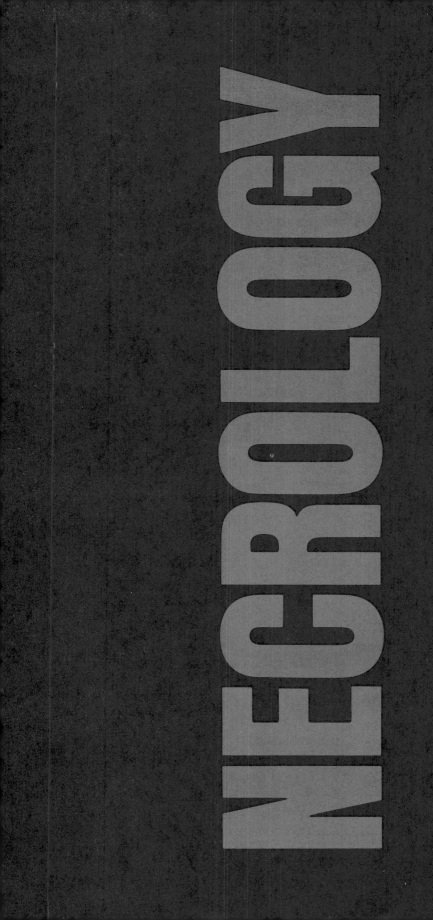

MANHATTAN

THE FINANCIAL DISTRICT

U.S. Office Building/originally **Aldrich Court,** 45 Broadway, bet. Morris St. and Exchange Alley, W side. 1886. Young & Cable.

A Romanesque Revival structure whose nine stories towered over its neighbors when built, and were towered over, in turn, by the time of its removal, in the 1970s.

71 Pearl Street (commercial building), bet. Broad St. and Coenties Alley. N side. Foundations, 1641. Walls, 1700. Facade, 1826. ★

The facade of this official landmark, whose foundations were claimed to be those of the Dutch Stadt Huys, New York's first city hall, was carefully dismantled to be reerected at South Street Seaport.

Seamen's Church Institute, 25 South St. SW cor. Coenties Slip. 1907. Additions, 1913, 1929. Warren & Wetmore.

The only part of this structure not destroyed to build the 55 Water Street office tower was the verdigris "lighthouse" memorializing the sinking of the *Titanic.* It can now be seen in a park at South Street Seaport, at Fulton and Water Streets.

55, 57, 61 Front Street, bet. Coenties and Old Slips. S side. **54, 56, 62, 64 Front Street,** bet. Cuylers Alley and Old Slip. N side. **96–110 Front Street,** bet. Gouverneur Lane and Wall St. N side. **142 Front Street,** NW cor. Depeyster St. All 1830s.

Such warehouses, almost entirely gone from the scene, formed the core of commercial Lower Manhattan in the early 19th century.

The Singer Tower on a 1912 postcard

Orig. Ger. Amer. Insur. Co. (1971 photo)

The Singer Tower, 149 Broadway, NW cor. Liberty St. 1907. Ernest Flagg.

One of the city's great Beaux Arts monuments, demolished for 1 Liberty Plaza.

Aetna Insurance Company, 100 William St., bet. John and Platt Sts. E side. ca. 1890.

Elegantly clad 100 William Street now occupies the site.

Originally **German-American Insurance Company,** 1 Liberty St., N side at Maiden Lane. 1907. Hill & Stout.

This magnificently corniced triangular structure was removed by the city to allow a street widening to accommodate a greater volume of traffic!

LOWER WEST SIDE

Originally **Laing Stores,** 258-262 Washington St. and 97 Murray St., NW cor. 1848. James Bogardus. ★

Stolen in the dead of night, much of one of the country's earliest prefabricated cast-iron facades was awaiting reerection nearby as part of the Washington Market Urban Renewal Project.

CIVIC CENTER/CHINATOWN

Fordham University, City Hall Division/formerly **Vincent (Astor) Building,** 302 Broadway, SE cor. Duane St. 1899. George B. Post.

Sixteen terra-cotta-trimmed stories demolished to make way for an ill-fated project: a new municipal office building.

H. Bowker & Co. (lofts), 101–103 Duane St., bet. Broadway and Church Sts. N side. 1870. Thomas Little. **317 Broadway (lofts),** SW cor. Thomas St. 1865. **10–12 Thomas Street (lofts),** bet. Broadway and Church Sts. S side. 1870. Thomas Little. **64–66 Thomas Street (lofts),** bet. Church St. and W. Broadway, S side. 1867. **43–45 Worth Street (lofts),** bet. Church St. and W. Broadway, N side. 1860. S. A. Warner. **54 Worth Street (lofts),** S side, ca. 1860. William Field & Son. **58–60 Worth Street (lofts),** S side. 1869. Griffith Thomas. Rebuilt, 1879, J. Morgan Slade. **66–68 Worth Street (lofts),** S side. ca. 1870.

Cast-iron "gray ghosts" that are now *truly* ghosts.

LOWER EAST SIDE

Originally **Olive Branch Baptist Church**/later **Congregation Beth Haknesseth Anshe Sineer (synagogue),** 290 Madison St., SW cor. Montgomery St. 1856.

Destroyed by fire.

Mills Hotel No. 2, 16 Rivington St., NW cor. Chrystie St. 1897. Ernest Flagg.

A lesser-known Flagg work built as a hostel for low-income guests. It is survived by a larger cousin, now The Atrium in the Village [see Greenwich Village 18.].

GREENWICH VILLAGE

Harout's Restaurant, 14 Waverly Place, bet. Greene and Mercer Sts. 1961. Haroutiun Derderian.

It recognized the values of leaving the original architecture pretty much alone.

Women's House of Detention, 10 Greenwich Ave., bet. Christopher and W. 10th Sts., NE side. 1931. Sloan & Robertson.

Not the architecture, Art Deco, but its ungainly bulk and ear-piercing conversations screamed from barred windows to friends in the street below caused this jail's demise.

Sutter's French Café, 18 Greenwich Ave., N cor. W. 10th St.

Croissants, brioches, and all manner of other caloric temptations, a touch of Paris, disappeared when inflation got the better of the proprietors (and their landlord).

Church of St. John's-in-the-Village (Protestant Episcopal)/originally **Hammond Street Presbyterian Church,** 220 W. 11th St., SW cor. Waverly Place. 1846.

The original Greek Revival church was destroyed by fire and then replaced [see Greenwich Village 77.].

Miller Elevated Highway/better known as **The West Side Highway,** Rector St. to W. 72nd St. Canal to W. 22nd Sts., 1931. W. 59th to W. 82nd Sts., 1932. W. 22nd to W. 38th Sts., 1933. W. 38th to W. 46th Sts., 1934. W. 46th to W. 59th Sts., 1937. Sloan & Robertson, architects for these sections. Canal St. bridge, 1939. Rector to Canal Sts., 1948.

Potholes, rust, and many other indications of the impact of rock salt, heavy traffic, and "deferred maintenance" were visible along the elevated

West Side Highway before December 15, 1973, when the combined weight of an asphalt-laden dump truck and a car finally caused a major collapse—near the Gansevoort Market—thus sealing its doom.

ASTOR PLACE/EAST VILLAGE

153 Crosby Street (warehouse), bet. E. Houston and Bleecker Sts. E side. ca. 1840.

Once a splendid Greek Revival commercial building.

Originally **Southern Hotel**/later **Grand Central Hotel**/later **Broadway Central Hotel,** 673 Broadway, bet. Bleecker and W. 3rd Sts. 1871. Henry Engelbert.

When this great lady went, she did so in dramatic fashion—not so much a peaceful demise as a mighty collapse into the center of Broadway.

Old Church of The Nativity, 46 Second Ave., bet. 2nd and 3rd Sts. 1832. Town & Davis (A. J. Davis, J. H. Dakin, and James Gallier).

A decayed church, now replaced.

CHELSEA

Cavanaugh's Restaurant, 256 W. 23rd St., bet. Seventh and Eighth Aves. 1876.

For many decades the steak and other Irish and American fare served here satisfied the appetites of the likes of Diamond Jim Brady.

Model Tenement, 441 W. 28th St., bet. Ninth and Tenth Aves. 1916.

It had originally been built as demonstration housing by the Hudson Guild.

403–405 West 28th Street (row houses), near Ninth Ave.

Two houses which possessed rare, vine-covered verandas.

FOUR SQUARES

Originally **DeMilt Dispensary**/later **American Musical and Dramatic Academy,** 245 E. 23rd St., NW cor. Second Ave. 1851.

A great display of carefully crafted masonry displaced by a lesser work.

Orig. DeMilt Dispensary: restrained Romanesque Revival brickwork (1967 photo)

Originally **Leonard Jerome Residence**/later **Manhattan Club,** 32 East 26th Street. SE cor. Madison Ave. 1859. T. R. Jackson. ★

At one time famous as the mansion of Winston Churchill's grandfather, later famous as one of New York's very few demolished official landmarks.

71st Regiment Armory, N.Y. National Guard, Park Ave. bet. E. 33rd and E. 34th Sts. E side. 1905. Clinton & Russell.

The first edition of the *AIA Guide* called it a "burly brick mass topped by a medieval Italian tower," now replaced by a combined high school and office tower [see Murray Hill 1.].

144 East 39th Street (carriage house), bet. Lexington and Third Aves. **143, 148, and 152 East 40th Street (carriage houses),** bet. Lexington and Third Aves. All late 19th century.

These four carriage houses once afforded passersby a variety of building styles and modest scale among newer monoliths.

Originally **Tiffany & Co. Stables,** 140 E. 41st St., bet. Lexington and Third Aves. 1904. McKim, Mead & White.

The stables are gone but the old Tiffany's on Fifth Avenue and 37th Street (in another guise) lives on [see Herald Square 18.].

113 and 115 East 40th Street (residences)/formerly **The Architectural League of New York,** bet. Lexington and Park Aves.

For decades these connected buildings, one a carriage house, sheltered the New York Chapter of the AIA, the Architectural League, and other art and architectural organizations.

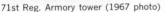

71st Reg. Armory tower (1967 photo)   Orig. Knoedler Gallery (1967 photo)

TIMES SQUARE AREA

Franklin Savings Bank, 658 Eighth Ave. SE cor. W. 42nd St. 1899. York & Sawyer.

This was one of the firm's earliest banks, in a massive Classical style.

FIFTH AVENUE: 47TH–57TH STREETS

Schrafft's (restaurant)/formerly **Knoedler Gallery,** 558 Fifth Ave., bet. E. 45th and E. 46th Sts. 1911. Carrère & Hastings.

Facade cosmetized via radical plastic surgery into the Philippine Center (1974. Augusto Comacho).

Olivetti-Underwood Showroom, 584 Fifth Ave., bet. W. 47th and W. 48th Sts. W side. 1954. Belgiojoso, Peressutti & Rogers. Wall relief, Constantino Nivola.

Olivetti's elegant office equipment roosted on green marble pedestals growing out of the green marble floor.

Spanish National Tourist Office, 587 Fifth Ave., bet. E. 47th and E. 48th Sts. E side. 1964. Javier Carvajal.

This austere white stucco and oak cave was often obscured by tourist come-ons.

Santiago Shoe Salon/later **T. Jones,** 697 Fifth Ave., bet. E. 54th and E. 55th Sts. 1965. Morris Ketchum, Jr., & Assocs.

Giant glass "shoe boxes," just off the sidewalk, were used to display its wares.

Lederer de Paris (leather goods), 711 Fifth Ave., bet. E. 55th and E. 56th Sts. E side. 1939. Morris Ketchum, Jr., architect. Victor Gruenbaum (Victor Gruen), associate. **Ciro of Bond Street (jewelry),** 713 Fifth Ave., bet. 55th and 56th Sts. E side. 1939. Morris Ketchum, Jr.

These were thirties showroom showpieces.

The Olivetti Showroom (1954 photo)   La Fonda del Sol interior (1960 photo)

Ciro of Bond Street/Lederer de Paris: elegant specialty shops (1939 photo)

ROCKEFELLER CENTER AREA

Japan Airlines Ticket Office, British Empire Building at Channel Gardens. 1956. Raymond & Rado; Junzo Yoshimura, associate architect.

A tiny, semiprecious jewel.

La Fonda del Sol (restaurant), Time-Life Building, 123 W. 50th St., bet. Sixth and Seventh Aves. 1960. Alexander Girard.

An exuberant design, but one in which the forms, spaces, and materials were impeccably controlled.

DRY DOCK COUNTRY

RKO 58th Street Theater, 964 Third Ave., bet. E. 57th and E. 58th Sts., W side.

One of central Manhattan's last movie palaces.

UPPER WEST SIDE

Litho City, W. 59th St. to W. 72nd St., West End Ave. to the Hudson River. Proposal, 1963. Kelly & Gruzen.

This aborted riverfront project would have placed 15,000 people—along with shopping, park, piers, an international student center, and a new headquarters for the *New York Times*—over the existing freight yards and piers.

UPPER EAST SIDE

Acquavella Building, 119 E. 57th St., bet. Park and Lexington Aves. N side.

An enchanting Tudor jewel replaced by an even more enchanting baguette [see Upper East Side 2f.].

L'Étoile (restaurant), 3 E. 59th St., bet. Fifth and Madison Aves. 1966. Alexander Girard. Lee Schoen, associated architect.

L'Étoile's design was "French" modern: austere, polished, and with elegant graphics.

Paraphernalia boutique (1967 photo)

The Presbyterian Home (1967 photo)

Mrs. M. Hartley Dodge Residence, 800 Fifth Ave., NE cor. E. 61st St. 1923. R. S. Shapter.

Although undistinctive and unused, it was one of the avenue's few remaining freestanding mansions.

7 East 67th Street (town house), bet. Fifth and Madison Aves. 1900. Clinton & Russell.

9 East 67th Street (town house), bet. Fifth and Madison Aves. 1913. Hiss & Weeks.

Paraphernalia, 795 Madison Ave. bet. E. 67th and E. 68th Sts., E side. 1966. Ulrich Franzen.

A neat adaptation of a womenswear boutique to an existing situation.

Elihu Root Residence, SE cor. E. 71st St. and Park Ave. 1903. Carrère & Hastings.

This was a freestanding neo-Georgian manor built for the distinguished statesman.

Presbyterian Home, 49 E. 73rd St., bet. Madison and Park Aves. 1869. Joseph Esterbrook.

An invigorating mansard-roofed institution.

James Stillman House, 900 Park Ave., NW cor. E. 79th St.

Replaced by a ubiquitous apartment tower.

Cherokee Club, 334 E. 79th St., bet. First and Second Aves. ca. 1885. James Gavigan.

Having lost a tardy battle for landmark designation, the ornately carved facade of this Romanesque Revival building, once a Democratic Party clubhouse, was then mutilated.

RKO 86th Street Theater, 137 E. 86th St., NW cor. Lexington Ave. 1920s.

Another movie palace gone, this one for Gimbels East.

Ruppert Brewery, Second to Third Aves., E. 90th to E. 93rd Sts. 1870s and later.

A grand old brewery complex removed for urban renewal [see Yorkville 12. and above.].

Squadron A (Eighth Regiment) Armory, N.Y. National Guard (east section), Park Ave., bet. E. 94th and E. 95th Sts. 1895. John R. Thomas.

The east part was removed in favor of a modern echo, I. S. 29 Manhattan, now Hunter High School—the west part survives as a "ruin" [see Upper East Side 36c.].

Lewisohn Stadium, City College of New York, during summer concert (1957 photo)

Ellis Island National Park: model of proposed unbuilt project (1966 photo)

THE HEIGHTS AND THE HARLEMS

Lewisohn Stadium, City College, Convent Ave., bet. W. 136th and W. 137th Sts. through to Amsterdam Ave. 1915. Arnold W. Brunner.

Most famous and warmly remembered for its summer concerts, not its architecture, the colonnaded stadium was demolished in favor of academic expansion.

THE OTHER ISLANDS

Ellis Island National Park, Proposal, 1966. Philip Johnson Assocs.

A monumental proposal to create a Boullée-inspired donut-shaped pavilion within which the names of all those who passed through the immigration station would have been inscribed.

THE BRONX

SOUTHERN BRONX

Mott Haven Reformed Church, 350 E. 146th St., W. of Third Ave. 1852.

This church, now replaced by a modern edifice, was destroyed by fire.

Richard Hoe & Company, Printing Machinery and Saws/originally **DeLavergne Refrigerating Machine Company,** 910 E. 138th St., from Locust Ave. to W of Walnut Ave. S side. ca. 1875.

Lost without warning in 1977 [see Port Morris 8.].

Old Bronx Borough Hall, Crotona Park, as portrayed on a postcard, circa 1907

CENTRAL BRONX

Old Bronx Borough Hall, in Crotona Park, Tremont Ave., SE cor. Third Ave. 1895, 1897. George B. Post.

Situated on a high bluff, the old local seat of government was irreparably damaged by fire while efforts were underway to find an adaptive reuse.

EASTERN BRONX

Formerly **Rectory of St. Peter's Church (Protestant Episcopal)**/later **Westchester-Bronx YMCA,** 2244 Westchester Ave., bet. Castle Hill and Havemeyer Aves. S side. 1850.

A neglected red brick Victorian country residence, one of the last of its type in New York, was replaced by a spanking new Y [see E Bronx 3.].

BROOKLYN

WEST CENTRAL BROOKLYN

Gilbert School, 341 Bridge St., bet. Myrtle Ave. and Willoughby St. E side. ca. 1845.

A Greek Revival building, drastically altered over the years.

RKO Albee Theater, 1 DeKalb Ave. at Albee Square. ca. 1924.

Not just Manhattan is losing its movie palaces. This one was removed on behalf of the shopping area's revitalization [see Civic Center/Downtown Brooklyn 10a.].

Ch. of Messiah/Incarnation (1967 ph.)   212 Gates Avenue (1967 photo)

Orig. Temple Israel (1967 photo)   Orig. A. Abraham Res. (1967 photo)

Hoagland Laboratory, Long Island College Hospital, 335 Henry St., SE cor. Pacific St. 1888. John Mumford.

Devastated by fire and later demolished, this eclectic Romanesque Revival building was the first privately founded laboratory in the country devoted to bacteriological, histological, and pathological research. Its early Art Nouveau copper signs were glorious.

Church of the Messiah and Incarnation (Protestant Episcopal), 80 Greene Ave., SE cor. Clermont Ave. 1865. James H. Giles. Redesigned, 1892. R. H. Robertson.

Until the church was engulfed by flames and then torn down, it was hard to miss its 130-foot-tall brick and terra-cotta beehive-capped tower.

Oriental Pavilion, Prospect Park, 1874. Calvert Vaux.

Fire ravaged yet another of the Vaux gems which graced Prospect and Central Parks. Will it be rebuilt?

374–376 Franklin Avenue (double house), SW cor. Quincy St. ca. 1865.

This house looked as though it came right out of Andrew Jackson Downing's Victorian country-house sketchbooks.

212 Gates Avenue (country house), bet. Franklin and Classon Aves. S side.

Victim of a fire and subsequent "renovations," this Carpenter Gothic, Victorian house is today barely recognizable.

Originally **Temple Israel (synagogue)**/then **Brooklyn Traffic Court**/then **Bergen Tile (store),** 1005 Bedford Ave., NE cor. Lafayette Ave. 1893. Parfitt Bros.

When this Byzantine Romanesque house of worship was dedicated by its affluent German-Jewish congregation, it rated two front-page columns in the *Brooklyn Daily Eagle.*

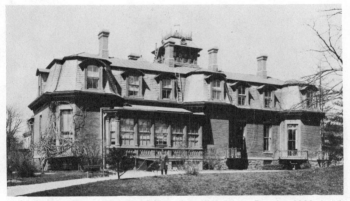

Old Brooklyn Children's Museum, S Bldg., Orig. W.N. Adams Res. (ca. 1890 photo)

Originally **Abraham Abraham Residence,** 800 St. Marks Ave., bet. New York and Brooklyn Aves. S side. ca. 1890.

Built as a proper mansion for one of Brooklyn's most prominent philanthropists, the founder of A & S. It was demolished for a nursing home [See Crown Heights 9. and below].

Originally **Ludwig Nissen Mansion,** 814 St. Marks Ave., bet. New York and Brooklyn Aves. S side. ca. 1905.

Also torn down for the nursing home, the *AIA Guide's* first edition called it "a miniature of the Potsdam Palace."

820 St. Marks Avenue (residence), bet. New York and Brooklyn Aves. S side ca. 1890.

Another mansion removed for the nursing home.

Old Brooklyn Children's Museum, in Brower Park, Brooklyn Ave., bet. St. Marks Ave. and Park Place. North Bldg: L. C. Smith Residence, ca. 1890. South Bldg: William Newton Adams Residence, 1867.

The museum's new facility replaces its original buildings, two Victorian mansions that were long familiar landmarks in Brower Park [see Crown Heights 13. and below].

Loehmann's (women's apparel), 1476 Bedford Ave., NW cor. Sterling Pl.

Until it went out of business at this location, Loehmann's was a chaotic store wrapped in Oriental details and filled with unbelievable fashion bargains.

NORTHERN BROOKLYN

Joseph Schlitz Brewing Co./originally **Leonard Eppig's Germania Brewery**/then **Interboro Cereal Beverage Co.** (during Prohibition)/then **George Ehret's Brewery,** 24–44 George St., SE cor. Central Ave. ca. 1877.

A richly worked brick behemoth gone to rest, together with the other once-world-renowned Brooklyn brewing industries.

Originally **Joseph F. Knapp Residence**/later **a dancing academy**/later **Yeshiva Umesivta Torah V'Yirah D'Satmar,** 554 Bedford Ave., NW cor. Ross St. 1894.

Replaced for a more modern Williamsburg.

Originally **First Reformed Dutch Church of Williamsburg**/later **Congregation Tifereth Israel (synagogue),** 491 Bedford Ave., SE cor. Clymer St. 1869.

Destroyed by fire and replaced by a new, matter-of-fact synagogue.

Dr. Charles A. Olcott Residence/later **Entre Nous Club,** 489 Bedford Ave., NE cor. Clymer St.

Orig. Eppig's Brewery (1967 photo)   Orig. Williamsburg Gas Light Company

Originally **Williamsburg Gas Light Company**/later **Brooklyn Union Gas Co.,** 324 Bedford Ave., NW cor. S. 2nd St. ca. 1866.

A fine work of architecture, needlessly demolished—cast-iron facade and all.

SOUTHWESTERN BROOKLYN

Cropsey Residence, 1740 84th St., SE cor. Bay 16th St.

A Victorian frame house replaced by a mundane facility for the elderly.

SOUTHERN BROOKLYN

Shatzkins' Famous Knishes, 1500 Surf Ave., SE cor. W. 15th St.

The knish was raised to a high art: here one could devour these pastry-covered delicacies—filled with apple, blueberry, cherry, cheese, kasha (groats), or, of course, potato.

EASTERN BROOKLYN

Belmont Avenue Baths, 15 Belmont Ave., bet. Thatford Ave. and Osborn St. N side. ca. 1915.

The handsome facade which once sported a fine lettered sign, **Russian and Turkish Baths,** is totally unrecognizable.

Parish House, New Lots Reformed Dutch Church, 620 New Lots Ave., SE cor. Schenck Ave. 1823.

The shingled parish house, a fitting complement to the church, was superseded by a new building [see East New York 14.].

QUEENS

NORTHWESTERN QUEENS

26–35 and 26–41 Fourth Street (residences), bet. 26th and 27th Aves. E side. ca. 1835.

Two of the last of Astoria's palatial Greek Revival mansions built by entrepreneurs in shipping and lumber during the mid-19th century.

NORTHEASTERN QUEENS

First Congregational Church of Flushing and Parish House, Bowne St., bet. 38th and Roosevelt Aves. W side.

Until destroyed by fire, these dignified 19th-century wood-frame structures enhanced the community, set as they were on a green carpet of grass.

Parish House, The First Congregational Church of Flushing (1967 photo)

St.Thomas Hall (school)/later St. Joseph's Academy (Roman Catholic), Kissena Blvd., NE cor. Sanford Ave. 1839.

A dour Victorian institutional structure; today the site of a busy shopping complex.

Bell Homestead, 38–08 Bell Blvd., bet. 38th and 39th Aves. W side. ca. 1845.

Replaced by Prudential.

CENTRAL QUEENS

United States Pavilion, 1964–65 New York World's Fair, Flushing Meadows Park, 1964. Charles Luckman Assocs.

As happens with pavilions at world expositions, this immense, elevated square donut was razed, in 1977, long after the rest of the fair.

St. James Episcopal Church, 87–07 Broadway, NE cor. Corona Ave., Elmhurst. 1849.

This mid-19th century church, now destroyed by fire, was an outgrowth of the earlier one, which remains [see Central Queens 8.].

STATEN ISLAND

Brooks House, 414–418 Richmond Terrace, SE cor. Westervelt Ave., New Brighton. 1835.

A common saga: a mansion first allowed to deteriorate and then demolished.

Planter's Hotel, 360 Bay St., NW cor. Grant St., Tompkinsville.

Once a fashionable hotel, it was patronized by wealthy Southerners during the 19th century.

Horrmann Castle, 189 Howard Ave., opp. Greta Place, E side. Grymes Hill. ca. 1915.

A fantasy castle, it was Bavarian, French Renaissance, Flemish, Spanish, and English Queen Anne all heaped together, and topped by a crow's nest with an onion-shaped cupola.

26–35 Fourth St., Queens (1967 photo) Nathaniel Marsh Res. (1967 photo)

Nathaniel Marsh Residence, 30 Belair Rd., bet. Bay St. and Wingham Home Ave., S side. ca. 1860.

This pink brick, wisteria-covered mansion sat elegantly atop a shady hill enjoying superb harbor views. Removed to build a residence for the elderly.

Holmes Cole House, 3425 Hylan Blvd., SW cor. Justin Ave., Great Kills. ca. 1730.

An early 18th century house, bulldozed for a tacky subdivision.

Old Church of St. Joachim and St. Anne (Roman Catholic), Mount Loretto Home for Children, Hylan Blvd., bet. Sharrott and Richmond Aves., N side. ca. 1882.

The towers and main facade of this imposing edifice, destroyed by fire, were saved; the badly damaged nave was demolished and replaced by a modern substitute [see Staten Island 22b.]

THAR SHE GROWS

Population of New York City

	Within Present Limits of N.Y.C.	Manhattan
1790	49,401	33,131
1800	79,216	60,515
1810	119,734	96,373
1820	152,056	123,706
1830	242,278	202,589
1840	391,114	312,710
1850	696,115	515,547
1860	1,174,779	813,660
1870	1,478,103	942,292
1880	1,911,698	1,164,673
1890	2,507,414	1,441,216
1900	3,437,202	1,850,093
1910	4,766,883	2,331,542
1920	5,620,048	2,284,103
1930	6,930,446	1,867,312
1940	7,454,995	1,889,924
1950	7,891,957	1,960,101
1960	7,781,984	1,698,281
1970	7,894,862	1,539,233

Area

	Square Miles	Acres
The City	319.8	204,681
Manhattan	22.6	14,478
The Bronx	43.1	27,606
Brooklyn	78.5	50,244
Queens	114.7	73,406
Staten Island	60.9	38,947

The Bronx	Brooklyn	Queens	Staten Is.
1,781	4,495	6,159	3,835
1,755	5,740	6,642	4,564
2,267	8,303	7,444	5,347
2,782	11,187	8,246	6,135
3,023	20,535	9,049	7,082
5,346	47,613	14,480	10,965
8,032	138,882	18,593	15,061
23,593	279,122	32,903	25,492
37,393	419,921	45,468	33,029
51,980	599,495	56,559	38,991
88,908	838,547	87,050	51,693
200,507	1,166,582	152,999	67,021
430,980	1,634,351	284,041	85,969
732,016	2,018,356	469,042	116,531
1,265,258	2,560,401	1,079,029	158,346
1,394,711	2,698,285	1,297,634	174,441
1,451,277	2,738,175	1,550,849	191,555
1,424,815	2,627,319	1,809,578	221,991
1,471,701	2,602,012	1,986,473	295,443

The City of New York in 1970 had a population greater than the combined total of 12 states:

Alaska	302,173
Delaware	548,104
Hawaii	769,913
Idaho	713,008
Maine	993,663
Montana	694,409
Nevada	488,738
New Hampshire	737,681
North Dakota	617,761
South Dakota	666,257
Vermont	444,732
Wyoming	332,416
	7,264,915

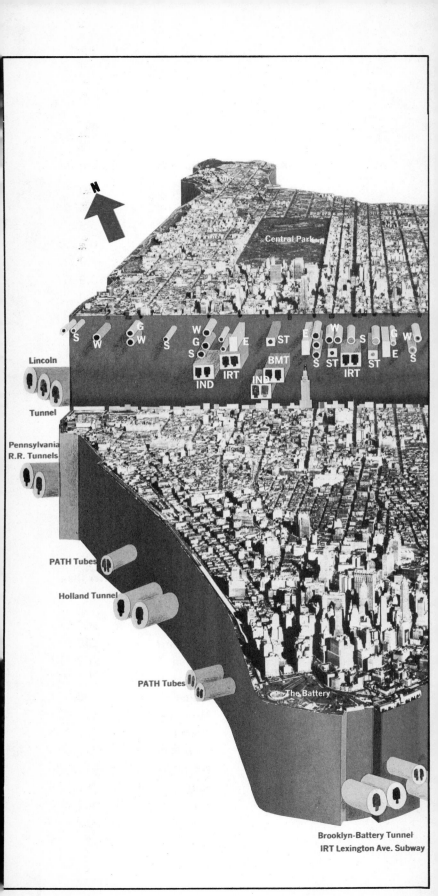

NEW YORK UNDERGROUND

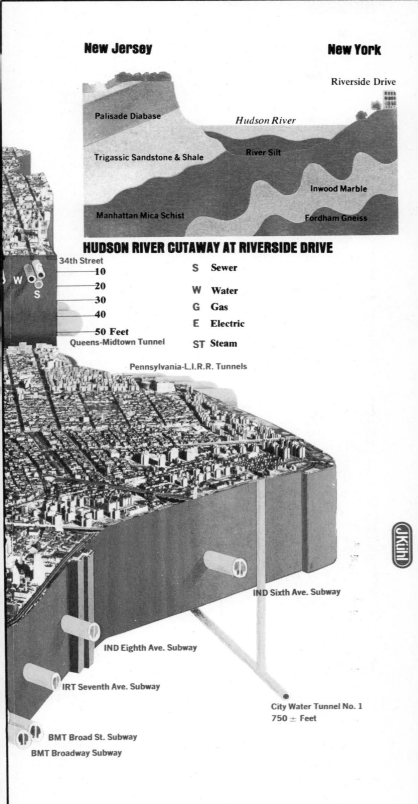

New Jersey

New York

Riverside Drive

Palisade Diabase

Hudson River

Trigassic Sandstone & Shale

River Silt

Inwood Marble

Manhattan Mica Schist

Fordham Gneiss

HUDSON RIVER CUTAWAY AT RIVERSIDE DRIVE

34th Street
10
20
30
40
50 Feet

Queens-Midtown Tunnel

Pennsylvania-L.I.R.R. Tunnels

S   Sewer

W   Water

G   Gas

E   Electric

ST Steam

IND Sixth Ave. Subway

IND Eighth Ave. Subway

IRT Seventh Ave. Subway

City Water Tunnel No. 1
750 ± Feet

BMT Broad St. Subway

BMT Broadway Subway

BRIDGES

	Type	Bridge	Water-crossing	Between or In
1	S	George Washington	Hudson River	Manhattan-N.J.
2	S	Throgs Neck	East River	Bronx-Queens
3	S	Bronx-Whitestone	East River	Bronx-Queens
4	F	Rikers Island	East River	Queens-Rikers Is.
5	S	Triborough	East River	Queens-Wards Is.
	L		Harlem River	Man.-Randalls Is.
	F		Bronx Kills	Bx.-Randalls Is.
6	A	Hell Gate	East River	Queens-Wards Is.
7	L	Wards Is. (Ped.)	East River	Man.-Wards Is.
8	L	Roosevelt Island*	East R./E. Channel	Qns.-Roosevelt Is.
9	C	Queensboro	East River	Man.-Queens
10	S	Williamsburg	East River	Man.-Brooklyn
11	S	Manhattan	East River	Man.-Brooklyn
12	S	Brooklyn	East River	Man.-Brooklyn
13	S	Verrazano-Narrows	The Narrows	Bklyn.-Staten Is.
14	A	Henry Hudson	Harlem River	Man.-Bronx
15	L	Broadway	Harlem River	Manhattan
16	S	University Heights	Harlem River	Man.-Bronx
17	A	Washington	Harlem River	Man.-Bronx
18	A	Alexander Hamilton	Harlem River	Man.-Bronx
19	A	High Bridge	Harlem River	Man.-Bronx
20	S	McCombs Dam	Harlem River	Man.-Bronx
21	S	145th Street	Harlem River	Man.-Bronx
22	S	Madison Avenue	Harlem River	Man.-Bronx
23	S	Third Avenue	Harlem River	Man.-Bronx
24	S	Willis Avenue	Harlem River	Man.-Bronx
25	T	174th Street	Bronx River	Bronx
26	B	Westchester Avenue	Bronx River	Bronx
27	B	Eastern Boulevard	Bronx River	Bronx
28	B	Unionport	Westchester Creek	Bronx
29	B	Eastchester	Eastchester Creek	Bronx
30	B	Hutchinson R.P. Ext.	Eastchester Creek	Bronx
31	B	Pelham	Eastchester Bay	Bronx
32	S	City Island	Pelham Bay Narrows	Bronx
33	B	Whitestone Expwy.	Flushing River	Queens
34	B	Flushing	Flushing River	Queens
35	B	Roosevelt Avenue	Flushing River	Queens
36	F	Little Neck	Alley Creek	Queens
37	B	Hunter's Point Ave.	Dutch Kills	Queens
38	F	Midtown Highway	Dutch Kills	Queens
39	R	Borden Avenue	Dutch Kills	Queens
40	F	Hawtree Basin (Ped.)	Hawtree Basin	Queens
41	B	Nolins Avenue	Shell Bank Basin	Queens
42	B	North Channel	North Channel	Queens
43	B	Cross Bay	Jamaica Bay	Queens
44	F	Hook Creek	Hook Creek	Queens-Nassau
45	B	Pulaski	Newtown Creek	Queens-Bklyn.
46	B	Greenpoint Ave.	Newtown Creek	Queens-Bklyn.
47	F	Kosciusko	Newtown Creek	Queens-Bklyn.
48	S	Grand Street	Newtown Creek	Queens-Bklyn.
49	B	Metropolitan Ave.	English Kills	Brooklyn
50	B	Union Street	Gowanus Canal	Brooklyn
51	R	Carroll Street	Gowanus Canal	Brooklyn
52	B	Third Street	Gowanus Canal	Brooklyn
53	F	Third Avenue	Gowanus Canal	Brooklyn
54	B	Ninth Street	Gowanus Canal	Brooklyn
55	B	Hamilton Avenue	Gowanus Canal	Brooklyn
56	B	Mill Basin	Mill Basin	Brooklyn
57	B	Cropsey Avenue	Coney Island Cr.	Brooklyn
58	S	Stillwell Avenue	Coney Island Cr.	Brooklyn
59	F	Ocean Avenue	Sheepshead Bay	Brooklyn
60	L	Marine Parkway	Rockaway Inlet	Bklyn.-Queens
61	A	Bayonne	Kill Van Kull	Staten Is.-N.J.
62	T	Goethals	Arthur Kill	Staten Is.-N.J.
63	T	Outerbridge Cross'g	Arthur Kill	Staten Is.-N.J.
64	R	Lemon Creek	Lemon Creek	Staten Is.
65	B	Fresh Kills	Richmond Creek	Staten Is.

TUNNELS

	Tunnel	Water-crossing	Between
1	Lincoln N. tube	Hudson River	Manhattan-N.J.
	C. tube		
	S. tube		
2	Holland N. tube	Hudson River	Manhattan-N.J.
	S. tube		
3	Brooklyn-Battery	Upper N.Y. Bay	Manhattan-Bklyn.
4	Queens-Midtown	East River	Manhattan-Queens

Year Compl.	Max. Span (feet)	Max. Clear. Above M.H.W. (feet)	Engineer/Architect	Operating Agency	
1931	3,500.	212.	O.H. Ammann/Cass Gilbert, Inc.	PA	1
1961	1,800.	142.	O.H. Ammann	TBTA	2
1939	2,300.	150.	O.H. Ammann/Aymar Embury II	TBTA	3
1966		52.		DPW	4
1936	1,380.	143.	O.H. Ammann/Aymar Embury II	TBTA	5
1936				TBTA	
1936	383.	55/135		TBTA	
1917	1,087.	135.	G. Lindenthal/H. Hornbostel	NYCRR	6
1951	312.2	55/135	Madigan/Hyland	DPW	7
1955	418.	40/103		DPW	8
1909	1,182.	135.	G. Lindenthal/Palmer & Hornbostel	DPW	9
1903	1,600.	135.	Leffert L. Buck.	DPW	10
1909	1,470.	135.	G. Lindenthal/Carrère & Hastings	DPW	11
1883	1,595.5	133.	J.A. & W.A. Roebling	DPW	12
1964	4,260.	228.	O.H. Ammann	TBTA	13
1936	800.	142.5	E.H. Praeger, C.F. Loyd	TBTA	14
1962	304.	24.3/135		DPW	15
1908	264.5			DPW	16
1888	508.8	133.5		DPW	17
1963	1,526.0	103.0		DPW	18
1848	322.0±	102.		DP	19
1895	408.5	29.2		DPW	20
1905	300.	25.2		DPW	21
1910	300.	25.		DPW	22
1898	300.	25.8		DPW	23
1901	304.	25.1		DPW	24
1928	190.	30.5		DPW	25
1938	83.	17.2		DPW	26
1953	118.7	26.6		DPW	27
1953	75.	17.5		DPW	28
1922	127.7	12.5		DPW	29
1941	160.5	35.		DPW	30
1908	80.	17.5		DPW	31
1901	164.8	12.3		DPW	32
1939	174.	35.		DPW	33
1939	107.	25.		DPW	34
1925	212.	25.6		DPW	35
1931	44.5	7.3		DPW	36
1910	71.5	88.	(Closed)	DPW	37
1940	126.5	90.		DPW	38
1908	82.	4.		DPW	39
1963	72.	18.		DPW	40
1925	43.	10.	(Closed)	DPW	41
1925	123.	26.3		DPW	42
1939	131.	17.5		TBTA	43
1931	34.17	4.1		DPW	44
1954	176.6	55/135		DPW	45
1929	180.	27.4		DPW	46
1939	300.	125.		DPW	47
1903	227.	9.		DPW	48
1933	111.	10.72		DPW	49
1905	56.	8.3		DPW	50
1889	45.2	4.7		DPW	51
1905	56.	7.3		DPW	52
1889	40.3	13.		DPW	53
1905	56.	7.3		DPW	54
1942	66.3	19.		DPW	55
1940	165.	35.		DPW	56
1931	155.	11.25		DPW	57
1929	250.	5.7		DPW	58
1917	46.2	7.8		DPW	59
1937	40.	55/150		TBTA	60
1931	1,675.	150.	O.H. Ammann/Cass Gilbert, Inc.	PA	61
1928	672.	135.	O.H. Ammann	PA	62
1928	750.	135.	O.H. Ammann	PA	63
1958	34.	4.	(Closed)	DPW	64
1931	81.	11.74		DPW	65

Legend:

A = Arch   L = Lift
B = Bascule   R = Retractile
C = Cantilever   S = Suspension
F = Fixed   T = Truss

*Originally, Welfare Island Bridge

M.H.W. = Mean High Water
Ped. = Pedestrian
DP = N.Y.C. Department of Parks and Recreation
DPW = N.Y.C. Department of Transportation
PA = Port Authority of New York and New Jersey
NYCRR = New York Connecting Railroad (Penn Central)
TBTA = Triborough Bridge and Tunnel Authority

Year Compl.	Length of Tube (feet)	Engineer	Operating Agency	
1945	7,482.		PA	1
1937	8,216.			
1957	8,006.			
1927	8,558. N. 8,371. S.	C.F. Holland, Ole Singstad.	PA	2
1950	9,117.	Ole Singstad.	TBTA	3
1940	6,414. N. 6,272. S.	Ole Singstad.	TBTA	4

GEOGRAPHY OF THE CITY

Latitude at City Hall: 40°42′26″ North

Longitude at City Hall: 74°0′23″ West

Elevation above sea level at City Hall: 37 feet

New York is a water city: It is situated at the confluence of a major river and the ocean, waterways that have played a major role in establishing the fundamental form of the city. Through the years they have also influenced its growth.

New York is a port city: Not only is there an abundance of shoreline but also natural deep channels and a harbor well protected from the vicissitudes of an open sea.

New York is an island city: Appropriately, all of New York's boroughs except one, The Bronx, are located on islands: Manhattan, Long Island (shared with two suburban counties), and Staten Island. In addition, the city is encrusted with other bits of land that poke up from its waters: Governor's, Roosevelt, and Riker's Islands, to name just a few, and the extensive and convoluted collection in Jamaica Bay, some of which forms a wildlife preserve.

Geology: Throughout the city the signposts of its geological development are everywhere apparent. The very location of its skyscrapers, divided into two distinct areas on Manhattan Island, the Financial District and Midtown, reflects the places where bedrock comes closest to the surface. Less abstract indications of the city's geology can be found in the New Jersey Palisades along the Hudson opposite Riverside Drive, in Manhattan's Fort Tryon or Morningside Parks, or in the hilly areas of the West Bronx and central Brooklyn and Queens.

New York's relative youth as a city is in strong contrast to its geological age. Fordham gneiss, which makes up the ridge of the West Bronx and along whose spine the Grand Concourse winds its way, dates from the earliest period of all, the archeozoic. Inwood limestone and marble are next in age. Their white substances are clearly visible in the stone cliffs of a community appropriately named Marble Hill (best viewed from a 'round-Manhattan boat tour, just as you leave the Harlem River for the Hudson). Next in age is the Manhattan schist, a mass of metamorphic rock covering the deeper limestone stratum, which is the firm bedrock providing the superb foundations for the city's skyscrapers.

The general physical form of the city and its immediate region, the form we recognize today, dates from a much later period, that of the Triassic Age. The Palisades, the lowlands, the gorge of the Hudson, and the brown sandstone so ubiquitous in the city's row houses, its brownstones, are all a product of this period.

The coming of the Ice Age 20,000 to 25,000 years ago provided the finishing touches to the pattern of the city. The glacier pushed ahead of it a mound of gravel, rock, and other debris. This mound is still visible as the terminal moraine which runs from the southern tip of Staten Island (and forms its backbone) to the Narrows, where it is interrupted, only to rise again to form Long Island's spine as well.

South of these hills, particularly in Brooklyn and Queens, is the sandy outwash deposited by the melted glacier, to this day giving rise to such descriptive place names as Flatlands. This melting of the glacier converted the once deeper gorge of the Hudson River into an estuary and filled the shallow depressions with water to form the East and Harlem Rivers (actually tidal straits), Long Island Sound, and the shallow bays of Jamaica and Gravesend.

The geological accidents of history have provided the city with some 578 miles of waterfront, innumerable beaches and overlooks, and, perhaps most important of all, a substratum to support its upward-reaching skyscrapers.

New York Underground: Within the geological strata and below the city's 6,000 miles of streets and its many miles of waterways are a variety of underground channels which most New Yorkers take for granted. A trip on the subway or through a vehicular or railroad tunnel is only a small indication of the vastness and complexity of New York's underground networks. The subways account for 134 miles of below-the-surface routes; the other publicly accessible tunnels for perhaps an additional 10 miles. The magnitudes for other such underground systems, however, are of an entirely different order: 62,000 miles of electrical wires and services; 7,800 miles in gas mains; 20 million miles of wire (in cables) for telephones; over 50 miles of steam mains that heat fully one-seventh of Manhattan's buildings; not to mention water mains, sewers, coaxial cable for television, and the now-unused pneumatic tubes that once sped mail between post office branches at 30 MPH *below* the streets (rather than 8 MPH *on* them).

If one were to calculate the amount of space invested in the subsurface facilities necessary to make the metropolis function, carved through its primeval rock and muck, enough area to support a small city would result. And within New York there are such underground "cities" even now, in Rockefeller Center, at Grand Central Terminal with its below-grade passages to adjacent buildings, and in the World Trade Center.

Though this underground empire is there, though it functions amazingly well, it remains an enigma, even for those who regularly patrol and repair the subworld mazes; the diagram on pages 578–579 gives some indication of their phenomenal complexity.

PARADES AND STREET SPECTACLES

New York City's Special Events Telephone Number is 755-4100. This handy service of the Department of Parks and Recreation offers both live information and recorded messages depending upon the time of day and availability of personnel.

Event	Dates	Location	Phone
January/February			
Chinese New Year Celebration	Lunar New Year	Chinatown along Mott and nearby streets	962-2798
March/April			
St. Patrick's Day Parade (Irish)	March 17	Fifth Avenue, 44th–86th Sts.	371-6100
Easter Parade	Easter Sunday, midday	Fifth Ave., vic. of 44th to 57th Sts.	
Ringling Bros. Barnum & Bailey Circus Parade	Day before or morning of first performance	From Twelfth Ave. and W. 34th St. to Madison Sq. Garden	867-8500
Cherry Blossoms	April into May	Brooklyn Botanic Garden	622-4433
May/June			
May Day Parade	May 1 if at all	Union Square	924-0550
Martin Luther King, Jr., Memorial Parade	First Sunday in May, afternoon	Fifth Avenue, 44th–86th Sts.	926-5800
Hungarian Independence Day Parade	May 15	First Ave. and E. 82nd St. to Riverside Dr. and West 98th St.	UN 1-8500
Ninth Avenue International Festival	Weekend in mid-May	Ninth Avenue, 37th to 59th Sts.	869-3610
Armed Forces' Day Parade	Third Sunday in May, afternoon	Fifth Avenue, 96th–62nd Sts.	682-1655
Norwegian Constitution Day Parade	Third Sunday in May	Fifth Ave., 90th St. to 67th St. (Brooklyn)	
Greek Independence Day Parade	Usually a Sunday in mid-May, afternoon	59th–79th Sts., then east to Second Avenue and E. 74th St.	628-2500

Event	Dates	Location	Phone
Washington Square Outdoor Art Exhibit	Late May thru June	Around Washington Square Park	982-6255
Memorial Day Parades	Memorial Day	All boroughs	Call your local veterans' org.
Salute to Israel Parade	First or second Sunday in June, afternoon	Fifth Avenue, 54th–86th Sts.	391-2030
Puerto Rican Day Parade	First or second Sunday in June, afternoon	Fifth Avenue, 44th–86th Sts.	993-3000
St. Anthony of Padua Feast and Parade (Italian)	First two weeks in June, evenings	Sullivan and West Houston Sts.	SP 7-2755
Blessing of the Fleet (Greek)	Fourth Sunday in June, morning	Emmons Ave. (Sheepshead Bay, Brooklyn)	322-2200
San Juan's Day (Puerto Rican)	Last weekend in June	Downing Stadium (Randall's Island)	
St. Paul of Nola Feast and Parade	Weekend near June 22	11th St. and 36th Ave. (L.I.C., Queens)	361-1884

July/August

Event	Dates	Location	Phone
Independence Day Parade	July 4	All boroughs	
Our Lady of Mt. Carmel and St. Paul of Nola Feasts and Parade (Italian)	First two weeks in July. Sunday parade carries towering giglio.	North 8th and Havemeyer Sts. (Williamsburg, Brooklyn)	EV 4-0223
Our Lady of Mt. Carmel Feast (Italian)	Mid-July	E. 187th St. and Belmont Ave. (Bronx)	295-3770
Feast of O-bon (Japanese)	Saturday night in July closest to full moon	Riverside Park play area at W. 103rd St.	RI 9-8719
Feast of the Assumption and Parade (Italian)	Week near August 15	Bedford Pk. Blvd. and Villa Ave. (Bronx)	733-3200
St. Stephen's Day Parade & Picnic (Hungarian)	Sunday nearest August 20	Call for information	UN 1-8500
Washington Square Outdoor Art Exhibit	Late August thru mid-September	Around Washington Square Park	982-6255
Medieval Festival	Second or third Saturday in August	The Cloisters Fort Tryon Park	923-3700

September/October

Event	Dates	Location	Phone
West Indian Festival and Parade	Labor Day weekend	Eastern Parkway E. of Grand Army Plaza (Brooklyn)	783-4469
Feast of San Gennaro (Italian)	Week of September 19	Mulberry St., Little Italy	CA 6-6427
Steuben Day Parade (German)	Third or last Saturday in September, afternoon	Fifth Avenue, 44th–86th Sts.	GL 4-1771
Atlantic Antic Street Festival	Usually third Sunday in September, all day	Atlantic Avenue bet. Hicks St. and Flatbush Ave. (Brooklyn)	875-1000
Pulaski Day Parade (Polish)	October 5 or nearest Sunday, afternoon	Fifth Avenue, 26th–52nd Sts.	MU 6-5420

Event	Dates	Location	Phone
Columbus Day Parade (Italian)	October 12, midday–afternoon	Fifth Avenue, 44th–86th Sts.	249-9923
United Hispanic American Parade (Puerto Rican)	Second Sunday in October, afternoon	Fifth Avenue, 44th–70th Sts.	242-2360
November/December			
Veterans' Day Parade	November 11, morning	Fifth Avenue, 36th–24th Sts.	
Macy's Thanksgiving Day Parade	Thanksgiving Day, morning	Central Pk. W. and Broadway from W. 77th to W. 34th Sts.	OX 5-4400
Rockefeller Center Tree-Lighting Ceremony	Second Thursday in December, at dusk	Rockefeller Plaza	489-4300
New Year's Eve Celebration and Fireworks	December 31, night	Bethesda Fountain, Central Park	755-4100
Traditional New Year's Eve Celebration	December 31, midnight	Times Square and W. 43rd St.	354-8860

OUTDOOR MURALS

Location	Facing	Artist, Title (If Any)	Year of Completion, Sponsor
Lower Manhattan			
110 Trinity Place NW cor. Cedar St.	E toward Trinity Pl.	Jay Rosenblum	1972, CW
140 Church St. NW cor. Warren St.	E toward Church St.	Jason Crum, *Revoluted Pushcart*	1967, CW
92 Reade St. W of Church St.	E toward Church St.	Robert Wiegand	1969, CW
Little Italy			
128 Mulberry St. S of Hester St.	N toward Hester St.	Marina Stern	1976, CW
132–138 Mulberry St. bet. Hester and Grand Sts.	W toward Mulberry St.	Richard Haas	1976, CW
Lower East Side			
80 Catherine St. S of Cherry St.	N toward playground	Cityarts Workshop, *Black Women of America Today*	1971, CA
465 Water St. E of Catherine Slip (rear of *N.Y. Post* Bldg.)	N toward Water St.	Cityarts Workshop (Italian Mural)	1974, CA
140 Madison St. E. of Market St.	W toward Market St.	Tony Rodriguez and Cityarts Workshop, *Destruction of Nature*	1973, CA

CW = City Walls, Inc.   P = private sponsor
CA = Cityarts Workshop, Inc.

Location	Facing	Artist, Title (If Any)	Year of Completion, Sponsor
109 East Broadway SW cor. Pike St.	E toward Pike St.	Cityarts Workshop, *Chinatown Today*	1973, CA
189 Madison St. E of Allen St.	W toward P.S. 2 playground	Cityarts Workshop, *Chi Lai/ Arrivá/Rise Up*	1974, CA
57 Rutgers Place (pedestrian walk) nr. Jefferson St. N of Cherry St. (Rutgers Indoor Pool)	W toward playground	Cityarts Workshop (Puerto Rican Heritage Mural)	1975, CA
165 East Broadway SE cor. Rutgers St.	W toward Rutgers St.	Cityarts Workshop, *Wall of Respect for Women*	1974, CA
236 East Broadway E of Clinton St. (Bialystoker Home)	E toward parking area	Cityarts Workshop (Jewish Ethnic Mural)	1973, CA
8–20 Ludlow St. N of Canal St.	W toward Ludlow St.	Cityarts Workshop (7th Pct. Youth Council Mural)	1973, CA
46 Forsyth St. bet. Canal and Hester Sts. (J.H.S. 65)	W toward Forsyth St. and Sara Delano Roosevelt Pk.	Cityarts Workshop, *Let Our People Grow*	1976, CA
464 Grand St. NE cor. Pitt St. (Henry St. Settlement)	W toward Pitt St.	Cityarts Workshop, *Arise from Oppression*	1972, CA
73 Delancey St. SE cor. Allen St.	W toward Allen St.	Mark Newman and Cityarts Workshop, *Art as an Alternative to Violence*	1974, CA
142 Forsyth St. N of Delancey St.	S toward Delancey St.	Cityarts Workshop, *Seeds for Progressive Change*	1975, CA
181 Chrystie St. N of Rivington St.	S toward Rivington St.	Cityarts Workshop, *New Birth*	1974, CA
Along both sides of the Bowery bet. E. 4th and Delancey Sts.		Murals advertising various businesses	1970s, P

Houston Street Corridor

Location	Facing	Artist, Title (If Any)	Year of Completion, Sponsor
135 Mangin St. S of E. Houston St. nr. FDR Dr.	N toward E. Houston St.	Cityarts Workshop, *Por Los Niños*	1976, CA
14 Second Ave. NE cor. E. Houston St.	S toward E. Houston St.	Cityarts Workshop, *Una Sociedad Nueva*	1976
304 Mulberry St. N of E. Houston St. (St. Barnabas Mission)	S toward E. Houston St.	Mel Pekarsky	1971, CW
325 Lafayette St. N of E. Houston St.	N toward Bleecker St.	Mel Pekarsky	1970, CW
136 Crosby St. S of E. Houston St.	N toward E. Houston St.	Mel Pekarsky	1972, CW
599 Broadway S of W. Houston St.	N toward W. Houston St.	Forrest Myers	1973, CW

Location	Facing	Artist, Title (If Any)	Year of Completion, Sponsor
171 Mercer St. SW cor. W. Houston St.	N toward W. Houston St.	Dorothy Gillespie	1975, P
475 West Broadway SE cor. W. Houston St.	N toward W. Houston St.	Jason Crum	1969, CW
East Village			
50 Avenue C SE cor. E. 4th St.	N toward E. 4th St.	Cityarts Workshop (Afro-Latin Mural)	1973, CA
121 E. 3rd St. W of Avenue A (P.S. 63)	E toward Avenue A	Cityarts Workshop, *Women Hold Up Half the Sky*	1975, CA
198 W. 7th St. E of Avenue B	W toward Avenue B	Jason Crum, *Tammuz*	1969, CW
340 E. 9th St. bet. 1st & 2nd Aves.	W toward empty lot	Allan D'Arcangelo	1967, CW
317 E. 9th St. bet. 1st & 2nd Aves.	S toward E. 9th St.	Robert Wiegand, *Juliette*	1967, CW
324 E. 9th St. bet. 1st & 2nd Aves.	W toward empty lot	Jason Crum, *Angus Special*	1967, CW
E. 10th St. NW cor. Avenue D	One wall of park building	Cityarts Workshop (Tito Rodriguez Memorial Mural)	1977, CA
441 Lafayette St. S of Astor Pl.	N toward Astor Pl.	Robert Wiegand, *At the Astor Bar*	1968, CW
SoHo and Greenwich Village			
114 Prince St. W of Greene St.	E toward Greene St.	Richard Haas (Trompe l'Oeil of Cast Iron Bldg.)	1975, CW
685 Broadway Rear wall on E. 3rd St.	W toward Mercer St.	Tania	1970, CW
173 Spring St. bet. W. Broadway and Spring St. (Gem Lumber Co.)	S toward Spring St.	James Januzzi, James Buckley, Mario Green, Phoenix Murals Co.	1976, P
Midtown (west)			
550 W. 20th St. SE cor. Eleventh Ave.	S toward Eleventh Ave.	Knox Martin, *Venus*	1971, CW
234 W. 27th St. E of Eighth Ave.	E toward Fashion Institute of Technology	Hugh Kepets	1976, CW
103 W. 42nd St. W of Sixth Ave.	E toward Sixth Ave.	Alvin Loving	1973, CW
258 W. 42nd St. E of Eighth Ave.	W toward Eighth Ave.	Cityarts Workshop, *Phoenix*	1975, CA
430 W. 46th St. W of Ninth Ave.	W toward playground	Arnold Belkin & Cityarts Workshop	1972, CA
620 W. 47th St. E of Twelfth Ave.	W toward Twelfth Ave.	Nassos Daphnis	1971, CW
840 Eighth Ave. N of W. 50th St.	S toward W. 50th St.	Richard Anuszkiewicz	1972, CW
Midtown (east)			
360 Park Avenue South Rear wall on E. 26th St.	W. toward Madison Ave.	Nassos Daphnis	1969, CW

Location	Facing	Artist, Title (If Any)	Year of Completion, Sponsor
529 Second Ave. N of E. 29th St.	S toward playground	Jason Crum, *Haven*	1968, CW
557 Third Ave. SE cor. E. 37th St.	N toward E. 37th St.	Mel Pekarsky	1973, CW
49 W. 53rd St. W of Park Ave.	E toward Lever House	Robert Wiegand, *Leverage*	1970, CW

Upper West Side

236 W. 64th St. W of Amsterdam Ave.	E toward playground	Allan D'Arcangelo	1970, CW
509 Amsterdam Ave. N of W. 84th St.	S toward playground	Helen de Mott	1975, CW
250 W. 89th St. W of Broadway (New Yorker Theater)	N toward 89th St.	West 89th Street Block Association competition	1975, P

Harlem

159 W. 127th St. E of Seventh Ave.	S toward W. 127th St.	Norman Messiah, James Buckley, and Thierey Kuhn	ca. 1975, P
Lenox Ave. NW cor. W.139th St.	E toward Lenox Ave.	Children's Art Carnival	1971 P, 1976 P

Bronx

841 Bryant Ave. N of Lafayette Ave.	S toward Lafayette Ave.	Tania (mural damaged)	1968, CW
Hart Island (not open to public)		Jason Crum 3 murals: *Dynamo, Surge, Phoenix*	1970–1971, CW

Brooklyn

221 Ryerson Walk S of Willoughby Ave. (Pratt Institute)	N toward Willoughby Ave.	Bruce McCloskey	1970, P
240 Livingston St. W of Bond St.	E toward Bond St.	Todd Williams	1970, CW
530 Dean St. E of Sixth Ave.	W toward playground	Todd Williams	1973, CW
531 Bergen St. E of Sixth Ave.	W toward playground	Todd Williams	1974, CW
389 Douglass St. E of Fourth Ave.	W toward Fourth Ave.	Cityarts Workshop	1976, CA
84, 92, 96; 110, 114 Prospect Pl. W of Flatbush Ave.	E toward Flatbush Ave.	Richard Haas	1976, CW
110 Weirfield St. S of Evergreen Ave.	N toward Evergreen Ave.	Tania (mural deteriorated)	1967, CW

Queens

90–36 Parsons Blvd. N of Jamaica Ave. (N.Y.C. Dept. of Health Addition)	N away from Jamaica Ave.	Nicholas Krushenick	1975, CW
160th St. & Archer Ave. (on LIRR embankment)	N toward Jamaica Ave.	Florence Siegel	1975, CW
161–04 Jamaica Ave. opp. 161st St. on side wall (Old Jamaica Savings Bank)	W toward 160th St. and Archer Ave.	Errol Dopwell	1975, CW
90–14 161st St. N of Jamaica Ave. (Con Edison)	N away from Jamaica Ave.	Pierre Clerk	1975, CW

Location	Facing	Artist, Title (If Any)	Year of Completion, Sponsor
162–04 Jamaica Ave. E of Union Hall St. (Reliance Federal Savings Bank)	W toward Union Hall St.	Robert Wiegand	1972, CW
89–64 163rd St. N of Jamaica Ave. (Marine Midland Bank)	N away from Jamaica Ave.	Jay Rosenblum	1975, CW
164–01 Jamaica Ave. on rear wall along 164th St. (Goodwin's)	N away from Jamaica Ave.	Janet Henry (mural deteriorated)	1975, CW

Sponsors

City Walls, incorporated in 1970, is a nonprofit organization whose efforts date back to 1967 when painter Allan D'Arcangelo painted the exterior wall of the tenement at 340 East Ninth Street, left exposed when the adjacent building was demolished. The group, led by Doris C. Freedman, identifies sites, chooses the artist for the mural, and coordinates landlord-contractor-community-governmental interests.

Cityarts Workshop, incorporated as a nonprofit group in 1971, stems from a concept developed in 1968 by Susan Shapiro Kiok, its first director. This organization's exterior murals are cooperative ventures of artists and community participants whose joint efforts contribute to the finished paintings. Since 1974 the workshop has been directed by Susan Caruso-Green. The group also sponsors exterior mosaics [see V Manhattan/Greenwich Village 7, and H Manhattan/Morningside Heights 20] and large-scale indoor murals.

CORRECTIONS AND ADDITIONS

If you think we've noted something incorrectly or left something out, let us know! Send the information via this form or on a separate sheet of paper to:

Elliot Willensky
c/o Macmillan Publishing Co., Inc.
866 Third Avenue
New York, N.Y. 10022.

Page_____ Entry no. [_____] Name of building_____

_____

Correction/Addition: _____

_____

_____

_____

_____

_____

_____

Your name: _____

Your address: _____

PHOTO AND LITERARY CREDITS

Location of photos is noted in the following manner. Where all photographs on one page are credited to the same source, only the page number is listed. Where photographs on a page are from multiple sources, the position on the page has been abbreviated: T, top; B, bottom; L, left; R, right. NW and EW stand for Norval White and Elliot Willensky, respectively.

Introduction: xvi-xvii courtesy Skyviews. **Manhattan:** P.2 courtesy Long Island Historical Society; 6 by NW; 9 TL by Margaret Latimer; 9 TR/B by NW; 10 by NW; 12 by NW; 13 by NW; 15 by NW; 16 by NW; 17 by NW; 19 by NW; 20 by NW; 21 by NW; 23 TL/TR by NW; 23 B courtesy Skidmore, Owings & Merrill, by Alexandre Georges; 24 L by NW; 24 R courtesy Port Authority of New York and New Jersey; 26 collection NW; 27 by NW; 29 by NW; 30 courtesy Long Island Historical Society; 31 collection NW; 32 by NW; 33 by NW; 34 by NW; 35 TL courtesy William Lescaze and Matthew Del Gaudio, by Joseph Molitor; 35 TR/BR/BL by NW; 36 by NW; 38 courtesy Library of Congress; 39 by NW; 40 by NW; 41 by NW; 42 by NW; 43 by NW; 44 by NW; 48 L by John Edstel; 48 R by Peter Blake; 49 by NW; 51 courtesy National Archives (Public Housing Administration); 53 by EW; 54 by EW; 56 courtesy Prentice & Chan, Ohlhausen, by Nathaniel Lieberman; 57 by NW; 58 TL by NW; 58 TR courtesy Edgar Tafel; 58 B courtesy Gruzen & Partners; 62 by Margaret Latimer; 64 by Margaret Latimer; 65 by Margaret Latimer; 67 L by Margaret Latimer; 67 R courtesy Warner Burns Toan & Lunde, by Gil Amiaga; 68 L by Ann Douglass; 68 R by EW; 69 L by EW; 69 R by Ann Douglass; 70 L courtesy I.M. Pei & Assocs., by George Cserna; 70 R by EW; 71 by EW; 72 by EW; 73 L by Ann Douglass; 73 R courtesy Margot Gayle; 75 L by Ann Douglass; 75 R by Margaret Latimer; 76 T/BL by Margaret Latimer; 76 BR courtesy Whittlesey & Conklin; 79 TL/TR by Margaret Latimer; 79 B courtesy Edgar Tafel & Assocs., by Alexandre Georges; 80 collection EW; 81 by Margaret Latimer; 82 by Ann Douglass; 83 L by Ann Douglass; 83 R by Margaret Latimer; 84 by Margaret Latimer; 85 by Margaret Latimer; 86 TL by Ann Douglass; 86 TR/BL/BR by Margaret Latimer; 88 L by Ann Douglass; 88 R by Margaret Latimer; 90 by Margaret Latimer; 94 courtesy Ketchum, Gina & Sharp, by Lionel Freedman; 95 by NW; 96 by NW; 97 by NW; 98 courtesy Giorgio Cavaglieri; 99 by NW; 100 by NW; 103 courtesy Long Island Historical Society; 105 L by John Dixon; 105 R collection EW; 110 by John Dixon; 113 by NW; 114 by NW; 117 L by NW; 117 R courtesy Long Island Historical Society; 118 by NW; 121 by NW; 123 L by NW; 123 R courtesy New York Public Library; 125 TL by Bill Rothschild; 125 TR by NW; 125 B courtesy Davis, Brody & Assocs., by Robert Gray; 126 L courtesy Davis, Brody & Assocs., by Robert Gray; 126 R by NW; 128 L courtesy Macy's Inc.; 128 R by John Dixon; 131 L by John Dixon; 131 R collection EW; 132 L courtesy Shreve, Lamb & Harmon Assocs., by Gil Amiaga; 132 R by John Dixon; 133 L by John Dixon; 133 R by NW; 134 by Ann Douglass; 137 L courtesy New York Public Library, by Bob Serating; 137 R by Ann Douglass; 140 L collection EW; 140 R by Ann Douglass; 141 L by Ann Douglass; 141 R by John Dixon; 142 TL courtesy Mayers & Schiff; 142 TR/B by Margaret Latimer; 144 by Margaret Latimer; 146 L by Margaret Latimer; 146 R by EW; 147 courtesy New-York Historical Society; 149 L by J. Alex Langley; 149 R by Ben Schnall; 151 TL by J. Alex Langley; 151 TR by Schechter Assocs.; 151 B by NW; 152 L by George Cserna; 152 R courtesy Skidmore, Owings & Merrill, by Ezra Stoller © ESTO; 153 courtesy Emery Roth & Sons; 154 courtesy Abraham Geller & Assocs.; 156 by John Dixon; 157 T by John Dixon; 157 BL/BR courtesy Ford Foundation, by Ezra Stoller © ESTO; 158 T courtesy the United Nations; 158 BR by John Dixon; 158 BL by NW; 160 courtesy Goldstone, Dearborn & Hinz; 161 L courtesy William Lescaze, by Ralph Streiner; 161 R courtesy Philip Johnson; 163 L by John Dixon; 163 R courtesy Lester Tichy, by Ben Schnall; 164 by Ann Douglass; 165 L by John Dixon; 165 R by Ann Douglass; 167 TL courtesy Edward D. Stone & Assocs.; 167 TR courtesy Harrison & Abramovitz, by Gottscho-Schleisner; 167 B collection NW; 168 L by Beta Csen; 168 R courtesy Victor Lundy; 169 courtesy Rockefeller Center, Inc.; 170 L courtesy Judith Kovis Stockman, by Norman McGrath; 170 R courtesy CBS; 172 TL/TR/BL by John Dixon; 172 BR by NW; 173 L by Ann Douglass; 173 R by John Dixon; 176 L courtesy Skidmore, Owings & Merrill, by Ezra Stoller © ESTO; 176 R courtesy Horace Ginsbern & Assocs., by Gil Amiaga; 177 courtesy Lincoln Center for the Performing Arts, by Morris Wormen; 178 L courtesy Lincoln Center for the Performing Arts; 178 R by EW; 181 courtesy Hausman & Rosenberg; 183 by Margaret Latimer; 184 by EW; 186 L courtesy N.Y.C. Department of Parks and Recreation; 186 R by EW; 187 L by EW; 187 R collection EW; 190 L courtesy the Museum of the City of New York (Byron Collection), photo by Byron; 190 R by EW; 193 TL by EW; 193 TR courtesy Kaminsky & Shiffer; 193 B by Margaret Latimer; 194 L by EW; 194 R by Roger Feinstein; 197 by EW; 199 by EW; 200 L courtesy the Museum of the City of New York (Collection of Albert M. Behrens); 200 R by EW; 204 by EW; 205 by EW; 209 by EW; 210 by John Albox; 213 L by T. Roberta Wayne; 213 R courtesy Abraham Rothenberg; 216 TL/BL/BR by NW; 216 TR courtesy Edward D. Stone Assocs.; 218 L by NW; 218 R by Ezra Stoller © ESTO; 219 L courtesy Ezra Stoller; 219 R courtesy New York Association for the Blind, by Norman McGrath; 222 L courtesy Philip Johnson, by Joseph Molitor; 222 R courtesy Edward Durell Stone; 223 by

NW; 224 by NW; 225 by NW; 227 by NW; 228 by NW; 231 by NW; 232 L courtesy Brown, Lawford and Forbes, by George Cserna; 232 R courtesy Marcel Breuer & Assocs., by Ezra Stoller © ESTO; 235 by NW; 236 TL courtesy Gruzen & Partners; 236 TR/B by NW; 238 by NW; 239 by NW; 240 L by NW; 240 R courtesy William N. Breger Assocs.; 243 by NW; 244 L courtesy Samuel Paul & Seymour Jarmul, by Louis Reens; 244 R by NW; 246 TL by NW; 246 TR courtesy Park East Synagogue, by John Kraif; 246 B courtesy Whittlesey & Conklin, by Salvatore Cavalastro; 248 by NW; 249 courtesy Conklin & Rossant; 254 collection EW; 256 T/BL courtesy Columbia University, Columbiana Collection, by A. Tennyson Beals; 256 BR courtesy Mitchell/Giurgola Assocs.; 259 TL by EW; 259 TR courtesy Frost Assocs., by Alexandre Georges; 259 B courtesy Teachers College; 261 collection EW; 263 collection EW; 264 courtesy City College, by Conrad Waldinger; 265 L courtesy City College; 265 R by EW; 268 courtesy Abraham Geller, by Louis Reens; 270 by Roger Feinstein; 273 courtesy Gruzen & Partners, by David Hirsch; 274 TL by EW; 274 TR/B by Roger Feinstein; 275 L courtesy Mt. Olivet Baptist Church, by Bro. David McAdams; 275 R by EW; 276 L by EW; 276 R courtesy Curtis & Davis, by Louis Reens; 279 by EW; 281 courtesy Percival Goodman, by Norman McGrath; 282 by Roger Feinstein; 284 courtesy Davis, Brody & Assocs., by David Hirsch; 285 by EW; 287 L courtesy Smotrich & Platt, by Norman McGrath; 287 R by Roger Feinstein; 289 courtesy The Hodne/Stageberg Partners, by Norman McGrath; 291 by Richard Dattner; 292 by Richard Dattner; 293 by Richard Dattner; 295 T by Richard Dattner; 295 B courtesy Port Authority of New York and New Jersey; 296 courtesy Yeshiva University; 297 courtesy Armand Bartos; 298 by NW; 300 L by Margaret Latimer; 300 R courtesy U.S. Coast Guard; 302 courtesy Johansen & Bhavnani, by Norman McGrath; 305 L courtesy Sert, Jackson & Assocs., by Steve Rosenthal; 305 R courtesy Kallmann & McKinnel, by Steve Rosenthal. **Bronx:** P. 310 collection EW; 311 collection EW; 313 courtesy Ciardullo-Ehmann; 314 by Roger Feinstein; 315 by EW; 316 L courtesy Facilities Development Corp., by Rothschild; 316 R by EW; 317 by EW; 318 by EW; 321 courtesy New York Botanical Garden; 322 courtesy New York Zoological Society; 323 L courtesy New York Zoological Society, by Bill Meng; 323 R courtesy Davis, Brody & Assocs., by Robert Gray; 325 courtesy Fordham University; 326 by EW; 328 by EW; 333 by EW; 334 L by EW; 334 R courtesy Davis, Brody & Assocs., by Lloyd Goldfarb; 337 L courtesy Hall of Fame for Great Americans; 337 R by Roger Feinstein; 339 by EW; 340 L courtesy Schuman, Lichtenstein & Claman, by Gil Amiaga; 340 R courtesy Facilities Development Corp., by Rothschild; 343 T courtesy Ferdinand Gottlieb; 343 BL courtesy Percival Goodman, by Alexandre Georges; 343 BR by EW; 345 L courtesy Vincent A. Claps; 345 R by EW; 346 courtesy Caudill Rowlett Scott; 347 courtesy College of Mount St. Vincent; 349 courtesy Metropolitan Life Insurance Co.; 350 TL collection EW; 350 TR by EW; 350 B courtesy Gruzen & Partners, by Bill Rothschild; 351 courtesy Reynolds Metals Co., by Ezra Stoller © ESTO; 353 L courtesy Pomerance & Breines, by Jack Horner-Pennyroyal; 353 R by EW; 354 courtesy Paul W. Reilly; 355 L courtesy William A. Hall & Assocs., by John R. Kennedy; 355 R by EW; 356 by EW; 359 L courtesy Davis, Brody & Assocs., by Norman McGrath; 359 R by EW; 360 L by EW; 360 R collection EW. **Brooklyn:** P. 364 courtesy Long Island Historical Society; 366 collection EW; 367 by NW; 368 L courtesy N.Y.C. Landmarks Preservation Commission; 368 R courtesy Samuel Lebowitz; 369 by NW; 371 L courtesy Davis, Brody & Assocs., by David Hirsch; 371 R by EW; 375 TL courtesy Brooklyn Union Gas Co.; 375 TR/BL/BR by NW; 376 by NW; 377 courtesy Joseph and Mary Merz, by Gil Amiaga; 378 L courtesy Long Island Historical Society, 378 R by NW; 379 L by NW; 379 R courtesy Long Island Historical Society; 381 by NW; 382 by NW; 383 by NW; 384 TL/TR courtesy Long Island Historical Society; 384 BL by EW; 384 BR by NW; 386 T courtesy Conklin & Rossant; 386 B courtesy Ulrich Franzen & Assocs., by George Cserna; 388 L collection EW; 388 R by NW; 389 by NW; 391 TL/B courtesy Long Island Historical Society; 391 TR courtesy Pomeroy, Lebduska Assocs.; 392 by EW; 393 L by NW; 393 R by EW; 394 courtesy Long Island College Hospital; 397 courtesy Long Island Historical Society; 399 by EW; 400 by Margaret Latimer; 404 L by NW; 404 R by EW; 405 by NW; 406 by EW; 408 by NW; 410 by NW; 412 by NW; 413 by NW; 415 by NW; 417 by NW; 418 by NW; 419 by NW; 421 courtesy the U.S. Navy; 422 by EW; 423 courtesy Long Island Historical Society; 424 by EW; 425 by EW; 429 TL/TR/BL by EW; 429 by BR by John Dixon; 430 L by EW; 430 R by NW; 431 courtesy Long Island Historical Society; 432 L by NW; 432 R by EW; 434 courtesy Long Island Historical Society; 435 courtesy N.Y.C. Department of Parks and Recreation; 436 courtesy Long Island Historical Society; 437 by NW; 438 courtesy N.Y.C. Department of Parks and Recreation; 439 by EW; 440 by EW; 441 courtesy Brooklyn Botanic Garden; 442 courtesy Brooklyn Museum; 443 by NW; 446 L by EW; 446 R by NW; 448 T courtesy Long Island Historical Society; 448 BL courtesy William N. Breger Assocs.; 448 BR by EW; 449 by EW; 450 by NW; 451 by EW; 452 L by NW; 452 R by EW; 453 by EW; 454 courtesy Hardy Holzman Pfeiffer Assocs., by Norman McGrath; 456 by NW; 457 courtesy Long Island Historical Society; 460 by EW; 461 by EW; 462 by EW; 464 by EW; 465 by EW; 467 L by EW; 467 R courtesy N.Y.C. Housing Authority, by Louis Marinoff; 468 courtesy Facilities Improvement Corp., by H. Bernstein Assocs.; 469 by EW; 470 by EW; 471 courtesy Long Island Historical Society; 473 by EW; 474 by EW; 475 by EW; 476 by EW; 477 L by EW; 477 R courtesy Max O. Urbahn & Assocs.; 478 by EW; 481 by EW; 482 L by EW; 482 R by Louis Reens; 483 courtesy Long Island Historical Society;

484 by EW; 485 by EW; 486 by Ben Schnall; 487 T by Ezra Stoller © ESTO; 487 B courtesy Goldstone, Dearborn, by Bill Rothschild; 488 TL by EW; 488 TR/B by NW; 491 TL/B by EW; 491 TR by NW; 492 by NW; 493 by NW; 494 L by EW; 494 R by NW; 495 by EW; 496 T courtesy N.Y.C. Department of Parks and Recreation; 496 B by NW; 497 L by EW; 497 R by NW; 498 courtesy Facilities Development Corp., by Bill Rothschild; 498 R by Ben Schnall. **Queens:** P. 503 by EW; 504 by EW; 506 by EW; 507 courtesy Ulrich Franzen & Assocs., by Ezra Stoller © ESTO; 508 by NW; 509 by EW; 511 by EW; 512 by NW; 513 by EW; 514 by NW; 515 by NW; 517 by NW; 518 by NW; 521 TL/TR by NW; 521 B courtesy Abraham Geller; 522 by NW; 523 by NW; 525 by EW; 526 courtesy Pan Am; 527 TL courtesy Port Authority of New York and New Jersey, by Ezra Stoller © ESTO; 527 TR by NW; 527 B courtesy TWA, by Ezra Stoller © ESTO; 528 T courtesy Skidmore, Owings & Merrill, by Gottscho-Schleisner; 528 BL courtesy Port Authority of New York and New Jersey, by Ezra Stoller © ESTO; 528 BR courtesy Port Authority of New York and New Jersey, by Ezra Stoller © ESTO; 530 by NW. **Staten Island:** P. 534 collection EW; 538 collection EW; 539 T by Mina Hamilton; 539 B collection EW; 542 courtesy Staten Island Historical Society, by Alice Austen; 543 courtesy Municipal Art Society of New York; 545 by EW; 546 L by EW; 546 R by Mina Hamilton; 548 by Mina Hamilton; 550 by Mina Hamilton; 551 by Mina Hamilton; 554 collection EW; 555 courtesy Davis, Brody & Assocs., by Norman McGrath; 557 collection EW; 560 courtesy Charles Luckman Assocs. **Necrology:** P. 562 L collection EW; 562 R by Margaret Latimer; 564 by EW; 565 L by John Dixon; 565 R by Ann Douglass; 566 TL courtesy Olivetti Corp.; 566 TR courtesy Restaurant Assocs., Inc., by Dan Wynn; 566 B courtesy Morris Ketchum, Jr., by Underwood & Underwood; 567 L courtesy Paraphernalia; 567 R by NW; 568 T courtesy City College of New York; 568 B courtesy Philip Johnson, © Louis Checkman; 569 collection EW; 570 TL by NW; 570 TR/BL/BR by EW; 571 courtesy Brooklyn Children's Museum; 572 L by EW; 572 R courtesy Brooklyn Union Gas Co.; 573 by EW; 574 L by EW; 574 R by Mina Hamilton.

Literary Credits   Page 269: Hughes, Langston, *The Sweet Flypaper of Life*. New York: Simon and Schuster, 1955. **Page 295:** Jeanneret-Gris, Edouard (Le Corbusier), *When the Cathedrals Were White* (trans. Francis E. Hyslop, Jr.). New York: Reynal & Hitchcock, 1947. New York: Harcourt, Brace & World, 1947. **Page 408:** Syrett, Harold C., *The City of Brooklyn, 1865–1898*. New York: Columbia University Press, 1944. **Page 537:** Millay, Edna St. Vincent, from "Recuerdo," from *Collected Poems*. New York: Harper & Row, copyright 1922, 1950 by Edna St. Vincent Millay. By permission of Norma Millay Ellis.

GLOSSARY

A

air rights Permission to fill airspace with building volume under zoning laws. Schools, for example, usually build much less volume than zoning permits: air rights are the rights to the additional unbuilt volume, as for an apartment house built over a school, e.g., Confucius Plaza apartment complex.

anthemion A stylized honeysuckle ornamentation of Greek, Greek Revival, and neo-Greek architecture.

archaeology The study of artifacts and, in particular, buildings of a lost or poorly recorded culture.

architrave The "chief beam" of a Classical entablature, spanning directly above and between columns, and, in turn, supporting frieze and cornice.

archivolt The decorated band around an arch.

arcuated Composed of arches.

Art Deco A modern style first presented by the Paris Exposition of 1924 and rehonored in the late seventies: a style of geometric ornament, rather than form.

articulate To set off and/or emphasize by means of a joint, as a brick is articulated by deeply incised mortar, or a building's wing is articulated by the link that connects it with its parent.

Art Moderne A modern style: streamlined stucco and chromium, as if buildings traveled at the speed of automobiles. Inspired by the Paris Exposition of 1937.

ashlar Stone cut for a wall; either regular and in courses, or "random." It implies a rough and variegated stone (as in Manhattan schist or Fordham gneiss), as opposed to the smooth and monolithic sawn granite, limestone, or polished marble.

atrium A center courtyard within a house.

avant-garde The cultural front-runners—artists and architects ahead of the pack.

B

Baroque The exuberant late Renaissance style supported by the Jesuits in their attempt to lure the flock back to Rome in the face of Luther's Reformation: extravagant architectural stagecraft for the Counter-Reformation.

battlements The toothy parapet atop a castle or would-be castle: crenellations.

Beaux Arts Literally "fine arts," from the Parisian architectural school (École des Beaux Arts) that served as fountainhead for formal American architectural education. The progeny of the school produced grand (sometimes pompous) public architecture: the Paris Opéra, Grand Central Station, the Chicago World's Fair of 1893, the New York Public Library, and so forth.

board and batten Flat boards with square trim covering their joints that gave "verticality" to the Gothic Revival wood cottage. Modern architects have used boards and battens on occasion more to be different than meaningful.

bollard A short, fat, round masonry pier, set freestanding into the street, that constrains wheeled traffic but allows pedestrians to pass.

broken pediments Pediments broken apart explosively as in Baroque and neo-Baroque architecture.

brownstone Brown sandstone from the Connecticut River Valley or along the Hackensack River. Soft, porous, and perishable.

Brutalism The bold concrete architecture inspired by Le Corbusier's work and his followers.

C

campanile The freestanding belltower of an Italian church.

cantilever A stationary lever, the arm of which supports a load, as in a fishing pole.

casement A window that opens out or in, like a door.

castle Now largely a romantic idea. Strictly speaking, a fortified royal residence.

catacomb A chambered cellar serving as a cemetery in, particularly, ancient Rome.

catenary The natural curve of a hanging string (or a cable, or a suspension bridge), supported at both ends. A discrete mathematical shape.

chamfer To dull, or cut off the edge of, say, a rectangular column.

chateau A French country castle, with or without fortifications.

Chicago School The early modern style of Louis Sullivan, John Wellborn Root, William Le Baron Jenney, and company: birthschool of the skyscraper.

clapboard Linear shingles that clad (clap) each other in courses. In Federal, Greek Revival, and other Victorian stylistic ventures.

classic Of a superior and/or eternal design.

Classical Of and/or relating to the Classical period of architecture and civilization, i.e., Greek and Roman.

Classical Revival A literal revival of Greek and Roman architecture, rather than the Renaissance arrangement of Classical detail in a new fashion.

Colonial The architecture of, particularly, America, when it was a colony. (Strictly speaking before July 4, 1776.) In Manhattan only one extant building can claim the Colonial title, St. Paul's Chapel of 1766. Other Colonial buildings, now encompassed by an expanded New York, were rural outposts when built.

colonnade A row of columns usually supporting a beam, architrave, or series of arches.

colonnettes Little columns for decorative purposes.

column The vertical sticklike support of a building or structure as opposed to the fatter "pier" or the archaic "pillar." Columns may range from matter-of-fact supports, such as a modern steel column, to those participating in ornate orders of Classical architecture: Doric, Ionic, and Corinthian.

Composite Mixed orders, where Doric and Ionic might share the same column.

concrete Particularly Portland Cement concrete: a chemical coalescense of materials (sand, water, and an aggregate such as crushed stone) into an artificial stone. Reinforced with steel bars, it becomes the structure of buildings, roads or bridges; plain, it fireproofs steel buildings by encasing the structure protectively.

console bracket The enscrolled bracket that supports many a Renaissance and neo-Renaissance cornice.

corbeled Bracketed out; in masonry, bricks are corbeled when each succeeding layer (course) projects slightly over the one below.

Corinthian The late Greek (Hellenistic) and early Roman order of architecture that produced acanthus-leaved capitals (as opposed to Ionic "rams' horns" and Doric austerity).

cornice The crown of a building, its edge against the sky; particularly part of a Classical order's entablature.

course Layer of masonry or wood; brick, block, board, or stone.

crenellated Crowned with a cornice of solid teeth (merlons) that protect the warrior, and voids that allow space for his shooting.

cresting The cast-iron filigreed crest atop a Victorian mansard roof.

crocket The teat on a Gothic finial.

cul-de-sac A dead-end street, alley, or road.

D

distyle With two columns, as in a temple.

distyle-in-antis Two columns flanked by two blank walls.

Doric The austere and elegant set of parts (called an "order") developed in the sixth and fifth centuries in Greek architecture (particularly Athenian, and of Athenian colonies).

Dutch Colonial The simple house style of New Amsterdam and environs, including those deep-eaved gambrel-roofed rural farmhouses (see Brooklyn's various Wyckoff houses) and the stepped gables of town houses at the tip of Manhattan. The former are numerous; the latter have totally vanished; one needs to view Amsterdam to see their equivalents.

E

eclectic In architecture the use of assorted styles and parts in a single building.

Egyptian Of, or relating to, Egypt from approximately 3000 B.C. to the time of Alexander the Great, 353 B.C.

entablature The set of roof parts in a Classical building that the columns support: i.e., architrave (or first beam over the columns), frieze, and cornice, or top-ending. The frieze is an opportunity for cartoon-graphics, as in the animal frieze at the Parthenon (the Zoophorus) or that at Brooklyn's zoo (also animals).

esplanade A linear walking park along the water's edge, like that at Brooklyn Heights or Carl Schurz Park.

exedra A large semicircular alcove (annex) to a central space (particularly in Classical architecture).

F

Federal The first "American" style of architecture, based on English Georgian (George III was the Germanic villain).

festoon A pendant wreath; it also describes any exuberant decoration.

Flamboyant Used to describe the flamelike tracery of late French Gothic; later, to describe anything that is ostentatiously ornate.

frieze The bas relief (or painting) in a band that decorates the top of a room or participates in a Classical entablature.

G

gable The triangular ending of a two-way pitched roof.

gambrel roof The double-pitched roofs employed by Dutch and later Victorian architects.

garland A collection of flowers, as in a wreath, or festoon.

Georgian Of the Georges, those imported German kings of England who were in charge when the best of English urban design was around. Simple, but elegant, brick and limestone.

Gothic Revival The romantic revival of largely Gothic detail in the 1840s. Some felt (like John Ruskin) that the Mediaeval period was filled with good and good people, and a revival of that architecture might make those of the 1840s equally good. Bad psychology, but it left some smashing architecture.

granite The hard, fine-textured igneous (i.e., solidified from a liquid state) stone of mixed quartz, mica, and other ingredients. Sedimentary stones (limestone, brownstone) erode, wear out; granite is forever.

Greek Revival The Greeks were revived for both archaeological and political honors (the 1821 revolution liberating them from Turkey). In America in the 1820s and 1830s, houses were decorated with Greek parts, and occasionally whole buildings took on Greek temple form: cf. New York's Federal Hall National Memorial.

H

hammer beam The bracketed wood structure of a Gothic or neo-Gothic hall: a kind of wood super-corbeling.

headers The short ends of bricks in a wall used as ties to connect (bond) two thicknesses (wythes) of brick together.

I

incunabulum A precocious affair; strictly speaking a book printed from movable type before 1501, but implying equivalent childlike precocity in any activity, including architecture.

Ionic The elegant voluted order of Greek architecture. Its capitals are sometimes compared to rams' horns.

Italianate Of an Italian character, particularly in mid-19th century villas copied from Italian prototypes.

J

jerry-built Slang for shoddy construction.

L

limestone Sedimentary stone, mostly from ancient seabeds; the silted and pressed product of sand and seashells. Soft, workable, and subject to erosion in time.

M

machicolation The stepped-out cornice of a Gothic place that allows the protected to pour boiling oil on an enemy.

maisonette A British term for duplex apartments within an apartment house: a little house.

mansard The steep, story-high roofs developed by the French 17th-century architect François Mansart, co-opted by Victorian architects of the 19th century (particularly in Paris, where they squeezed in an extra illegal floor).

marble Pressed and heated (metamorphized) limestone, pressed for extra eons to a harder, finer texture. It can be polished to bring out its striations; in its purest form it is without veins, as in the Pentelican marble of the Parthenon, or Carrara marble from Italy.

mastaba The battered (sloped walled) tombs of early Egyptian nobles subordinate to the pyramids which they surrounded (cf. Gizeh).

merlon The tooth of a crenellated wall; a solid between two voids (the warrior behind a merlon shoots between the merlons).

mullion The vertical member supporting a glass wall, as in a storefront, or between repetitive windows.

muntin A small bar that divides a window's sash into panes: the little sticks that make up the framing of six-over-six and so forth.

N

nave The central space of a Christian church: the space for people, as opposed to the space for clergy (chancel), or monastic brethren (transepts).

neo-Renaissance A revival of Renaissance buildings and parts, in New York mostly those of England and Italy, but with an occasional French example. (The New York County Lawyers' Association, The Metropolitan Club, and the Towers Nursing Home, respectively.)

New Brutalism A second coming, in the 1960s, of Brutalism (q.v.).

O

oculus An eye-like round window.

ogee The double-curved arch of both Moorish and French Flamboyant Gothic.

order The set of parts of Classical architecture, as in a Doric, Ionic, Corinthian, Tuscan, or Composite order.

P

palazzo The super town house of Italian nobility (i.e., palace); later a description of any big, urbane place in an Italian town.

Palladian Of and/or relating to Palladio (Jefferson went bananas over Palladio): particularly used in reference to the paired columns flanking an arch used at the Basilica, Vicenza, and later advertised by the contemporary writer Sebastiano Serlio.

parapet The wall around a building's roof (literally a "breast guard").

pediment The triangular gable end of a Classical temple and part of its architecture's order: later used separately as a decorative part of Renaissance architecture.

permastone Artificial stone or brick made from scored and colored cement stucco.

Philistines The smug who know not and attack what they fear.

piazza The Italian word for plaza. And sometimes an American word for porch (particularly in the Midwest).

pilaster The flat remembrance of a column that articulates a wall, and frequently repeats the rhythm and parts of an adjacent colonnade. Usually decorative and nonstructural.

pinnacle The tower atop a Gothic buttress.

plaza The English (and now American) version of the Italian piazza: an outdoor space contained by different buildings. New York has few, and only two publicly created ones: The Plaza at 59th Street and Central Park; and the Police Plaza next to the Brooklyn Bridge.

plinth The base that holds it all up, as in a column or a wall.

polychromy Of many colors, particularly in architecture.

porte cochère The horse and carriage port to a house or public building.

Q

Queen Anne Style The pre-Georgian style of Queen Anne's reign (1702–1714). In American architecture the style is that of a mixture of medieval and Classical parts: Tudor, Federal, and Greek Revival grown fat, bulbous, rich, and encrusted. Eclectic extravaganzas of delight.

quoin Cornerstone of a building that articulates that corner; frequently in a different material, as in the limestone quoins of a brick Georgian building.

R

rectory The dwelling of a priest (whether Catholic or Episcopalian).

reentrant corner An interior corner.

Renaissance The rediscovery of the individual, his creative powers, and his rights: in art, architecture, and law, ostensibly returning to the individual humanism of the Classical world, as opposed to the communal Church-dominated life of the Middle Ages.

reredos The background of an altar, and, occasionally, a major art object itself, like the reredos by Frank Freeman in Brooklyn Heights' Trinity Church.

rockface Rock made more rocky by artful sculpture: neat stones faced with hewn-rock forms.

Roman The imperial organizers of the Classical world who brought engineering to architecture, creating great public works—vaulted, domed baths and temples, arched aqueducts—all decorated and ordered with the parts developed by fifth-century Greece.

Romanesque The round-arched and round-vaulted early Mediaeval architecture of Europe that was succeeded by the more elegant and sinuous Gothic. Its revived forms were highly popular in the late 19th century (e.g., Jay Street Firehouse, Brooklyn).

row house Houses that share common walls and form a row, or what the English term terraces. Town house is the elegant social promotion of the same physical place.

Ruskinian Relating to the ideas of the 19th-century English writer and historian John Ruskin. *See* Gothic Revival.

rusticated Stones that have deeply incised joints to exaggerate their weight and scale. A Renaissance device.

S

schist Laminations of rock, the product of hot geology, as a napoleon or baklava has layers of pastry. Manhattan island's skyscraper core is founded on Manhattan schist.

serpentine Anything that is serpentlike in its undulating form. Stone called serpentine has such striations.

Shingle Style The romantic and picturesque style of the 1880s and 1890s that brought the architecture of freestanding America to a special apogee: the plastic forms resulting were clad in wood shingles. But the style's name extended to wood-less buildings, based on the same picturesque forms.

spandrel The space between the window head of one floor and the window sill of the floor above: opaque masonry or paneling that conceals the floor construction behind. In Renaissance architecture it was the triangular space between two adjacent arches.

swag A draping of cloth, frequently remembered in stone, and also termed a festoon.

T

tenement A 19th-century, low-rise walk-up apartment house that covers most of its site: now a pejorative term, because of the decayed state of the survivors.

terrace A group of row houses (English).

terra cotta Literally "cooked earth" in Italian, Terra cotta is baked clay. A hard, red-brown material used for pottery, paving, shingles, statuary, and, in late 19th century New York, the fireproofing of steel (by encasing it in terra cotta blockwork).

town house Originally the secondary residence of the English country gentleman. Now not necessarily a house in town but one in an urban arrangement: i.e., row house. *Town house* is a classier term—to increase sales. New York has, of course, town houses of the 19th and early 20th centuries equivalent to the Italian palazzo.

Tuscan The smooth unfluted columns in a Roman adaptation of Doric.

V

verandah The airy porch imported from India, partially screened for outdoor living, not just rocking.

verdigris The green patina (oxide) on weathered copper, brass, or bronze, particularly near the sea. It is the handsome equivalent on copper of iron's rust.

vernacular The ordinary architecture of a culture without benefit of architect, as in the stuccoed houses of the Mediterranean's rim (Greece, Capri, North Africa) or the verandahed farmhouses of 19th-century rural America.

viaduct An elevated roadway that is the trafficked equivalent of an aqueduct, supported on many columns or piers; as opposed to a bridge that spans the space in question.

Victorian A loosely defined catchall word. The architecture of the Industrial Revolution was largely coincidental with the reign of Victoria, 1837–1901; 64 years that spanned from carpenter Greek Revival to the steel-framed skyscraper.

villa A country house for a well-to-do city dweller (Italian).

volutes The scroll-like cresting of, for example, an Ionic capital.

voussoir The wedge-shaped stones or radial bricks of an arch, cut to fit its shape, whether circle, ellipse, or ogee.

W

water table The level of water underground (that may affect a building's foundations); or the deflecting molding that skims water away from a building like a skirt near the ground on the building's perimeter.

wrought iron More easily wrought and less brittle than cast iron, it now serves for railings and decoration and once served as structural beams and railroad rails, before the more refined steel was invented.

wythe A single plane of brick (usually 4 inches); part of a wall composed of two or more wythes bonded together by metal ties or brick "headers." A cavity wall is composed of two wythes with an air space between.

Z

ziggurat The stepped or spiral pyramidal holy places of ancient Babylon.

zoning The legal constraint of building to protect one's neighbors and oneself from noxious uses, to preserve or ensure one's quota of light and air, and to prevent overbuilding.

INDEX

Virtually every building described in the Guide is listed as a primary entry in the Index, either by name or by street address. Police precincts are indexed by precinct numbers. Firehouses are indexed by the names of their engine companies.

Numbered streets designated as "East" or "West" are listed under those designations, in numerical sequence; all other numbered streets are indexed alphabetically. Numbered streets and avenues located outside Manhattan are differentiated as to borough or community; for those in Manhattan the borough name is usually omitted.

The names of those involved in creating the works listed in the Guide appear in large and small capital letters. Unless otherwise indicated, these are architects or landscape architects. A (?) following a building's name indicates questionable attribution.

A page reference in **boldface** type indicates that a picture of the specified building or other work will be found on that page.

610   **Index**

Gorham Building, 130, **131**
GORI, OTTAVIO, stonemason
A. T. Stewart Dry Goods Store, 44
Gotham Book Mart, 163
Gotham Hotel, **168**
Gottesman Playground, 206-7
GOTTLIEB, ADOLF, stained-glass artist,
236, 237
GOTTLIEB, ALBERT S.
Cartier Bldg. (former), 168
GOTTLIEB, FERDINAND
Victor residence, **342**
Gould, Jay, 340
Gould, Joe, 63, 69
Gould family, 164
Gould Memorial Library,
N.Y.U./B.C.C., 336, **337**
Gouverneur Hospital, 52
GOVE, GEORGE
Parkchester, 348-**349**
Government House, 8-9
Governor Alfred E. Smith Houses, 36
Governor's House, Governors Is., 301
Governors Island, 2, 6, 11, **300**-301,
535
Gowanus, 365, 406-7, 434
Gowanus Canal, **406**-407, 426
Grace, W. R., and Co., **15**-16
Grace, W. R., Building, 136
Grace Chapel/Dispensary, Manh., 124
Grace Church, Bklyn., 374
Grace Church, City Is., **356,** 357
Grace Church, Manh., **99,** 124, 378
Grace Court, Bklyn., 374
Grace Court Alley, Bklyn., 374
Grace Episcopal Church/Graveyard,
Jamaica, 524
Grace United Methodist Church,
Bklyn., 431
Grace United Methodist Church,
Manh., 208
Gracie, Archibald, 243
Gracie Mansion, **243**
Gracie Square Gardens, 243
GRAHAM, BRUCE CAMPBELL
235 E. 78th St., 247
GRAHAM, ERNEST R.
Equitable Bldg., **20**
GRAHAM, THOMAS
America Press Bldg., 189
GRAHAM, ANDERSON, PROBST &
WHITE
Equitable Bldg., **20**
Graham Court Apartments, 272
Graham Home for Old Ladies, 419
Gramercy Park, 112, 120
Gramercy Park East, Nos. 34 and 36:
120
Gramercy Park Historic District,
120-21
Gramercy Park West, Nos. 3 and 4:
121
Gramercy Towers, 121-22
Grammar School No. 91, Bronx, **334**
Granados Restaurant, 68
GRAN, WARREN W., & ASSOCS.
Schermerhorn-Pacific Housing, 403
Tompkinsville Water Pollution
Control Facility, 540
see also WEINER & GRAN
Grand Army Plaza, Bklyn., 426, 434-
435
Grand Army Plaza, Manh., 214-16,
332
Grand Central Depot (1871), 116, **147**
Grand Central Hotel, 564
Grand Central Oyster Bar, 148
Grand Central Terminal (1903-13),
147, 148, 310, 583
Grand Concourse, 310, 330-32, 338
No. 888: 331
Grandma's Table, Stapleton, 537
Grand Opera House (site), 105
Grand St., Bklyn., 466-67
Grand St., Manh., 54
Nos. 83-87: 45
No. 165: 49
Grand St. Market, 463
Grant, Ulysses S., 260, 555
sculptures, 434, **452**

Grant's Tomb, 260
GRAVES & DUBOY
Ansonia Hotel, **190,** 191
Gravesend, 365, 483-85
Gravesend Bay, 479, 582
Gravesend Cemetery, 485
Gravesend Reform Church, 485
Graymore Friars' Residence, 80
Great Building Crack-Up, 90
Great Depression bathhouses, 540
Greater Bethel AME Church, 276
Greater Ridgewood Historical Society,
523
Great Fire (1835), 15, 16
Great Palm House, Kew, Eng., 321
Greek Consulate, 234
Greeley, Horace, 556
statues, 30, **33,** 129
Greeley Square, 127, 129
GREEN, MARIO, painter, 587
Greenacre Park, **160**
GREENBERG & AMES
Wyckoff Gardens, 406
Greenbrook development, 552
Greene St. cast-iron buildings, 45, 46
GREENMAN, WILLIAM B.
848 Carroll St., 428
Greenpoint, 457, 469-72, 507
Greenpoint Branch, Corn Exchange
Bank, 471
Greenpoint Branch Library, 471
Greenpoint Reformed Church
(former), Kent St., **471,** 472
Greenpoint Reformed Church, Milton
St., 472
Green Tree, The, 255
Greenwich Hotel, **69**
Greenwich House, 81-82
Greenwich Savings Bank, Herald Sq.,
127
Greenwich St., No. 767: **88,** 89
Greenwich Village, 59-92, 563-64
Greenwich Village Historic District,
63-66, 73-78, 79-85, 87-88, 89-90
Greenwich Village Improvement
Society, 82
Greenwich Village Walking Tours
8th St./Washington Sq./South
Village, 64-72
14th St., 91-92
Jefferson Market Library-University
Place, 73-78
Lower West Village, 79-87
West Village, 87-91
Green-Wood Cemetery, 365, **423**-424,
473
GREER, SETH, builder
Colonnade Row, Manh., 98, **99**
Gregory the Great, Saint (statue), 195
Greyston Conference Center, 344,
345, 346
GRIFFIN, PERCY
18-52 W. 74th St., 201
Griffith, D. W., 357
GRIMSHAW & MORRILL
Lafayette Ave. Presb. Church, 410
GRINNELL, WILLIAM G.
Excelsior Power Co. bldg., 13
Grolier, Jean, 220
Grolier Club buildings, **132,** 220
GROPIUS, WALTER
Pan Am Bldg., 148-**149**
Grosvenor, The, Bklyn., 380
Grotta Azzurra, 50
Ground Floor (restaurant), 171
Grove Court, 84-85
Grove St., Bklyn., 461
Grove St., Manh.
Nos. 4-10: 85
Nos. 14-16 and 17: 84
GRUEN ASSOCS.
Albee Square Mall, 370
Queens Center, 520
GRUENBAUM (GRUEN), VICTOR
Ciro of Bond St., **566**
GRUPPE, KARL, sculptor, 343
GRUWE, EMIL
The Evelyn, 192
GRUZEN, BARNEY
Chatham Green, **35**